Lecture Notes of the Institute
for Computer Sciences, Social Informatics
and Telecommunications Engineering   44

Thanasis Korakis   Michael Zink
Maximilian Ott (Eds.)

Testbeds and Research Infrastructures

Development of Networks and Communities

8th International ICST Conference, TridentCom 2012
Thessaloniki, Greece, June 11-13, 2012
Revised Selected Papers

 Springer

Volume Editors

Thanasis Korakis
Polytechnic Institute of New York University
Brooklyn, NY 11201, USA
E-mail: korakis@poly.edu

Michael Zink
University of Massachusetts
Amherst, MA 01003, USA
E-mail: zink@ecs.umass.edu

Maximilian Ott
NICTA Australia
Eveleigh, NSW 2015, Australia
E-mail: max.ott@nicta.com.au

ISSN 1867-8211   e-ISSN 1867-822X
ISBN 978-3-642-35575-2   e-ISBN 978-3-642-35576-9
DOI 10.1007/978-3-642-35576-9

Springer Heidelberg Dordrecht London New York

Library of Congress Control Number: 2012953704

CR Subject Classification (1998): C.2.1-5, C.4, B.8.1, D.2.5

Typesetting: Camera-ready by author, data conversion by Scientific Publishing Services, Chennai, India

Printed on acid-free paper

Springer is part of Springer Science+Business Media (www.springer.com)

Message from the General Chair

It is my pleasure to welcome you to the proceedings of TridentCom 2012, the 8th International ICST Conference on Testbeds and Research Infrastructures for the Development of Networks and Communities. I was truly honored to organize Tridentcom 2012 in Thessaloniki, Greece, during June 11–13, 2012, with the vision bringing together technical experts and researchers from academia, industry, and government from all around the world to discuss experimental research infrastructures of the Future Internet.

This year's Tridentcom was very exciting. We set up a single-track technical program with 21 high-quality paper presentations on experimentation and testbeds in the field of wired and wireless networks, cloud, measurements, routing, and sensors. Apart from the regular paper presentations, Tridentcom 2012 featured a rich variety of other activities. A record number of 33 demos and posters were hosted in the demo section of the conference, presenting live the last trends on experimentation activities all over the world. Two keynote speakers, Piet Demeester from University of Ghent in Belgium and Jeff Chase from Duke University in the US, gave very interesting talks on research infrastructures and deployment platforms. The program included a fascinating tutorial on state-of-the-art tools for accessing and using federated research testbeds in a systematic way. Last but not least, the Infinity workshop was collocated with Tridentcom 2012, with the aim of gathering information on the existing research testbeds in Europe.

Tridentcom 2012 would not have been a success without the invaluable efforts of the Organizing Committee. I would like to thank Max Ott from NICTA and Michael Zink from the University of Massachusetts in Amherst for putting together an excellent technical program. Ivan Seskar from Rutgers University did a great job setting up a demo and poster section full of innovative ideas and implementations. I am grateful to Leandros Tassiulas from University of Thessaly for his significant support on several organization issues. Timur Friedman from UPMC and Aki Nakao from University of Tokyo worked hard on the publicity of the conference. The very nice website of this year's Tridentcom was a result of the creative work of Stratos Keranidis from CERTH. Gentian Jakllari from the University of Toulouse helped really in putting together the proceedings of the conference right on time. A big thank you to Stavroula Maglavera from CERTH for her tireless help with the complicated but exciting local arrangements. This year, for the first time, we launched student travel grants for Tridentcom. I would like to thank Serge Fdida from UPMC for his enormous work to secure resources in order to make these travel grants a success. Finally, I would like to thank Ruzanna Najaryan and Elisa Mendini from EAI for their collaboration on the organization of the conference.

Thanasis Korakis

Preface

Welcome to the proceedings of the 8th International ICST Conference on Testbeds and Research Infrastructures for the Development of Networks and Communities, which was held in Thessaloniki, Greece. The conference comprised four days of workshops, conference sessions, keynote presentations, poster discussions, networking, and most importantly, a good time among fellow researchers.

Every year Tridentcom grows in reputation and stature and has become a very selective venue for research publications in the broad area of methods and techniques for experimental-based networking research, After a careful and rigorous review process, 21 high-quality papers were selected among submissions from Europe, North America, Africa, Australia, Brazil, China, Japan, Korea, and Singapore.

The conference program this year consisted of six single-track sessions covering a diverse range of very timely topics such as wireless, clouds and networks, measurements, sensor networks, routing, and testbeds.

The main conference also featured two excellent and thought provoking keynotes from Piet Demester and Jeff Chase. Given the nature of the Tridentcom community, the poster and demo session, organized by Ivan Seskar, was one of the highlights of the conference and showcased the latest achievements in the field of testbeds and experimentation.

The technical program is the result of the dedicated and hard work of many people. We are most grateful to the authors who submitted their work to TridentCom 2012, as well as to the reviewers, who generously contributed their time and expertise to the review process. We also want to thank the conference Steering Committee and the General Chair for their guidance as well as the local Organizing Committee members in Thessaloniki for the smooth running of the conference.

It was a privilege to work with so many excellent and knowledgeable people leading up to the conference and a joy to engage in so many interesting conversations throughout the conference.

Max Ott
Michael Zink

Conference Organization

Executive Committee

General Chair

Thanasis Korakis — Polytechnic Institute of NYU, USA - University of Thessaly, Greece

TPC Chairs

Max Ott — National ICT Australia
Michael Zink — University of Massachusetts Amherst, USA

Poster/Demo Chair

Ivan Seskar — Rutgers University, USA

Workshop Chairs

Leandros Tassiulas — University of Thessaly, Greece
Tanja Zseby — Fraunhofer Institute FOKUS, Germany

Student Travel Grant Chair

Serge Fdida — UPMC, France

Publication Chair

Gentian Jakllari — University of Toulouse, France

Publicity Chairs

Timur Friedman — UPMC, France
Aki Nakao — University of Tokyo, Japan

Web Chair

Stratos Keranidis — CERTH, Greece

Local Arrangements Chair

Stavroula Maglavera — CERTH, Greece

EAI Conference Manager

Ruzanna Najaryan — EAI, Italy

Steering Committee

Imrich Chlamtac   Create-Net, University of Trento, Italy
Thomas Magedanz   TU Berlin, Fraunhofer Fokus, Germany
Csaba A. Szabo   BUTE, Hungary

Technical Program Committee

Sudhir Aggarwal   Anastasius Gavras   Eugen Mikoczy
Jeannie Albrecht   Deniz Gurkan   Paul Mueller
Ilia Baldine   Jason Hallstrom   Max Ott
Paolo Bellavista   Marco Hoffmann   Pablo Serrano
Prasad Calyam   David Irwin   Ivan Seskar
Justin Cappos   Henry Jerez   Mineo Takai
Emmanuel Cecchet   Jongwon Kim   Kurt Tutschku
Spyros Denazis   Andre Koenig   Scott A. Valcourt
Serge Fdida   Koutsopoulos Iordanis   Yang Yang
Stefan Fischer   Rick McGeer   Sun Yi
Alex Galis   Ruben Merz   Michael Zink

Table of Contents

Infinity Workshop

Wireless

Clouds and Networks

Measurements

Sensor Networks

Routing

Testbeds

Posters

Demos

A Satellite Network Emulation Platform
for Implementation and Testing of TCP/IP Applications

Michele Luglio, Cesare Roseti, and Francesco Zampgnaro

Univeristà di Roma Tor Vergata –Electronics Engineering Dpt.
Via del Politecnico, 1 – 00133 Roma, Italy
{luglio,cesare.roseti,francesco.zampognaro}@uniroma2.it

Abstract. In order to assess the performance of TCP/IP based applications and protocols for communication over heterogeneous networks, simulation and emulation activities are of great importance. In particular, real time emulation provides the opportunity to reproduce realistic environment thanks to the implementation in laboratory of real architectures and protocols, avoiding utilizing real networks and in a controlled environment. We developed a broadband satellite real-time emulation platform called SNEP, designed to match the DVB-RCS European standards. The SNEP reproduces with great details the architecture and behavior of a real satellite broadband network, where it is possible to attach end-user PCs and use real protocols and applications. In this way, real network applications can be benchmarked in laboratory as in the real scenario of broadband satellite communications, at the same time proposing alternative solutions and optimizations. Furthermore with the SNEP the integration of satellite platforms with further terrestrial networks is also possible, both real and simulated/emulated, in order to extend the scope for testing.

Keywords: DVB-RCS, Broadband Satellite networks, IP, testbed emulation.

1   Satellite Network Emulation Platform (SNEP)

The SNEP is a cluster of PCs designed to reproduce the characteristics of access to a real Satellite Broadband Network, compliant with the DVB-RCS standards [1]. In particular, one side of the SNEP contains the Network Control Center (NCC)/Gateway-HUB functionalities of the satellite network, and can be connected to the Internet. The other side includes emulated Satellite Terminals (ST, or satellite modems) and user terminals, where applications and real protocols and external hardware are installed. A simplified architecture of the testbed is presented in fig. 1. The whole emulator is built with several virtual machines into a Virtual Environment, and can fully emulate several concurrent Satellite Terminals. Each machine can be connected to resemble the Satellite System real architecture (star/mesh), and performs the same logical operations to recreate the behavior of the real system (e.g., ST is performing login and sync operations, bandwidth on demand and traffic classification/shaping). All lower layers models (e.g., physical delay, interferences, etc.) has been evaluated offline and included in the platform as IP level operations.

T. Korakis, M. Zink, and M. Ott (Eds.): TridentCom 2012, LNICST 44, pp. 1–2, 2012.

Satellite Network Emulation Platform

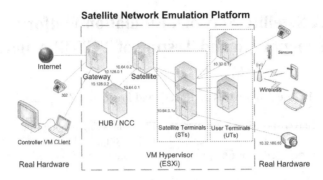

Fig. 1. SNEP logical architecture with real hardware interconnections

The SNEP in particular reproduces all signaling and effects of Bandwidth on Demand used in DVB-RCS to optimize the bandwidth utilization at the cost of introducing additional access delays (which can be much greater than 1 s). The Bandwidth on demand (called DAMA) and all other simulated blocks (error model, QoS, MAC framing and encapsulation, etc.) greatly impact on TCP/IP applications and protocols, than can underperform or misbehave in such challenging environment.

2   TCP/IP Applications Testing on the SNEP Platform

Since the SNEP testbed gives the possibility of controlling and monitoring all the system parameters (not only at network layer, but also below), one of its application can be the execution of real commercial applications (e.g., teleconferencing with Skype), to be assessed and validated before the use on a real system. In addition, the platform has been lately used to verify the impact of cyber-attacks (e.g., malware, eavesdropping, DoS from external STs, etc.) to a satellite network. Using the SNEP makes possible to install ad-hoc malware, which is producing TCP/IP unwanted traffic, or alter the behavior of some nodes. In this way it is possible to better understand possible anomalies in the network propose countermeasures and verify their validity. In particular one of the attacks tested deals with security for heterogeneous and inter-operable networks including a satellite segment. The mandatory presence of Performance Enhancing Proxies (PEPs [2]) at the edges of satellite links, justified to improve TCP performance, opens the way to several proxy-related classic attacks. In this case the focus has been on how to implement an Intrusion Detection System (IDS) and develop software countermeasure in strict relation to the emulated satellite environment.

References

1. ETSI, Digital Video Broadcasting (DVB); Interaction Channel for Satellite Distribution Systems, DVB-RCS standard EN 301 790 (2003), http://www.etsi.org/deliver/etsi_en
2. Interoperable Performance Enhancing Proxy, SatLabs Group, ESA, Air Interface Specifications (2005),
   http://satlabs.org/pdf/I-PEP_Specification_Issue_1a.pdf

GAIA Extended Research Infrastructure: Sensing, Connecting, and Processing the Real World

Pedro Martinez-Julia, Antonio J. Jara, and Antonio F. Skarmeta

Department of Communication and Information Engineering
University of Murcia, 30100, Murcia, Spain
{pedromj,jara,skarmeta}@um.es

Abstract. The GAIA Extended Research Infrastructure is located at the southeast of Spain. It targets the research of Future Internet architectures and comprises several facilities from the University of Murcia and the Spanish government. It offers a vertical infrastructure, composed of a backend with high capacity of data storage, communication, and processing, together with a frontend with an extended set of multidisciplinary testbeds, deployments, and living labs for the ubiquitous monitoring, sensing, and processing. That said, it offers a highly flexible framework for experimentation with architectures and protocols for the Future Internet. In fact, it has been used in many research projects to evaluate their outputs from the communications and telematics point of view.

Keywords: Research, Experimentation, Testbed, Living Labs, Future Internet.

1 Infrastructure Description

The GAIA Extended Research Infrastructure, as illustrated in Figure 1, is composed of several deployments, living labs, and multidisciplinary scenarios based on mobile communications, ubiquitous computing and Internet of Things (IoT). All of them are focused on the Future Internet and supported by our backend infrastructure.

The backend, as depicted in the inner sub-figure of Figure 1, is built by a computer cluster of 22 nodes with high processing capacity, connected to a storage area network (SAN) to provide high capacity/speed remote storage based on the Fiber Channel technology. The SAN is provisioned with a total capacity of 2 TiB.

In addition, the GAIA infrastructure offers many experimentation machines, interconnected by a Gigabit Ethernet (GE) network. Moreover, the experimentation infrastructure has a dedicated CWDM network to evaluate elements destined to backbone networks. Furthermore, the infrastructure also has a WiMAX network deployed throughout the university campus and connected to the main network by dedicated VLANs.

Apart from the central GAIA facilities, the research infrastructure is extended with a set of multidisciplinary deployments focused on sensor networks and monitoring platforms. They target Intelligent Transport Systems, environmental monitoring, mobile health, and buildings automation. Specifically, these deployments are:

- Building Automation: Many facilities, including a complete building from the Fuente Alamo Technology Park (FATP), are managed by over 50 multiprotocol cards developed by our research lab. These platforms are focused on energy sustainability to reach positive-net building with the deployed solar power plants.

T. Korakis, M. Zink, and M. Ott (Eds.): TridentCom 2012, LNICST 44, pp. 3–4, 2012.

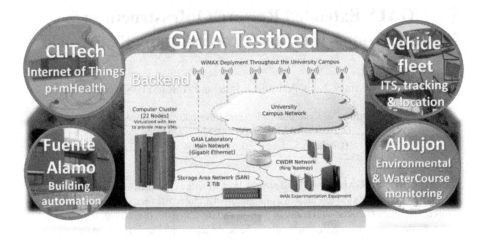

Fig. 1. GAIA extended infrastructure with the living labs and deployments

- Internet of Things (IoT): Our building at FATP also presents an IoT network with a weather station, 20 parking spots, 20 air-quality sensors located at the streetlights, 50 environmental sensors (temperature, humidity, pressure), and 50 activity sensors.
- Environmental Monitoring: We have a real-time monitoring system for the main drainage basin of the watercourse (in Albujon), covering an area of $550km^2$. These platforms are mainly focused on watercourse improvement and flood forecast.
- Clinical Technology: The clinical research lab is also located at FATP, in two dedicated rooms: an Ambient Assisted Living room with 15 personal and wearable clinical devices, and a hospital room with 5 patient monitors.
- Vehicle fleet: The vehicle fleet of the University of Murcia, composed of 48 cars destined to personnel mobility and various internal services of the university, has integrated a platform for location and tracking developed and interconnected with our research lab. For instance, this permits us to track the vehicles when experimenting with WiMAX mobility scenarios.

Finally, it is worth to mention that this infrastructure has been used for many EU projects, like SWIFT and DAIDALOS, and it is currently used for experimentation within the IoT6 project and prospectively within the OpenLab project.

Acknowledgments. This work is partially supported by the European Commission's Seventh Framework Programme (FP7/2007-2013) project GN3, by the Ministry of Education of Spain under the FPU program grant AP2010-0576, by the Program for Research Groups of Excellence of the Séneca Foundation under grant 04552/GERM/06, and the European Regional Development Fund (ERDF) in the frame of Proces@2 (PCT-430000-2010-006) and LABCONECT@2 (PCT-430000-2010-005) grants.

MTT CropInfra

Ari Ronkainen, Frederick Teye, Markku Koistinen, Jere Kaivosoja, Liisa Pesonen,
and Pasi Suomi

MTT Agrifood Research Finland, Vakolantie 55, FI-03400 Vihti, Finland
ari.ronkainen@mtt.fi

Abstract. CropInfra is a development and testing platform for future agricultural production, information and knowledge management infrastructure.

1 History and Motivation of MTT CropInfra

Farmers around the world and especially in the western world have for decades faced growing pressure to increase the efficiency of their production, because of rising prices in production inputs and environmental requirements. Administrative tasks have also increased the work load of the farmer. Recently also the food processing and retail industry and consumers are imposing new and continuous requirements for producers to produce more sustainable products and to provide information about the products for the food production chain as well as to consumers.

To manage resources efficiently, the ideology of precision farming was formed. In precision farming each production unit, is treated individually according to its needs. Precision agriculture has not made a true breakthrough. A reason for this is the lack of efficient data management, equipment interoperability and knowledge models to take advantage of precision agriculture machinery.

A Nordic InfoXT project studied the infrastructure needs for agricultural production and precision farming. The project proposed a web based distributed and networked production infrastructure. [1] The description of this infrastructure laid the ground work for CropInfra platform.

2 Description of MTT CropInfra

CropInfra is constructed at MTT Vakola's farm, which is a research farm located in the Southern Finland. MTT Vakola's farm has 150 ha arable farm that produces cereals and silage grass. CropInfra infrastructure consists of MTT Vakola's research and testing infrastructure; MTT Vakola's fields and farming machinery, Soil weather sensor network and the local monitoring sensor networks.

Research outputs produced in MTT are implemented into CropInfra platform to be tested in, and used in actual farming operations. These implementations include outputs from the machine automation research as well as results of information and knowledge management research.

T. Korakis, M. Zink, and M. Ott (Eds.): TridentCom 2012, LNICST 44, pp. 5–6, 2012.

CropInfra platform is used to gather and store information about field operations and environment, like the fertility of the land, the state of the land, meteorological information, water flows, and nutrients in leaching waters. CropInfra platform is also used to plan farming operations. Specific services are created to merge, aggregate and utilize the collected farm data, an example is the plant decease forecast and alarm service. CropInfra platform also assists in execution of farming operations. CropInfra platform stores and distributes work tasks to farm machinery, monitors and documents the execution of given tasks, creating data to be used in planning of the future farming operations. The massive work-data collection makes it possible to simulate, test and develop different data modeling, proofing, refining, filtering and aggregation methods and systems. Also, the level of information and performance accuracy can be studied.

Principles of networked systems in farm management information systems were further studied in European FutureFarm project. The Project concluded that the future system will be distributed system of services and repositories. [2]

CropInfra's information management is built according to SOA-principles as a distributed networked system, as suggested by research views. In CropInfra data is collected into databases and a web service layer is built on top of these databases. Web services are tailored and used to create assisting services for planning, development and execution of farming operations, which are required for enabling precision agriculture practices. Figure 1 illustrates structure and functionalities of MTT CropInfra information infrastructure.

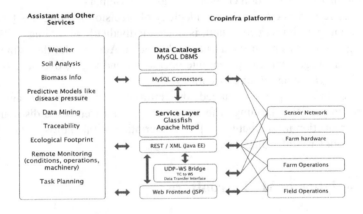

Fig. 1. MTT CropInfra platform information infrastructure and services

References

1. Pesonen, et al.: InfoXT - User-centric mobile information management in automated plant production. Nordic Innovation Centre (2008)
2. Pesonen, et. al.: Final report and documentation specifications of FMIS, FutureFarm Deliverable (2011), http://www.futurefarm.eu/system/files/ FFD3.7_Final_Rep_Doc_Spec_Final_0.pdf

The IBBT w-iLab.t: A Large-Scale Generic Experimentation Facility for Heterogeneous Wireless Networks

Stefan Bouckaert, Bart Jooris, Pieter Becue,
Ingrid Moerman, and Piet Demeester

IBBT - Ghent University, Gaston Crommenlaan 8 Bus 201, 9050 Ghent, Belgium
stefan.bouckaert@intec.ugent.be

Abstract. The w-iLab.t is a large-scale generic wireless experimentation facility. Over 260 wireless nodes are installed at two different locations. Every single wireless node is equipped with multiple wireless technologies, namely IEEE 802.15.4, Wi-Fi a/b/g(/n), and on some devices also Bluetooth. Additionally, w-iLab.t provides access to software defined radio platforms and also uses them to characterize the wireless environment during an experiment. The w-iLab.t flexibility and its tools enable experimenters to design and schedule a wide range of wireless experiments, and to collect and process results in a user-friendly way.

Keywords: experimentation, wireless, sensor, mesh, Wi-Fi, cognitive, testbed.

1 Hardware and Tools Available in w-iLab.t

There are two operational testbed locations in w-iLab.t. The biggest installation, w-iLab.t Office, hosts wireless hardware on 200 locations spread across three floors of an office environment in Ghent, Belgium. In a more recent deployment in Zwijnaarde (close to Ghent), another 60 fixed and 20 mobile nodes are located in an unmanned utility room. A schematic overview of the Zwijnaarde architecture is provided in Figure 1. The w-iLab.t Office has a similar architecture but uses power over Ethernet in the control network. The figure shows the hardware available at every location: an embedded PC that doubles as Wi-Fi node with two wireless interfaces, (at least) one 802.15.4 sensor node, and a so-called 'environment emulator', which can be used for advanced control and monitoring of the sensor node (including power emulation, analog/digital IO, synchronized logging of results). The nodes in the Zwijnaarde testbed are additionally equipped with a Bluetooth 3.0 interface. Experimenters can choose to use any one of the available interfaces of the wireless nodes (or use of multiple interfaces simultaneously) during their experiments, in any way (e.g. for Wi-Fi: station, client, ad-hoc, custom driver,...). In the scope of the FP7-CREW project [www.crew-project.eu], a number of cognitive radio platforms and spectrum scanners have been made available in Zwijnaarde. While in the office environment, the wireless medium is also used for day-to-day activities of the employees (wireless LAN, DECT, microwave ovens), there is very limited or no wireless activity in Zwijnaarde.

T. Korakis, M. Zink, and M. Ott (Eds.): TridentCom 2012, LNICST 44, pp. 7–8, 2012.
© Institute for Computer Sciences, Social Informatics and Telecommunications Engineering 2012

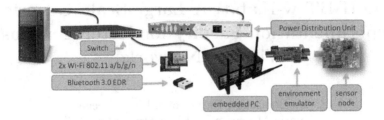

Fig. 1. Architecture of the w-iLab.t Zwijnaarde (simplified; only 1 node is shown)

In addition to the hardware, w-iLab.t offers a set of tools to experimenters, supporting the entire experimentation lifecycle: installation of the devices (images for the embedded PC and/or firmware for the sensor nodes), configuration of the wireless nodes, scheduling experiments, event-based interaction during experiments (e.g. emulate power failure, shut down node, trigger an event on the I/O pins of the sensor node), collecting and storing of results (this is a generic system, configurable by the experimenter), and processing and visualizing results (2D graphs and/or visualization on a testbed map). The w-iLab.t Office tools are based on Motelab software [http://motelab.eecs.harvard.edu/] but were extended to support more advanced sensor node through support for the environment emulator, and to support Wi-Fi enabled experiments. The Zwijnaarde testbed tools are based on OMF [http://omf.mytestbed.net/]; OMF and the w-iLab.t OMF updates are available as open source software.

2   Use of w-iLab.t and Access Info

While it is impossible to list all possibilities of w-iLab.t in this abstract, it is important to understand that the w-iLab.t is called a generic testbed, because the configuration possibilities allow the experimenter to use the testbed for 'any' (wireless) application. As a rule of thumb: whatever experiment an experimenter would be able to execute using the testbed hardware and his/her own laptop on his/her desk, can also be executed on the w-iLab.t in an organized way. Similarly, any type of data that could be collected from a wireless networking set-up e.g. during a small-scale experiment on an experimenter's desk, can in nearly all cases also be effortlessly collected from a large-scale set-up on the w-iLab.t testbed.

The w-iLab.t testbed control interface, nodes and tools are remotely accessible over the Internet via an OpenVPN connection. Use of w-iLab.t is free of charge for non-commercial use. Commercial use is possible, but other terms may apply. For more information and to apply for an account, please consult the iLab.t homepage http://ilabt.ibbt.be, the CREW project's information portal at www.crew-project.eu/portal/wilabdoc, or contact the authors.

The research leading to these results has received funding from various national funds, and from the European Union's Seventh Framework Programme (FP7/2007-2013) under grant agreements nr 258301 (CREW) and nr 287581 (OpenLab).

UMA Testing Facility

Almudena Díaz Zayas[1], Francisco Javier Rivas[2], and Pedro Merino Gomez[1]

[1] Dpto. de Lenguajes y Ciencias de la Computación, University of Malaga, Spain
almudiaz,pedro@lcc.uma.es
[2] AT4 Wireless, System Division, Malaga, Spain
fjrivas@at4wireless.com

Abstract. UMA (University of Malaga) is developing a testing facility to provide support for the complete development process of Internet services in mobile networks. The platform enables the execution of data services on instrumented mobiles and will offer a remote access to carry out unattended measurement campaigns in commercial and emulated cellular networks. The facility mainly targets data connectivity and performance over cellular networks (GSM, GPRS, UMTS, HSPA and LTE), mobility procedure analysis, IP traffic monitoring, energy consumption and location.

Keywords: cellular networks, performance measurements, quality of service, experimental testbed.

1 Introduction

In this paper we introduce the experimental testbed implemented by our research group[1] to carry out mobile experiments in a real context and to extract the correlation between radios access configurations and QoS parameters perceived at the application level. The execution of exhaustive measurements campaigns using this testbed will enable the identification of specific performance counters and used cases for QoS and QoE optimization in mobile networks [1].

Concretely UMA testbed is expected to be used in the following scenarios:

- to measure KPI (Key Performance Indicators) related to radio access, applications performance and QoS perceived by final users
- to support the testing of new radio access configurations
- to deploy experiments in live cellular network to test the performance of new services, applications and mobile application protocols
- to evaluate the performance of LTE as radio access technology in FI-PPP scenarios.

2 Testbed Configuration

As we can see in Figure 1, the testbed include an eNodeB emulator which provides high performance protocol and radio capabilities to emulate a LTE access

---

[1] This work has been funded by Spanish projects TIN 2008-05932 and WITLE2 IDI-20090382, by the Andalusian project P07-TIC3131 and ERDF from the European Commission.

T. Korakis, M. Zink, and M. Ott (Eds.): TridentCom 2012, LNICST 44, pp. 9–10, 2012.

network, COST mobile devices where new applications, services and protocols can
be deployed, servers for deploying services, monitoring tools and post-processing
facilities.

The emulator supports the connections of real LTE devices and the transport
of IP traffic generated by commercial applications.It also includes features such
as emulation of channel propagation that allows modeling fading and additive
white gaussian noise impairments and configuration of cell load, in addition to
a high degree of configurability of the LTE stack. The COST devices includes
monitoring tools developed by UMA. The monitoring software is available for
Symbian [2], Android[3] and Blackberry OS platforms. Current functionality
focuses on the monitoring of network parameters, data traffic, battery and location. Mobile devices can be connected to commercial cellular networks deployed
in Spain or to the LTE base station emulator.

Post-processing tools available at the UMA facility enable the testing and
identification of IP connectivity issues in cellular connections, objectives and
subjective performance parameters.

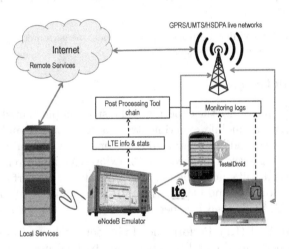

Fig. 1. UMA testing facility setup

References

1. Díaz, A., Merino, P., Rivas, F.J.: Test Environment for QoS Testing of VoIP over
   LTE. In: IEEE/IFIP Network operations and management Symposium (NOMS)
   (April 2012)
2. Díaz, A., Merino, P., Rivas, F.J.: Mobile Application Profiling for Connected Mobile
   Devices. IEEE Pervasive Computing, 54–61 (January-March 2010)
3. Alvarez, A., Díaz, A., Merino, P., Rivas, F.J.: Field measurements of mobile services
   with Android smartphones. In: IEEE Consumer Communications and Networking
   Conference, CCNC (2012)

Infrastructure Overview with Focus on Experimental Facility

Rudolf Vohnout, Lada Altmannova, Stanislav Sima, and Pavel Skoda

CESNET z.s.p.o., Optical Networks Department,
Zikova 4, 1600 Prague, Czech Republic
{rudolf.vohnout,lada.altmannova,stanislav.sima,
pavel.skoda}@cesnet.cz

Abstract. CESNET's main role is to run, maintain and provide services for users of Czech NREN called CESNET2. It has more than 5 thousand kilometres of leased fibres of which 360 kilometres are represented by the Experimental Facility. Connection to other NRENs (mostly represented by GÉANT members) has capacity of 10Gbit, with exception of cz.NIC, where CESNET has 2x 10Gbit. Beyond this, CESNET also operates single fibre bidirectional transmission lines and offer several advanced services, mostly coming from its R&D activities. One example could be photonic service, based on pure fibre optic network advantages. Services such as wireless, security, storage, grid and others are mostly represented by particular CESNET departments.

Keywords: Experimental Facility, Testbed, CESNET, Optics, Networking, NREN, Czech, Photonic, Research.

1 Introduction

CESNET was established in 1996 as non-profit association of legal entities (represented by all public Universities and Czech Academy of Sciences). It operates Czech NREN and Dark Fibre Experimental Facility. It has high optical fibre density among NRENs of about 65 fibre meters per square kilometre. Production network covers more than 4700 km of all leased fibres. The rest belongs to the Experimental Facility, which will be explained in greater detail later on. About one thousand kilometres of all leased fibres are single bidirectional transmission fibres. For the detailed topology scheme see Figure 1. CESNET also offers some advanced services based on photonic transmissions (see chapter 3).

2 CESNET Infrastructure

Main connection to GÉANT, which node CESNET hosts directly in its HQ in Prague has capacity of 10Gbit. Other key NRENs have the same connection speed to Czech NREN, including SANET (.sk), ACONET (.at) and PIONIER (.pl). To another Czech ISPs, CESNET is peering with 2x 10Gbit through NIX.cz association. CESNET

T. Korakis, M. Zink, and M. Ott (Eds.): TridentCom 2012, LNICST 44, pp. 11–17, 2012.

experimental facility connection to GLIF has also 10Gbps. GLIF helps CESNET not only to promote advantages and importance of photonic services but also with research in lambda networking. Overseas connection to US has capacity of 2,5Gbps at the time of writing. CESNET infrastructure is made of leased dark fibres. They are lighted up by Open DWDM system designed and developed in CESNET (CzechLight family) or by Cisco.

Big advantage of the fully leased fibre network is that CESNET does not have to maintain and take care of the fibres. But of course CESNET has its 24/7 monitoring services, which supervises the link states.

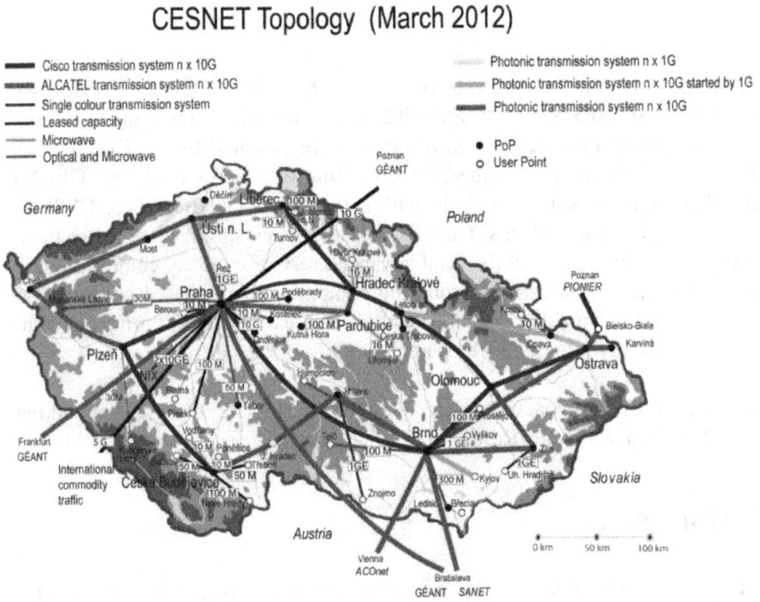

Fig. 1. CESNET Topology

CESNET was also one the first propagators of single fibre bidirectional transmission (hereafter "SFBC"), saving costs up to 40%, while keeping the same performance for typical NREN traffic. This approach can be used in case of lack of fibres and also as a backup solution to access provider's POPs. There are more than 1000 km of these lines in the topology. CESNET started with SFBC back in 2002, when proved its functionality for the first time.

Cross border fibres started back in 2004, while making significant contribution on cross border experiments such as atomic clock synchronization.

NREN infrastructure project is called CESNET large infrastructure, which will be connected to other e-infrastructure projects like those which are part of ESFRI infrastructure roadmap. Because of this, CESNET infrastructure is under improvement, started with upgrading of its national GRID infrastructure and PoPs main DWDM devices. One example could be ESFRI infrastructure for biological data called project called ELIXIR.

2.1   CzechLight Devices and Optical Lab

CzechLight (hereafter "CL") is a trademark for CESNET's devices intend to use in optical networks. It is outcome of its optical R&D activities. They include range of optical amplifiers (based on EDFA), CL Raman amplifiers (only for long distances and not widely used), fully tuneable chromatic dispersion compensators and photonics cross-connects (optical switches).

Department of Optical Networks also has two optical labs for its research purposes. Here the newly developed devices are tested and also this lab is used to do real network simulations, signal quality, chromatic dispersion and signal attenuation monitoring. This lab could be considered as a part of CESNET's Experimental Facility (more in chapter 4).

3   Advanced Services

In cooperation with GEÁNT CESNET started to promote term "photonic service" which leads to the new type of advanced service based on pure photonics. It covers critical and "real-time" applications in areas of metrology, seismology, remote instrument control and other emergency usage. Generally all advanced services that need fixed and low latency. Another example of new type services can be "lit fibre", which is based on CL devices family. Customer can order lit fibre, fully lighted up by CL devices and can use it for various tests and new technology prototypes verification. The photonic services could be user controlled by using fully tuneable CL devices.

The application area where CESNET network could benefit in and use its gained experience from GN3 activities is ENVIROFI case project (its Atmospheric Condition part respectively) of FI-PPP. However, CESNET its self does not have experience in "smart" project scenarios. Its infrastructure is prepared for these issues, but in most cases these applications also require mobile network. CESNET does not own or lease such kind of networks. On the other hand, it is an issue that is being under consideration at the time of writing.

Other services focus on transparent L2 like Carrier Ethernet. Common services includes Eduroam wireless network[1], data storage infrastructure and network security group called CSIRT. This security group monitors and resolves security incidents in whole AS 2852. Some of common security issues are:

- Intensive Scanning.
- Spam.
- Copyright issues.
- Phishing

---

[1] http://eduroam.cz/doku.php?id=en:start

CESNET also has its dedicated GRID infrastructure called "Metacentrum"[2]. At the time of writing it consists of more than 4000 cores overall. Approximately half of them belong to CESNET, half to connected organizations. Its purpose is to offer computation power and software resources to CESNET users and members. Software installations cover those which allow parallelism and other functionalities which could be beneficial in various research areas (bioinformatics, computation chemistry etc.). Hardware equipment is heterogeneous to be more flexible to user and software needs. Metacentrum infrastructure and its connected institutions can be found in the following figure.

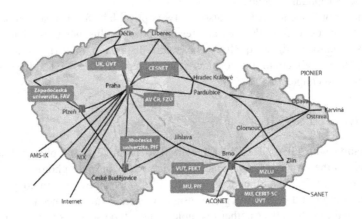

Fig. 2. Metacentrum Infrastructure

3.1   Certain Experiments

Highly accurate clock synchronization has been demonstrated to show potential of modern photonic networks. As written in [1], accuracy of 1 ns has been archived over distance of more than 500 km without OEO in the path and over production DWDM network. This Czech-Austrian experiment has been done between CESNET and its counterpart ACOnet and relied on prototypes of time signal transfer adapters developed by CESNET. Involved national time and frequency labs in Prague and Vienna: IPE (Institute of Photonics and Electronics of Academy of Sciences of the Czech Republic) and BEV (Bundesamt für Eich- und Vermessungswesen). The development of methods for accurate time signal transfer and the research into all-optical networks are parts of research activities put through by CESNET within the framework of its research project Optical National Research Network and Its New Applications.

Another demonstration of low-latency photonic service was unique real-time 3D Full HD stereo broadcast of a kidney surgery performed by a "da Vinci robot" [2].

---

[2] http://www.metacentrum.cz/en/

This experiment has been made between Masaryk Hospital in Ústí nad Labem and CESNET headquarter in Prague. The broadcast went through 10-gigabit link with fibre distance over 130 km and it was a part of standard production infrastructure. Signal delay along the transmission stream was less than 1 ms, enabling a truly real-time 3D Full HD stereo broadcast. In this experiment the images from the surgery were produced by CESNET's F10 AS3D ProjectionDesign stereo-projector.

4   Experimental Facility

CESNET testbed[3] consists of fully leased open dark fibres for experimental usage and testing of new technologies. They are lighted up by CL devices and the infrastructure has connection of 10Gbps to GLIF. It also has 10G connection to Netherland's Netherlight, which is one of GLIF Open Lightpath Exchanges. CESNET also provides dedicated Experimental Facility (hereafter "EF") for Physicists and thank to its Large Infrastructure project it is open and ready to provide means for interconnection of any modern European infrastructure project.

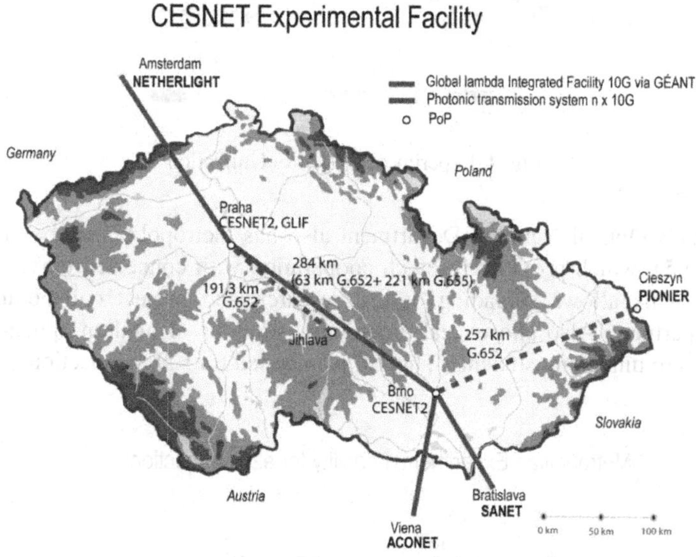

Fig. 3. Experimental Facility

The facility is now mainly used for testing of new photonic devices developed by CESNET and also for testing of new network technologies in cooperation with our partners and in international research projects. 100Gbps Alcatel-Lucent transmission system has been tested recently [3]. These test proved that CESNET optical

---

[3] CESNET prefers to use term "Experimental Facility", which refers to multi-purpose, long term and less technology/vendor dependent than regular testbed.

infrastructure is prepared to adopt 100GB signal speed, not only on its backbone lines [4].

CESNET uses EF for:

- Testing of new CL devices and new photonic products.
- Building and operation of testbeds.
- Disruptive experiments with new services and products before deployment.
- Support of experiments with new applications and research.
- Collaboration.
- First mile solutions testing.

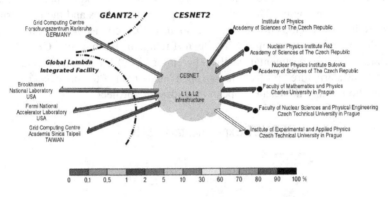

Fig. 4. Experimental Facility Utilization

CESNET's Optical Network Department also has metropolitan testbed in Prague (see Figure 5), which provides research cooperation with connected universities and their labs. This allows spreading optical research and project collaboration with CESNET partners. Also allows real-time demonstrations of modern optical network possibilities to university students. This EF is intended for E2E connections.

Metropolitan Experimental Facility for e2e connections

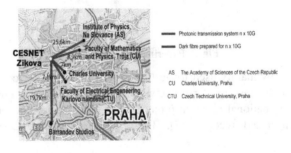

Fig. 5. Metropolitan Experimental Facility in Prague

References

[1] A new method of accurate time signal transfer demonstrates the capabilities of all-optical networks [online]. Press Release, (c) 1996–2012 CESNET z. s. p. o., Prague (January 04, 2010), http://www.ces.net/doc/press/2010/pr100401.html (cit. May 10, 2012)

[2] 3D Full HD Broadcast from a Robotic Surgery [online] Press Release, © 1996–2012 CESNET z. s. p. o., Prague (June 18, 2010), http://www.ces.net/doc/press/2010/pr100618.html (cit. May 11, 2012)

[3] Parallel 100 Gbps transmissions in CESNET2 network [online]. Press Release, © 1996–2012 CESNET z. s. p. o., Prague (September 9, 2011), http://www.ces.net/doc/press/2011/pr110909.html (cit. May 12, 2012]

[4] Pavel, Š., Radil, J., Vojtěch, J., Hůla, M.: Tests of 100 Gb/s [online]. CESNET Technical Reports 4/2011. © 1996–2012 CESNET z. s. p. o., Prague (2011), http://www.cesnet.cz/doc/techzpravy/2011/tests-100g/ (cit. May 13, 2012)

[5] Vojtěch, J., Lada Altmannová, M., Hůla, J., Radil, Síma, Š.,Škoda, P.; Single Fibre Bidirectional Transmission [online]. WDM Systems Summit 2011. © CESNET (April 07, 2011), http://czechlight.cesnet.cz/documents/publications/fiber-optics/2011/10_CESNET_Vojtech-SingleFibreBidirectionalTransmission.ppt

LTE Emulation over Wired Ethernet

Roman Chertov, Joseph Kim, and Jiayu Chen

The Aerospace Corporation
2310 E. El Segundo Blvd
El Segundo CA 90245, USA
{Roman.O.Chertov,Joseph.Y.Kim,Jiayu.Chen}@aero.org

Abstract. Long-Term Evolution (LTE) standard merges an all IP voice and data communications with dynamic spectrum resource scheduling. The resource scheduler must balance the QoS requirements, traffic demands, and physical channel conditions to create desirable wireless end-user performance. The purpose of our research and the focus of this paper is a development of a unified testbed platform based on Emulab that can be used to examine the key aspects of an LTE system in realtime, including real time uplink and downlink scheduling, QoS parameters, and Android end-user applications. Our validation studies demonstrate that the testbed is capable of achieving delay, loss, and jitter that can be associated with an LTE communication system, and can be easily used to study a variety of LTE scheduling algorithms.

1 Introduction

Over the past several years, mobile carriers began the transition towards the 3rd Generation Partnership Project (3GPP) Long-Term Evolution (LTE) standard. The LTE standard relies on Orthogonal Frequency-Division Multiple Access (OFDMA) for the downlink radio access. The uplink in LTE utilizes the Single-Carrier FDMA (SC-FDMA) radio access scheme. Both the uplink and the downlink can support multiple users concurrently by allowing the users to be partitioned in time and frequency. A centralized resource scheduler is required to create the time and frequency mappings for the users and the base station for the uplink and the downlink. LTE differs from the previous 3GPP standards as all of the communications are Internet Protocol (IP)-based, including the regular phone calls. The all-IP based nature of the communications requires Quality of Service (QoS) to ensure that realtime traffic such as voice gets priority over non-realtime traffic such as HyperText Transfer Protocol (HTTP). This feature of LTE means that the scheduler must be cross-layer-aware and must consider physical channel conditions as well as the Layer 3 QoS requirements.

A great breadth of research has been conducted regarding LTE up and downlink scheduling. However, the majority of works rely either on pure simulation [1,2] or on specialized hardware emulators [3]. The problem with simulation approaches is that the simulation does not allow the complete high-fidelity simulation of a real-world LTE system (end users, services, base station, etc.) as

T. Korakis, M. Zink, and M. Ott (Eds.): TridentCom 2012, LNICST 44, pp. 18–32, 2012.

the complexity severely impacts validation and simulation times. In addition, a simulation approach requires rewriting the handset and server applications for the simulation environment. Naturally, this approach requires extensive validation to ensure that the rewritten applications follow the same behavior as their real-world counter parts. The hardware-based emulation solutions can emulate the entire system, but the hardware settings might be closed to the experimenter because of the proprietary nature of the hardware emulator. Hardware emulation systems typically suffer from scalability problems as they are primarily designed for testing and troubleshooting. Finally, the emulation hardware can be prohibitively expensive to some experimenters. In order to address these two limitations, we sought to create an LTE emulation system that incorporates (1) end-user handset IP stacks and applications, (2) QoS management, (3) real-world services, and (4) up/downlink LTE scheduling. Finally, the emulation system must allow for repeatable and reproducible experiments, use commodity hardware, and scale to several hundred or more users.

An LTE network is a system of systems, where the individual systems can have a direct impact on other systems. Hence, we were interested in creating a complete LTE emulator that could support the following types of scenarios: "How would an Android application, or the cloud service X react to the QoS or scheduler changes on the up/down LTE link?" "What is an impact of application Y in a heavily congested cell?" "What are the measurable impacts of multicast video distribution in an LTE network?" "What is an optimal QoS and pricing strategy for a carrier for a given network and end-user applications?"

As the foundation for the emulator, we have chosen to use the Emulab (http://www.emulab.net) [4] testbed platform from University of Utah. The testbed is composed of several hundred commodity PCs with multiple network cards and Cisco 6000 series enterprise switches. The high degree of connectivity between the commodity PCs coupled with custom switch Virtual Local Area Network (VLAN) management software allows experimenters to create arbitrary networks. Because of this capability, the Emulab testbed is well known in the networking community for its flexibility in creating arbitrary network topologies and its ability to conduct repeatable and reproducible experiments. Another notable feature of Emulab is that the testbed management source code is freely available for download, meaning that anybody can create an Emulab instance given sufficient hardware.

The other components of our LTE emulator were built around the Click Modular Router [5] (referred as Click from now on), Android Software Development Kit (SDK), and the Linux operating system. All of the chosen components are open source, thus allowing us to perform any necessary modifications. The resulting LTE emulation system is capable of running Android-based "soft" handsets, using highly configurable QoS settings, utilizing any Linux-based service (httpd, Session Initiation Protocol (SIP) proxy, etc.), and performing realtime uplink and downlink LTE scheduling duties. The majority of this paper focuses on the emulator architecture and the validation of the emulator. However, we did perform several showcase experiments that demonstrate the interaction between the LTE uplink scheduling, QoS settings, and the end-user application performance.

The remainder of the paper is organized as follows. Section 2 provides an overview of the related work. Section 3 describes our emulation architecture. Section 4 tests the fidelity of the emulation. Section 5 presents the results of our experiments. Finally, Section 6 concludes this paper.

2 Related Work

Several prominent scientific instrumentation companies such as Rohde & Schwarz, Agilent Technologies, and Nomor Research provide products that can integrate LTE hardware-based emulators with the user-supplied equipment to test end-to-end performance in the LTE environment [6,7,8]. The two main drawbacks of the hardware-based testers are the high price of the devices and the closed nature of the equipment. From a research standpoint, the proprietary nature of the LTE testers can possibly prevent experimenters from implementing and testing their own scheduling algorithms.

The closest works in the literature that is comparable to our LTE emulator is the Mobility Satellite Emulation Testbed (MSET) developed by Chertov et al. [10] and the OpenAir LTE emulator [9]. MSET was primarily designed to emulate single-carrier satellite Time Division Multiple Access (TDMA) links and did not implement a dynamic scheduling scheme that could operate on 10 ms time boundaries. Additionally, MSET did not provide a highly configurable QoS management system that is supported by our LTE emulator. The OpenAir LTE emulator developed by EURECOM is capable of emulating LTE physical and Media Access Control (MAC) layers over Ethernet, but it is more geared towards modeling the radio channel, while our system makes more emphasis on the scheduling aspects of LTE.

3 Architecture

The following section describes the components of the architecture that we have developed to run a complete emulated LTE network on The Aerospace Corporation testbed. Our testbed is based on Emulab [4] and utilizes 150 nodes. Emulab control software allows an experimenter to reserve a number of nodes and create an arbitrary network via Virtual Local Area Network (VLAN) manipulation on the experimental switches, which interconnect the testbed nodes. In addition, each reserved node is solely dedicated to the experiment owner who has root privileges. On Emulab, Base Stations (BSs) and end-user handsets can be implemented by using testbed nodes connected by a Local Area Network (LAN), as shown on Figure 1. In addition, all of the nodes utilize a separate 1 Gbps network interface for control traffic only to ensure that experimental and control packets do not interfere with each other. The rest of the section described the individual components that are necessary to turn an Emulab-type testbed into an LTE emulator.

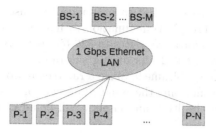

Fig. 1. Emulated LTE topology, where the base station and the end-user handset functions are performed by commodity PCs

3.1   LTE Radio Emulation

Radio emulation is the foremost critical component of our framework. The radio emulator is what allows the access point or the end-user handsets to control the bandwidth, jitter, and latency of the LTE network. In Figures 2(a) and 2(b), the LTE Radio Emulator component is responsible for the LTE radio emulation. Currently, the radio emulator does not model any physical layer parameters such as noise, multipath, etc. The primary function of the radio emulator is to ensure that the right number of bits is sent during an appropriate time slot. However, the radio emulation element can be easily modified to read from scenario files that specify Block Error Rate (BLER) for a given time instance in order to determine if packets need to be corrupted or not. The BLER scenario files can be derived by running physical layer simulations that take into account fading, multipath, antenna parameters and interference over a given time period.

Figure 3 shows a sample 10-subframe LTE uplink schedule where the dark gray blocks denote Transport Block (TB) allocations to a particular user. In an LTE schedule, if a user is assigned a set of K TBs in a frame, then the sum of the transmitted bits can be computed by adding up the usable bits for each

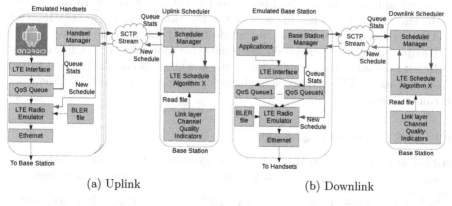

(a) Uplink   (b) Downlink

Fig. 2. End-user handset and base station emulation

TB in the set K. Lets assume that each assigned TB uses the 16 Quadrature Amplitude Modulation (16QAM) modulation with a code rate of $\frac{1}{2}$. This coding when using an LTE waveform translates to 336 bits per TB[1]. This would imply that the user can transmit 672 bits during subframe 0, 1008 bits during subframe 5, and 1344 during subframe 9. Since a radio emulator permits the user or the base station to transmit only the assigned number of bits during the allotted subframes, the bandwidth, jitter, and latency will be affected as a result.

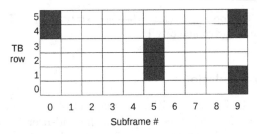

Fig. 3. Sample LTE schedule

We implemented the LTE radio emulation as Click element just like in the previous work on satellite TDMA emulation [10]. The radio emulation element in the emulated handset dequeues bits from an upstream queue only if the current LTE scheduler assigned TB(s) to the current user. The queues in Click are packet-based, hence we implemented an accounting scheme to keep track of how many bits of the current packet have been sent. Once all of the TBs assigned to the current packet have been "sent", the packet is dequeued from the queue and sent over the Ethernet. This accounting approach allows a packet to span several TBs, subframes, or even schedules. Alternatively, a single TB can hold multiple packets if its usable bit volume is high enough. It is easy to see that the time it takes to transmit a given packet is entirely dependent on the LTE scheduler and the allocations it creates for a given user. Therefore, the radio emulator can influence the network effects such as delay and jitter solely based on the schedule allocations just like the real-world LTE network. In this version of the emulator, we did not implement the Hybrid Automatic Repeat Request (HARQ) retransmission scheme, but we do plan to add it in the future.

The downlink can be emulated using the same radio emulation Click element such that the base station emulates only the downlink (packets to be transmitted to the end users). This arrangement allows for a complete LTE emulated network to run on the testbed.

3.2   QoS Queue Management

Instead of using a simple drop-tail Queue, we opted to develop a highly customizable queue management Click element, which is labeled as QoS Queue in

---

[1] $7\frac{symbol}{subcarrier} \times 12\frac{subcarrier}{RB} \times 4\frac{bits}{symbol} * \frac{1}{2} * 2\frac{RB}{TB} = 336\ bits$, (each TB is composed of two Resource Blocks (RB)).

Figures 2(a) and 2(b). The queue management element was designed to allow priority queues based on Differentiated Services Code Point (DSCP) values. The queue management element permits any user-specified mapping of DSCP code points into N priority queues, where queue zero is the highest priority and queue $N-1$ is the lowest. The queues have an adjustable queue depth. Finally, each priority queue can be configured to delete packets that have been enqueued for more than X seconds. This feature can be useful when experimenting with real-time traffic, where packets that have experienced severe queuing delays might as well be dropped. Since the end-user handsets send packets to the base station, the queue management element maintains a set of priority queues only for the base station, as shown in Figure 2(a). On the base station, however, the queue management element creates a set of priority queues for each individual end user as shown in Figure 2(b).

The queue management element is tied to the LTE radio emulator element, such that the radio element pulls the packets out of the highest priority queue first, when the user has been allocated LTE resources. Alternatively, the LTE radio emulator can specify from which queue to dequeue if such information is provided in the schedule. Finally, the queue manager can provide a variety of statistics, such as queue depth, bytes seen, bytes dropped, etc., via the Click read handler.

3.3   Schedule Management

One of the key aspects of an LTE network is the centralized scheduler that creates up and downlink schedules. The scheduler is responsible for responding to user demands and assigning non-overlapping frequency and time resources to the users. In the real-world LTE network, the control channels are used to convey user channel quality conditions and traffic demands to the scheduler. In our emulated LTE architecture, we also utilize a control channel in the form of an Ethernet LAN that is separate from the experimental Ethernet LAN. Figure 2(a) shows the relationship between the end-user emulated handsets and the uplink scheduler. The emulated handsets submit the queue statistics to the uplink scheduler by accessing the Click read handler of the queue management element. The uplink scheduler aggregates all of the individual queue reports and submits them to the currently selected uplink scheduling algorithm. The uplink scheduler considers the aggregated queue statistics, Channel Quality Indication (CQI) values, scheduler parameters (end-user priorities, traffic type preferences, etc.) and then creates a global schedule that is transmitted to the emulated end-user handsets. The emulated end-user handsets in turn install the new schedule such that the LTE radio emulator can follow the new schedule. The downlink schedule management functions in exactly the same fashion. Figure 2(b) shows the relationship between the base station and the downlink scheduler. The CQI values for uplink and downlink can be derived in the same off-line simulation fashion as the BLER values used by the radio emulation element.

The schedule management system is created by using a client and server architecture that relies on Stream Control Transmission Protocol (SCTP) for communication. The handset or the base station managers can interact with the Click elements via the read/write handlers. The scheduler manager's primary goal is to aggregate the data from the clients and then submit the data to a scheduling algorithm. The output of the scheduling algorithm can then be disseminated to the handset or the base station managers. The scheduler manager architecture allows for the scheduling algorithm to be chosen at startup via a command line argument. This feature allows the user to rapidly experiment with a variety of schedulers just by restarting the scheduler manager. We have opted to use SCTP over Transmission Control Protocol (TCP) to ensure that queue aggregation, schedule creation, and schedule dissemination cycle can occur in under 10 ms. Additionally, we disabled the delayed transmissions to force SCTP to transmit the data immediately. This setting change was necessary to achieve the aggregation of end-user traffic demands and creation of a new LTE schedule in the 10 ms time frame.

The schedule management system also has the ability to time-synchronize the handset managers (not applicable for the downlink as there is only one base station). The time synchronization uses a technique similar to the Network Time Protocol (NTP) to measure the offset between the scheduler and the clients [11]. However, the clients do not change their local clocks to match the clock of the server. The clients adjust the start time of the next schedule based on the offset between the server by telling the LTE radio emulation element to either increase or decrease the start time of the next LTE frame. Such an approach can ensure that the clients synchronize their packet transmissions according to the global uplink schedule.

3.4   "Soft" Handsets

As one of the primary goals of our emulation effort was to run real-world cell phone applications, we have installed the Android emulator SDK on our testbed nodes. The Android emulator runs the actual Android firmware on a Qemu (http://www.qemu.org) Advanced RISC Machine (ARM) emulator. When running, the Android soft handset uses Qemu to send packets via the Linux IP stack. Using Click, we created a fake Ethernet device[2] called LTE, which receives all of the packets from the Linux IP stack destined for the experimental IP subnet. In turn, the fake Ethernet device injects packets into the kernel-level Click, which then uses our QoS queue and LTE radio elements to emulate the LTE MAC layer (see Figures 2(a) and 2(b)).

3.5   Admission Control and Mobility

Admission control can be accomplished by having a scheduler for a given base station deny a connection attempt by an end user in case there is a resource shortage. If the experimental scenario specifies that the end user is in reach of

---

[2] `FromHost` Click Modular Router element.

several base stations, then end user can be scripted to try the base stations in order until a connection can be established.

Our architecture allows for creating experiments where the users can migrate from one base station to another and the schedulers for the base station can admit or not admit new users. In our system, base station migration is nothing more than establishing a connection to a scheduler instance that manages a particular base station. In addition, the handset emulator needs to start utilizing an Ethernet MAC that corresponds to a new base station. MAC addressing ensures that the packets will be delivered only to the newly associated base station.

4   Emulator Validation

It was important to ensure, prior to conducting the experiments, that the emulation components produced the expected results. This required running a suite of calibration experiments to ensure that the specified delay, loss, and jitter of a given LTE network were achieved.

4.1   Experimental Layout

For our validation experiments, we have used the topology shown in Figure 1. The topology has 40 testbed nodes that run Fedora14 and use the Android emulator with Android firmware version 2.3.3. Even though the testbed supports 150 nodes, only 40 nodes were available to us as other nodes were down for maintenance or were used by other experimenters. One node serves as a base station. All of the nodes use Click Modular Router 2.0 and use our custom Click elements described in Section 3. For the validation experiments, we have chosen to concentrate on the uplink as it is more challenging from the emulation perspective: forty nodes must perform in unison to abide by the global uplink schedule versus just the base station shaping its own downlink. The schedule manager was configured to check the timing offsets between the base station node and the handset nodes every 500 ms and could adjust the frame offset by as little as 0.01 ms. In addition, an Exponential Moving Average (EMA) was used to keep track of the time offset between the handset node and the base station.

4.2   Validation Results

The uplink LTE emulator can be deemed successful if it achieves timing synchronization between the participants and the correct delay and jitter effects are produced. To test the uplink emulation, we have used a proportional schedule (equal allocation to each handset), shown in Figure 4. The proportional schedule evenly divides an LTE 10-ms frame with 6 TB rows among 30 handsets. Each handset gets two TBs ($\frac{60}{30} = 2$). The schedule in Figure 4 also shows to which

TB row	0	1	2	3	4	5	6	7	8	9
5	2	5	8	11	14	17	20	23	26	29
4	2	5	8	11	14	17	20	23	26	29
3	1	4	7	10	13	16	19	22	25	28
2	1	4	7	10	13	16	19	22	25	28
1	0	3	6	9	12	15	18	21	24	27
0	0	3	6	9	12	15	18	21	24	27

Subframe #

Fig. 4. Proportional LTE schedule that assigns two TBs per handset

handset ID the TBs are assigned. For example, handset IDs 12, 13, and 14 can transmit bits only during the fifth millisecond of the 10-ms frame.

We have used the 16QAM modulation with a code rate of $\frac{1}{2}$ (one of the allowed LTE uplink settings), which equates to 672 bits per handset per frame (see Section 3.1). With a 672-bit allotment, each handset can transmit an 84-byte packet every 10 ms. Even though a proportional scheduler is used, every handset submits its queue statistics to the uplink scheduler, which disseminates the global schedule. This was done to ensure that all parts of the emulation were active.

The nodes that emulated the handsets were configured to transmit 84-byte UDP packets (includes Ethernet/IP/UDP headers) at 200 packets per second to the base station node for 100 seconds. The packet transmission rate was intentionally set too high, to determine if the LTE emulation shaping would take effect. The base station node used Click's `StoreUDPTimeSeqNum` element to embed time stamps into the packets as soon as they arrived and then used `ToDump` element to save the captured packets to disk in Packet CAPture (PCAP) format.

The packet inter-arrival times computed from the base station node's time reference point have the following statistics: mean – 10.0 ms, 5th percentile – 9.97 ms, 50th percentile – 9.985 ms, and 95th percentile – 10.036 ms. The inter-arrival statistics do indeed show that LTE emulation allowed only one packet per handset every 10 ms.

A much more interesting test is to determine if all the 30 handset nodes were synchronized on the uplink, and if the packet arrival times coincided with the global uplink schedule. The packet arrival times of the individual handset nodes were compared against a static repeating 10 ms schedule shown in Figure 4. We computed the time delta between the observed packet arrival time and its logical slot location in the schedule. The time deltas for all 30 handset nodes have the following statistics: mean – 0.279 ms, 5th percentile – 0.108 ms, 50th percentile – 0.23 ms, and 95th percentile – 0.623 ms. Visually, the data can be represented as shown in Figure 5. The numbers and their position represent the IDs of the handset nodes and the time of the packet arrival from that node, the solid vertical lines signify start/end of a 10-ms frame, and the dashed vertical lines signify 1-ms subframes. The data almost exactly matches the schedule shown in Figure 4 except for the time shift of around 0.23 ms (50th percentile time delta). Even though there is a small violation in the schedule, the fact that 30 handset nodes were able to almost exactly synchronize with the global schedule shows great promise in the emulator's capability. In the future, we can improve the timing by using Precision Time Protocol (PTP) or by coupling Global Positioning System (GPS) devices to the testbed nodes [10].

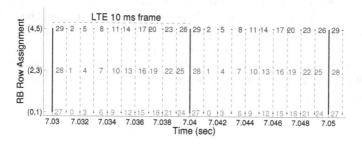

Fig. 5. Packet arrival times overlaid with an uplink LTE schedule

5   Experiments

In this section, we present several uplink experiments that show the interaction between scheduling, QoS, and end-user application performance. For the experiments, we used all 40 handset nodes and used the same LTE parameters as in Section 4, which equates to an uplink capacity of just over 2 Mbps. The primary goal of the experiments was to show that the interactions can be quite significant and warrant more detailed future studies.

5.1   HTTP Performance

To study the performance of HTTP from the end user's perspective, we have written a simple Android application that can time how long it takes to load a given webpage. Using this application and the Android Debug Bridge (ADB), we created a framework where we could instruct a handset to visit a web page, wait until it loads, and log the result to a log file.

As we were using a closed test environment, we developed a suite of nine synthetic web pages that included graphics and text. The pages were sized to mimic the webpage distribution observed by Google crawlers [12]. The base station node was configured to run an Apache web server and was loaded with the synthetic web pages. The handset nodes were configured to visit the web pages at random for 900 seconds, and used an exponential "reading" time with a mean of 30 seconds before visiting the next web page. The "reading" time distribution was taken from the IEEE C802.16m-07/074r1 evaluation document [13].

For this test, we have used two LTE uplink schedulers: proportional and on-demand round robin. Just like in the validation section, the proportional scheduler simply allocates $\lfloor \frac{60}{40} \rfloor$ TBs per handset and does consider the queue reports. On the other hand, the on-demand round robin scheduler allocates the resources to the handsets only if they report non-zero queues. The allocations are performed in a first fit fashion such that the first subframe must get filled before the TBs in the next subframe can be allocated. Finally, the handset scanning order is round robin to ensure fairness.

Figure 6 shows the average, min, and max web page load times when using only 1 Gbps Ethernet, LTE uplink proportional scheduling, and LTE uplink round robin on demand scheduling. It is interesting to see that the web page load times for on-demand LTE scheduling is comparable to the no-emulation results. Not surprisingly, the proportional scheduling does not perform as well, primarily because the resources are assigned to the handset nodes even when no HTTP get requests are issued, thus disallowing active handset nodes to take advantage of the unused resources.

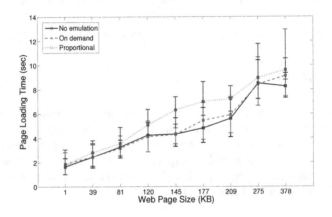

Fig. 6. Web page loading times

5.2   VoIP Performance

As cellular networks are primarily used for voice communications, we have performed several experiments with only VoIP calls. In our experiments, we used a Constant Bit Rate (CBR) application to generate UDP packets such that the packet size and the packet rate was representative of the G.711 codec [14]. The G.711 codec averages around 87 Kbps on Ethernet and the packets cover 20 ms of voice data, which equates to 50, 217-byte (including headers) packets per second. We chose the G.711 codes as it offers relatively high fidelity and can occupy a significant part of the uplink bandwidth.

To generate realistic call duration times observed by a single base station, we used the lognormal distribution with $\mu = 3.287$ and $\sigma = 0.891$, as was observed by F. Barcelo and J. Jordan [15]. We chose the lognormal instead of the recommended lognormal-3 distribution as we wanted to utilize the readily available Perl probability packages. For the call arrival times, we have chosen a Poisson distribution and varied the $\frac{1}{\lambda}$ (inter arrival mean) parameter between

60, 30, and 20 seconds. The expected number of concurrent calls can be derived from the following equation:

$$E[C] = N \times \frac{E[D]}{E[D] + \frac{1}{\lambda}}$$

where $E[D] = e^{\mu + \frac{1}{2}\sigma^2}$. The $\frac{1}{\lambda}$ values of 60, 30, and 20 equate to 16, 22.85, and 26.66 expected concurrent calls, respectively, for our 40-node topology.

Prior to conducting experiments with the LTE uplink emulation, we ran the voice scenario on the testbed for 10 minutes without any emulation using the arrival $\frac{1}{\lambda} = 60$ to measure jitter and loss values. As the VoIP protocol is most sensitive to jitter (inter arrival times) and packet loss ratios, we primarily concentrated on these network statistics. The inter arrival times for the VoIP packets were measured and the following statistics were recorded: mean – 20 ms, 5th percentile – 19.967 ms, 50th percentile – 20.017 ms, and 95th percentile – 20.018 ms. Just as expected, the inter arrival times were almost exactly 20 ms (50 pps) and there were no losses.

Next, we enabled LTE uplink emulation with an on-demand round robin scheduler and configured the queue manager to drop voice packets that sat in the uplink queue for more than one second. Additionally, the uplink queues were sized to hold 64 packets as it is a typical size for many network cards. Table 1 shows the obtained inter arrival times for call arrival $\frac{1}{\lambda}$ values of 60, 30, and 20. It is interesting to note that some losses occurred and that even though the mean inter-arrival values are almost 20 ms, the 5th, 50th, and 95th percentile values indicate increased levels of jitter compared to the pure Ethernet scenario. Scheduling is one of the primary reasons for jitter, as packets cannot be sent from a handset node until the scheduler grants the resources, and this can take 10 ms at a minimum. Additionally, even though the average call volume bandwidth does not exceed the 2 Mbps up link capacity, there can be instances when too many calls are in the system, thus leading to queue-based delays and queue overflows.

5.3 HTTP and VoIP

For the final set of experiments, we have combined HTTP and VoIP traffic. The handset nodes were configured to browse web pages and make VoIP calls as was described in the above sections. The HTTP and VoIP calls were allowed to occur independently of each other to mimic users that can browse and call at the same time.

As the handset nodes were allowed to browse and call at the same time, we have conducted two sets of experiments where we have given priority to VoIP over HTTP and where VoIP and HTTP were treated equally. Just like before, we ran the experiments for 10 minutes where 40 handset nodes requested webpages and made phone calls. To ensure a heavily loaded up link, we have used the call arrival $\frac{1}{\lambda}$ value of 20 sec. Also, the uplink LTE scheduler was configured to provide on-demand round robin allocations, and the queue manager was set to time-out

Table 1. VoIP Inter-Packet Delays (ms)

	Call arrival $\frac{1}{\lambda}$		
	60 sec	30 sec	20 sec
5th	0.998	0.999	0.998
50th	19.968	19.967	19.967
95th	38.968	39.985	40.031
mean	20.344	20.316	20.257
loss ratio	0.015	0.015	0.012

Table 2. VoIP Inter-Packet Delays (ms) in the Presence of HTTP

	Priority	No Priority
5th	0.997	0.995
50th	17.972	19.02
95th	42.979	41.032
mean	20.257	20.505
loss ratio	0.012	0.021

priority traffic after one second. Both of the priority and best-effort queues were configured to allow 64 packets before dropping any additional incoming packets.

Table 2 shows the VoIP packet inter arrival times when VoIP was given priority and when it was treated the same as HTTP. The jitter values for priority and non priority cases are quite similar. The main difference between priority and non priority cases was the loss ratios. As expected, the non priority experiment produced more VoIP packet losses on the uplink. Also, the results in Table 2 are similar to the results in Table 1. The slightly lower 50th percentile values in Table 2 can be attributed to a somewhat higher volume of random VoIP traffic during the experimental runs, which led to an increased amount of jitter.

Figure 7 shows the web page loading times when no VoIP is present, VoIP is given priority, and VoIP has the same priority as HTTP. When VoIP is given priority, the web page load times are considerably longer compared to when no VoIP is present. In addition, HTTP page load times experience a large amount of variance as HTTP get requests can be processed only after all of the VoIP queues have been drained. The HTTP page load times when VoIP was not given priority are similar to when no VoIP was used. This is the case because HTTP traffic on the uplink is primarily composed out of TCP SYN/ACK and HTTP get request messages. Since the HTTP uplink traffic is light, the VoIP loss ratios and jitter values are not significantly impacted, as Table 2 demonstrates. Based on this observation, a cellular provider can choose not to prioritize voice-over HTTP in order to significantly improve web page loading times while not significantly affecting VoIP communications.

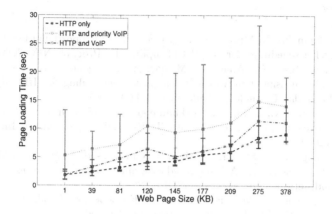

Fig. 7. Web page loading times in the presence of VoIP

6 Conclusion

In this paper, we have described an Emulab-compatible LTE emulation system that relies on commodity PCs and wired Ethernet. The emulation system is capable of emulating the LTE radio, LTE scheduler, QoS management, and the Android handsets and scales with the number of the available PC nodes. The all-encompassing aspect of the system permits experimentation with a wide variety of components: (1) end-user handset IP stacks and applications, (2) QoS management, (3) real-world services, and (4) up/downlink LTE scheduling. Our validation experiments have shown that the LTE emulation system can accurately produce network-level effects that are expected from an LTE setting including data transmissions on 10 ms time boundaries. Finally, our limited set of experiments has shown that scheduling and QoS settings can have a significant impact on end user performance. In our future work, we plan to investigate scheduling approaches that take into consideration CQI and BLER values, expected traffic arrival rates, and QoS settings. We plan to extend the emulator to allow mobility, an HARQ mechanism, and increase the number of possible end users by four fold via Xen virtualization (http://xen.org). Finally, we plan to run experiments that utilize several base stations and allow for user mobility between the stations.

Acknowledgments. This work was supported under The Aerospace Corporation's Independent Research and Development Program. In addition, we would like to thank David Blumenfeld for creating the synthetic web sites used in this paper.

All trademarks, service marks, and trade names are the property of their respective owners.

References

1. Lee, S., Pefkianakis, I., Meyerson, A., Xu, S., Lu, S.: Proportional fair frequency-domain packet scheduling for 3GPP LTE uplink. In: Proc. of INFOCOM (2009)
2. Calabrese, F., Rosa, C., Anas, M., Michaelsen, P., Pedersen, K., Mogensen, P.: Adaptive transmission bandwidth based packet scheduling for LTE uplink. In: Proc. of Vehicular Technology Conference (VTC) (2008)
3. Tappayuthpijarn, K., Liebl, G., Stockhammer, T., Steinbach, E.: Adaptive video streaming over a mobile network with TCP-friendly rate control. In: Proc. of IWCMC (2009)
4. White, B., Lepreau, J., Stoller, L., Ricci, R., Guruprasad, S., Newbold, M., Hibler, M., Barb, C., Joglekar, A.: An integrated experimental environment for distributed systems and networks. In: Proc. of OSDI (2002)
5. Kohler, E., Morris, R., Chen, B., Jannotti, J., Kaashoek, M.F.: The Click Modular Router. Transactions on Computer Systems 18(3) (2000)
6. Rohde, Schwarz, R&S CMW500-PT HSPA+ and LTE Protocol Tester (2011), http://www2.rohde-schwarz.com/product/CMW500-PT.html
7. A. Technologies, E6621A PXT Wireless Communications Test Set (2011), http://www.home.agilent.com/agilent/product.jspxcc=US&lc=eng&ckey=1314599&nid=-33762.752176.00&id=14599cmpid=zzfindpxt
8. N. Research, LTE HSPA WiMAX application tester (2011), http://www.nomor.de/home/solutions-and-products/products/application-tester
9. EURECOM, OpenAir interface (2011), http://www.openairinterface.org
10. Chertov, R., Havey, D., Almeroth, K.: MSET: A mobility satellite emulation testbed. In: Proc. of INFOCOM (2010)
11. Mills, D.L.: Internet time synchronization: the Network Time Protocol. Transactions on Communications 39 (1991)
12. Google, Web metrics: Size and number of resources (2011), https://code.google.com/speed/articles/web-metrics.html
13. Novak, R., et al.: Proposed text for evaluation methodology and key criteria for p802.16m. IEEE C802.16m-07/074r1 (2007)
14. Cisco, Voice over ip - per call bandwidth consumption (2011), https://www.cisco.com/en/US/tech/tk652/tk698/technologies_tech_note09186a0080094ae2.shtml
15. Barcelo, F., Jordan, J.: Channel holding time distribution in cellular telephony. Proc. of Wireless Communications (1997)

Environment-Independent Virtual Wireless Testbed

Hiroshi Mano

Interdisciplinary Graduate School of Medicine and Engineering,
University of Yamanashi, 4-4-37 Takeda, Kofu, Yamanashi 400-8510, Japan
hiroshi@manosan.org

Abstract. Current digital packet-switching communications involves more cross-layer trade-offs than legacy wireless communications. Conventionally, each network layer is studied separately, and then the total system is evaluated in field tests. However, the results are always specific to the particular environmental conditions during the test and are not reproducible. Here we propose an architecture for an environment-independent virtual wireless testbed. We describe the implementation and validation results for a programmable wireless propagation emulator—the key component of the testbed. It was found that the system could emulate wireless propagation over at least 10 wireless nodes in real time using 10 field-programmable gate arrays with programmable parameters consisting of the channel model, path loss model, antenna model, and emulation scenario. Thus, the system is promising as a replacement for conventional field tests.

Keywords: Wireless testbed, Wireless emulator, Virtual networking.

1   Introduction

Today, digital broadband communication systems often rely on a combination of wireless and wired network technologies. Furthermore, systems are rapidly switching from single-purpose (such as voice specific) to general-purpose (IP) services by adopting packet switching. These packet-switching systems employ more cross-layer collaboration than conventional networks, such as TCP retransmission for quality of service (QoS) control and Mobile IP for transparency.

Conventionally, the wireless layer is evaluated without taking into consideration the upper-layer protocols, which are largely evaluated with wireless simulators or specific existing wireless technologies (i.e., LTE, Wi-Fi, or Wi-MAX). Therefore, a comprehensive evaluation of any new network technology requires a complete field test. However, the results of any field test are always specific to the environmental conditions during the test (geographic location, physical specifications, MAC, link-layer protocols, radio licensing terms, etc.) and are therefore not easy to reproduce.

Here we describe an environment-independent virtual wireless testbed that is fully programmable, from the physical layer to the application layer, and can interface with external network devices in real time while allowing easy reproducibility. In this section, we describe the current state of today's wireless testbed and the advantages of

T. Korakis, M. Zink, and M. Ott (Eds.): TridentCom 2012, LNICST 44, pp. 33–47, 2012.
© Institute for Computer Sciences, Social Informatics and Telecommunications Engineering 2012

an environment-independent system. Then, in Sections 2 and 3, we describe the proposed architecture and an implementation of the main component, the programmable wireless propagation emulator. Section 4 presents the results of an evaluation of the emulator, and Section 5 lists our conclusions.

1.1   Current State of the Art

In the field of network research, several wireless testbeds have been developed, but none allow complete environment-independent evaluation without a field test. GNURADIO [1], for example, is a software-defined radio (SDR) that provides programmable capability for the PHY and MAC layers. However, it has specific RF units. This necessitates the use of a propagation simulator or a field test for total evaluation. The ORBIT Radio Grid Testbed [2] provides an evaluation environment for upper-layer protocols such as for mesh networks comprising established IEEE802.11 wireless LANs and IEEE802.16 Wi-MAX stations on a grid. However, only a fixed environment is provided for path loss and delay spread, and the lower network layers (MAC and PHY) are not reconfigurable. In addition, the CMU wireless emulator [3] includes a digital signal processor (DSP) for user-defined propagation between specific wireless units in real time, but it does not include wireless radios.

Thus, the existing wireless testbeds are restricted to particular environments (propagation, channel, etc.), device characteristics (frequency, power, modulation/demodulation, antenna, etc.), and upper-layer protocols (multiplex, duplex, packet congestion control, etc.). The consequences of these restrictions are quite significant in practice. For example, we spent much time and money to test a high-speed hand-over protocol over Wi-Fi at an actual motor sports course with a professional driver and a racing car. However, this only demonstrated the performance under a particular set of conditions (2.4 GHz, DSS, single vehicle, and closed-circuit environment). If we needed to perform the same evaluation using different preconditions (OFDM, 5.8 GHz, multiple vehicles, etc.), we would have to spend the same amount of resources again.

1.2   Advantages of Virtual Wireless Testbed

The proposed environment-independent virtual wireless testbed is fully programmable from the physical layer to the application layer and can interface with external network devices in real time for easy reproducibility. Because of the wide adaptability of the proposed architecture, there are numerous prospective uses with no regulatory limitations. This will allow users to evaluate their own new concepts without requiring radio licenses and test fields. The use case shown in Fig. 1 is one possible example. The testbed is a typical use case of network virtualization.

Most new ideas on the future of the Internet are evaluated over the testbed that has been deployed over a layer provided by virtual technologies.

The adaptivity of the virtual network provides an effective evaluation environment. However, only the wireless part depends on particular technologies.

Therefore, we hope to use this virtual wireless testbed as part of a virtual network that provides network service functions such as flow control, mobility control, and authentication.

For example, with a heterogeneous network system with a different wireless network, a user can configure each wireless node to employ different wireless technologies. In addition, the propagation environment is also programmable; this makes it easy to evaluate systems in different environments such as urban, rural, and indoor settings.

Although this system does not dispense with all experimental tests, the user can reproduce the experimental environment by inputting the data gathered during the experiment. In addition, and most importantly, the user only needs to program or configure the target part to be evaluated—all other parts would be described by ideal parameters. For example, if a user wants to evaluate a new concept for an antenna, it is only necessary to program the antenna characteristics, while selectable predetermined values are provided for all of the other layers: PHY, MAC, LINK, and transport.

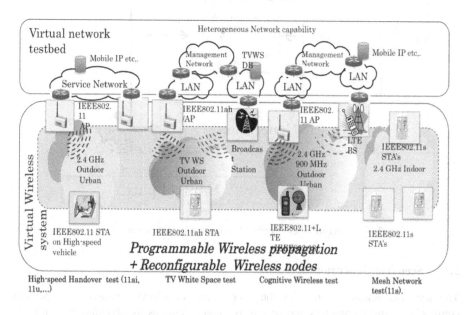

Fig. 1. Prospective use case for proposed virtual wireless testbed

2 Proposed Architecture

As shown in Fig. 2, the proposed testbed incorporates a scenario generator, several reconfigurable wireless nodes, and a programmable wireless propagation emulator.

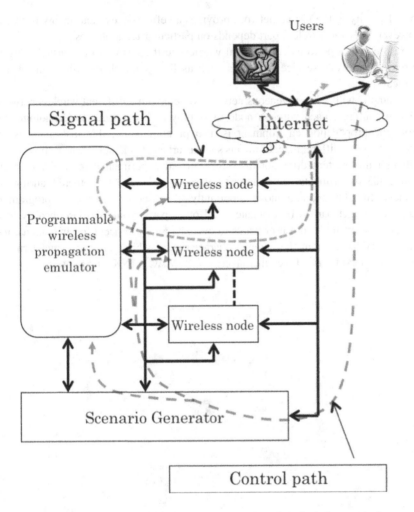

Fig. 2. Architecture of environment-independent virtual wireless testbed

2.1   Scenario Generator

The scenario generator provides the user interface, allows resource management (setting/selecting parameters and scenarios), and calculates the dynamic propagation scenario that would be executed by the emulator. A commercial off-the-shelf personal computer is used as the scenario generator.

2.2   Wireless Nodes

The wireless nodes, as shown in Fig. 3, are implemented on field-programmable gate arrays (FPGAs) and provide a fully reconfigurable PHY, MAC, and Frontend (roll-off

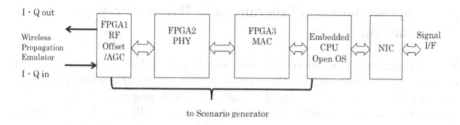

Fig. 3. Reconfigurable wireless node

filter, AGC, etc.). In addition, they incorporate an embedded computer, which is used for the Link or higher-layer control. For a virtual network, a user may also implement a virtual host on this embedded computer.

2.3 Programmable Wireless Propagation Emulator

As shown in Fig. 4, this system emulates the propagation path between wireless nodes. The channel and path loss models are implemented using a finite impulse response (FIR) filter on FPGA hardware. All wireless propagation behavior can be described as a combination of delay, amplitude, and phase. The channel model is implemented with a seven-tap FIR that also emulates frequency-selective fading. The multiplication value (Kn and dn in Fig. 4) for the signal is calculated beforehand using the scenario generator, and the values are updated based on the time and the user-defined scenario. All the wireless nodes are connected to each other through this propagation emulator using I/Q complex signals. Therefore, $\left(2^{n}-n\right)$ propagation paths are required for this propagation emulator.

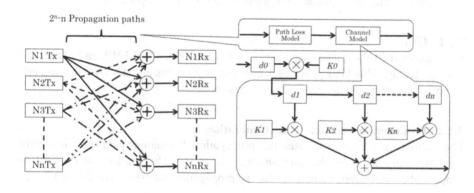

Fig. 4. Programmable wireless propagation emulator

3   Implementation of Programmable Wireless Propagation Emulator

We implemented the scenario generator and programmable wireless propagation emulator for 10 wireless nodes. The scenario generator was implemented in software on a Linux system, and the programmable wireless propagation emulator was implemented using a hardware board that integrates FPGAs. Gigabit Ethernet connects the scenario generator and programmable wireless propagation emulator, as shown in Fig.5.

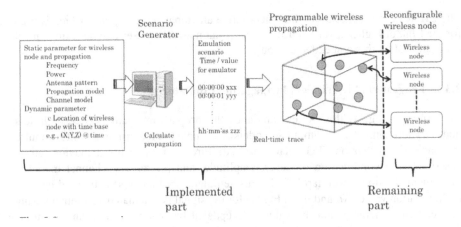

Fig. 5. System overview

3.1   Scenario Generator

The scenario generator software comprises the following components:

3.1.1   GUI

We implemented the entire user interface in Adobe Flash and PHP, and considered system sharing. This GUI provides a user-friendly interface that shows the scenario behavior and all the parameters of the wireless nodes.

3.1.2   Propagation Characteristics Generation

The scenario generator calculates the propagation fluctuation parameter using the conditions provided by the user through the GUI. The implemented prototype supports the configurable conditions for the propagation path shown in Table. 1.

Table 1. Configurable conditions

Path loss model	Channel ITU-R M.1225	Fading Model	Antenna
Two-way ray	Indoor A/B	Classic	Isotopic
COST-231Hata	Pedestrian A/B	Flat	Dipole
	Vehicular A/B	User defined	ITU-R M.2135
	PDSekm		ITU-R M.1245
	User defined		User defined

3.1.3 Path Loss Calculation

The scenario generator calculates the path loss between nodes using the conventional formulas described in the following. In the case of the two-ray model, the path loss is given by (1) for sufficiently short distances and by (2) otherwise.

$$L = 20\log_{10}\left(\frac{4\pi d}{\lambda}\right) \tag{1}$$

$$L = 40\log_{10}(d) - 20\log_{10}(h_t) - 20\log_{10}(h_r) \tag{2}$$

For the COST-231 Hata model, the path loss is given by

$$L = 46.3 + 33.9\log(f) - 13.82\log(h_t) - a(h_r) + \left[44.9 - 6.55\log(h_t)\right]\log(d) + 3$$
$$a(hr) = (1.1\log(f) - 0.7)h_r - (1.56\log(f) - 0.8) \tag{3}$$

where L represents the path loss in decibels; d represents the distance, λ represents the wavelength, and h_t and h_r are the antenna heights all in meters; and f denotes the frequency in megahertz.

3.1.4 Fading Calculation

The scenario generator calculates the vector data for the Rayleigh fading wave $r(t)$ as

$$r(t) = x(t) + j*y(t)$$
$$= \left[\sqrt{\frac{2}{N_1+1}}\sum_{n=1}^{N_1}\sin\left(\frac{\pi n}{N_1}\right)\cos\left\{2\pi f_d\cos\left(\frac{2\pi n}{N_1}\right)t\right\} + \frac{1}{\sqrt{N_1+1}}\cos\left(2\pi f_d t\right)\right]$$
$$+ j\sqrt{\frac{2}{N_1}}\sum_{n=1}^{N_1}\sin\left(\frac{\pi n}{N_1}\right)\cos\left\{2\pi f_d\cos\left(\frac{2\pi n}{N_1}\right)t\right\} \tag{4}$$

where d is the maximum fading frequency in hertz and N_1 is the number of FIR taps.

3.1.5 Emulation Scenario

The emulation scenario is defined by the time and location (x, y, z, and azimuth) of the wireless nodes using the GUI, as shown in Fig. 6. The scenario generator calculates the time-based fluctuation of the propagation using the process described above.

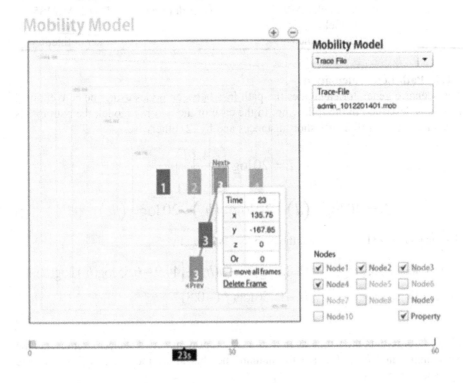

Fig. 6. Emulation scenario GUI

3.2   Programmable Wireless Propagation Emulator

The programmable wireless propagation emulator was implemented in hardware using 10 FPGAs (Vertex-6 XC6VLX130T, 1156 pin, 200 MHz). We implemented this 10-node capability in the virtual wireless space with a 49% slice, 74% DSP, and 60% RAM consumption.

After calculating the vector data of the path loss and channel model using the scenario generator, the data were transferred to the programmable wireless propagation emulator over Gigabit Ethernet. The programmable wireless propagation emulator operates in real time by combining the delay memory and complex multipliers, as shown in Fig. 7.

In this proposed architecture, 215 adders and 360 multiplexers emulate wireless propagation with 200-MHz clocks. In addition, the required number of I/O pins P between the wireless nodes and propagation emulator is given by

$$P = n \times N \times k \tag{5}$$

where n is the number of wireless nodes, N is the bit depth or signal resolution, and $k = 4$ (I,Q, +,-).

In other words, the scalability of the proposed architecture depends on the clock speed of the FPGA, signal resolution, and the number of I/O pins.

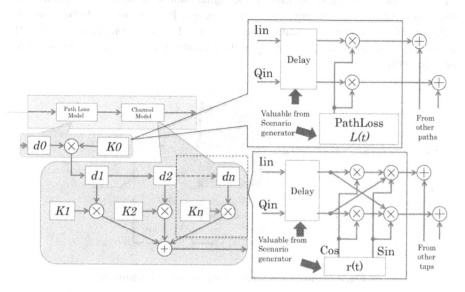

Fig. 7. Block diagram of programmable wireless propagation emulator

4   Evaluation of Programmable Wireless Propagation Emulator

We evaluated the accuracy, process delay, and behavior of the implemented programmable wireless propagation emulator. In this section, the evaluation methodology is explained first, and then the results of the evaluation are described.

4.1   Evaluation Methodology

Here we used existing legacy radio measurement equipment such as a spectrum analyzer, signal generator, and commercial Wi-Fi products. Because the programmable wireless emulator only had digital I/Q interfaces, it was not amenable to visible inspection. Therefore, we employed analog-digital (A/D) and digital-analog (D/A) converters for use between the measurement equipment and programmable wireless emulator. In addition, the throughput was measured with iPerf on a personal computer connected to the both ends of the wireless LAN device.

4.2   Path Loss Characteristics

We measured the throughput between 2.4-GHz wireless LAN access points (AP) and stations (STA) using the emulator and an RF attenuator, as shown in Fig. 8. The results of this measurement showed that differences exist between the emulator and RF attenuator, as pointed in Fig.9.

The difference in the low-attenuation range is caused by saturation of the analog circuit, and the difference in the high-attenuation range is caused by noise in the analog circuit. As a result, we confirmed that the implemented emulator can replace the RF circuit in adding attenuation to the signal path with the desired scenario but does not have the characteristics of analog circuits. Further, we confirmed that the accuracy of attenuation to a static signal was +/- 1.0dB in comparison to the RF attenuator. In addition, the signal delay of the emulator was confirmed to be only 1 μs by pulse reply.

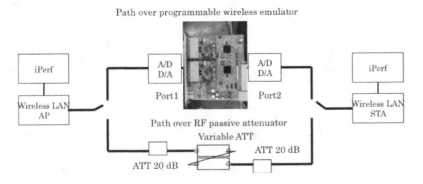

Fig. 8. Measurement scheme for path loss characteristics

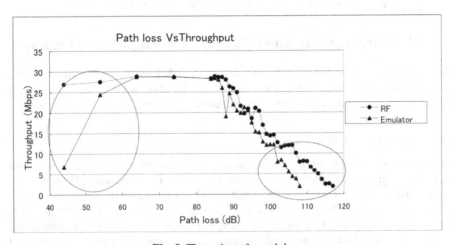

Fig. 9. Throughput for path loss

4.3　Desired/Undesired Signal Characteristics

We measured the desired/undesired (D/U) ratio at 10% outage throughput of a wireless LAN link with an added undesired CW or OFDM signal, as shown in Fig. 10. From the measurement results shown in Fig. 12, we see that the D/U characteristics over the emulator and RF attenuator are in close agreement. In addition, it was confirmed that the emulator added signals with different propagation paths.

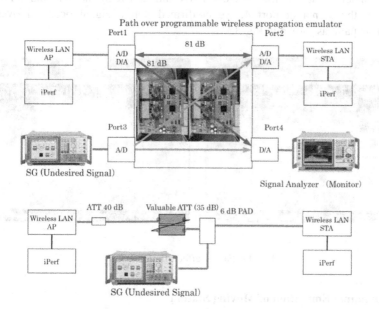

Fig. 10. Measurement scheme for D/U signal ratio

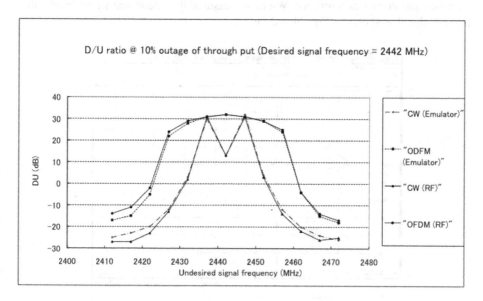

Fig. 11. D/U signal ratio over programmable wireless propagation emulator

4.4   Fading Signal Characteristics

Using the same measurement scheme as that shown in Fig. 10, we added a particular fading channel model to the wireless LAN link between the AP and STA. By monitoring the signal at port 4, we confirmed that a signal occurred over the propagation path, as shown in Fig. 13.

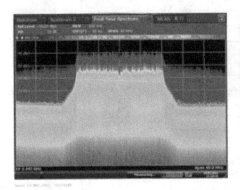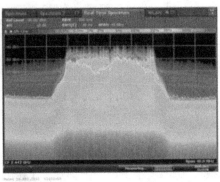

Fig. 12. Fading effect: flat/classic

4.5   Dynamic Emulation of Moving Station

We programmed a vehicle scenario in which the distance between two wireless nodes increases and decreases with time. We then measured the attenuated signal level with the CW signal as shown in Fig. 14 and Fig. 15.

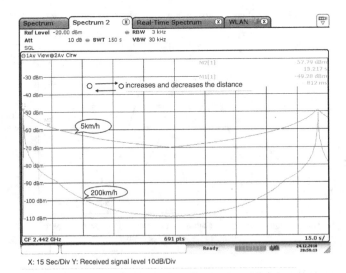

X: 15 Sec/Div Y: Received signal level 10dB/Div

Fig. 13. Signal output level for vehicle scenario with two-way ray model

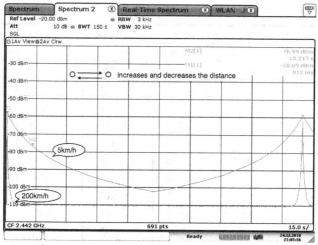

X: 15 Sec/Div Y:Received signal level 10dB/Div

Fig. 14. Signal output level for vehicle scenario with COST-231 Hata model

4.6   Error Vector Magnitude Measurement

We measured the internal effect on the error vector magnitude (EVM) using an ideal OFDM signal. Table 2 lists the measured EVM data for the original signal and the signal after passing through the emulator path shown in Fig. 16. As seen from these measured data, the EVM indeed degraded. However, it is reasonable to assume that these changes were caused by the characteristics of the analog conversion because the emulator performs only digital operations, and the typical digital operation error is not as small as that measured. In addition, the results showed that there was no significant quality change that would violate the IEEE802.11 standard.

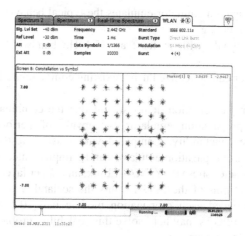

Fig. 15. EVM through programmable wireless propagation emulator

Table 2. EVM of programmable wireless propagation emulator

Item	Measurement point		Difference	Unit	IEEE802.11 Limit
	Input	Output			
EVM All Carr.	1.03	2.95	+1.92	%	5.62
	-39.76	-30.61	-9.15	dB	-25.00
EVM Data Carr.	1.04	2.98	+1.90	%	5.62
	-39.69	-30.53	-8.84	-25.00	-25.00
EMV Pilot Carr	0.91	2.57	-1.6	%	39.81
	-40.77	-31.80	-9.46	dB	-8.00
IQ Offset	-69.50	-58.08	-11.42	dB	-15.00
Gain Imbalance	-0.09	-0.07	-0.02	%	-
	-0.01	-0.01	0	dB	-
Quadrature Err.	0.00	-0.04	0.02		
Freq Err	-149.13	-152.60	-3.60	Hz	+/-48840
Symb Clock Err.	0.09	-0.03	0.12	ppm	+/-20

5   Conclusions

In this paper, we proposed an environment-independent virtual wireless testbed architecture and reported the implementation of a wireless propagation emulator.

The results of the actual implementation of the programmable wireless propagation emulator showed the following:

- The wireless propagation emulator emulates wireless propagation with sufficient accuracy (±1.0 dB).
- The emulation delay is small enough for this system to be used as a real-time air interface (1.0 µs).
- The wireless propagation emulator emulates the typical behavior of flat fading and frequency-selective fading.
- Complex vector signals with at least an 85-MHz bandwidth can be emulated simultaneously.
- A 10-node emulator can be realized using existing commercial FPGA products.

The results of this implementation demonstrated that the combination of a scenario generator and the propagation emulator is capable of performing propagation emulation with wide adaptability. Compared with existing testbeds, the proposed programmable wireless propagation emulator can be implemented without depending on wireless node characteristics (PHY, MAC, Link, and upper layers).

The number of I/O pins of the FPGA limits the scalability to a large number of nodes because we divided each propagation module into 10 FPGAs. However, a greater integration of FPGAs may help solve this scalability problem by reducing the number of discrete components.

In conclusion, the technical feasibility of the proposed architecture for an environment-independent virtual wireless testbed was demonstrated through an actual implementation. The performance of the programmable wireless propagation emulator was sufficient for real-time applications. The reconfigurable wireless node, the last remaining part of the proposed testbed, will be implemented in subsequent work. In addition, we intend to evaluate our concept for a fast initial link setup protocol, which will be proposed as IEEE802.11ai, using the virtual wireless testbed. For IEEE802.11ai, we must evaluate a large number of STA-to-AP connections using a vehicle model, which is the typical use case for a virtual wireless testbed.

Acknowledgments. The assistance received from Tetsuya Shigeyasu, Hiroshi Matsuno, Akihiro Nakao, Marc Emmelmann, Masanori Hanawa, and Eiko Torkai in the preparation of this manuscript is gratefully acknowledged.

The author is grateful to Toshihisa Yamada, Satoshi Funada, Masanori Uno, Mineo Takai, Shigeru Kaneda, and Fred Okuma for their assistance with the implementation of the programmable wireless propagation emulator.

References

1. Blossom, E.: GNU Radio: Tools for exploring the radio frequency spectrum. Linux Journal 122 (June 2004)
2. Raychaudhuri, D., Seskar, I., Ott, M., Ganu, S., Ramachandran, K., Kremo, H., Siracusa, R., Liu, H., Singh, M.: Overview of the ORBIT Radio Grid Testbed for Evaluation of Next-Generation Wireless Network Protocols. In: Proceedings of the IEEE Wireless Communications and Networking Conference, WCNC 2005 (2005)
3. Judd, G.: Using Physical Layer Emulation to Understand and Improve Wireless Networks, PhD Thesis, Department of Computer Science, Carnegie Mellon University, Also published as technical report CMU-CS-06-164 (October 2006)
4. Harada, H., Prasad, R.: Simulation and Software Radio for Mobile Communications. Artech House, Norwood (2002)
5. Mano, H., Yamada, T., Funada, S., Uno, M., Takai, M., Kaneda, S.: Wireless propagation emulator for virtual wireless testbed. In: IPSJ DPS Workshop (2011)

FPGA-Based Wireless Link Emulator
for Wireless Sensor Network

Wei Liu[1], Luc Bienstman[2], Bart Jooris[1], Opher Yaron[1], and Ingrid Moerman[1]

[1] Ghent University - IBBT, Gaston Crommenlaan 8 Bus 201, B-9050 Gent, Belgium
wei.liu@intec.ugent.be, luc.bienstman@groept.be
[2] GroepT University College Leuven, Vesaliusstraat 13, B-3000 Leuven

Abstract. Wireless sensor testbeds lack the flexibility for topology control and the accuracy for interference generation. Once the testbed is set up, the topology becomes fixed. Due to the nature of the wireless environment, experimenters often suffer from unpredictable background interference, while at the same time, find it hard to get accurate and repeatable interference sources.

The wireless link emulator addresses these issues by replacing the uncontrollable wireless link by a well-controlled and programmable hardwired medium. A radio interface is then made to behave according to the link configuration, thus offering flexibility for both topology and interference control. This paper describes the implementation of the wireless link emulator based on a number of low-cost Xilinx FPGAs. The system is verified experimentally and compared to existing emulation systems.

Keywords: Topology control, interference control, FPGA, wireless link emulation.

1 Introduction

Over the years, more and more researchers have realized that simulation results alone are not sufficient to guarantee the proper function of wireless network applications in a real-life environment. Hence many universities and research groups have setup their own testbeds [1] [2]. Such a testbed often consists of a large number of actual sensor nodes which can be programmed remotely. It is a common practice to install the sensor nodes at fixed locations. Therefore once the testbed is setup, the topology of the network is fixed. In addition, many testbeds are deployed within the office environment, the experiments often suffer from unpredictable interference, such as WIFI, Bluetooth or even microwave oven.

Network simulators are generally flexible and predictable, however, they ignore many aspects of the real hardware platforms. A testbed offers real hardware behavior but lacks flexibility and controllability. Is there a way to combine the advantages of both systems? The answer is yes: use emulation instead of simulation and at the lower level, emulate only the wireless ether behavior, not the sensor node itself. This is the solution integrated into WiLab — the wireless sensor network testbed of Gent University [4].

T. Korakis, M. Zink, and M. Ott (Eds.): TridentCom 2012, LNICST 44, pp. 48–63, 2012.

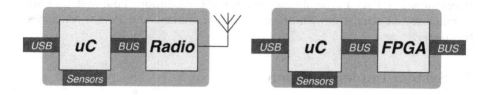

Fig. 1. The original TelosB node   **Fig. 2.** The modified TelosB node

The WiLab testbed is deployed in an office building of 12x80m and is spread out of three floors. It consists of more than 200 sensor nodes. The sensor node is based upon the TelosB mote [3] (Fig 1). The TelosB mote is an ultra low power wireless module for use in sensor networks. It mainly consists of integrated sensors, a microcontroller and a radio module (Fig 2). The radio module is based on the Chipcon CC2420 radiochip [5]. The CC2420 is a true single-chip 2.4 Ghz IEEE802.15.4 compliant RF transceiver designed for low-power and low-voltage wireless applications. On the TelosB mote, the CC2420 is controlled by TI MSP430 microcontroller.

We extend the WiLab testbed with a group of special nodes. These nodes are also TelosB compatible, however, they communicate via an emulated network instead of the wireless ether (Fig 3, Fig 4). In another word, we introduce a group of nodes with their "private ether" into the testbed. An interface is offered to control the "private ether". For the experimenters of the testbed, those special nodes can be programmed in an identical way as the original nodes.

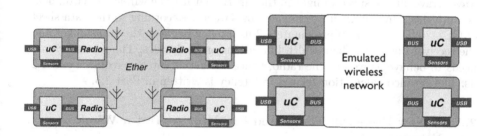

Fig. 3. The wireless network   **Fig. 4.** The emulated wireless network

To implement the wireless link emulator three steps are needed : first, separate the radio from the rest of the hardware on the sensor node. Second, a radio interface is made to maintain the radio functionality. Finally, a hardwire programmable link to other nodes is implemented to replace the ether. In reality this is realized by replacing the radio and its antenna with an interface that connects the MSP430 processor to this private ether. All the ether behavior is emulated with low cost FPGA .

The remaining part of the paper is organized as follows: Part 2 discusses the system implementation in detail. Part 3 describes the principles of physical layer emulation. Part 4 presents the experimental validation of our system. Part 5 compares our emulator with other emulation systems and Part 6 concludes this paper.

2 System Implementation

2.1 Requirements for a Wireless Network Emulator

The emulator of WiLab takes a different approach compared to most existing emulation systems. The idea is to remove the wireless ether completely, and replace it by a well-controlled programmable medium. The requirements for such an emulator are :

- The software running on the modified sensor node should behave exactly the same as if it was executed on the original TelosB mote.
- The electrical characteristics of the radio (CC2420) should be maintained, including the SPI commnication to the local processor and the interface signals (CCA, SFD, FIFO,FIFOP, Vref, RST).
- The transmitting and receiving functionality of the radio should be maintained.
- Similar latency as the radio physical layer is mandatory for the emulator.
- Programmable topology.
- Programmable interference.

Among all the requirements, the latency is the most challenging. Electromagnetic waves travel at the speed of light in the air. By nature, the wireless environment is a broadcast medium with extremely low latency. According to the data sheet of CC2420 [5], there is approximately 2 us latency between the transmitter and the receiver due to the bandwidth limitations on both sides. The emulator only needs to behave as well as the radio, hence the actual latency requirement is 2 us. The detailed calculation related to latency is written in Part 2.5.

2.2 A New Proposal: The Wired Emulator to Test a Wireless Network

In order to achieve reliable low level interconnection, wires are used as the physical medium for the emulator. The "private ether" is now a wired network in which all nodes are connected together by wires. The question is, what is the most suitable physical topology for the emulator to meet all the requirements? One option is to use a full meshed topology, where every node can communicate to every other node, Figure 5 . A Master node is required to control the communication parameters of the mesh while the effective data is directly transmitted between the slaves. The definition of the Master node (to manage the ring) and the Slave node (the real transceiver) is used all over in this paper.

It is obvious that such a topology offers the largest bandwidth, but at the same time it also has the largest amount of connections. For a network of N nodes,

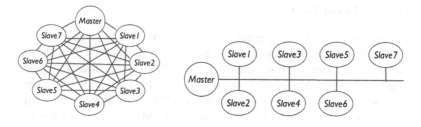

Fig. 5. Full mesh topology   **Fig. 6.** Bus topology

a total $N \times (N-1)/2$ connections are required. This could be a considerable number for a complex emulator.

Another option is to connect all the nodes in a common bus topology (Figure 6). All nodes can still communicate to each other, but a complex arbitrator on the bus is required. This could be a serious limitation to the system bandwidth. From a electrical point of view, the more nodes present on the bus, the higher the parasitic capacitance (every node adds some capacitance), and accordingly the lower the switching speed of the bus will be.

The star topology (Figure 7) is a point-to-point network that does not suffer from the accumulation of parasitic capacitance. However, the master node needs to have enough processing power to handle all the incoming and outgoing data to meet the low latency requirement.

   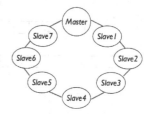

Fig. 7. Star topology   **Fig. 8.** Ring topology

The ring topology of Figure 8 has some appealing features. It is a point-to-point network, so every link can run at high speed. Although it does not offer direct link between every single node (Slave), the available high speed and an appropriate protocol can compensate for it. The ring topology has an inherent pipelined behavior, which further increases the total network bandwidth. The pipelined architecture allows for simultaneous data transfer between every two neighboring nodes. For example, at the same time instant, while Slave 2 is communicating with Slave 3, Slave 3 can also communicate with Slave 4. This offers a huge advantage over the bus topology. Therefore, we decide to take the ring topology as the physical topology of the emulator.

2.3   The Low Level Protocol

A flow of packets are circulating unidirectionally through the ring. At any moment every single node is receiving a frame from its left neighbor and at the same time is transmitting a frame to its right neighbor. The packet flow is formed by frames (Figure 9). Each frame is allocated to one node (Master, Slave). A node is only allowed to write data into its own frame. When receiving a frame from another node, the content of the frame is retransmitted; when receiving a frame from the node itself, either new data or a dummy empty frame is transmitted. Hence a given frame can circulate only once on the ring. Thanks to the frame structure and inherent pipelining, the ring effectively behaves as multi-access medium without collision, which is exactly what we wanted for the physical connection on the emulator.

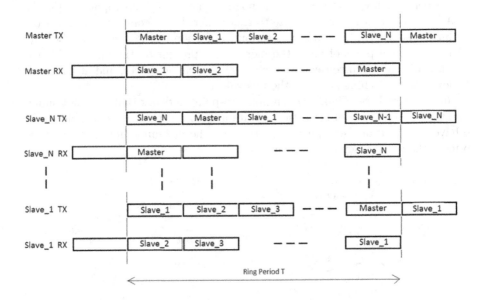

Fig. 9. Frame sequence

A frame is a 32 bit value and can have several formats. Figure 10 shows the normal data frame. A normal data frame is used to transfer data from one slave to the other slaves. The bit D0=1 indicates the normal data frame. The bits D1-D7 contain the source address, which serves as the identifier of the frame on the ring. The D8-D15 bits contain the parameter Channel ID, indicating at which "frequency" the node is transmitting, compatible to the Zigbee channel index. The bits D16-D23 are the transmit power (TX Power) in dBm unit. And the Lower 4 bits of D24-D31 contains the 4-bit actual data, comparable to the 4-bit symbol formed on the real radio, the extra 4 bits are reserved for future extension. The parameters Channel ID and Tx Power cover all the physical property of a symbol. According to the 802.15.4 standard, a symbol stays on the ether for 16

Normal data frame

0	1-7	8-15	16-23	24-31
1	source address	channel ID	Tx Power	Symbol

Configuration or node status reporting/logging data frame

0	1-7	8-15	16-23	24-31
0	destination address	parameter ID	parameter value	parameter value

Fig. 10. Normal data frame   **Fig. 11.** Configuration or status frame

us. To emulate the symbol period, the data frame is only transmitted via the ring every 16 us, however, the actual duration for a frame to circle around the ring is much shorter. This is covered in Part 2.5.

Besides connections to the ring, the Master node also has connections to a Web Server and a LAN connection to the Wilab Database. Via the Web Server the user can configure the "virtual ether". Parameters for a specific node, such as the noise floor, or path loss, can be programmed via the Master. This is realized by generating a master configuration frame on the ring (Fig 11). This frame circulates through the ring and the addressed slave will copy the data internally. Broadcasting configuration, i.e. addressing several slave nodes with one frame, is possible. Besides configuration, if requested, a slave node can send status reports to the Master. The Master fetches the report and writes it into the WiLab database. The status reports usually contain information related to GPIO activities on the radio interface, or commands received from the local processor. Therefore it is a powerful tool for monitoring the radio activity and software debugging.

Broadcasting is straightforward. A transmitting node will write its frame with a given Channel ID on the ring. Any other node with the same channel ID should read out this frame.

2.4   The Physical Implementation

A connection between two nodes is made by a standard UTP cable (4 twisted pairs) Fig 12. Low voltage differential signaling (LVDS) is the IO standard on the ring. This ensures good signal integrity at high transmission speed. Among the 4 twisted pairs, one pair is used as clock signal, two pairs are used for data, the last pair is used for synchronization. The Sync signal travels along with the Master frame. It can be considered as the Master frame flag. This Sync signal is essential for the synchronization of the whole ring structure. A node that is receiving a frame while the sync is active is for sure receiving the Master frame.

The two data lines allow to double the transmit speed. Hence to transmit 32 data bits only 16 clock pulses are needed. Three extra clock pulses are needed for internal processing. This results in a total of 19 clock pulses to transmit a 32 bit frame. The timing diagram of the ring is shown in Figure 13. Every frame on the ring corresponds to a time slot of 19 clock pulses.

As mentioned earlier, all the logic needed to implement the ring structure and to emulate the radio module is implemented on the FPGA. Every node (master, slave) has one FPGA board. More specifically, the slave node is built

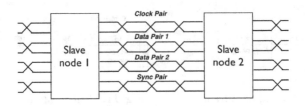

Fig. 12. The 4 pair UTP cable connection between nodes

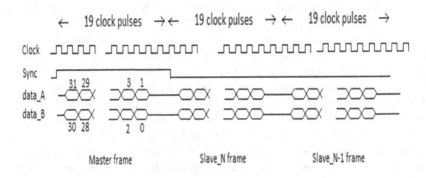

Fig. 13. Detailed timing diagram of the data on the ring

on the Xilinx Spartan-3A-400 FPGA [7], while the master is built on the Xilinx Spartan3E-500 FPGA [6]. The FPGA chip has a large amount of logic gates available to build all types of dedicated logic, on top of that a powerful 32 bit "soft" microprocessor (microBlaze [15]) is also available as an IP core(intellectual property). To implement the low level ring protocol, a dedicated ring transmitter is built with VHDL(hardware description language).

The radio interface is a combination of software and customized hardware on the FPGA, with the software part running on the "soft" processor — microBlaze, mainly responsible for connecting the ring transceiver and the radio interface. In addition, the software also performs processing needed for physical layer emulation, to be explained in Part 3. The core of the hardware part of the radio interface is a dedicated finite state machine, which takes care of the SPI communication towards the MSP processor, generating necessary interrupt towards software and partially controls the GPIO signals on the radio interface. The block diagram of a slave is shown in Figure 14.

Special care is taken to maintain the quality of the clock signal. The Xilinx Spartan-3A FPGA has on-board high-speed LVDS transceivers to drive the ring. The clock recovery is executed by the PLL inside the FPGA. The Master node is generating the clock while each slave node is reconstructing the clock on its output with minimal phase delay with respect to the input. This recovered clock is used in the ring transceiver logic. Thanks to this structure, the clock quality is maintained through the entire ring. This enables the ring clock to run at very high speed.

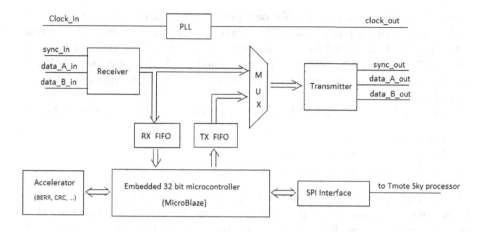

Fig. 14. Block diagram of the slave node

2.5 Timing Considerations

The clock speed of the ring is 100 MHz. A complete 32-bit frame requires 19 clock pulses. We currently only implement a ring with 6 slave nodes and one master. When a frame passes a node, it is first received completely and then transmitted. Hence the duration for a frame to reach all the other nodes on the ring equals:

$$T_1 = 6 \times 19 \times 10nSec = 1.14us \tag{1}$$

The duration for one frame to completely circulate through the ring is :

$$T_2 = (6 + 1) \times 19 \times 10nSec = 1.33us \tag{2}$$

Be aware that not one but seven frames do travel around the ring during the 1.33 uSec. Hence a node can get access to the ring every 1.33 us.

The latency on the ring is defined as the time between transmitting a frame by a given node and receiving that frame by another node. The best case is when a node is transmitting to its left neighbor, the worst case is when a node is transmitting to its right neighbor. The equation (1) shows that our worst case latency is 1.14 us, smaller than the 2 us latency of CC2420 chip. Hence this design meets the initial requirement.

3 Physical Layer Emulation

In wireless systems, bit errors occur during the decoding of received symbols. When the received signal is much stronger than the local noise floor, the received symbol is almost always correctly decoded, hence hardly any bit error can appear. On the other hand, if the received signal is not strong enough to decode, frequent bit errors will appear. In between the two extremes, there is a "gray zone" where the bit error rate varies . We now focus on this zone. It is known that for each modulation technique, there is a given relationship between the bit error rate(BER) and the signal to noise ratio(SNR). The 802.15.4 standard features the OQPSK and DSSS modulation. The theoretical BER curve for 802.15.4 is shown in Figure 15, [13]. Once the SNR is known, we can generate the bit error accordingly.

To enable the calculation of SNR, several parameters need to be considered:

- The transmit power
- The path loss between transmitter and receiver
- The local noise floor and interference level at the receiver

The transmit power accompanies with each symbol as explained in Part 2.4. Each slave has a path-loss table which contains the path loss to all the other nodes. The local noise floor is also a parameter configured by the Master. All the parameters are stored in dB scale. For each incoming symbol, the SNR can be calculated as

$$SNR = TxPower - PathLoss - NoiseFloor \qquad (3)$$

If there are multiple senders active at the same time on the same channel, receivers can only recognize the symbol from one sender, the symbols of the other senders are treated as interference. To emulate the interference from other nodes, the strongest interference is used instead of the noise floor in the calculation of SNR. In this case the SNR is actually the same as SINR (signal to interference and noise ratio), for simplicity, we use the term SNR throughout this paper.

3.1   Quantized SNR and Its Link to Bit Error Rate

Once the SNR value is obtained, theoretically we could calculate the corresponding BER, however, practically this would give too much processing load on the embedded FPGA system. Hence we quantize the BER vs SNR curve and store the most interesting part into a local look-up table. As explained above, the "gray zone" of SNR is closely related to the bit error. So the first step is to quantize this "gray zone". This is illustrated in Figure 15. The SNR value can be expressed by the formula below:

$$SNR = SNR_{offset} + SNR_{step} \times n \qquad (4)$$

SNR_{offset} and SNR_{step} are two important parameters. SNR_{offset} represents the lowest SNR value at which data can still be received, albeit with errors. Below this value packets are completely corrupted. SNR_{step} is the quantization step. Thus SNR becomes a function of n. The maximum value of n represents a threshold set by the user. When the SNR value is above the selected threshold, the data is processed without introducing bit error. The value n is also used as the index to look for the proper BER in the look-up table. In the remainder of the paper, the value n is referred as SNR_{index}.

3.2   Bit Error Generation

The bit error is generated in software. BER value by nature is a fraction number, however, calculation based on floating point and fraction number is slow and expensive. Therefore we express BER as $1/X$, the X is the nearest integer of the BER value's reciprocal. Only X is stored in the look up table. For instance, when BER is 0.1%, the value 1000 will be stored in the look-up table. The software counts the total number of received bits, and will toggle one bit every X bits. The toggle location is generated randomly. When X bits are received, the bit count is cleared to zero, and a new cycle starts with a new random toggle location generated. Such a cycle is called a bit-error cycle.

This solution is simple to implement, but has one major drawback, when transmitting a fixed number of packets with a fixed packet size, the packet error rate(PER) becomes a constant. To avoid this situation, another parameter is introduced — run-length of the bit error. This parameter defines the maximum number of bit errors that can appear in a roll. Thus in the beginning of one bit-error cycle, the random toggle location and the run-length of bit error are generated. When the bit count reaches the toggle location, it will continue to toggle the received bits until the number of toggled bits reaches the run-length. When more than one bits are toggled in a bit-error cycle, there will be none toggled in the following cycles. Hence eventually bit error rate stays the same. The run length parameter effectively characterizes the burst behavior of the bit error.

The random generator used here is based on a 32-bit hardware CRC shift register. So it is actually a pseudo random generator. We admit this can cause certain level of distortion. However, during experiments (see Part 4), we are able to obtain emulation results that are compatible with real measurements, the distortion introduced here is considered to be insignificant.

3.3   Topology Control and Interference Generation

Until now the link between bit error rate and SNR is established. In summary, the topology control is directly achieved by specifying path loss between each node. The path loss will affect several parameters, namely, RSSI and SNR, and eventually affect the bit error rate of the received packet. By configuring the path-loss table in each node inside the "virtual ether", an arbitrary logical topology can be formed, with no impact from the physical ring topology. When the path-loss table is configured in real time, the logical topology becomes dynamic. This allows us to emulate a network with mobile nodes.

As for interference generation, there are two options. One option is to directly generate interference configuration from the Master. This is realized by configuring the local noise floor parameter in all the Slave nodes. The noise configuration can be based on a simple pattern, as illustrated by experiment in Part 4.2. Another possibility is to record the interference in a certain environment and replay it by the Master afterwards. The quality of this approach depends on the time resolution of the recorded interference.

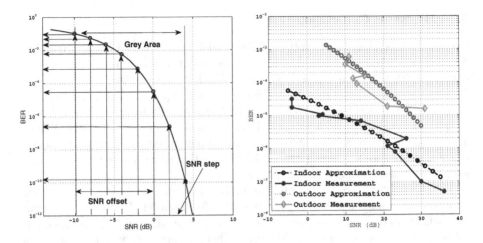

Fig. 15. Quantized BER curve   **Fig. 16.** Approximated BER curve

The second option is done by estimating the BER curve. Sometimes interference does not have a simple pattern. Recording interference with high resolution consumes a large amount of memory. Hence direct interference generation is not always a good option. If we can obtain the BER vs SNR curve under a certain environment, an appropriate amount of bit errors can be generated. The amount of generated bit errors should be equivalent to what is caused by the interference in the given environment. Therefore the desired amount of interference is obtained.

The measurement of BER is usually not that straightforward. It can be done in many ways. Here for simplicity, we assume every bit inside a packet is independent, for a packet of N bits, the BER and PER have the following relationship:

$$1 - PER = (1 - BER)^N \tag{5}$$

Therefore BER can be derived from PER when the packet size is known. The measurement of PER is usually simple. When combine the PER measurement with a simple energy recording, the BER vs SNR curve can be derived. This is further explained with experiment, Part 4.1.

4   Experiments

4.1   Emulation of Indoor and Outdoor Environment by BER Estimation

In this experiment we aim to emulate different environments by the proper estimation of BER curve. We used the experiment result in [13] as input, where a set of packet error rate(PER) measurements are performed in function of the distance between the transmitter and the receiver. The measurement is performed both indoor and outdoor. In addition to PER, RSSI (received signal strength indicator) is also recorded. The indoor experiment is performed multiple times. Each time a different packet size is used. We only selected the measurement with packet size of 127 bytes for the indoor emulation. The PER in the outdoor environment is measured only with a packet size of 20 bytes. For details of the experiment, readers are referred to [13]. We derived the path loss from the measured RSSI, the result is shown in Figure 17. These derived path loss is used as the direct input for the link configuration.

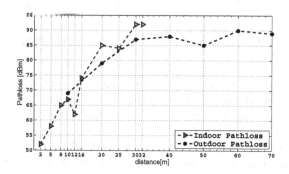

Fig. 17. Path loss vs distance

The next step is to estimate the BER curve. We first calculate the measured BER based on the PER measurement (Fig 18, Fig 19) and Equation (5). We measured the indoor noise floor in our office with Airmagnet [9], which is around -88 dBm. For the outdoor environment, -100 dBm is the selected average noise level based on calculations [17]. Given the transmit power (0 dBm), path loss, and local noise floor, SNR can be calculated according to Equation (3). These lead us to the measured BER curve, shown in Figure 16. Based on the theoretical relationship of SNR and BER, the approximation of measured BER curves are derived (Figure 16). These estimated BER curves are stored in the look-up table for our emulation. The results of the emulated PER for both indoor and outdoor environments are plotted in Figure 18 and Figure 19 respectively.

In general, the emulated PER approaches the measured PER very well for both indoor and outdoor scenarios. There are some deviations at certain locations, these are most likely caused by inaccurate RSSI or simply fluctuations of measurements.

Hence, we prove that by estimating the BER curve properly, we are able to emulate different environments. The PER increase with the distance, which also prove that our methodology for topology control works as expected.

4.2 Emulation of Microwave Oven Interference by Direct Configuration

In this experiment, we generate the interference configuration directly from the Master. We aim to compare our emulation result with JamLab [12]. JamLab

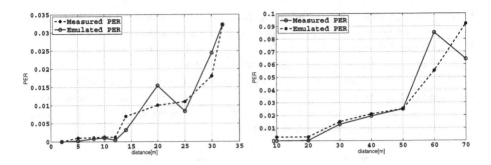

Fig. 18. PER indoor   **Fig. 19.** PER outdoor

focuses on interference emulation based on existing testbed facilities, such as TelosB nodes. According to [12], the interference of microwave oven has a simple on-off pattern with 20 ms period time and 50 % duty cycle. We decide to use this simple pattern to emulate the interference of microwave oven. The experiment scenario is identical as in JamLab. One node sends 400 packets to another node at 1 pkt/sec. The transmitter and receiver are placed about 3 meters apart with no obstacles in between. According to the widely-used path loss model[16], path loss at distance d from the transmitter equals:

$$PL(d) = PL(d_0) + 10\lambda \log \frac{d}{d_0} \tag{6}$$

The path loss at 2 meter is known to be 46 dB [12]. The path loss coefficient λ for indoor environment is typically 2.5. When substitute these values into equation (6), we get 50 dBm as the path loss at 3 meter. Thus the topology can be configured.

The only difference between our emulator and JamLab is how the interference is generated. JamLab used another TelosB node to generate the interference. In our system, Master transmits a configuration frame every 10 ms via the broadcast configuration channel, thus the interference is turned "on" or "off" every 10 ms.

We only emulated for NULL MAC with packet size of 100 bytes. The emulated packet receiving rate (PRR) from our emulator is 44.1%, from JamLab is 43.6%. We can see, that both emulation results are compatible to each other. However, in JamLab, the location of the interferer has to be carefully chosen, the transmit power also needs to be adjusted in order to obtain the right level of interference. If interference is required in a large area, the coverage becomes an issue. When multiple interference sources are present, JamLab needs a careful planning to avoid cross talk between different interference areas. Compared to JamLab, we only need to configure the Master. Every node gets the exact amount of interference as configured, which is much more accurate and flexible.

4.3   Testing at MAC Layer

There is always a concern that the physical topology of the ring will influence the network behavior on the higher level. In this experiment we further prove the reliability of the emulator by performing a throughput test at MAC layer.

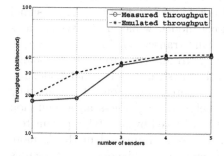
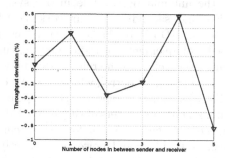

Fig. 20. Throughput vs Senders   **Fig. 21.** Deviation vs physical topology

We emulate the throughput experiment presented in [10]. The original experiment is performed on a set of TelosB motes. The receiver is situated in the center while a set of 1 to 10 senders are placed 1 meter away from the receiver. To emulate the same topology, we configured the receiver to have identical path loss to all the senders. The path loss value is calculated based on Equation (6). The senders sent packets to the receiver as fast as permitted by the MAC layer. The receiver counted the number of packets received successfully over the duration of 60 seconds. We only performed the test for XMAC[14] with 1 to 5 senders. The software is downloaded from [11], identical as used in [10]. The result is shown in Figure 20. In general, the throughput increases with the number of senders. The emulated throughput curve fits well with the measurements.

We also take an extra step to exclude the influence of the physical topology. In case of only one sender and one receiver, we change the sender and receiver's physical location, from being neighbors on the ring till 5 hops apart. The deviation of the throughput in percentage is plotted in Figure 21. The deviations do not show a trend related to the physical topology, and the value itself is also very small, less than 1% of the total throughput. Hence we conclude the impact of the physical ring topology on the performance of higher level protocol is neglectable.

5   Related Work

Many efforts have been made to overcome the limitations associated with wireless testbeds. For example, the solution presented in [12]. This solution focuses on generating interference with existing off-the-shelf hardware in a testbed. The transmit power and the location of the interferer have to be carefully set up in order to obtain desired interference coverage and low cross-talk between interference sources. Our solution, on the other hand, does not require such kind of physical deployment. Both topology and interference are controlled by software parameters, and can be realized in real-time.

The work presented in [18] is comparable to our work in the sense that they also use FPGA to replace the wireless media. However, there are three major differences: first at hardware level, they actually intercept the analog RF signal at the antenna port, while in our system, the data is never modulated into RF signal; secondly, in their work the FPGA is used to perform digital signal processing(DSP) based on a certain channel model, while in our system it is used to implement the radio interface and ring transceiver; Finally in essence, our system relies on the relationship between SNR and BER to achieve topology and interference control, while they rely on the physical layer channel model and DSP. From a user perspective, the topology and interference control is realized by tuning DSP parameters of the selected channel model, eg large-scale attenuation or fine grain fading. While for our system it is achieved by specifying parameters such as pathloss and noise level directly. The work presented in [18] is more suitable to emulate certain physical layer phenomena, while our system focuses more on general network performance. Also we believe our system is more user-friendly for researchers without DSP and physical layer background.

6   Conclusion and Future Work

We implemented a wireless link emulator based on low-cost Xilinx FPGA. This emulator differs from previous work by its unique hardware aspects, including the customized radio interface and the ring transceiver. The high speed hardware design is the key enabler for the concept of physical layer emulation.

We introduced the methodology used by our system to emulate various environments, and demonstrated experimental results that are compatible with real-life measurements.

Nevertheless, many interesting directions remain for further research. For example, the real-time topology control can be used to emulate a network with mobile nodes, and the real-time interference control creates the possibility to replay interference from recordings.

Our solution is a low cost yet very powerful and flexible test facility, that can be extended to other radio chips and wireless technologies. The scale of the emulated network can be further increased by using the newest FPGA family (Spartan6) yielding higher speeds clock on the ring. In the future, we aim to enhance the ring clock speed by a factor of eight, resulting in 48 nodes in the emulated network.

Acknowledgment. The research leading to these results has received funding from the European Union's Seventh Framework Programme FP7 under grant agreements number 258301 (CREW project) and number 287581 (OpenLab project).

The authors would also like to thank Piet Cordmans, Yang Yang, Stefan Schipper, Libo Li and Peter Ruckebusch for their contribution to this work.

References

1. Werner-Allen, G., Swieskowski, P., Welsh, M.: Motelab: A wireless sensor network testbed. In: 4th Annual Conference on Information Processing in Sensor Networks, IPSN (2005)
2. Handziski, V., et al.: TWIST: a scalable and reconfigurable testbed for wireless indoor experiments with sensor networks. In: Proceedings of the 2nd International Workshop on Multi- Hop Ad Hoc Networks: From theory to Reality (REALMAN 2006), Florence, Italy, May 26, pp. 63–70 (2006)
3. Tmote sky: ultra low power IEEE 802.15.4 compliant wireless sensor module (2006)
4. Tytgat, L., Jooris, B.: WiLab: a real-life Wireless Sensor Testbed with Environment Emulation (2009)
5. Chipcon. CC2420 datasheet (March 2007), http://focus.ti.com/lit/ds/symlink/cc2420.pdf
6. Xilinx, UG331 Spartan-3 Generation FPGA User Guide, www.xilinx.com
7. Avnet, Spartan-3A Evaluation Kit, User Guide, www.avnet.com
8. Digilent, Spartan-3E Starter Kit, www.digilent.com
9. Fluck Corporation AnalyzerAir User Manual. Rev. 2 (2006)
10. Kevin, K., et al.: A Component-Based Architecture for Power-Efficient Media Access Control in Wireless Sensor Networks. In: SenSys (2007)
11. http://tinyos.cvs.sourceforge.net/tinyos/tinyos-2.x-contrib/wustl/upma/
12. Carlo Alberto, B., et al.: JamLab: Augmenting Sensornet Testbeds with Realistic and Controlled Interference Generation. In: IPSN 2011, Chicago, Illinois, April 12-14 (2011)
13. Petrova, M., Riihijarvi, J., Mahonen, P., Labella, S.: Performance study of IEEE 802.15.4 using measurements and simulations. In: Wireless Communications and Networking Conference, WCNC 2006. IEEE (2006)
14. Buettner, M., Yee, G.V., Anderson, E., Han, R.: X-MAC: a short preamble MAC protocol for duty-cycled wireless sensor networks. In: SenSys (2006)
15. MicroBlaze Processor Reference Guide: Embedded Development Kit EDK 10.1i, http://www.xilinx.com
16. Zuniga, M., Krishnamachari, B.: Analyzing the Transitional Region in Low-Power Wireless Links. In: SECON 2004 (2004)
17. Haykin, S.: Communication Systems, 4th edn., p. 61. Wiley, New York (2001)
18. Borries, K., Wang, X., Judd, G., Anderson, E., Steenkiste, P.: Experience with a Wireless Network Testbed based on Signal Propagation Emulation. In: IEEE European Wireless 2010 Lucca, Italy, April 12-15 (2010)

Implementation and End-to-end Throughput Evaluation of an IEEE 802.11 Compliant Version of the Enhanced-Backpressure Algorithm*

Kostas Choumas, Thanasis Korakis,
Iordanis Koutsopoulos, and Leandros Tassiulas

Department of Computer and Communication Engineering,
University of Thessaly, Greece
Centre for Research and Technology Hellas, CERTH, Greece
{kohoumas,korakis,jordan,leandros}@uth.gr

Abstract. Extensive work has been done in wireless multihop routing with several ideas based on shortest path or load balancing routing algorithms, that aim at minimizing end-to-end delay or maximizing throughput respectively. Backpressure is a throughput-optimal scheme for multihop routing and scheduling, while Enhanced-Backpressure is an incremental work that reduces end-to-end delay without sacrificing throughput optimality. However, the implementation of both theoretical schemes is not straightforward in the presence of 802.11 MAC, mainly because of their requirement for centralized scheduling decisions that is not aligned with the aspects of CSMA/CA.

This paper proposes a novel scheme, named Enhanced-Backpressure over WiFi (EBoW), which is compatible with the decentralized operation of WiFi networks and efficiently utilizes the benefits of Enhanced-Backpressure design, combining throughput optimality with low end-to-end delay. EBoW router is implemented relying on Click framework for routing configuration. The performance of EBoW is evaluated both on a medium-scale outdoors wireless testbed as well as through experimentations in NS-3 simulator tool. The protocol has been compared against other state of the art routing protocols and we argue that EBoW is much more throughput efficient than the others, while succeeding similar end-to-end delay.

Keywords: Backpressure, wireless mesh, multi-path routing, testbed.

1 Introduction

As the demand for seamless connection increases, the use of wireless multihop networks as a communication infrastructure becomes more and more popular. The efficiency of a multihop mesh network is directly related to the routing protocol. On the one hand, shortest path routing algorithms achieve minimum end-to-end delay. On the other hand, when efficiency is measured in terms of

* This work was supported by European Commission under Marie Curie IRSES grant PIRSES-GA-2010-269132 AGILENet.

T. Korakis, M. Zink, and M. Ott (Eds.): TridentCom 2012, LNICST 44, pp. 64–80, 2012.

throughput, the routing protocol should utilize multiple paths connecting a source-destination pair, avoiding the dominant shortest path approach.

A scheme that achieves throughput optimality is the well-known Backpressure (BP) algorithm, which operates on a time-slotted and centralized schedule and introduces scheduling and routing policies. Enhanced-Backpressure (EBP) is an improved mechanism that can be configured with an appropriate bias that inclines packets to move in the direction of their shortest paths. EBP provides lower delay than BP, without sacrificing throughput efficiency. The seminal work of Tassiulas and Ephremides [1] constitutes the core of BP and EBP, first introduced in the work of Neely et al. [2] as Dynamic Routing and Power Control (DPRC) and Enhanced-DPRC respectively. The work of Georgiadis et al. [3] offers a comprehensive survey.

Although both schemes are throughput optimal, they have not been implemented, mainly because of the centralized scheduling policy and the time-slotted assumption. These features do not fit with the dominant wireless communication protocols. In this paper we propose an 802.11 compliant version of EBP, named Enhanced-Backpressure over WiFi (EBoW), which implements the EBP aspects in a manner that is compatible with WiFi networks. The experimentation results of the proposed scheme show that EBP principles can be efficiently applied to contemporary WiFi mesh networks.

The novelty of the proposed algorithm is twofold: i) it provides a distributed load balancing scheme, which connects nodes through multiple paths and optimizes throughput efficiency keeping low end-to-end delay, while ii) it is applicable to WiFi ad-hoc meshes that support parallel flows, where a flow defines a stream of packets with specific source and destination. We prove that EBP principles could be well adapted so as to be efficient even if a central scheduling mechanism cannot exist. Particularly, we introduce a scheme in which every node attempts to forward packets to less loaded and closer to the destination neighbors, in a similar way that EBP scheme schedules. If there is no less loaded neighbor that is closer (or at least at the same distance) to the destination, then the node stops forwarding. This feature enables a simultaneously activated scheduling policy that offers more transmission opportunities to other neighboring nodes that experience collisions.

In order to evaluate the proposed routing and scheduling scheme in realistic conditions, we implement it using the Click modular router [4]. By conducting experiments in a realistic wireless testbed, named NITOS [5], we compare our algorithm to other well-known schemes, and we show that it sometimes gains significant throughput increase due to load-balancing inherent characteristics. We also explore and verify our experimentation results in identical setups using NS-3 [6] simulator integrated with Click development.

The rest of the paper is organized as follows. In Section 2 we introduce related work, while in Section 3 we describe BP and EBP schemes in detail. Section 4 describes our proposed scheme and Section 5 presents the implementation features. The numerical results are provided in Section 6, while Section 7 concludes the paper.

2   Related Work

The main part of BP and EBP [3] is the scheduling policy that requires a central node responsible for collecting information about the whole network. According to these schemes, each packet is related to a particular *commodity*, which may be defined by its destination or its source-destination pair or something more specific. For the rest of the paper, we assume that each commodity represents a particular destination, and there is a one-to-one correspondence between sets of commodities and destinations. Furthermore, each node maintains a set of internal network layer (layer 3 of OSI model) queues, while each queue corresponds to a commodity and stores all associated packets with this commodity. The length of a commodity queue is named as commodity *backlog*.

The scheduling policy of both schemes is actually a *maximum weight matching*[1] algorithm that chooses to transmit packets corresponding to particular commodities through specific links, so as to maximize the aggregate *link-commodity weight*. In contrast to traditional schemes where each link is assigned a single weight, BP and EBP assign multiple weights to a link, corresponding to different commodities. BP utilizes a link-commodity weight that is linear to the difference among the commodity backlogs of the adjacent nodes of the corresponding link, which is denoted as *differential backlog*. In case of EBP, the relative weight is also linear to the difference of the distances between the adjacent nodes of the link and the destination of the commodity, which similarly is denoted as *differential distance*.

Finally, the routing decision of each node is implied by the centralized scheduling policy, as each node transmits a packet associated with the commodity and through the link of the corresponding scheduling choice. Unlike traditional routing mechanisms for wired and wireless networks, BP and EBP routing does not perform any explicit path computation from source to destination.

Several algorithms based on BP aspects have been proposed, which mainly require heuristic modifications of BP principles and sometimes introduction of new MAC protocols. XPRESS [7] is a well designed cross-layer architecture, which implements accurately most of the BP designs. Actually, it forces the wireless network to act like a hypothetical wireless switch, operating on a TDMA MAC, as it is originally proposed in theory. On the other hand, ad-hoc wireless environments without centralized control are commonly used, and a TDMA MAC is not applicable in such environments.

Backpressure-based Rate Control Protocol (BRCP) [8] is an approach of BP scheduling over a predefined routing tree of sensors with a single commodity (or destination) related to the root of the tree. It is actually a distributed version, where each sensor decides the prioritization of its current transmission based on the current differential backlog. Obviously, this scheme does not apply on a wireless mesh with multiple commodities.

---

[1] Matching is a set of pairwise non-adjacent links and the maximum weight matching has the maximum aggregate weight.

DiffQ [9] is a different scheduling approach for wireless mesh networks that support multiple commodities. It enables packet transmissions of commodities through links with positive differential backlog and gives higher priority to those with larger differentials. This design requires changes of the 802.11 MAC layer. Furthermore, the routing decision depends on a shortest path routing protocol that does not feature load balancing characteristics and therefore does not take advantage of these BP inherent features.

The Backpressure Collection Protocol (BCP) [10] is a remarkable implementation and experimentation of BP design in wireless sensor networks over 802.15.4. In sensor networks there is only one commodity, since all packets have the same destination. So sensors include only one network layer queue, a feature that differentiates BCP from the BP scheme. Furthermore, BCP uses a BP related weight that is enriched with a penalty mechanism, while the use of an EBP oriented weight seems to be more efficient.

Horizon [11] is another system design for distance-vector routing in wireless multihop networks, which is inspired by the BP principles and it is compatible with 802.11 MAC and TCP. It is the first system architecture that implemented these principles in a wireless system design. However, Horizon uses an inexplicably simplified forwarding algorithm that actually depends on backlogs and not on differential backlogs, as BP does. Congestion Diversity Protocol (CDP) [12] is another distance-vector routing protocol that is queue length aware and not BP inspired. In like manner, it does not depend on differential backlogs and moreover does not keep different queues for different commodities. Both protocols, Horizon and CDP, do not include scheduling policies. The proposed EBoW scheme is compared with these implementations.

In contrast, SouRCe Routing (SRCR) is a shortest path routing protocol implemented in Roofnet [13]. It uses Expected Transmission Time (ETT) [14], which is the state of the art for defining wireless link weight for forwarding packets, and applies Dijkstra algorithm to explore the shortest route from a source to a destination. Since several evaluation works show that SRCR efficiently routes packets in mesh networks, the proposed algorithm will be compared to SRCR to measure the efficiency of the load balancing feature that comes as inherent characteristic in BP.

Summarizing, the most remarkable implemented routing protocols for WiFi ad-hoc meshes with multiple flows are these of Horizon, CDP and SRCR. Horizon and CDP are two notable distance-vector routing schemes that attempt to use multiple paths for packet forwarding using BP principles. Their common feature is their effort to avoid overloaded paths. On the other hand, SRCR uses always the shortest path ignoring alternative less loaded routes.

3   Enhanced-Backpressure Explained

Before starting the description we will introduce the main terminology of BP and EBP. A throughput vector includes the throughputs of all network flows, where a flow throughput is the average packet delivery rate of this flow. Furthermore,

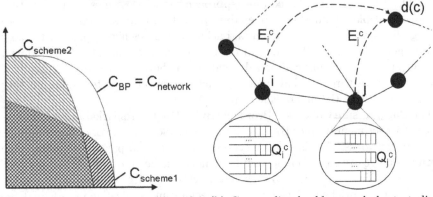

(a) Capacity region of a network with two flows

(b) Commodity backlogs and shortest distances of two adjacent nodes

Fig. 1. Capacity region and Network snapshot

the capacity region of a certain scheme consists of the throughput vectors that this scheme is able to manage, while the capacity region of a network is the union of the capacity regions of all possible schemes. Figure 1(a) illustrates the above mentioned regions for a network with two flows. Tassiulas and Ephremides [1] proved that under a slotted environment, the capacity region of a network is the same as the capacity region of the BP scheme, which is superset of the capacity region of any other scheme. Neely *et al.* [2] also showed that EBP has the same capacity region with BP. The goal of the proposed scheme is to succeed an extended capacity region similar to that of the BP and EBP schemes.

Before proceeding, we introduce also some notations. We consider a multihop wireless network with node, link and commodity sets denoted as $\mathcal{N}, \mathcal{L}$ and $\mathcal{C}$ respectively. If $i, j \in \mathcal{N}$ are two adjacent nodes in the network, then $l = (i, j) \in \mathcal{L}$ is a directional link. Furthermore, if $c \in \mathcal{C}$ denotes a commodity, then $d(c) \in \mathcal{N}$ is the destination node that corresponds to commodity c. Finally, as it is shown in Figure 1(b), Q_i^c symbolizes backlog of commodity c at node i and E_i^c stands for the length of the shortest path (or the distance) from node i to destination $d(c)$. Consequently, differential backlog and differential distance of commodity c through link (i, j) are denoted as $\Delta Q_{i,j}^c = Q_i^c - Q_j^c$ and $\Delta E_{i,j}^c = E_i^c - E_j^c$ respectively. In addition, $R_{i,j}$ is the actual data rate of link (i, j).

The core of BP and EBP schemes is the maximum link-commodity weight matching algorithm. The BP link-commodity weight for a commodity $c \in \mathcal{C}$ and a link $(i, j) \in \mathcal{L}$ is either zero or the positive product of the actual data rate $R_{i,j}$ of the specific link and the differential backlog $\Delta Q_{i,j}^c$, as it is given in equation 1. Furthermore, EBP can be configured so as to incline packets to move in the direction of their shortest paths, using another appropriately defined link-commodity weight. More specifically, in EBP differential distance $\Delta E_{i,j}^c$ is added to the above mentioned differential backlog, as it is defined in equation 2. The distance should be estimated using hop count or another more sophisticated approach for measuring the shortest path length. Finally, the EBP scheme succeeds the same throughput optimality as the BP scheme, while at the same time it reduces packet delivery time.

$$w_{i,j}^c = \max\{\varDelta Q_{i,j}^c \cdot R_{i,j}, 0\} \tag{1}$$

$$\bar{w}_{i,j}^c = \max\{(\varDelta Q_{i,j}^c + \varDelta E_{i,j}^c) \cdot R_{i,j}, 0\} \tag{2}$$

4 EBoW Design

4.1 Algorithm Description

The goal of the Enhanced-Backpressure over WiFi (EBoW) scheme is to improve throughput efficiency of wireless mesh networks, adopting the EBP principles, while simultaneously succeeding low delay, similar to the shortest path routing schemes. Due to its characteristics, this scheme can dynamically avoid overloaded paths, create parallel routes and therefore balance the traffic load in the network, increasing in this way its throughput efficiency.

Below we describe the main principle behind EBoW explaining the practices adapted, in order to achieve the benefits mentioned. Consider a network with multiple nodes that operate in a multihop environment. In such a setup, EBoW runs in every node that can act as source, destination or relay. Every node maintains a set of internal network layer queues, where each queue corresponds to a commodity, as specified in the BP and EBP schemes (further details in Section 2 and Section 3).

When a node receives or generates a packet that needs to be forwarded, it identifies the related commodity, recognizing the destination of the packet, and pushes the packet to the corresponding network layer queue. Moreover, each node that has packets in its queues, initiates a procedure to schedule the transmission of a packet. The most important part of this procedure is the calculation of the link-commodity weights of equation (3).

$$\hat{w}_{i,j}^c = (\varDelta Q_{i,j}^c + \varDelta E_{i,j}^c) \cdot R_{i,j} \tag{3}$$

Next, the node finds the link-commodity pair with the maximum weight, with positive differential backlog $\varDelta Q_{i,j}^c > 0$ and non-negative differential distance $\varDelta E_{i,j}^c \geq 0$. If there is at least one link-commodity pair that satisfies these conditions, the node selects the one with the maximum weight and transmits a packet from the corresponding queue. Then, the packet is passed down to the data-link layer (layer 2 of OSI model), while it is tagged to be transmitted through the link that is related with this pair. This algorithm is the routing policy of the EBoW scheme. On the other hand, in case there is no pair that meets these requirements, the node remains inactive and does not schedule transmissions. These requirements constitute the scheduling policy of the EBoW scheme.

The first scheduling condition requires a positive differential backlog $\varDelta Q_{i,j}^c > 0$ and exists because of the remark of Li *et al.* [15], who explained why the capacity of a chain of nodes is reduced due to the inherent characteristics of 802.11. Nodes centrally located in the chain experience more collisions than border nodes. This is due to the fact that border nodes inject more packets into the chain than the subsequent nodes can forward, so these packets are eventually dropped. The time that border nodes spend to send those extra packets decreases the overall throughput, since it prevents transmissions of subsequent nodes. Our proposed algorithm takes this observation into account and therefore introduces the positive differential backlog condition to prevent it. So, in EBoW if a node observes that an adjacent node features a higher backlog than itself, it refrains from forwarding packets to it, thereby providing more transmission opportunities to this node. In this way, the capacity per hop is allocated more efficiently.

The second scheduling condition namely non-negative differential distance $\Delta E_{i,j}^c \geq 0$ exists in order to avoid excessively long routes of packets towards their destinations. Eventhough the EBP scheme takes into account distance to destination by incorporating it into the link weights, it often allows a packet to move further away from its destination. However, this is a typically undesired feature for traditional wireless applications, where users are interested in experiencing low end-to-end delay and jitter. This observation explains why the non-negative differential distance is a necessary condition for packet forwarding in our proposed scheme, which takes practical WiFi applications into consideration.

In essence , the main differentiation of EBoW with respect to the original EBP scheme is that it is structured around a distributed architecture, which makes it more suitable for real WiFi applications. EBP is a centralized algorithm which assigns non-negative weights to all link-commodity pairs and schedules packet transmissions based on the maximum weight matching principle. In contrast, in EBoW each node makes its forwarding decisions independently, according to the algorithm described before. More specifically, each node $i \in \mathcal{N}$ finds neighbor $j \in \mathcal{N} : (i,j) \in \mathcal{L}$ and commodity $c \in \mathcal{C}$ that maximize $\hat{w}_{i,j}^c$ (ties broken arbitrarily) subject to $\Delta Q_{i,j}^c > 0$ and $\Delta E_{i,j}^c \geq 0$, and pushes down from the

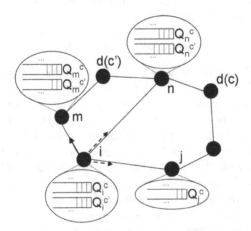

Fig. 2. Network example illustrating EBoW design

network to the data-link layer a packet that corresponds to commodity c for transmission through link (i, j). If there are no neighbor j and commodity c that satisfy these conditions, the node remains inactive.

For example, in Figure 2, considering that the path length is measured in hops and the data rate of each link is equal to unit, then $\hat{w}_{i,j}^c = ((3-2)+(2-2))\cdot 1 = 1$ and $\hat{w}_{i,m}^{c'} = ((3-2)+(2-1))\cdot 1 = 2$, while $\Delta Q_{i,n}^c = 3-3 = 0$, $\Delta E_{i,m}^c = 2-3 < 0$, $\Delta E_{i,j}^{c'} = 2-3 < 0$ and $\Delta Q_{i,n}^{c'} = 3-4 < 0$. As a result, node i forwards to neighbor m a packet that corresponds to commodity c'.

4.2   Distance Calculation and Broadcast Packets

The way that the algorithm estimates the distance between two nodes is another important point to mention. In the previous example, we used hop count for simplicity. In fact, the proposed algorithm uses a more sophisticated technique of distance measurement. The distance E_i^c between node i and destination $d(c)$ is expressed as a scale factor θ of the aggregate expected transmission time of a packet (queuing and processing delay is ignored), which is routed through the shortest path from source i to destination $d(c)$. The scale factor is adjusted so that $\Delta E_{i,j}^c$ and $\Delta Q_{i,j}^c$ to have the same range of values. The expected transmission time through a link is given by the well known formula of the Expected Transmission Time (ETT) metric [14]. According to this formula:

$$ETT = \frac{1}{d_f \cdot d_r} \cdot \frac{S}{B} \qquad (4)$$

where d_f and d_r are the expected forward and reverse link delivery probabilities (the product of these two is the probability of a successful acknowledged transmission), S is the average packet size and B is the average packet rate that the rate controller assigns. So, if $e_{i,j}$ stands for the ETT weight of link (i, j), then

$$E_i^c = \theta \cdot \sum_{\forall (k,l) \in \mathcal{L} \text{ in the shortest path } i \rightsquigarrow d(c)} e_{k,l} \qquad (5)$$

Every node needs to know all commodity backlogs of its neighbors, as well as the aggregate ETT of the shortest paths from itself and its neighbors to every destination. The ETT calculation for every link, especially of the forward and reverse probabilities d_f and d_r, is based on a probing mechanism that periodically forces nodes to send broadcast packets and inform neighbors about the number of the broadcast packets they have received. Due to this mechanism, each node estimates the ETT weights of its outgoing links, while simultaneously learning about the commodity backlogs of its neighbors, which are included in the broadcast packets.

However, nodes need to know ETT weights of links that are located multi-hops away from them. So, before a source starts forwarding a packet, it initiates a broadcast query flooding the network in order to reach the destination of the packet. While the query packet is passing through network links, it is tagged with the path that it followed until that point. The destination receives these queries and replies through all paths that the query flood explored. Similarly, each reply packet is tagged with the ETT weights of all links that this packet passed through. In this way, once the source (or a relay) receives the reply packets, it learns about all necessary ETT weights in order to estimate the distances from itself and its neighbors to the destination.

5   Implementation Details

The software development of EBoW scheme is based on the Click modular router framework [4], a novel software architecture for building flexible and configurable routers, that lie on network nodes and forward packets. A Click modular router consists of packet processing modules called elements. Individual elements implement simple router functions like packet classification, queuing and interfacing with network devices. Complete router configurations are built by connecting elements into a graph, where packets flow along the graph's edges. Most of these elements are given by the existing framework, while it is possible to construct additional and more specific elements.

The Click modular router is able to run as a linux-kernel module or a user-level executable on top of linux operated boxes. The Click framework includes a package of elements and a configuration of a user-level SRCR router (designed by the Roofnet [13] team). The configuration of the EBoW router shares a lot of common features with the corresponding one of the SRCR router, as it is illustrated in Figure 3. So, a brief description of the SRCR router follows, and then it is presented how the EBoW router is differentiated from this.

The User-Level SRCR Click Router (see Figure 3(a)) uses a *pseudo*-interface that connects the application layer with the underlying network layer and a *wireless* interface that receives and transmits packets over the air. Once a packet is received from the application layer (through the *pseudo*-interface), it is forwarded to the *SRQuerier* element. The main goal of this element is to estimate the shortest path from this node to the final destination of the packet. If *SRQuerier* does not have already the information for this packet (through past investigation for the shortest path of another packet with the same destination), it forwards the packet to the *MetricFlood* element. This element initiates a broadcast query flooding the network in order to reach the destination of the particular packet.

The query packets of the flood visit the *MetricFlood* elements of the relays until the destination. Once the destination is reached, the query packet is forwarded from *MetricFlood* to the *SRQueryResponder* element. *SRQueryResponder* initiates a reply packet that follows the shortest path to the initial node, visiting the corresponding element of each relay until the source. The shortest path is recognized by *SRQueryResponder* in the following way: the destination receives multiple query packets that were transmitted through the flooding method, through multiple paths. Each query packet is tagged with the path that it followed, as well as with the ETT weights of the intermediate links. So the destination explores the intermediate link weights and finds the shortest route applying Dijkstra algorithm.

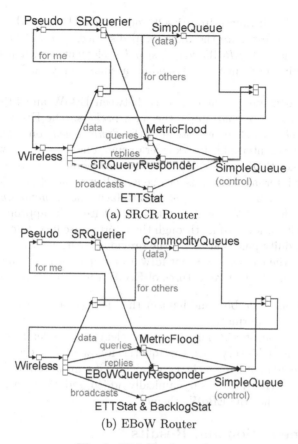

(a) SRCR Router

(b) EBoW Router

Fig. 3. Click Configurations

Once the source receives the reply packet, it learns also about the shortest path to the destination, because the reply packet is similarly tagged with the path that it followed. So *SRQuerier* has the relative information for the following packets with the same destination. Therefore, the following packets are forwarded to the *SimpleQueue* element, which is able to store up to 50 packets, and implements the network layer queue. There is also another *SimpleQueue* element that stores the control packets, like query, reply and broadcast packets. The broadcast packets are generated and processed by the *ETTStat* element, for estimation of the ETT weights of the outgoing links, as it was described earlier in Subsection 4.2. Both queues store the packets, and forward them to the *wireless* interface on demand.

The User-Level EBoW Click Router (see Figure 3(b)) uses the same underlying probing mechanism (*ETTStat*) that estimates the ETT weights of the network links, while it features an additional probing mechanism (*BacklogStat*) for broadcasting commodity backlogs of each node to its neighbors. Furthermore, as it was mentioned in Subsection 4.2, either the source or the relay of a packet needs to know the distances from itself and its neighbors to the destination, so as to be able to estimate the differential distances. So, *SRQueryResponder* is replaced by the new *EBoWQueryResponder* element, which responds with a broadcast reply flood, instead of sending a single reply packet through the shortest path.

Finally, the most important difference between EBoW and SRCR configurations, is the structure that stores the data packets. The EBoW router uses the *CommodityQueues* element instead of the *SimpleQueue* one. This structure includes a variety of internal network layer queues, one for each known commodity. Once a packet that corresponds to a new commodity arrives, the structure produces a new internal network layer queue. When a packet is to be forwarded from *CommodityQueues* to the *wireless* interface, the *CommodityQueues* element estimates the EBoW weights, pulls a packet from the appropriate internal queue and tags it for forwarding through the appropriate link. In case that there is no link-commodity pair that meets the previous mentioned requirements (see Section 4), then the element does not forward any packet to the interface.

In summary, the distinctive features of EBoW router are three:

- The extension of probing mechanism that is used also to propagate commodity backlog information.
- The modification of *SRQueryResponder* element in order to respond more than once through every path that queries followed until the destination.
- The replacement of *SimpleQueue* element with an appropriate *CommodityQueues* one, that includes dynamically added and removed network layer queues and applies the EBoW scheme.

6   Experimentation and Results

In this section, we present evaluation experiments of the implemented scheme under various scenarios. For the purposes of the experimental evaluation, we used the realistic medium-scale NITOS testbed.. Experimentation with implemented mechanisms in realistic infrastructure, may lead to results that depend on varying traffic, interference conditions and topology settings that cannot be fully controlled. In order to arrive at solid results regarding the evaluation of our protocol, we decided to run multiple executions of each experimental scenario that is presented in this section. More specifically, each experiment is run 5 times and lasts 10 minutes. The reported results present average values. Moreover, we decided to run the same experiments under fully controlled settings in a simulation environment and for this purpose we used the NS-3 platform. Comparison between the results obtained through experimentation on the different platforms, enhances the validity of the followed evaluation approach.

Through our experiments, we compare EBoW with SRCR, Horizon and CDP, which are considered as state of the art routing protocols for WiFi networks. For comparison reasons, we also implemented the Horizon and CDP mechanisms based on the Click framework and the SRCR Click configuration. Performance comparison between EBoW, SRCR, Horizon and CDP, is presented in terms of throughput and end-to-end delay. Our experiments are organized in two parts, where in the first part the execution of an experimental scenario in a simple proof-of-principle network is presented, while in the second part we conduct a complex experiment in a topology of 20 nodes that introduces randomness and approximates realistic conditions. Details about the experimentation platform used in each case follow.

6.1 Experimentation Platforms

NITOS is a wireless outdoor testbed deployed across several floors and thus it provides for easy setup of multi-hop routes (Figure 4(a)). It is a non-RF-isolated wireless testbed, so we used 802.11a to eliminate interference, since commercial 802.11 products in Greece use only 802.11bg. The nodes used for the experiments feature a 1GHz VIA C3 processor and a Wistron CM9 wireless card. These wireless cards come along with a special version of the open source MAD-WiFi driver that enables the Click router to transmit and receive packets. The main features of the nodes and their software specifications are depicted in Table 1.

Table 1. Basic Configuration of NITLAB nodes

Model	Orbit radio nodes
CPU / Memory	1 GHz VIA C3 processor / 512 MB RAM
Operating system	Debian GNU/Linux 4.0r8 "etch" / kernel ver 2.6.16
Wireless card	Wistron CM9 mini-pci / chipset Atheros AR5213A
Wireless driver	madwifi-old r846 2005-02-16 (modified)

NS-3 is a valid simulation framework that is able to simulate network topologies under accurately controlled conditions. The experimenter has the flexibility to decide about the preferred OSI layer protocols. We exploited this feature to run our experiments using specific routing protocols. We decided to use the NS-3 simulator, because of its ability to be integrated with the Click framework, in order to be able to test the developed Click configurations in a simulation environment. As a result, we were able to use the same Click configuration in both real and simulated experiments.

6.2 Measurement Methodology

The traffic on the real testbed is generated using Iperf [16], a powerful tool for traffic generation and measurement. The experimental setup consists of several pairs of nodes that initiate UDP traffic flows by running Iperf clients at the sources and Iperf servers at the destinations. We also use the Iperf tool to collect throughput performance in each experiment. In order to monitor end-to-end delay performance per packet, we developed a custom timestamp mechanism

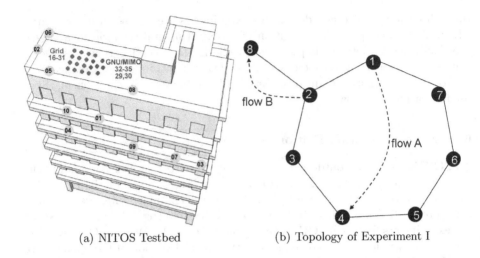

(a) NITOS Testbed   (b) Topology of Experiment I

Fig. 4. Experimental Setup

using the Click framework. For experiments conducted in the NS-3 platform, we used the same mechanism to gather delay measurements, while traffic generation and throughput monitoring were performed using the *OnOffApplication* and *PacketSink* NS-3 application modules. Description of the conducted experiments and discussion about the obtained results follow.

6.3   Experiment I

The topology and connectivity map of our first experiment are illustrated in Figure 4(b). A ring topology of 7 nodes is designed, enabling a 3-hop and 4-hop path with the same source (node 1) and destination (node 4) nodes. Each network node is able to communicate through single-hop transmissions with each one of the two nodes that exist before and after it in the ring topology. In the presented topology, an extra node (node 8) also exists, which is able to communicate directly only with node 2.

The experiment consists of two parallel active flows, namely flow A and flow B, where through flow A node 1 transmits to node 4, and through flow B node 2 transmits to node 8. We conduct experiments of varying traffic rate for both of these flows, in order to estimate the capacity region supported by the network across the different protocols. Results obtained through experimentation in NITOS testbed and NS-3 simulator are very close, and for this reason we present in the following figures only the realistic testbed results. In Figure 5(a), we illustrate the capacity regions of the examined schemes. For example, the throughput vector $[6Mbps, 15Mbps]$ that indicates throughputs $6Mbps$ and $15Mbps$ for the flows A and B respectively, exists inside the capacity region of EBoW, while it is outside the capacity region of the SRCR scheme.

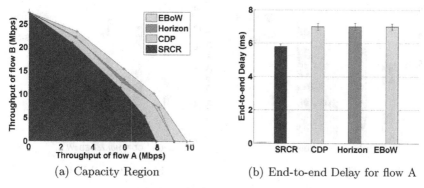

(a) Capacity Region   (b) End-to-end Delay for flow A

Fig. 5. Results of Experiment I

SRCR as a shortest path routing algorithm indicates the shortest route for each flow. Due to the symmetric nature of the designed topology, nearly equal ETT weights are reported for each link. As a result, SRCR obviously selects the shortest 3-hop path 1-2-3-4 that features the lowest aggregate ETT weight, in comparison with the 4-hop path 1-7-6-5-4. As SRCR does not feature any load balancing mechanism, it is not able to detect simultaneous ongoing transmissions, as these of flow B in this scenario. Under the SRCR approach, node 2 acts as a bottleneck that significantly reduces the throughput for both flows.

On the other hand, the rest of the schemes under consideration, better exploit the existence of two paths between the source and destination nodes of flow A. Although the 4-hop path is longer in terms of ETT weight, it features less traffic load in comparison with the 3-hop path due to the simultaneous transmissions of node 2. As a result, the 4-hop path is able to provide higher throughput performance. In addition, we notice that EBoW approach features an extended capacity region compared to the regions of the other two distance vector routing protocols. The main reason for this phenomenon comes from the inherent scheduling policy of the EBoW scheme, through which nodes that feature non positive differential backlogs are scheduled not to forward packets, while relay nodes that follow are provided with more transmission opportunities (see more details in Section 4).

Another important factor that has to be considered is end-to-end delay performance. We notice that end-to-end delay reported for flow B is equal for all schemes, as they all use the same 1-hop route for packet forwarding. The end-to-end delay performance for flow A yielded in each approach, is depicted in Figure 5(b). As clearly shown in this figure, end-to-end delay performance for flow A is reported quite similar for all load balancing schemes. Another observation is that the SRCR scheme outperforms all the other schemes in terms of end-to-end delay. The lower end-to-end delay measurements reported for SRCR are expected, as this approach is based on the shortest path principle. However, end-to-end delay performance of SRCR is not significantly lower, which is due to the collisions that occur frequently in the heavy loaded 3-hop path and negatively affect delay performance.

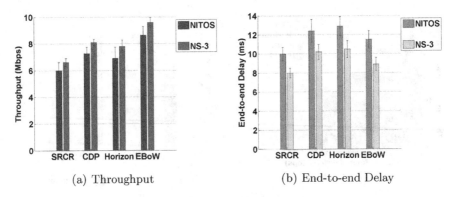

(a) Throughput   (b) End-to-end Delay

Fig. 6. Results of Experiment II

6.4   Experiment II

In the second experiment we extend our validation in a random setup that in-cludes 20 nodes and 3 randomly selected 4-hop flows. Figure 6(a) shows the average throughput achieved for the 3 flows under each approach, on top of the two different platforms. As we can see, the proposed scheme features significant throughput improvement compared with the other schemes, across both plat-forms. Under EBoW, transmitter nodes are able to utilize multiple paths and moreover refrain from forwarding packets to nodes that feature high backlogs and thus result in network capacity improvement. In addition, EBoW performs better even in cases where the source-destination node pair is connected through a unique path, as it provides more transmission opportunities to nodes that fea-ture higher backlogs.

Figure 6(b) demonstrates end-to-end delay measurements obtained during experimentation in the extended topology, across the different environments. According to these results, we notice that SRCR provides the lowest delay val-ues among the compared approaches. An observation of notable importance is that the EBoW scheme outperforms the rest load balancing schemes. This re-sult is obtained under experimentation in more generic topologies compared with the simple ring topology used in the previous experiment. More complex topologies provide larger paths in terms of aggregate ETT, which are avoided by the proposed scheme based on the non-negative differential distance forwarding requirement, but not by the rest load balancing schemes.

Results obtained between the different platforms are quite close but have some characteristics that provide for further discussion. First of all, we notice that real testbed experiments yield lower throughput and higher delay performance in comparison with simulation results. This comes from the fact simulation envi-ronments are not able to accurately estimate performance of realistic networks. However, experimentation in each platform aids in arriving at relative conclu-sions, regarding the superiority of our protocol. At this point we also remark the higher deviation values observed during testbed experimentation, which result because of the volatile nature of the realistic testbed environment.

7   Conclusions and Future Work

In this paper we propose an implemented EBP inspired scheme that exploits multi-path flow forwarding and outperforms the state of the art routing protocols in terms of throughput, while it keeps low packet delay close to the delay of the shortest path routing protocols. The new scheme features significant throughput benefits comparing to other routing protocols with load balancing efforts. We intent to extend the current work towards two directions: The first one is to compare the proposed protocol with centralized EBP based implementation approaches, and to see the advantages and disadvantages of the distributed VS the centralized version. The second one is to combine the proposed scheme with more sophisticated scheduling EBP inspired policies that will be implemented in a distributed manner and will allow the scheduling of transmissions in the neighborhood based on the load difference of the contenting hops. The scheduling will be based on prioritization schemes of 802.11 such as those proposed in 802.11e (different AIFS or different back-off values based on traffic queues).

References

1. Tassiulas, L., Ephremides, A.: Stability properties of constrained queueing systems and scheduling policies for maximum throughput in multihop radio networks. IEEE Transactions on Automatic Control 37(12), 1936–1948 (1992)
2. Neely, M.J., Modiano, E., Rohrs, C.E.: Dynamic power allocation and routing for time varying wireless networks. In: IEEE INFOCOM, vol. 1, pp. 745–755 (April 2003)
3. Georgiadis, L., Neely, M., Tassiulas, L.: Resource allocation and cross layer control in wireless networks. Foundations and Trends in Networking 1(1), 1–149 (2006)
4. Morris, R., Kohler, E., Jannotti, J., Frans Kaashoek, M.: The click modular router. ACM SOSP 34(5), 217–231 (1999)
5. NITLab: Network Implementation Testbed Laboratory, http://nitlab.inf.uth.gr/NITlab/index.php/testbed
6. ns-3: Network Simulator, http://www.nsnam.org
7. Laufer, R., Salonidis, T., Lundgren, H., Guyadec, P.L.: Xpress: a cross-layer backpressure architecture for wireless multi-hop networks. In: ACM MobiCom, pp. 49–60 (2011)
8. Sridharan, A., Moeller, S., Krishnamachari, B., Hsieh, M.: Implementing backpressure-based rate control in wireless networks. In: IEEE ITA, pp. 341–345 (February 2009)
9. Warrier, A., Janakiraman, S., Ha, S., Rhee, I.: Diffq: Practical differential backlog congestion control for wireless networks. In: IEEE INFOCOM, pp. 262–270 (April 2009)
10. Moeller, S., Sridharan, A., Krishnamachari, B., Gnawali, O.: Routing without routes: The backpressure collection protocol. In: ACM/IEEE IPSN, pp. 279–290 (April 2010)
11. Radunović, B., Gkantsidis, C., Gunawardena, D., Key, P.: Horizon: Balancing tcp over multiple paths in wireless mesh network. In: ACM MobiCom, pp. 247–258 (2008)

12. Bhorkar, A.A., Javidi, T., Snoereny, A.C.: Achieving congestion diversity in wireless ad-hoc networks. In: IEEE INFOCOM, pp. 521–525 (April 2011)
13. Bicket, J., Aguayo, D., Biswas, S., Morris, R.: Architecture and evaluation of an unplanned 802.11b mesh network. In: ACM MobiCom, pp. 31–42 (2005)
14. Draves, R., Padhye, J., Zill, B.: Routing in multi-radio, multi-hop wireless mesh networks. In: ACM MobiCom, pp. 114–128 (2004)
15. Li, J., Blake, C., De Couto, D.S.J., Lee, H.I., Morris, R.: Capacity of ad hoc wireless networks. In: ACM MobiCom, pp. 61–69 (2001)
16. Iperf: The TCP/UDP Bandwidth Measurement Tool,
    http://dast.nlanr.net/Projects/Iperf/

BonFIRE: A Multi-cloud Test Facility
for Internet of Services Experimentation

Alastair C. Hume[1], Yahya Al-Hazmi[2], Bartosz Belter[3], Konrad Campowsky[4],
Luis M. Carril[5], Gino Carrozzo[6], Vegard Engen[7], David García-Pérez[8],
Jordi Jofre Ponsatí[9], Roland Kűbert[10], Yongzheng Liang[11], Cyril Rohr[12],
and Gregory Van Seghbroeck[13]

[1] EPCC, University of Edinburgh, King's Buildings, Mayfield Road, Edinburgh, UK
A.Hume@epcc.ed.ac.uk
[2] Chair of Next Generation Networks, Technical University Berlin, Berlin, Germany
[3] Poznan Supercomputing and Networking Center (PSNC), Poznan, Poland
[4] Next Generation Network Infrastructures, Fraunhofer FOKUS, Berlin, Germany
[5] Centro de Supercomputación de Galicia (CESGA), Santiago de Compostela, Spain
[6] Nextworks s.r.l., Pisa, Italy
[7] IT Innovation Centre, Southampton, UK
[8] Atos Research and Innovation Group, Barcelona, Spain
[9] Distributed Applications and Networks Area, i2CAT Foundation, Barcelona, Spain
[10] High Performance Computing Center Stuttgart (HLRS), Stuttgart, Germany
[11] Computing Center, University of Stuttgart, Stuttgart, Germany
[12] INRIA Rennes - Bretagne Atlantique research center, Rennes, France
[13] Department of Information Technology, Ghent University, IBBT, Ghent, Belgium

Abstract. BonFIRE offers a Future Internet, multi-site, cloud testbed,
targeted at the Internet of Services community, that supports large scale
testing of applications, services and systems over multiple, geographically
distributed, heterogeneous cloud testbeds. The aim of BonFIRE is to
provide an infrastructure that gives experimenters the ability to control
and monitor the execution of their experiments to a degree that is not
found in traditional cloud facilities.

The BonFIRE architecture has been designed to support key functionalities such as: resource management; monitoring of virtual and physical
infrastructure metrics; elasticity; single document experiment descriptions; and scheduling.

As for January 2012 BonFIRE release 2 is operational, supporting
seven pilot experiments. Future releases will enhance the offering, including the interconnecting with networking facilities to provide access
to routers, switches and bandwidth-on-demand systems. BonFIRE will
be open for general use late 2012.

Keywords: Multi-cloud, Future Internet, Internet of Services, Testbed,
Bandwidth on Demand.

1 Introduction

BonFIRE offers a multi-site cloud testbed that supports large scale testing
of applications, services and systems over multiple, geographically distributed,

T. Korakis, M. Zink, and M. Ott (Eds.): TridentCom 2012, LNICST 44, pp. 81–96, 2012.
© Institute for Computer Sciences, Social Informatics and Telecommunications Engineering 2012

heterogeneous cloud testbeds. BonFIRE targets the Internet of Services community and offers a test infrastructure that is ideal for performing experiments relating to distributed applications and services. BonFIRE's aim is not to provide a production environment for cloud applications, but instead to provide an infrastructure that gives experimenters the ability to control and monitor the execution of their experiments to a degree that is not found in traditional cloud facilities.

By targeting the Internet of Services community, BonFIRE aims to extend the reach of Future Internet experiment testbeds into the area of distributed applications and services. To further appeal to that community, BonFIRE adopts a cloud-based model that is familiar to many Internet of Services experimenters.

One of the key features of BonFIRE is to give experimenters the ability to control some of the many variables that affect the performance of distributed applications. For example, BonFIRE allows users to control network quality-of-service parameters such as latency, delay and packet loss using the Virtual Wall [1] network emulation facility. Further control of network performance between geographically distributed infrastructures is anticipated through future interconnection with FEDERICA [2] and GÉANT AutoBAHN [3,4].

Apart from network characteristics there are many other variables that can affect performance of an application running on a cloud infrastructure; examples include the load of the VMs running on the physical machine as well as disk and memory contention. BonFIRE supports exclusive access to physical machines and allows experimenters to directly control the placement of VMs on physical machines. These features give experimenters the control required to reduce contention or even ensure an explicit level of contention required for the experiment.

Where BonFIRE cannot control variables, it provides low- level infrastructure metrics that can be used to monitor the infrastructure at a level that is typically hidden from users of cloud systems. Examples of infrastructure metrics include the load on a physical CPU, network throughput and disk I/O metrics. Experimenters are to use this low-level infrastructure monitoring data to understand, and account for, the impact of these variables on their experiment results.

By adopting a cloud-model to access the multi-cloud facility, BonFIRE provides a convenient resource-level interface for managing compute, network and storage resources on any of the BonFIRE testbeds. Thus BonFIRE supports geographically distributed experiments over multiple heterogeneous cloud testbeds including the ability to elastically adjust the resources used during an experiment. BonFIRE also supports a higher experiment-level interface that provides users with the ability to describe the whole experiment in a document. Additionally, BonFIRE provides built-in support for commonly used experiment functionality such as monitoring collectors and publishers.

2   The Testbeds

At the core of BonFIRE are five geographically distributed cloud testbeds that together offer 350 cores, with 700GB of RAM and 30TB of storage. An additional

2,300 multi-core nodes can be added to BonFIRE on specific request. Additionally, BonFIRE is working to interconnect with several external facilities to enhance the offering.

2.1   Core Testbeds

The BonFIRE core testbeds can be divided into two groups: OpenNebula based testbeds located at EPCC (UK), INRIA (France) and HLRS (Germany) and non-OpenNebula based testbeds located at IBBT (Belgium) and HP (UK). All testbeds are different from one another regarding structure, networking and resources. This heterogeneity is a key feature of the BonFIRE system.

The common point of the testbeds of EPCC, INRIA and HLRS is that they use OpenNebula as a cloud management solution and are currently running the Xen hypervisor. Apart from that, the sites are quite different: EPCC provides 96 cores on two nodes, INRIA 36 cores on 9 nodes and HLRS a total of 44 cores: 20 cores on five nodes at 2GB RAM and 24 cores on six nodes at 8 GB RAM.

IBBT's Virtual Wall is based on the Emulab network emulation software. Tight integration of Emulab's capabilities and the BonFIRE functionality makes it very much suited for network related experiments. The IBBT Virtual Wall consists of 100 nodes, of which 8 are available permanently to BonFIRE users throughout the project's lifetime. Each node has 4 cores at 4GB RAM and 4 to 6 Gigabit Ethernet interfaces, all of them connected to a non-blocking switch.

The HP infrastructure provides a virtual machine execution service. The virtual machines will be running in a Xen environment, augmented with network and storage virtualization.HP's infrastructure is set up with the current stable release of HP Cells [5] as a Virtual Infrastructure Manager. The HP facility provides 32 4-core nodes permanently dedicated to BonFIRE with access to up to 96.

2.2   On-Request Resources

On-request resources are resources that are not part of the BonFIRE facility on a permanent basis, but they are provided to users for large- scale experiments. Typically, a substantially larger collection of resources is available on-request than is offered by the pemanent infrastructure. The operation and investments of these facilities are too high to be exclusively provided for experiments but are operated as production level facilities. In order to allow large scale testing, these resources can be made available for a specific experiment for a limited time.

As with the permanent resources, the kind and amount of on-request resources differs from site to site. In total, there will be around 2,200 cores available through on-request resources across all sites.

2.3   External Facilities

Integration of the internal multi-site cloud facilities and their interconnection with external (FIRE) facilities is key in BonFIRE. Horizontal integration is achieved through the integration of the different testbeds facilities as described in Section 2.1. Conversely, the vertical integration of the facilities (Cloud-and-Network) enables cross-layer testing to propagate service-level requirements down to the connectivity levels. BonFIRE will initially interconnect with two external facilities to provide vertical integration to the network level. These are GÉANT's Bandwidth-on-Demand (BoD) system and FEDERICA's slice-based infrastructure that gives access to routes, switches and servers.

A major challenge in the vertical federation of cloud and network is the need to provision on-demand network connectivity services among multiple cloud resources and sites by interfacing to multi-domain heterogeneous production networks. In this framework, BonFIRE integrates with Bandwidth- on-Demand (BoD) provisioning systems that have been developed by network operators to provide their end-users with dynamic and efficient systems for their on-demand network connectivity services. Due to the research-driven mission of the BonFIRE project and the positioning of the overall FIRE initiative, national Research and Education networks (NREN) and GÉANT are the preferential connectivity providers for BonFIRE. It is planned to inter-connect some of the available sites (PSNC, EPCC, HLRS) through their NRENs - PIONER, JANET and DFN respectively - and through the GÉANT network. This will enable to perform and demonstrate a cloud-to-network proof-of- concept prototype utilizing GÉANT BoD service implemented with AutoBAHN for establishing and monitoring dedicated high capacity connections between sites.

FEDERICA [2] was a European Project of the 7th Framework Program. Its main goal was to deploy an e-Infrastructure for researchers on Future Internet. Resources of this e-Infrastructure can be allocated to independent slices and assigned to different experimenters allowing them to have the complete control of the resources in their slice. This infrastructure is physically distributed around the whole of Europe and it is composed by routers, switches and servers. By interconnecting with a subset of FEDERICA's infrastructure, BonFIRE users will be able to perform new kinds of experiments over a controlled network. This includes configuring network topologies and routing protocols and setting quality of service (QoS) parameters.

3   Architectural Principles

The following architecture principles have been used to drive the design of the BonFIRE architecture. By explicitly specifying these key principles we aim to ensure a consistent architectural vision throughout the BonFIRE system by applying these key principles when making any architectural decisions. The principles are as follows:

1. It must always be possible for the BonFIRE multi-cloud facility to include testbeds over which BonFIRE has no control.
2. Always provide APIs to BonFIRE functionality, in addition to any BonFIRE graphical user interfaces (GUIs). These APIs will allow third parties to better integrate BonFIRE into their systems.

3. Allow experimenters full access to the specific functionality of particular testbeds. The heterogeneous testbeds within the BonFIRE multi-cloud differ for good reasons.
4. Allow higher-level functionality to exclude specific functionality of a testbed if this makes common tasks easier to achieve. Thus BonFIRE will give experiments the opportunity to choose the best approach for their specific task.
5. Support incremental adoption of the BonFIRE system by experimenters. Some experimenters will come to BonFIRE fresh and will be happy to invest effort learning the whole system in order to utilize its full power. Other users may wish to incrementally integrate BonFIRE functionality into existing experiments.
6. Support declarative specification of experiments as far as possible. Experimenters need only focus on what they want to deploy as an experiment and on the relevant conditions.

4   Architectural Functionality

This section presents an overview of the BonFIRE architectural functionality. These are the key functionalities of the BonFIRE architecture and are expressed independently of the architectural components needed to implement them.

4.1   Resources

BonFIRE allows experimenters to execute experiments that create and use various resources on the BonFIRE testbeds. BonFIRE supports three types of resources: compute, network and storage.

Compute resources are virtual machines (VMs) that are created and run for some part of the duration of an experiment. All BonFIRE virtual machines are created as part of an experiment and have a lifetime that does not exceed the lifetime of the experiment. Compute resources can be configured with application-specific contextualization information that can provide important configuration information to the virtual machine; this information is available to software applications after the machine is started.

To support the degree of control required by experimenters, BonFIRE allows users to reserve exclusive access to some physical machines. The experimenter can then explicitly specify the placement of VMs on these physical machines in order to control the desired level of contention between VMs.

Network resources can be used to connect the VMs to networks to allow the VMs to communicate with each other and possibly with the wider Internet. BonFIRE provides one network that any VM on any BonFIRE site can connect to. This network is also used by the BonFIRE services to manage and monitor the VMs in the experiment. Experiment-specific networks can be configured on the testbeds, according to the experiment's needs.

Storage resources are disks that can store data associated with an experiment. It is often important to decouple the lifetime of the storage resources from the lifetime of the experiment. This provides a persistence of data that allows experiment data to be written to a storage resource and be retrieved at a convenient time after the experiment has completed. BonFIRE supports two types of storage resource: operating system (OS) storage resources, and data block storage resources.

All BonFIRE compute, network and storage resources reside on the testbeds on which they are created and BonFIRE makes no attempt to hide this location information from the end user. End users are expected to plan their experiments with a detailed understanding of how they wish to distribute their resources among the various testbeds.

BonFIRE supports dynamically creating, updating, reading and deleting resources throughout the lifetime of an experiment. In order to aid the end user in managing the resources within an experiment, BonFIRE provides the concept of experiment resources that can be used as containers for the resources whose lifetime is limited to the duration of the experiment.

4.2   Monitoring

BonFIRE includes an extensible monitoring framework that allows users to log and monitor various metrics associated with an experiment's progress. There are three types of metrics that may be monitored according to the experiment's needs: VM metrics, application metrics and infrastructure metrics.

VM metrics provide system information regarding the status of the VM from the perspective of CPU, memory, disk space.

Application metrics can be defined by the experimenter according to the specific software applications being used by the experiment, for example the number of open database connections, or the value of an application counter.

Infrastructure metrics provide detailed information about the underlying hypervisor's system performance. For example, some experiments may need to monitor the hypervisor's CPU, how many VMs run on the same CPU, or what the load is on a specific CPU. This level of monitoring is typically not provided by production cloud systems but it is an essential feature of the BonFIRE experimental facility.

Users, and user-agents such as software systems, can access an integrated view of an experiment's monitoring information giving access to all three levels of metrics from a single source. BonFIRE provides an API to access monitoring information and also a graphical tool to display metric values and metric value graphs in real time while an experiment is executing.

4.3   Elasticity

Elasticity is the ability to create and delete resources, typically virtual machines with associated storage and networking, while an experiment is running. Usually elasticity actions are performed when specific conditions occur. For example, a new VM may be created when the overall system load is high. The BonFIRE monitoring functionality can be used to detect when these experiment-specific conditions occur. BonFIRE aims to provide three levels of elasticity support:

- Manual: where experimenters manually observe the monitoring system and create or delete resources as desired.
- Programmed: where the experimenter writes a program that uses the monitoring API to detect when specific conditions occur and programmatically creates or deletes the resources as desired. According to the experimenter's preferences this program may be executed either on a BonFIRE virtual machine or on a machine outside of the BonFIRE infrastructure.
- Managed: where the user specifies the elasticity policies in a high- level experiment descriptor and BonFIRE creates or deletes the resources according to the specified rules.

The BonFIRE resource API supports the control of resources on all testbeds in the BonFIRE infrastructure. It is therefore possible for an control program running on a VM on one testbed to create resources on another testbed. This support for cross-site elasticity is a key feature of BonFIRE.

4.4   Experiment Descriptors

Experiments can interact with the BonFIRE system at two different granularities: resource level and experiment level granularity.

When using resource level granularity, experimenters explicitly send a request to BonFIRE for each resource create, update, read or delete operation. With the experiment level granularity the experimenter describes the experiment in a single document and sends one request to BonFIRE to submit the experiment. Once submitted, the experiment is managed by BonFIRE and the individual resource level operations are performed by BonFIRE.

BonFIRE provides resource level operations through an implementation of the Open Cloud Computing Interface (OCCI) [6]. OCCI provides create, read, update and delete operations to compute, storage and network resources.

With experiment level granularity the experimenter describes their experiment in a single document that we call the Experiment Descriptor (ED). There are five parts to an experiment descriptor:

1. Specification of the initial deployment of compute, storage and network resources.
2. Specification of the monitoring metrics.
3. Specification of elasticity rules containing both trigger conditions (specified with respect to the monitoring metrics) and the actions to perform when the conditions are met.
4. Specification of general rules that specify trigger conditions and actions to perform that are not necessarily related to elasticity.
5. Specification of a shutdown sequence for stopping the experiment.

BonFIRE uses Open Virtualization Format (OVF) [7] as its primary experiment descriptor. OVF is a standard for the specification of the deployment of virtual resources and being developed within the Distributed Management Task Force (DMTF).

OVF will support the first part of the experiment descriptor described above. Parts 2, 3, 4 and 5 will require extensions to standard OVF in several directions. Other projects have already extended OVF to support specific cloud requirements such as elasticity [10] and BonFIRE will aim to adopt the same extensions where possible.

Release 2 of BonFIRE supports experiment descriptors that specify the initial deployment of compute, storage and network resources, but does not support the specification of monitoring metrics or elasticity rules in one document. This does not mean that experiments requiring monitoring and elasticity are nor supported by BonFIRE. Such experiments simply have to configure the monitoring metrics and elasticity rules separately within the virtual machine images used by the experiment, rather than specifying them within an experiment descriptor.

As an alternative to the OVF format, BonFIRE will also support a very simple experiment descriptor format that provides the core functionality of specifying compute, network and storage resources in a single document.

4.5   Scheduling

Many commercial cloud facilities present a model of almost-infinite resource availability: the user gets as many resources as they apply for. Most BonFIRE testbeds, however, offer a small number of compute nodes as part of the permanent infrastructure. BonFIRE therefore operates at a different end of the resource spectrum from commercial cloud facilities and hence must operate in a different way regarding the scheduling of resources.

The problem is made interesting by the fact that BonFIRE combines cross-site deployment with the notion of the experiment. It is possible that the user may have a preference to start specific compute resources on specific sites; if one site cannot fulfill its requirements, while the others can, experiments may fail to run as expected. Also, BonFIRE will allow the user to leave the location unspecified, so the system needs a mechanism to resolve this in a way that the resources can be deployed.

This leads to the idea of *Atomic Experiment Scheduling*, whereby BonFIRE considers an experiment in its entirety before attempting deployment. The intention is that BonFIRE does not attempt deployment of any experiment resources until all involved BonFIRE sites indicate that they can allocate the required resources.

Future releases of BonFIRE will provide atomic scheduling over all the OpenNebula-based facilities. This will require BonFIRE-specific extensions to OpenNebula.

5   Architectural Components

The architectural components of BonFIRE can be seen in the architecture overview diagram show in Fig 1. The BonFIRE architecture consists of five layers each building on the functionality of the layer below it. Each layer exposes its functionality via a set of APIs. The APIs of the lowest two layers, the Testbeds and the Enactor, can only be used by the layer above them. The APIs of the next two layers, the Broker and the Experiment Manager, can be used by end users, agents acting of behalf of end users, and the layer above them.

5.1   Testbeds

The lowest layer of the BonFIRE architecture are the testbeds. The testbeds are the cloud infrastructures that provide compute, network and storage resources that can be used by BonFIRE experiments. Currently BonFIRE has three different types of testbeds: the Cells cloud infrastructure provided by HP; the Virtual Wall network emulation infrastructure provided by IBBT; and three cloud infrastructures implemented using the OpenNebula toolkit for cloud computing and offered by EPCC, HLRS and INRIA.

Theoretically testbeds may expose their functionality via any API they choose but to simplify the initial implementation all testbeds currently expose their basic resource manipulation functionality using a version of the Open Cloud Computing Interface (OCCI) [6].

5.2   Enactor

The role of the Enactor is to shield the technical details of how to communicate with each specific testbed from the higher level Broker. The Enactor receives OCCI requests from the Broker and transforms them onto suitable requests for the appropriate testbeds. The transformed request is then sent to the testbeds and the response received. The response is then transformed into a common format and passed to the Broker.

5.3   Broker

The Broker is the lowest layer of the BonFIRE architecture that may be accessed by end users and provides the entry point for experimenters to interact with BonFIRE at the resource level granularity.

The Broker maintains the current set of experiment resources and all the compute, storage and network resources currently used by the experiment. User operations on the compute, storage and network resources are passed to the Enactor and then onto the appropriate testbed. User operations, such as create and read, on the experiment resource are typically executed at the Broker because

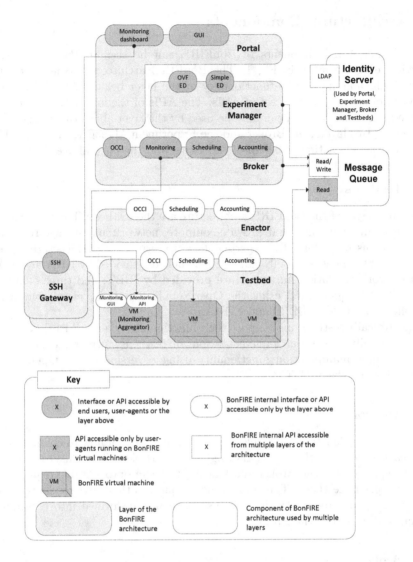

Fig. 1. BonFIRE architecture. The accounting and scheduling APIs shown here are not supported by the current version of BonFIRE.

the testbeds know nothing about the concept of an experiment. Some operations such as deleting an experiment require the Broker to interact with the testbeds via the Enactor.

The Broker currently exposes two APIs: OCCI for managing resources; and a Monitoring API. The OCCI interface is used to create, read, update and delete compute, network and storage resources. The OCCI is extended from the proposed standard to include BonFIRE specific requirements related to the experiment resource, explicit indication of the location at which a resource must be created, and also additional network elements to specify the bandwidth, loss rate and latency for emulated networks on the Virtual Wall.

5.4   Experiment Manager

The role of the Experiment Manager is to take a description of an experiment as described in an experiment descriptor and manage its execution through multiple calls to the Broker. Experimenters can create new managed experiment resources and specify the corresponding experiment descriptor.

BonFIRE supports two different formats of experiment descriptor, OVF and the BonFIRE simple experiment descriptor. For each format the Experiment Manager contains a parser that maps the experiment descriptor onto a common data model that describes the experiment. This allows the rest of the Experiment Manager architecture to be decoupled from the choice of experiment descriptor format.

The data model is then validated to check that it is consistent and that the labels used to identify locations, templates, etc. are valid. When an experiment descriptor request is sent to BonFIRE, the validator is the last component to execute before the response is returned. This response indicates whether or not a valid experiment descriptor was provided, but cannot indicate whether it could be successfully deployed as deployment is carried out later in a background task. It is therefore important that the validator detects as many errors in the experiment descriptor as it possibly can.

The managed experiments are then placed in a queue, and deployed in turn in a background task. In a future version, the testbeds will be polled to check resource availability, before either deploying each experiment or holding in the queue until the necessary resources become available. At present, the Experiment Manager attempts to deploy every experiment in the queue. If the location of any resources is left unspecified in the experiment descriptor, the scheduler will choose a suitable location.

Next, the planner plans the order in which the various resources should be created. Network and storage resources will need to be created before the compute resources that use them. Additionally, property constraints between virtual machines may also influence the order in which compute resources must be created. For example, if a client virtual machine must be configured at boot time with the IP address of the server virtual machine, then the server virtual machine must be created first in order to determine its IP address.

Once the initial deployment of resources has been planned, the resources are created in the appropriate order via calls to the OCCI API of the Broker. Property values are also passed to VMs on creation, for example to ensure the server's IP address is written to the appropriate contextualisation section when the client virtual image is created.

5.5 Portal

The Portal offers the experimenter a graphical interface to the BonFIRE capabilities. It has a view of the experimenter's data, the running experiments, and the available platform capabilities (for example, the list of sites). The Portal is the aggregated view of the whole platform, and is the simplified entry point for the experimenter. It is also a way to present to the experimenter information from the Broker or the cloud sites, for example, to monitor experiment progress.

5.6 SSH Gateways and the BonFIRE WAN

The availability of publicly addressable IP addresses varies across the various BonFIRE testbeds. Some testbeds have very few, or even zero, such IP addresses to allocate. This obviously creates a challenge when one VM in a experiment must communicate with another that does not have a publicly addressable IP. To overcome this problem BonFIRE implements a WAN to which all VMs can be connected. This WAN can be used for both BonFIRE's control data and experimenters' application data. The WAN is implemented using VPN technology. The BonFIRE WAN can be a major bottleneck and should not be used for large scale inter-testbed communication that is crucial to an experiment. Instead in such cases publicly addressable IPs should be used wherever possible.

The SSH Gateways provide a means for experimenters to SSH into virtual machines that are not publicly addressable. Each BonFIRE site provides an SSH gateway that experimenters can connect to using SSH. From these gateways experimenters can then SSH to their VMs over the BonFIRE WAN.

5.7 Identity Server

The Identity Server provides BonFIRE's identity management functionality. User credentials are stored in a central LDAP database. To avoid a single point of failure the database is cloned on a master-slave approach on each site. The slaves on the sites are also used for user authentication on the sites. The web interface of the Identity Management allows users to manage their credentials. There is also an administrative web- interface which gives the BonFIRE administrators full control of all existing user accounts. The passwords are never seen in clear text by the administrators, as they are stored in hash format. For each user the Identity Server stores the username, password, groups and also optionally the user's SSH public key. If available, the testbeds use this public key to preconfigure all virtual machines such that only that user can SSH to them.

6 Experiments

BonFIRE is currently being used by seven experiments. This section gives an overview of two of these experiments and explains why BonFIRE is particularly suited to the task.

6.1   QoS-Oriented Service Engineering for Federated Clouds

This experiment is one of the three driving experiments in the BonFIRE project, which is carried out by the IT Innovation Centre at the University of Southampton. The experiment investigates techniques to better understand and predict the Quality of Service (QoS) achieved by service based applications when running on cloud infrastructures. The complexities of determining QoS requirements for service based applications in the cloud has given rise to a new class of service engineering tools within the Platform-as-a-Service (PaaS) layer for modelling, analysing and planning. While it is in the interest to a PaaS provider not to over- provision, it is important that the application performance is stable and the user experience is acceptable. This is not trivial since service based applications are often highly interactive and the usage patterns may fluctuate significantly depending on user demand.

QoS terms are typically set out in a Service Level Agreement (SLA) based on low level infrastructure terms such as CPU speed, disk space, etc. However, the customers (typically the application users) are often more interested in application-level parameters, e.g., the number of dropped frames for a multimedia streaming application. The gap between the terms infrastructure providers offer and what the users are interested in can be large. This results in a complex relationship between application performance and resource parameters, which is greater still for applications deployed across federated clouds.

Several service engineering tools have been developed in the EU IST IRMOS project to address the challenges above [8]. This experiment focuses on prediction of application performance based on a generic description of infrastructure resources (based on application benchmarking scores), to enable transferability across different providers, particularly with federation in mind. The hypothesis put to test in the experiment is that such a description of resources not only allows for prediction of application performance, but may enable more accurate predictions compared with using typical infrastructure parameters. Moreover, we hypothesize that using QoS terms in SLAs will improve overall efficiencies for all cloud stakeholders due to increased accuracy of requirements achieved by a simplification of service planning and adaptation models, and increased market adoption and flexibility due to the simplification of the federation between Platform and Infrastructure stakeholders.

The heterogeneous resources and federated testbeds in BonFIRE is essential to this experiment to be able to address the above hypotheses. The resource control offered in BonFIRE ensures repeatable experimentation, and the built-in monitoring facilities allow a more in-depth analysis than what is possible elsewhere; particularly infrastructure monitoring as that allows for correlation of results obtained on the virtual resources with what actually happened on the physical infrastructures. This is important for addressing resource reliability in the cloud, which is a factor one needs to consider when predicting application performance to estimate QoS. For more details about the experiment and initial results, please refer to [9].

6.2   Virtual Clusters on Federated Sites

The *Virtual Clusters on Federated Sites* experiment is funded through the first BonFIRE open call and is being carried out by Centre of Supercomputing of Galicia (CESGA). The aim of this experiment is to research the feasibility of using multiple cloud environments for the provision of services which need the allocation of a large pool of CPUs or virtual machines to a single user (as High Throughput Computing (HTC) or High Performance Computing (HPC)). The use case covers dose computation for radiotherapy treatments based on Monte Carlo methods, developed in the eIMRT project [11].

The experiment studies questions related to the usage of virtual clusters in a distributed cloud environment. A first set of questions are related to the time that the deployment and enlargement of such cluster need to be operational and the influence other simultaneous operations have in the process. Previously in other experiments in grids, local clusters and even commercial cloud providers, interferences with other users and processes have been observed which affect the final quality of service. The objective is to understand better how to manage these virtual clusters to guarantee a low time to solution or latency (this means, the time since the cluster has been requested to the end of the service). Also, the elasticity functionality will be analyzed, using the application performance monitoring as a trigger for the change in the size of the cluster.

A second set of experiments will investigate the usage of the distributed capability of cloud providers (federated or multi- site) in order to protect the service against failures. A virtual cluster will be deployed divided in two sets, and the characteristics of the network (latency, bandwidth and packet loss rate) will be changed to study the effects in the performance of the cluster. The radical situation of losing part of the cluster will be simulated changing the bandwidth to zero, when the other part should recover from it to guarantee that the customer receives the solution on time.

The main metric to measure in the experiments is the time to execute one operation as function of the factors which can affect this time, as the number of machines that compose the cluster, the size of each virtual machine, etc.

Because clouds are shared environments which are not completely under control of the experimenter, several measurements must be done. To automate the process of executing the experiments, an Experiment Agent should be developed. This agent will communicate with the BonFIRE infrastructure and will control the execution as well as record the data locally to make analysis later.

The results and data acquired during the experiment should permit CESGA to develop the policies and business rules to include in the applications under development at the institution which use the Software as a Service model. This new model will be developed after the end of the experiment.

An experiment like this needs the BonFIRE infrastructure because the usage of commercial providers does not guarantee enough control of the factors which can affect the results. Installing a local infrastructure for executing it is too complex and time consuming. Additionally, BonFIRE includes a site where the network can be controlled. This is a facility that CESGA can not deploy currently. BonFIRE, therefore, offers a unique cloud infrastructure where new cloud concepts and applications can be experimented with.

7   Current Status and Future Work

As of January 2012 release 2 of BonFIRE is operational and is being used by the three embedded experiments and the four experiments funded by BonFIRE's first open call. These open call experiments are feeding back comments and requirements that will be addressed in subsequent releases of BonFIRE. A new set of experiments funded by a second open call are planned to begin using the BonFIRE facility in September 2012. Subsequently, it is planned to open BonFIRE up to a wider set of users later in 2012.

The resource-level API provided by the Broker is working very well and will continue to provide the core functionality of BonFIRE. The higher-level functionality offered by the Experiment Manager will be extended to support all five levels of the experiment descriptor as described in Section 4.4.

The ability to obtain exclusive access to a physical machine and specify the placement of VMs on these machines has given BonFIRE experimenters the means of controlling their experiment infrastructure to a degree that is not supported by typical cloud infrastructures. This functionality has shown good promise in allowing experimenters to control the degree of contention experienced by a VM. Further research is planned to investigate if BonFIRE can provide a set of typical contention templates that can be easily applied to VMs under test. Where such contention cannot be controlled, BonFIRE allows it to be monitored via the infrastructure monitoring functionality. This ability to monitor infrastructure metrics and easily correlate them with application or VMs metrics is proving of great use to experimenters.

BonFIRE will expand vertically to support the dynamic interoperation among some BonFIRE sites through the GÉANT network. This will automate the network control for real multi-site experiments and offer network as primary resource for the experiments with its key configuration parameters (bandwidth, delay, etc.). In release 3, the BonFIRE system will be interfaced to the GÉANT AutoBAHN system (Automated Bandwidth Allocation across Heterogeneous Networks). The user/cloud (BonFIRE) to network (GÉANT) interface will be based on the AutoBAHN User Access Point interface(UAP): the AutoBAHN client will be integrated into the BonFIRE Enactor to issue BoD request and implement consequent actions on the respective LAN sides (end-point). Also other BonFIRE system components will be adapted to cope with the new WAN network resources: in particular, the Portal will require new tabs/pages to describe the new resources; the OCCI will be extended to include specific fields for BoD network resources; the Experiment Manager and Broker will require data model adaptations. These near-future BonFIRE architecture and components modifications will make available on-demand network connectivity services between selected sites/resources bound to the experiments: user-controlled network QoS parameters and possibility to reserve actual (i.e. not emulated) network resources both in immediate-permanent and advance reservation mode will definitely enhance the Future Internet (FI) experiment coverage area.

Additional vertical expansion and the ability to federate with other FI testbeds will be demonstrated by connecting BonFIRE with a subset of the FEDERICA facility. This will require BonFIRE to connect to the Slice-based Facility Architecture (SFA) used by many of the networking-focused FI testbeds.

Acknowledgements. BonFIRE is funded by the European Union Seventh Framework Programme (FP7/2007-2013) under grant agreement number 257386. The authors wish to acknowledge the contributions of: Frédéric Gittler (HP Labs), Kostas Kavoussanakis (EPCC), David Margery (INRIA), Josep Martrat (Atos), Eilidh Troup (EPCC), Constantino Vázquez Blanco (Universidad Politécnica de Madrid), Celia Velayos (i2CAT) and Tim Wauters (IBBT).

References

1. Virtual Wall, http://www.ibbt.be/en/develop-test/ilab-t/virtual-wall
2. FEDERICA Project, http://www.fp7-federica.eu/
3. GÉANT2 Bandwidth on Demand (BoD) User and Application Survey (DJ.3.2.1), http://www.geant2.net/upload/pdf/GN2-05-086v11.pdf
4. Definition of Bandwidth on Demand Framework and General Architecture (DJ3.3.1), http://www.geant2.net/upload/pdf/GN2-05-208v7_DJ3-3-1_GEANT2_Initial_Bandwidth_on_Demand_Framework_and_Architecture.pdf
5. HP Labs cloud-computing test bed projects - Cells as a Service, http://www.hpl.hp.com/open_innovation/cloud_collaboration/projects.html
6. Open Cloud Computing Interface, http://occi-wg.org/
7. Open Virtualization Format (OVF), http://www.dmtf.org/standards/ovf
8. Metzger, A., Boniface, M., Engen, V., Phillips, S., Zlatev, Z.: Towards Critical Event Monitoring, Detection and Prediction for Self-adaptive Future Internet Applications. In: Proc. of the 1st Int. Workshop on Adaptive Services for the Future Internet (2011)
9. Phillips, S., Engen, V., Papay, J.: Snow White Clouds and the Seven Dwarfs. In: Proc. of the IEEE Int. Conf. and Workshops on Cloud Computing Technology and Science (2011)
10. Rodero-Merino, L., Vaqueroa, L.M., Gil, V., Galán, F., Fontán, J., Montero, R.S., Llorente, I.M.: From Infrastructure Delivery to Service Management in Clouds. Future Generation Computer Systems 26, 1226–1240 (2010)
11. González-Castaño, D.M., Pena, J., Gómez, F., Gago-Arias, A., González-Castaño, F.J., Rodríguez-Silva, D.A., Gómez, A., Mouriño, C., Pombar, M., Sánchez, M.: eIMRT: A Web Platform for the Verification and Optimization of Radiation Treatment Plans. J. Appl. Clin. Med. Phys. 10(3), 2998 (2009)

ExoGENI: A Multi-domain Infrastructure-as-a-Service Testbed*

Ilia Baldine, Yufeng Xin, Anirban Mandal, Paul Ruth, Chris Heerman,
and Jeff Chase

RENCI

Abstract. NSF's GENI program seeks to enable experiments that run within virtual network topologies built-to-order from testbed infrastructure offered by multiple providers (domains). GENI is often viewed as a network testbed integration effort, but behind it is an ambitious vision for multi-domain infrastructure-as-a-service (IaaS). This paper presents ExoGENI, a new GENI testbed that links GENI to two advances in virtual infrastructure services outside of GENI: open cloud computing (OpenStack) and dynamic circuit fabrics. ExoGENI orchestrates a federation of independent cloud sites and circuit providers through their native IaaS interfaces, and links them to other GENI tools and resources.

The ExoGENI deployment consists of cloud site "racks" on host campuses within the US, linked with national research networks and other circuit networks through programmable exchange points. The ExoGENI sites and control software are enabled for software-defined networking using OpenFlow. ExoGENI offers a powerful unified hosting platform for deeply networked, multi-domain, multi-site cloud applications. We intend that ExoGENI will seed a larger, evolving platform linking other third-party cloud sites, transport networks, and other infrastructure services, and that it will enable real-world deployment of innovative distributed services and new visions of a Future Internet.

1 Introduction

ExoGENI is a new testbed at the intersection of networking and cloud computing, funded through NSF's Global Environment for Network Innovation (GENI) project. GENI is the major US program to develop and deploy integated network testbeds. The ExoGENI testbed is designed to support research and innovation in networking, operating systems, distributed systems, future Internet architectures, and deeply networked, data-intensive cloud computing. The testbed can also serve as a platform for novel applications and services, e.g., for the US IG-NITE initiative. The initial deployment is scheduled to become operational in late 2012.

---

* This work is supported by the US National Science Foundation through the GENI initiative and NSF awards OCI-1032873, CNS-0910653, and CNS-0720829; by IBM and NetApp; and by the State of North Carolina through RENCI.

T. Korakis, M. Zink, and M. Ott (Eds.): TridentCom 2012, LNICST 44, pp. 97–113, 2012.
© Institute for Computer Sciences, Social Informatics and Telecommunications Engineering 2012

ExoGENI is based on an extended Infrastructure-as-a-Service (IaaS) cloud model with orchestrated provisioning across sites. Each ExoGENI site is a private IaaS cloud using a standard cloud stack to manage a pool of servers. The sites federate by delegating certain functions for identity management, authorization, and resource management to common coordinator services. This structure enables a network of private clouds to operate as a hybrid community cloud. Thus ExoGENI is an example of a *multi-domain* or *federated* cloud system, which some have called an intercloud.

ExoGENI combines this structure with a high degree of control over networking functions: OpenFlow networking within each site, multi-homed cloud servers that can act as virtual routers, site connectivity to national circuit backbone fabrics through host campus networks, and linkages to international circuits through programmable exchange points. The project aims to enhance US research cyberinfrastructure capabilities in four inter-related ways:

- **The missing link.** ExoGENI interconnects clouds to dynamic circuit fabrics, enabling a range of networked cloud applications and services, including data-intensive interaction, distributed data sharing, geo-replication, alternative packet networks, and location-aware services.
- **On-ramps to advanced network fabrics.** ExoGENI shows how to use campus clouds to bridge from campus networks to national transport network fabrics, overcoming a key limitation identified by NSF's CF21 vision. ExoGENI cloud sites can act as *virtual colocation centers* that offer on-demand cloud services adjacent to fabric access points. Sites at fabric intersection points can also act as *virtual network exchanges* to bridge "air gaps" between fabrics stemming from lack of direct connectivity or incompatible circuit interfaces.
- **Cloud peering and data mobility.** ExoGENI enhances the potential for peering and sharing of private clouds. It offers a means to bring data and computation together by migrating datasets to compute sites or placing computation close to data at rest.
- **Networking as a service.** ExoGENI brings flexible network configuration to cloud computing. It also enables experimental deployments of new packet networking models over a flexible link substrate. Built-to-order virtual networks can implement routing overlays using IP or other packet-layer protocols. Testbed users may deploy custom node operating systems with alternative networking stacks into their nodes, and use OpenFlow datapaths and/or virtual routers to implement new network services at the cloud edge and at network intersection points.

This paper gives an overview of the ExoGENI testbed and its control software. The research contribution of this paper is to summarize the design principles of ExoGENI resulting from our experience in developing the testbed software (Section 2). Section 3 explains the rack site structure and interconnection architecture for the testbed. Section 4 outlines the integration of multi-domain IaaS with the GENI architecture as it currently stands. The software described in this paper has been implemented, deployed and demonstrated at various events.

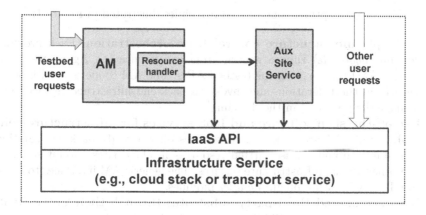

Fig. 1. Structure of a resource provider or *aggregate*. Each provider runs a native infrastructure service (IaaS) of its choice, which may serve requests from local users through a native API. To join a federation the aggregate is fronted with a generic Aggregate Manager (AM) service. The AM validates user requests against local policy and serves them by invoking the native IaaS API through resource-specific plugin *handlers*. A handler may rely on other auxiliary services for some functions, e.g., image loading, OpenFlow authorization, or network proxying.

2 A Testbed of Federated IaaS Providers

ExoGENI supports virtual infrastructure resources, which are instances of "fundamental computing resources, such as processing, storage, and networks" according to the NIST definition of Infrastructure-as-a-Service [17]. Testbed users may instantiate and program a virtual topology consisting of virtual machines (VMs), programmable switch datapaths, and virtual network links based on Ethernet standards. The deployment is based on an evolving set of technologies including point-to-point Ethernet circuits, OpenFlow-enabled hybrid Ethernet switches, and standard cloud computing software—OpenStack and xCAT [8].

The "Exo" (outside) prefix reflects our view of how GENI will evolve and what capabilities are needed to deliver on the promise of GENI to "explore networks of the future at scale". GENI is evolving alongside cloud technologies and open network control systems whose functions and goals overlap with GENI. The rate of investment in developing and deploying these systems is quite a bit more than an order of magnitude larger than the GENI effort.

One purpose of ExoGENI is to define a path to leverage these technologies and substrates in the GENI project. At the same time, GENI control software offers new ways to combine and extend them as a unified deployment platform for advances in network science and engineering. ExoGENI shows how GENI control software can leverage IaaS advances in a way that addresses important orchestration challenges for networked cloud computing.

The Exo prefix captures four related principles illustrated in Figure 1:

E1 **Decouple infrastructure control from orchestration.** Each provider domain (*aggregate*) runs a generic front-end service (an Aggregate Manager or AM) that exports the testbed APIs. The AM cooperates with other services in the federation, and invokes a back-end infrastructure service to manage the resources in the domain.

E2 **Use off-the-shelf software and IaaS services for infrastructure control.** Standard IaaS software and services offer a ready back-end solution to instantiate and release virtual resources in cloud sites, circuit services, and other virtual infrastructure services. The generic AM interfaces to these standard APIs using plugin *handler* modules.

E3 **Leverage shared third-party substrates through their native IaaS interfaces.** This compatibility with standard back-end infrastructure control services offers a path to bring independent resource providers into the federation. The provider deploys an off-the-shelf IaaS service and "wraps" it with an AM to link it into the testbed federation.

E4 **Enable substrate owners to contribute resources on their own terms.** Participating providers are autonomous: they are empowered to approve or deny any request according to their policies. Providers allocate virtual resources with attached QoS properties for defined intervals; the callers determine what resources to request and how to expose them to applications. Resource allotments are visible to both parties and are controlled by the providers. These principles are similar to those put forward for the *exokernel* extensible operating system [15] developed at MIT in the 1990s; the exo name also pays homage to that project [13].

Based on these principles ExoGENI provides a framework to incorporate "outside" resources and infrastructure services into a federation and to orchestrate their operation. For example, providers may deploy new cloud sites using open-source cloud stacks, such as Eucalyptus [18] or OpenStack, which support the de facto standard Amazon EC2 IaaS cloud API. Common APIs such as OS-CARS [10] are also emerging for transport network circuit services. Providers may deploy these and other systems independently; once a system is deployed we can install a front-end orchestration service (AM) to link it into the federation without interfering with its other functions and users. The AM may be operated by the provider itself or by a delegate or authorized client.

2.1 ExoGENI Control Software

The control software for ExoGENI was developed and refined in an ongoing collaboration between RENCI and Duke University to create a GENI testbed "island" around the Breakable Experimental Network [1] (BEN), a multi-layer optical testbed built by the State of North Carolina and managed by RENCI. The project grew into a more comprehensive effort to support a federated IaaS system linking BEN and other infrastructure systems under orchestrated control

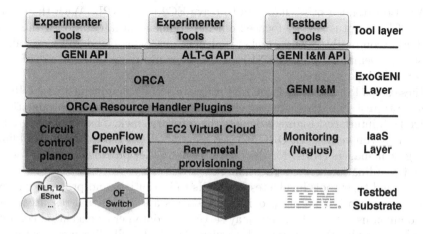

Fig. 2. Conceptual view of the ExoGENI software stack. An IaaS layer consists of standard off-the shelf software and services for server clouds, network transport services, and OpenFlow networking, which control the testbed substrate. Testbed users and tools access the testbed resources through GENI APIs and an alternative API (labeled Alt-G in the figure) based on semantic resource models. The ORCA resource leasing system tracks resource allocation and orchestrates calls to *handler* plugins, which invoke the APIs for services in the IaaS layer. The monitoring system has a similar structure.

and a common authorization framework. Some early results from the project have been reported in previous publications [3,2,24,16].

An initial goal of the project (2008) was to build a native circuit service for BEN based on the Open Resource Control Architecture (ORCA [5]). ORCA is an outgrowth of earlier projects in networked cloud computing at Duke, funded by NSF and IBM. It is based on the SHARP federation model [9] and the plugin architecture of the Shirako resource leasing core [14], with extensions for automated control policies added for Automat [25]. The project developed a set of plugin modules for ORCA, which are used in ExoGENI.

Building the native BEN circuit service presented an interesting test case for the ORCA control framework. We built policy plugins that plan requested paths through the BEN network by issuing queries on *semantic resource models*, which are logic-based declarative descriptions of the network expressed in an extended variant of the Network Description Language (NDL [11,7,12]). We also built handler plugins that manage paths by forming and issuing commands to network devices over the BEN management network, based on path descriptions generated by the queries.

BEN is one of several circuit providers for ExoGENI. We later implemented new ORCA plugins to interface to external circuit APIs: National LambdaRail's Sherpa FrameNet service and OSCARS, which is used in the national circuit fabrics ESnet and Internet2 ION.

We also extended other handlers to drive EC2 cloud APIs. With the emergence of Eucalyptus [18] we focused our development on integration with standard EC2-compatible cloud stacks, replacing our older cloud software called Cluster-on-Demand [6]. ExoGENI rack sites now use these plugins to drive the OpenStack cloud service.

These steps led us to the ExoGENI software architecture, which uses ORCA to orchestrate a set of participating virtual infrastructure providers through their native IaaS interfaces. Figure 2 depicts the software stack. The ORCA portions of the stack run in different ORCA-based servers: ORCA is a toolkit for building aggregate managers (AMs) for the rack sites and other providers, together with related coordination services (Section 4).

Users and their tools invoke testbed APIs to instantiate and program virtual resources from participating providers. A *slice* is a set of virtual resources under common user control. A slice may serve as a container or execution context to host an application or network service. An ExoGENI slice may contain a network topology with programmable nodes and links—a virtual distributed environment [21]. The links in the topology comprise the slice *dataplane*. Software running within a slice may manage its dataplane as a private packet network using IP or alternative protocol suites at the discretion of the slice owner.

A slice may span multiple sites and link to other GENI resources or other external resources as permitted by peering and interconnection agreements. ExoGENI slices are isolated: they interact with the outside world through controlled interfaces, and the resources in a slice may have quality-of-service properties defined by the providers.

2.2   Relationship to Other GENI Testbeds

ExoGENI is significant in part because it offers our first opportunity to evaluate the federated IaaS model in a production testbed. The ExoGENI principles represent a departure in the GENI effort, whose current standards evolved from testbeds that were established and accepted by the research community at the start of the GENI program in 2007: PlanetLab [19], Emulab [23], and ORBIT [20]. Each testbed developed its own control software to manage substrates that are permanently dedicated to that testbed and under the direct control of its central testbed authority.

The ExoGENI testbed is the first GENI-funded substrate whose control software departs from that model and instead uses standard virtual infrastructure services, which may be deployed and administered independently and/or shared with other uses. We intend that ExoGENI will serve as a nucleus for a larger, evolving federation that encourages participation from independent cloud sites, transport networks, and testbed providers, beyond the core GENI-funded substrate. An important goal of the project is to provide a foundation for organic and sustainable growth of a networked intercloud through a flexible federation model that allows private cloud sites and other services to interconnect and share resources on their own terms.

The ExoGENI model offers potential to grow the power of the testbed as infrastructure providers join and their capabilities continue to advance. In time these advances may enable not just real deployment of innovative distributed services but also new visions of a Future Internet.

This goal requires an architecture that supports and encourages federation of sites and providers and exposes their raw IaaS capabilities, including QoS capabilities, to testbed users through common APIs. It requires a different structure from the GENI predecessors, whose primary uses have been to evaluate new ideas under controlled conditions (for Emulab and ORBIT) and to measure the public Internet as it currently exists (for PlanetLab). PlanetLab has enabled development of innovative distributed services in the real world, but it is limited as a deployment platform because it supports only best-effort resource allocation, limits use of modified kernel software to user-mode virtualization, and depends on the existing Internet for its dataplane.

3   ExoGENI Services and Interconnections

Each ExoGENI cloud site includes a packaged rack with a small cloud server cluster and an integrated OpenFlow network, built by our industry partner IBM. The initial funding will deploy 14 rack sites at universities and research labs across the United States. Each of the sites is capable of supporting about 100 virtual machines, based on an EC2-compatible IaaS cloud service (OpenStack with Linux/KVM).

Figure 3 depicts the rack components and connections. The nodes in the initial racks are x3650 M3 and M4 IBM servers. The *worker nodes* are the server substrate for dynamic provisioning of nodes for slices. A single *management node* (head node) runs the control servers for the site, including the OpenStack head and ORCA servers. The rack also includes an iSCSI storage appliance for images, instrumentation data, and other needs.

All components are connected to a *management switch*, which has an L3 connection to the campus network and from there to the public Internet. This switch is used for intra-site access to the iSCSI storage, for remote management by the testbed operator (RENCI) through a VPN appliance (not shown), and for slice connectivity to the public Internet. Each worker has multiple 1Gbs ports for these uses.

A separate *dataplane* switch carries experiment traffic on the slice dataplanes. It is the termination point for L2 links to external circuit providers and to VLANs or subnets on the host campus network, if permitted by the host campus. The initial racks have an IBM/BNT G8264R 10G/40G OpenFlow-enabled hybrid L2 switch with VLAN support. Each worker node has two 10Gbps links to the dataplane switch.

Slice owners can access their nodes over public IP through a management interface. Access is by root *ssh* with a public key specified by the slice owner.

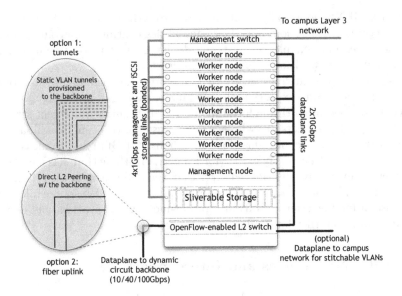

Fig. 3. Structure of an ExoGENI site rack for the initial deployment. Each rack has low-bandwidth IP connectivity for management and a high-bandwidth hybrid OpenFlow switch for the slice dataplanes. The site ORCA server controls L2 dataplane connections among local nodes and external circuits.

Nodes may also have public IP addresses if permitted by the host campus. Public IP access is managed by OpenStack and proxied through its head node.

3.1   Circuit Backbones

Each circuit provider offers a point-to-point Ethernet service among specified points-of-presence on its network. ExoGENI can use dynamic circuit services offered by major national fabrics (NLR, Internet2, ESnet) through their native APIs (e.g., OSCARS). Two rack sites (RENCI and the *exo-dev* development cluster at Duke University) have direct links to the BEN network, which connects to 10Gbps ports on NLR FrameNet and I2/ION.

Rack sites connect to the circuit backbones either through dedicted fiber or a static pool of pre-provisioned VLAN tunnels that traverse campus networks and/or regional networks (RONs). The host campus presents these circuit VLANs to the rack dataplane switch. ExoGENI coordinator services use these various L2 capabilities to construct end-to-end circuit paths requested for a slice dataplane, passing through intermediate network exchange points as needed to remap VLAN tags or bridge gaps between multiple circuit providers (Section 3.2). Authorized slices may also link to other VLANs entering the dataplane switch from the campus network or backbone, such as the GENI Meso-Scale OpenFlow Waves on Internet2 and NLR.

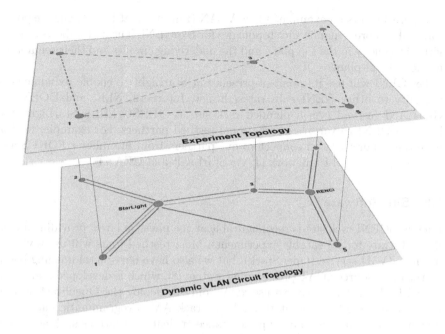

Fig. 4. A virtual topology mapped to a circuit fabric substrate with network exchange points. The exchanges are ExoGENI aggregates that stitch adjacent circuits into end-to-end paths with VLAN tag remapping. The exchanges bridge gaps among multiple circuit providers and reduce the need for common VLAN tags for circuits that span rack sites.

3.2   Network Exchange Points

ExoGENI has connectivity to a wider range of circuit providers through two network exchange points: a RENCI-operated exchange on BEN and the StarLight facility in Chicago, which lies at the intersection of various national and international networks. RENCI has deployed switches with VLAN tag translation (Cisco 6509) to these exchange points, each controlled by an AM.

We use the exchange points to stitch end-to-end circuits that span multiple transport networks with no common inter-domain circuit service, i.e., an "air gap" between circuit fabrics. The exchanges can also remap VLAN tags to link end-to-end circuits between edge sites, for use when no tag remapping option is available along the direct path and the sites have no common VLAN tags available in their static pools. We have demonstrated use of the exchanges to bridge connections among different circuit providers and to interconnect member sites of GENI's "Cluster-D" through various regional networks and NLR. Some sites without NLR access have dedicated connectivity to StarLight through regional or commercial providers and can bridge circuits to other networks through StarLight.

Figure 4 shows an example of how VLAN translation at fixed exchange points can enable more dynamic slice topologies for ExoGENI. The figure shows a slice's virtual topology in the top plane and the underlying circuits and their remapping in the bottom plane.

ExoGENI will use its point-of-presence at StarLight to enable dynamic connectivity to other GENI substrates, ESnet, Internet2, NLR, and DOE's 100 Gbps ANI testbed (via a planned rack site at NERSC/LBL). StarLight also links ExoGENI to various international testbed partners. For example, we will have the opportunity to connect to our partners from Fraunhofer FOKUS and their Teagle control framework [4] via StarLight and GEANT.

3.3   Site Software

Each ExoGENI rack site is reconfigurable at the physical layer, providing a flexible substrate for repeatable experiments. Most testbed users will use a virtual machine (VM) service (OpenStack), but we also have bare-metal imaging based on the open-source xCAT provisioning system [8], which is developed and maintained by IBM. Currently we use xCAT only to deploy the OpenStack worker nodes, and do not expose it through the rack AM. Programmatic bare-metal imaging is on our roadmap for performance-critical applications such as virtual routers.

The head node runs the OpenStack head and various network proxies and auxiliary services for GENI and ORCA. These services include a native ORCA-based AM for the site, and a second ORCA-based server that proxies the GENI APIs (Section 4). Each rack AM includes a cloud handler plugin to invoke EC2/OpenStack APIs and an *ImageProxy* server to obtain node images named by a URL in the request. An *image* file specifies a canned operating system and application stack selected by the user. ImageProxy is a stand-alone caching server that enables the cloud site to import images on demand from the network (Section 3.4).

The ORCA cloud handler also invokes a cloud service extension with a command set to instantiate dataplane interfaces on VMs when they are requested, stitch interfaces to adjacent virtual links, and configure interface properties such as a layer-3 address and netmask. This extension is known as *NEuca*: we implemented it for Eucalyptus before porting it to OpenStack/Nova. We plan to integrate it with the OpenStack/Quantum framework as it develops. Both NEuca and ImageProxy are independent of ORCA.

Each rack also runs OpenFlow control services, including a FlowVisor [22] proxy to mediate access from OpenFlow controllers to OpenFlow datapaths on the rack dataplane switch. An ExoGENI slice may designate an OpenFlow controller to manage traffic on its local dataplane links; the ORCA cloud handler invokes the proxy to authorize the controller to manage traffic on VLANs assigned to those links.

3.4   Image Management

A key orchestration challenge for multi-domain networked clouds is uniform management of images to program the node instances. With standard IaaS cloud stacks following the Amazon EC2 model each cloud site requires some local user to pre-register each image with the site's cloud service, which then generates an image token that is local to that site. Networked clouds need a way to manage images across the member sites of a federation.

In our approach the creator of an image registers it at some shared image depository and names it by a URL. A request to instantiate a VM names the image by a URL and a content hash for validation. The AM's cloud handler plugin passes the image URL and hash to the local *ImageProxy* server. The ImageProxy fetches and caches any image components if they are not already cached, and registers the image with the local cloud service if it is not already registered. It then returns a local token that the AM cloud handler may use to name the image to the local cloud service when it requests a VM instance.

In principle, ImageProxy can work with any image server that supports image fetch by URL, e.g, the various Virtual Appliance Marketplaces operating on the web. It also supports BitTorrent URLs to enable scalable content swarming of images across many cloud sites.

4   ExoGENI and the GENI Federation

ExoGENI may be viewed as a group of resource providers (aggregates) within a larger GENI federation. ExoGENI itself is an instance of the GENI architecture and supports GENI APIs, and also supports additional native ORCA interfaces and capabilities that are not yet available through standard GENI APIs. This section outlines how ExoGENI integrates with GENI and extends the GENI federation model.

4.1   Aggregates

GENI aggregates implement standard GENI APIs for user tools to request resources. The ExoGENI AMs, as described in this paper, are orchestration servers built with the ORCA toolkit. They support internal ORCA protocols rather than the standard GENI aggregate APIs. The GENI APIs are evolving rapidly to support more advanced control and interconnection of slices and rich resource representations and credential formats. Rather than implementing the GENI API directly in the AMs, the initial ExoGENI deployment proxies them through a GENI plugin for separate ORCA-based servers called *Slice Managers* (SM), as described below.

This approach enables ExoGENI to present a secure and flexible interface to the GENI federation and to support standard user tooling for GENI. At the same time ExoGENI supports end-to-end slice construction across the ExoGENI aggregates, based on native ORCA capabilities. The AM operator interface also

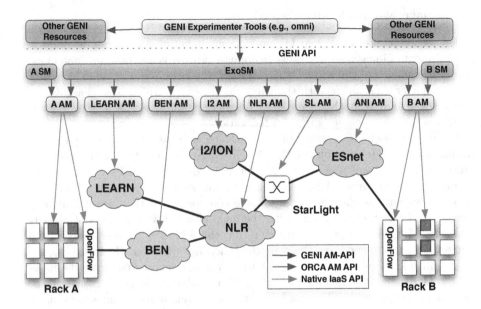

Fig. 5. ExoGENI as a set of GENI aggregates. There is one ORCA Aggregate Manager (AM) for each ExoGENI site or other provider. For third-party IaaS services the AM authenticates using an ExoGENI-linked identity as a registered customer of the provider. Each ExoGENI site also runs an ORCA Slice Manager (SM) that proxies the GENI API, exposing the site as an independent aggregate within GENI. One or more ExoGENI-wide SMs (ExoSM) expose the entire ExoGENI testbed to GENI as a single GENI aggregate. The ExoSM uses native ORCA brokering, slicing, and stitching features to construct complete virtual topologies within ExoGENI slices.

allows local policies that limit the local resources available to the testbed over time. This feature enables ExoGENI providers to hold back resources from the testbed for other uses, according to their own policies.

4.2   GENI Federation: Coordinators

GENI aggregates delegate certain powers and trust to *coordinator* services. The coordinators help aggregates to cooperate and function as a unified testbed. For example, GENI currently defines coordinators to endorse and monitor participating aggregates, authorize and monitor use of the testbed for approved projects, and manage user identities and their association with projects. The GENI coordinators are grouped together under the umbrella of a GENI *Clearinghouse*, but they act as a group of distinct services endorsed by a common GENI root authority.

The GENI federation architecture allows participating aggregates to choose for themselves whether to accept any given coordinator and what degree of trust to place in it. These choices are driven by federation governance structure. GENI has opted for a hierarchical governance structure for its initial trial deployment, for reasons of safety and simplicity. To join the GENI federation an aggregate must enter into certain agreements, including compliance with various policies and export of monitoring data to GENI coordinators.

The aggregates in the initial ExoGENI deployment will enter into mandated agreements with GENI and accept and trust all GENI coordinators. Specifically, ExoGENI trusts GENI-endorsed coordinators to certify users, issue keypairs to users, authorize projects, approve creation of new slices for projects, authorize users to operate on approved slices, and endorse other aggregates in GENI. The GENI coordinators in turn delegate some identity management functions to identity systems operated by other GENI testbeds and participating institutions (Shibboleth/inCommon).

4.3   ExoGENI Coordinators

ExoGENI provides additional coordinators and APIs for managing resources and configuring end-to-end virtual topologies within the ExoGENI testbed itself. The ExoGENI services are based on the ORCA control framework. Figure 5 depicts some of the key services and their interactions.

User requests enter an ORCA control system through a server called a *Slice Manager* (SM), which invokes the AMs to obtain the requested resources. In general, an ORCA slice manager runs on behalf of slice owners with no special trust from other services: the SM is in essence an extensible user tool that runs as a recoverable server. However, in ExoGENI the SMs function as coordinators that provide a trusted interface to the rest of the GENI federation. The ExoGENI AMs accept requests only from trusted SMs endorsed by the testbed root. The SMs run plugins that expose the GENI standard APIs for GENI users and tools. They are responsible for validating the GENI authorization for the slice and the user identity in each request, and translating between GENI RSpec-XML resource descriptions and the logic-based semantic resource models used in ORCA.

Internally to ExoGENI the SMs interact with other ORCA coordinators called *brokers*, which collect and share information about ExoGENI aggregates, including their advertised resources, services, and links to circuit providers. Each ORCA broker is trusted by some set of aggregates to advertise and offer shares of their resources. A broker may also coordinate resource allocation across its aggregates and guide or limit the flow of requests to the aggregates, e.g., based on scheduling policies and capacity constraints, as described in previous work on SHARP resource peering [9,14]. Each request for resources is approved by a broker before the SM passes it to an AM.

There are two distinct SM configurations in ExoGENI. Each ExoGENI rack site runs an SM called a *site SM*. Each site SM exposes its rack site as a distinct GENI aggregate. Requests to a site SM can operate only on the local rack: each site SM uses a local broker with a share of local site resources.

In addition, a global ExoGENI SM called an *ExoSM* can access all aggregates within the ExoGENI testbed. There may be any number of ExoSMs, but the initial deployment has a single ExoSM. The ExoSM exposes ExoGENI as a single GENI aggregate. The ExoSM offers a unified view of the testbed, and supports virtual topology mapping and circuit path planning across the ExoGENI aggregates, including the circuit providers and network exchanges. User requests to ExoSM may request a complete slice topology spanning multiple sites and circuit providers. The ExoSM coordinates construction and stitching of the end-to-end slice.

An ExoSM plans and sequences the resource requests and stitching actions to the AMs based on declarative semantic models that advertise the resources and capabilities of the participating aggregates [3,24,2]. The ExoSM obtains these domain models from a common testbed-wide broker (*ExoBroker*) that is accepted by all ExoGENI aggregates and receives all of their advertisements. The ExoBroker also facilitates allocation of common VLAN tags from static tunnel pools when needed.

4.4   Integration with GENI

GENI users and their tools choose for each slice whether to access the ExoGENI testbed as a single aggregate (through the ExoSM) or as a collection of distinct site aggregates (through the site SMs). External GENI tools can interact with ExoGENI site aggregates based on the current GENI architecture and API, in which aggregates are loosely coupled except for common authorization of users and slices. Each ExoGENI slice may also link to other GENI resources to the extent that the standard GENI tools and APIs support that interconnection.

At the same time, the ExoSMs and ExoBroker allow ExoGENI to offer capabilities for automated cross-aggregate topology embedding, stitching, and resource allocation within the ExoGENI testbed. These capabilities are currently unique within GENI. They are based on coordinator services, APIs, resource representations, and tools that are not part of a GENI standard. In particular, GENI defines no coordinators for resource management, so cooperation among GENI aggregates is based on direct interaction among AMs or exchanges through untrusted user tools. GENI is developing new extensions that would offer similar capabilities for automated configuration of cross-aggregate virtual networks.

ExoGENI also differs from current GENI practice with respect to the usage model for OpenFlow networks. GENI views an OpenFlow datapath as a separate aggregate that allocates the right to direct network traffic flows matching specified packet header (flowspace) patterns, which are approved manually by an administrator. In ExoGENI, OpenFlow is an integrated capability of the ExoGENI rack aggregates, rather than a distinct aggregate itself. ExoGENI slices may designate OpenFlow controllers to direct network traffic within the virtual network topology that makes up the slice's dataplane. ExoGENI is VLAN-sliced: each virtual link corresponds to a unique VLAN tag at any given point in the network. The handler plugins of the ExoGENI rack AMs authorize the controllers automatically, so that the designated controllers may install flow entries in the datapath for VLANs assigned to the slice's dataplane. We believe that this approach can generalize to other OpenFlow use cases in GENI and cloud networks.

5 Conclusion

This paper describes the design of the ExoGENI testbed, which addresses the goals of GENI by federating diverse virtual infrastructure services and providers. This approach offers a path to leverage IaaS advances and infrastructure deployments occurring outside of GENI. At the same time, it offers a path to bring GENI technologies to bear on key problems of interest outside of the GENI community: linking and peering cloud sites, deploying multi-site cloud applications, and controlling cloud network functions.

ExoGENI offers an architecture for federating cloud sites, linking them with advanced circuit fabrics, and deploying multi-domain virtual network topologies. The initial deployment combines off-the-shelf cloud stacks, integrated OpenFlow capability, linkages to national-footprint research networks and exchange points with international reach.

ExoGENI and its ORCA control framework enable construction of elastic Ethernet/OpenFlow networks across multiple clouds and circuit fabrics. Built-to-order virtual networks are suitable for flexible packet-layer overlays using IP or other protocols selected by the owner. IP overlays may be configured with routed connections to the public Internet through gateways and flow switches. ExoGENI can also serve a broader role as a model and platform for future deeply networked cloud services and applications.

Acknowledgements. We thank RENCI, NSF, IBM, and the GENI Project Office (GPO) at BBN for their support. Many colleagues at GPO and other GENI projects have helped work through issues relating to ExoGENI.

References

1. Baldine, I.: Unique Optical Networking Facilities and Cross-Layer Networking. In: Proceedings of IEEE LEOS Summer Topicals Future Global Networks Workshop (July 2009)
2. Baldine, I., Xin, Y., Evans, D., Heermann, C., Chase, J., Marupadi, V., Yumerefendi, A.: The Missing Link: Putting the Network in Networked Cloud Computing. In: ICVCI: International Conference on the Virtual Computing Initiative (an IBM-sponsored Workshop) (2009)
3. Baldine, I., Xin, Y., Mandal, A., Heermann, C., Chase, J., Marupadi, V., Yumerefendi, A., Irwin, D.: Autonomic Cloud Network Orchestration: A GENI Perspective. In: 2nd International Workshop on Management of Emerging Networks and Services (IEEE MENS 2010), in Conjunction with GLOBECOM 2010 (December 2010)
4. Blum, N., Magedanz, T., Schreiner, F., Wahle, S.: A Research Infrastructure for SOA-based Service Delivery Frameworks. In: Proceedings of the 5th International Conference on Testbeds and Research Infrastructures for the Development of Networks and Communities (TridentCom), Washington DC, USA (April 2009)

5. Chase, J., Grit, L., Irwin, D., Marupadi, V., Shivam, P., Yumerefendi, A.: Beyond Virtual Data Centers: Toward an Open Resource Control Architecture. Selected Papers from the International Conference on the Virtual Computing Initiative (ICVCI) (May 2007)

6. Chase, J.S., Irwin, D.E., Grit, L.E., Moore, J.D., Sprenkle, S.E.: Dynamic Virtual Clusters in a Grid Site Manager. In: Proceedings of the 12th International Symposium on High Performance Distributed Computing (HPDC) (June 2003)

7. Dijkstra, F.: Framework for Path Finding in Multi-Layer Transport Networks. PhD thesis, Universiteit van Amsterdam (2009)

8. Ford, E.: From Clusters To Clouds: xCAT 2 Is Out Of The Bag. Linux Magazine (January 2009)

9. Fu, Y., Chase, J., Chun, B., Schwab, S., Vahdat, A.: SHARP: An Architecture for Secure Resource Peering. In: Proceedings of the 19th ACM Symposium on Operating System Principles (October 2003)

10. Guok, C., Robertson, D., Thompson, M., Lee, J., Tierney, B., Johnston, W.: Intra and Interdomain Circuit Provisioning Using the OSCARS Reservation System. In: Proceedings of the 3rd International Conference on Broadband Communications, Networks and Systems, BROADNETS (2006)

11. Ham, J., Dijkstra, F., Grosso, P., Pol, R., Toonk, A., Laat, C.: A Distributed Topology Information System for Optical Networks Based on the Semantic Web. Journal of Optical Switching and Networking 5(2-3) (June 2008)

12. Ham, J.V.: A Semantic Model for Complex Computer Networks. PhD thesis, University of Amsterdam (April 2010)

13. Irwin, D., Chase, J., Grit, L., Yumerefendi, A.: Underware: An Exokernel for the Internet? Technical report, Duke University Department of Computer Science (January 2007)

14. Irwin, D., Chase, J.S., Grit, L., Yumerefendi, A., Becker, D., Yocum, K.G.: Sharing Networked Resources with Brokered Leases. In: Proceedings of the USENIX Technical Conference (June 2006)

15. Kaashoek, M.F., Engler, D.R., Ganger, G.R., Briceno, H.M., Hunt, R., Mazieres, D., Pinckney, T., Grimm, R., Janotti, J., Mackenzie, K.: Application Performance and Flexibility on Exokernel Systems. In: Proceedings of the Sixteenth Symposium on Operating Systems Principles (SOSP) (October 1997)

16. Mandal, A., Xin, Y., Ruth, P., Heerman, C., Chase, J., Orlikowski, V., Yumerefendi, A.: Provisioning and Evaluating Multi-Domain Networked Clouds for Hadoop-Based Applications. In: Proceedings of the 3rd International Conference on Cloud Computing Technologies and Science 2011 (IEEE Cloudcom 2011) (December 2011)

17. Mell, P., Grance, T.: The NIST Definition of Cloud Computing. Special Publication 800-145, Recommendations of the National Institute of Standards and Technology (September 2011)

18. Nurmi, D., Wolski, R., Grzegorczyk, C., Obertelli, G., Soman, S., Youseff, L., Zagorodnov, D.: The Eucalyptus Open-Source Cloud-Computing System. In: Proceedings of the 9th IEEE/ACM International Symposium on Cluster Computing and the Grid (CCGRID) (May 2009)

19. Peterson, L., Bavier, A., Fiuczynski, M.E., Muir, S.: Experiences Building PlanetLab. In: Proceedings of the 7th Symposium on Operating Systems Design and Implementation (OSDI) (November 2006)

20. Raychaudhuri, D., Seskar, I., Ott, M., Ganu, S., Ramachandran, K., Kremo, H., Siracusa, R., Liu, H., Singh, M.: Overview of the ORBIT Radio Grid Testbed for Evaluation of Next-Generation Wireless Network Protocols. In: Proceedings of the IEEE Wireless Communications and Networking Conference, WCNC (2005)
21. Ruth, P., Jiang, X., Xu, D., Goasguen, S.: Virtual distributed environments in a shared infrastructure. Computer 38(5), 63–69 (2005)
22. Sherwood, R., Gibb, G., Yap, K.-K., Appenzeller, G., Casado, M., McKeown, N., Parulkar, G.: Can the Production Network Be the Testbed? In: Proceedings of the Symposium on Operating System Design and Implementation (OSDI) (October 2010)
23. White, B., Lepreau, J., Stoller, L., Ricci, R., Guruprasad, S., Newbold, M., Hibler, M., Barb, C., Joglekar, A.: An integrated experimental environment for distributed systems and networks. In: Proceedings of the 5th Symposium on Operating Systems Design and Implementation (OSDI), pp. 255–270 (December 2002)
24. Xin, Y., Baldine, I., Mandal, A., Heermann, C., Chase, J., Yumerefendi, A.: Embedding Virtual Topologies in Networked Clouds. In: 6th ACM International Conference on Future Internet Technologies (CFI) (June 2011)
25. Yumerefendi, A., Shivam, P., Irwin, D., Gunda, P., Grit, L., Demberel, A., Chase, J., Babu, S.: Towards an Autonomic Computing Testbed. In: Workshop on Hot Topics in Autonomic Computing (HotAC) (June 2007)

Experimental Demonstration of Network Virtualization and Resource Flexibility in the COMCON Project*

Michael Duelli[1], Sebastian Meier[2], David Wagner[2], Thomas Zinner[1],
Matthias Schmid[3], Marco Hoffmann[4], and Wolfgang Kiess[5]

[1] Institute of Computer Science, University of Würzburg
[2] Institute of Communication Networks and Computer Engineering,
University of Stuttgart
[3] Infosim GmbH & Co. KG
[4] Nokia Siemens Networks GmbH & Co. KG
[5] DOCOMO Communications Laboratories Europe GmbH

Abstract. In the recent past, *Network Virtualization* (NV) received much attention. Nevertheless, *Virtual Networks* (VNs) are still not available on the market. The consortium of the *COntrol and Management of COexisting Networks* (COMCON) project examines the potential interactions in vertically and horizontally divided markets and evaluates the applicability of existing technologies, like *Generalized Multi-Protocol Label Switching* (GMPLS), for automated virtualization-enabled network management. To promote the manifold research, a selected scenario was demonstrated at the EuroView 2011 comprising a *Video on Demand* (VoD) service using a *Scalable Video Codec* (SVC). All necessary components have been implemented and the selected scenario was performed on a real network based on Linux PCs. In this paper, we describe the components, the scenario, and the gained insights in detail.

Keywords: network virtualization, automated provisioning, GMPLS, VoD, SVC.

1 Introduction

From a business perspective, there are several reasons for the virtualization of network resources. On the one hand, established network operators and service providers would like to profit from the new opportunities opened by network virtualization, like consolidation of resources and resource flexibility. On the other hand, newcomers get more and easier possibilities to enter vertical and horizontal markets in network and service provisioning.

* This work was funded by the Federal Ministry of Education and Research of the Federal Republic of Germany (Förderkennzeichen 01BK0915, 01BK0916, 01BK0917, 01BK0918, 01BK0919, GLab). The authors alone are responsible for the content of the paper.

T. Korakis, M. Zink, and M. Ott (Eds.): TridentCom 2012, LNICST 44, pp. 114–129, 2012.

Today, virtualization focuses on computation or storage clouds while the virtualization of fully configurable networks has not yet become reality. This is partly due to the lack of standardized interfaces as well as missing best practices for integrating a complete *Network Virtualization* (NV) environment [1]. Our consortium of the G-Lab [2] phase 2 project *COntrol and Management of COexisting Networks* (COMCON) [3] identified key functions in a potential vertical market based on the first definition of a vertical role model of the *Architecture and Design for the Future Internet* (4WARD) project that gives a framework for intercommunication of physical resource owners, brokers, and renters. Based on these concepts, we revised the role model [4] and investigated how the different players could fill their roles and how the interaction with respect to the provisioning of *Virtual Network* (VN) is supposed to work. Therefore, we consider the complete control loops of the different players and investigate monitoring mechanisms as well as the role of decision components. On this foundation, we implemented an exemplary scenario of service provisioning on a virtual infrastructure integrating monitoring and dynamic adaptation. The scenario was integrated in a testbed and successfully demonstrated [5]. In this work, we present an elaborated view of the set-up as well as details on the individual steps.

The remainder of this work is organized as follows. In Section 2, we describe the background of our work and our goals. In Section 3, we give detailed information on implementations and their capabilities. In Section 4, we describe the scenario we selected and the run of proof-of-concept experimentations with respect to automated network provisioning and service flexibility reacting on dynamically changing demands. In Section 5, we summarize the lessons learned in the course of our implementation and give an outlook on future work. In Section 6, we draw final conclusions.

2   Background and Requirements

In this section, we present related work and give details on the background of our implementation as well as an overview of our architecture.

2.1   Related Work

The impact of NV on the traditional *Internet Service Provider* (ISP) role model is described in [6]. The authors propose to split up the ISP role into an infrastructure provider managing the physical resources and a service provider deploying enabler services such as routing, *Domain Name System* (DNS) as well as end-to-end services.

The 4WARD project refined this role model in [7]. Furthermore, 4WARD introduced interfaces for role interaction with the focus on virtual network deployment and end-user attachment. We further refined these approaches to include end-users in the role model and to be less static with regard to the protocols used in the virtual networks, especially non-IP. The latter requires the consideration

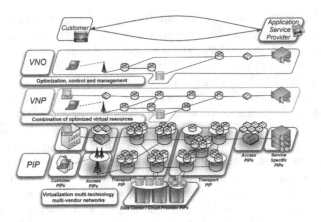

Fig. 1. An overview of the roles and architecture considered in the COMCON project

of arbitrary virtual nodes. In [4], we introduce a business role model, which structures the core functions to be fulfilled by the cooperating players. Furthermore, the interactions and dependencies between these roles are outlined.

For instantiation of virtual networks with *Quality of Service* (QoS) guarantees, the authors of [8] propose a virtualization architecture based on DiffServ/*Multi-Protocol Label Switching* (MPLS) enabled transport networks. To translate between different QoS parameters across several roles, a multi-tier architecture for *Service Level Agreement* (SLA) management is proposed.

The *Dynamic Resource Allocation by GMPLS Optical Networks* (DRAGON) project presents an architecture for inter-domain virtual path provisioning [9]. The mechanisms for path computation and resource reservation are based on *Generalized Multi-Protocol Label Switching* (GMPLS). However, their implementation of *Resource Reservation Protocol with traffic engineering extensions* (RSVP-TE) is focused on controlling Ethernet switches while we target arbitrary network technologies.

The project on *Generalized Architecture for Dynamic Infrastructure Services* (GEYSERS) [10, 11] defines an architecture to instantiate virtual networks for interconnecting IT resources that relies on GMPLS. In contrast to our approach where VNs are *custom-tailored* to meet the requirements of one particular application service, in GEYSERS a VN is set up independently of the services that might be deployed on it later on. We also integrate individual monitoring on each role's scope as an integral part of our architecture since we consider the ability to verify SLA conformance to be critical for the economic acceptance of VN. Additionally, the approach of *service-tailored* VNs means that every role has to be able to monitor all relevant information.

2.2   Business Role Model

The different roles and their interaction assumed in the COMCON architecture are illustrated in Figure 1. The role model comprises *Physical Infrastructure*

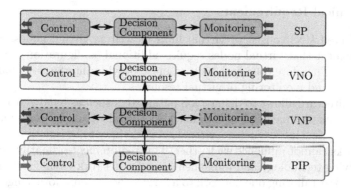

Fig. 2. The loop of monitoring, decision, and control between the different roles

Providers (PIPs), *Virtual Network Providers* (VNPs), *Virtual Network Operators* (VNOs), and *Application Service Providers* (ASPs).

A PIP is the owner of its physical resources and uses virtualization techniques to rent shares of these physical resources to VNPs. These virtual topologies provided to a VNP include links as well as virtual nodes providing storage and computation resources. The PIP also provides means to configure and control these virtual nodes. A VNP is a broker and an aggregator that typically acquires resources from multiple PIPs while delivering a single contiguous VN to a VNO. A VNO designs the VN, defining its topology and the functionality to be provided by each node. During operation, the VNO configures the functionality of the nodes in a VN using the control means forwarded from the PIPs. Thus, the VNO defines the shape as well as the inner configuration of the VN and, thereby, tailors the network to the needs of the service envisaged by the ASP.

The clear definition of these four roles allows to identify potential and necessary interaction and cooperation. Nevertheless, the modeled roles do not need to be actually represented by different players, in real scenarios several roles may also consolidate in one entity.

To set up a new VN, the roles interact as follows. The ASP formulates its demands and mandates the VNO that makes the best and most suitable offer to realize the requested service. In turn, the VNO requests a VNP who contacts PIPs. As we consider automation to be a key enabler for future networks, all communication for the set-up as well as the operation of a VN is assumed to use standardized interfaces and corresponding protocols.

Due to the layered and multi-party business, trust and monitoring play an even more important role than in today's networks. Therefore, monitoring is needed in different roles and on different levels to verify compliance with requested criteria such as QoS parameters. In turn, monitoring allows all roles to reconsider and redesign the VN taking into account the monitored internal state. Thus, each role may implement a control loop that comprises monitoring, decision making, and execution. These control loops as well as the relations of the different roles are illustrated in Figure 2.

2.3   Technical Requirements

The considered VNs consist of virtual links as well as virtual nodes. Furthermore, we expect that virtual nodes require additional configuration after initial provisioning. Therefore, our architecture must provide interfaces to hand over configuration and monitoring of virtual resources.

Our architecture allows to define QoS parameters such as bandwidth or delay for a virtual link that have to be guaranteed. As several virtual networks may share a common physical infrastructure, virtual networks have to be isolated so that virtual networks cannot influence each other. This requirement primarily influences the underlying technology and implementation for network virtualization.

As we aim at tailoring one network to a service, we account for changes in this service or its demands by dynamically adapting the underlying virtual network. This includes simple modifications such as increasing the bandwidth of virtual links as well as more complex adaptations such as changing the virtual network topology at runtime.

Today's transport network technologies like GMPLS and *Next Steps in Signaling* (NSIS) already support QoS guarantees and isolation for links. Those technologies not only allow dynamic instantiation and tear-down of virtual links, but also support adjustments, e.g., of link capacity, during ongoing operation. Therefore, our approach is reusing existing technologies and enabling them for network virtualization by prototypic extensions. In our implementation presented in the following sections, we show how we use the well-established GMPLS control plane framework, cf. Section 3.3, for link virtualization.

3   Implementation and Integration of Building Blocks

In this work, we focus on resource flexibility – a use case purely enabled by NV – that allows networks to "breath", i.e., dynamically grow or shrink. The resources are assumed to be requested by a *Video on Demand* (VoD) service whose video content ist to be streamed using the *Scalable Video Codec* (SVC) format, described below. In the following, we describe the building blocks as well as the split-up of their functions.

3.1   Multi-path SVC Framework

The newly gained resource flexibility can be combined with additional flexibility provided on application layer by SVC streaming to realize a VoD service.

Multi-path Transmission. The split-up of a data flow on multiple paths towards a common sink, has recently attracted a lot of attention since it allows to utilize different access networks, e.g., 3G and WLAN available on today's smart phones, and to enable a virtualization of the transport resource [12], i.e., flexibly use parallel network resources. A multi-path transmission is initiated by a *splitting* component that splits up the data on disjoint paths. In contrast to

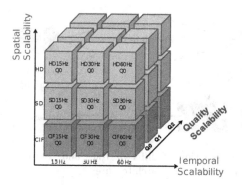

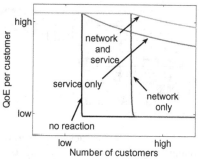

Fig. 3. Illustration of the possible scalability dimensions for an SVC video

Fig. 4. Qualitative comparison of the benefit of different types of adaptation

Equal-Cost Multi-Path (ECMP), the splitter is not bound to simple packet-wise load balancing but might be able to make use of knowledge on the structure of the transmitted data, i.e., video streams in our case. Finally, the multiple transmission paths end in an *assembling* component. Thereby, the assembler not only has to join but also needs to synchronize corresponding data streams by means of buffering and has to prevent reordering of packets [13].

Scalable Video Coding. The H.264/SVC is an extension of the widely used H.264/*Advanced Video Coding* (AVC) codec, which was specified by the ITU-T [14]. SVC provides a way to shift the balance between quality and consumed bandwidth of an encoded video clip by selecting frame rate, resolution, and image quality. These three dimensions are called *temporal*, *spatial*, and *quality* scalabilities. Figure 3 illustrates a video containing all three scalabilities. Therein, the left "sub-cube" at the bottom is the *base layer*, which is necessary to play the video file at *Common Intermediate Format* (CIF) resolution, 15 Hz frame rate, and quality Q0. Based on this layer, different additional *enhancement layers* permit a better video experience with a higher resolution, better *Signal-to-Noise Ratio* (SNR), or higher frame rate. Enhancement layers can be omitted to reduce the required bandwidth without interrupting the video stream. However, their omission also decreases the video quality. As different layers are separately packeted, they can be sent via multiple paths.

Cross-Layer Benefit. As mentioned before SVC quality is assembled of different blocks, cf. Figure 3, that increase the quality of the video and also the required bandwidth. By means of NV, the VNO, which is given full control on the video transmission in our case, is able to make use of these SVC properties by splitting different quality layers among multiple paths. Thus, the service is able to make use of changes to the underlying VN. The ability to adapt both, network resources and service, has proven to outperform individual adaptations of either network or service. This is illustrated in Figure 4, which is computed based on the results taken from [15].

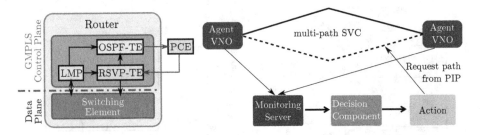

Fig. 5. GMPLS protocol stack and
components

Fig. 6. Interaction of different roles and components to an integrated architecture

Investigations on the impact of the SVC scalabilities on the user perceived
quality as well as the influence of insufficient network resources on SVC video
streaming were published recently. In [16], the authors showed that spatial adaptation should be preferred compared to temporal adaptation. This results from
spatial adaptation allowing higher bandwidth savings and lower decrease in video
quality than temporal adaptation. Packet loss rates of about 2% already have a
severe impact on the user perceived quality, as indicated by [17]. However, it was
shown that packet loss on enhancement layers has a lesser impact on *Quality of
Experience* (QoE) than packet loss on the base layer. Thus, we conclude that
in case of multi-path video streaming with different path QoS parameters, the
enhancement layers should be transmitted via the paths with lower QoS.

3.2   Monitoring

To be able to react on increasing load, e.g., to change the topology of a VN
and to split the SVC video stream to off-load paths, monitoring is required.
In the considered scenario, performing monitoring solely by the VNO is sufficient since we presume trust between the roles and the VNO has full control
on the video transmission. As we consider a distributed architecture, we require distributed measurement points. Thereby, data is collected by, so called,
agents that send information to a data collection point, a database server. We
use the *StableNet* software [18], which uses *Simple Network Management Protocol* (SNMP) amongst others for monitoring the state of network resources and
provides interfaces to trigger decision making for certain network situations such
as high load. Furthermore, StableNet is multi-tenant capable. This opens up the
possibilities to use a single monitoring solution to individually monitor different
ASPs or VNOs with a single StableNet server.

3.3   Control Plane Framework

As presented in Section 2, a PIP has two core tasks. Firstly, a PIP operates and
manages a physical network consisting of nodes and links. Secondly, a PIP creates
virtual resources on top of the physical resources. In our demonstration, we focus

on the virtualization of links. Due to the dynamic nature of virtual networks, we expect a PIP to rely on a control plane to automate virtual link management. This includes virtual link establishment, modification, and tear-down. Figure 5 depicts the functional blocks and protocols of the GMPLS framework [19] that are involved in virtual link setup. We will shortly introduce those components in the following.

To verify whether a virtual link can be embedded into the physical network, a PIP needs an up-to-date view on its physical links, their properties, and their utilization. The *Link Management Protocol* (LMP) and in particular the *Open Shortest Path First protocol with traffic engineering extensions* (OSPF-TE) provide this information. Currently, *Traffic Engineering* (TE) extensions are defined for bandwidth information. Additional metrics such as link delay are currently taken into account by emerging protocol extensions [20]. Relevant information on resource usage is stored in a *Traffic Engineering Database* (TED).

Algorithms for constraint-based path computation can operate on this TED to find possible embeddings of a virtual link into the physical network. Embedding can be a complex task, in particular for large networks and many constraints. Therefore, the GMPLS framework comprises a dedicated *Path Computation Element* (PCE) for constraint-based path computation.

Once an embedding solution is computed, signaling protocols such as RSVP-TE are used to instantiate the virtual link accordingly. In case of RSVP-TE, a hop-by-hop signaling is performed to allocate resources on each node that the virtual link traverses. During this setup every node verifies that the requested QoS parameters can be satisfied and reserves resources for the virtual link.

3.4   Integration

The starting point for designing software integration in NV environments is the generic role interactions as depicted in Figure 2. Obviously, each role has access to monitoring information but on different levels: the PIP has access to all monitoring based on the physical devices while the VNO only gets information regarding its VN. This monitoring information defines the foundation of the decision making components of each player. These decision making components represent the players' intelligence, their decisions are based on internal policies and strategies. Therefore, they also cannot be standardized or even predicted, so we decided to define the decisions to be taken beforehand. In the considered scenario, the decisions of the PIP concern where to place paths and *Virtual Machines* (VMs). The decisions of the VNO are the layout of the VN and the configuration of the VMs. In the selected use case, this includes where to install splitting and assembling functionalities, to configure the routing of the different video layers but also to dimension the links and nodes of this VN. An overview of the control process in the VNO is given in Figure 6.

4   Demonstration

We developed a sophisticated scenario to show the flexibility in service provisioning that can be achieved using the capabilities of an automated Network Virtualization Infrastructure and of a elaborated service provisioning architecture. We demonstrate automated network management and resource control for virtual networks in the use case of a high quality VoD service over virtual networks. This scenario was integrated in a real network and was demonstrated at EuroView 2011 [5]. In the following, the technical realization, the starting situation and the run of events are presented in detail.

4.1   Testbed

The scenario has been implemented using seven off-the-shelf PCs running Ubuntu Linux 10.04 equipped with 4-port Gigabit Ethernet network interface cards. These nodes have been configured with distinct IPv4 networks for each link and a manually configured routing table. In order to separate data plane and control plane in the set-up, an additional GRE-tunnel [21, 22] was set up on each GMPLS-controlled physical link and provided with its own IPv4 addresses. Nevertheless, the data plane implementation is not complete: there are no labels added and there is no scheduling enforcing the confirmed bandwidth. Five of the seven nodes represent the PIP's network infrastructure while the other two represent the neighboring PIPs hosting source and destinations of the video streaming service. Additionally, there is one remote machine hosting the StableNet server process representing the VNO's service monitoring. Thus, there are seven local hosts in the testbed and one remote host representing three PIP domains and one VNO domain in total.

4.2   Starting Situation

As a starting point the PIP in focus is assumed to have its physical components virtualized and offering them via the VNP to VNOs. The PIP already deployed virtual routers without special functionality within the network. An ASP has developed a business plan for a VoD service and requests the VNO to design the required network and to deliver the service. The VNO decides for a SVC solution as it provides the VNO with the most adaptable solution while transmitting the video. Based on this decision and the business plan of the ASP, the VNO plans the network for the assumed customer base.

The network provided by the VNP includes a part provided by the PIP in focus. In Figure 7, the PIP's topology can be seen in the upper right part of the demonstration GUI, which integrates the PIP's and the VNO's view for demonstration purposes. The PIP's network consists of the ring formed by nodes A to E and the links in between. For the sake of clarity, we additionally depict the nodes and links that the PIP uses for peering, i.e., node G connecting to the data center and node F connecting to the users. To guarantee the QoE requested by the ASP, the VNO monitors the virtual resources which is indicated in the demo control GUI   topology of the PIPs (weathermap)

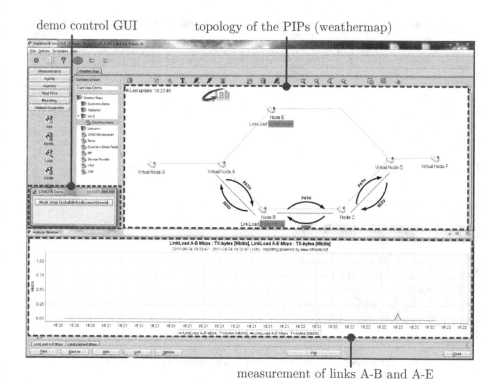

measurement of links A-B and A-E

Fig. 7. Annotated illustration of the initial set-up of the VN

lower part of Figure 7. The VNO is prepared to trigger actions with regard to the SVC set-up as well as by requesting changes to the VN from the VNP that communicates with the PIP.

4.3   Course of Events

The VNP requests the PIP to create a VN consisting of a connection from node G to F with virtual nodes at the domain borders (nodes A and D). For the demo, we use a simple GUI element to trigger the request (visible on the middle left). After receiving the request, the PIP's network management has to determine how to fulfill the request, which heavily depends on business policies and strategies. We define the path A-B-C-D as the selected solution. Having the request mapped to physical resources, the PIP triggers an RSVP-TE signaling session to set up the virtual link. In the demo, the signaling PATH and RESV messages establish a *Label Switched Path* (LSP) with the requested bandwidth as can be seen in Figure 7.

When the signaling is complete, the VNO takes over control of the VN and sets up the VoD service. This includes setting up the streaming server in the data center, but also deploying monitoring agents in the VN. In this case, that

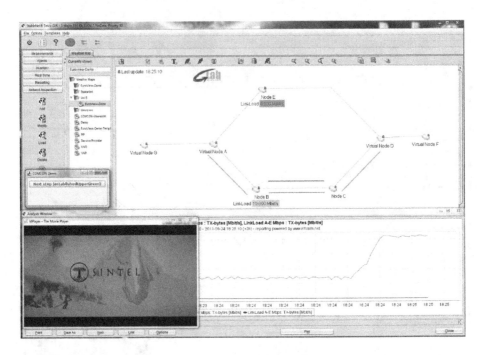

Fig. 8. VoD service running and serving an increasing number of clients

means StableNet agents on nodes B and E. The VNO's monitoring shows the current usage of the requested virtual link from node A to D as depicted at the bottom of Figure 8.

Since the PIP provides virtual resources for other VNs as well, resource usage on the physical infrastructure may change without changes in the selected VN. In our scenario, the remaining bandwidth of the link between nodes B and C is assigned to another VN indicated by a red line as shown in Figure 8. But also the resource consumption within the VN changes and may call for adaptation. In our scenario, more and more customers join the VoD service inducing an increasing bandwidth consumption, which we emulated by a traffic generator on node G.

The VNO's StableNet agents keep track of this as virtual link utilization is monitored constantly. At a predefined link utilization level of 75%, the StableNet monitoring issues a warning to the VNO, shown by the yellow background color in Figure 8. Due to the history of the link utilization the VNO's network management system reacts.

One possible reaction is a request to the VNP and then to the PIP to increase the bandwidth of the existing virtual link. As there is no remaining capacity on the link B-C, the PIP has to decline this request. However, the PIP may set up a second virtual path via node E although this path is known to have a higher packet loss probability than the first one. We therefore assume that these paths cannot be transparently aggregated. Nevertheless, the PIP offers the VNO to

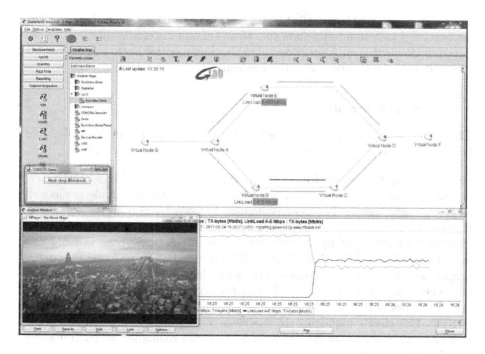

Fig. 9. Enhancement layers successfully transferred to second path

adopt the VN by adding a second virtual path between nodes A and D with higher packet loss probability.

When evaluating this offer the VNO has to consider the SLAs in force for this service. We assume that the VNO cannot simply serve new users using this second path due to the links' characteristics and its service guarantees with the ASP. Nevertheless, due to the flexible SVC framework the VNO can maintain high QoE for all users despite the lower QoS characteristics of the second virtual path. As described in Section 3.1, packet loss on the base layer result in a higher impact on the perceived quality than on the enhancement layers, which may be separated and routed differently using this enhanced framework. Therefore, the VNO can configure its components to transmit the base layer for all users on the reliable path and the less important ones on the second path. So the VNO accepts the proposal of the PIP and activates a demuxer daemon on node A and a muxer daemon on node D. As a result there is no perceivable quality degradation of the video streams that are delivered to the customers. The resulting changes in traffic on the two paths are illustrated in the lower part of Figure 9.

5   Lessons Learned and Next Steps

The process of integrating and setting up the scenario described in Section 4 provided insights on how interaction between different roles and also between functional components controlled by one role have to be designed. Anyway, this integration is just an intermediate step to an extended scenario that is to be designed, implemented, and integrated in the coming months. Both, lessons learned and next steps, are presented in the following.

5.1   Lessons Learned

This section details the lessons learned during the implementation of the building blocks and their integration into the discussed demonstration scenario.

Control Loop Coordination. The experimentation provided us a holistic view on several phases of the operation of a selected VN. It revealed challenges as well as promising solutions. The most prominent lesson learned from the scenario is that possessing flexibility in network and service does pay off in certain scenarios. Moreover, it may pay off by various ways: when designing this scenario in order to use all capabilities of the Virtualization Platform and SVC, we found that many simpler scenarios, that would cause serious problems when using today's network and service architecture, can be alleviated or significantly improved by each of the two actors (PIP and VNO) alone given either the advanced features of NV or SVC. This clearly highlights the challenge how these independently managed control loops can be coordinated in order to avoid redundant or contradicting actions and oscillation.

VN Descriptions. In order to establish such VN-provisioning relationship as presented in the scenario and to allow for automatic topology changes, description of VNs have to be exchanged in a negotiation process. These descriptions express requests or offers of VNs to be created or changes to existing VNs. The work on this topic is ongoing, some general requirements were identified.

- *Description methodology*: The information model needs to support all needed network elements and has to support embedding of information on control access.
- *Negotiation protocol*: Although a simple take-it-or-leave-it approach could be used, the flexibility often incorporated by complex topologies would be neglected and the solutions are expected to be far from optimal.
- Definition of responsibilities. This depends on a solution for challenge described above but since all players do have capabilities to react to external events from the start, it would make sense to include agreements on responsibilities in the VN negotiations from the very beginning.

Multi-path SVC Streaming. Multi-path transmission implemented in the network requires additional functional blocks, namely a flow splitter and a flow assembler. We implemented these functionalities and also mechanisms to cope with out-of-order packets and assure a valid byte stream for the video player. We used the capabilities of a SVC stream to split the flow into base and enhancement layers and transmit them via different paths. This extends pure round-robin packet scheduling techniques. However, we had to extend the flow assembler to be able to identify base and enhancement layers in order to reassemble the complete stream or forward only a part of the stream if parts are missing. Due to SVC dependencies we could not forward the video clip frame by frame but buffered a *Group of Pictures* (GOP) before we forwarded the best available video quality stream to the destination. Thus, we had to provide a larger buffer at the assembler compared to the case of round-robin packet scheduling.

The splitter transmits packets via different paths and the assembler receives the packets and forwards them to the destination. In order to guarantee the original sequence of the packets, this entity has to buffer out-of-order packets and re-sequence the packets if necessary [12]. This introduces additional waiting times in the magnitude of the current round trip time. However, by tailoring multi-path transmission to work together with SVC streaming we had to care on additional issues. First, the splitter has to be able to identify base and enhancement layers and transmit them via different paths. This extends techniques like round-robin based scheduling approaches. In order to exploit the capabilities of SVC, the assembler also is able to identify the different quality layers. We took into account, that switches between resolutions can be performed on a GOP basis. Thus, we first assemble all parts of the current GOP, identify whether a quality switch was performed and then forward the best available video quality stream to the destination.

5.2 Next Steps

The scenario presented in Section 4 shows flexibility and dynamic in terms of "breathing" of the VN and the service. Nevertheless, instantiated components remain at their physical host throughout the VN's life time. But there are incentives for both the PIP and the VNO to relocate virtual resources.

Motivations for the PIP to move a VM from one physical host to another range from utilization optimization, maintenance, data center migration, consolidation, or even disaster avoidance [23]. On virtualization level today a VM can be migrated without noticeable service interruption from one physical host to another (live migration) but these mechanisms are Ethernet and IPv4-focused and come with several constraints. The integration of VM-management with a virtualization-enabled network control plane, e.g. based on GMPLS, promises to ease live migration of VMs and to reduce constraints.

The VNO itself may have motives to restructure its service provisioning VN by relocating resources, e.g., to cope with changed (technical) requirements that cannot be met at the old location or in order to save money by moving to another VNP. In any case, this approach needs service or application specific knowledge and possibly even built-in support. Therefore, the scenario can be extended by relocation of virtual resources by virtualization or application specific means.

Another important topic to be addressed is the control loop coordination, in particular the cooperation of PIP and VNO. There are events that are evident from the infrastructure layer monitoring of the PIP, the network monitoring within the VN performed by the VNO as well as from the application level monitoring performed by the ASP. If such network situation changes happen and PIP and VNO and ASP use simple independent control mechanisms, they all might trigger reactions to this condition which might prove to be redundant or even contradicting. E.g., a link failure should normally just trigger the resilience mechanisms provided by the PIP. Anyway, if these mechanisms fail or do not exist, possibly the VNO could improve the situation by changing the VN-internal routing or even the ASP could reduce the currently needed bandwidth by service-specific means. Thus, it is not only required to define responsibilities between the roles but also to develop means to coordinate them dynamically.

6   Conclusion

In this paper, we presented a complete scenario using NV. It is based on a market model comprising PIPs, VNPs, VNOs and ASPs, defining a vertically and horizontally divided market. We presented our implementations namely an SVC framework, a GMPLS control plane, and a monitoring framework. For the selected use case of VoD delivery using a VN, the scenario shows the variety and power of interaction between different roles. In the scenario, the cooperation of the PIP and the VNO, i.e., coordination of virtualization and service layer, guarantee unaffected QoE for the end-users despite of unexpected demand and limited network resources.

One prerequisite for successful coordination is an efficient monitoring infrastructure that allows to react on changing conditions as well as to verify SLA accordance of consumed and provided services. The second prerequisite is an ability to handle the dynamic of each player in its own responsibility domain: the PIP has to be able to adapt instantiated VNs as well as a VNO should be able to adapt its service to changing demands. A future challenge is the coordination of these independent but overlapping control loops.

In short, we showed that NV is able to bring benefits for all parties but the coordination of the different control loops needs to be further investigated.

References

1. Chowdhury, N., Boutaba, R.: Network virtualization: state of the art and research challenges. IEEE Communications Magazine 47, 20–26 (2009)
2. German-Lab (G-Lab), Project Web Page (December 2011), http://www.german-lab.de
3. COntrol and Management of COexisting Networks (COMCON), Project Web Page (December 2011), http://www.german-lab.de/phase-2/comcon/
4. Meier, S., Barisch, M., Kirstädter, A., Schlosser, D., Duelli, M., Jarschel, M., Hoßfeld, T., Hoffmann, K., Hoffmann, M., Kellerer, W., Khan, A., Jurca, D., Kozu, K.: Provisioning and Operation of Virtual Networks. Electronic Communications of the EASST, Kommunikation in Verteilten Systemen 37 (March 2011)
5. Schlosser, D., Duelli, M., Zinner, T., Meier, S., Wagner, D., Barisch, M., Hoffmann, M., Kellerer, W., Schmid, M.: Service Component Mobility Enabled by Network Virtualization. In: EuroView 2011, Würzburg, Germany (August 2011)

6. Feamster, N., Gao, L., Rexford, J.: How To Lease The Internet In Your Spare Time. SIGCOMM Comput. Commun. Rev. 37(1), 61–64 (2007)
7. Bless, R., Werle, C.: Network virtualization from a signaling perspective. In: IEEE International Conference on Communications Workshops, pp. 1–6 (June 2009)
8. Cheng, Y., Farha, R., Tizghadam, A., Kim, M.S., Hashemi, M., Leon-Garcia, A., Hong, J.-K.: Virtual network approach to scalable ip service deployment and efficient resource management. IEEE Communications Magazine 43(10), 76–84 (2005)
9. Yang, X., et al.: Policy-based resource management and service provisioning in gmpls networks. In: First IEEE Workshop on Adaptive Policy-based Management in Network Management and Control (2006)
10. Figuerola, S., García-Espín, J.A., Riera, J.F.: An optical network and it infrastructure virtualisation framework from geysers project. Local event in Catalonia (2010)
11. Generalized Architecture for Dynamic Infrastructure Services (GEYSERS), Project Web Page (December 2011), http://www.geysers.eu
12. Zinner, T., Tutschku, K., Nakao, A., Tran-Gia, P.: Using Concurrent Multipath Transmission for Transport Virtualization: Analyzing Path Selection. In: Proceedings of the 22nd International Teletraffic Congress (ITC), Amsterdam, Netherlands (September 2010)
13. Zinner, T., Klein, D., Tutschku, K., Zseby, T., Tran-Gia, P., Shavitt, Y.: Performance of Concurrent Multipath Transmissions - Measurements and Model Validation. In: of the 7th Conference on Next Generation Internet Networks (NGI), Kaiserslautern, Germany (June 2011)
14. ITU-T Recommendation, H.264 : Advanced video coding for generic audiovisual services, http://www.itu.int/rec/T-REC-H.264
15. Hoßfeld, T., Fiedler, M., Zinner, T.: The QoE Provisioning-Delivery-Hysteresis and Its Importance for Service Provisioning in the Future Internet. In: Proceedings of the 7th Conference on Next Generation Internet Networks (NGI), Kaiserslautern, Germany (June 2011)
16. Zinner, T., Hohlfeld, O., Abboud, O., Hoßfeld, T.: Impact of Frame Rate and Resolution on Objective QoE Metrics. In: International Workshop on Quality of Multimedia Experience, Trondheim (June 2010)
17. Singh, K.D., Ksentini, A., Marienval, B.: Quality of Experience Measurement Tool for SVC Video Coding. In: IEEE International Conference on Communications (ICC), Kyoto, Japan, pp. 1–5 (June 2011)
18. Infosim, StableNet (December 2011), http://www.infosim.net/index.php/products
19. Mannie, E.: Generalized Multi-Protocol Label Switching (GMPLS) Architecture. RFC 3945 (Proposed Standard), Updated by RFC 6002 (October 2004)
20. Fu, X., Betts, M., Wang, Q., McDysan, D., Malis, A.: GMPLS extensions to communicate latency as a traffic engineering performance metric. draft-wang-ccamp-latency-te-metric-03 (Proposed Standard) (2011)
21. Hanks, S., Li, T., Farinacci, D., Traina, P.: Generic Routing Encapsulation (GRE). RFC 1701 (Informational) (October 1994)
22. Hanks, S., Li, T., Farinacci, D., Traina, P.: Generic Routing Encapsulation over IPv4 networks. RFC 1702 (Informational) (October 1994)
23. Joint whitepaper from VMware and Cisco, Virtual Machine Mobility with VMware VMotion and Cisco Data Center Interconnect Technologies (2009), http://www.cisco.com/en/US/solutions/collateral/ns340/ns517/ns224/ns836/white_paper_c11-557822.pdf

A Passive Measurement System
for Network Testbeds

Charles Thomas, Joel Sommers, Paul Barford, Dongchan Kim, Ananya Das,
Roberto Segebre, and Mark Crovella

University of Wisconsin, Colgate University and Boston University
{cthomas,dkim24}@wisc.edu, {jsommers,adas,rsegebre}@colgate.edu,
{crovella,pb}@cs.bu.edu

Abstract. The ability to capture and process packet-level data is of
intrinsic importance in network testbeds that offer broad experimental capabilities to researchers. In this paper we describe the design and
implementation of a passive measurement system for network testbeds
called GIMS. The system enables users to specify and centrally manage packet capture on a set of dedicated measurement nodes deployed
on links in a distributed testbed. The first component of GIMS is a
scalable experiment management system that coordinates multi-tenant
access to measurement nodes through a web-based user interface. The
second component of GIMS is a node management system that enables
(i) local processing on packets (*e.g.,* flow aggregation and sampling),
(ii) meta-data to be added to captured packets (*e.g.,* timestamps), *(iii)*
packet anonymization per local security policy, and *(iv)* flexible data
storage including transfer to remote archives. We demonstrate the capabilities of GIMS through a set of micro-benchmarks that specifically
highlight the performance of the node management system deployed on
a commodity workstation. Our implementations are openly available to
the community and our development efforts are on-going.

1 Introduction

Network testbeds are designed to offer environments to researchers and prac-
titioners in which experimental systems, configurations and protocols can be
carefully tested and evaluated. Network testbeds in use today can be differentiated by the specific systems, level of control and "realism" that they offer
users. While the strengths and weaknesses of different testbed types have been
well documented, the utility of each depends directly on the ability to gather
measurements from the infrastructure.

Measurements in network testbeds can be broken into two categories: active
and passive. Active measurements are based on sending and receiving specifically crafted packet probes through the infrastructure (*e.g.,* `traceroute` measurements). These probes enable a variety of characteristics to be measured such
as end-to-end delay, loss and jitter [22]. While active probe-based measurements
are important and widely used in testbeds and operational networks, they may

T. Korakis, M. Zink, and M. Ott (Eds.): TridentCom 2012, LNICST 44, pp. 130–145, 2012.
© Institute for Computer Sciences, Social Informatics and Telecommunications Engineering 2012

lack detail or precision or be entirely unable to capture aspects of behavior that are critical for experiments.

Passive measurements are based on using specialized counting or capture mechanisms that are built into software and systems deployed in network testbeds. Standard examples are log files from servers, flow-export logs [17, 26] or the diverse measurement information bases (MIBs) that are available from networked devices via the Simple Network Management Protocol (SNMP) [15]. One of the most compelling types of passive measurement is the ability to capture packet information from transmissions on links in a testbed. Information from packet traces can be critical to experiments with new network applications, protocols and security techniques, as well as for day-to-day management and troubleshooting of the testbed infrastructure itself.

There are a myriad of challenges to enabling packet capture capability within a network testbed. First, packet capture almost always requires dedicated systems since measurements on high-bandwidth links can result in overheads that are beyond the capability of standard hardware. This means that sufficiently capable systems must be acquired, configured, deployed and (securely) managed alongside the experimental systems. Further, if packet capture is meant to be available to concurrently running experiments, the measurement systems must be able to log data such that multiple tenants have exclusive access to their own data. Finally, packet capture always has security and privacy implications since packets can contain personally identifiable and private information. Depending on the size and diversity of the testbed, these challenges can become quite significant.

In this paper we describe a packet capture management environment for network testbeds called GIMS (GENI Instrumentation and Measurement Systems). The system was designed for deployment within the GENI infrastructure [4], however it has evolved into a system that can be independent from that environment. GIMS provides the capability to (i) configure packet capture measurements (typically associated with an experiment on the testbed) on a deployed set of dedicated packet capture devices, (ii) manage measurements from simultaneous users, (iii) enforce local security and privacy policies, and (iv) summarize and archive captured data to remote storage devices.

The architecture of GIMS is divided into three major components. The first is the GIMS front end, which includes web-based user interfaces for GIMS administrators and users, and allows the user access to monitoring capabilities during the experiment and access to results after an experiment is over. The second component of the architecture is the GIMS backend, which instantiates and facilitates control of measurements, and coordinates activities between the front end (i.e., admins and users) and the GIMS packet capture devices. The backend also includes a monitoring system that gathers and stores system information and logs from running experiments. The third component is the packet capture control system that runs on the packet capture devices that are deployed within the testbed. This control system includes the capability to enforce privacy policies, summarize and aggregate packet data, and archive data in a variety of ways for multiple simultaneous experiments. Communication throughout GIMS is facilitated through an XML/RPC-based command language. The system is designed for scalable and extensible deployment and to simplify tasks of deploying capture devices, and managing and using the system. The GIMS components were implemented in run on commodity PC hardware and UNIX-based operating systems.

We describe the implementation of GIMS and include a screenshot of the front-end user interface, and show results from a set of micro-benchmarks on the packet capture control system. The former highlights some the capabilities of the system from the user perspective. The latter is critical for understanding the behavior and capabilities of the components that will actually be capturing experiment data in the testbed. Our microbenchmark results show that the packet capture system performs well under high offered packet rates, with zero or nearly zero packet loss under a load of 200K packets/sec. In a configuration with realistic TCP traffic offered at an average rate of 500 Mb/s and in which the capture system produced flow export records, we observed zero packet loss.

The GIMS software distribution is openly available to the community [9]. It has been running in a prototype deployment within the Wisconsin Advanced Internet Lab [8] for nearly a year. We are currently in the process of identifying locations for deployment of packet capture nodes in different parts of the GENI infrastructure.

The remainder of this paper is organized as follows. In Section 2, we provide details on the GIMS architecture. In Section 3, we provide details on the implementation of GIMS. We evaluate the packet capture system through a set of micro-benchmarks in Section 4. Studies and projects related to GIMS are described in Section 5. We summarize, conclude and describe our future work in Section 6.

2   System Requirements and Architecture

In this section, we describe the requirements and design of GIMS. At the highest level, development of GIMS was motivated by the recognition that the ability to capture packets on links (*i.e.,* passive measurement) in a network enables a broad range of network research experiments and network operations activities. These include experiments with new networking protocols, experiments in network security, experiments with new network applications, experiments with new measurement tools, etc. From a network operations perspective, passive packet capture enables network performance tuning and network troubleshooting. However, this capability is not common in network testbeds and coordinated management of packet capture devices is complex.

2.1   GIMS Relationship to GENI

GIMS was developed as a measurement infrastructure that would be deployed within GENI [4]. To that end, the primary requirements beyond specific experimental functionality is that it be consistent with the GENI authorization and credentialing mechanisms and that it interface with one of the GENI control frameworks.

GIMS currently implements interfaces for the ProtoGENI control framework as discussed in Section 3. However, during the development process, every effort was made to make the implementation general and to modularize components such that interfaces to additional control frameworks could be easily developed, and so that the system could be used in a standalone fashion. A standalone version of the system is nearing completion.

2.2 Passive Measurement System Requirements

The requirements for the GIMS environment are based on the GENI Instrumentation and Measurement Systems Specification [18]. That document specifies a broad vision for instrumentation and measurement, and discusses the trade-offs and challenges for different types of instrumentation and measurement within GENI. Our focus is specifically on the objective of developing a *passive packet capture* capability *i.e.,* the ability to gather, save and analyze packets from taps on links in a network testbed.

The general requirements of the GIMS environment include (a number borrowed from [18]):

- Full or partial packet capture at line rate with zero packet loss,
- No (or at least measurable) impact on experiments,
- Extensibility (*i.e.*, the ability to add new measurement synthesis capability),
- High availability (*e.g.*, at least as available as testbed systems on which experiments are conducted),
- Large capacity (*i.e.*, the ability to support a diverse set of simultaneous activities from a large number of experiments),
- Remote management and monitoring capability,
- Access control (*i.e.*, the ability to specify what data is available from a particular device or collection of devices, to whom, and for how long),
- Flexible storage including the ability to house data locally and to stream to a remote archive,
- Measurement nodes that are secure from unauthorized external access,
- Ease of use for both administrators and users of the system,
- Deployment on commodity PC's and UNIX-based operating systems.

Specific requirements for the packet capture systems include:

- Support for IPv4 (IPv6 support is future work),
- Support for IPv4 header capture only,
- Support for specifying individual fields of interest in the IPv4 header,
- Support for on-the-fly prefix preserving anonymization of specified fields,
- Support for no-loss packet capture at line rate of at least 1 Gbps,
- Support for up to 256 simultaneous active experiments per node.

Satisfying these requirements entails the development of a packet capture management environment that bears many similarities to network testbeds themselves and can easily be thought of as a parallel experimental infrastructure. We are aware of no other packet capture management systems that fully satisfy these requirements.

2.3   Architectural Specification

The design space for GIMS makes several assumptions. First, dedicated measurement hardware will be deployed in a network testbed as illustrated in Figure 1.

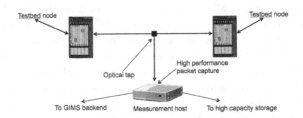

Fig. 1. The basic physical components that support a GIMS deployment

These measurement host systems are connected to target links via taps (optical splitters or active devices) or SPAN ports on switches. The systems are commodity PC hosts running a UNIX-based OS and may include high performance packet capture cards (*e.g.*, such as Endace [3]), or specialized software to improve packet capture efficiency (*e.g.*, [14, 16]). These systems are remotely accessible via a management network interface and include a separate network interface for streaming captured data to remote, high capacity storage systems. While not an explicit part of the GIMS requirements, attaching high precision timestamps to packets is highly desirable for different types of experiments. This is most effectively accomplished with specialized hardware and GPS support, although there are emerging software solutions [28]. Adding high precision timestamps is a future objective for GIMS deployments but does not require any specific capability from our software.

The GIMS design is three-tiered and divided into components as shown in Figure 2. The first component is the *front end*. This component of the system includes the interface mechanisms for both GIMS users and administrators that enable access to the measurement infrastructure. The interfaces enable users to configure their packet capture measurements. This includes specifying the set of nodes that will be monitored [1], IP aggregates that will be captured, remote data

---

[1] Users currently must have out-of-band knowledge of the links their experimental traffic will use. Coordinating links that have packet capture nodes with testbed experiments requires specific coordination with the testbed management infrastructure.

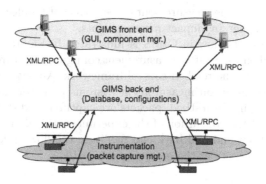

Fig. 2. The key components in the GIMS architecture

storage targets (*e.g.*, Amazon S3) and local packet processing (*e.g.*, sampling or flow aggregation). The admin GUI enables access to and configuration of remote measurement nodes. The front end also includes the *component manager*. This system enables coordination and integration of GIMS with a network testbed control system such as ProtoGENI. The component manager facilitates authenticated access to GIMS and control of GIMS systems from the testbed system should the GIMS GUI's not be required. In short, it makes GIMS more broadly useable across diverse testbed infrastructures. The front end can run on a single system or on multiple systems in a distributed testbed.

The second component in the GIMS design is the *back end*. This component of the system is responsible for coordination of front end systems and the distributed measurement nodes; it is, in a sense, the "nerve center" of GIMS. The back end provides information about the availability and status of measurement nodes via GIMS control messages to the front end. It also facilitates all communication via GIMS control messages with measurement nodes, including registration with the infrastructure, administrative configuration, and configuration of packet capture activities for individual users. The core component of the back end is a database system that maintains all state information about the configurations of GIMS systems. This component can be distributed to enhance robustness and to enables GIMS to scale to support a large infrastructure.

The third component in GIMS design is the *packet capture management system* that runs on each of the measurement nodes that are deployed on links in the testbed. Fundamentally, these nodes run some kind of packet filter (*e.g.*, libpcap) that enables packets to be captured from a network interface, locally processed, and stored. The packet capture management system runs on these nodes and *(i)* facilitates multi-tenant use of measurement systems, *(ii)* enforces local privacy policies, *(iii)* provides data summarization and aggregation capability, and *(iv)* provides data streaming to a designated remote storage device. Remote storage recognizes the fact that packet capture on high speed links can quickly fill disks, thus each user is only allocated a fixed local storage volume. It is also critical that the packet capture management system impose a very low processing overhead on the measurement nodes so as not to affect packet capture and processing and thereby impact measurements.

The control and data flow in GIMS is illustrated in Figure 3. Users specify experiments and their associated measurement configurations through the GIMS GUI or an interface in the testbed control framework. Among other things, this results in filters deployed on measurement systems and storage allocation. As experiments are run in the testbed, packets are captured and stored in the user-specified archive. At the conclusion of the experiment, the filters and storage are deallocated. The front end and back end facilitate the flow of control data and maintain the current state of the measurement systems.

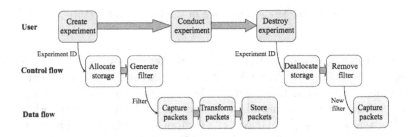

Fig. 3. Control and data flow in GIMS

Finally, the security and access control are critically important in GIMS since measurement nodes may be deployed on live links. Measurement nodes are therefore only accessible to authorized users or administrators. Data collection on the measurement nodes enforces local privacy policies by only capturing designated fields of packets (*e.g.*, header fields) and applying any required anonymization before transmitting to either local or remote storage. The front end, back end and measurement systems themselves are secured from unauthorized external access by only allowing access on specified ports from specified systems and from users with the correct credentials.

3   Implementation Details

In this section we describe implementation aspects of GIMS. We first discuss the management and control components of GIMS (the front-end and back-end components), followed by the packet capture subsystem implementation.

Figure 4 depicts the GIMS system components and interfaces among them. These components are consistent with the architectural specification described in Section 2. The user-facing components offer web-based views for users to manage, configure, and control testbed measurements. These front-end components communicate with the back-end, which coordinates all of the activities in the GIMS infrastructure. As such, the back-end performs remote procedure calls to

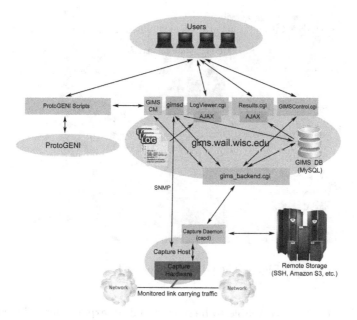

Fig. 4. The GIMS system components

configure and control capture daemon components, and to manage the database of users and device configurations in response to user and administrator actions initiated from the front-end.

3.1 GIMS Front End

The most prominent of the front-end components, the GIMS control GUI, is implemented using AJAX and runs from a web server in the testbed (in this case gims.wail.wisc.edu). The GUI allows users to create device configurations, assign names to specific configurations, and store them in the GIMS database for retrieval. A screenshot of the control GUI is shown in Figure 5. A new set of device configurations can be created automatically when an experiment in the network testbed is created (*e.g.,* a GENI slice), or it can be manually generated. Each configuration can be saved in the GIMS database for future retrieval and modification.

To obtain the status of a set of measurements, or an ongoing measurement session, a GIMS user can view a separate results page, which can either show the full results of a measurement session after it has ended, or display some (near-)real-time information. The view of an ongoing measurement allows a user to see a status log, as well as the results of querying the capture daemons for basic statistics of packet or flow capture.

A separate administration GUI allows authorized users of GIMS to add, delete and edit devices in the GIMS back-end database. A device must be added to the

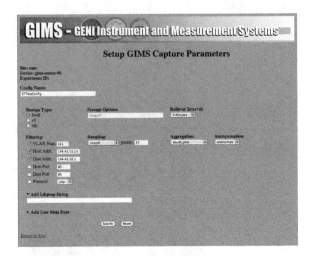

Fig. 5. The GIMS control GUI

database before it will be available to be selected for an experiment. The user is prompted for information about the device such as location, device name, device type, hostname, port and description. The capabilities of the device also need to be entered so that the correct options can be displayed to the user during the creation of device configurations.

3.2   GIMS Back-End

The GIMS back-end implements various functions to coordinate user actions with the capture daemon systems deployed in a testbed. There are also a number of functions to support generation, update, and retrieval of users' device configurations in the GIMS database, and it performs a variety of sanity-checking, error-checking and logging functions.

The GIMS database is a core back-end component and is built on MySQL. It contains tables to keep track of experiment state, location and type of devices, which devices are being used in a given experiment, the configuration of experiment devices, and statistics for each experiment.

Lastly, the "gimsd" monitoring daemon uses SNMP to monitor GIMS capture devices that are currently running and collecting data on behalf of users. It takes a snapshot of system performance every 15 seconds and stores the results in the GIMS database. These results are available to the user via the GIMS Results tool during and after experiment execution.

3.3   GENI Integration

GIMS currently includes a collection of scripts that forms a modular interface to facilitate interaction with the ProtoGENI control framework. These interfaces enable integration with the GENI testbed, and their modular construction enables additional control frameworks to be added without affecting other GIMS components. These scripts are used to control and query various aspects of the ProtoGENI system from GIMS. Likewise, the GIMS component manager is a GIMS front-end component that translates ProtoGENI control instructions into GIMS-specific control actions. In general, these components deal with translation of GENI contructs of "slices" and "slivers" into GIMS components and configurations. Because of the modular design of this part of the back-end, it is fairly straightforward to integrate with different external control frameworks. As noted above, GIMS can also operate autonomously (*i.e.*, without an interface to a specific control framework).

3.4 Packet Capture Subsystem

The core measurement capabilities of GIMS are implemented in a subsystem called the *capture daemon*. This subsystem consists of three components: the capture daemon controller, which handles requests from the GIMS backend to configure and control packet capture processes, the storage controller, which handles storage interactions, and the capture daemon itself, which performs the packet capture, aggregation and transformation of packets, and creation of metadata. The capture daemon subsystem is depicted in Figure 6.

The capture daemon controller implements a set of XML/RPC handlers to accept requests from the GIMS back end for configuring packet capture system parameters and storage parameters, for starting, stopping, and pausing capture daemon processes, and for gathering some statistics on the progress of packet

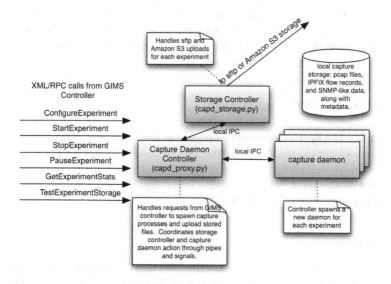

Fig. 6. GIMS capture daemon architecture

capture. It is implemented in Python as a single process, and communicates with the storage controller and capture daemon processes through standard UNIX inter-process communication mechanisms (pipes and signals). It also performs detailed logging, which the GIMS backend relays to users if they want to gain detailed runtime information about the capture system.

The storage controller is also implemented in Python as a single process, and utilizes various modules to interact with sftp and Amazon S3 servers. As new files are produced and become available for transfer, the storage controller initiates upload to user-specified directories, in the case of sftp, or a user-specific bucket, in the case of S3. Since there may be multiple capture processes running simultaneously we must take care to avoid blocking operations in the storage daemon. Thus, the files generated from each configuration are handled by separate threads in the storage controller.

Lastly, the capture daemon process implements the actual passive measurement collection and processing. It is implemented in C, and uses the standard libpcap API for packet capture. As a result, it can leverage any modified versions of libpcap that are available for accelerating packet capture, e.g., [3, 16]. To perform aggregation into flow records, the capture daemon uses the open source libfixbuf and yaf libraries, and for anonymization, we use the well-known prefix-preserving IP address anonymization algorithm of Fan et al. [19].

As data files are created (either packet traces or flow record traces), the capture daemon generates metadata in an easily processed XML format. The metadata include information about the experiment configuration (obtained through the initial configuration call from the GIMS back-end) as well as user-specific metadata (specified in the GIMS front-end GUI). Finally, experiment-specific details related to the runtime performance of the experiment are added periodically as an experiment proceeds. For example, the number of received packets and bytes are added periodically to the metadata, as well as information about any interface packet drops that libpcap reports. These packet and byte counters are also relayed to the GIMS back end, so that a user can gain (near-)real-time information about his or her experiment as it runs.

4   System Microbenchmarks

Understanding the performance of the packet capture system is important to ensure that it does not skew measurements e.g., by inadvertently dropping packets. In this section we describe a set of micro-benchmark experiments to evaluate the performance of the GIMS capture daemon system. We also discuss operational aspects of other parts of the GIMS system.

4.1   Experiments

The goal of our microbenchmark experiments was to evaluate the impact of different configuration parameters on the performance of the GIMS capture daemon. Since the capture daemon can perform optional transformation and aggregation of packets, we sought to understand the implications of different options. Our testbed consisted of four identical commodity workstations, each with Intel Xeon E5530 quad-core processors, 8 GB of RAM, and dual-port Intel Gigabit Ethernet card dedicated to experiment traffic. A fifth workstation had similar CPU and memory specs, but two dual-port Intel Gigabit Ethernet cards. The four identical hosts were wired directly to the fifth host with cross-over cables, creating a star topology. Each host ran Linux 2.6.32.

On the fifth (center of the star) host, we installed and ran the GIMS capture daemon software. We additionally installed the PF_RING [16] kernel module, as well as the modified Intel Gigabit Ethernet (igb) driver to improve raw packet capture performance. While experiments were running, we monitored CPU load and collected information (from the capture daemon, and also directly from PF_RING) about packet drops. We used three of the other hosts to generate traffic, and the fourth as a traffic sink. The packet capture daemon was configured to monitor traffic on the interface connected to the traffic sink node.

We used iperf to generate uniform streams of UDP packets [1], from 64 bytes through 1000 bytes, and the Harpoon traffic generator to generate more realistic TCP traffic [27]. Due to limitations of using iperf for generating traffic, we were only able to generate up to 210,000 packets per second (210 Kpps). This rate is approximately the maximum rate of 512 byte packets that can be generated at 1 Gb/s. We configured Harpoon to generate an average load of about 500 Mb/s.

The capture daemon was run in four configurations. In the first, we captured the first 64 bytes of packets and did not perform any other transformations to the packets. In the second, we configured the capture daemon to do uniform sampling of 10% on received packets (i.e., 90% of received packets were discarded). Again, we captured and stored the first 64 bytes of the packets that remained after sampling. In the third configuration, we collected simple SNMP-like packet and byte counters on the received traffic, and in the fourth, we collected and stored flow-level information in the IPFIX format [26]. In each configuration, data was stored on the local system and not streamed to remote storage. We used the iperf traffic generator for the first three configurations, and Harpoon in the flow-oriented configuration.

4.2   Results

We first note that in all experiments, CPU load on the capture daemon host was quite low (around 10%). This result is consistent with other measurements that have been performed with PF_RING-enabled systems [11, 14], and suggests that the capture daemon does not impose significant processing overhead.

Table 1 shows the percent of packets captured (i.e., not dropped) for the three experiments involving the iperf traffic generator. Results are shown for each of the three capture daemon configurations, and five different iperf configurations. As noted above, due to limitations of iperf we could only generate, at maximum, about 210 Kpps. We see from the table that there was zero or close to zero packet drops in all cases except for experiments in which we collected 64 byte packet headers with 64 byte and 128 byte packet traffic. In our Harpoon experiment with collecting flow records at the capture daemon, reported packet drops were also nearly zero (less than 0.5%).

In both our CPU utilization measurements and packet drop measurements, our results are consistent with prior work that has studied the performance of PF_RING-based systems. As a result, we expect the capture daemon to exhibit scaling properties similar to other systems that use PF_RING, and perform well under high-load situations. We also note that the capture daemon can also take advantage of hardware-accelerated packet capture platforms such as the Endace DAG cards [3] to scale to higher speeds, since these platforms often offer modified versions of the libpcap software.

Table 1. GIMS capture daemon system performance in different configurations using the iperf traffic generator. Table values show percent of packets captured.

| Packet size | 64 | 128 | 256 | 512 | 1024 |
Offered packet rate	200 Kpps	201 Kpps	201 Kpps	208 Kpps	100 Kpps
Packet header capture	96.9	98.9	100	100	100
Header capture; 10% sampling	100	100	100	100	100
SNMP-like counters	100	100	100	100	100

5   Related Work

Passive network measurements are instrumental to operators and researchers for gaining insight into network behavior and performance. As such, there have been many protocols and systems developed over the years to facilitate passive collection of network measurements.

The most ubiquitously deployed measurement capability today is defined by the Simple Network Management Protocol (SNMP) [15]. The SNMP standards define a set of counters and configuration variables arranged in a hierarchical structure, called the Management Information Base, as well as protocols to retrieve counters and set device configurations. For example, many network operators utilize basic byte and packet interface counters that are available through SNMP to gain a coarse view of traffic characteristics in their networks. Operators and scientists also use software packages such as the Multi-router Traffic Grapher (MRTG) [24] to visualize these basic SNMP counters in appealing and useful graphics, and to track traffic patterns over time.

Although SNMP counters are widely available, they cannot provide insight into application traffic patterns or other traffic details. As a result, many routers have the ability to export *flow records*, which contain more detailed information on individual application flows, and there have been other efforts within the IETF to define flexible traffic flow measurement mechanisms, *e.g.*, RTFM [12]. For example, the *de facto* standard Cisco Netflow formats [2, 17] are supported on many devices, and it is likely that the flexible flow record formats provided by the recent IPFIX standard [26] will see broad adoption.

Packet traces provide one of the most detailed views of network traffic, at the cost of higher CPU and I/O load to perform the data collection. There are many standard tools and libraries available to facilitate capture and processing of packet data, *e.g.*, [7,13,23], and specialized hardware platforms that enable efficient packet capture at multi-gigabit speeds [3].

A number of efforts within the research community have focused on improving packet capture efficiency on commodity hardware systems. For example, the PF_RING system can be compiled and installed in a Linux kernel to enable packet capture at very high rates [16], and the related vPF_RING system facilitates high-speed capture in Linux-based virtual machine environments [14]. There are PF_RING-based modifications available to the standard libpcap API, enabling applications to transparently take advantage of the performance improvements provided by PF_RING. Since the GIMS packet capture daemon is built on top of the libpcap interface, it can also transparently take advantage of these performance improvements. Still, tuning a commodity operating system and hardware platform to achieve best performance can be difficult. Braun *et al.* evaluated packet capture bottlenecks on FreeBSD and using PF_RING and PF_PACKET on Linux in order to provide guidelines for achieving optimal performance [11].

There have been a number of systems developed to improve passive packet measurement capabilities by making it easier for network managers and/or researchers to initiate, collect, process and/or analyze the collected data. For example, the pktd system provides authorized users with an API to initiate packet capture on an end host while not having to give the user privileges to directly open a network interface card in promiscuous mode [20]. Building on the capabilities of pktd, Agarwal, *et al.* developed a system to remotely initiate packet capture at specific vantage points within an enterprise network for the purpose of debugging performance problems. In a similar vein, Hussain, *et al.* describe a system for passive packet capture based on using Endace DAG cards that also provides automated storage for packets [21]. These systems have similarities with the capture daemon back-end of GIMS. However, GIMS includes a much broader set of capabilities in terms of the kinds of data that can be collected and how data can be transformed prior to storage.

Two systems that are specifically designed with measurement capabilities for testbed environments include the MINER system [10] and the OMF management framework [25]. The MINER system allows a user to initiate both active and passive measurement tools on testbed hosts. A primary goal of MINER is to provide a unified API for using arbitrary measurement tools. As a result, it requires some code to be written to adapt existing measurement tools to the MINER framework. OMF is more broadly a management and control framework for network testbeds, but includes integrated capabilities to collect and store experiment-specific measurements. GIMS has some similarities with these systems, but is geared specifically toward providing high-performance passive measurement capabilities. It is also control framework agnostic: it can either be run in an independent manner, or easily interface with an existing testbed or network management platform.

6   Summary and Future Work

The ability to capture packets traversing links in a network testbed is of central importance to many different types of experiments. However, the costs and complexity of deploying and managing a packet capture measurement infrastructure within a testbed can be very high. In this paper, we describe a packet capture management environment for network testbeds that we call GIMS. The key objective of GIMS is to reduce the complexities associated with managing and using a distributed packet capture infrastructure.

The design of GIMS is divided into three components. The *front end* includes a set of GUIs that facilitate management and use of distributed packet capture devices. The *back end*, controls configurations of packet measurement and facilitates communication between the front end and the packet capture devices. The *packet capture control system* enforces privacy policies, summarizes and aggregates packet data, and archives data for multiple simultaneous experiments on packet capture devices.

GIMS was developed to run within the GENI infrastructure and has interfaces to directly interact with the ProtoGENI control framework. However, it has also capable of running autonomously outside of ProtoGENI. It was implemented to run on commodity PC hardware with UNIX-based operating systems. It has been running in the WAIL testbed for nearly a year and the software distribution is openly available to the community.

Our on-going efforts are focused in three areas. First, we are in the process of deploying GIMS nodes within the GENI infrastructure. This will enable the system to be used by researchers in that environment. We are also adding additional capabilities for results analysis and reporting. This recognizes the fact that the process of running experiments does not stop with packet capture and requires standardized tools to make use of that data. Finally, to enable the system to be more broadly used, we plan to add new interfaces for other GENI control frameworks such as Orbit [5] and PlanetLab [6].

References

1. Iperf 2.0.5 – the TCP/UDP bandwidth measurement tool (2012), http://iperf.sourceforge.net/
2. Cisco IOS Netflow (2012), http://www.cisco.com/en/US/products/ps6601/products_ios_protocol_group_home.html
3. Endace, Inc. (2012), http://www.endace.com
4. GENI — Global Environment for Network Innovations (2012), http://www.geni.net/
5. The Orbit Testbed (2012), http://www.orbit-lab.org/
6. The Planetlab Testbed (2012), http://www.planet-lab.org/
7. Wireshark — go deep (2012), http://www.wireshark.org/
8. Barford, P.: The Wisconsin Advanced Internet Laboratory (2012), http://groups.geni.net/geni/wiki/MeasurementSystem
9. Barford, P., Sommers, J., Crovella, M.: Instrumentation and Measurement for GENI (2012), http://www.schooner.wail.wisc.edu

10. Brandauer, C., Fichtel, T.: MINER — A measurement infrastructure for network research. In: Proceedings of Tridentcom 2009 (2009)
11. Braun, L., Didebulidze, A., Kammenhuber, N., Carle, G.: Comparing and improving current packet capturing solutions based on commodity hardware. In: Proceedings of ACM Internet Measurement Conference (2010)
12. Brownlee, N.: Using NeTraMet for production traffic measurement. In: Proceedings of IEEE/IFIP International Symposium on Integrated Network Management (May 2001)
13. CAIDA. Coralreef software suite (2012), http://www.caida.org/tools/measurement/coralreef/
14. Cardigliano, A., Deri, L., Gasparakis, J., Fusco, F.: vPFRING: Towards Wire-Speed Network Monitoring using Virtual Machines. In: Proceedings of ACM Internet Measurement Conference (2011)
15. Case, J., Fedor, M., Schoffstall, M., Davin, J.: RFC 1157: A Simple Network Management Protocol (SNMP) (May 1990), http://www.ietf.org/rfc/rfc1157.txt
16. Deri, L.: Improving passive capture: Beyond device polling. In: Proceedings of SANE (2004)
17. Claise, B. (ed.): RFC 3954: Cisco Systems NetFlow Services Export Version 9 (October 2004), http://tools.ietf.org/html/rfc3954
18. Barford, P. (ed.): GENI Instrumentation and Measurement Systems (GIMS) Specification, GDD-06-012 (2006), http://groups.geni.net/geni/wiki/GeniInstMeas
19. Fan, J., Xu, J., Ammar, M., Moon, S.: Prefix-Preserving IP Address Anonymization. Computer Networks 48(2) (October 2004)
20. Gonzalez, J.M., Paxson, V.: Pktd: A packet capture and injection daemon. In: Proceedings of Passive and Active Measurement Workshop (2003)
21. Hussain, A., Bartlett, G., Pryadkin, Y., Heidemann, J., Papadopoulos, C., Bannister, J.: Experiences with a continuous network tracing infrastructure. In: Proceedings of the ACM SIGCOMM Workshop on Mining Network Data (2005)
22. Sommers, J., Barford, P., Duffield, N., Ron, A.: Multi-objective monitoring for sla compliance. IEEE/ACM Transactions on Networking 18(2) (2009)
23. Jacobson, V., Leres, C., McCanne, S., et al.: Tcpdump (1989), http://www.tcpdump.org/
24. Oetiker, T.: MRTG: The Multi Router Traffic Grapher. In: Proceedings of USENIX LISA 1998 (1998)
25. Rakotoarivelo, T., Ott, M., Jourjon, G., Seskar, I.: OMF: a control and management framework for networking testbeds. ACM SIGOPS Operating Systems Review 43(4) (2010)
26. Sadasivan, G., Brownlee, N., Claise, B., Quittek, J.: RFC 5470: Architecture for IP Flow Information Export (March 2009), http://tools.ietf.org/html/rfc5470
27. Sommers, J., Barford, P.: Self-configuring network traffic generation. In: ACM SIGCOMM Internet Measurement Conference (October 2004)
28. Veitch, D., Babu, S., Pasztor, A.: Robust Synchronization of Software Clocks Across the Internet. In: Proceedings of ACM SIGMETRICS (2004)

Monitoring Pairwise Interactions to Discover Stable Wormholes in Highly Unstable Networks

Luis C.E. Bona, Elias P. Duarte Jr., and Thiago Garrett

Federal University of Paraná - Dept. Informatics
P.O. Box 19018 Curitiba PR 81531-980 Brazil
{bona,elias,garrett}@inf.ufpr.br

Abstract. Users of large-scale testbeds often need a group of nodes with a reasonable level of stability to execute applications and experiments. Although monitoring the stability of nodes themselves is certainly part of the solution, it is important to classify and select groups of nodes according to their ability to communicate among themselves. In this work we call such groups of nodes "stable wormholes", and describe strategies to find those wormholes based on monitoring end-to-end pairwise interactions. Data acquired is used to find five different types of wormholes, each with a different stability pattern. The system was implemented in PlanetLab. Extensive experimental results are reported evaluating the proposed strategies. A comparison with another tool that selects nodes based on node stability alone is also presented. The execution of a MapReduce application shows that nodes selected with the proposed strategy ran the application significantly faster.

Keywords: Testbed Monitoring, PlanetLab, Testbed Node Selection.

1 Introduction

Uncertainty is arguably the major obstacle for developing dependable distributed systems. As even in static systems it is impossible to solve agreement problems when communication and computing time bounds are unknown and at least one node may crash [10], the situation can only get worse in more unstable networks. It is not difficult to see that depending on the level of instability it may be impossible for a distributed application to complete successfully.

As Veríssimo points out in [22], current network environments often present an spectrum of synchrony, that varies from components that present perfectly predictable behavior to those that have a completely uncertain behavior. These properties can be found in time, i.e. during the timeline of their execution systems become faster or slower, presenting lower or higher bounds to execute. The properties can also be found in space: some components are more predictable and/or faster than others, actions performed in or amongst on these nodes have better defined and/or smaller bounds. Veríssimo defined a hybrid distributed system model, Wormholes [21], in which different loci of the system have different properties which correspond to different sets of assumptions.

T. Korakis, M. Zink, and M. Ott (Eds.): TridentCom 2012, LNICST 44, pp. 146–161, 2012.
© Institute for Computer Sciences, Social Informatics and Telecommunications Engineering 2012

In this work we describe a monitoring strategy for finding wormholes in hybrid distributed systems, i.e. those that cannot be classified either as synchronous nor as asynchronous. Several different types of wormhole selection criteria are proposed, all of them based on the ability of pairs of nodes to communicate among themselves. At the heart of this strategy, end-to-end interactions between pairs of nodes are monitored, i.e. the response times, measured at the application level. All pairs are monitored, from each node to each other node.

Acquired data is used to build a graph that represents the system from the point of view of the different nodes. This graph is called *stability graph*. An edge of a stability graph indicates a stable communication - according to a criterium - between the corresponding nodes on which the edge is incident. Based on the obtained graph it is possible to find wormholes, i.e. groups of nodes that together have behaved in a stable way. Several wormhole selection strategies were defined, each with a different stability pattern.

We employed the global research testbed, PlanetLab [5] in order to evaluate the proposed monitoring and wormhole selection approaches. In our previous experience of running HyperBone [4] in PlanetLab we had found out that several nodes of this important testbed presented a very unstable behavior. HyperBone is an overlay network that allows the execution of distributed applications on a virtual hypercube. In order to execute parallel and distributed tasks, HyperBone requires a set of nodes that present a reasonably stable behavior. We found out that it is not trivial to find such a large set of such nodes in PlanetLab. Sometimes it is not easy even to find a set of nodes each of which can communicate with all others. At a given time, a large set consisting of such nodes might not even exist. Another characteristic we found out is that a communication channel is frequently not symmetric: if a node considers another to be stable, the opposite might not be true. Moreover, a given node might consider two other nodes to be stable, but those two nodes may not consider each other stable. All communication patterns are possible in this environment.

Although there are tools for monitoring and selecting PlanetLab nodes for the execution of experiments [19,15,6,17,13,3], they employ criteria on the stability of the nodes themselves, such as processing load or available memory, for example. None of them selects groups of nodes also considering their ability to communicate among themselves.

We describe extensive experimental results of our wormhole selection strategies obtained from monitoring PlanetLab. The first set of experiments consists in evaluting the different wormhole selection strategies, also checking how predictable each wormhole is, i.e. how it behaves as time passes. We also checked experimentally how nodes of a wormhole selected by our tool fared when executing an experiment. We compared the performance of the wormhole with the performance of nodes selected by another PlanetLab node selection tool, SWORD. Both sets of nodes executed a MapReduce application. Results show that in most cases the wormhole nodes ran the application significantly faster.

The rest of this paper is organized as follows. Section 2 describes related work. Section 3 defines the online monitoring strategy, as well as the stability graphs and the wormhole selection strategies. Section 4 presents experimental results obtained in PlanetLab. Conclusions follow in section 5.

2   Related Work

The original Wormholes hybrid distributed system model was proposed by Veríssimo [22,21]. This is a realistic model that is based on the fact that networks often present an spectrum of synchrony, that varies from components that present perfectly predictable behavior to those that have a completely uncertain behavior. Wormholes correspond to a subsystem - defined in time or space - that behaves in a predictable way.

In [18] the authors report the development of end-to-end dependable distributed applications and mobility-aware services in ubiquitous communication scenarios. They assume the use of off-theshelf components (COTS) and unreliable wireless communication links. The proposed strategy is based on a hybrid system architecture, which considers the existence of wormholes: subsystems with better properties than the rest of the system. A wormhole provides specialized timeliness and trustworthiness services that may be used to construct more dependable and resilient applications. The implementation of an embedded wormhole is reported.

The Partitioned Synchronous Distributed System Model [12] is another hybrid model that assumes that a subsystem is timely, i.e. provides known upper bounds on communication and computation times. In [16] the authors describe how to implement perfect failure detectors in this system. The implementation assumes the existence of a timeliness oracle, that classifies processes and channels as timely or untimely.

Another work that employs similar ideas for selecting supernodes in P2P nodes is reported in [14]. The superpeer selection problem is hard because in a P2P network a large number of superpeers must be selected from a huge and dynamically changing network in which neither the peer's characteristics nor the network topology are known a priori. A set of superpeers has similarities with a wormhole. The supernodes must be well-dispersed throughout the network, and must fulfill additional requirements such as load balance, resource needs, adaptability to churn, and heterogeneity.

We applied our proposed wormhole selection strategies to PlanetLab. There are other tools that aim at selecting PlanetLab nodes for the execution of experiments. CoMon [19] is a monitoring system specifically designed for PlanetLab. The objective is to provide information about the environment to users and administrators. CoMon collects information about the nodes themselves, such as CPU and memory usage, for example. All the information gathered by CoMon helps finding "problematic" nodes and slices. Also, CoMon provides a tool for selecting nodes which satisfy given restrictions. This work differs from Comon in respect to the monitored data and the way nodes are selected. CoMon monitors just attributes related to the nodes themselves, while the monitoring strategy presented in this work monitors the interaction between pairs of nodes. The node selection in CoMon uses just the last data obtained from nodes, while the node selection strategies proposed in this work can use data relative to any period of time.

Vivaldi [6] is a fully distributed synthetic coordinate system whose objective is to predict the RTT between hosts, i.e. determine the RTT between two hosts without having one host effectively communicating with the other. Vivaldi's algorithm assign synthetic coordinates to each host, in such a way that the distance between the coordinates of two hosts corresponds to the RTT between them. The monitoring strategy described in this work is similar to Vivaldi as both employ the RTT as the basic monitoring metric. But in Vivaldi the RTT is an estimation that, even with good precision, does not consider faults and network problems. Furthermore, in our strategy the RTT is measured in both ways, i.e. we do not consider the RTT to be symmetric.

SWORD [3] is an application for resource discovery. It allows users to describe the desired resources with requirements related to nodes themselves and their interaction. In this way, SWORD is a tool for selecting nodes which satisfy various criteria specified by the user. But SWORD itself performs just the node selection. It is necessary to obtain the node's monitoring data from another system. Using that data SWORD is capable of selecting the best nodes that satisfy the given restrictions. There is an implementation of SWORD in PlanetLab which uses data from CoMon.

SWORD is similar to the work described in this paper, as both are strategies or selecting nodes in which applications experiments will be run. Experiments comparing the nodes selected by SWORD and by the proposed node selection strategies were executed and are described. Since it uses data from CoMon, the version of SWORD available for use in PlanetLab has the same differences to our strategy as CoMon, i.e. it uses only data related to the nodes themselves, not their interaction. Furthermore, the data corresponds to the last measurement obtained from nodes, while we considered data sampled during a whole time frame.

In [9] we describe results of our observation of PlanetLab based on a offline monitoring strategy, based on which we extracted cliques of stable nodes. In the current work we present a different, on line monitoring strategy and formally define both the monitoring strategy and five different wormhole selection strategies, one of which is the clique.

3   Online Monitoring and Node Selection

This section describes the proposed monitoring strategy. We then define the stability graph that is built by applying a stability criterium to the monitoring data, and finally define five different types of stable wormholes that can be obtained from the stability graph.

3.1   Monitoring Pairwise Interactions

Consider a network, represented as directed graph $G = (V, E)$, where V is the set of vertices corresponding to network nodes, and E the set of edges such that the ordered pair (i, j) is an edge if node i communicates directly with node j, i.e. without employing intermediate nodes.

The purpose of the proposed monitoring strategy is to provide data that can be used to select a set of nodes W, called a stable wormhole, such that for any two nodes $r, s \in W$, $W \subseteq V$, the communication initiated by r with s can be considered stable. In other words, wormhole nodes are able to communicate among themselves in stable way, which of course depends on the stability criteria defined below.

Every node of the monitored network executes a monitoring daemon, specified as follows. Periodically, $\forall i \in V$, node i sends a message to each other node and waits for a reply. Upon receiving the reply message, the Round Trip Time (RTT) is computed using the local clock, and tuple $(i, j, rtt_{i,j}, timestamp)$ is stored. The *timestamp* corresponds to the local time instant at which the measure was obtained. We assume that clocks are roughly synchronized, for example with the level of accuracy that is obtained with the Network Time Protocol (NTP) [2] in the Internet.

Monitoring is supposed to run at the application level, thus RTT measurements vary not only because of network issues, but also due to the situation of the node himself, for instance the number of processes on the scheduler's queue and CPU usage.

Even if a daemon stores recently colleted measurements locally, at some point data is sent to a *central monitor* that eventually collects measured data from all daemons. Due to the large amount of data that this strategy generates, and the fact that recent data is more important that previous samples, the central monitor summarizes sequences of tuples for predefined time frames. For example, in our PlanetLab experiment described in the next section, we summarized data per hour, day, month and year. Summarization computes both the mean and standard deviation of measurements for a given pair of nodes within a given time frame. Thus, the summary for ordered pair (i, j) for a given time frame $T = [t_0, t_1]$ and set of tuples $(i, j, rtt_{i,j}, timestamp)$ is the average $\mu_{i,j,T} = < rtt_{i,j} | t_0 \leq timestamp \leq t_1 >$, plus the standard deviation $\sigma_{i,j,T}$ used as a measurment of the dispersion.

Given two consecutive time frames it is also possible to compute the average and standard deviation of the most recent timeframe taking into account the summary obtained for the previous time frame.

3.2 Building the Stability Graph

From the monitoring data acquired, the central monitor builds a so called *stability graph* S for time frame $T = [t_0, t_1]$. Before the stability graph is formally defined, we give the definition of "stability" itself, i.e. we define the criteria used to classify a given pairwise interaction as stable or unstable. Consider the ordered pair of nodes (i, j) monitored as described above. A threshold θ is defined as the maximum value allowed for an RTT sample. We then compute the frequency in which the round trip times fall below θ, considering the two sets of tuples $(i, j, rtt, timestamp)$ and $(j, i, rtt, timestamp)$, such that $t_0 < timestamp < t_1$.

Node i is said to consider node j to be stable if at least a fraction p of the obtained $rtt_{i,j} \leq \theta$. The analogous procedure is used to check whether node j considers node i to be stable. In our PlanetLab experiments we employed $p = 90\%$. Stability Graph $T = (V_T, E_T)$ is an non-directed graph defined as follows. An edge $(i, j) \in E_T$ (thus node $i \in V_T$ and node $j \in V_T$) if an only if both node i considers node j to be stable within T, and node j considers node i to be stable within T.

3.3   Finding Stable Wormholes

After the stability graph S is built, we reach the final stage, i.e. searching for wormholes, i.e. a connected set of nodes with a reasonable level of stability, that could be employed to run distributed applications that require a "reasonable" level of stability. Although at first we assumed that finding a wormhole was equivalent to finding a clique in S, i.e. there should be an edge between any two vertices in V_T of S, experience taught us less strict criteria could lead to more stable, more predictable wormholes. In particular, the clique represents an overly restricted criteria, and the number of nodes (wormhole size) is often not large enough. In this subsection we present the five different types of stable wormholes we defined and evaluated: Minimum Degree, Highest Minimum Degree, K-Core, Core and Stable Clique.

Minimum Degree. The least strict strategy for finding wormholes is the one based on Minimum Degree. This strategy returns a stable wormhole W, such that node $i \in W$ if the degree of node i in S $deg_S(i) \geq d_{min}$, for a given minimum degree d_{min}. Thus the Minimum Degree strategy filters nodes by their degrees in the stability graph. Only nodes with degree higher than the minimum degree which is entered as an input parameter are selected.

The rationale behind this strategy is that it may suffice to find nodes that can communicate in a a stable fashion with a large number of other nodes. However it is possible that two nodes in a Minimum Degree wormhole are not able to communicate with each other in a stable way.

Highest Minimum Degree. The Highest Minimum Degree strategy receives as input parameter the desired number of nodes in the stable wormhole, m. Given that parameter, an algorithm is executed on stability graph S to find such a group of m nodes with the highest possible minimum degree, D_{min}. This strategy thus selects a wormhole with a specified minimum size (number of nodes) and with the highest possible minimum degree for that size. A trivial polynomial algorithm can be used to find a Highest Minimum Degree wormhole.

k-Core. The k-Core strategy finds a k-core on the graph representing the system. A k-Core is the largest group of nodes that form a subgraph C of the stability graph S that has minimum degree equal to k. In other words, this strategy selects a group of nodes that have a minimum degree among themselves, i.e. each selected node has a degree higher than or equal to k within the wormhole. The input parameter in this case is the minimum degree k. This strategy is more restrictive than the Minimum Degree and Highest Minimum Degree, since the degrees in those two other strategies may involve nodes not in the wormhole.

The algorithm to compute a k-core from S is polynomial. It starts by building subgraph $S_1 = (V_1, E_1)$, such that node $i \in S_1$ iff $deg_S(i) \geq k$. Note that an edge $(i, j) \in E_T$ is also in E_1 if both $i, j \in S_1$. The process is then repeated: create subgraph $S2 = (V_2, E_2)$ selecting from all nodes of S_1 those that have degree greater than or equal to k. Eventually the resulting subgraph is equal to the original graph, this is the k-core, the largest set of nodes in the stability graph S that have minimum degree k among themselves.

Core. The Core strategy finds the stability graph core. A *core* is the largest group of nodes that form a subgraph with the highest minimum degree possible; i.e. the core of a graph is the k-Core with the highest value of k that is not empty. This strategy thus returns the largest set of nodes that have the highest minimum degree among them.

In order to find the Core wormhole the algorithm described above in the k-Core strategy is executed on a binary search for the largest k that returns a non-empty set of nodes. Initally $k = n/2$, half the number of nodes in the system; the lower bound (b_l) is 0 and the upper bound (b_u) is n. If the k-core is non-empty, then k is set to $(b_u + k)/2$ otherwise k is set to $(b_l + k)/2$. This process is repeated until an empty set of nodes is returned; the core is the last non-empty k-core.

Stable Clique. The Stable Clique strategy finds a clique [8] - a complete subgraph - of the stability graph. In a clique there is an edge between every pair of nodes. Finding cliques is a NP-hard problem [11]. Therefore finding the largest clique in a graph with a large number of edges, such as the graphs created by the strategy described in this work, is impracticable, since the nodes - in which experiments will be run - must be selected quickly. To address this problem, the Stable Clique strategy uses two parameters: the minimum size of the clique and the maximum processing time. We employed a well-known depth-first search algorithm for generating all maximal cliques of an undirected graph, that employs pruning and is feasible in practice [20]. The algorithm is executed until a clique with a size higher than or equal to the specifed minimum size is found. Alternatively, if such clique is not found within the specified time limit, the largest clique found so far is selected. This strategy is the most restrictive one, since there must be an edge between every pair of selected nodes.

4   Experimental Results

This section describes experimental results obtained from a PlanetLab implementation of the wormhole selection strategies. When the experiments were executed in 2011, PlanetLab consisted of 983 nodes. Although the complete set of nodes were monitored, the number of nodes that actually ran the system varied from 500 and 600 nodes. This was because a large number of nodes continuously alternated being online and offline, and some other nodes remained unreachable during the whole period of the experiments. In all experiments described in this section each node measured the RTT to each other node every 5 minutes.

Two groups of experiments were conducted. The first group consisted of an evaluation of the node selection strategies. Several stability graphs were built using monitoring data obtained during continuous periods each consisting of 3 weeks. The second group of experiments, described in subsection 4.2, aimed at comparing nodes selected by our strategy with nodes selected by another Planet-Lab monitoring tool. This comparison was performed by executing a MapReduce application on nodes selected both with our tool and with the other tool.

4.1   Evaluation of the Wormhole Selection Strategies

This experiment was based on monitoring data collected from January 30, 2011 at 00:00, to February 19, 2011, at 23:59 (UTC -3), for a total of 21 days. Stability graphs were built at each hour during this period. The RTT thresholds employed for generating the stability graphs were 0.05s, 0.1s, 0.15s and 0.2s; 4 graphs were built per hour, for a total of 2016 graphs. Both the average and maximum degrees of all stability graphs were computed. Figure 1 shows the average and maximum degrees observed considering a threshold of 0.1s. Figure 2 shows the analogous results when a threshold of 0.2s was employed. It is not difficult to see that the values for both the average and maximum degrees were significantly higher when the threshold was 0.2s. For instance, the average degree was about 60 during the whole period in which the threshold was 0.1s; as the threshold was increased to 0.2s, the average degree increased to 130. Higher threshold values are not reported because the return meaningless results: a very high threshold does not filter nodes and interactions which are highly unstable (variations fall within the threshold).

After the stability graphs were generated, we executed the several wormhole selection strategies. Each strategy was executed to find wormholes on the stability graphs. The purpose of this experiment is to evaluate the performance of the different strategies as time passes.

The Minimum Degree is the simplest strategy: we counted the number of nodes in the stability graphs with degree greater than or equal to the minimum specified. The minimum degrees evaluated were 50, 100, 150 and 200. Figure 3 shows the number of nodes selected with the Minimum Degree strategy for several days period using a RTT threshold of 0.1s. For minimum degree 50, for example, the number of nodes selected remained close to 450 during the observation time, note that this is about 80% of the total number of monitored nodes, which ranged from 500 to 600 nodes.

Next we evaluated the performance of the Highest Minimum Degree strategy. In this strategy we specify the number of nodes, and verify the maximum degree of any such group in the stability graphs. Figure 4 shows, for a threshold of 0.1s, the highest minimum degree identified over 21 days for groups of 50, 100, 150,

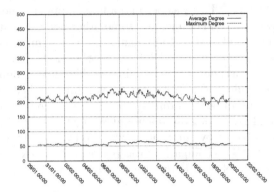

Fig. 1. Average and maximum degrees of the stability graphs built with threshold of 0.1s

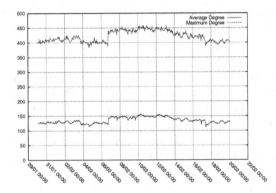

Fig. 2. Average and maximum degrees of the stability graphs built with a threshold of 0.2s

200 and 300 nodes. For 300 nodes, for example, the highest minimum degree was about 100; for groups of 50 nodes the highest minimum degree was about 180.

In order to evaluate the Core strategy, cores were extracted from all stability graphs. The number of selected nodes and the minimum degree among them were recorded. Figure 5 shows the results for a threshold of 0.1s, considering the whole observation period. We can observe that the number of varied widely, while the minimum degree presented a low variability. Furthermore, frequently the mininum degree was close to the number of nodes selected, thus the subgraph induced by the selected nodes presents high density, i.e. there are edges between most node pairs, which means that in the graph cores obtained each node considers the majority of the others to be stable.

Our main purpose in evaluating the Stable Clique strategy was to check whether a Stable Clique maintains itself as time passes. Three Stable Cliques were computed on the first stability graph considering a 1-day monitoring

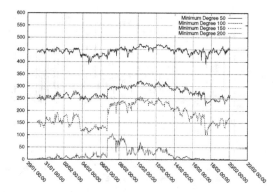

Fig. 3. Number of nodes selected with the Minimum Degree Strategy for a threshold of 0.1s

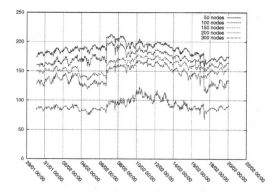

Fig. 4. Highest Minimum Degree for groups of different sizes, threshold of 0.1s

period. During that day we computed for each of the remaining stability graphs if that Stable Clique was still there. The RTT threshold used to compute the initial clique was equal to 0.05s; in order to check whether the clique was still there we used a threshhold of 0.1s. The reason we computed the initial clique with this low threshold (the most strict of all thresholds employed in all experiments, employed to find both an initial clique as well as a initial core in the next experiment we report below) was that it would allow us to initially select nodes that were interacting in a very stable pattern. Then when checking the clique we would employ a larger threshold to allow for some variation.

Figure 6 shows how each of the three fared during a representative time frame (one day). We show for each group of nodes, the number of nodes that remained fully connected among themselves. The threshold was of 0.1s. It is possible to see that only one group of nodes remained as a clique for most of the time (not all the time though). From our observations we reached the conclusion that the Stable Clique employs a criterium that is too restrictive, and the selected group of nodes most probably will not hold the desired properties for long.

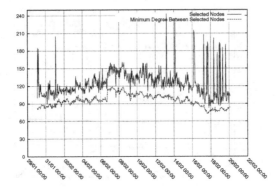

Fig. 5. Minimum degree and number of nodes selected with the Core strategy, threshold 0.1s

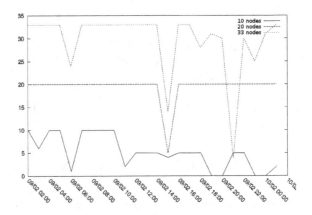

Fig. 6. The performance of Stable Cliques during one representative day

The Core strategy - which is less restrictive than the Stable Clique - proved to be a better choice for selecting a group of nodes that presented among themselves a stable communication pattern for a longer time frame. In order to check how the nodes selected using the Core strategy behave as time passes, we selected nodes using this strategy the first stability graph of a one day period. Again for the initial selection we employed a strict threshold of 0.05s. 62 nodes were selected. Figure 7 shows the average, minimum and maximum degree for these 62 nodes during a 1-day observation period, with threshold equal to 0.1s. Note that as in the Stable Clique experiment above here we employed a larger threshold to monitor the core, in comparison with the original threshold with which the core was selected at first. This makes room for some fluctuation in the stability among nodes.

The average degree had a very low variation during the whole observation period, as well as the maximum degree - which remained constant. The minimum

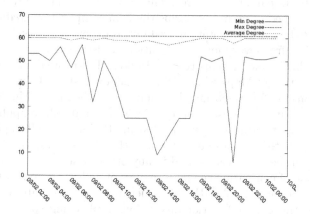

Fig. 7. Average, minimum and maximum degrees of nodes selected with the Core strategy

degree, however, had a much higher variation. However, even when the minimum degree varied this did not impact the average degree. This indicates that few nodes were affected by some instability. Also, the average degree was close to the maximum degree during the whole period, showing that the majority of the nodes in the cores presented a stable behavior among themselves during the whole period.

Discussion. Although the Minimum Degree and Highest Minimum Degree strategies consistently return a larger number of nodes, these strategies do not guarantee that the group of nodes all present a stable communication pattern among themselves. On the other hand, the Stable Clique strategy only selects a group of nodes such that *all* of them are able to communicate in a stable pattern with all others. However this proved to be too restrictive, and difficult to sustain as time passes. The results show that the Core strategy is the best: it selects good sized groups of nodes that are able to interact among themselves in a pretty stable way and remained so for longer.

4.2   Comparison with Another Tool

In order to compare the performance of nodes selected with the proposed strategies and those selected with another tool, we executed experiments using MapReduce. MapReduce [7] is a software framework aimed at distributed computing on large data sets. MapReduce requires the definition of a mapping function, which transforms the data in key/value pairs, and a reduction function, which gathers the key/value pairs to obtain the final result. A MapReduce application can be automatically parallelized and executed in a set of hosts. A node divides the input data between several other nodes, each of which then repeats the process. The set of nodes form a tree. When a node completes its mapping, the result is sent back to its parent in the tree. This process continues until the first node receives all mapped data and performs the final computation (reduction).

The MapReduce implementation used in this experiment was Apache Hadoop [1]. Hadoop is a framework for the execution of distributed applications. It provides a distributed file system, HDFS (Hadoop Distributed File System), and an implementation of MapReduce. When Hadoop is started the HDFS and the system responsible for executing the applications (including MapReduce ones) are instantiated in all nodes. In order to execute MapReduce applications with Hadoop, the input data must be inserted in HDFS, since all applications will be run on top of this file system. All nodes then have access to any part of the data, which can be effectively stored in any other node.

For the sake of comparing the performance of nodes selected by the proposed strategies we employed SWORD [3], which was described above in section 2, and provides the closest functionality to our tool, being specifically designed for selecting PlanetLab nodes for running experiments. We selected our Core strategy for this comparison, since it gave our best results when all strategies were compared. The values chosen for all parameters used, both for SWORD and for the Core strategy, were as restrictive as possible. The attributes used in SWORD for selecting nodes were the response time of the nodes (based on the CoMon server), and the one minute load which should be less than or equal to 10 in all experiments.

The MapReduce application used was a *wordcount*, which counts how many occurences of each word appear in an input file. The text file used in the experiments had size 1GB, and was created randomly. The experiment consisted in executing this application several times, both using nodes selected by SWORD and selected by the Core strategy. For every measured metric we computed the mean and the standard deviation, as well as the maximum median, and minimum value.

Two different experiments were conducted, in both cases we employed 100 PlanetLab nodes. After the nodes were selected, Hadoop was started on all nodes. The input file was then inserted in HDFS. Then, the MapReduce application was run 15 times, one after the other. After these executions completed, measurements were recorded. This procedure was performed twice (for a total of 30 runs), each time using a group of nodes selected differently.

The first experiment was executed on July 15th 2011. 100 nodes were first selected using SWORD at 10:50 (UTC -3), after that the experiment was run on those nodes. Later 100 nodes were selected using the Core strategy at 18:00 (UTC -3) and the experiment was executed again. Table 1 shows the results obtained from the 30 executions (15 using each set of nodes). Nodes selected by the Core strategy ran the application significantly faster. Except for the standard deviation, all values corresponding to the nodes selected by SWORD were about two times the values obtained for the nodes selected by the Core strategy.

The second experiment was executed on July 18th 2011. This experiment consisted of the same procedures employed for the first one, but with an important difference: we first executed the application on the nodes selected by the Core

Table 1. Comparison results (first experiment): execution time

	SWORD	Core
Average	22min 59s	9min 25s
Standard Deviation	12min 18s	6min 3s
Median	18min 54s	7min 34s
Lowest	6min 47s	4min 21s
Highest	58min 19s	28min 49s

Table 2. Comparison results (second experiment): execution time

	SWORD	Core
Average	20min 17s	8min 18s
Deviation	17min 33s	1min 49s
Median	16min 57s	8min 23s
Lowest	7min 46s	5min 10s
Highest	83min 25s	11min 42s

strategy. This was done to check whether there was an impact of the period of the day in which the experiments were run. In this experiment, 100 nodes were first selected using the Core strategy at 11:28. After the execution finished, 100 nodes were selected using SWORD at 14:40 and the experiment was run again. Table 2 shows the results obtained from the 30 executions (15 per set of nodes). As in the first experiment, nodes selected by the Core strategy ran the application significantly faster, but in this experiment the standard deviation was much higher for nodes selected by SWORD. Also, the highest execution time for nodes selected by SWORD was by far higher than the highest execution time for nodes selected by the Core strategy. The low standard deviation might indicate that the nodes selected by the Core strategy presented a "good" stability during the whole experiment duration.

Discussion. In both experiments, nodes selected by the Core strategy ran the application significantly faster than nodes selected by SWORD. These results show that even on a highly unstable network such as PlanetLab, the strategies described in this paper were able to select nodes that presented a reasonable stable communication pattern among themselves.

5   Conclusions

Based on the fact that current network environments often present a spectrum of synchrony, that varies from components that present perfectly predictable behavior to those that have a completely uncertain behavior, in this work we described strategies to find sets of nodes that can be considered to be stable according to various criteria. Such groups of nodes are called stable wormholes and the criteria for discovering wormholes are based on monitoring end-to-end pairwise interactions. Monitoring data is used to build stability graphs which in turn are used to find five different types of wormholes, each with a different stability pattern, ranging from cliques to sets of nodes with a minimum degree. The system was implemented in PlanetLab, and we report results of a comparison between different wormhole selection strategies. Experiments comparing the performance of nodes selected by the proposed strategies with nodes selected by a tool that is based on node stability alone are also presented. The execution of a MapReduce application on those nodes show that, in most cases, nodes selected by the proposed strategies ran the application significantly faster.

Future work includes developing a tool for PlanetLab users that accepts more input parameters, such as the size of a desired wormhole. Developing new strategies for finding wormholes, such as the connectivity of the subgraph is also a new research direction. Another issue that can be expanded in the future is the classification of stability using other criteria such as an for instance adaptive thresholds.

Acknowledgments. This work was partially supported by grant 308692/2008-0 from the Brazilian Research Agency (CNPq).

References

1. Apache Hadoop, http://hadoop.apache.org (accessed at July 29, 2011)
2. NTP: The Network Time Protocol, http://www.ntp.org/ (accessed em April 18, 2011)
3. Albrecht, J., Oppenheimer, D., Vahdat, A., Patterson, D.A.: Design and Implementation Trade-offs for Wide-area Resource Discovery. ACM Trans. Internet Technol (2008)
4. Bona, L.C.E., Fonseca, K.V.O., Duarte Jr., E.P., Mello, S.L.V.: HyperBone: A Scalable Overlay Network Based on a Virtual Hypercube. In: Proc. of the 8th IEEE Int. Symp. Cluster Computing and the Grid, CCGRID (2008)
5. Chun, B., Culler, D., Roscoe, T., Bavier, A., Peterson, L., Wawrzoniak, M., Bowman, M.: PlanetLab: An Overlay Testbed for Broad-coverage Services. SIGCOMM Comput. Commun. Rev. (2003)
6. Dabek, F., Cox, R., Kaashoek, F., Morris, R.: Vivaldi: A Decentralized Network Coordinate System. In: SIGCOMM 2004: Proceedings of the 2004 Conference on Applications, Technologies, Architectures, and Protocols for Computer Communications, New York, NY, USA. ACM (2004)
7. Dean, J., Ghemawat, S.: MapReduce: simplified data processing on large clusters. In: Proceedings of the 6th conference on Symposium on Opearting Systems Design & Implementation, Berkeley, CA, USA, vol. 6. USENIX Association (2004)
8. Diestel, R.: Graph Theory, 3rd edn. Springer (2005)
9. Duarte Jr., E.P., Garrett, T., Bona, L.C.E., Carmo, R.J.S., Zuge, A.: Finding Stable Cliques of PlanetLab Nodes. In: The 40th Annual IEEE/IFIP International Conference on Dependable Systems and Networks, DSN 2010 DCCS (2010)
10. Fischer, M.J., Lynch, N.A., Paterson, M.S.: Impossibility of distributed consensus with one faulty process. Journal of the ACM (1985)

11. Garey, M.R., Johnson, D.S.: Computers and Intractability: A Guide to the Theory of NP-Completeness. W.H. Freeman (1979)
12. Gorender, S., de Araújo Macêdo, R.J., Raynal, M.: An Adaptive Programming Model for Fault-Tolerant Distributed Computing. IEEE Transactions on Dependable and Secure Computing (2007)
13. Liang, J., Ko, S.Y., Gupta, I., Nahrstedt, K.: MON: On-demand Overlays for Distributed System Management. In: Proceedings of USENIX WORLDS (2005)
14. Lo, V., Zhou, D., Liu, Y., GauthierDickey, C., Li, J.: Scalable Supernode Selection in Peer-to-Peer Overlay Networks. In: Proceedings of the 2005 Second International Workshop on Hot Topics in Peer-to-Peer Systems, HOT-P2P 2005 (2005)
15. Londoño, J., Bestavros, A.: netEmbed: A Network Resource Mapping Service for Distributed Applications. In: Proceedings of the IEEE/ACM IPDPS High-Performance Grid Computing Workshop, Miami, Florida, USA (2008)
16. Macedo, R.A., Gorender, S.: Perfect Failure Detection in the Partitioned Synchronous Distributed System Model. In: International Conference on Availability Reliability and Security, ARES (2009)
17. Massie, M.L., Chun, B.N., Culler, D.E.: The Ganglia Distributed Monitoring System: Design, Implementation And Experience. Parallel Computing (2003)
18. Ortiz, H., Casimiro, A., Veríssimo, P.: Architecture and Implementation of an Embedded Wormhole. In: Proceedings of the 2007 Symposium on Industrial Embedded Systems. IEEE Industrial Electronics Society (2007)
19. Park, K., Pai, V.S.: CoMon: A Mostly-scalable Monitoring System for PlanetLab. SIGOPS Oper. Syst. Rev. (2006)
20. Tomita, E., Tanaka, A., Takahashi, H.: The worst-case time complexity for generating all maximal cliques and computational experiments. Theoretical Computer Science (2006)
21. Veríssimo, P., Casimiro, A.: The Timely Computing Base model and architecture. IEEE Transactions on Computers. SIGACTN: SIGACT News (ACM Special Interest Group on Automata and Computability Theory) (2006)
22. Veríssimo, P.: Travelling through Wormholes: a new look at Distributed Systems Models. SIGACTN: SIGACT News (ACM Special Interest Group on Automata and Computability Theory) (2006)

DNEmu: Design and Implementation of Distributed Network Emulation for Smooth Experimentation Control

Hajime Tazaki[1] and Hitoshi Asaeda[2]

[1] National Institute of Information and Communications Technology (NICT), Japan
[2] Keio University, Japan

Abstract. Conducting a realistic network experiment involving globally distributed physical nodes under heterogeneous environment introduces a requirement of experimentation control between the real world network and emulated/simulated networks. However, there is a gap between them to deploy network experiments. In this paper, we propose the *Distributed Network Emulator* (DNEMU) to fill the gap for the requirements of a planetary-scale network experiment. DNEMU addresses the issue of real-time execution with message synchronization through distributed processes, and enables us to evaluate protocols with actual background traffic using a fully controlled distributed environment. Through evaluation with micro-benchmarks, we find that our DNEMU prototype implementation is similar in terms of packet delivery delay and throughput to the existing non-virtualized environment. We also present a use-case of our proposed architecture for a large distributed virtual machine service in a simple control scenario involving actual background traffic on the global Internet. DNEMU will contribute to research in protocol evaluation and operation in a huge network experiment without interfering with the existing infrastructure.

Keywords: distributed emulation, real-time simulation, ns-3.

1 Introduction

Designing novel network protocols aiming to replace the current Internet architecture (i.e., clean-slate designs [6]) requires showing feasibility on the existing network before replacing it. Alternatively, analyzing the vulnerability of current protocols or unrevealed incidents (such as an outage for the popular site YouTube caused by inappropriate route announcement from Pakistan Telecom [1]) is important to avoid the accident happening in the future. As the demand for methods of studying communication is growing, a variety of network environments is necessary to be produced for the purpose of evaluating current and future protocols or architectures.

Network simulators greatly facilitate various network experiments. Researchers can create experimental scenarios and evaluate network architectures or protocols on simulated networks, without preparing large-scale and global wide network infrastructures or complex communication environments such as mobile and wireless

T. Korakis, M. Zink, and M. Ott (Eds.): TridentCom 2012, LNICST 44, pp. 162–177, 2012.

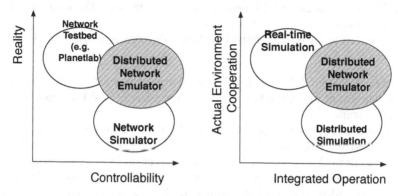

Fig. 1. Our work aims to fill the gap between network testbed and network simulator (left), and the gap between real-time simulation and distributed simulation (right). Both gaps are caused by lack of *smooth experimentation control*.

network experiments. However, as network simulators work with pre-defined communication models, it is impossible to evaluate protocols with unpredictable active traffic that occurs in the actual global Internet. This condition often precludes realistic evaluation and reduces the evaluation quality.

As an alternative solution, a planetary-scale network testbed such as Planet-Lab [15] has recently been used for experimenting with active traffic on the global Internet. The scale of the number of nodes in the experiment, however, is limited to the number of physical nodes in the testbed. Moreover, the cost of the experiment controlling multiple nodes is regrettably high, especially when the number of nodes and complexity of the experimental scenario in the experiment grow.

More realistic experimental results have been gained by using ns-3, which is a novel network simulator [9]. Thanks to numerous contributions by researchers, ns-3 now has capabilities such as the ability to import actual traffic with a real-time scheduler, parallel distributed network simulation by Message Passing Interface (MPI) [7] for synchronized operation under a distributed environment, and Direct Code Execution (DCE) [11] to execute active running code in the simulation. Such functionalities help researchers conduct a realistic experiment for the evaluation of network protocols in a single toolset of software. However, it still lacks the key functionality for satisfying the requirements: the implementation of current distributed simulation in ns-3 cannot carry out simultaneous execution with the real-time simulation. It was impossible to perform an integrated operation by distributed simulation and cooperate with external traffic by real-time simulation simultaneously.

By considering the current picture of network experiments without *smooth experimentation control* as illustrated in Figure 1, our motivation for this work is filling the gaps in order to conduct planetary-scale network experiments. We introduce a novel distributed, real-time network emulation architecture, called DNEMU (Distributed Network Emulator), to satisfy the following requirements for the network experiment.

- R1: The experiment should incorporate live traffic with the simulated background traffic.
- R2: We should have fully control of the experiment in a distributed environment.

Our design choice for DNEMU involves exploiting the existing MPI-based network simulation of **ns-3**, while considering the issue of real-time execution involving live traffic.

The contributions of this paper are two-fold. First, we have designed a distributed real-time emulation on a novel network simulator, ns-3, to achieve a global-scale network experiment with easier operation in a single toolset of the software. In the design phase of this study, we identified the issue of distributed simulation in real-time execution. Second, we have implemented a prototype of our proposed design and evaluated the similarity of basic network performance between the proposed architecture and a non-virtualized environment. To the best of our knowledge, no such architecture exists based on the combination of these two distinct simulation algorithms.

2   Background

This section briefly introduces two important functionalities of network simulation: *real-time simulation* and *distributed simulation*. Both help users of network simulators conduct network experiments in the distributed environment, but they are mutually exclusive, which motivates the pursuit of a solution in this paper.

2.1   Real-Time Simulation

In contrast to traditional discrete event simulation, simulation synchronized with wallclock time of a computation node (called real-time simulation) was proposed by Fall [5] and implemented on the ns-2 network simulator, which is the primary network simulator of ns-3. As depicted in Figure 2, instead of conventional discrete event scheduling, *real-time scheduling* allows us to wait for the next pending event until wallclock time corresponds to time in the simulator, and thus the clock inside the simulation is synchronized with the outside the simulator, allowing communication. By using this enhanced scheduler, the application in the simulator is able to include live traffic from the outside (e.g., the Internet).

While real-time scheduling provides external interoperability to the network simulator, it does not schedule events in real time. When a large number of events attempt to execute at the same time t, the next pending event will be delayed and the clock will then be desynchronized. Performance improvement in the simulation core will help us to ensure that the event scheduling meets these deadlines [13].

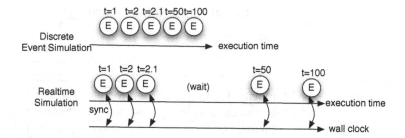

Fig. 2. Real-time simulation. The event at simulation time t waits until the wallclock time reaches t.

2.2   Parallel and Distributed Simulation

Parallel and distributed network simulation [18] has been studied with the requirement of rapid execution of complex and large-scale network simulation. By utilizing multiple logical processes (LPs) distributed to multiple nodes, the simulation has accelerated execution time, while ensuring the same results with a synchronized clock among the distributed processors.

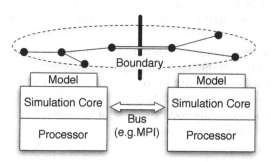

Fig. 3. Parallel and distributed simulation. Using several processors or physical nodes distributes the load of simulation processes and accelerates execution with coordination of time synchronization.

As shown in Figure 3, the topology on the simulated model could be shared among the different processors or physical nodes. When the message (or event) goes across the simulation boundary in the shared topology, a time-stamped message is exchanged via the message bus between the different simulation cores and processed at the second processor. The result then goes back to the original simulation core without adding to the original processor's workload and the final execution time of the simulation will be thereby shortened.

Though the previous studies in the distributed simulation have focused on the performance improvement of the network simulation, it is also necessary to study the environmental synchronization among the distributed nodes, for an integrated network experiment with simple operation.

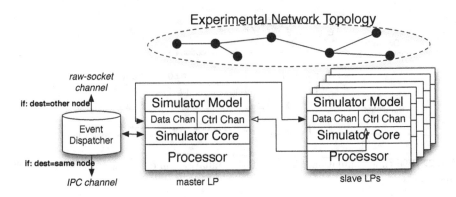

Fig. 4. The DNEmu architecture for distributed real-time emulation

2.3   What Is Missing?

Although the above two simulation algorithms are distinct, both of these algorithms will contribute to the execution of a network experiment at distributed locations. Controlling a complex experimental topology in a single scenario script allows for easier deployment of the network experiment into hundreds of nodes, and actual traffic generated by actual applications improves the quality of the simulation.

However, the current implementation of the distributed simulation in ns-3 does not allow external traffic to be imported via a real-time scheduler. Further, designing additional functionality for real-time execution in the distributed simulation is also not straightforward, because of the timescale differences within the simulation. The following sections detail a framework for filling the gap of the current simulation architecture.

3   The Architecture

In this section, we present our proposed architecture, DNEMU for distributed real-time network emulation satisfying the above requirements.

3.1   Overview

As stated in Section 1, the goal of this paper is to provide a network experiment framework, which both involves live traffic, and also uses a distributed environment.

Our design choice to accomplish this goal is to extend existing frameworks of distributed simulation and real-time simulation, and be able to utilize them simultaneously. Current distributed simulations require time synchronization between distributed processors (or systems), but our proposed architecture does not require any such synchronization, since the time should "walk along" with the wallclock time of each system in the real-time scheduler (details are discussed in Section 3.3).

In addition, we do not use MPI as an *inter-connect* for data transfer between logical processes. Instead, we use the usual *raw-socket* based communication via the usual network interface cards (or tunnels in some physical network environment cases). We do this because the buffering strategy of MPI for optimized message synchronization does not allow the exchange of real-time messages between the LPs (details are discussed in Section 3.3). This separation of control channel and data channel allows us to use a distributed real-time scheduler in a network simulator.

Figure 4 shows the overview of the DNEMU architecture. While MPI is used as a control channel between distributed logical processes, the real-time scheduler handles external traffic coming from outside the simulator, and also appropriately schedules the traffic on the data channel at the simulation boundary (i.e., the link between logical processes). A simulation scenario among the distributed nodes can be shared, and execution is handled only at the master node and synchronized with all of the distributed slave nodes.

3.2 Principles

During the design phase of our architecture, the following principles for design choice, from several directions, were considered.

Less Dependency on Hardware Environment: The architecture and its implementation should not be restricted to any particular hardware environment (e.g., dedicated cluster computers for distributed simulation) in order to allow distribution all over the world. It should use standard hardware with a common operating system.

Less Dependency on External Toolsets: Dependency on external toolsets is minimized to reduce the complexity of the operation of network experiments. Since the architecture is a framework for any network experiments, and could be utilized in many different ways, it should be able to tolerate for future extensions of the architecture.

3.3 Functional Components

This section explains the functional components required for the DNEMU architecture.

Event Dispatcher: We introduce a new simulated event dispatcher for distributed real-time emulation. Existing distributed simulation transfers events (i.e., packets) to the other endpoints via the MPI library if the events cross the simulation boundary. Instead, in our architecture, the events are translated and transferred to an emulated *raw-socket* (or tap device), and delivered to the other endpoints over a connected network when distributed emulation is defined in the simulation scenario. If the destination node of an event transfer is the same as the original node, it conducts inter-process communication (IPC) for the event transfer instead of *raw-socket* based communication.

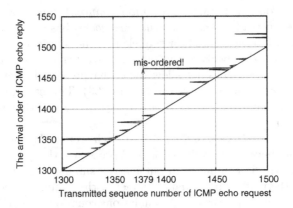

Fig. 5. The order of the arrival of echo reply packets at Tx (in Figure 7). The protruded point presents mis-ordered arrival of echo reply packets. The buffering effect of the MPI library reveals mis-ordered ping results.

Message Passing between LPs: In addition, the function of the message passing in a time-stamped order at the boundary of LPs is removed since we do not have to synchronize the simulation clocks, as the real-time scheduler uses wallclock instead. However, we still use the MPI library, because it easily enables to control distributed nodes by providing the initial rendezvous, bootstrapping, and to assign of MPI *rank*, which is the unique number of each logical process. We then utilize existing raw-socket based communication at the simulation boundary for data transfer between simulated nodes. During the implementation of our prototype, we found that using MPI as a data channel of the *inter-connect* is not suitable since the buffering behavior of the MPI message transfer prevents real-time traffic delivery to another node. For example, the order of arrival of ICMP echo request packets at a destination is different from the order of transmitted packets. Figure 5 shows the order of arrival of ICMP Echo reply packets in function of the transmitted sequence number from our prototype implementation based on an MPI-based *inter-connects*. We can see that the packet transmitted with sequence number 1379 was echoed backed in 1465th place. Such a non-negligible effect for real-time simulation should be removed. One possible solution to this issue is using a high-performance cluster computer with remote direct memory access (RDMA) to reduce the delay on the *inter-connect*. However, such hardware environments are not commonly available and restrict the use of our architecture. We therefore do not use it in our design principles.

Figure 6 depicts the bootstrap sequence of distributed real-time emulation with a pseudo-scenario script. When the simulation is executed at a node, the node is the master LP ($rank = 0$), others are slave LPs, then:

(1) The MPI handles the execution of the program at remote (i.e., slave LPs), and assigns *rank* using a static configuration for the MPI executable as usual.

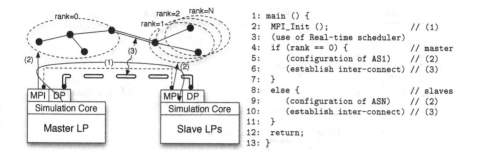

Fig. 6. The sequence of bootstrapping using DNEmu

(2) Decide the behavior of each simulated node based on their assigned *ranks* (e.g., each AS (Autonomous System) setup in the network).

(3) Configure the *inter-connect* link between simulation boundaries at each LP.

When a packet in the simulation reaches the boundary node of each LP, and is going to forward to another LP, this *inter-connect* is used for the data channel between distributed emulation. The sequence of (1) and (2) is the same as in the standard distributed simulation, while (3) is introduced by our DNEmu architecture.

In the architecture of DNEmu, the separation of the control and data channels allows the real-time execution of the distributed simulation. While the MPI only takes care of control messages for distributed logical processes as a *control channel*, raw-socket based *inter-connects* work as a *data channel*. Such a design choice fulfills our requirement of distributed real-time emulation.

4   Evaluation

In this section, based on our prototype implementation of DNEmu on `ns-3`, we present a performance measurement using micro-benchmarks on our proposed architecture, with the Linux container-based CORE (Common Open Research Emulator) distributed network emulator [2] as an alternative. The objectives of this evaluation are to show the proof of the concept of DNEmu and the similarity of our approach in terms of packet delivery with alternative network emulators. We then give a possible use-case of DNEmu over globally distributed virtual machines.

4.1   Setup

All of our experiments were conducted on two Linux systems, Node A and B as shown in Figure 7, which were equipped with an Intel Core i7-2600 (3.4GHz) and an AMD Opteron 6128 (2.0 GHz) processor. Two distributed nodes were located in Tokyo and Kanagawa in Japan respectively, with nine hops between them. Both systems ran with Ubuntu 10.04 64-bit with kernel versions 2.6.32.29 and

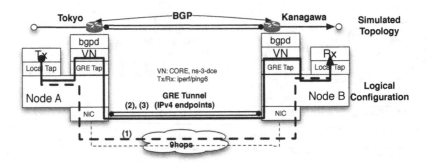

Fig. 7. Experimental setup of micro-benchmark

2.6.39.4. We then installed the modified version of ns-3-dce-quagga-umip[1] with our distributed real-time emulation extension. We also used a CORE network emulator version 4.2svn2 (20110919) on both systems.

By using two distributed nodes, we configured the experimental network as illustrated in Figure 7. In the case of **ns-3**, we set up one simulated node in each distributed physical node and configured Zebra BGP routing, based on Direct Code Execution (DCE) [11], to exchange their owned route information at the virtual node (VN), as shown in Figure 7. The forwarding processes in **ns-3** were also configured with the modified version of DCE, Linux kernel integration (i.e., **ns-3-linux**[2]), and **DlmLoader**. Each simulated node was connected via a **tun/tap** interface (i.e., Local Tap) configured in the underlying operating system in order to inject traffic from outside the simulation. The simulated node was also configured with a GRE tunnel via a **gretap** interface (i.e., GRE Tap) for the *inter-connection* of distributed nodes. The entire configuration is described in a single simulation script of **ns-3** with DNEMU.

In this experimental network, we used **ping6** and **iperf** to measure the experimental traffic. All traffic was generated by Node A's underlying operating system (i.e., Tx), directed to the VN via Local Tap, and forwarded to Node B's VN according to the routing information exchanged by BGP, then delivered to Node B's underlying operating system (i.e., Rx) via Local Tap.

In the case of CORE network emulation, we also configured the same network topology and VN as configured in **ns-3** above.

4.2   Micro-benchmark

By using the previous setup, we conducted round-trip time (RTT) and available throughput measurements. We first measured the performance of direct communication between Node A and B (as shown in (1) in Figure 7) without involving

---

[1] Original version is downloaded from
  http://code.nsnam.org/thehajime/ns-3-dce-quagga-umip/
[2] Original version is downloaded from
  http://code.nsnam.org/mathieu/ns-3-linux/

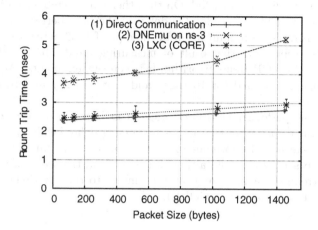

Fig. 8. Packet delivery delay in function of packet size with standard deviation, from 5000 replications

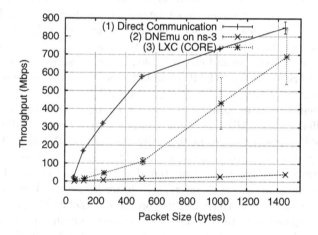

Fig. 9. Throughput (TCP) in function of packet size

any virtualized node, in order to show the performance baseline of the network environment. We then measured the performance via our DNEmu architecture (2) and the CORE network emulator (3).

Figure 8 represents the RTT between two endpoints with an interval of 10 milliseconds in function of the size of packets (64, 128, 256, 512, 1024, and 1452 bytes) with standard deviation, from 5000 repetitions of the ping6 command. As shown in the result of direct communication, the base RTT in this network environment in this experiment was around 2.5 milliseconds. The CORE emulator based on Linux Containers (LXCs) scored with an additional $0.1 - 0.2$ millisecond delay on which to the base RTT. This minimum amount of overhead is achieved by lightweight virtualization of LXC. On the other hand, ns-3 with distributed real-time emulation added considerable delay to the base performance: almost twice as much as direct communication in the case of 1452 bytes packet.

Figure 9 also represents the result of measuring bandwidth by the iperf command using the TCP Reno algorithm between two endpoints. We recorded the bandwidth every second for 10 times and plotted the standard deviation from repetitions.

We can see the performance disadvantage of DNEmu in delivery delay and throughput. This comes from the packet processing delay inside ns-3 via *raw-sockets* and *tap-devices*. Performance improvement of such functionality is required to obtain accurate results although it is beyond the scope of this paper. However, the trend of packet size growth is similar to that in direct communication and other emulators (i.e., CORE).

4.3   Use-Case: Experiment Using a Globally Distributed Virtual Machine Service

One possible use-case of DNEmu is that of network experiments in a distributed network testbed based on a virtual machine service provider. Due to the limitation of the number of nodes in the network experiment with such a virtual node, a network simulator contributes to increasing the number of experimental nodes on the testbed with a simple and controllable scenario description. This section presents a NEtwork MObility (NEMO) handoff experiment involving distributed located home agents maintained by BGP and OSPFv3.

Figure 10 depicts our experimental network configuration for this use case using three different sites. MR is a mobile router operated with NEMO software, MNN is a mobile network node moving with the MR, BS0 and BS1 are base stations equipped with IPv6 router functionality, HA is a home agent, ARs are access routers bridging three distributed networks via a tunnel, and CN is a correspondent node. Access routers, which are located at the boundary of each site, operate using the BGP routing protocol of Zebra to exchange route information in the network. In addition to the experiment shown in Section 4.2, we used a globally distributed virtual machine operated by the WIDE cloud service, which is organized by the WIDE project[3] and composed of Kernel-based virtual machines (KVM) [10] located at nine distributed sites. We used a single KVM node located in San Francisco and configured with a GRE tunnel and an IP6-in-IP6 tunnel as *inter-connects* between each distributed sites.

In node A, the HA was operated with an Usagi-patched Mobile IPv6 implementation (UMIP)[4], and Linux kernel[5] to provide mobile networks for the MR. In node B, two base stations served Wi-Fi access points to the MR and created

---

[3] http://www.wide.ad.jp
[4] USAGI-patched Mobile IPv6 for Linux: http://umip.linux-ipv6.org/, downloaded Jul 7 2010 version.
[5] http://git.kernel.org/?p=linux/kernel/git/davem/net-next-2.6.git, downloaded Aug 19 2010 version.

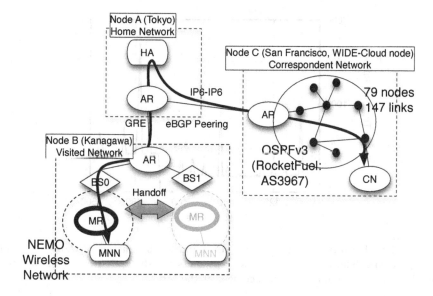

Fig. 10. Experimental use-case of an all IPv6 mobile network with a WIDE Cloud (VM cloud) node as a complex network configuration with a single controlled emulation scenario script

different wireless cells. The MR switched its point of attachment to the base station and obtained a different network prefixes to change its Care-of-Address, while the MNN followed and used the same address served by the upper MR. In node C, the reachability to the CN was managed by the OSPFv3 protocol executed by the Zebra `ospf6d` daemon using **ns-3** DCE functionality. The operated network was created by the RocketFuel topology dataset [19] and we used an Exodus (AS3967) database, which consists of 79 nodes and 147 links.

During this experiment, the MR and the MNN moved around between BS0 and BS1 with re-registration of binding to its home agent, and the MNN continuously sent ICMPv6 echo requests to the peer node (CN in Figure 10) to measure the duration of the disrupted communication during a handoff.

All of the above experimental scenarios were configured in a single **ns-3** script and controlled at the master node (node A) with our DNEmu architecture.

Figure 11 shows the result of handoff during this experiment. In this figure, the MR switched its point of attachment from BS0 to BS1 involving the handoff procedure with the HA, creating nine-second disruption of the `ping6` command. At around 460 seconds, the MR changed the IP address of the egress interface of the mobile router, re-registered the binding information to the home agent, and updated the bidirectional tunnel between the MR and HA. After that, the `ping6` command continuously recovered without changing the MNN's address insured by NEMO. We can see longer RTT after the handoff since BS1 adds a 100-millisecond delay in its simulation scenario. The fluctuating RTT is also seen because of path characteristics between Tokyo and San Francisco.

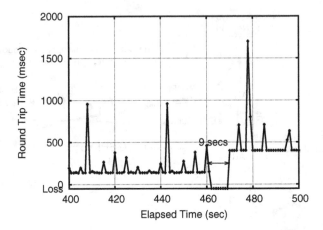

Fig. 11. Round trip time value between MNN and CN in function of elapsed time of the experiment. The RTT value "Loss" represents the disruption of communication caused by changing the point of attachment at the MR.

Such an experiment could be executed without involving existing environmental modifications. Neither network configurations (IP address and prefix allocation) nor operating system and kernel modifications are required.

5   Discussion

This section discusses the results of the above evaluation and future directions for this work.

From an architectural design point of view, the proposed architecture is not a *simulator*, because there is no reproducibility of the experimental result: time synchronization is not performed among the distributed nodes, un-modeled behavior at wallclock based timescales always produces different result, and background traffic at the *inter-connect* always changes. However, the fully integrated control via a network simulator greatly helps the easier operation of network experiments with our DNEmu architecture. We therefore focused on a network simulator as a toolset of network experiment.

Moreover, the architecture only relies on common features of the current operating systems and does not require upgrading the system, which sometimes would be a constraint in network experiments (e.g., the case of PlanetLab [3]). Such a design choice will help with global-scale deployment without the obstacle of software dependency.

The performance of the real-time scheduler plays an important role in this architecture. If events are not finished before the deadline of the wallclock time, the clock will be desynchronized, as mentioned in Section 2.1. Performance improvement in the simulation core is required, and would be a future direction of this work.

6 Related Work

The architecture proposed in this paper is related to two areas of work: integrated emulators and external testbed controllers. This section highlights the relations with the existing work.

Integrated emulators here refers to the experimental tool that is able to emulate various environments from operating systems (by virtualization) to network conditions (by, for example, Wi-Fi emulation on a wired link). This enables researchers to experiment in advance with their proposed protocols, architectures, or operations without wholesale deployment of the environment. CORE (Common Open Research Emulator) [2] exploits the lightweight virtualization technology of the operating system (i.e., IMUNES [16], netns [4]) and allows us to execute existing applications over emulated links. This tool supports describing the arbitrary topology with a GUI and executing on a distributed environment from a single controller. While CORE is able to automate the flow of a network experiment in a realistic environment, it requires the operating system's support to execute it. By contrast, the architecture proposed in this paper virtualizes everything in the user-land application based on ns-3 and requires no extension to the kernel. PrimoGENI [20] and ROSENET [8] are both integrated network simulators with an emulation facility via an emulation gateway, and achieving flexible and scalable network experiments. However, due to the number of components involved in an experiment, the potential complexity will increase. Our DNEMU architecture achieves distributed emulation involving only with a single toolset of the software and can control everything in a single simulation scenario. This is the strength of our architecture compared to alternatives.

An external testbed controller is a tool (or toolset) to help the execution of network experiments allowing easy operation and repeatability of the experiment. OMF (cOntrol and Management Framework) [17] is a toolset of the software to control experiments, manage the experimental component, and conduct measurement via a unified controller. These have been successfully deployed into an ORBIT testbed [14] to operate on hundreds of physical nodes. NEPI (Network Experiment Programming Interface) [12] has been proposed as a general framework for network experiments with a python programming interface. It can operate across multiple types of network testbeds such as PlanetLab, EmuLab [21], or ORBIT etc. While these testbed controllers provide an abstract model of the network experiments, our DNEMU architecture only targets at a specific network simulator (i.e., ns-3) in order to reduce external software dependencies of the toolset.

7 Conclusion

In this paper, we have designed the DNEMU architecture based on the combination of a distributed simulation and real-time simulation. To the best of our knowledge, there is no other such architecture based on the combination of these two distinct scheduling algorithms. The architecture has satisfied our requirements for a network experiment within a single toolset of software. Through the prototype implementation of our architecture, micro-benchmarking has shown similar trends with packet delivery delay and throughput, and a use-case has been presented on top of a globally distributed cloud service with a distributed synchronized network experiment. Yet the implementation is at an early stage and we have already found some performance drawbacks. However, our architecture will benefit the user who is going to deploy network experiments with globally distributed nodes, without being concerned about a complex toolset for the experiment.

The contributions of this paper are two-fold. First, we have designed a distributed real-time emulation on a novel network simulator ns-3 to achieve a global-scale network experiment with easier operation in a single toolset of the software. Second, we have implemented a prototype of DNEmu and evaluated the similarity of basic network performance between our proposed architecture and a non-virtualized environment.

Acknowledgment. The authors wish to thank the WIDE Cloud Computing Working Group of WIDE project for their support of our experiment. We also thank Clare Horsman for her comments to improve the paper.

References

1. Pakistan hijacks YouTube, `http://www.renesys.com/blog/2008/02/pakistan-hijacks-youtube-1.shtml` (accessed October 17, 2011)
2. Ahrenholz, J., Danilov, C., Henderson, T., Kim, J.: CORE: A real-time network emulator. In: Proceedings of Military Communications Conference, pp. 1–7 (November 2008)
3. Bhatia, S., Di Stasi, G., Haddow, T., Bavier, A., Muir, S., Peterson, L.: Vsys: a programmable sudo. In: Proceedings of the 2011 USENIX Annual Technical Conference, USENIX ATC 2011, Berkeley, CA, USA. USENIX Association (2011)
4. Bhattiprolu, S., Biederman, E.W., Hallyn, S., Lezcano, D.: Virtual servers and checkpoint/restart in mainstream linux. SIGOPS Oper. Syst. Rev. 42(5), 104–113 (2008)
5. Fall, K.: Network emulation in the VINT/NS simulator. In: Proceedings of International Symposium on Computers and Communications, pp. 244–250. IEEE (July 1999)
6. Feldmann, A.: Internet clean-slate design: what and why? SIGCOMM Comput. Commun. Rev. 37(3), 59–64 (2007)
7. Gropp, W., Lusk, E., Doss, N., Skjellum, A.: A high-performance, portable implementation of the MPI message passing interface standard. Parallel Computing 22(6), 789–828 (1996)
8. Gu, Y., Fujimoto, R.: Applying parallel and distributed simulation to remote network emulation. In: Proceedings of the Winter Simulation Conference, WSC 2007, pp. 1328–1336 (December 2007)
9. Henderson, T.R., Roy, S., Floyd, S., Riley, G.F.: ns-3 project goals. In: Proceedings of the 2006 Workshop on ns-2: the IP Network Simulator, WNS2 2006. ACM (2006)
10. Kivity, A.: Kernel Based Virtual Machine, `http://www.linux-kvm.org/` (accessed December 17, 2010)

11. Lacage, M.: Experimentation Tools for Networking Research. PhD thesis, Universite De Nice-Sophia Antipolis (2010)
12. Lacage, M., Ferrari, M., Hansen, M., Turletti, T., Dabbous, W.: NEPI: using independent simulators, emulators, and testbeds for easy experimentation. ACM SIGOPS Operating Systems Review 43(4), 60–65 (2010)
13. Mahrenholz, D., Ivanov, S.: Real-Time Network Emulation with ns-2. In: Proceedings of International Symposium on the Distributed Simulation and Real-Time Applications, DS-RT 2004, pp. 29–36 (October 2004)
14. Ott, M., Seskar, I., Siraccusa, R., Singh, M.: ORBIT testbed software architecture: supporting experiments as a service. In: Proceedings of the First International Conference on Testbeds and Research Infrastructures for the Development of Networks and Communities, TridentCom 2005, pp. 136–145 (February 2005)
15. Peterson, L., Anderson, T., Culler, D., Roscoe, T.: A blueprint for introducing disruptive technology into the Internet. SIGCOMM Comput. Commun. Rev. 33(1), 59–64 (2003)
16. Puljiz, Z., Mikuc, M.: IMUNES Based Distributed Network Emulator. In: Proceedings of the International Conference on Software in Telecommunications and Computer Networks, pp. 198–203 (October 2006)
17. Rakotoarivelo, T., Ott, M., Jourjon, G., Seskar, I.: OMF: a control and management framework for networking testbeds. SIGOPS Oper. Syst. Rev. 43, 54–59 (2010)
18. Riley, G., Fujimoto, R., Ammar, M.: A generic framework for parallelization of network simulations. In: Proceedings of the 7th International Symposium on Modeling Analysis and Simulation of Computer and Telecommunication Systems, pp. 128–135 (October 1999)
19. Spring, N., Mahajan, R., Wetherall, D., Anderson, T.: Measuring ISP topologies with rocketfuel. IEEE/ACM Transactions on Networking (TON) 12(1), 2–16 (2004)
20. Van Vorst, N., Erazo, M., Liu, J.: PrimoGENI: Integrating Real-Time Network Simulation and Emulation in GENI. In: Proceedings of the Workshop on Principles of Advanced and Distributed Simulation, PADS 2011, pp. 1–9. IEEE (June 2011)
21. White, B., Lepreau, J., Stoller, L., Ricci, R., Guruprasad, S., Newbold, M., Hibler, M., Barb, C., Joglekar, A.: An integrated experimental environment for distributed systems and networks. In: Proceedings of the 5th Symposium on Operating Systems Design and Implementation, OSDI 2002, pp. 255–270 (2002)

Implementation and Performance Evaluation of a New Experimental Platform for Medium Access Control Protocols

Francisco Vázquez Gallego[1], Jesús Alonso-Zarate[1], Danica Gajic[2],
Christian Liss[2], and Christos Verikoukis[1]

[1] Centre Tecnològic de Telecomunicacions de Catalunya (CTTC)
Parc Mediterrani de la Tecnologia (PMT), Av. Carl Friedrich Gauss, 7
08860 Castelldefels (Barcelona), Spain
{francisco.vazquez,jesus.alonso,cveri}@cttc.es
[2] InnoRoute GmbH, P.O. Box 260114
80058 Munich, Germany
{gajic,liss}@innoroute.de

Abstract. OpenMAC is presented in this paper as an innovative experimental platform suitable for field testing and performance evaluation of Medium Access Control (MAC) protocols developed in C++. The concept design of OpenMAC avoids the use of hardware-specific code or Hardware Description Language (HDL), softening the learning curve and accelerating the implementation process. This paper describes the OpenMAC hardware/software architecture and shows its benefits with a design example of a Carrier Sense Multiple Access (CSMA) protocol. Finally, the paper provides the implementation details and presents performance results of a practical test to demonstrate how OpenMAC can fulfill strict MAC timing specifications and thus perform as a device backwards compatible with standards.

Keywords: MAC protocol, rapid prototyping, flexibility, cross-layer.

1   Introduction

The Medium Access Control (MAC) layer defines the rules to access a shared communication medium, indicating when and how a specific node is granted access to transmit or receive data. Several MAC protocols have been proposed in the literature due to their key impact into the performance and energy-efficiency of communication networks. However, most of these works present only theoretical analysis or simulation, and just in very few cases they have been actually tested in the field. Experimental prototyping and real testing are essential processes for evaluating the protocols under realistic physical (PHY) layer conditions due to the fact that the inclusion of real-world effects in theoretical models often leads to intractable problems and computer-based simulation techniques are affected by the variability and, usually lack PHY layer accuracy [1].

The requirements for a MAC experimental platform are tightly related to the key functions of the MAC layer, which are briefly described as follows:

T. Korakis, M. Zink, and M. Ott (Eds.): TridentCom 2012, LNICST 44, pp. 178–193, 2012.

1) Provide access to PHY layer information, e.g., to monitor the channel status for Clear Channel Assessment (CCA) in order to know whether the channel is idle or busy.
2) Enable PHY layer re-configuration to select various PHY parameters such as data-rate, modulation, transmit-power, frequency-channel, etc.
3) Enable precise scheduling and timing, e.g., to ensure that transmissions occur during time-slots in Time Division Multiple Access (TDMA) protocols.
4) Guarantee fast identification of received control packets which have to be quickly processed to generate answers and make decisions rapidly.
5) Guarantee fast packet transmission, e.g., in contention-based protocols packets must be transmitted with minimum delay when the channel is detected to be clear.

In addition, an ideal platform should also:

1) Smooth the learning curve to create a prototype from a protocol concept design.
2) Guarantee the fulfillment of the protocol time-specifications to ensure backwards compatibility with standards in case it is required.
3) Provide flexible interfacing to experiment with different PHY layers.

A number of research projects have addressed the implementation of experimental platforms to test MAC protocols [2]. Two categories of platforms have been identified in the literature: platforms based on commercial Network Interface Cards (NIC) and platforms based on custom hardware.

Commercial off-the-shelf 802.11 NIC-based platforms [3]-[5] split the implementation of the MAC layer functions between the firmware on the networking card, which implements the time-critical functions, and the software-driver running on the computer hosting the card, which implements the time-tolerant functions. NIC-based solutions constitute an inexpensive prototyping approach and facilitate reprogramming the MAC protocol functions by modifying the software-driver. However, the interface between the host-computer and the NIC introduces unpredictable delays which may compromise the precise scheduling and the compliance with strict timing requirements of the MAC protocol. For this reason, time-critical functions are programmed in the NIC firmware, which usually cannot be easily reconfigured, thus limiting the flexibility to efficiently customize certain MAC functions. This limitation is extended to the access to information and configuration of the PHY layer, thus not allowing for MAC-PHY cross-layer designs.

Several custom hardware platforms [6][7] have been implemented as an alternative to NIC-based platforms, e.g., TUTWLAN [8], Universal Software Radio Peripheral (USRP) [9] and GNU Radio [10], Wireless Open-Access Research Platform (WARP) [11], CalRadio [12], OpenAirInterface [13], among others. Custom hardware platforms are equipped with an analog Radio-Frequency (RF) front-end connected to a built-in computing subsystem by means of analog-to-digital and digital-to-analog converters. The computing subsystem performs both the PHY digital base-band processing (BBP) and the MAC functions. These solutions are based on Field-Programmable-Gate-Arrays (FPGAs), embedded processors, or Digital-Signal-Processors (DSP). They offer full control over the MAC and the PHY layers. The implementations based on FPGA allow partitioning the MAC into software and custom hardware-accelerators, offering even more processing power. In addition, they enable to experiment with different PHY layers and to design MAC-PHY cross-layer optimizations.

On the other hand, state of the art custom-hardware platforms have some disadvantages. Their implementation cost is very high and they show a steep learning curve to start prototyping. The protocol designer needs to understand the hardware details to develop hardware-specific C-code in order to fulfill the tightest protocol time-constraints. However, MAC designers are typically familiar with high-level programming languages, e.g., C++, which may endanger the implementation of time-critical functions. While the use of FPGAs allows hardware-acceleration and may relax the software optimization requirements, it forces the protocol designer to learn a Hardware Description Language (HDL). This is the main motivation for the development of the OpenMAC platform, which intends to bring MAC prototyping capabilities closer to the research community. OpenMAC introduces a special hardware/software partitioning of the MAC protocol that eases the task to fulfill the most challenging MAC timing-specifications with non hardware-specific code. The protocols can be entirely designed in C++ and hardware is transparent to the designer.

The contribution of this paper is threefold. Firstly, it describes the implementation of the OpenMAC platform architecture presented in [14], which is summarized in this paper to make it self-contained. Secondly, it provides a comprehensive description of the measurement procedure and performance evaluation of the platform. Thirdly, it provides an example of implementation of a contention-based protocol.

The remainder of this paper is organized as follows. Section 2 briefly describes the hardware/software architecture of OpenMAC. Section 3 provides a code example for a MAC protocol. The hardware implementation of OpenMAC is described in Section 4. The performance results of the OpenMAC platform are reported and discussed in Section 5. Finally, Section 6 concludes the paper.

2   OpenMAC Platform Architecture

The architecture of the OpenMAC platform is depicted in Fig. 1. The implementation of a MAC protocol is split into the Software (SW) MAC and the Hardware (HW) MAC modules. The reason for this HW/SW partitioning is to enable the use of *non-hardware-specific C/C++ code* for protocol prototyping and to *fulfill the MAC protocol time specifications*.

The SW MAC implements non time-critical MAC functions in C++ code. The SW MAC is prevented from accessing long data payloads in order to minimize non-deterministic software latencies. Instead, the SW MAC only needs to access the packet headers and packet-descriptors to make simple MAC decisions.

The HW MAC executes time-critical MAC operations and heavy computation functions by means of hardware acceleration, e.g., Clear Channel Assessment (CCA), packet error control, encryption, etc. In addition, the HW MAC provides an efficient hardware mechanism to guarantee precise and deterministic MAC scheduling, e.g., time slots in reservation-based protocols, and back-off periods and inter-frame spacing in contention-based protocols.

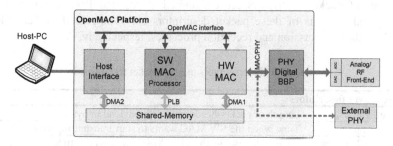

Fig. 1. Hardware/Software architecture of the OpenMAC platform

The HW MAC interfaces to the PHY digital BBP through the MAC/PHY interface, which supports fast transfer of packets and control parameters. The HW MAC configures various PHY parameters on the BBP such as the data-rate, modulation, transmit power, and carrier selection. In a similar way, the HW MAC monitors some variables that are read from the PHY layer, e.g., Received Signal Strength Indicator (RSSI). Access to PHY layer information at the MAC and upper layers is important in order to support cross-layer optimizations.

The layers above the MAC are integrated in a host computer (Host-PC) connected to the OpenMAC platform through the Host Interface. However, the upper layers can also be integrated in the SW MAC processor when stand-alone operation is required. The current design of the Host Interface has the same architecture as the HW MAC.

The shared-memory is a common storage place for accelerating the packet transactions among the SW MAC, HW MAC, and the Host-PC by means of a Direct Memory Access (DMA). The SW MAC accesses the shared-memory through the Processor Local Bus (PLB). The HW MAC stores in the shared-memory the packets received from the PHY, and it reads the ones to be transmitted through the PHY. Similarly, the Host-PC stores in the shared-memory the packets coming from upper layers and reads the ones stored by the HW MAC in the reception process.

Each packet is referenced by a packet-pointer that identifies the base address where the packet is located in the shared-memory. The SW MAC exchanges packet-pointers with the HW MAC and with the Host-PC through the OpenMAC interface.

The remainder of this section is organized as follows. Section 2.1 describes the structure of the packets in the shared-memory. The operation of the HW MAC blocks is detailed in Section 2.2. Finally, Section 2.3 describes the SW MAC functionalities and details the functions of the Hardware Abstraction Layer of OpenMAC.

2.1 Packet-Descriptors

A packet in the shared-memory is comprised of three components:

1) The packet-header contains control information related to the MAC protocol.
2) The data-payload contains the actual useful data of the packet.
3) The packet-descriptors contain control and status information required for transmission and reception.

Two types of packet-descriptors are considered: MAC and PHY descriptors. The structure and contents of these packet descriptors are summarized in Table 1 and Table 2 for the transmission and reception processes, respectively.

Table 1. Packet-descriptors used in packet transmission

MAC Layer descriptors	
PacketLength	Length of packet-header and data-payload in bytes
TimeStamp	Time when the SW MAC wants to start transmitting a packet
EnableRxTimeOut	To enable/disable the HW MAC to detect a time-out event in packet-reception after a packet is transmitted
EnableBackoff	To enable/disable the HW MAC to perform backoff process
RxTimeOut	Time-out interval to be used by the HW MAC to receive a new packet just after a packet-transmission if EnableRxTimeOut is enabled
Backoff	Max. duration of the backoff period to be used by the HW MAC for the transmission of a packet when EnableBackoff is enabled
PHY Layer descriptors	
Modulation	Modulation type used for a transmission
DataRate	Data-rate used for transmission at the PHY layer
TxPower	Transmission power
Carrier	Frequency band and carriers used for transmission

Table 2. Packet-descriptors used in packet reception

MAC Layer descriptors	
PacketLength	Length of packet-header and data-payload in bytes
TimeStamp	Time when the packet was received from the PHY layer
CRCresult	Indicates if the current packet was received without error
PHY Layer descriptors	
Modulation	Modulation type used for the reception of a packet
DataRate	Data rate at which the packet was received at the PHY layer
RSSI	The RSSI is a measure of the RF energy received

The SW MAC can read or write the packet-descriptors by accessing directly to the packets' structures in the shared-memory. The HW MAC transfers the PHY layer packet-descriptors among the shared-memory and the PHY layer.

2.2   Hardware MAC

The HW MAC is a digital module designed in VHDL. It has been created to support any time-critical function that can be required by any type of MAC protocols (i.e., contention-based, reservation-based, and hybrid MAC protocols), and to avoid re-design efforts for adapting the HW MAC to new functions.

In this section, the functionalities and the interaction among the HW MAC elements are described. A block diagram of the HW MAC is shown in Fig. 2.

The connection between the HW MAC and the SW MAC modules is implemented with the two interfaces shown in the left hand side of the diagram: the DMA bus to the shared-memory and the OpenMAC interface directly to the SW MAC.

The transfer of packets is performed through the shared-memory using the DMA bus. In the transmission process, packets are read from the shared-memory by the Tx DMA block and then parsed to extract the packet-descriptors at the Tx Packet Parsing block. In the reception process, the packet-descriptors are first collected and registered by the Rx Packet Formatting block, and then the packets are written into the shared-memory by the Rx DMA block.

The SW MAC exchanges packet-pointers (PP) with the Tx PP Manager and Rx PP Manager blocks through the OpenMAC interface. The packet-pointers are temporarily buffered in the TxPP FIFO and RxPP FIFO blocks, respectively, for transmission and reception. In the transmission process, the SW MAC sends the packet-pointers to the Tx PP Manager block. In the reception process, the Rx PP Manager notifies to the SW MAC when a new packet has been stored in the shared-memory. In the case that the RxPP FIFO is empty, the Rx PP Manager block notifies to the SW MAC, which sends one or more available packet-pointers. This approach overcomes possible latencies introduced by the SW MAC and guarantees that packets received from the PHY layer can be stored into the shared-memory immediately.

As shown in Fig. 2, the OpenMAC interface is connected to the internal registers of the Channel State Monitor and the Configuration BBP/RF blocks. In their turn, these two are connected to the PHY layer through the MAC/PHY interface, shown in the right hand side of the diagram. This interface supports hardware-accelerated transfers of data and control parameters between the HW MAC and the PHY layer. The Channel State Monitor block periodically senses the channel status (e.g., RSSI, busy, or idle) provided by the PHY layer. The channel status is read by the Backoff Controller block, or by the SW MAC, to implement CSMA.

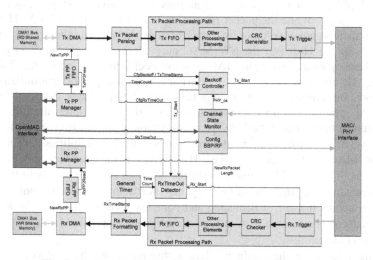

Fig. 2. Hardware MAC Module Functional Block Diagram

The Configuration BBP/RF block configures the PHY layer (i.e., the Digital BBP and the Analog RF Front-End) by transferring the contents of its configuration registers (e.g., modulation, transmit power, carrier selection, etc). The configuration registers can be updated at any time from the SW MAC through the OpenMAC interface. In addition, the PHY configuration can be performed in a packet by packet basis by sending the PHY packet-descriptors (detailed in Table 1) at the beginning of each packet transmission.

The HW MAC includes two packet processing paths devoted to the execution of time-critical functions in packet transmission and reception, e.g., Cyclic Redundancy Code (CRC), encryption, packet aggregation, etc. Packets are fetched from the shared memory, processed, and transferred to the MAC/PHY interface, and inversely with packets received from PHY.

Finally, the HW MAC includes three hardware blocks devoted to provide simple, precise and deterministic scheduling and timing to the MAC layer:

1) The General Timer block provides a time indication signal (TimeCount) to the other blocks with a time resolution of 1 μs.
2) The RxTimeOut Detector block detects when no packet is received within a time period (i.e., RxTimeOut packet-descriptor in Table 1) after the last transmission, e.g., acknowledgement (ACK) is lost for the previous data-packet transmission.
3) The Backoff Controller block determines the time instants to trigger the packet transmission by comparing the TimeCount signal with the TimeStamp packet-descriptor. It can be configured to execute a backoff process using the Backoff packet-descriptors, detailed in Table 1, and the channel status (PHY_cs) provided by the Channel State Monitor block.

2.3   Software MAC

The SW MAC is a C++ program that runs on an embedded processor without operating system. While the packet-processing load is concentrated on the HW MAC, which transfers great volumes of data through the shared-memory to exchange packets with the Host-PC, the SW MAC only accesses the packet-descriptors and packet-headers to make simple MAC protocol decisions (e.g., check the destination address, identify the packet type, determine time-stamps for transmission, etc). Therefore, by avoiding the need to access long data-payloads from software, the OpenMAC platform reduces software latencies and thus facilitates the fulfillment of strict timing constraints of the MAC protocol without using hardware specific code.

The use of packet-descriptors (described in Section 2.1) simplifies the access from the SW MAC to the hardware, i.e., HW MAC, Host Interface, and PHY layer parameters. The SW MAC simply performs fast read or write access to the packet-descriptor stored in the shared-memory that needs to monitor or configure. This approach avoids the use of dedicated and complex software functions to access the PHY, reduces the complexity in the development of the MAC protocol, and minimizes delays.

In order to make the hardware details transparent to the protocol designer, a Hardware Abstraction Layer (HAL) is included in OpenMAC. The HAL is comprised of a set of software functions which ease the access to the HW MAC and the Host interface. A HAL function is a very short piece of C-code that executes read/write accesses to the hardware internal registers through the OpenMAC interface.

The functions of the OpenMAC HAL are described in Table 3. The input argument named *channel* used in all the HAL functions allows selecting among the channels connected to the OpenMAC interface bus: the PHY channel (HW MAC) and the HOST channel (Host interface). Both channels have basically the same architecture as the HW MAC module described in Section 2.2.

Table 3. Functions of the OpenMAC Hardware Abstraction Layer

Function: `packet_pointer get_packet(char channel)`
Description: It returns the packet-pointer of a new packet that has been received from *channel* and has been stored in the shared-memory.
Function: `void send_packet(packet_pointer tx_pointer, char channel, unsigned int timestamp)`
Description: It writes the packet-pointer *tx_pointer* of the next packet to transmit through the *channel*. The transmission will start at the time indicated by the packet-descriptor *timestamp*, passed as an argument.
Function: `unsigned int check_send_packet(char channel)`
Description: It returns the integer number of packets that are still pending to be transmitted through the *channel*. The packets are buffered in the Tx FIFO of the *channel*.
Function: `unsigned int check_get_packet(char channel)`
Description: It returns an integer value that can be mapped into the state of the reception process: (1) a new packet has been received from the *channel* and stored in the shared-memory, (2) the *channel* needs packet-pointers for the reception of new packets, and (3) a time-out event has been detected after the last transmitted packet.
Function: `void pointer_allocation(char channel, char n, packet_pointer *rx_pointer)`
Description: It writes into the RxPP FIFO of the *channel* a list of *n* packet-pointers, *rx_pointer*, which will be used to store in the shared-memory new packets received.
Function: `unsigned int get_phy_cs(char channel)`
Description: It returns the status (RSSI, busy, idle) of the PHY layer connected to channel.
Function: `void config_phy(char channel, unsigned short modulation, unsigned short data_rate, unsigned short tx_power, unsigned short carrier_select)`
Description: It writes the parameters, passed as input arguments, to configure the channel.
Function: `unsigned int get_timer(char channel)`
Description: It returns the current TimeCount value of the General Timer shown in Fig. 2.
Function: `void reset_timer(char channel)`
Description: It resets the General Timer block of the *channel*.

3   Example of CSMA Protocol

This section presents an example of implementation of a CSMA protocol in the SW MAC processor. The aim of this description is to demonstrate how simple the design of a MAC protocol using OpenMAC can be.

In CSMA, a node that has data to transmit first senses the channel. In the case that the channel is clear, the node starts transmitting. Otherwise, the node initiates a random backoff and waits for the channel to be idle. The backoff timer is decremented along time; it is frozen when the channel is busy, and it is resumed when the channel becomes idle again. When the backoff timer expires, i.e., gets to zero, the packet is transmitted if the channel is idle, otherwise the backoff is reinitiated. When a data-packet is sent, the transmitting node waits for an ACK from the intended destination. If the ACK is not received within a timeout, the packet is retransmitted.

The SW MAC code for CSMA is shown below. It is divided in two parts:

(1) Transmission of Data-Packets from Host-PC to PHY. The data-packets transmitted from the Host-PC to the PHY are temporarily stored in the variable *buffer_HOST2PHY* of type packet. A new packet can only be stored in the *buffer_HOST2PHY* when it is free, i.e., an ACK has been received for the previously transmitted data-packet. The hardware Backoff Controller implements the backoff process and the RxTimeOut Detector generates the ACK time-out events. Therefore, the SW MAC has only to configure the associated packet-descriptors (i.e., EnableBackoff, Backoff, EnableRxTimeOut, and RxTimeOut) on each data-packet transmission. If an ACK time-out event is detected, the data-packet is re-transmitted.

(2) Reception of Packets from PHY to Host-PC. The packets received from PHY are temporarily stored in the *buffer_PHY2HOST*, of type packet, to be later transferred to the Host-PC. Since the throughput among the Host-PC and OpenMAC can be assumed higher than the throughput among OpenMAC and PHY, the *buffer_PHY2HOST* is always ready to store new received packets. The SW MAC first checks the Cyclic Redundancy Code (CRC) descriptor of the received packet. Then, the SW MAC checks the destination address and the packet type. If it is a data-packet, it is transferred to the Host-PC and the SW MAC starts the transmission of an ACK to the PHY delayed a Short Inter Frame Space (SIFS) from the time-stamp of the received packet. If an ACK is received, the *buffer_HOST2PHY* is released.

Example code of a CSMA protocol implemented in the SW MAC processor.

```
packet_pointer TxPP, RxPP;
packet buffer_HOST2PHY, buffer_PHY2HOST, ACK;
unsigned int status_HOST = 0, status_PHY = 0; char buffer_ready = 1;
while(1){
/* PART 1: transmission of data-packets from Host-PC to PHY */
    status_HOST = check_get_packet(HOST);
    /* Packet-pointer requested for data-packet reception from HOST? */
    if ((status_HOST & RxPP_REQUEST) && buffer_ready)
        pointer_allocation(HOST, 1, &buffer_HOST2PHY);
    /* Data-packet stored in buffer_HOST2PHY by the HOST_IF? */
    if (status_HOST & RxPACKET_RDY) {
        buffer_ready = 0; /* buffer_HOST2PHY is busy with new packet */
        TxPP = get_packet(HOST); /* get the packet-pointer */
        /* write some of the MAC and PHY packet-descriptors */
        TxPP-> EnableRxTimeOut = ENABLED; /* enable Rx time-out */
        TxPP-> RxTimeOut = ACKTIMEOUT; /* time-out to receive ACK */
        TxPP-> EnableBackoff = ENABLED; /* enable backoff */
        TxPP-> Backoff = CW; /* Contention-Window for backoff process */
```

```
        TxPP-> TxPower = TX10dBm; /* configure PHY tx power */
        send_packet(TxPP, PHY, 0); /* transfer the packet to HW MAC */
        }
  /* Time-out detected after the last data-packet sent to PHY? */
  if (status_PHY & RxTIMEOUT) send_packet(TxPP, PHY, 0);/* tx again*/

/* PART 2: reception of packets from PHY to Host-PC */
  status_PHY = check_get_packet(PHY);
  /* Packet-pointer requested for packet reception from PHY? */
  if (status_PHY & RxPP_request)
      pointer_allocation(PHY, 1, &buffer_PHY2HOST);
  /* Packet stored in buffer_PHY2HOST by the HW MAC? */
  if (status_PHY & RxPACKET_RDY){
      RxPP = get_packet(PHY); /* get the packet-pointer */
      if (RxPP->CRCresult == OK){ /* check that CRC is correct */
          for (i=0; i<6; ) /* check the destination MAC address */
              if (RxPP->DstAddr[i] == my_Addr[i]) i++; else break;
          if (i==6){ /* destination MAC address is correct? */
              send_packet(RxPP, HOST, 0); /* transfer to HOST */
              if (RxPP->Type == DATA){ /* is it a data-packet? */
              /* calculate time-stamp to transmit an ACK */
              TxTimeStamp = RxPP->TimeStamp + SIFS;
              /* transfer ACK to HW MAC */
              send_packet(&ACK, PHY, TxTimeStamp);
              } /* is it an ACK? then release the buffer_HOST2PHY */
              else if (RxPP->Type == ACK) buffer_ready = 1;
          }
      }
  }
}
```

4   Hardware Implementation

The OpenMAC platform architecture has been implemented and tested on a Commercial Off-The-Shelf (COTS) FPGA-based development board. The technical features of this board are detailed in Table 4. It contains a Xilinx Virtex-5 FPGA [15] which integrates two PowerPC440 processors. One of the processors is used to run the code of the SW MAC and the other is left unused for future applications, e.g., development of high-performance upper layers for standalone OpenMAC nodes. The rest of the FPGA implements the following digital modules: the HW MAC, the Host Interface, the OpenMAC interface bus, the shared-memory, and the MAC/PHY interface.

Table 4. Features of the FPGA-based Development Board

Board part-number	HTG-V5-PCIE-100-2 (from HiTech Global, LLC [16])
FPGA	Xilinx Virtex-5 XC5VFX100T-3
Processors	2 PowerPC 440 (hard cores)
RAM Memory	512MB DDR2-SDRAM, expandable up to 2GB
Flash Memory	4 MB
Interface with Host	8-lanes PCI Express End-Point connector. 2 Gigabit Ethernet ports.
Interface with PHY	2 connectors (QSE type) with 64 pairs of Low Voltage Differential Signals (LVDS) or 128 single-ended signals. Outputs of 5V and 3.3V supply for add-on PHY modules.

The shared-memory module is implemented using on-chip Random Access Memory (RAM) blocks of the FPGA. The Double Data Rate-Synchronous Dynamic RAM (DDR-SDRAM) module, included in the FPGA-based board, is left unused for future extensions with huge memory requirements.

The PowerPC440 processor clock has been set to 400MHz in order to provide high speed to the SW MAC. For the processor peripheral cores (i.e., HW MAC, Host Interface, and shared-memory) and for the communication buses (i.e., OpenMAC interface, PLB, and DMA buses) the clock frequency has been selected as low as 100MHz in order to facilitate and speed-up the FPGA implementation process.

The FPGA-based board includes one Peripheral Component Interconnect (PCI) bus and two Gigabit Ethernet PHY ports based on the Alaska 88E1111 transceiver from Marvell. One of the Ethernet ports is used to connect the OpenMAC platform with the Host-PC. The PCI bus is foreseen to plug the board into a desktop computer in applications with greater bandwidth and throughput requirements.

The expansion connectors of the FPGA-based board allow the implementation of a flexible MAC/PHY interface with external PHY layer boards. Two different PHY layer solutions can be implemented:

1) A complete PHY which incorporates the BBP and the Analog RF Front-End.
2) The BBP can be implemented inside the FPGA and an external Analog RF Front-End can be used for the RF operation.

So far, a Gigabit Ethernet PHY has been used for the proof-of-concept of OpenMAC. The use of a wired solution is mainly motivated by the lack of availability on the market of low-cost high-performance wireless PHY solutions which do not require great implementation efforts.

5   Performance Evaluation

The aim of this section is to show the ability of the OpenMAC platform to meet the time-constraints of a standardized MAC protocol. As an example, in the context of the IEEE 802.11 Standard for Wireless Local Area Networks [17], the data-packet reception and post processing to decide whether to transmit an ACK or not, and the initialization of the transmission of the ACK, must be done within less than a SIFS interval, i.e., tens of microseconds, in order to be able to tolerate non-negligible propagation delays as well.

The remainder of this section is organized as follows. First, Section 5.1 details the performance metrics. The experimental setup is briefly described in Section 5.2 and, finally, the performance results are discussed in Section 5.3.

5.1   Performance Metrics

The following metrics have been considered for the performance evaluation of OpenMAC. The time metrics are shown in the timing diagram of Fig. 3.

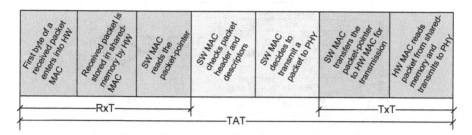

Fig. 3. Timing diagram of the HW MAC and SW MAC processes within TxT, RxT, and TAT

- **Transmission Time (TxT)** is defined as the time elapsed from the moment when the SW MAC initiates the transfer of the associated packet-pointer to the HW MAC, until the moment when the HW MAC finishes the transmission of the packet to the PHY.
- **Throughput in transmission** is defined as the length of transmitted packets divided by the corresponding TxT (assuming a constant packet length).
- **Reception Time (RxT)** is defined as the time elapsed from the moment when the first byte of a received packet enters into the HW MAC, until the moment when the SW MAC reads the packet-pointer.
- **Throughput in reception** is defined as the length of the received packets divided by the corresponding RxT (assuming a constant packet length).
- **Turn-Around Time (TAT)** is defined as the time elapsed from the moment when the first byte of a received packet enters into the HW MAC, until the moment when the HW MAC finishes the transmission of an answer packet (ACK) to the PHY. During this time, the SW MAC reads the packet-pointer, checks the packet header and descriptors, and transfers the ACK packet-pointer.

It is worth noting that the processing delays introduced by the PHY layer are not considered in the definition of TxT, RxT, and TAT. The TAT is the most critical time parameter for those protocols which rely on handshaking of control packets, e.g., the ACKs used in the IEEE 802.11 Standard, as it defines the capability to respond to received packets in due time. This parameter is the key to ensure backwards compatibility with current standards.

5.2   Experimental Setup

The performance of the OpenMAC platform architecture has been assessed using the board described in Section 4. The wired Gigabit Ethernet PHY layer has been used for the setup shown in Fig. 4, which does not include the Host Interface for simplicity. One of the Ethernet transceivers has been connected through its Gigabit Media Independent Interface (GMII) to the MAC/PHY interface in the FPGA. Then, the OpenMAC platform has been connected to a Gigabit Ethernet port of a computer.

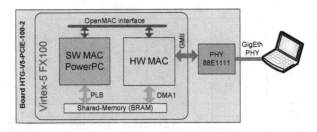

Fig. 4. Experimental setup used for the performance tests of OpenMAC

The following procedure has been used to measure the TxT, RxT, TAT, and the different throughput values.

1) The OpenMAC platform transmits or receives packets to/from the computer through the Gigabit Ethernet PHY.
2) The following HAL functions, described in Section 2.3, are included in a test program to receive, to transmit, to monitor the status, and to allocate packet-pointers:
   get_packet(), *send_packet()*, *check_get_packet()*, *check_send_packet()*, and *pointer_allocation()*.
3) The *get_timer()* function is utilized to measure time periods between two different instants. In this way, the time measurements are simplified by employing the time-base provided by the HW MAC.
4) In order to transmit Ethernet packets with a controlled length to the OpenMAC platform, the *ping* command is executed on the desktop computer as:
   ping -t -l length ip_address_openMAC .
5) The transmission and reception throughput values have been computed by dividing the packet length by the TxT and RxT measurements, respectively.

5.3   Experimental Results

The experiments have been performed with different data-packet lengths (100, 500, 1000, and 1500 bytes) and ACK packets of 46 bytes, which is the minimum data field length in Ethernet frames. Fig. 5 shows the results for TxT, throughput in transmission, RxT, throughput in reception, and TAT.

In terms of throughput, OpenMAC performs close to the maximum available throughput in Gigabit Ethernet with long data-packets (1000 to 1500 bytes), which is 1Gbps. As far as the turn-around-time values are concerned, OpenMAC achieves values of the TAT that are below 16 µs for short packets (46 to 500 bytes) and below 20 µs for long packets (1000 to 1500 bytes). It is worth noting that, for short packets, and if the PHY layer device connected to OpenMAC was changed to one compliant with the IEEE 802.11 Standard [17], OpenMAC would fulfill the SIFS time (16 µs) specified in the standard for OFDM PHY layer using a bandwidth of 20MHz. Similarly, for long packets, OpenMAC is in compliance with the SIFS time (32 µs) using a bandwidth of 10MHz. In addition, the TAT could still be reduced by increasing the clock frequency of the processor peripheral cores (i.e., HW MAC, and shared-memory) and of the communication buses (i.e., OpenMAC interface, PLB, and DMA buses) above the currently utilized 100MHz. This frequency adjustment could yield a reduction of more than 20% of the TxT, RxT, and TAT results obtained in the current implementation.

The measurements that have been carried out on the FPGA board demonstrate that the OpenMAC platform fulfils the strictest timing specifications of the IEEE 802.11 Standard.

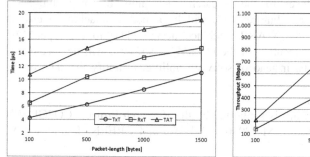
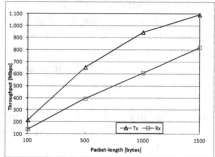

Fig. 5. (a) TxT, RxT, TAT, and (b) throughput in Tx/Rx (with respect to the packet-length)

6   Conclusions

OpenMAC has been presented in this paper as an innovative platform suitable for the development and experimental testing of MAC protocols. It has been implemented using a COTS FPGA-based board with a processor integrated in the FPGA. OpenMAC provides full flexibility and re-configurability to develop any MAC protocol, to change the PHY layer, and to do research with cross-layer optimizations. The main objectives considered in the design of OpenMAC have been:

1) To speed-up the development process of a MAC protocol by simplifying the conversion from the theoretical model down to implementation,
2) To fulfill the protocol time-constraints, and
3) To attain precise scheduling.

Regarding the complexity of the protocol development cycle, OpenMAC allows implementing MAC protocols entirely designed in C++, without operating system in the embedded processor, and with hardware fully transparent to the protocol designer, who does not have to optimize hardware-specific C, assembly or HDL code.

OpenMAC integrates a set of software HAL functions that abstract the accesses to hardware. In addition, it delegates the packet processing to hardware accelerators and prevents software from accessing high-volume data-payloads. The software accesses only short packet-descriptors and packet-headers, which facilitate the fulfillment of MAC time constraints. Moreover, OpenMAC contains hardware accelerators devoted to configure and monitor the PHY layer, and to perform backoff processes, which avoids software to fast access to PHY. Regarding scheduling and timing, OpenMAC includes hardware elements to accurately control time events.

The performance of the OpenMAC platform has been tested experimentally using Gigabit Ethernet PHY. It performs at maximum throughput of 1 Gbps and yields turn-around-times below 20 μs for long packets (1000 to 1500 bytes) and below 16 μs for short packets (46 to 500 bytes). Hence, OpenMAC can fulfill strict MAC timing specifications such as the ones of the IEEE 802.11 Standard.

OpenMAC achieves successfully the aforementioned objectives and brings prototyping capabilities closer to the research community by overcoming the limitations of state of the art. Future work will be aimed at attaching a custom wireless PHY layer (e.g., the WARP reference design [11]) to the OpenMAC platform. Furthermore, the execution of the OpenMAC software will be accelerated by using hardware interrupts, instead of software polling, to notify the state of the OpenMAC hardware modules.

Acknowledgements. This work is supported by the Research Projects CO2GREEN (TEC2010-20823), GREEN-T (TSI-020400-2011-16), and GREENET (PITN–GA–2010-264759).

References

1. Kotz, D., Newport, C., Gray, R.S., Liu, J., Yuan, Y., Elliott, C.: Experimental evaluation of wireless simulation assumptions. In: Proceedings of MSWiM (2004)
2. Vázquez Gallego, F., Alonso-Zarate, J., Alonso, L., Verikoukis, C.: A Survey on Prototyping Platforms for the Development and Experimental Evaluation of Medium Access Control Protocols. IEEE Wireless Communication Magazine 19(1), 74–81 (2012)
3. Korakis, T., Knox, M., Erkip, E., Panwar, S.: Cooperative Network Implementation Using Open-Source Platforms. IEEE Communications Magazine 47(2), 134–141 (2009)
4. Lu, M.H., Steenkiste, P., Chen, T.: Using Commodity Hardware Platform to Develop and Evaluate CSMA Protocols. In: Proceedings of the Third ACM International Workshop on Wireless Network Testbeds, Experimental Evaluation and Characterization, San Francisco, pp. 73–80 (2008)
5. Verikoukis, C., Pérez-Neira, A., Alonso-Zárate, J., Skianis, C.: Experimental Performance Evaluation of a MAC Protocol for Cooperative ARQ Scenarios. In: Proc. of the IEEE GLOBECOM, Hawaii (2009)
6. Pawelczak, P., Nolan, K., Doyle, L., Oh, S.W., Cabric, D.: Cognitive radio: Ten years of experimentation and development. IEEE Communications Magazine 49(3), 90–100 (2011)
7. Chowdhury, K.R., Melodia, T.: Platforms and Testbeds for Experimental Evaluation of Cognitive Ad Hoc Networks. IEEE Communications Magazine 48(9), 96–104 (2010)
8. Tikkanen, K., Hännikäinen, M., Hämäläinen, T., Saarinen, J.: Advanced Prototype Platform for a Wireless Multimedia Local Area Network. In: 10th European signal processing conference (EUSIPCO), Tampere, pp. 2309–2312 (2000)
9. Nychis, G., Hottelier, T., Yang, Z., Seshan, S., Steenkiste, P.: Enabling MAC Protocol Implementations on Software-Defined Radios. In: Proceedings of the USENIX NSDI, Boston (2009)

10. Blossom, E.: Exploring GNU Radio (2004), http://www.gnu.org/software/
    gnuradio/doc/exploring-gnuradio.html
11. Hunter, C., Camp, J., Murphy, P., Sabharwal, A., Dick, C.: A flexible framework for
    wireless medium access protocols. In: Asilomar (2006)
12. Manfrin, R., Zanella, A., Zorzi, M.: Functional and Performance Analysis of CalRadio 1
    platform. In: 8th IEEE International Symposium on Network Computing and Applications,
    Cambridge, pp. 300–305 (2009)
13. OpenAirInterface, http://www.openairinterface.org/
14. Vázquez Gallego, F., Alonso-Zarate, J., Liss, C., Verikoukis, C.: OpenMAC: A New
    Reconfigurable Experimental Platform for Energy-Efficient Medium Access Control
    Protocols. IET Science, Measurement & Technology Journal (in press)
15. Xilinx, Virtex-5 FXT FPGAs,
    http://www.xilinx.com/products/virtex5/fxt.html
16. HiTech Global LLC, http://www.hitechglobal.com/
17. IEEE Std. 802.11-2007, Part 11: Wireless LAN Medium Access Control (MAC) and
    Physical Layer (PHY) specifications (2007)

MagicLink: Weaving Multi-site Wireless Sensor Networks for Large-Scale Experiments

Xinxin Liu[1], Li Yu[2], Di Wang[1], and Xiaolin Li[1]

[1] Scalable Software Systems Laboratory
University of Florida, Gainesville, FL 32611, USA
xinxin@cise.ufl.edu, wdiyou@ufl.edu, andyli@ece.ufl.edu
[2] Google, Moutain View, CA 94043, USA
yyuy@cs.okstate.edu

Abstract. Despite the promising vision of pervasive sensor networks of thousands of nodes, conducting such large-scale experiments on demand is still far from reality due to the limitations of resources, space, and maintenance. To address such challenges, we propose the MagicLink middleware to "magically" weave geographically distributed sensor networks into a large-scale sensor network testbed. MagicLink is a key part of the OKGems remotely programmable cyber-physical system project under the GENI (Global Environment for Network Innovation) initiative; and MagicLink is designed to enable shared "clouds" of sensors for sensor network research and experiments at scale and on demand. Specifically, MagicLink has the following salient features: (1) seamless integration of multi-site sensor networks offering elastic and scalable testbeds; (2) online adaptive simulation that adopts a realistic radio model making the cross-site Internet connection behave like a one-hop sensor network link in real environment; (3) component-based design allowing easy integration with user applications. To the best of our knowledge, MagicLink is the first solution to enable "almost-real" large-scale sensor network experiments across sites. In this paper, we present MagicLink's system architecture and subsystem design. We demonstrate the usability and fidelity of MagicLink through experimental results with representative applications on a two-site testbed.

1 Introduction

The rapid evolution of ubiquitous sensing and pervasive computing paradigm has spurred increasing demand for Wireless Sensor Networks (WSNs) that consist of thousands of sensor nodes and span over large geographic territories. Due to the high cost of sensor motes and lack of testing environment, simulation has been the primary method for researchers to test their sensor network protocol and application design before actually deploying it on a real system. Although simulators provide users the flexibility of acquiring various sizes of virtual networks on demand and reproducing their experiments under different settings, they cannot provide satisfactory performance for both large-scale and high fidelity sensor network simulations. On one hand, some unrealistic abstractions used in simulation hinders the studying of protocol performance under real world constraints. On the other hand, high-fidelity simulation of every event on a sensor mote dissipates computation resources, thus makes it extremely unscalable [1].

T. Korakis, M. Zink, and M. Ott (Eds.): TridentCom 2012, LNICST 44, pp. 194–209, 2012.

With the accelerating development of WSNs, using experimental testbeds for proto-typing and validating protocols and applications becomes a preferred method, because it allows for investigating program performances in diverse hardware platforms and various environmental settings. There has been an explosive deployment of sensor network testbeds in the past few years. Numerous small scale testbeds, typically from 20 to 40 sensor nodes, have been deployed and used in many research laboratories. However, the scales of these individual testbeds are insufficient for future WSN applications. To work around this issue, one alternative is to remotely deploy experiments on publicly accessible large-scale sensor platforms, e.g., MoteLab [2], MistLab [3], KanseiGenie [4] and NetEye [5]. Users access sensor resources through assigned accounts and program the sensor motes using customized end-to-end programming tools. However, these platforms suffer from two major problems: First, the scale of such platform is limited to a single site, and is hard to be extensible in terms of resource federation. Second, the provider-dependent interfaces and data logging methods at various platforms hinder the users from reusing their programs. Thereafter, there is a urgent demand for large scale and high fidelity experimental testbeds.

Some recent studies have proposed to create federated sensor networks across multiple sites [4, 6–8]. However, these federated testbeds lack high-fidelity radio models for virtual links across sites. Although these platforms offer connections for data collections and disseminations, they are not suitable for large-scale experiments across multiple sites for protocol design that require realistic radio properties in the virtual links across sites.

We propose the MagicLink system as a hybrid approach to overcome both deficiencies of inaccurate radio abstraction in simulators and inflexible sensor resource acquisition in testbeds. MagicLink aims at fully utilizing isolated sensor resources to enable large-scale sensor network experiments. To accomplish this goal, MagicLink first establishes message tunnels on top of the intermediate Internet connections of the distributed sensor resources. Then, MagicLink restores the original radio link properties over the Internet connections by employing an adaptive radio model to highlight the essential the features of wireless radio links in sensor networks.

The following design features make MagicLink stand out from other projects:

1. MagicLink is highly elastic and scalable in that it weaves isolated small sensor networks. The federated testbed provides not only data sharing, but also means for cross-layer network protocol design and testing.
2. MagicLink features a unique adaptive radio model that preserves the lossy, anisotropic, and dynamic properties of a real radio link in sensor networks deployed in real world environments.
3. MagicLink is component-based, thus is easy to customize and integrate with user applications.

The rest of this paper is organized as follows. Section 2 defines scope and presents system architecture overview. Section 3 elaborates on the core component of MagicLink. Section 4 presents resource initialization and updating functionalities. Section 5 illustrates cross-site communication details. Section 7 summarizes state-of-the-art related works. Finally, Section 8 concludes this paper and discusses potential future work.

2   MagicLink Design

The motivation behind MagicLink is to unite massive small-scale sensor testbeds prevalent in many research laboratories for large-scale experiments. Sensor nodes in these small scale platforms usually have continuous power supply for long-term usage and connections to computers for easy reprogramming. The rationale of MagicLink is analogous to cloud computing, or peer-to-peer desktop systems [9, 10], which harvest geographically distributed computing resources for computationally intensive applications. Similarly, MagicLink enables a "cloud" of sensor networks that federates multi-site of sensor resources and presents itself as a single large sensor network testbed. Through testbed federation, MagicLink enables researchers to access to diverse resources that are hard to acquire in a single site deployment and can also include and mix real world sensor networks deployed for precision agriculture [11, 12] and habitat monitoring [13]. It can be viewed as a middleware to jointly connect physically separated small sensor networks together, as shown in Figure 1(a). Challenges, however, arise not only in the process of building up connections among the gateway computers of these sensor testbeds, but also in smoothing the Internet gaps to achieve near identical radio link features in a real large-scale sensor testbed.

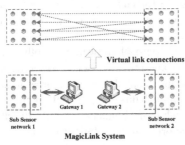
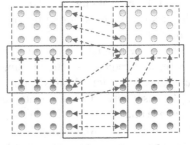

(a) Illustration of construction of virtual links over wired connection.

(b) Large-scale testbed constructed by MagicLink System.

Fig. 1. MagicLink system illustration. Colored circles represent sensor nodes; squared areas indicate geographically separated testbeds. Using MagicLink for sensor resource federation results in a large-scale, smoothly connected sensor testbed that includes real and virtual radio links.

MagicLink primarily addresses two challenges: (1) **Scalable resource federation**: the system should be able to support federation of many sub sensor networks to form a large scale experiment platform. (2) **High-fidelity one-hop virtual link connection simulation**: to construct a seamless connection, the simulated virtual links should hide Internet connection features, e.g., packet loss ratio and round trip delay, but simulate high-fidelity characteristics of radio links in a sensor network. Further, the interfacing functionality should mimic radio communication properties for investigating protocol behaviors in real world settings.

Use Case: To better illustrate the necessity of the high-fidelity virtual link connection simulation, let us consider the scenario of running the Surge application [1] that builds a

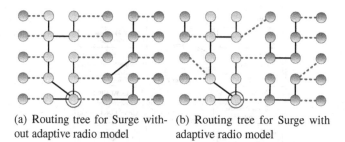

(a) Routing tree for Surge with-   (b) Routing tree for Surge with
out adaptive radio model   adaptive radio model

Fig. 2. Routing tree for the Surge application on a federated testbed of four sites. Each sub sensor network is highlighted with different colors. Double circled nodes represent root nodes, black solid lines represent radio connections, and green dashed lines represent virtual links across sites. (a) Without adaptive radio model, Internet-based virtual links are always preferred over real radio links as next-hop in the routing path. (b) With adaptive radio model, Internet-based "magic" virtual links and real radio links are treated similarly. Either a magic link or a radio link is selected as next-hop based on their runtime link qualities. This results in a real large testbed rather than simply "connected" but actually "partitioned" multiple testbeds.

routing tree on a federated testbed consisting of four sites. A sensor node running Surge will actively probe its neighbors and select the one with the most reliable link as its routing path. Figure 2(a) depicts the resulting tree on a rigidly connected four-site testbed. In this case, no radio model is applied and the raw Internet connections are used. Since Internet connections are more reliable than radio links (especially when certain reliable transmission protocol such as TCP is adopted), they are most likely to be chosen as the routing path. This is undesirable because it lacks the essential characteristics, e.g., heterogeneity and dynamics, of real radio links. Without these features, the reliability, robustness, and self-adaptive qualities of a protocol cannot be thoroughly investigated. On the other hand, MagicLink employs an adaptive radio model to connect testbeds. As shown in Figure 2(b), a more realistic routing tree is constructed, because the intermediate Internet connections preserve the essential features of radio links. Hence, protocol reliability and robustness can be better investigated.

To ease our presentation, we use the following terminologies throughout the rest of this paper:

- *Sub Sensor Network (SSN)*: a small sensor testbed that are federated into MagicLink.
- *Edge nodes*: those sensor nodes that are at the edge of a SSN.
- *Virtual links*: the virtual connections among the edge nodes from different SSNs.
- *SSN Gateway*: a computer that provides Internet connection interface of a SSN.

System overview: The design of MagicLink system is centered around a set of virtual link specifications called *virtual link pool*, as shown in Figure 3. All the cross-site connection information is maintained in this virtual link pool. Four types of operations are performed on the virtual link pool to achieve distributed resource weaving: *system initialization, system monitoring, virtual link adaptation,* and *message dispatching* as illustrated in Figure 3.

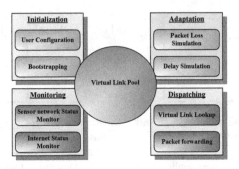

Fig. 3. Component based design of MagicLink System

Virtual link pool contains the information about each individual link constructed by MagicLink system. In its simplest form, it is a list of all source and destination sensor node pairs and their properties, such as transmission delay and packet reception rate. The following key functionalities are implemented:

- Interact with users for testbed configuration and result retrieving
- Locate distributed sensor resources (e.g. SSNs) and establish a connections between their gateway computers
- Build virtual links for each edge sensor node with appropriate setups
- Provide status monitoring service for updating virtual link properties
- Dispatch cross-site messages to their destination
- Customize communication methods for edge nodes to transmit to both radio and wired interfaces

These functionalities are encapsulated in different components and are decoupled from each other as shown in Figure 3. Such a component-based design offers flexibility and easy integration with user applications. The basic functionalities are wrapped into four components: *resource initialization*, which includes (1) interacting with users for system configuration; (2) bootstrapping the system and initializing various parameters for virtual link pool; *monitoring* of resources, which involves (1) keeping tracking locally connected sensor nodes and (2) establishing and maintaining remote gateway computer connections; *message dispatching*, which responsible for (1) providing joint messaging interface between radio links and Internet, (2) performing virtual link lookup and forwarding packets to appropriate virtual links; *adaptation*, which indicates the operations for emulating radio link behavior by adaptively adjust message dispatching operations on virtual links.

3   Virtual Link Pool

Virtual link pool is the central component of MagicLink and maintains virtual links' information. Its primary purpose is to manage edge nodes' communication radius as well as connection qualities. Each virtual link between a pair of edge nodes is represented as a source/destination pair with certain link quality metrics in the virtual link pool. Since radio links are inherently asymmetric, individual gateway computer maintains a separate virtual link pool connecting its local edge nodes to remote edge nodes. The quality of a virtual link is measured in terms of packet reception rate and transmission delay. As MagicLink's target is to seamlessly weave multi-site sensor networks into one large-scale experiment platform, an adaptive radio link model is essential for determining virtual link properties in cross-site message transmission.

It is well-known that radio communications are irregular and unpredictable. To construct a realistic radio model in MagicLink, we not only consider the property of **radio signal path loss and shadow fading**, but also further incorporate a link quality adjustment component to reflect the **anisotropic transmission** and **dynamically changing** property of a radio link. For initial link quality setup, MagicLink uses analytical model to calculate packet reception rate at user specified distance and transmission power. During the execution of the user application, virtual link qualities are periodically updated in accordance to the edge node's real link qualities.

Radio signal path loss and shadow fading: There has been extensive studies on radio propagation under different constraints [14]. In MagicLink, two radio signal path loss models, namely free-space model and two-ray ground model, are provided for ideal line-of-sight communication and single ground reflection scenarios. Users can determine the virtual link distances and choose the desired environment parameter settings for their experiment.

Besides radio signal attenuation, noise on wireless channels as well as other shadowing factors, such as reflecting and scattering, also result in degradation in received signal strength. The most commonly used statistic model for describing this shadowing effect is *log-normal* distribution [14–17]. Therefore, the final received power P_f is the summation of the attenuated transmission power P_r and the shadowing effect, and it also follows the *log-normal* distribution $P_f \sim Logn(P_r, \sigma)$. We use the subscript "dB" to indicate the decibel form of a variable from now on, thus the final received power $P_{f\mathrm{dB}} \sim \mathcal{N}(P_{r\mathrm{dB}}, \sigma_{\mathrm{dB}})$. The variance σ_{dB} of this distribution is a environment related factor, and it is preset by the users to represent the characteristics of different environments.

MagicLink uses a threshold value ξ to infer the correlation between packet reception and final received transmission power. Based on the threshold, we can calculate the probability of a packet being successfully received using:

$$p(P_{f\mathrm{dB}} > \xi_{\mathrm{dB}}) = Q(\frac{\xi_{\mathrm{dB}} - P_{r\mathrm{dB}}}{\sigma_{\mathrm{dB}}}), \tag{1}$$

where the Q-function is defined as the probability that a Gaussian random variable X with mean 0 and variance 1 is greater than certain value.

Anisotropic radio propagation: Anisotropic radio propagation is another significant property to model radio transmission. It should be carefully preserved when building up virtual link connections between two SSNs. Many modeling methods have been proposed in previous studies, e.g., [18], herein we describe the anisotropic property of a sensor node's radio transmission in terms of the *degree of irregularity* metric defined in [18]. The degree of irregularity parameter ϑ of a node is defined as *the maximum path loss percentage variation per unit degree change in the direction of radio propagation,* and is used to calculate the virtual link status based on its relative digression from a predefined direction. The value of ϑ is typically a small number (e.g., 0.005) and it is preset by users for desired radio irregularity degree. Using the metric of irregularity degree requires that the testbed topology is preconfigured, and all the gateway computers know the network topology in advance. This information can be easily obtained via bootstrapping phase. Without the knowledge of testbed topology, a pre-calculated ϑ value can also be obtained from a radio's specification sheet (e.g., Telosb's specification sheet [19]).

Once ϑ is set, the theoretical received transmission power between two edge sensor motes at a relative angle can be adjusted using:

$$P'_r = (1 \pm \vartheta) \times P_r. \tag{2}$$

With Equation 1 and 2, and using dB form of the final adjusted received transmission power P'_f as previously mentioned, the theoretical packet delivery ratio P_{prr} of a virtual link can be calculated as:

$$P_{prr} = p(P'_{f\mathrm{dB}} > \xi_{\mathrm{dB}}) = Q(\frac{\xi_{\mathrm{dB}} - P'_{r\mathrm{dB}}}{\sigma_{\mathrm{dB}}}). \tag{3}$$

Using the radio propagation models enables the users to test their algorithms under different settings, and provides a starting point for virtual link simulation. However, the general free-space and two-ray models may not be able to accurately describe the radio link path loss or fading parameters due to reasons such as occasional obstacles or temporary interferences from other sources. Hence, in MagicLink design, we further adjust the packet reception ratio P_{prr} using the measured data.

Dynamically changing radio link quality: Since wireless links are extremely sensitive to environmental changes, capturing the dynamically changing behavior of a wireless link becomes an indispensable task for link simulation. Although the causes of a link quality fluctuation can be complex, we observed that when all radio links surrounding one sensor node exhibit sudden changes of packet reception ratio, it is highly possible that problem occurs at that sensor node, i.e., low battery level or presence of physical obstacles in the near vicinity. Based on this observation, we can safely infer that the virtual link should also be affected and adjust its link quality accordingly. In order to make our model reflect this temporal property of a link, we introduce a link quality coefficient ψ to adjust virtual link quality. ψ is calculated as *the percentage changes between current link quality and link quality of previous period.* When the motes surrounding a sender all experience link quality degradation or improvement, given the theoretical packet delivery success rate, P_{prr}, we have the adjusted packet reception rate P'_{prr} over virtual link as:

$$P'_{prr} = \psi \times P_{prr}. \tag{4}$$

By integrating the anisotropic and dynamic properties, MagicLink's adaptive radio model can emulate the radio communication in high-fidelity, and user applications' reliability and robustness can be thoroughly investigated.

4   Resource Mediation

Resource mediation is a collection of operations that maintains and updates sensor nodes and virtual link information. These operations mainly take place on gateway computers. Resource mediation functionalities corresponds to the initialization and monitoring components on the left hand side of virtual link pool in Figure 3. Initialization of testbed is a static, one-time operation, which includes user configuration and bootstrapping, while monitoring is a periodically executed procedure, which can be further categorized as sensor and Internet status monitoring. New status report message will trigger a virtual link records update in the virtual link pool. This update is essentially an adjustment of the theoretical link quality values in accordance to measured real link status. We elaborate these operations in this section and illustrate them in the order of temporal execution sequence within the lifetime of the testbed.

4.1   User Configuration

To setup MagicLink across multiple sites, as shown in Figure 1(b), users are asked to provide the following parameters through a user interaction interface to establish the initial platform topology:

- Information about how these SSNs to be connected, especially the gateways' network locations.
- Virtual link distances and environmental parameters, this information is used for initialize the adaptive radio connection models. The orthogonal distance of two adjacent SSNs, e.g., SSN 1 and SSN 2 in Figure 1(b), are provided by users to initialized the basic topology.
- Sensor status monitoring frequency, this parameter is adjustable depending on the specific user application features.

At this point, we assume that user has already obtained privilege of accessing these SSNs to construct their testbeds. We will not elaborate on the associated resource discovery and authentication mechanisms. The information provided by users will be used to evaluate the initial link qualities. By default, local SSN topology and transmission power information will be used.

4.2   Bootstrapping

Since users may not have all the sensor mote connection information, a bootstrapping phase is necessary to assist virtual link pool initialization. Based on the testbed federation information specified by a user, the procedure of bootstrapping includes: (1) identifying which locally connected sensor motes are selected as edge nodes for cross-site communication; (2) calculating the relative distances of edge nodes according to user defined orthogonal testbeds distance; (3) evaluating the default values for each link's quality metrics according to MagicLink's radio model. After bootstrapping, each sensor node in a local testbed will establish connections to several remote edge nodes as its neighbors in the federated platform.

4.3   Status Monitoring

The status monitoring component contains two parts running on different hardware: the *sensor network status monitor* running on each edge node and *Internet status monitor* running on each gateway computer.

Sensor network status monitor: In order to facsimile the important properties of radio links, Sensor network Status Monitor (SSM) is employed to assist virtual link simulation. The packet reception rate metric P_{prr} is of primary concern, whereas average transmission latency τ_s is protocol related and can be helpful in some cases, such as real-time communication [20]. SSM runs periodically and measures the aforementioned metrics to provide a reference for simulating physical channel characteristics.

One advantage of designing SSM as a configurable component is that it can easily be adjusted in accordance to different application contexts. First, depending on various usage scenarios, users can choose to enable or disable SSM at any time. Take a data gathering application for example, when the primary concern of the user application is to collect sensed data, rather than to investigate the network protocol behavior, SSM is unnecessary and can be safely turned off. On the other hand, if user application requires link status monitoring, SSM can either be reused by the user application to alleviate programming burden, or simply be replaced by user's own monitoring program as long as the same status report message format is used. SSM can also be customized in terms of scheduled execution time and frequency in accordance to user needs.

Once the SSM component is configured, it measures packet delivery rate by sending out probing message during the "idle" time of an application. During each probing period, a fixed number of messages are sent out, and the packet delivery ratio of a link is estimated by dividing the number of received packets by the expected packet number. To elaborate, for each edge node n_i, packet reception rates between each of its neighbors are measured. Given P_{prr}^{ij} as the reception rate between n_i and n_j, the average reception rate for edge node n_i with m neighbors is: $\sum_{j=0}^{m} P_{prr}^{ij}/m$.

Although transmission latency is a relatively less significant factor in sensor networks comparing to packet reception ratio (many simulators simply ignore this factor), in a hybrid system like MagicLink, transmission latency can be useful to some extent. The measurement for latency τ_s is provided as an optional function, and is evaluated by subtracting the time when a packet is sent from the time when an acknowledgement is received by the sender. Assume τ_s^{ij} is the packet transmission latency between sensor node n_i and n_j. For edge node n_i with m neighbors, its average one-hop transmission latency is: $\sum_{j=0}^{m} \tau_s^{ij}/m$

Internet status monitor: Similar to SSM, Internet Status Monitor (ISM) measures Internet link qualities between gateway computers at a user configured frequency. Packet reception rate and packet transmission latency are also relevant metrics we use to quantify link qualities. Depending on the underlying protocol used, Internet connections can be very reliable, thus measuring Internet reception rate is primarily used for preventing extreme cases, such as loss of connection.

As to packet transmission delay, there is a rich literature on accurately measuring transmission delays between Internet host computers, e.g, [21, 22]. We adopted the algorithm proposed in [22]. For gateway computers within the same Internet domain, average transmission delay τ_i is usually within 10 milliseconds. This is about the same delay as typical one-hop radio transmission without using any MAC or other protocols. If the SSM measured radio transmission delay τ_s is significantly larger than τ_i, which implies possible heavy data traffic or large packet size, the message forwarding component of MagicLink will interfere accordingly. On the other hand, for cross-domain Internet connection, a longer delay may present. If this is the case, a notification to users will generate for proper settings of timeout thresholds, if applicable.

5   Adaptation and Dispatching

Virtual link adaptation and message dispatching is the core operation that actually achieves resource stitching among distributed sensor network sites. It establishes a virtualization layer that hides the underlying geographical and connection heterogeneity. The objectives of link adaptation and messaging dispatching are manifold: (1) providing joint messaging interface between radio links and Internet; (2) performing virtual link lookup and forwarding packets to appropriate virtual links; (3) emulating radio link behavior by adaptively adjust message dispatching operations on virtual links according to real radio link environments and conditions.

5.1   Send/Receive Interface

On the edge sensor nodes of each SSN, whenever a radio message is broadcasted, both the radio interface and serial/USB interface should be involved such that local and remote neighboring nodes can hear this transmission. A customized send/receive interface, which is implemented on top of TinyOS, is provided in MagicLink to handle this job. Users invoke this interface the same way as the built-in radio send and receive functions in nesC, with the same destination address format.

5.2   Message Forwarding

A message queue is implemented as a container to store sensor network application messages on a gateway computer. In addition to the raw messages transmitted within the sensor networks, time information is also included in each message stored in the message queue for referencing purpose by certain applications. Once an edge node transmission is heard by the gateway, which means the transmitted message should be forwarded onto the virtual links, the gateway will insert this message into the message queue. Messages are popped out and forwarded by the message dispatcher. Virtual link lookup operation is implemented to guarantee messages are forwarded to the proper destination. In addition, different virtual links may have different packet reception rates according to the adaptive ratio model explained in Section 3. Packet forwarder processes each message based on the adaptation rules and forwards it to the virtual links selected by the link lookup operation.

5.3 Adaptation

Virtual link adaptation refers to emulating the properties of wireless radio links on the Internet connections. Based on the virtual link quality measurements, some messages in the message queue may be intentionally dropped to simulate a packet loss. In other words, the time to forward packets on the virtual link is dependent on the adaptation policy configured by the end user in MagicLink. If a user turns on the transmission delay adaptation in MagicLink configuration, the packets forwarding time will be affected accordingly. Particularly, when the gateway connections delays are much less than radio transmission latency, the packet forwarding operation is intentionally postponed. If the latency on the Internet is similar to that on the radio links, packets are forwarded immediately.

6   Performance and Usage Cases

To validate our implementation of MagicLink system and demonstrate the effectiveness of the radio model used, we tested two representative usage scenarios, single hop communication and multihop communication, on a federated testbed constructed by MagicLink. The testbed is configured as follows: a total of 32 sensor nodes are deployed at University of Florida and Oklahoma State University. Each site configured 4×4 Telosb sensor motes arranged in a grid topology with a node to node distance of 9 feet. At each site, there is one gateway computer (fitPC2) connected to these sensor motes for reprogramming and power supply. Four motes from each site were configured as edge nodes. They all had SSM installed and communicated through the send and receive interface provided by MagicLink. Virtual links are set as 9 feet in distance as well, and use the same transmission power level as radio communications. The variance σ is set to 7.6 as adopted by NS-2 to indicate office environment with soft partitions.

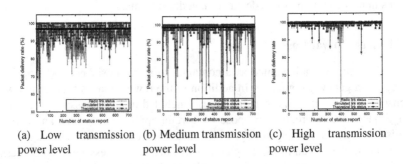

(a) Low transmission power level   (b) Medium transmission power level   (c) High transmission power level

Fig. 4. Single hop link quality comparison: real radio link quality versus virtual link quality

6.1   Single Hop Communication

One advantage of using MagicLink is to achieve smooth cross-site communication; we tested the performance of MagicLink's radio model by comparing the quality of real

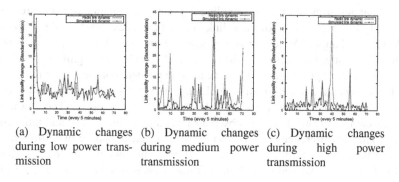

(a) Dynamic changes during low power transmission

(b) Dynamic changes during medium power transmission

(c) Dynamic changes during high power transmission

Fig. 5. Single hop transmission dynamics: real radio link versus virtual link

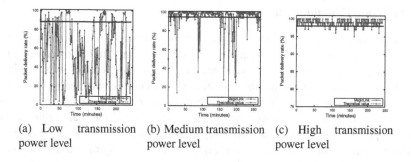

(a) Low transmission power level

(b) Medium transmission power level

(c) High transmission power level

Fig. 6. Multihop communication across two sites at different transmission power levels

radio link with the virtual link. We randomly selected one edge node at each site to form a virtual link. Packet reception rate (PRR) is used as the comparison metric here. By letting one edge node send probe messages via the send interface at the frequency of 120 messages per second, both neighbors at the local site and the virtual neighbors at the remote site can hear this transmission. Upon receiving a message, an acknowledgement is transmitted back to the sender in order to collect status information. Three transmission power levels were tested, and virtual link adjustment was twice per second. This experiment was conducted continuously for 6 hours to thoroughly exploit the dynamic property of our radio model. We plot the results in Figure 4 and 5.

In these figures, the red lines show the fluctuation of radio link qualities, the straight blue lines stand for the theoretical packet reception rate, a constant value calculated by the methods used in NS-2 [23] and some other simulators, and the green lines represent the virtual link variations in MagicLink. From Figure 4 one can observe that the adaptive radio model used in MagicLink vividly emulates the lossy and dynamic behavior of radio transmissions, which is hard to manifest by the previously proposed theoretical radio simulation model in other projects. In addition, with the increase of transmission power, radio communication becomes more reliable, and both MagicLink and the constant model show a better result in approximating link quality. Figure 5 quantifies the dynamic changes of radio links by sampling the standard deviation of packet reception rate in every five minutes. Both radio link and virtual link exhibit similar fluctuation of link quality changes. At some rare cases, e.g., time 40 in Figure 5(c), one can observe that the standard deviations of virtual link and radio link are significantly different comparing to other approximations. This can be explained that the radio link dynamic created by the adaptation method in MagicLink is probabilistic in nature (refer to Equation 4), and the virtual link is also affected by the anisotropic property. Therefore, some cases may deviate greatly from the observed variations of the nearby real links. Similarly, this kind of difference appears also in two real radio links or two different time periods of the same radio link under identical environments, making our MagicLink virtual links behave like real radio links in these aspects too. However, MagicLink is designed to be flexible that with proper configurations, user can acquire the desired level of link emulation.

6.2 Multihop Communication

Multi-hop communication is one of the key features in many applications targeted at large-scale sensor networks. In this set of validation, we set up a multi-hop configuration implemented by MagicLink and recorded packet delivery rates at different transmission power levels. The implementation of a multi-hop configuration enabled by MagicLink is depicted as follows: from the federated testbed, we randomly selected one sensor node at each site to form a 4-hop communicate path, three of them are radio connections while the rest one is virtual link. We plotted the end-to-end packet delivery rate at different transmission power levels in Figure 6. From the figure we draw two conclusions. First, MagicLink successfully accomplishes cross-site communication. The pattern of the end-to-end packet transmission path agrees with many theoretical analysis, e.g., [24]. When transmission power level is low, end-to-end link quality is very poor and shows significant dynamics over time. With the increase of transmission power level, the overall link quality is improved. Again, the constant blue lines in all three figures show that the theoretical link simulation is not capable of capturing the dynamic changing link property. In contrast, the mixture multi-hop model represented by the red lines suggests that MagicLink seamlessly stitches the two simulation sites by rendering similar multi-hop communication patterns as within the same local sensor testbed.

7 Related Work

The maturing of sensor network technologies has resulted in increasing demand for large-scale sensor experiment platforms for fast prototyping and experimentation. Due to the high cost of sensor motes and computation/memory limitations for high-fidelity simulation, existing approaches for providing such experiment platform mainly fall into two categories: hybrid simulation and testbeds virtulization.

Hybrid simulation approach emphasizes on using real sensor network data, such as radio link status measurements and sensed data, as the input to simulators to improve simulation quality. This approach is adopted by SensorSim [26] and Kansei [25]. In SensorSim, real sensed data from a limited number of sensor motes are collected as input to the simulator in order to test applications' response to environmental changes. In Kansei, the sensor network simulator on a computer is connected to real sensor nodes, and the radio communication is performed by real radio hardware on these sensor nodes. Their methods are viable to small-scale simulations, but may not be applicable to large-scale simulations due to message congestion.

Testbeds virtualization, on the other hand, focuses on creating a mapping between deployed real testbeds and virtual nodes in a computer to visualize testbeds topology and communication paths. Typically, in a virtualized testbed, there are more simulated sensor nodes than real sensor nodes. For example, in NetTopo [7] the authors created avatars for each real sensor node in a simulator. The WISEBED project [8] and [6] proposed a testbed federation method that is conceptually similar to MagicLink's design. However, despite the conceptual similarity, a high-fidelity radio model that is critical for seamless cross-site communication is missing from all these existing approaches, and MagicLink is the essential missing piece for accomplishing smooth testbeds federation and virtualization.

An essential component for sensor network experiment platform is its radio communication module. To better reflect the communication performances, there exist a rich literature on modeling of radio link properties. Two broad classes for modeling are widely used in simulation of radio transmission behaviors in WSNs, namely analytical models and empirical data based models.

For analytical modeling of radio signal attenuation, the physical layer features of a wireless link are captured by the radio signal attenuation formulas. It provides a simplified and straightforward description of wireless communication between sensor nodes. Many simulators adopt this approach to build up connections in a simulated network. NS-2 [23] calculates received power at a receiver according to a user defined distance. This power level is compared to (1) the receive threshold (RT), and (2) the carrier sense threshold (CST). If it falls below CST, the packet is discarded as noise. If the received power is between CST and RT, the packet is marked as an error packet. Otherwise, if received power is above RT, the packet is conceived normal. Similar approaches that using theoretical model to determine packet transmission rate are also adopted by GloMoSim [27], ATEMU [28], and SWAN [29]. In MagicLink, we leverage the analytical models to setup initial values for each virtual link. However, to reflect dynamic features of radio communications, MagicLink periodically adjusts virtual link quality metrics and values at runtime. This continuous refreshing process is a great leap forward towards more realistic radio model, and makes Magiclink suitable for investigating the reliability and robustness of real-world sensor applications.

An alternative approach to model radio links is to use empirical data. With the help of radio quality trace files, simulators can provide diverse environment settings for radio link simulations, making it a more favorable approach to many simulator implementations. In TOSSIM [30], the simulator loads the empirical data files to generate statistical models for each link. Although this approach offers more flexibility, it consumes huge memory space for simulating a network (e.g., 10MB per node), which hinders its application to large-scale network simulation. Several researches used smoothing and fitting methods to statistically analyze the experimental data samples, e.g., [31] and [32]. Instead of using the one-time-gathered trace data, MagicLink's radio link model includes an online algorithm that is capable of dynamically adjusting virtual link status based on the monitored real links. since anisotropic property is also important for building a convincing radio link model. Zhou et al. [18] proposed a radio irregularity parameter, Degree of Irregularity (DOI), to quantify radio propagation patterns in sensor networks. MagicLink incorporates this DOI metric and assimilates the anisotropic feature to build a topology-aware virtual link for comprehensive radio transmission simulation.

8   Conclusion and Future Work

We proposed the MagicLink middleware system for building large-scale sensor network testbeds from distributed small sensor networks. MagicLink features an elastic infrastructure that flexibly integrates multiple sites of sensor networks. In order to help investigation of network protocol performance, we further proposed an adaptive radio communication model that embodies lossy, dynamic, and irregular properties of radio links. We experimentally tested representative sensor network applications on a testbed constructed by MagicLink, and showed that MagicLink possesses the desired features and reflects real radio dynamics and heterogeneity. Under the GENI initiative, using MagicLink, we are building a federated large-scale sensor network testbed that integrates multiple sensor networks across the nation with friendly web interfaces, visualization and debugging utilities. This large-scale testbed with high-fidelity "magic" virtual links is an ideal platform for evaluating and testing next-generation Internet protocols that consider sensor networks and mobile devices as first-class citizens.

References

1. TinyOS, http://docs.tinyos.net/index.php/TOSSIM
2. Werner-Allen, G., Swieskowski, P., Welsh, M.: Motelab: A wireless sensor network testbed. In: IPSN, pp. 483–488. IEEE (2005)
3. MistLab, http://mistlab.csail.mit.edu/
4. Sridharan, M., Zeng, W., Leal, W., Ju, X., Ramnath, R., Zhang, H., Arora, A.: From Kansei to KanseiGenie: Architecture of Federated, Programmable Wireless Sensor Fabrics. In: Magedanz, T., Gavras, A., Thanh, N.H., Chase, J.S. (eds.) TridentCom 2010. LNICST, vol. 46, pp. 155–165. Springer, Heidelberg (2011)
5. Sakamuri, D.: NetEye: A wireless sensor network testbed, Ph.D. dissertation, Wayne State University (2008)
6. Baumgartner, T., Chatzigiannakis, I., Danckwardt, M., Koninis, C., Kröller, A., Mylonas, G., Pfisterer, D., Porter, B.: Virtualising Testbeds to Support Large-Scale Reconfigurable Experimental Facilities. In: Silva, J.S., Krishnamachari, B., Boavida, F. (eds.) EWSN 2010. LNCS, vol. 5970, pp. 210–223. Springer, Heidelberg (2010)
7. Shu, L., Wu, C., Zhang, Y., Chen, J., Wang, L., Hauswirth, M.: NetTopo: beyond simulator and visualizer for wireless sensor networks. ACM SIGBED Review (2008)
8. The WISEBED project web page, http://www.wisebed.eu/
9. Foster, I., Iamnitchi, A.: On Death, Taxes, and the Convergence of Peer-to-Peer and Grid Computing. In: Kaashoek, M.F., Stoica, I. (eds.) IPTPS 2003. LNCS, vol. 2735, pp. 118–128. Springer, Heidelberg (2003)

10. Michael, A., Armando, F., Rean, G., Anthony, D., Randy, K., Andy, K., Gunho, L., David, P., Ariel, R., Ion, S., et al.: Above the clouds: A berkeley view of cloud computing. EECS Department, University of California, Berkeley, Tech. Rep. UCB/EECS-2009-28 (2009)

11. Li, Z., Wang, N., Franzen, A., Li, X.: Development of a wireless sensor network for field soil moisture monitoring. In: ASABE (2008)

12. Liu, X., Zhao, H., Yang, X., Li, X., Wang, N.: Trailing Mobile Sinks: A Proactive Data Reporting Protocol for Wireless Sensor Networks. In: Proc. of MASS (2010)

13. Mainwaring, A., Culler, D., Polastre, J., Szewczyk, R., Anderson, J.: Wireless sensor networks for habitat monitoring. In: Proc. of the 1st ACM International Workshop on Wireless Sensor Networks and Applications, pp. 88–97. ACM (2002)

14. Goldsmith, A.: Wireless communications. Cambridge Univ. Pr. (2005)

15. Chipara, O., Hackmann, G., Lu, C., Smart, W., Roman, G.: Practical modeling and prediction of radio coverage of indoor sensor networks. In: Proc. of the ACM/IEEE International Conference on Information Processing in Sensor Networks (2010)

16. Stoyanova, T., Kerasiotis, F., Prayati, A., Papadopoulos, G.: Evaluation of impact factors on RSS accuracy for localization and tracking applications. In: Proc. of the 5th ACM International Workshop on Mobility Management and Wireless Access, pp. 9–16. ACM (2007)

17. Zamalloa, M., Krishnamachari, B.: An analysis of unreliability and asymmetry in low-power wireless links. ACM Transactions on Sensor Networks, TOSN (2007)

18. Zhou, G., He, T., Krishnamurthy, S., Stankovic, J.: Models and solutions for radio irregularity in wireless sensor networks. ACM Transactions on Sensor Networks, TOSN (2006)

19. CC2420 radio datasheet 2nd ed. Texas Instruments (October 2005)

20. He, T., Stankovic, J., Lu, C., Abdelzaher, T.: SPEED: A stateless protocol for real-time communication in sensor networks. In: Proc. of ICDCS (2003)

21. The IDMaps web page, http://idmaps.eecs.umich.edu/

22. Gummadi, K., Saroiu, S., Gribble, S.: King: Estimating latency between arbitrary internet end hosts. In: Proc. of the 2nd ACM SIGCOMM Workshop on Internet Measurment. ACM (2002)

23. NS-2, http://www.isi.edu/nsnam/ns/

24. Zhao, J., Govindan, R.: Understanding packet delivery performance in dense wireless sensor networks. In: Proc. of SenSys. ACM (2003)

25. Ertin, E., Arora, A., Ramnath, R., Nesterenko, M., Naik, V., Bapat, S., Kulathumani, V., Sridharan, M., Zhang, H., Cao, H.: Kansei: a testbed for sensing at scale. In: IPSN. IEEE (2006)

26. Park, S., Savvides, A., Srivastava, M.: SensorSim: a simulation framework for sensor networks. In: Proc. of the 3rd ACM International Workshop on Modeling, Analysis and Simulation of Wireless and Mobile Systems. ACM (2000)

27. Ben Hamida, E., Chelius, G., Gorce, J.M.: Impact of the physical layer modeling on the accuracy and scalability of wireless network simulation. Simulation (2009)

28. Polley, J., Blazakis, D., McGee, J., Rusk, D., Baras, J.: Atemu: A fine-grained sensor network simulator. In: IEEE SECON (2004)

29. Liu, J., Perrone, L., Nicol, D., Liljenstam, M., Elliott, C., Pearson, D.: Simulation modeling of large-scale ad-hoc sensor networks. In: Proc. of European Interoperability Workshop (2001)

30. Levis, P., Lee, N., Welsh, M., Culler, D.: TOSSIM: Accurate and scalable simulation of entire TinyOS applications. In: Proc. of SenSys. ACM (2003)

31. Cerpa, A., Wong, J., Kuang, L., Potkonjak, M., Estrin, D.: Statistical model of lossy links in wireless sensor networks. In: IPSN (2005)

32. Sundresh, S., Kim, W., Agha, G.: SENS: A sensor, environment and network simulator. In: Proc. of the 37th annual symposium on Simulation. IEEE Computer Society (2004)

Data Filtering and Aggregation in a Localisation WSN Testbed

Ivo F.R. Noppen[2], Desislava C. Dimitrova[1], and Torsten Braun[1]

[1] Universität Bern, Bern, Switzerland
{dimitrova,braun}@iam.unibe.ch
[2] Universiteit Twente, Enschede, The Netherlands
i.f.r.noppen@alumnus.utwente.nl

Abstract. The main challenge in wireless networks is to optimally use the confined radio resources to support data transfer. This holds for large-scale deployments as well as for small-scale test environments such as test-beds. We investigate two approaches to reduce the radio traffic in a test-bed, namely, filtering of unnecessary data and aggregation of redundant data. Both strategies exploit the fact that, depending on the tested application's objective, not all data may be of interest. The proposed design solutions indicate that traffic reduction as high as 97% can be achieved in the specific case of test-bed for indoor localisation.

Keywords: WSN, filtering, aggregation, WiFi, bluetooth.

1 Introduction

Wireless sensor networks provide excellent means for monitoring and data gathering in a large range of application areas. One such application is the use of radio-enabled sensor nodes for (indoor) positioning in which the sensor nodes collect signal measurements of user devices using radio transmissions, e.g., Bluetooth. Among the most frequently used radio standards are the IEEE 802.11 (with commercial name WiFi) and Bluetooth standards. Processing of the collected measurements can derive the location coordinates of the transmitting device. Potential use cases of a positioning application include, but are not limited to, analysis of visitor behaviour in shopping malls, tailored discount dissemination in attraction parks and evaluating staff efficiency in hospitals.

Inspired by the many use case opportunities, the Location Based Analyser (LBA) project addresses the indoor localisation challenge by leveraging radio frequency (RF) based technologies, namely WiFi and Bluetooth. More specifically, we use multiple sensor nodes at known positions to collect measurements on the received signal strength indicator (RSSI) from personal devices on the premises. The collected measurements are periodically sent to a central database server where they are sorted per observed device and processed to determine the current position of each device. There are various techniques to map RSSI to distance, the most often cited being (multi)lateration and fingerprinting.

T. Korakis, M. Zink, and M. Ott (Eds.): TridentCom 2012, LNICST 44, pp. 210–223, 2012.

As part of the development process of the localisation system we set up a test-bed for the purpose of testing and performance evaluation. Early in the design and testing phase we stumbled across the problem of rapidly growing sensor data. Although test-beds are designed typically at a smaller scale than the finally deployed system, challenges related to congestion of the wireless medium may arise. In addition, data storage may prove another affected aspect. In order to ensure non-disrupting operation and system scalability one needs to take care when managing the radio resources. We chose for an intuitive approach that classifies the wireless traffic and identifies what data is pertinent for the needs of the application. Possible data reduction strategies include filtering of unnecessary data, aggregation of redundant data and data compression. Data aggregation in WSNs has been largely studied [5,9,12] and evaluated in WSN testbeds [1,3,10] for the purposes of reducing traffic volume and energy consumption.

This paper describes how we adopt filtering and aggregation to minimise wireless traffic in a test-bed. Contrary to other studies, e.g., [9], which address hierarchical aggregation in the network, we are only interested in a local (on a single node) aggregation. We take as an example the case of a localisation application but the discussed data reduction strategies can be applied to a larger set of applications by modifying parameters of switching functionality on or off.

The rest of the paper is organised into the following sections. Section 2 describes the specific test-bed that we use and the encountered traffic challenges, given the application's needs. Next, Sections 3 and 4 discuss the implementation and performance of filtering and aggregation respectively. Their combined use is analysed in Section 5. Finally, Section 6 summarises the paper.

2   Localisation WSN Test-Bed

2.1   Localisation of User Devices

We designed an indoor localisation system that relies on sensor nodes at known positions, which collect signal measurements from personal devices. A central server processes the collected measurements to derive the location of the personal devices. We are interested in signals from personal devices and in signals from the sensor nodes. These signals are used to monitor the quality of the radio channel and to improve the performance of the system.

In order to test and evaluate the localisation system we built a test-bed inside a single room, which reflects the system design. Its objective is to collect measurements of signals from personal devices and reference sensor nodes. The test-bed contains 16 sensor nodes, which form a 4x4 grid at 0.5 meter below the room ceiling, see Figure 1. The sensor nodes scan continually for WiFi and Bluetooth signals and record the RSSI levels. Periodically, each sensor node sends its measurements to a gateway node, which collects all measurements and forwards them to the database server. At the server the measurements are stored and analytically processed. In the rest of the paper the term sensor node and sensor are used interchangeably.

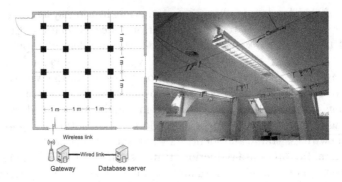

Fig. 1. LBA test-bed architecture: multiple sensor nodes (SNs), connected over WiFi to a gateway (GW). Measurements are stored in a database server (DB).

In our proposed localisation system the amount of wireless traffic depends on the number of deployed sensor nodes, the frequency at which measurements are reported, and on the number of detected or tracked devices. Additionally, there is interfering traffic from other devices that may use the same wireless medium. Since the test-bed is located in the Computer Science building of the University of Bern, there are other experimental wireless networks and wireless access infrastructures that use the same radio channels. We consider traffic from such networks and WiFi access points, e.g., beacons, as non-informative since measurements regarding these devices contribute neither to the localisation of devices nor to the radio channel monitoring. Therefore, these are unnecessary measurements and while we cannot always avoid their collection we can prevent their transmission to the central server. To this end we apply filtering.

Another factor that directly affects the busyness of the radio channel is the proportion of collected measurements per device. For each device several measurements may be collected by one sensor while a single measurement would suffice for localisation. Clearly, reporting all measurements would be redundant and we would like to minimise the radio channel utilisation. This can be achieved by decreasing the amount of data to send. Therefore, we explore the use of data aggregation.

2.2   Test-Bed Implementation

As sensor nodes we used Gumstix Overo Fire devices [2] with integrated on-board Bluetooth and WiFi interfaces, which support the scanning of the wireless medium. Moreover, we attached an additional WiFi card, which is used for communication between the sensor node and the gateway. On the sensor nodes, we run a light Linux kernel and several lightweight packages to keep the sensor as lightweight as possible. This sensor software is built using the Administration and Deployment of Adhoc Mesh (ADAM) framework [11] which includes the custom packages needed for running the Bluetooth and WiFi scanners. WiFi measurements are collected by capturing packets on the wireless interface with *libpcap*, an application programming interface for capturing network traffic, and by hopping through the WiFi channels with an interval of one second. Bluetooth measurements are recorded by using output from the *bluez* Linux Bluetooth library. When the measurement buffer is full or a predetermined period has ended, the measurements are flushed to the gateway. All the sensor nodes and the gateway are situated in the same local network.

The gateway and the database server both run on a regular Linux distribution. The gateway can reside on both a desktop machine or a sensor node, as long as there is a wired connection available for the communication to the database server. The communication is through a SOAP web-service. At the database server, we use a regular MySQL databases.

3   Filtering

One strategy to decrease traffic in the test-bed (and any other wireless network) is to transmit only data that is pertinent. Filtering is a method that can successfully omit the collection and transmission of unnecessary measurements. The choice of an appropriate filtering solution needs an answer to three *design questions*: what to filter, where to filter and how to filter.

What to filter. A filtering solution is needed that can identify unnecessary measurements and only allow the transmission of measurements on user devices (used for localisation) and reference sensor nodes (used for channel estimation). As discussed earlier, we consider measurements on signals from experimental wireless networks and WiFi infrastructure, e.g., access points (APs), as unnecessary. We refer to the former group as 'always-on devices' and to the latter - as 'fixed infrastructure'. Each group requires different filtering strategies as it is explained later.

Where to filter. Three places can be identified in our system where we can employ filtering: the sensors, the gateway and the database server. Filtering at the sensors has a direct impact on buffer occupation and on wireless traffic but is challenging due to their limited resources while the decision what to exclude needs large sets of measurements. The only benefit of filtering at the gateway is the decreased traffic towards the database server. However, often bandwidth is not a problem since wired connections are used generally. Moreover, the gateway also does not have knowledge on long-term data. On the database server, we have both the capacity and the measurements at our disposal to support a decision making for filtering. Hence, it is a more appropriate system for the filtering decision process.

How to filter. Filtering can be based on black- or whitelisting of certain MAC addresses. When a certain MAC address is blacklisted, all measurements of that MAC address are discarded. When a MAC is whitelisted, all measurements related to it are collected. The choice of strategy depends entirely on the application's objective. In a controlled environment, when the target group of devices to monitor is well defined, whitelisting is the better choice since we are only interested in measurements from a limited set of known MAC addresses. In realistic environments, where we have no control over the target devices, whitelisting is not feasible because the targeted MAC addresses are not known beforehand. In such case blacklisting is the better choice.

Another classification criterion is how the decision what to filter is taken. If we collect the MAC addresses and enter them manually into the filtering system we call this *static filtering*. Static filtering is time consuming, requires effort and does not scale well. A better alternative is *dynamic filtering*, which introduces certain intelligence in the system. Such a system integrates decision making processes to analyse incoming measurements and decides what MAC addresses to filter out.

3.1   Filtering Solution

Taking into account the requirements of the current experimental test-bed we chose a dynamic blacklisting strategy with static elements and static whitelisting support, which we term combi-listing.

Static Blacklisting. Static blacklisting refers to the filters that are directly installed at the sensor to filter out signal measurements from the fixed infrastructure (APs). An AP contributes significantly to the wireless traffic because (i) it typically sends a beacon message every 100ms and (ii) it serves multiple clients in parallel. Note that measuring this kind of traffic is undesirable, independently of the specific WSN application.

Filtering of the fixed infrastructure is quite easily done at the sensor nodes using the two distribution system (DS) flags in a WiFi packet [4] that indicate sender (first bit) and receiver (second bit): 0 for mobile device and 1 for AP. Hence, since they already use *libpcap* to capture packets at the WiFi interface, we only need to create an additional rule to discard all packets with the type 'Beacon' or DS flags 10 or 11 (first bit 1 indicates AP originating traffic). Static blacklisting is implemented using the existing *libpcap* functionality.

Dynamic Blacklisting. Static blacklisting on top of *libpcap* is not feasible for the identification of always-on devices that behave as any other device but are active continually or for long periods of time. Instead we use a dynamic blacklisting technique that combines a decision making process, which periodically generates blacklists, and a dissemination process, which distributes the blacklists to the sensor nodes.

Decision making. The decision making process is situated on the central server and is responsible for the generation of the blacklists - one for each sensor node. The process relies on one commonality between all always-on devices, namely, they are generally connected 24/7. Therefore, if we analyse the collected measurements over a long period we should be able to identify always-present MAC addresses that correspond to always-on devices.

Formally a device in our test-bed can be identified by its MAC address and *activity level*, i.e., the percentage of time in which measurements of its MAC address were received. The activity level is calculated over a specific *evaluation period*, which is the timespan over which the list of blacklisted MAC addresses is generated. For example, if a device was active for two hours within an evaluation period of eight hours it has an activity level of 25%. If we define an activity level threshold and a device's activity level is above this level we can deduce that this is an always-on device. The choice of the threshold is very important and related to the duration of the evaluation period. For instance, it is fair to say that a threshold of 80 or 90% should allows the identification of always-on devices.

An easy way to implement the proposed decision making is to count the number of distinct timestamps for a specific MAC address and divide this by the total number of seconds in the evaluation period. However, there are disadvantages to that in our test-bed. First, our WiFi-scanner hops channels every second. Second, if an always-on device is only connected to the network and not actively transmitting it will have only few measurements. To correct for this, we divide the evaluation period into equal-length *activity periods*. Per MAC address, we check within each activity period whether there is at least one measurement of this address. If this is the case we mark the period as true, otherwise we mark it as false. If we now count the number of activity periods marked as true and divide that by the total number of activity periods in the evaluation period (equation 1) we will get the percentage of time that this MAC address has been active. We can derive the number of activity periods by dividing the evaluation period by the activity period, both measured in seconds.

A simple comparison of the activity level threshold with the activity levels of all MAC addresses detected within the evaluation period will give us the MAC addresses to include in the blacklist.

$$ActivityLevel = \frac{count(ActivityPeriod\_True)}{EvaluationPeriod/ActivityPeriod} \qquad (1)$$

Dissemination. The dissemination of blacklists is pull-based. The procedure is shown in Figure 2. The sensors request the blacklists from the central database server via the gateway node. The server can answer, also via the gateway, either with a new blacklist, when available, or with an empty message, when the sensor polled too early and no update is available yet. Note that the new blacklist from the server can contain no MAC addresses when there are none to filter out. If a sensor should blacklist certain MAC addresses it filters out their measurements but keeps statistics for each of the blacklisted address. Periodically this information is sent back to the server, where it is used to re-evaluate whether the MAC address should stay blacklisted. Without these statistics the decision support process will loop into a repetitive adding and removing of MAC addresses to the blacklist.

The dissemination procedure is implemented by extending the test-bed functionality and introducing three new message types, namely, blacklist request, blacklist update and blacklist aggregate messages. Either on start-up or after a timer expires, the sensor nodes request a blacklist through the gateway using a *blacklist request* message. The message contains a *timestamp* of the current

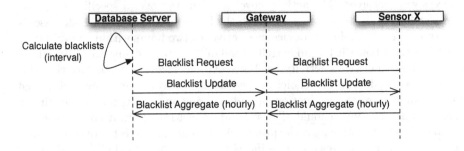

Fig. 2. Message exchange between sensors, gateway and database server regarding the blacklist

blacklist at the sensor and the *type* of blacklist the node is requesting (Bluetooth or WiFi).

The server answers with a *blacklist update* message, which contains the *timestamp* of the list in the update, or the timestamp of the blacklist request if no newer update is available. The *checkback-time* field suggests how many seconds will pass between the timestamp and the time a new blacklist will be available. The *list size* field tells us how many MAC addresses the complete blacklist contains. The *update* flag indicates if a new list is sent (flag 1) or if the sensor polled and there is no update (flag 0). When there are no MAC addresses to blacklist the flag is 1 (true) but the list size is zero and the MAC addresses field is empty. The length of the MAC addresses field for a non-empty list depends on the list size field.

Upon receiving the blacklist update message the sensor replaces the old blacklist with the new one and resets the timer according to the checkback-time field. For each blacklisted MAC address the sensor collects statistics and reports them hourly back to the server in a *blacklist aggregate* messages. The blacklist aggregates message contains one or more structures depending on the number of blacklisted MAC addresses. Each structure contains the MAC address of the blacklisted device along with the first-seen and last-seen timestamp, the number of measurements between the two timestamps and the average RSSI. The count is used to make a decision whether a MAC address has to remain blacklisted.

Static Whitelisting. Static whitelisting is used to ensure the collection of measurements on the reference sensor nodes which are used for channel evaluation in the test-bed. For that purpose the MAC addresses of all reference sensor nodes are identified and a specific whitelist for each sensor is kept at the central server. The server is responsible to check that a MAC address from the whitelist does not become blacklisted.

Alternative Solutions. The proposed distribution of node-specific blacklists uses many unicast connections, which may lead to depletion of radio resource if a large-scale sensor network is considered. Therefore, the realisation of the filtering solution may need modifications in order to scale down service traffic. One possible approach is to broadcast the blacklist, that is the same for all sensor nodes in a specific area (the area size depends on the communication range of the radio technology). In addition, each sensor can pull its specific whitelist from the central server when coming online.

3.2   Experimental Analysis

In this section we present results on the data reduction that filtering can bring but first we discuss some parametrisation issues.

Parametrisation. Integrating the proposed filtering solution requires setting up some parameters such as the blacklist evaluation period and the activity period. For our purposes we selected an evaluation period of 24 hours, which aligns easily with human activity. Choosing a good value for an activity period is more challenging. In order to analyse this, we set up a test, where we included a fixed WiFi device (laptop) in idle mode in the test-bed. The device was only connected to a wireless network with no data traffic exchange. We let the sensor nodes collect measurements over 65 hours and calculated the activity level of the idle and the most frequently seen device at each of the sensor nodes for an activity period of 60 and 300 seconds. Corresponding box plots over all sensors are given in Figure 3.

A successful deployment should be able to filter out the idle device's MAC address as well as other high activity MAC addresses (most frequently seen device). As we can see in Figure 3, an activity period of 60 seconds will not lead to a successful identification of the idle device as 'always-on' since its activity level reaches only about 42% on average. When we change the activity period to 300 seconds the activity period of the idle devices rise up to 90% and it can be easily identified for blacklisting. The reason for the above behaviour is the idle status of the device in which case it communicates to the networks once every few minutes. Note that the most seen device is less vulnerable to short activity periods and easily reaches 80-90% of activity because it is actively transmitting.

Traffic Reduction. To quantify the gains in terms of reduced number of measurements we conducted the following experiment. First, the testbed ran for full 24 hours, after which both Bluetooth- and WiFi blacklists were generated for each node. Then, in a second 24 hours run no filtering was directly applied but the generated blacklists were used to calculate, for the same data set, what the measurement reduction would have been. This provides us a common base for comparison since we are using the same data set. In the filtering decision the parameters are: *activity level* > 0.8, *activity period* $= 300$ seconds, *evaluation period* $= 86400$ seconds (24 hours).

Table 1 provides detailed statistics on the measurement reduction per sensor node. The reduction is the percentage of measurements that will not be transmitted if using filtering. Interestingly, the size of the generated blacklist is rather small although the test-bed location would suggest much larger wireless activity.

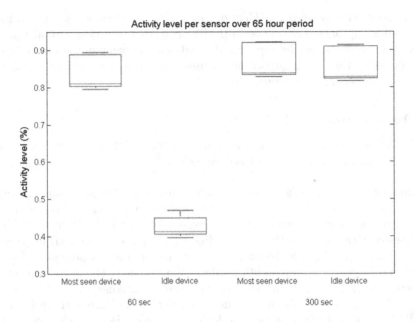

Fig. 3. WiFi: Activity level over all sensors for the most active MAC address and an idling device when the activity period is 60 seconds

We explain that with the fact that the experiments were conducted on a weekend when there are significantly less people, and hence always-on devices, in the building.

In terms of reduced measurement values the results show that the effect of filtering is significant. The reduction with combi-listing includes whitelisting of the MAC addresses of the other sensor nodes for reasons discussed earlier. For deployments where whitelisting is not needed the gains in reduction would be even bigger. This trend is better visible in Figure 4 for WiFi - the mean measurement reduction per sensor without whitelisting is about 93%, more than 10 percentage points higher than the mean reduction with combi-listing, i.e., the combined use of black- and whitelists.

For Bluetooth we registered even higher measurement reduction with 99.76% on average. We explain that with the smaller (six times) proportion of Bluetooth devices in our test-bed environment compared to the number of WiFi devices. As result one Bluetooth MAC address contributes more to the total number of measurements. In addition, the range of Bluetooth is smaller than for WiFi and therefore less devices will be detected in general. Note that whitelisting is not included because there are no addresses to be whitelisted for Bluetooth (we do not use Bluetooth signals in channel characterisation).

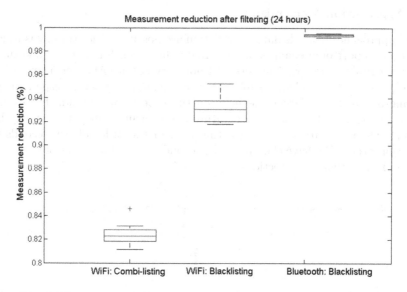

Fig. 4. Measurement reduction comparison over all sensors after filtering

Table 1. Overview of WiFimeasurements in the second 24 hour period in the experiment

Sensor	Total measurements	Reduced measure-ments	Reduction [%]	Blacklisted MACs
1	408.453	74.569	81.7%	26
2	458.547	83.204	81.9%	26
3	425.139	76.017	82.1%	26
4	416.985	72.839	82.5%	25
5	432.813	72.880	83.2%	27
6	404.987	71.233	82.4%	26
7	418.635	74.164	82.3%	25
8	412.666	76.420	81.5%	25
9	441.695	83.182	81.2%	26
10	390.836	70.235	82%	26
11	394.006	71.564	81.8%	26
12	441.728	78.060	82.3%	25
13	427.409	72.928	82.9%	26
14	364.902	62.817	82.8%	26
15	268.988	63.144	82.9%	25
16	414.818	63.914	84.6%	26

4   Aggregation

Aggregation of data (measurements) is another strategy that can improve the utilisation of the limited radio resource and decrease the chances of collision. Generally speaking aggregation is a technique to decrease the amount of measurements sent over the wireless channel while retaining the measurements credibility. In sensor networks aggregation has been proposed to decrease energy consumption [8,12] or network congestion [5]. We are interested in using aggregation to decrease network traffic and improve scalability since the current deployment of electrically powered sensor nodes does not face energy consumption challenges.

4.1 Aggregation Mechanism

Several approaches towards data aggregation are possible. One strategy is to let the sensors report only changes in measured values, which is not suitable since RSSI vulnerable to external factors and not very stable. Another aggregation method is to send a single measurement (e.g., mean, max) per timespan where the timespan duration largely depends on the type of application. For example, for monitoring of ambient temperature one measurement per hour may be sufficient while for target tracking a timespan in the order of few seconds is more appropriate. We have chosen for the second option; the choice of timespan duration is investigated in Section 4.2.

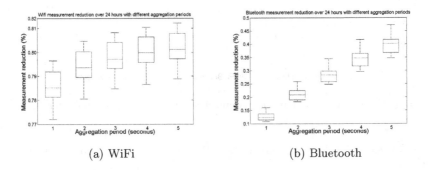

(a) WiFi   (b) Bluetooth

Fig. 5. Measurement reduction over different timespans of aggregation

In addition, we need to select which value to report. In the case of RSSI we expect that the maximum value would be best since it is the least affected by propagation conditions. The feasibility of other choices such as an average value or another statistic registered over the aggregation timespan are discussed in another study, namely [6].

An alternative approach to decrease wireless traffic is data compression [7]. Instead of using the redundancy in measurements data compression gains from redundancy in the data itself by applying appropriate encoding. Although beneficial it also requires additional processing.

To enable the chosen aggregation strategy in the test-bed two buffers are set at the sensor nodes - one that collects all raw measurements and another for the reported values. When the first buffer is full, or at the end of a reporting period, all measurements are processed and the maximum RSSI per MAC address is written into the second buffer. Then, it flushes the data to the gateway.

4.2 Experimental Analysis

To determine the measurement reduction we can achieve by applying aggregation, we used the same experiment setup as for the filtering experiment. We took measurements over the first 24 hours and calculated the measurement reduction if each sensor would apply aggregation. Given the mobility of the tracked device, we chose o aggregate over timespans of one to five seconds. We have chosen to report the maximum RSSI value since we believe they are least affected by propagation factors. The calculations were done for both WiFi- and Bluetooth signals.

Results for WiFi are shown in Figure 5(a), where boxplots of the reduction achieved by each sensor node (y-axis) are plot against the used timespan (x-axis). As expected, aggregation significantly affects the measurement traffic and in our cases leads to a reduction in the number of measurements by more than 79% on average for a one-second timespan. Increasing the timespan to five seconds does only marginally improve the reduction to 81%. The reason for this is twofold. On the one hand, not all devices are broadcasting every second. On the other hand, the WiFi-scanner hops the wireless channels every second. Since devices communicate with a network on a single channel, we will not see their MAC addresses after this second again until we completed the cycle of channel-hopping.

In Figure 5(b) the results for Bluetooth show different patterns - the measurement reduction has an almost linear increase when we increase the timespan. More notably the measurement reduction grows from 12% to 40%, a less dramatic improvement than in the case of WiFi. The number of measurements we collect for Bluetooth are far fewer than the measurements collected for WiFi, reflecting the ratio of devices that use the two technologies. Based on the results we can conclude that the optimal value of the aggregation period for Bluetooth depends on the application needs.

5   Combined Filtering and Aggregation

While the individual measurement reduction of both filtering and aggregation shows great promise, it will be interesting to know if we can gain even more by applying both techniques in the same sensor network. To analyse this, we again used the results of the estimated measurement reduction experiment for the filtering and calculated the total measurement reduction when we apply aggregation (with one-second timespan) on top of that.

Figure 6(a) shows the results for WiFi measurements. For comparison reasons we include the results for filtering as shown in Figure 4. Aggregation adds an additional gain on top of the reductions that can be achieved by black- and whitelisting. Differences between blacklisting and whitelisting are consistent with previous observations - disabling whitelisting leads to even higher reduction. In our specific case, given we chose to apply a combi-listing, the combined reduction will be on average just shy of 94%.

The results of combining filtering and aggregation for Bluetooth are shown in Figure 6(b). For reference, the results on using only blacklisting are included. The graphs show that aggregation only slightly improve performance, the reasons being the few Bluetooth devices that the system detects and the efficient filtering of always-on devices that already brings measurement reduction of almost 99.8%. Although we are aware that the results are sensitive to the specific system deployment, we expect that aggregation will lead to smaller reduction in

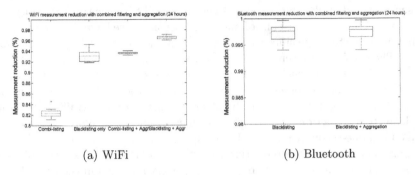

(a) WiFi   (b) Bluetooth

Fig. 6. Measurement reduction for combinations of blacklisting, whitelisting and aggregation

measurements for Bluetooth than for WiFi due to the typically lower number of Bluetooth devices. Note that there is no whitelisting for Bluetooth since in the current deployment it is not used for channel estimation.

6   Conclusion

This paper deals with radio traffic challenges arising in wireless sensor test-beds. We showed how the traffic volume can be greatly reduced by leveraging filtering and aggregation independently and combined. We achieved reductions of 80% on average with a peak above 95%, depending on used settings. Without this reduction in traffic, the testbed would not be able to scale well when extended to large testing sites due to the limited resources on the sensors and congestion of the radio medium.

The reductions were achieved for an experimental test-bed consisting of 16 sensor nodes deployed indoors for the purpose of testing a positioning system based on WiFi and Bluetooth technologies. Therefore, the chosen parameter setting were specifically tailored to the system. Still, the described approaches of filtering and data aggregation can fit to a diversity of WSN applications by simply alternating component combinations (filtering) or fine tuning of parameters (aggregation). For example, an environmental monitoring application can tolerate long aggregation periods, radio echo profiling can use only whitelisting the deployed sensors but an assisted/ambient living application may prefer pure blacklisting, since whitelisting requires human participation.

The presented evaluation and results have relevance beyond the scope of wireless test-beds. We are confident that filtering and aggregation strategies can also help real-world deployments to scale better and to make better use of the limited radio resources. We are aware that both mechanisms have a downside, e.g., wrongly identifying a device as always-on in filtering or loosing measurements details in aggregation, but we believe that a careful parametrisation can eliminate the effects. In addition, compression techniques could further bring the size of the transferred data down.

References

1. Greenorbs test-bed, `http://greenorbs.org` (accessed: January 27, 2012)
2. Gumstix overo, `https://www.gumstix.com/store/`
   `product_info.php?products_id=227` (accessed: January 27, 2012)
3. Honk kong university, internet and mobile computing laboratory test-bed,
   `http://www.comp.polyu.edu.hk/en/research/centres_labs/internet_and_`
   `mobile_computing_laboratory/index.phpm` (accessed: January 27, 2012)
4. IEEE 802.11-2007, Wireless LAN Medium Access Control (MAC) and Physical
   Layer (PHY) Specifications (2007),
   `http://standards.ieee.org/about/get/802/802.11.html`
5. Chen, Z., Shin, K.G.: Opag: Opportunistic data aggregation in wireless sensor
   networks. In: Real-Time Systems Symposium 2008, pp. 345–354 (2008)
6. Dimitrova, D.C., Alyafawi, I., Braun, T.: Experimental Comparison of Bluetooth and
   WiFi Signal Propagation for Indoor Localisation. In: Koucheryavy, Y., Mamatas, L.,
   Matta, I., Tsaoussidis, V. (eds.) WWIC 2012. LNCS, vol. 7277, pp. 126–137. Springer,
   Heidelberg (2012)
7. Dolfus, K., Braun, T.: An evaluation of compression schemes for wireless networks.
   In: International Congress on Ultra Modern Telecommunications and Control Systems, pp. 1–6 (2010)
8. Krishnamachari, L., Estrin, D., Wicker, S.: The impact of data aggregation in
   wireless sensor networks. In: Proc. of Distributed Computing Systems Workshops,
   pp. 575–578 (2002)
9. Kumar, V., McCarville-Schueths, J., Madria, S.: A test-bed for secure hierarchical data aggregation in wireless sensor networks. In: 2010 IEEE 7th International
   Conference on Mobile Adhoc and Sensor Systems (MASS), pp. 762–764 (November
   2010)
10. Murty, R.N., Mainland, G., Rose, I., Chowdhury, A.R., Gosain, A., Bers, J., Welsh,
    M.: Citysense: An urban-scale wireless sensor network and testbed. In: Proc. of
    IEEE Technologies for Homeland Security, pp. 583–588 (2008)
11. Staub, T., Morgenthaler, S., Balsiger, D., Goode, P.K., Braun, T.: Adam: Admin-
    istration and deployment of adhoc mesh networks. In: 3rd IEEE Workshop on Hot
    Topics in Mesh Networking (IEEE HotMESH 2011) (2011)
12. Taghikhaki, Z., Meratnia, N., Havinga, P.J.M.: Energy-efficient trust-based aggre-
    gation in wireless sensor networks. In: IEEE INFOCOM: Workshops, pp. 584–589
    (2011)

A Framework for Resource Selection in Internet of Things Testbeds

Michele Nati[1], Alexander Gluhak[1], Hamidreza Abangar[1],
Stefan Meissner[1], and Rahim Tafazolli[1]

University of Surrey, Guildford, GU2 7XH, UK
{m.nati,a.gluhak,h.abangar,s.meissner,r.tafazolli}@surrey.ac.uk

Abstract. As the scale and heterogeneity of experimental environments
increases, the selection of adequate testbed resources becomes a daunting task for the experimenter. Wrong choices or unexpected resource
behavior can significantly decrease an experimenters productivity. These
challenges are further amplified by the recent trend of moving testbeds
from isolated labs to unpredictable real world environments to favor experimental evaluation under realistic conditions. This paper presents a
framework for resource selection in large scale and heterogeneous Internet of Things testbeds, in order to support the experimenter with an
increased understanding of available testbed resources, their expected
behavior and topological relationships in the experimentation environment. Through an evaluation case study we demonstrate the effectiveness
of our proposed framework.

Keywords: Testbeds, Resource selection, Internet of Things, Wireless
Sensor Networks, Semantics.

1 Introduction

The promise of the Internet of Things (IoT) to bring new levels of efficiency
and increased real world insights to a variety of business domains has fueled
research in the recent years with the aim to make this vision become a reality.
However, the lack of understanding how existing solutions can operate in various real world environments as well as the missing consensus on technologies and
standards across different business sectors has hampered the wide scale deployment of IoT solutions. There is a growing need to evaluate, compare and bench-
mark emerging IoT solutions on larger scale and outside lab environments under
realistic operational conditions and to mature these solutions further through
experimentally driven research.

While suitable experimentation environments and testbeds are slowly emerging [1], there is still a lack of adequate tools in order to support user friendly
and efficient experimentation in such environments [2] with reduced management complexity. In particular features such as increased heterogeneity of these
testbeds and their scale represent severe challenges for the experimental users as
well as the testbed management tools that are necessary to manage efficiently

T. Korakis, M. Zink, and M. Ott (Eds.): TridentCom 2012, LNICST 44, pp. 224–239, 2012.
© Institute for Computer Sciences, Social Informatics and Telecommunications Engineering 2012

available testbed resources. For example the selection of an adequate set of experimentation resources for a planned experiment can be a daunting task in an environment of thousands of experimentation resources, with different capabilities and time-varying properties if the user is provided with non-intuitive user interfaces such as simple resource list which are commonly used in today's testbeds. Similarly testbed management tools must provide reduced complexity for testbed administrators to manage a potentially large number of experimentation resources. These tools must take into account the time-varying properties of testbed resources and their surrounding environment in order to provide users with reliable information for their selection and to optimize the re-use of the underlying testbed substrate for concurrent experiments.

In this paper, we present a framework for large scale and heterogeneous Internet of Things testbeds, which allows experimental users to efficiently select resources to fulfill specific experimentation requirements based on static and time varying properties of available testbed resources. More concretely we make the following specific technical contributions that are integrated into an holistic framework:

- We propose a mechanism that allows an experimental user to quickly verify whether there are suitable resources for an experiment based on static properties of the testbed. For this purpose an ontology for describing IoT testbed resources has been developed together with a semantic query mechanisms that identifies a suitable set of resources based on matching required properties to those of available IoT testbed resource description instances.
- We provide a tool that allows a user to visually explore the topology for the resource required for an experiment and further scope the exploration by specifying constraints such as time-varying properties of links between IoT resources.
- We provide mechanisms to efficiently update properties of resources in the system to closely match real world changes to the testbed infrastructure and surrounding environment.
- We describe an implementation of the above framework and evaluate its effectiveness on a case study in our testbed

The remaining paper is structured as follows. Section 2 surveys existing work, while section 3 provides an overview of our framework for resource selection, putting it into the context of IoT experimentation environments. Section 4 describes in more detail realization of our proposed framework components and underlying information models. In section 5 we evaluate the effectiveness of the proposed framework using a detailed case study and present conclusions in section 6.

2   Related Work

In the following section we briefly discuss related work in the field and how our work differs and improves on it. In particular we focus on how resource selection in existing Wireless Sensor Network and IoT testbeds is supported and how resources in these testbeds are described.

2.1   Resource Selection in Existing WSN and IoT Testbeds

The increasing trend in the field of Wireless Sensor Networks (WSNs) and IoT research to test the effectiveness of the proposed solutions on a real hardware deployments motivated the creation of a multitude of IoT testbeds and the development of numerous custom solutions for their management [2]. Most of the proposed solutions provide basic functions for executing experiments on top of a given set of resources, such as reprogramming resources with a given test image, resetting them in order to start and stop an experiment and to stream back debug messages generated at run-time by the selected resources to a central server, mainly through the use of a wired backbone infrastructure. Examples of such frameworks are MoteLab [3], TWIST [5] and their clones or evolutions, such as for instance the INDRIYA testbed [2]. These frameworks were mainly used to manage a set of homogeneous sensor nodes as experimentation resources and provided the user with little support in selecting suitable ones apart from a list-view providing not much more information than the unique identifier of the resource. Such approaches for resource selection put an increasing burden on the testbed user for larger testbeds with heterogeneous nodes.

In order to present topological relationships between nodes and environmental dependencies, some frameworks provide views to display a deployment map of the testbed resources, showing the hierarchy of the testbed infrastructure components [4] and/or physical links that may exist between different nodes [3]. While serving as decision aid for the experimental user, they are based on static information data bases that have been obtained through previous experiments or by manual user entry. Furthermore resource selection is still carried out manually through list-views, making it a tedious tasks for experimental users. In order to better capture the characteristics of heterogeneous resources, the WISEBED [6] framework defines an XML based language called WiseML able to describe testbed resources and topological links they may have. In order to select adequate experimentation resources, users must still either browse these WiseML descriptions or generated lists from these XML documents. Similarly, SWORD [17] represents an example of an XML based declarative resource discovery service for wide-area distributed systems, which successfully operates on top of overlay testbeds such as PlanetLab.

Our framework complements the above efforts by providing a holistic solution to simplify resource selection for large scale and heterogeneous IoT testbeds and corresponding framework management services.

2.2   Description of Testbed Resources

The increased heterogeneity in testbed hardware and the need to provide access to testbed resources in the context of federated testbeds has motivated more descriptive approaches of expressing resource capabilities inside of a testbed framework. Initial approaches made use of XML based description formats. Examples thereof are the aforementioned WiseML format or the RSpec [9] format of the ProtoGENI and PlanetLab control framework. The cOntrol, Management and Measurement Framework (OMF) developed within the ORBIT testbed, introduced a domain-specific language named OEDL [10], which allows to describe experiment specific resource requests through a Ruby based scripting language.

The potential of exploiting machine processing capabilities for the development of advanced testbed tools that increase the autonomy of testbed operation and productivity of the testbed users have seen semantic resource descriptions recently emerging. An early example is the Network Description Language (NDL) [11], its extension NDL-OWL and the Network Markup Language (NML).

There have been other attempts developing XML and RDF based resource descriptions for sensor networks, which are however not focused at modeling these as testbed resources. Examples are the Sensor Model Language (SensorML) [12], the Semantic Sensor Network specification of W3C [13] or OntoSensor [14]. These efforts mainly focus on the sensing capabilities and observations or how to expose sensors as service endpoints in web service architectures.

More closely to our work on semantic modeling of IoT testbed resources is the recent work of Ju et al. [7]. In their work the authors propose an ontology for describing heterogeneous resources of wireless sensor network called LENS (Language for Embedded Networked Sensing) which has been integrated within the testbed framework developed by KanseiGeni initiative [8]. In contrast, our approach does not propose an ontology model from scratch, but instead extends the recent W3C ontology on Semantic Sensor Network [13] by specifying further details pertinent to IoT testbed resources. While there are similarities in modeled concepts, there a differences in properties and how the relationships of concepts are expressed. Furthermore, the authors of [7] do not provide any details on the mechanisms to populate and maintain the static and dynamic properties of these models within the testbed framework during operation.

3   Overview of Framework Architecture

Experimentation on existing IoT testbeds typically follows an experimentation life-cycle that comprises different activity stages, including experiment specification, preparation of experimentation resources as well as the execution of experiments and the subsequent analysis of experimentation data [2].

One of the most critical task is the experimentation scenario design and the selection of appropriate testbed resources for the envisioned experiment. The latter is particularly challenging for large scale IoT testbeds such as the emerging SmartSantander facility [1] as the experimental user is confronted with thousands of possibly heterogeneous experimentation resources with different capabilities and specific connectivity characteristics, constraint by their deployment environment. This is further complicated by that fact that experimentation resources may fail or become temporarily unavailable for experimentation due to connectivity failure or other ongoing experimentation tasks. Furthermore time-varying interference levels at wireless experimentation resources due to ongoing experimentation at neighboring experimentation nodes or external sources may have an influence on the suitability of a particular experimentation resource.

Figure 1 shows a high level overview of the architecture of our proposed IoT experimentation framework. As can be seen from the figure, the framework functions and support tools are exposed through a graphical user interface called *TMON* towards the experimental users of the testbed. *TMON* allows simplified and user friendly access to a variety of different testbed services which are able to support the experimentation users during all stages of experimentation. This includes access to functions that assist the user during experiment specification and resource configuration phases but also during experiment execution and experimentation data analysis.

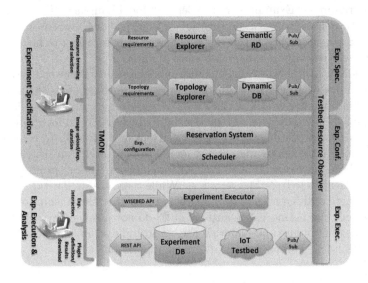

Fig. 1. Overview of the architecture of the proposed IoT framework for resource selection and management

For supporting the resource selection phase, the framework provides two dedicated functional components, the *resource explorer* and the *topology explorer* in order to assist the user with an exploration of available testbed resources and their static and dynamic properties and topological interdependencies. In our framework testbed resources and the preliminary static capabilities they provide are described by semantic resource descriptions, which are stored in a RDF data base. Through *TMON* a user can formulate visually queries for specific resource properties in order to satisfy the requirements for a particular experimentation scenario. The resource explorer evaluates these queries and performs a semantic matching against the semantic resource descriptions (RD), in order to provide the user with a selection of testbed resources fulfilling the desired properties. Once an initial subset of resources has been selected, the *topology explorer* allows a user to explore the topological relationships and characteristics of the links between nodes. As this information is quite dynamic and may change in particular for wireless links, it is updated regularly by the testbed management framework and kept in a separate database. This data base also includes other dynamic properties such as the interference levels experienced in different wireless channels. *Testbed resource observers* that are attached to each testbed resource are able to detect the availability of new testbed resources, as well as corresponding status and topology information and ensure that the information available to the proposed testbed framework functions are always up-to-date. The preliminary event based communication is realized through a publish subscribe messaging bus inside of the framework.

Once a user has selected a suitable set of experimentation resources, the experimentation specification is completed through *TMON* by provisioning of images for experimentation and the specification experimentation timing requirements. The experimentation configurations are passed to the reservation system and scheduler for execution of the experiment. An *experiment executor* controls the execution of experiments and allows testbed users to interact with the experiments. During the experimentation phase, experimentation results and traces are collected to an *experimentation database*. *TMON* provides the user with different views to the experimentation data, allowing quick visual inspection of the behavior of an experiment during execution or a detailed analysis after experimentation.

The discussions in the remaining paper will focus on the components and tools that allow efficient specification of testbed resources.

3.1   Resource Exploration

The purpose of the resource exploration tool is to simplify the discovery of available experimentation resources and the identification of a suitable sub-set for an envisioned experiment. The design of an adequate experimentation scenario is not an easy task and requires the user to have a thorough understanding of the underlying testbed resources, their capabilities and inter-relationships. For larger testbeds such information may be difficult to know or obtain upfront. Starting with a rough idea for an experimentation scenario an experimentation user will explore the availability of suitable resources and may iteratively adapt and refine the experimentation scenario to match the characteristics offered by a testbed environment. The availability of critical information for the resource selection process is crucial, so is the efficiency with which such information can be accessed and searched directly by the human experimenter or by tools supporting him.

In order to leverage the increased machine processing capabilities of the growing eco-system of the semantic web, one of our design decision has been to semantically describe our testbed resources. Instead of reinventing an ontology from scratch for our resource model, we have carefully evaluated existing state of the art ontologies in the sensor network and IoT domain and selected the Semantic Sensor Network (SSN) ontology [13] as a starting point. We have then extended

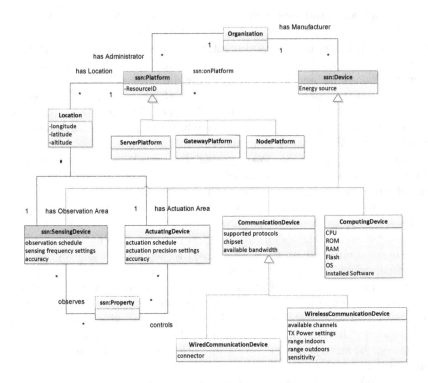

Fig. 2. UML diagram of the resource description model

the SSN ontology with concepts that are pertinent to IoT and sensor network testbed resources, including the most critical information that an experimenter may require for an adequate selection of testbed resources. Figure 2 provides an overview of the key concepts of SSN highlighted in grey and our proposed extensions.

Our proposed resource model takes into consideration the three possible device tiers that state of the art IoT facilities [2] are comprised of, by subclassing platforms for IoT node tier, gateway tier and server tier from the original SSN platform concept. A platform is deployed at a particular location, which has implication for most of the different devices that it hosts. Devices that are attached to a platform can be computing and communication devices and for the IoT node platforms often sensing and actuation devices. Communication devices can be wired or wireless. Sensing devices observe properties of their surrounding environment, which are constraint to a particular observation area. Likewise actuator may influence properties within their respective actuation area. The SSN ontology so far only specifies sensing devices.

For each of the concepts a variety of attributes have been defined that may be of relevance to the experimenter for resource selection. Experimentation code, e.g. a protocol implementation, is often developed based on a particular operating system, e.g. TinyOS and may have certain requirements on processing capabilities or available memory of the underlying node platform. It is therefore important to know whether there are nodes supporting the execution of the experimentation code. Some experiments may require specific sensing capabilities and/or cover specific geographic locations with these. In other cases experimenters may have a specific interest in communication devices available at IoT and GW nodes and what settings are possible for their configuration during experimentation. It is important to note that our proposed resource model is a starting point and will evolve as new hardware or software features become available or new experimentation use cases emerge.

The resource descriptions are created an maintained in a triple store, which can be queried through a SPARQL query engine. In order to hide the user from the details of constructing SPARQL queries, our resource explorer provides an front-end for visual query specification. These query specification contain the above described resource types available, constrained by desired properties and required numbers. The visual query specifications are then translated by the resource explorer into a set of SPARQL queries which are submitted to the query endpoint. Only those resources will be returned that satisfy the filters applied in the query. While gaining quickly effective feedback about availability of suitable resources, the user can use the identified subset as a starting point for further topology exploration.

3.2 Topology Exploration

Based on the nature of an experiment, an experimenter may be interested also to investigate the relationship among the resources and between the resources and the experimentation environment. The *topology explorer* provides the experimenter with an interface to explore these relationships based on an underlying physical network topology model as depicted in Figure 3 for IoT node platforms. A physical topology consists of node platforms and links. A link is defined between two communication devices that are hosted by a node platform. Each link is described by a source device and by a sink device, thus two links between to devices may exist with their specific properties. This is in particular the case for wireless interfaces where link behavior is inherently asymmetric. Furthermore in order to account for interference in an experimentation environment a corresponding interference module describes the perceived interference at the sink side of a link.

Examples of a topology visualization are provided in provided in figures 4 and 5. The topology explorer takes as input a node set and a particular setting configuration of the communication devices. For example, for an 802.15.4 based radio, the interface takes as input one of the 16 available channels and one of the transmission power level available for the radio chip featured by the respective resource. Based on this information, all the links connecting the selected resources are visualized. The topology explorer also offers the possibility to filter only the links with specific properties in terms of Packet Error Rate (PER), Link Quality Indicator (LQI), Receive Signal Strength Indicator (RSSI). A given

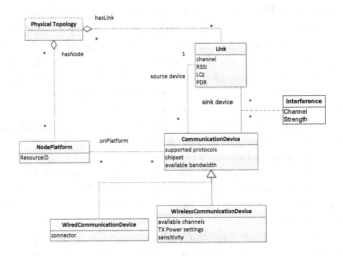

Fig. 3. UML diagram showing topological relationships between resources

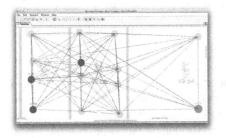 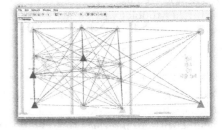

Fig. 4. TMON Topology Explorer, inter-ference free topology

Fig. 5. TMON Topology Explorer, inter-ference affected topology

pre-defined sets of topology exploration rules are also defined, implemented and accessible to the user in order to highlight nodes forming a connected component, nodes forming a clique, or all the nodes geographically connected to a selected destination sink. Further user-defined rules can be also easily defined based on a plug-in mechanism provided by the *TMON* interface, which offers APIs for accessing topology information and their visualization.

Figure 4 shows the nodes that are geographically connected (yellow nodes) to a selected sink (green node) with a path made by only nodes closer to the sink than the considered node and for a given selected configuration of channel (20), power level setting (7) and PER (0.9). Red nodes represent dead-end nodes in a geographic sense, while blue nodes (not present in the considered topology) are the disconnected ones, because no links between them and the rest of the topology exist for the selected parameter. All these provided information allow the user to gain a better understanding of the relations between resources and check if they match what it will expect to see during its experimentation phase in terms of topology connectivity, multi-hop path between a given source and destination nodes or other features.

Apart from displaying available links between nodes, a user can also explore existing interference affecting the links in an experimentation environment. For a scenario similar to that depicted above (channel 15, power 7, PER 0.9), Figure 5 shows the interference that was present during the characterization of the respective links by highlighting the occurrence of interference above a certain threshold level with exclamation mark symbols next to the affected links and by changing the node shape to a triangle. By adjusting channels and interference levels an experimenter can thus quickly determine where his experiment may be affected by an overlapping interferer in the environment. In our initial implementation, we consider as interference sources the presence of WiFi Access Point operating close to a resource in a range of frequencies overlapping with those selected by the user for its experiment. A range of configurable parameters for selecting the interfering sources based on the quality and power of the IEEE 802.11 signal affecting a given resource is also provided to the user. Our model can be extended to other interferer based on available detection mechanisms in the testbed.

The outcomes of both resource and topology exploration phase is a set of suitable experimentation resources that can be further reserved and configured for subsequent experimentation.

3.3 Resource Observation Plane

The resource and topology explorer are only effective, if the information kept in the underlying information models about the resources is up-to-date and reflects the current conditions in the testbed. This is the responsibility of the *testbed resource observer* in our framework. *Testbed resource observers* have two primary tasks. The first one is to keep track of the availability status of testbed resources in the testbed and detectable changes to resource properties and reflect those in the semantic resource descriptions. The second task is to keep continuously track of topology and environmental related information of the testbed, such as link characteristics or experienced interference levels in the surroundings and reflect those in the topology data base. In the following we describe the realization of each of the two functionalities in more detail.

The first time a new resource is added to the testbed, an administrator provisions a semantic resource description (possibly by customizing a pre-existing template for a resource type), which is added to semantic resource database. This ensures that only authorized resources are able to attach to the testbed framework. These descriptions are only removed, if an administrator decides to discontinue the use of a particular testbed resource.

Our assumption for our framework is that IoT testbeds follow a three tier architecture, which is the case for more advanced IoT testbeds of larger scale [2]. In such architectures, IoT nodes attach to GW tier devices which in turn attach to server tier devices. The *testbed resource observer* function is realized by a distributed process framework that is mainly deployed across nodes of the server and gateway tier. *Testbed resource observer* instances of the GW tier not only observe information about their own node, but also take care of observing directly attached IoT nodes. In the case of a two tier architecture with no GW tier, the testbed resource observer instances on the server tier take care of directly attached IoT nodes. Our design tries to minimize the reliance on IoT node tier as much as possible, due to the resource constraint nature of these devices to support a dedicated observation plane stack in parallel to experimentation code.

Availability information for testbed resources is kept as soft-state and requires periodic update from *Testbed resource observer* instances. Respective instances report the resource identifier of the corresponding testbed resources they are responsible for using registration messages, which are matched against the semantic resource descriptions in the data base. Only previously configured resources are considered. Resource identifiers are in the form of URNs composed of a testbed identifier prefix (preconfigured by an administrator at the testbed resource observer instance) and a unique resource identifier that can be discovered local at a resource. The latter can be the MAC address of the interface through which a node attaches to the testbed or a serial id for the case of some IoT devices, e.g TelosB.

While the update process for server tier and GW tier devices is straight forward, some more details for the IoT tier need to be explained. The *testbed resource observer* instances of the GW device discover directly attached IoT nodes either through implicit detection of their attachments or through an explicit registration of the IoT node instances. The first case works well for IoT nodes that are connected through a wired infrastructure. For example in our testbed all sensor nodes are attached via USB connections to the GWs, which can discover attachment and detachment of USB devices by observing the USB bus events or device maps of the underlying operating system. In the case only wireless links exist to IoT resources, each IoT resource must be configured with a bootstrap image that is able to communicate availability information and minimum device properties (such as the resource id) to the *testbed resource observer* instance of a gateway device. Apart from updating availability information or changes to properties that can be locally detected, e.g. energy levels, *testbed resource observer* instances also update discovered topology related information between IoT nodes and GW nodes.

A more complex process is the maintenance of IoT node related topology information and environmental characteristics such as interference for which the *testbed resource observer* relies on further support functionality. The update of the IoT node related topology information is coordinated across different testbed resource observer instances and requires the explicit installation of a profiling image on the IoT nodes. The outcomes of such characterization is then reflected by the resource observers in the topology database. Update of IoT node topology related information is carried out automatically at periodic intervals during idle time of the testbed resources or based when significant changes in interference are detected in the surrounding environment. In order to avoid interference with ongoing or scheduled experiments, the profiling activities are carefully coordinated using knowledge on utilized channels from the experiment specifications. The interference characterization of the environment requires interference detectors to be present at the gateway nodes. As our IoT nodes operate in the 2.4 GHz ISM band, WiFi interferer represent the major problem. Our current implementation characterizes interference caused by WiFi access points in the surroundings by frequently scanning available sources and recording the corresponding channels together with signal strength and quality indicators through a WiFi card attached to the gateway node. As a GW device and directly attached IoT nodes are physically close located in our testbed architecture, we make the simplifying assumption that the measured interference at the GW nodes caused by the presence of WiFi signals also affects the IoT nodes in the same manner. The *testbed resource observer* updates the corresponding information in the topology database. Interference characterization takes also place at the same time link characterization experiments are performed. As interference characterization does not rely on code executing on IoT nodes, it can take place more frequently, even during user generated experiments, and annotated to the corresponding experimentation data.

Finally the testbed resource observer instances communicate with framework services and between each other through a publish subscribe messaging bus. Our current implementation is based on an MQTT broker and client implementations. However details of the underlying communication framework is out of scope of this paper.

4 Evaluation Use Case

In the following we present a WSN protocol evaluation as an initial case study to demonstrate the usefulness of the resource selection framework in our IoT testbed. The evaluation is carried out in the SmartCCSR IoT testbed deployment, which is part of the SmartSantander experimental facility. The testbed consists of 250 freely programmable sensor nodes deployed in a real world office environment across the two floors of the CCSR building, at the University of Surrey, covering all the desks and communal areas of the research centre. The deployed IoT nodes consist of 200 TelosB based platforms and about 50 SunSpots, which are heterogeneous in their sensing capabilities. While the SunSpot platforms provide only on-board sensing capabilities (accelerometer, temperature, light), the TelosB platforms provide various sensing modalities varying from on-board sensors such as temperature, light and humidity to external sensors mounted on a custom board providing energy metering, noise and light levels, temperature and motion.

The WSN protocol utilized in this case study is a TinyOS implementation of a geographic routing protocol for wireless sensor networks [15]. The goal is to carry out an initial small scale evaluation of protocol behavior on a dense multi-hop connected network with approximately 15-20 nodes. Figure 6) shows an overview of all experimental resources on the first floor of the building.

A first challenge the experimenter is faced with is to find suitable testbed resources out of 250 available experimentation nodes inside of the building that match the expected node platform and topology requirements. While sensing modalities are not important for the experiment, the experimenter knows that all nodes with energy meters attached to it are currently utilized for a longer term study [16]. Furthermore the experiments must be run on TelosB motes as Sunspots do not support execution of his TinyOS based experimentation code. Through *TMON*, the user specifies desired resource properties in a visual query, indicating TelosB as node platform type and to use nodes with no energy meters as sensing devices. Figure 7 shows the result of the query, which identifies a subset of these nodes matching the requirements. Only 14 nodes are available, however a visual inspection with the topology explorer allows the user to verify that a suitable connected multi-hop topology exists, which will be otherwise a tedious process.

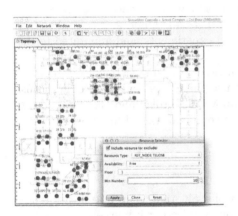 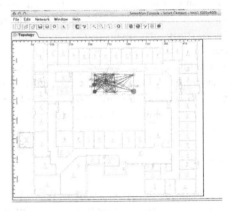

Fig. 6. TMON Topology Explorer, 1st floor testbed deployment

Fig. 7. TMON Topology Explorer, resource query result

Having identified a potentially suitable resource set, the experimenter now has to chose a suitable channel and power level for its planned experimentation. In order to have a fully connected multi-hop topology with the existing geographic distribution, the user requires to fine tune of the transmission power the selected set of nodes carefully. Using topology explorer, he can observer a fully connected topology at a transmission power level of 7. He further discovers potential dead-end nodes that are good experimentation cases for the behavior evaluation of the protocol.

However the protocol performance and behavior greatly depends on the behavior of the links between the experimentation nodes. Lack of detailed knowledge about the link behavior and environmental interference can lead to misinterpretation of the protocol behavior, which we will try to demonstrate in the following experimentation scenarios.

Table 1 summarizes 5 scenarios that show different channel that are affected by different levels of interference coming from WiFi access points in the surroundings. While the Scenarios 1 to 4 are derived using the knowledge gained by the system during the link characterization phase, the Scenario 5 is artificially created by modifying the testbed environment at experimentation time.

Table 1. Experiment scenarios

Scenario	802.15.4 Ch.	Interfering 802.11 Ch.	Affected nodes	Degree of Interference
1	11	1	14/14	High
2	15	2	11/14	Medium
3	16	6	5/14	Low
4	20	None	0/14	None
5	20	7	2/14	Very Low

We ran our geographic routing protocol 5 consecutive times, each over a period of 15 mins with an average generation packet rate of 1 packet every 2 seconds. In each of the considered scenarios, we compute the fraction of packet successfully delivered to the sink (PDR) and their end-to-end latency. During each run the *Testbed observer* characterizes the interference environment and we use this data for annotating each set of results. No deviations were observed to the interference previously captured in our resource models, apart for the Scenario 5 for with we intentionally turned on an new Access Point in the nodes proximity that operates on a new interfering channel (7). The results of the evaluation are reported in Table 2.

Table 2. Experiment results

Scenario	PDR	End-to-end Latency (s)
1	0	0
2	0.75	1.42
3	0.98	2.42
4	1.0	2.96
5	1.0	2.84

As expected, in an high interference scenario, such as 1, no packet are received. This is due to a characteristics of our protocol, that performs a Clear Channel Assessment of the channel based on energy level before each transmission. Due to the high interference strength affecting all the nodes in this scenario, all of them are prevent to transmit any packets. In order to exclude possible bug in the protocol, it has been tested with the same channel on a different set of nodes, not affected by this interference. The behavior of the other scenarios is quite predictable based on the collected interference information. The medium interference scenario performs better then the high interference one, with 75% of the packet delivered, but performs worse to the scenario 3 and 4 were less interference is experienced. This is due to the fact that interference prevents some node to deliver their packets, as they appear to be disconnected from the topology. As expected an higher PDR translates in an higher traffic for the network and in an higher latency experienced in delivering packets. Finally, as expected, Scenario 5 behaves very similar to Scenario 4, due to the very low interference the nodes are exposed.

Even for the small scenario that we presented for reason of simplicity, the experimenter would have had difficulties to explain the protocol behavior for randomly selected channels without such explicit knowledge of interference provided by our framework. He could have confused protocol behavior for an implementation bug or spent significant amount of time playing with channel setting in order to find a suitable topology characteristics. As the scale of experiments and testbeds grows, the benefits of our framework become even more evident.

5   Conclusions

Our initial evaluation shows that the proposed resource selection framework provides a useful tool when experimenting in unpredictable real world environments of larger scale with heterogeneous testbed resources. It allows experimenters to become more productive by providing an increased understanding of available testbed resources, their expected behavior and topological relationships in the experimentation environment. In the coming months, the proposed framework for resource selection will be integrated into the Santander testbed site, which represents a urban scale outdoor experimentation environment. We believe that such tools are essential for more productive experimentation in such challenging IoT testbed environments. While the initial focus of our work has been on catering towards the challenges of IoT environments, our framework could be applicable to testbeds of other Future Internet technologies. We have already started work on integrating mobile phone based experimentation devices into our framework and hope to investigate soon the required adaptations and the effectiveness of our framework in federated Future Internet testbeds.

Acknowledgment. This work has been partially supported by the European Union under contract numbers ICT- 2009-257992 (SmartSantander) and ICT-2009-257521 (IOT-A).

References

1. Smartsatander Project, http://www.smartsantander.eu/
2. Gluhak, A., Krco, S., Nati, M., Pfisterer, D., Mitton, N., Razafindralambo, T.: A survey on facilities for experimental internet of things research. IEEE Communications Magazine 49(11), 58–67 (2011)

3. Werner-Allen, G., Swieskowski, P., Welsh, M.: Motelab: a wireless sensor network testbed. In: Proceedings of the 4th International Symposium on Information Processing in Sensor Networks, IPSN 2005. IEEE Press, Piscataway (2005)

4. Sakamuri, D., Zhang, H.: Elements of sensornet testbed design. In: Yang Xiao, H.C., Li, F.H. (eds.) Handbook of Sensor Networks, ch. 35, pp. 1–36. World Scientific Publishing Co. (2009)

5. Handziski, V., Köpke, A., Willig, A., Wolisz, A.: Twist: a scalable and reconfigurable testbed for wireless indoor experiments with sensor networks. In: Proceedings of the 2nd International Workshop on Multi-hop Ad Hoc Networks: From Theory to Reality, REALMAN 2006, pp. 63–70. ACM, New York (2006)

6. Coulson, G., Porter, B., Chatzigiannakis, I., Koninis, C., Fischer, S., Pfisterer, D., Bimschas, D., Braun, T., Hurni, P., Anwander, M., Wagenknecht, G., Fekete, S., Kroeller, A., Baumgartner, T.: Flexible Experimentation in Wireless Sensor Networks. Communications of the ACM 55(1), 82–90 (2012)

7. Ju, X., Zhang, H., Zeng, W., Sridharan, M., Li, J., Arora, A., Ramnath, R., Xin, Y.: LENS: Resource Specification for Wireless Sensor Network Experimentation Infrastructures. In: Proceedings of the 6th International Workshop on Wireless Network Testbeds, Experimental Evaluation and Characterization (WinTECH), Las Vegas, Nevada (September 2011)

8. Sridharan, M., Zeng, W., Leal, W., Ju, X., Ramnath, R., Zhang, H., Arora, A.: Kanseigenie: Software infrastructure for resource management and programmability of wireless sensor network fabrics. In: K. M. S., et al. (eds.) Next Generation Internet Architectures and Protocols. Springer, New York (2010)

9. ProtoGENI RSpec, http://www.protogeni.net/trac/protogeni/wiki/RSpec

10. OEDL - The OMF Experiment Description Language, http://mytestbed.net/projects/omf/wiki/The_Experiment_Controller_API

11. Network Description Language, http://www.science.uva.nl/research/sne/ndl

12. Botts, M., Robin, A.: OpenGIS Sensor Model Language (SensorML) Implementation Specification

13. Semantic Sensor Network, http://www.w3.org/2005/Incubator/ssn/charter

14. Russomanno, D.J., Kothari, C.R., Thomas, O.A.: Building a Sensor Ontology: A Practical Approach Leveraging ISO and OGC. In: The 2005 International Conference on Artificial Intelligence, Las Vegas, NV (2005)

15. Casari, P., Nati, M., Petrioli, C., Zorzi, M.: Efficient Non Planar Routing around Dead Ends in Sparse Topologies using Random Forwarding. In: Proceedings of IEEE International Conference on Communications, ICC 2007, Scotland, UK (June 2007)

16. REDUCE project, http://info.ee.surrey.ac.uk/CCSR/REDUCE/

17. Oppenheimer, D., Albrecht, J., Patterson, D., Vahdat, A.: Design and implementation tradeoffs for wide-area resource discovery. ACM Transactions on Internet Technology 8(2) (May 2008)

Automated Deployment and Customization of Routing Overlays on Planetlab

Claudio Daniel Freire, Alina Quereilhac, Thierry Turletti, and Walid Dabbous

INRIA, Sophia Antipolis, France
{claudio-daniel.freire,alina.quereilhac,
thierry.turletti,walid.dabbous}@inria.fr

Abstract. PlanetLab testbed is widely used to evaluate protocols and applications under realistic Internet conditions, but this realism comes at the cost of uncontrolled topology and traffic behavior. The use of overlay networks on PlanetLab can solve this problem by giving more control to the experimenter. However, manually creating such overlays is far from simple, and existing solutions are either not available for all PlanetLab nodes, or lack support for low level overlays. Deployment and customization of overlay architectures are also poorly supported. In this paper we present a flexible solution to support overlay networks on Planet-Lab, providing deployment automation, tunneling, routing, and traffic shaping capabilities. By building our solution into NEPI, a general framework for network experimentation, which automates design, deployment, and management of experiments, we simplify the complexity of building overlays on PlanetLab, and foster reusability and extensibility though NEPI's modular structure.

Keywords: networking, overlays, PlanetLab, NEPI.

1 Introduction

PlanetLab[4] is a globally distributed testbed composed of many nodes connected to the Internet. It provides support for the development of new network technologies, enabling researchers to evaluate new protocols and applications under realistic Internet conditions. It is difficult, or even impossible, to achieve the same level of realism using alternative experimentation environments, such as simulators [22], and this is what makes PlanetLab so valuable. However, this realism comes at the cost of a lack of control over the many factors that influence the outcome of an experiment, such as links, nodes, and external traffic conditions, since the researchers have no control over the Internet itself.

The use of overlay topologies on top of the Internet can mitigate this problem by giving more control to the experimenters. Overlays can be used to force specific routing topologies [2], or to analyze real traffic conditions[1,3] with a degree of fault isolation.

Still, creating overlays on top of PlanetLab is a non-trivial task because of the constraints imposed by the type of network virtualization [16,7] used to

T. Korakis, M. Zink, and M. Ott (Eds.): TridentCom 2012, LNICST 44, pp. 240–255, 2012.

allow multiple experiments to run independently in the same nodes. Setting up routes, tunnels, or IP filters, cannot be achieved by simply invoking appropriate system calls as in classical (non-virtualized or fully virtualized) environments, but requires instead the use of PlanetLab-specific tools.

Previous efforts have been made to enable the creation of overlay networks on PlanetLab, which were mainly focused on the tunneling and routing aspects. Existing solutions like PL-VINI [5] are limited because they depend on extensions or infrastructure that is not available for all nodes, and thus they do not currently work on the whole PlanetLab network. Other alternatives like Splay [9], do not suffer from this limitation, but can only be used with application level overlays. While these solutions do provide enabling technology to build overlays on top of PlanetLab, they do not solve the heavy load of manual work involved in the customization and deployment of concrete overlay experiment scenarios. In general, they do not provide enough tools to easily customize overlays, and only perform a subset of the tasks needed to run and manage experiments on top of them.

In this paper we present a solution for automatic creation and customization of overlay experiment scenarios on PlanetLab, based on NEPI [12,13], the Network Experimentation Programming Interface. Similar to other tools, our work enables the creation of virtual links over the Internet, allowing both, layer-2 switching and layer 3-routing, between PlanetLab nodes. Nevertheless, by building our solution into NEPI, we provide support for the different steps involved in the construction of overlay experiment scenarios, integrating the design, configuration, and automatic deployment on top of PlanetLab in one single tool. We refer to this aspect of experimental overlay construction as *deployment automation*. Moreover, our solution provides all the necessary mechanisms for overlay customization, including custom queues and transmission mechanisms, and the functionalities required to run applications in the overlay, like IP routing.

Efficient and flexible *tunneling* between arbitrary PlanetLab nodes is accomplished by providing several tunneling alternatives. Like RiaS [6] and Trellis [8], we support layer-2 and layer-3 tunnels with options for UDP, TCP and GRE encapsulation. However, in contrast with previous work, our solution does not require specially tailored nodes, and can be deployed in any node in the PlanetLab network.

Routing table manipulation was not possible before due to the lack of an appropriate system interface. We enhanced *routing* capabilities in PlanetLab by extending the *vsys*[11] interface to allow scalable, secure, and cooperative manipulation of nodes' routing tables, a capability on top of which our solution builds application-transparent overlay networks.

Our solution was designed to enable the use of experimental queuing and aggregation methods with low implementation overhead. It allows the researcher to easily perform *traffic shaping* within experimental overlays.

Using these tools, researchers can experiment with routing overlays on PlanetLab with minimal effort, and through NEPI they can perform the experiments repeatedly and automatically in a controlled way.

The focus of this paper will be set on the techniques used to support deployment automation, tunneling, routing, and traffic shaping capabilities for the construction of routing overlays on PlanetLab using NEPI, which we consider the be the core contributions of this work.

The rest of the paper is organized as follows: we begin by discussing the challenges involved in the development of our solution, then we cover the implementation details of NEPI overlay construction and customization support for PlanetLab. We finally evaluate the solution with a concrete use case showing how the tools we develop can benefit to the evaluation of networking protocols with increased accuracy.

2   Related Work

Two of the most complete previous solutions for low-level overlay deployment in PlanetLab are PL-VINI [5] and RiaS [6]. Both have serious drawbacks that limit their usability.

PL-VINI is an implementation of a virtual network infrastructure on PlanetLab, that uses User Mode Linux virtual machines [17] to provide full network virtualization for independent experiments running in the same node. Contrary to the Linux-VServer [16] container-based virtualization approach used natively in PlanetLab, in PL-VINI, virtual machines in the same node have direct access to the kernel network stack, making it possible to trivially manipulate routing tables and create tunnels without interfering each other.

PL-VINI has a good performance and enables to easily create layer-2 overlay topologies, but only around 40 nodes out of the many (1040) nodes in PlanetLab support it. It depends on a set of extensions to PlanetLab that have not been deployed on all nodes, and access to dedicated infrastructure that is also not globally available, making it not suitable for big scale deployments in PlanetLab.

While PL-VINI allows the implementation of custom routing and queuing algorithms, this can only be done through the Click modular router [5,21], which precludes the possibility to reuse prototype code. In contrast, our solution was crafted upon the idea of easy re-usability and it does not relinquish overlay customization to a single application, thus it makes the researcher's task of testing prototype algorithms in realistic conditions easier. Furthermore, we provide methods to run the experimental code in any PlanetLab node, expanding available resources beyond what PL-VINI provides.

Trellis [8], is another platform for network virtualization which implements container based virtual machines by using Linux network namespaces [18]. Although being the most performant alternative out there, by constructing its tunnel implementation using GRE and kernel-mode switches, it suffers from scalability issues. It creates one bridge and four taps (at least) per tunnel, all connected via virtual (software) switches, stateful and expensive to maintain objects. If every experiment running in a PlanetLab node created such tunnels, the kernel would be overwhelmed very easily. Trellis also does not respect the administrative and fair share bandwidth limits that are imposed per node (and critical) to PlanetLab. Although it does provide bandwidth management, it is not integrated with PlanetLab's mechanism, so large-scale deployment of the technique would be impractical. Like PL-VINI, it also would require heavy changes in the PlanetLab system to enable its wide deployment, and thus it remains an unavailable solution on most PlanetLab nodes.

RiaS [6], on the other hand, is supported by all the nodes in PlanetLab. It is built upon an architecture of user-mode packet forwarders that create a network of *point-to-point* links with layer-2 tunnels. By operating in user-mode, it scales significantly more graciously than previous approaches under pressure, since it is subject to PlanetLab's fair-share scheduler. However, its support for layer-3 tunneling is limited because nodes with more than one interface (routers) in the overlay topology are required to be PL-VINI nodes, thus for layer-3 tunneling RiaS shares PL-VINI and Trellis limitations.

RiaS is heavily focused on layer-2 experiments, and because of this its architecture is ill-suited for layer-3 overlays. It only implements layer-2 routing techniques, to circumventing PlanetLab nodes' inability to set IP routes at the kernel level for one, and to support experimentation with arbitrary layer-2 protocols. It works more like a switch than a router. This imposes limitations on the experiments, since RiaS by itself provides no layer-3 routing, and nodes cannot reach other networks. Since RiaS does it all in user mode, it incurs heavy CPU overhead, resulting in artificial bandwidth and scalability limits, and packet loss well above that experienced in the underlying network. Rias does provide some support for overlay deployment automation, in the form of a Resource Allocator and Virtual Network Mapper tools. Although these tools consider the topology level of an experiment, they do not cover the application level.

Other solutions like Splay [9] and Plush [14], do not even support low level overlays (i.e. at layer 2 or 3), but rather they build application-level overlays. Splay [9] is a good example, as it automates deployment both at topology and application levels, has good performance, and is easy enough to use. However, it only handles packets at the application level. Even its packet loss models apply at the application level, which is an inaccurate rendition of link packet loss in most cases. It is also not able to handle all applications, since they must be written in Ruby using splay-specific support libraries.

PlanetLab support in NEPI was built to address the need to easily create and customize overlays, both at topology and application levels, a problem which current solutions do not fully address.

3 Challenges

PlanetLab [4] uses container-based virtualization to allow multiple experiments to run independently on the same node while sharing its resources. The implementation of network virtualization [7], however, has a cost: some tasks are made more complex than in a classical (non-virtualized or fully virtualized) environment. Slivers (isolation units for experiments running in PlanetLab) do not have full root privileges, so system calls to set up routes, tunnels, or IP filters, among others, are forbidden, requiring the use of PlanetLab-specific tools to perform these tasks. These limitations make many of the existing tools for overlay creation unusable within PlanetLab [10].

In order to build overlays on PlanetLab, the first challenge that needs to be addressed is tunneling. Packets have to be captured, encapsulated, and transmitted over the Internet to their destination in a way that is transparent for applications, and neutral for the intervening networks. Since PlanetLab nodes host many slivers, 300 in average, which are container-based virtual machines that share the same network stack, lower layer tunnels have to be implemented to respect network isolation, in an environment of high concurrency.

User mode tunnels have their own challenges too. Since only the kernel knows when a link is congested, and it will happily discard outgoing packets in this case. To avoid packet loss at the kernel's queue, which is undesirable when applying customized queuing, it is necessary to limit packet egress rate to match available bandwidth. But bandwidth can only be guessed, so user mode queues become delicate to use.

Routing packets is another key challenge. Kernel routing table virtualization is not able to handle as many slivers as are normally present in a node, so a technique that shares resources safely is key to achieve routing successfully.

Per-sliver routing, a technique designed for UMTS/3G-connected nodes in PlanetLab in [20] and embodied as a PlanetLab *vsys* script, allows slivers to create their own private routing tables. This technique has scalability issues since it only supports 150 concurrent slivers on each node, whereas the average on PlanetLab is around 300.

Another problem that requires special attention is the testbed's unstable and unreliable nature. Nodes can be brought up and down without any warning, or be overloaded and unresponsive, and their state is not always faithfully mirrored in the PLC API which we use for resource discovery. Our automation procedures had to be made resilient on these situations, otherwise deployment of big experiments resulted in unacceptably high failure rates.

4   PlanetLab Overlays in NEPI

NEPI [12,13] is a framework for network experimentation that automates experiment design, deployment, and control, providing a uniform way of interacting with different testbeds. NEPI provides an *experiment description* (ED) language that allows researchers to design experiments, both at topology and application levels, by adding and connecting testbed-specific component abstractions, such as nodes and links. New abstractions can be implemented to support other testbeds or to add new functionality.

An *experiment controller* (EC) entity is in charge of orchestrating the experiment from the given experiment description. The EC is responsible for allocating resources, configuring components, running applications, and retrieving experiment results. It also handles the coordination of the (possibly several) testbeds involved in the experiment. The EC is independent from any specific testbed, providing a large body of pre-existing automation functionality.

Because of these characteristics NEPI was an ideal choice to support automated deployment and overlay customization on PlanetLab. Our work was focused, then, on adding the PlanetLab specific functionality to allow NEPI to deploy experiments on PlanetLab. This not only included implementing the necessary abstractions on NEPI, but also modifying the available interface in PlanetLab to add the required routing and tunnel-enabling functionality.

In this section we will describe how overlays are created and customized on PlanetLab using NEPI. We will also explain the mechanisms developed to support network-level routing overlays in PlanetLab, that is, overlays that route IP or Ethernet packets. Other kinds of overlays are application-specific, and thus require application-specific abstractions that are beyond the scope of our work. The new mechanisms we contributed to PlanetLab to enable routing and tunneling, can be invoked by any user and application through the *vsys* interface. With them, any PlanetLab user can now easily set up GRE links, and manipulate routing tables.

4.1   Deployment Automation

In order to automate deployment of experiments involving overlays, an experiment must first be described in a machine-understandable way. NEPI provides

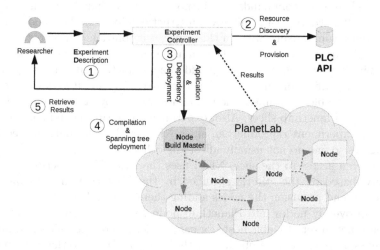

Fig. 1. NEPI-managed PlanetLab overlays. (1) The user creates the Experiment Description (ED) and passes it to the Experiment Controller (EC). (2) The EC uses the instructions in the ED to discover and provision available resources. (3) The EC instructs the allocated PlanetLab nodes to perform compilation and installation of applications. (4) Build masters prepare application data which is then distributed Peer-to-Peer among all nodes prior to experiment execution. (5) Results are relayed back to the researcher automatically upon completion.

an experiment description language based on interconnecting experiment component abstractions, called *boxes*. These boxes can be grouped into two categories: *topology*, and *application*.

To describe the topology-level of a PlanetLab experiment, we added boxes to represent PlanetLab *nodes*, *interfaces*, and *internet access*. Picking nodes is a critical design step. Since experiments can be affected by the presence of overloaded nodes, we allow researchers to specify constraints on various node metrics that will be resolved at deployment time. An experiment could accept any node, or it might require nodes with some amount of CPU or bandwidth unused. Or, the other way around, we might need overloaded nodes, perhaps, if they were trying to evaluate what happens when a node in the network is congested. All those criteria can be useful for reproducing previous experiments.

To describe the application level, we added *application* and *application-dependency* boxes, which can be connected to a node box, and represent an instruction to deploy the application or dependency, and run it on the specified node. Application boxes allow the specification of all the dependencies needed for deployment: packages they depend on, to be automatically installed in the nodes, and user programs to be launched, built and installed if necessary.

NEPI supports the concept of application traces, which capture the output of applications or even network traffic. NEPI can automatically gather all the traces at any point during execution, for inspection or analysis.

In contrast with Splay [9] and Plush [14], during experiment execution, NEPI acts as a PlanetLab controller which can manage PlanetLab slices (groups of slivers) and execute commands within nodes, rather than an agent that runs directly in PlanetLab. NEPI only gives instructions to PlanetLab nodes the way regular users would, using SSH. In this sense, our solution can be regarded as a big, specialized scripting engine. The main benefits of this approach arise from its flexibility: researchers can easily add functionality to it, and they do not require any modifications made to PlanetLab itself, making it very easy to build a range of reusable experimentation modules for deploying common topologies or utilities in PlanetLab slices. Also, experiments descriptions remain valid and usable for experiment reproduction, since NEPI and PlanetLab are decoupled and changes to one do not usually affect the other

Once given access to the slice, NEPI uses the PLC API to perform resource discovery, based on the criteria specified by the researcher in the experiment description, and provision the nodes adding them to the slice.

To map overlay nodes into PlanetLab nodes, we implemented an algorithm that constructs a set of viable hosts for each node, based on explicit and implicit constraints. Implicit constraints include the number of real interfaces as specified in the experiment description, and capabilities as required by the presence or absence of virtual interfaces and custom routing tables. After such a set is built for all nodes in the experiment, a simple backtracking procedure constructs a subset of all viable assignments. Not one solution, but a whole class of solutions are represented in a way that lets NEPI pick the best one in terms of *qualitative health* metrics, such as node load and reliability.

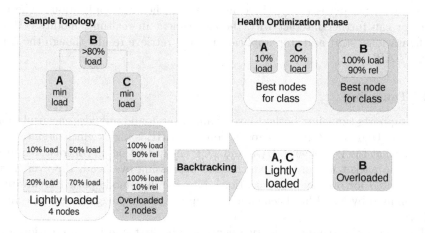

Fig. 2. Resource allocation strategy. Available nodes are partitioned into categories defined by the constraints derived from the experiment description. Each node will require assignment from one or more categories. A backtracking algorithm computes a set of solutions represented as an assignment node-to-category. Since each category contains more than one node, the final solution is built using only the healthiest nodes of the category (i.e. taking into account the node reliability).

NEPI obatins these node *qualitative health* metrics, tracked by the CoMon [15] tool, through the PLC API. If apparently healthy nodes turn out not to be so, NEPI adds those *"seemingly live"* nodes to a blacklist. With these precautions, allocation on nodes with unstable communication is minimized, and thus deployment success rates improve, which is a real problem when deploying large experiments consisting of a great many nodes.

In order to achieve a certain level of *reproducibility*, we had to take into account the constantly changing landscape of PlanetLab. The controller will record effective running parameters, like node load at the moment of deployment, physical locations, available bandwidth. When those parameters are not constrained by experiment design, effective execution values will provide all the information needed for posterior experiment reproduction, even when resource availability has changed. Later runs can use this information to constrain node selection in a way that resembles prior executions, or that ensures sufficient resource availability.

Once the nodes are successfully added to the slice and become responsive, NEPI coordinates the process of deploying applications and dependencies. Application resources, such as source code, are copied over to a few select nodes, called the build masters. These build masters take care of building applications, and downloading required rpm packages. In this way we avoid inefficient use of PlanetLab's resources - binaries only need to be built once per architecture, and bandwidth can be better utilized by sharing required downloads in a peer-to-peer fashion, preferring fast connections over slow ones. The rest of the nodes, the build slaves, wait for their master to be done to copy the resulting binaries and rpms from them.

When everything is ready, the controller launches the applications. The researcher can further interact with the experiment in realtime, modify certain configurations, start and stop applications, and retrieve results though the controller's API.

4.2   Tunneling

NEPI supports tunneling both at layer 2 and layer 3, and provides encapsulation over TCP, UDP, and GRE. Encapsulation over GRE is highly efficient since it is supported at the kernel level. UDP and TCP encapsulation, in contrast, requires user-mode packet forwarding, which adds processing overhead. However, it is better suited for overlay customization, since the user-mode packet forwarding daemon used by NEPI has been coded to support easily pluggable user-specified behavior.

The creation of tunnels has two aspects. The first one is the creation and configuration of the virtual interfaces, which is done through PlanetLab's *vsys* interface. We extended the existing interface to support creation of GRE links, which was previously only possible through Trellis [8], with all the scalability issues mentioned in Section 2. We also addressed potential conflicts related to concurrent use of GRE tunnels by many slivers, a problem present in Trellis, by marking all GRE packets between any two endpoints as belonging to the slice, and in this way allowing the kernel to de-multiplex traffic belonging to each slice both efficiently and securely, and allowing widespread adoption of GRE tunneling without interference.

We enhanced point-to-point links configuration in PlanetLab by allowing passing the remote endpoint to the kernel when appropriate, and automatically setting point-to-point routes, which is essential in the correct operation of many applications. The system as a whole, though, still needs network-level routes, so a mechanism for routing table manipulation is still necessary and will be discussed in 4.3.

The second aspect of tunnel creation, is the actual forwarding of packets. NEPI deploys a special purpose application for this, *tun_connect*. It creates UDP, TCP or GRE tunnels between two virtual interfaces, a basic building block of more complex topologies. GRE tunnels require no user-mode packet processing, so they perform best. But, when GRE links are inappropriate, such as when custom queues or stream filters are applied, user-space packet forwarding is performed. NEPI only performs packet encapsulation, routing and packet forwarding is done in the kernel, avoiding any kind of heavyweight packet processing that was a limiting factor in previous approaches.

4.3   Routing

Connecting network segments requires the presence of routing-capable nodes. That is, nodes that can forward packets to the intended destination IP, for which they need knowledge of the network's topology. There are two main ways to do this: static and dynamic routing.

In static routing, routes are predefined, either manually or automatically, but they do not change. This is the most common case, where routing tables are populated with fixed rules.

In dynamic routing, routing tables are present just as in static routing, but routers communicate with router-specific protocols to dynamically maintain optimum paths. There are many algorithms to do this, so the routing algorithms usually work in user space and are highly customizable, sending routing table updates to the kernel which does the actual forwarding. This mechanism is a compromise between flexibility and performance, with highly customizable routing daemons in user space, and packet forwarding taking place in the kernel, to avoid unnecessary copying and thus achieving higher performance.

In order to support both static and dynamic routing, a mechanism to manipulate the kernel's forwarding information base (FIB) is required. To this end we developed a new PlanetLab-specific interface, the *vroute vsys* script, that implements the standard IP routing manipulation system calls in a straightforward fashion while enforcing certain rules aimed at maintaining proper separation between slivers. *vroute* adds entries to the main routing table after validating that the routes will not interfere with other slivers. This is done by checking the private network address space assigned to the slice through the *vsys_vnet* tag. This tag can only be assigned by administrators, who are responsible of making sure that the assigned segments are non-overlapping.

Prior to our work, PlanetLab only provided the *sliceip* interface to create routing tables for slivers, which only supports 150 concurrent slivers per node, an insufficient amount for the average number of slivers in a node (see Section 2). By using both, the *sliceip* per-sliver routing, and the new *vroute* per-node routing methods, we solve the scalability problem and afford every sliver necessary control over the routing tables.

Using the main routing table has the benefit of being limited by the number of rules per node, rather than the number of slivers in a node. In fact, NEPI will pick the *vroute* method if it does not need many rules, and *sliceip* if the table is big enough to warrant a separate table, or the routes do not belong to the slice's private address space. With this we hope to make the system scale better to high number of users sharing resources on the same nodes.

In combination with *per-sliver routing* [20], our solution creates a scalable and secure way of configuring IP-routing at the kernel-level, that can be widely adopted without disrupting PlanetLab. This means userland routing daemons like *olsrd* are easily adaptable.

In this way, bandwidths up to 300Mbps have been achieved, enabling high-bandwidth, low-overhead, and highly-customized overlays, which were previously only possible in PL-VINI (using the handful PL-VINI-enabled nodes).

4.4 Traffic Shaping

In order to support overlay customization, including new queuing policies, userland packet forwarding and routing, like Xorp and Click, and even new tunnelling protocols like OverQoS[1], we introduced several hooks into the framework in or-

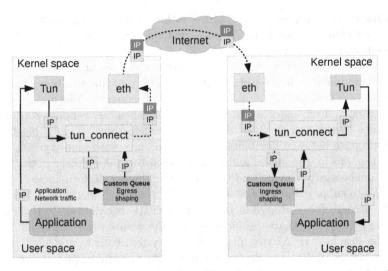

Fig. 3. Customizing overlay packet handling. Interprocess communication is used to send all packets through a user process. Custom queuing, filtering and aggregation algorithms can in this way be applied to the packet stream, both before encapsulation and transmission, and after reception and de-encapsulation. When this is used in combination with the built-in rate limiting options, arbitrary loss models, among other things, can be applied to the overlay.

der to let experiments process network packets without having to implement all the low-level details.

Stream filters can be arbitrary applications that process the packets flowing through the overlays. They can be used to implement custom queues, packet filters or transformations, tunnelling protocols. These modules can be provided to the *tun_connect* userland packet forwarder, to route all packets through user-specified code. The mechanism only works when userland forwarding is taking place, so it cannot be used with GRE tunnels.

The mechanism was designed so that even previous code not designed to work with NEPI could be used. It takes either Python or C code, and provides several ways in which experiments can process packets. Packets can be rejected by implementing a filtering predicate, or a customized queuing class can be provided that will be used instead of the primitive default FIFO. For more complex processing, a connection to an external process that filters packets can be made, covering most customization scenarios.

External filters can include piping all packets through a shell command, or forwarding them to separate daemons, as would be the case if we wanted to use Click. This is accomplished by writing a small module that returns two file descriptors (i.e. a socketpair) through which all packets are piped. Thus, no matter how a researcher decides to implement the prototype, the same code could be reused for testing within PlanetLab. All this provides a level of *flexibility* no other framework does.

The *tun_connect* module also performs user-land queuing. PlanetLab does not allow slivers to control virtual interface's queuing parameters, so queuing can be accomplished in user-land by specifying custom queuing sizes or classes. This allows researchers to very easily experiment with new queuing disciplines, as we will demonstrate in 5.1.

Implementing OverQoS in PlanetLab would be trivial with this framework, once the prototype has been written, significantly lowering the cost of experimentation. The only foreseeable drawback of this technique is performance, as the usage of stream filters incurs significant performance overhead.

5 Evaluation

In order to evaluate the solution in terms of ease of use, effectiveness and practicality, we present an experiment case conducted on PlanetLab using NEPI. We evaluate the practicality of our framework for real research cases by reproducing an experiment from a published paper: POPI [19], a tool for packet forwarding priority inference. It was originally validated in PlanetLab in a costly and laborious way, by probing routes between nodes and then manually requesting information from intermediate providers by contacting their administrators.

We re-validated POPI using NEPI in a controlled PlanetLab overlay, a possibility that was not available at the time the paper by Guohan et al[19] was published: by controlling routing behavior and comparing known overlay characteristics against POPI's inferred ones, we managed to achieve verifiable results, in an automated and effortless fashion.

5.1 POPI

POPI[19], which stands for Packet fOrwarding Priority Inference, is a tool that attempts to infer packet priorities in the intervening routers between two endpoints. In the paper by Guohan Lu et al, the tool is evaluated by simulation as a first step, and in PlanetLab as a second step. During the PlanetLab run, however, researchers had to ask ISPs about their routing policies, because they could not otherwise verify that the priorities reported by the tool corresponded to actual prioritization policies. Even then, their success was limited, because not every provider answered, and because the information so gathered was very rough.

We re-evaluated POPI, with the intention to evaluate NEPI's adequacy in creating controlled routing overlays for protocols and application validation. NEPI provides here the ability to create an overlay spanning lossy and congested links, while at the same time granting controllable packet prioritization at selected routing points by the use of customized queuing.

Designing the experiment was straightforward. NEPI already provided a reference queue class with TOS support [1], out of which a classifier queue based on

---

[1] NEPI provides a base queue implementation, which can be attached to network devices in PlanetLab, and defines queuing policies by inspecting the Type Of Service (TOS) field in the IPv4 header.

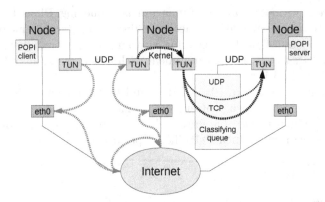

Fig. 4. POPI experiment concept. Three PlanetLab nodes connected physically by the Internet, on top of which a routing overlay provides a controllable environment in which to test POPI.

IP protocol was rather trivial to derive. We exploited our ability to control routing to introduce a mediating node between two arbitrary PlanetLab nodes. All traffic between the endpoints is routed through this mediating node, which applies a controlled class of queuing, and which should result in the application of recognizable statistical bias to the packet stream. Figure 4 shows the experiment design, which includes deployment of POPI, unmodified, in PlanetLab.

We ran the experiment with numerous queue configurations, with the help of a small script that leverages NEPI's programmatic API. The experiment was run in PlanetLab Europe (PLE) as well as a private PlanetLab-like cluster, allowing us to experiment with different environments with little effort. The experiment took 179 hours to run, but required no supervision. Of 325 runs, only 11 failed to be deployed, because of connectivity issues (the controller was operating from a domestic network), but were automatically retried or flagged as bad runs so they could be skipped when analyzing results.

Since any PlanetLab node would be able to run the experiment, we could have cut experiment run time significantly by running several configurations in parallel, using more nodes instead, and illustrating the convenience of not being limited to using only PL-VINI nodes for routing, as RiaS is. However, this would have undermined our ability to compare against our small, private cluster.

Table 1 shows execution details. We induced multiple connectivity glitches by connecting and disconnecting from the network, and joining and leaving VPNs to stress NEPI's failure recovery capabilities. Within the remaining runs, 32 failed because of problems with POPI's tool itself and produced no results. A vastly lower failure rate can be observed in our dedicated cluster, evidencing that the strain on PLE nodes does have an effect on experiment success. Our experiment was conducted at a particularly busy time of the year, yet failure rates are acceptable, due to NEPI's automated recovery procedures.

POPI could successfully infer queue prioritization in clear channels as long as the different classes had different rate limits, but in instances where protocols

Table 1. POPI experiment runs. Good runs are those where NEPI returned a successful code. Bad runs when it did otherwise. Failed runs are good runs that produced no output, in every case, because POPI could not establish the control connection due to connectivity glitches.

runs/sets	Good	Bad	Fail
PlanetLab Europe	142/30	8/0	16/0
Dedicated cluster	172/35	3/0	16/1

Table 2. POPI results, based on PLE runs only. Columns specify the bandwidth at the node with the classifier queue, while rows specify the classifier queue configuration. Marks show sets that contain cases (1) where the correct classification was detected (2) where there was underpartitioning (3) where there was overpartitioning. Marks are ordered according to predominance within the set. "4x TCP" represents a queue with 4 times as much bandwidth allocated to TCP traffic than other kinds.

config \ k	32	64	128	256	384
4x TCP	(3,2)	(1,2)	(1,2)	(3,1)	(1,3)
4x ICMP	(1,2)	(1)	n/a	n/a	(1)
4x UDP	(1,3)	(1)	(1)	(1,3)	(1)
4x TCP 16x I	(1)	(1,2)	(1)	(1,3)	(1)
4x U+T 16x I	(2,3)	(1)	(3)	(1)	(1)
4x T+I	(1)	(1)	n/a	(1,3)	(1)
indep. U,T,I	(2)	(2)	n/a	(1)	n/a

were assigned separate classes with equal bandwidth (fair share queuing), POPI could not tell the difference from a plain FIFO queue. There was a certain amount of overpartitioning (cases where POPI inferred more classes than in reality) and underpartioning (cases where POPI failed to infer a class), as expected, although somewhat more frequent than expected according to the original research paper. Table 2 summarizes our results.

In our experiment, 256k and 384k cases should not result in any classification, because other nodes were uniformly limited to 256k. Any partitioning there is considered overpartitioning, except when it detects the exact queue configuration. It is interesting to note that TCP priority detection is consistently less precise than with other protocols, as shown by the results of "4x TCP" and "4x U+T 16x I" at 128k. In the former, there was a tendency to overpartitioning, while in the latter TCP was consistently detected as having less priority than UDP. This, after checking the resulting packet captures, could most probably be due to reactive traffic generated by target nodes responding to POPI's synthetic TCP packets. This can interfere with the measurements, by exerting more pressure than expected on the bottleneck queue. This effect is even more prominent in our private cluster, where POPI is generally more precise due to the absence of background traffic. This only highlights the bias experienced in TCP measures, that is less evident when running in PLE.

All the required sources and scripts to reproduce the experiment have been made available on-line. With our tools, researchers can easily (assuming they do have access to PlanetLab) reproduce the experiment, and even build other experiments on top of it. NEPI's experiment description XML contains not only topology information, but also deployment instructions: where to get POPI sources, how to build it, how to patch it if it were required. NEPI's execution XMLs contain valuable details about the resources used to run the experiment. All this results in very strong reproducibility guarantees.

More details, and instructions on how to reproduce this experiment, can be found at: http://www.nepihome.org/wiki/nepi/popiExperiment.

6   Conclusions

In this paper we have presented a framework that increases control over experiments conducted using PlanetLab, allowing researchers to go beyond what previously available tools permitted.

Our solution is based on building flexible routing overlays on top of PlanetLab. We provide the ability to automate deployment of whole overlay experiment scenarios, and improve the flexibility and scalability of the tunnelling and routing techniques compared to previous approaches used in PlanetLab. Additionally, our solution supports custom traffic shaping and different traffic encapsulation and transmission methods, enabling easy customization of the overlays.

As part of this work, we extended PlanetLab's *vsys* interface to include scalable and secure mechanisms for routing table manipulation, and creation of GRE links. With these tools, we have shown how to implement low-overhead yet highly customizable routing overlays.

In our use case "POPI", we demonstrated the relevance of our contribution by showing how it enables the researcher to gather experimental information that was previously unavailable to him or her. By choosing to reproduce a previously published experiment case, we proved that our solution is relevant to real research cases, while providing additional value.

A comprehensive technical evaluation of our solution is needed to further validate the extent and limitations of our work. In future work, we will focus on evaluating metrics related to scalability, resource usage, and performance. To this end, we will consider node specific metrics, such as per node maximum bandwidth and resource consumption, as well as global performance and scalability metrics, such as maximum number of concurrent overlays and maximum number of nodes per overlay.

References

1. Subramanian, L., Stoica, I., Balakrishnan, H., Katz, R.: OverQoS: An Overlay based Architecture for Enhancing Internet QoS. In: NSDI 2004 (2004)
2. Jannotti, J., Gifford, D.K., Johnson, K.L., Kaashoek, F.M., O'toole, J.W., Frans, M., James, K.: Overcast: Reliable Multicasting with an Overlay Network. In: OSDI 2009 (2009)

3. Andersen, D., Balakrishnan, H., Kaashoek, F., Morris, R.: Resilient overlay networks. In: SOSP 2001 (2001)
4. Chun, B., Culler, D., Roscoe, T., Bavier, A., Peterson, L., Wawrzoniak, M., Bowman, M.: PlanetLab: an overlay testbed for broad-coverage services. In: SIGCOMM 2003 (2003)
5. Bavier, A., Feamster, N., Huang, M., Peterson, L., Rexford, J.: In VINI veritas: realistic and controlled network experimentation. In: SIGCOMM 2006 (2006)
6. Lischka, J., Karl, H.: RiaS: overlay topology creation on a PlanetLab infrastructure. In: SIGCOMM VISA 2010 (2010)
7. Mark, H.: VNET: PlanetLab Virtualized Network Access. PlanetLab Consortium (2005)
8. Bhatia, S., Motiwala, M., Muhlbauer, W., Mundada, Y., Valancius, V., Bavier, A., Feamster, N., Peterson, L., Rexford, J.: Trellis: a platform for building flexible, fast virtual networks on commodity hardware. In: CoNEXT 2008 (2008)
9. Leonini, L., Rivière, E., Felber, P.: SPLAY: distributed systems evaluation made simple (or how to turn ideas into live systems in a breeze. In: NSDI 2009 (2009)
10. Muir, S., Peterson, L., Fiuczynski, M., Cappos, J., Hartman, J.: Privileged operations in the PlanetLab virtualised environment. SIGOPS Oper. Syst. Rev. 40, 75–88 (2006)
11. Bhatia, S., Di Stasi, G., Haddow, T., Bavier, A., Muir, S., Peterson, L.: Vsys: A Programmable sudo. In: USENIX ATC (2011)
12. Lacage, M., Ferrari, M., Hansen, M., Turletti, T., Dabbous, W.: NEPI: using independent simulators, emulators, and testbeds for easy experimentation. SIGOPS Oper. Syst. Rev. 43, 60–65 (2010)
13. Quereilhac, A., Freire, C., Lavage, M., Turletti, T., Dabbous, W.: NEPI: An Integration Framework for Network Experimentation. In: SoftCom 2011 (2011)
14. Albrecht, J., Tuttle, C., Snoeren, A.C., Vahdat, A.: PlanetLab application management using plush. SIGOPS Oper. Syst. Rev. 40, 33–40 (2006)
15. CoMon, http://comon.cs.princeton.edu/
16. Linux-VServer, http://linux-vserver.org
17. User-mode Linux, http://user-mode-linux.sourceforge.net/
18. Linux network namespaces, http://lxc.sourceforge.net/index.php/about/kernel-namespaces/network/
19. Lu, G., Chen, Y., Birrer, S., Bustamante, F.E., Li, X.: POPI: a user-level tool for inferring router packet forwarding priority. IEEE/ACM Trans. Netw. 18, 1–14 (2010)
20. Botta, A., Canonico, R., Di Stasi, G., Pescape, A., Ventre, G.: Providing UMTS connectivity to PlanetLab nodes. In: CoNEXT 2008 (2008)
21. Kohler, E., Morris, R., Chen, B., Jannotti, J., Kaashoek, M.F.: The click modular router. ACM Trans. Comput. Syst. 18, 263–297 (2000)
22. Floyd, S., Paxson, V.: Difficulties in simulating the internet. J. IEEE/ACM Transactions on Networking (TON) 9 (2001)

A Real-Time Testbed for Routing Network

Kang Yao[1], Weiqing Sun[2], Mansoor Alam[1], Mingzhe Xu[2], and Vijay Devabhaktuni[1]

[1] Department of EECS, The University of Toledo, Ohio, USA
{kang.yao,mansoor.alam2,vijay.devabhaktuni}@utoledo.edu
[2] Department of ET, The University of Toledo, Ohio, USA
{weiqing.sun,mingzhe.xu}@utoledo.edu

Abstract. Existing network testbeds can enable developers to evaluate the performance of different routing protocols in a network and help students to enhance their hands-on experiences and understand complex and abstract concepts of routing protocols by allowing them to carry out real-world experiments, but they are either limited in features or expensive to establish and manage. To address the problem, this paper presents ARTNet - A Real-Time Testbed for Routing Network – which supports almost all the popular routing protocols for typical applications in a cost-effective manner. ARTNet has been implemented on a multiprocessor server for users to create and manage their routing networks. Performance and functionality evaluations on the ARTNet platform show that it is a promising approach.

Keywords: ARTNet, Network Testbed, Routing Protocols, Virtualization, Network Service.

1 Introduction

Network researchers and designers need to test different routing protocols under various conditions to determine whether they are robust or reliable. Students need to learn how to deploy routing protocols and manipulate their parameters in order to understand how these protocols actually work. However, it is not always possible to setup a live routing network testbed due to its high cost.

Two types of techniques, emulation and simulation, have addressed the problem. The main difference between the two techniques is that a simulator is a program focusing on modeling components of a network, while an emulator is the hardware, software, or both focusing on duplicating the behavior of a live network. For emulation, a computer system running software such as Zebra [1], Quagga [2], and XORP [3] functions as a part of emulated testbed. For simulation, only software is used to simulate a whole network. There are a few well-known simulators in the market, such as OMNeT++ [4], Ns-2 [5], Cisco Packet Tracer [6], and OPNET IT Guru [7].

An ideal testbed for routing protocols should comply with the following basic requirements:

T. Korakis, M. Zink, and M. Ott (Eds.): TridentCom 2012, LNICST 44, pp. 256–270, 2012.
© Institute for Computer Sciences, Social Informatics and Telecommunications Engineering 2012

1. It should provide a real-time, cost-effective, and realistic environment. Although the approach of emulation provides a real-time environment, it is expensive in terms of hardware cost. The approach of simulation, on the other hand, does not provide the real-time ability and the necessary realism.
2. It should enable users to study and evaluate the performance of the network under specified loads. The load could consist of HTTP, FTP, TFTP, SMTP, POP3, DNS, and so on.
3. It should be scalable and extensible. The testbed should scale well with an increasing number of routers, links and be able to inject real-world application traffic to the routing network. The approach of emulation allows users to inject real-world traffic, which is extensible. However, the scalability is constrained by its limited resources, management, and physical setup. Although the approach of simulation is used to perform large-scale routing experiments, it is hard to add non-built-in traffic.
4. It should support routing protocols used widely in real-world networks, including Intermediate System to Intermediate System (IS-IS), OSPF, Routing Information Protocol (RIP), EIGRP, Border Gateway Protocol (BGP), and so on. Among these, different Interior Gateway Protocols (IGP), OSPF and EIGRP have been considered as the pre-eminent routing protocols. However, because EIGRP is a Cisco proprietary protocol [8], most emulators or simulators do not support it.
5. It should provide a user-friendly environment for conducting routing experiments and performing analyses.

In this paper, we design a testbed ARTNet in an effort to meet all the requirements by providing all the above-stated features. The rest of the paper is organized as follows: Section 2 presents the architecture of ARTNet. Section 3 describes the implementation and evaluation of ARTNet. Section 4 presents related work. Finally, in Section 5, conclusions are drawn, and future work is proposed.

2   ARTNet Architecture

Based on the requirements, we design the ARTNet architecture as shown in Fig. 1. ARTNet consists of Web-based Interface (WBI), Initialization Module (IM), Real-time Configuration Module (RCM), ARTNet Database, Virtual Network (VN), Virtual Hosts (VHs), and Results Visualization Module (RVM).

The WBI is a part of the GUI developed for users to login and access the virtual networks. It also enables users to specify configuration options for a network including the topology, protocols along with their parameters, and various loads on VHs. Once IM receives the users' input through WBI, it is responsible for initializing the VN and VHs of their networks. Thus, these two components provide the configuration initialization capability of ARTNet. WBI, IM, and RCM can read and write configuration data into the ARTNet Database, which contains all the data related to the routing networks in the testbed. Users can also interact with ARTNet and their networks during the process of the experimentation, since RCM provides the real-time control to the VN and VHs. The RVM component provides the functionality

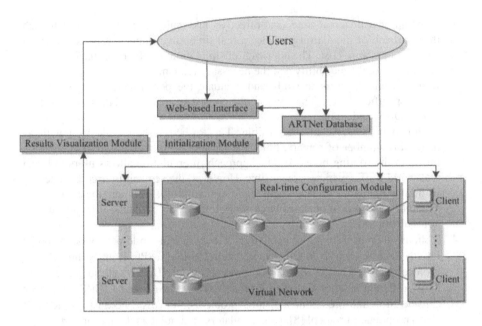

Fig. 1. Architecture of ARTNet

of capturing and analyzing the experimentation data. It is also equipped with a user-friendly interface for displaying the network statistics, deriving performance metrics, and makes it easy for users to analyze results and develop insights from the results.

2.1   Virtual Network

The VN consists of virtual routers, switches, and links. Our infrastructure is built on top of the real-time network simulator GNS3 [9]. It is an open-source Graphical Network Simulator that allows emulations of complex networks using Cisco Internetwork Operating Systems (Cisco IOSs) running on Windows, Linux and Mac OS X based computers. GNS3 was chosen because it has the following features:

- Users can interact with it during experimentations. If an unusual event occurs in a network, they can see the impact immediately and make prompt adjustments. It provides the basic real-time control ability needed by ARTNet.
- Cisco IOS software supports most of the routing protocols including ODR, RIP, IGRP, OSPF, EIGRP, IS-IS, and BGP [10]. These routing protocols will make a good set supported by ARTNet.
- GNS3 supports real-time interactions with the simulated network. It also allows a connection of the simulated network to real routers or computers. These features play a key role in the extensibility of ARTNet.
- It supports a realistic environment by using real Cisco IOSs and Command Line Interface (CLI), which is a powerful method for expert administrators to configure Cisco's devices.

There are two sides to every sword. Due to licensing restrictions, users have to buy Cisco IOSs from Cisco or its partners [11]. In addition, The IOSs cannot be modified. In other words, ARTNet is not programmable and new routing protocols will be supported only if Cisco IOSs update has this new feature.

Two sets of configuration files in GNS3 are supported and manipulated in ARTNet, one for routers' configurations, and the second file is used to store GNS3 network topology information such as name, location, and the IOS for each virtual router. When users start a virtual network, GNS3 will load these files for instantiating the topology and routers.

2.2   Virtual Host

A VH is a completely isolated duplicate of a real computer. In ARTNet, it provides the ability of generating real-world application traffic. VHs are connected to the virtual network through the Cloud device in GNS3. Users can manage how VHs connect to VN using WBI in ARTNet. Application servers are installed and run in VHs to provide the capability of traffic generation based on users' specifications. Hence, the network performance can be analyzed by measuring specific traffic on a particular network.

VMware Workstation is chosen to run virtual hosts because it provides seamless support for different guest OSs, manageability, and operational flexibility. VMware Workstation allows one physical PC to run multiple operating systems at the same time without rebooting or hard-drive partitioning. Physical hardware resources are mapped to the virtual machine's resources, so that each virtual machine has its own CPU, memory, disks, I/O devices and more [12].

There are some common application services used in today's networks, including HTTP, FTP, TFTP, Email, and DNS services. Table 1 lists the software that is commonly used to provide these services. User can also choose to incorporate other applications that produce various types of traffic into the network. Examples include Voice over IP (VoIP), and streaming video.

Table 1. Application Servers

Application Services	Software
HTTP	Apache HTTP Server
FTP	Vsftpd
TFTP	Tftpd
Email	Postfix
DNS	BIND

Currently, in ARTNet, Ubuntu is used for the guest operating system running on each VH. A few open-source application servers have been pre-installed in the guest OS, such as BIND and Postfix. With these services installed, VHs function as application servers. The desired application services can be easily specified using the ARTNet interface without users worrying about the installation or configuration of the services.

2.3   Web-Based Interface and Initialization Module

ARTNet consists of two GUI components, WBI and IM for researchers and students to create and manage their routing networks in ARTNet.

WBI provides an interface to specify configuration options. Only the authenticated users can login and manage their networks remotely. Users can configure the VN or VHs in a visual way. For example, possible specifications for a router include which routing protocol to deploy, the IP address for each interface on the router, and so on. After configurations are made, IM generates the corresponding configuration files. ARTNet will then power on the specified network automatically by using the respective configuration files. Fig. 2 shows a screenshot of the WBI for configuring a virtual EIGRP network.

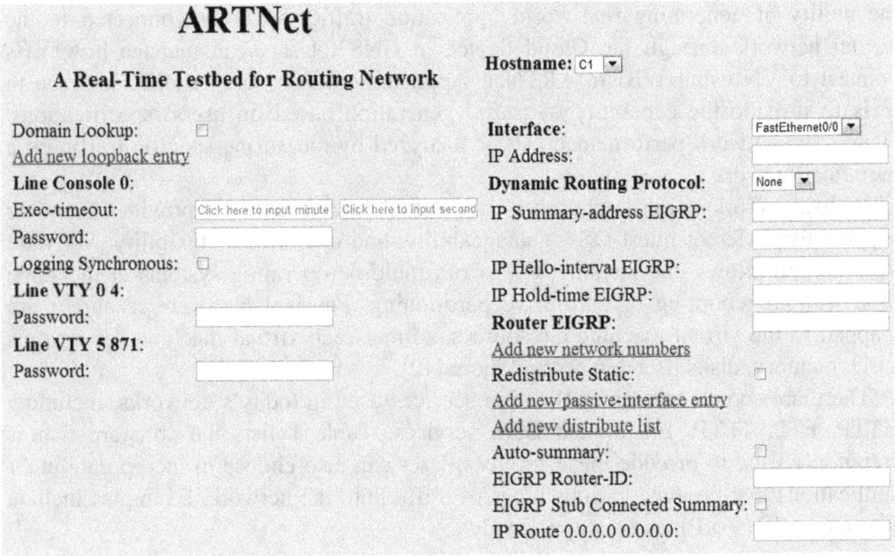

ARTNet

A Real-Time Testbed for Routing Network

Hostname: C1 ▼

Domain Lookup: ☐	Interface: FastEthernet0/0 ▼
Add new loopback entry	IP Address:
Line Console 0:	**Dynamic Routing Protocol:** None ▼
Exec-timeout: [Click here to input minute] [Click here to input second]	IP Summary-address EIGRP:
Password:	
Logging Synchronous: ☐	IP Hello-interval EIGRP:
Line VTY 0 4:	IP Hold-time EIGRP:
Password:	**Router EIGRP:**
Line VTY 5 871:	Add new network numbers
Password:	Redistribute Static: ☐
	Add new passive-interface entry
	Add new distribute list
	Auto-summary: ☐
	EIGRP Router-ID:
	EIGRP Stub Connected Summary: ☐
	IP Route 0.0.0.0 0.0.0.0:

Fig. 2. Screenshot of WBI for a sample network

For example, if a user wants to configure a virtual router C1 in an existing virtual network, he can choose C1 from the drop-down menu and then configuration changes may be made to this router. As can be seen, users do not need to fill in the complete information, and default values will be used for the rest. After pressing the save button, the configuration changes will be sent to IM, which will populate the configuration file named C1.cfg for router C1.

By using the GUI interfaces, it is more efficient and easier for users to configure their networks and specify routing options when compared to text or command-line based methods. And it also helps to avoid making configuration mistakes.

2.4   ARTNet Database

ARTNet stores all of the information needed to run the routing networks in a central database. The stored data consists of three parts: User & Login (U & L) data, General Configuration Data (GCD), and Protocol Dependent Configuration Data (PDCD). Each type of data will be handled by its corresponding module.

The U & L data consists of users' names, passwords, and activity logs. A user can access ARTNet from any computer connected to the Internet using WBI. User name and password are checked against the authentication information stored in the database. The administrator can pre-register the network for each user. And users may also register by themselves.

GCD and PDCD are used to store data regarding routers' configurations in a routing network. GCD stores some common configurations such as router name, static route, loopback interface or access-list. PDCD stores data about routing protocols, such as router ID, redistribution, Hello/Dead interval, and more.

WBI locates the network configuration data in ARTNet Database upon a successful user login. Then IM will extract the data and generate different configuration files to instantiate the network.

2.5   Real-Time Configuration Module

Networks hosted by ARTNet can also be configured and controlled dynamically using RCM. For instance, they can dynamically adjust the routing parameters in real-time, when the whole network is powered on.

RCM enables users to start, stop, restart and login to a virtual router. For instance, users are able to interrupt the primary link for a subnet during the experimentation by shutting down the network interface of the router.

RCM can also be used to control a specific VH or a group of VHs. It is capable of performing the following operations: start and stop a VH, run an executable program within a VH, copy a file from a VH to the host computer or vice versa, and assign an IP address to a VH. For example, the packet file stored in a VH can be copied from the guest VH operating system to the host operating system for further analysis.

2.6   Results Visualization Module

RVM is responsible for monitoring networks, capturing, filtering and visualizing packets, and displaying traffic statistics. Because the raw packet capture files usually include a large amount of data, it is important for users to be able to display and analyze only those packets of their interest. In addition, RVM provides key performance metrics such as convergence duration, throughput, end-to-end delay, delta time, number of retransmission packets, and service response time, which are used to measure the performance of routing protocols.

The RVM consists of two different components. The first parts is a packet analyzer, which is used to caputre all the packets over a network interface. The second is a GUI frontend which will display the statistics about the performance metrics. As VMware Workstation or GNS3 has no built-in packet capturing functionality, we use the open-source Wireshark [13] as the basic packet capturer/analyzer. After an experiment is completed, RVM will import the files captured by Wireshark, and then generate the statistics about these metrics from the packet files. Users can then compare them across different routing protocols in a visual way with just a few clicks.

3   Implementation and Evaluation of ARTNet

This section describes the hardware and software components used to implement the ARTNet platform. In addition, performance and functionality evaluations are performed on ARTNet.

3.1   Implementation of ARTNet

ARTNet is currently hosted on a multiprocessor server with 16×Intel® Xeon® E5620 @2.40GHz processor, 48 GB memory, 500 GB hard drive, and six gigabit Ethernet interfaces.

The open-source software bundle, LAMP (Linux, Apache, MySQL, and PHP5), is used to implement the ARTNet platform as described in Section 2. The operating system is Ubuntu 11.10 64-bit desktop version which has the built-in GUI support. The ARTNet Database is created and managed by MySQL 5.5. The Apache Web Server is used to host WBI and IM, and PHP 5.4.0 is used to implement the server side functionality as required by the WBI and IM components of the architecture. In particular, two PHP scripts are developed to realize the functionality to enable users to initialize routing networks in ARTNet. The first one is used to interact with users to provide authentication and dumping users' configuration options into the database. The second script is responsible for reading from the database and generating corresponding configuration files.

ARTNet uses the stable version GNS3 v0.7.4, which supports 1700, 2600, 3600, and 3700 serials routers for constructing routing networks. In our current setup, we use router model 3640 and the corresponding IOS is c3640-ik9o3s-mz.124-25b.bin.

VMware Workstation 8 is used to create and manage VHs in ARTNet. The OSes for guests are the same as the OS for the workstation. Several virtual network interfaces (vmnets) are created and set up as host-only networks.

3.2   Evaluation of ARTNet

The ARTNet can run multiple instances of the routing networks for different users at the same time. This is especially useful in a class setting, when each student (or group of students) is assigned a dedicated routing network for experimentations. The number of instances supported is dependent on the size of routing network and the available resources on the physical server. The performance evaluation will shed light on this aspect. In addition, a comparative routing protocol study is performed on ARTNet to show its usability. Both the evaluations are conducted based on a campus routing network.

The campus network segregates the functions of the network into three layers: Access, Distribution, and Core Layers [14]. According to the Cisco recommended hierarchical campus design [15], routers at different layers play distinct roles. Routers at the Access Layer are intended to forward traffic only to and from the locally connected subnets. They ensure that the packets are delivered to end-user devices. The Distribution Layer acts as an aggregation point for all Access Layer devices. Routers at this layer implements policies, such as route filter or summarization. The Core Layer provides the high capacity transport between the attached Distribution Layer routers. Routers at this layer focus on speed and ensure reliable delivery of packets.

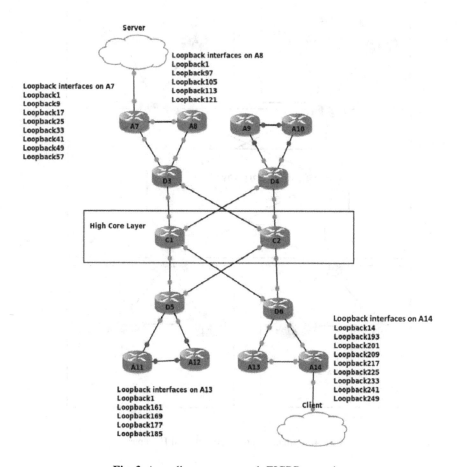

Fig. 3. A small campus network-EIGRP scenario

3.2.1 Performance Evaluation

First, two small campus network scenarios including 14 routers and 2 Cloud devices (in the form of VHs) as shown in Fig. 3 and Fig. 4 are created in ARTNet. D3, D4, D5, and D6 belong to the Distribution Layer. C1 and C2 belong to the Core Layer. Other end-user devices in a LAN are represented by the loopback interfaces on the Access Layer routers. The performance evaluation is done by running an increasing number of instances of the two scenarios until the workstation runs out of CPU or RAM resources.

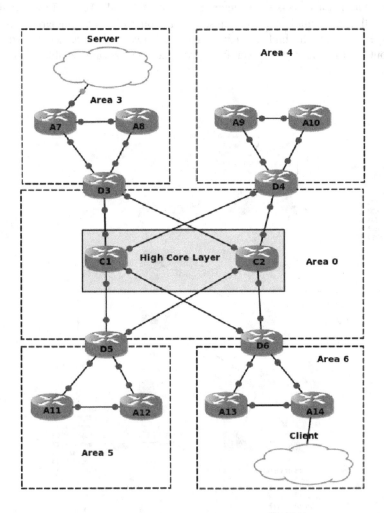

Fig. 4. A small campus network-OSPF scenario

As shown in Fig. 5, Fig. 6, Fig. 7, and Fig. 8, the CPU runs at 100% temporarily when a new routing network instance starts. Then the CPU usage drops after 3-7 seconds. This happens after the idlepc values have been set. It sleeps the virtual router occasionally while virtual routers are idle. This significantly reduces the CPU consumption on the server. 25% of the CPU resources are reserved for the virtual routers and VHs to perform their tasks. For our specific setup, ARTNet supports about 15 routing network instances concurrently without significant performance degradation.

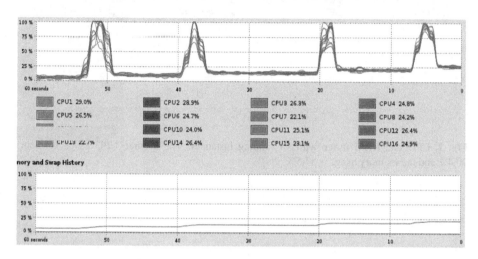

Fig. 5. CPU and RAM usage with 4 running instances. The average CPU usage is about 25.4% and the memory usage is 20.5%.

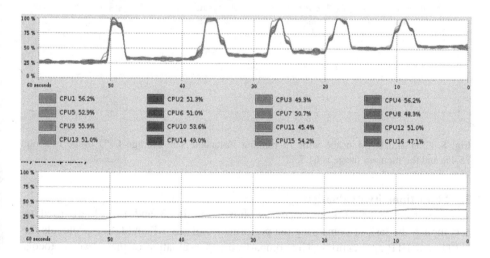

Fig. 6. CPU and RAM usage with 9 running instances. The average CPU usage is about 51.4% and the memory usage is 39.0%.

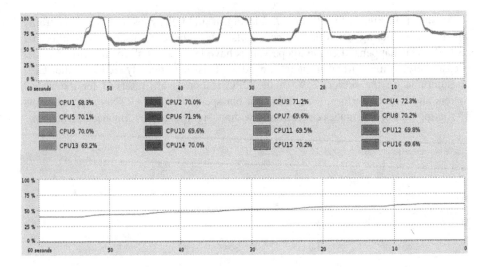

Fig. 7. CPU and RAM usage with 14 running instances. The average CPU usage is about 70.4% and the memory usage is 57.5%.

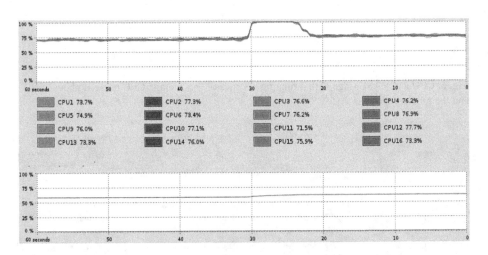

Fig. 8. CPU and RAM usage with 15 running instances. The average CPU usage is about 75.4% and the memory usage is 61.2%.

3.2.2 Functionality Evaluation

The two routing network instances as shown in Fig. 3 and Fig. 4 are used to accomplish the task of comparing the performance of EIGRP and OSPF protocols for HTTP and FTP applications. The comparison and evaluation of these two protocols are done based on performance metrics, packet loss and delta time.

Packet loss occurs when packets of data travelling across the network fail to reach the destination. It can be caused by a number of factors, so it is normal in a stable network. HTTP and FTP sessions were performed from the Virtual Host Server to the Client to transfer a large video file whose size is 27,580,668 bytes. Table 2 lists the number of packet loss generated by RVM. Recovery means that while the primary link is shut down (by using RCM) for the subnet between the Server and A7 at about 45 second marks, the routings will converge again after certain time periods.

Table 2. Packet Loss

	HTTP/Recovery	FTP/Recovery
EIGRP	65 packets / 90 packets	58 packets / 76 packets
OSPF	87 packets /164 packets	83 packets /137 packets

The following formula is used to compare the rate for the increasing packet loss:

$$Rate = \frac{Recovery\ Packet\ Loss}{Packets\ Loss}$$

For HTTP in EIGRP network,

$$Rate_{HE} = \frac{90}{65} = 1.385$$

For HTTP in OSPF network,

$$Rate_{HO} = \frac{164}{87} = 1.885$$

This indicates that the rate for the increasing packet loss is smaller in EIGRP network than that in OSPF network under HTTP traffic.

For FTP in EIGRP network,

$$Rate_{HE} = \frac{76}{58} = 1.310$$

For FTP in OSPF network,

$$Rate_{HO} = \frac{137}{83} = 1.651$$

Similarly, this indicates that the rate for the increasing packet loss is smaller in EIGRP network than that in OSPF network under FTP traffic or HTTP traffic.

Delta time is the time between the captured packets. Recovery delta time means the time between the last packet, which is captured before the primary link is interrupted, and the first packet, which is captured after the backup link becomes active. ARTNet RVM generates graphs like Fig. 9 and Fig. 10.

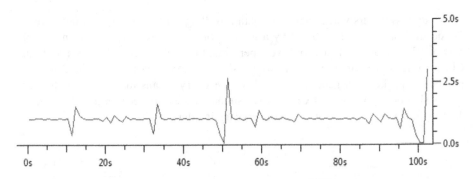

Fig. 9. Recovery delta time for HTTP in EIGRP scenario

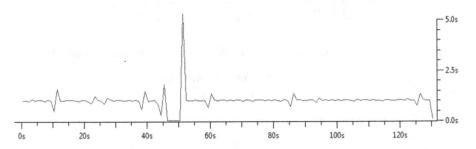

Fig. 10. Recovery delta time for HTTP in OSPF scenario

By comparing recovery delta time, most of the recovery delta times for both scenarios are the same. The spike in OSPF scenario (5.0 second) is larger than the spike in EIGRP scenario (2.5 second). In other words, EIGRP converges faster than OSPF.

These experiments demonstrate that ARTNet can be used to effectively perform the necessary quantitative comparisons between different routing protocols.

4   Related Work

A number of previous researches have been done to evaluate the performance of interior protocols with application data flows by using either a live network testbed or a simulator. The way of employing a live testbed which consists of real routers, switches and computers provides the most realistic results, but is costly to establish and manage. On the other hand, the pure simulator based approach reduces cost, but the results obtained are less realistic.

Some studies have used simulator OPNET to compare EIGRP, OSPF or other protocols for different applications. Kaur and Sharma [16] evaluated the performance of a hybrid network implementing EIGRP, OSPF and BGP routing protocols for different applications in a campus network using the OPNET IT GURU Academic Edition simulator. The applications included Email, FTP, Remote Login, and HTTP

& Print Server. Yehia, Aziz, and Elsayed [17] compare EIGRP and OSPF performances for voice, HTTP, and FTP using OPNET modeler. They measured convergence duration, voice packets delay, and throughput. Lucio, Paredes-Farrera, Jammeh, Fleury and Reed [18] presented a comparative study of two simulators OPNET Modeler and NS-2. Simulator outputs are compared to the output from a live network testbed in a sample network. They used CBR-type traffic and FTP sessions. OPNET is a powerful tool for administrators and researchers to design, secure, analyze, troubleshoot and improve large-scale networks. However, both OPNET and NS-2 lack the real-time control functionality as provided in the ARTNet testbed presented in this paper.

Knežević, Schubert and Kostić [19] proposed a testbed named MX to emulate programmable routers running over a realistic topology on multi-core servers. MX used XORP for the control plane and one physical computer was allowed to behave as multiple routers. Li, Liu and Rangaswami [20] integrated PRIME and XORP. This design used a forwarding plane offloading approach to reduce the I/O overload. A case study using OSPF to demonstrate its capability to conduct elaborate routing test was also provided. Petac and Musat [21] built a platform which includes Cisco routers and computers running GNU Zebra and Quagga. They studied the convergence time by interrupting various links in a hybrid network. Nguyen, Roughan, Knight, and Falkner [22] described AutoNetkit to auto-configure the complex emulation network. Quagga was used to provide the implementation of routing protocols. Platforms using XORP, Zebra, and Quagga software, provide programmable routers and allow rapid introduction of new protocols, but they do not include the popular proprietary routing protocols which ARTNet supports.

5   Conclusions and Future Work

In this paper, we present ARTNet, a cost-effective, realistic testbed for routing networks. It is scalable, extensible and user-friendly. It supports popular routing protocols and allows users to easily configure networks, control networks during real time and analyze the results after experimentations.

We use ARTNet to evaluate the performance of two popular routing protocols, EIGRP and OSPF based on quantitative metrics (packet loss and delta time) for standard application services. The comparative analysis demonstrates that EIGRP converges faster for HTTP and FTP applications, when the primary link for a subnet is interrupted.

For future work, we plan to combine IM with RCM to make ARTNet more user-friendly and develop an intelligent results analysis module to help users to develop insights from their experimentations.

References

1. GNU Zebra, http://www.gnu.org/software/zebra/
2. Quagga Software Routing Suite, http://www.quagga.net/

3. XORP Routing Platform, http://www.xorp.org/
4. OMNeT++, http://www.omnetpp.org/
5. Ns-2, http://www.isi.edu/nsnam/ns/
6. Cisco Packet Tracer, http://www.cisco.com/web/learning/netacad/course_catalog/PacketTracer.html
7. OPNET IT Guru, http://www.opnet.com/university_program/itguru_academic_edition/
8. Introduction to EIGRP, http://www.cisco.com/en/US/tech/tk365/technologies_tech_note09186a0080093f07.shtml
9. Graphic Network Simulator-GNS3, http://www.gns3.net/
10. IP Overview, http://www.cisco.com/en/US/docs/ios/12_0/np1/configuration/guide/1covervw.html#wp4585
11. Software License Agreement, http://www.cisco.com/public/sw-license-agreement.html
12. VMware Workstation Datasheet, http://www.vmware.com/files/pdf/VMware-Workstation-Datasheet.pdf
13. Wireshark, http://www.wireshark.org/
14. Hucaby, D.: CCNP SIWTCH 642-813 Official Certification Guide. Cisco Press, Indianapolis (2010)
15. Campus Network for High Availbility Design Guide, http://www.cisco.com/en/US/docs/solutions/Enterprise/Campus/HA_campus_DG/hacampusdg.html
16. Kaur, I., Sharma, M.: Performance Evaluation of Hybrid Network Using EIGRP & OSPF for Different Applications. International Journal of Engineering Science and Technology (IJEST) 3(5), 3950–3960 (2011)
17. Yehia, M.A., Aziz, M.S., Elsayed, H.A.: Analysis of IGP Routing Protocols for Real Time Applications: A Comparative Study. International Journal of Computer Applications 26(3), 11–17 (2011)
18. Lucio, G.F., Paredes-Farrera, M., Jammeh, E., Fleury, M., Reed, M.J.: OPNET Modeler and Ns-2: Comparing the Accuracy of Network Simulators for Packet-Level Analysis using a Network Testbed. In: 3rd WEAS International Conference on Simulation, Modeling and Optimization, vol. 2, pp. 700–707 (2003)
19. Knežević, N., Schubert, N., Kostić, D.: Towards a Cost-Effective Networking Testbed. SIGOPS Operating Systems Review 43(4), 66–71 (2009)
20. Li, Y., Liu, J., Rangaswami, R.: Toward Scalable Routing Experiments with Real-Time Network Simulation. In: Proceedings of the 22nd Workshop on Principles of Advanced and Distributed Simulation, pp. 23–30 (2008)
21. Experimental results about Multiprotocol Routing and Route Redistribution. In: 6th RoEduNet International Conference, Craiova, Romania, pp. 83–88 (November 2007)
22. Nguyen, H.X., Roughan, M., Knight, S., Falkner, N., Maennel, O., Bush, R.: How to Build Complex, Large-Scale Emulated Networks. In: Proc. 6th International Conference on Testbeds and Research Infrastructures for the Development of Networks & Communities, pp. 3–18 (2010)

VF2x: Fast, Efficient Virtual Network Mapping
for Real Testbed Workloads

Qin Yin and Timothy Roscoe

Systems Group, ETH Zürich,
Universitätstrasse 6, CH 8092, Zürich
{qyin,troscoe}@inf.ethz.ch

Abstract. Distributed network testbeds like GENI aim to support a potentially large number of experiments simultaneously on a complex, widely distributed physical network by mapping each requested network onto a share or "slice" of physical hosts, switches and links. A significant challenge is *network mapping*: how to allocate virtual nodes, switches and links from the physical infrastructure so as to accurately emulate the requested network configurations.

In this paper we present the VF2x virtual network mapping system. Based on the VF2 subgraph isomorphism detection algorithm designed for matching large graphs, VF2x incorporates several novel algorithmic improvements. These and careful implementation make VF2x perform more than two orders of magnitude faster than the fastest previously published algorithm.

In evaluating our algorithm, we generated an extensive test workload based on analysis of a 5-year trace of experiments submitted to the popular Emulab testbed, and using the current ProtoGENI topology. We use this test workload to evaluate the performance of VF2x, showing that it can allocate resources to virtual networks on a large testbed in a matter of seconds using commodity hardware.

Keywords: Network testbeds, virtual network mapping, subgraph isomorphism.

1 Introduction

Network testbeds are used by networking researchers to experiment with new protocols, applications, and systems, and are generally shared between users to reduce the considerable capital cost involved. A testbed consists of a set of physical resources – compute nodes (usually PCs), switches, links, etc. – together with a control plane which allocates resources. Users submit "requests" in the form of specifications of particular network configurations (nodes, topology, etc.) they would like to experiment with, when they require the resources, and for how long. In response, the control plane allocates, if possible, a set of resources to the users at the requested time.

Resources can be physical machines or links, but are often virtual "slices" of real resources. Multiplexing enables a plurality of diverse virtual networks to coexist on a shared physical network infrastructure [1–3]. Widely distributed testbeds like GENI [4] aim to support a potentially large number of experiments simultaneously by mapping each requested network onto a share or "slice" of physical hosts, switches and links.

A significant challenge in the context is *virtual network mapping:* how to map a virtual network (VN) topology with resource constraints to specific nodes and links in

T. Korakis, M. Zink, and M. Ott (Eds.): TridentCom 2012, LNICST 44, pp. 271–286, 2012.

a given physical network (PN) infrastructure so as to accurately emulate the network configurations requested by users. This mapping problem is difficult in theory and in practice due to the four properties summarized in [5]: *diverse topologies, resource constraints, online requests* and *admission control*. Even simplified variants of the mapping problem with relaxed properties turn out to be difficult: assigning nodes in a switched Ethernet-connected testbed without violating bandwidth constraints can be reduced to the NP-hard multiway separator problem [6], and even when the nodes are pre-selected, the link mapping problem for VN requests with link constraints is still NP-hard [5].

In this paper we present a new algorithm, VF2x, based on the VF2 subgraph isomorphism algorithm for matching large graphs [7]. VF2x performs network mapping more than two orders of magnitude faster than the previously-published vnmFlib (also based on VF2) but reduces solving time for near-worst-case problem instances through more careful implementation and several novel algorithmic changes: constructing a candidate queue, applying heuristic sorting, and introducing a new "timeout-and-relax" strategy.

In the rest of this paper, we first provide some background and related work of the problem, and then in Section 3 we describe the VF2x algorithm, discuss the implementation issues and algorithmic improvements, and evaluate its effectiveness through simulation. In Section 4.1 we explain the generation of a more realistic test workload derived from a 5-year trace of experiments submitted to the Emulab testbed. Using the generated test workload, we evaluate the performance of VF2x in Section 4. In Section 5 we make a conclusion.

2   Background and Related Work

Until recently, most testbeds supporting specification of network properties were centralized, such as Emulab [8] and DETER [9]. These testbeds emulate a variety of network topologies using a small number of high-port-count, high-capacity switches to approximate a physical crossbar between machines. This testbed mapping problem with bandwidth constraints has been proven to be NP-complete [10]. Simulated annealing has been successfully applied to this situation [11], but does not work well for large-scale virtualized network testbeds [12].

Other recent virtual network mapping algorithms make different assumptions in order to apply efficient heuristics to make the problem tractable.

Zhu and Ammar [13] assume unlimited physical network resources and then try to achieve low and balanced load on both physical nodes and links. Their algorithm, VNA-I, subdivides the general topology in the VN request into multiple small star topologies, and then exploits the flexibility of these small topologies.

Lu and Turner [14] consider the offline problem of mapping a virtual network with a backbone-star topology to the physical network with the aim of getting sufficient capacity to accommodate any traffic pattern specified by traffic constraints.

Yu et al. [5] propose a two stage solution to the problem. They first map the virtual nodes, and then map the virtual links using shortest path and multi-commodity flow (MCF) algorithms. The authors focus on improving the link mapping through *substrate support* for path splitting and migration. Razzaq and Rathore [15] also propose a two stage solution, but without the assumption of substrate support: virtual nodes are first mapped as closely as possible to the physical network, then virtual links are mapped to the shortest paths which satisfy the demands.

Chowdhury et al. [16] propose algorithms which provide better coordination between the two stages. The virtual nodes are mapped to the physical nodes in a way that facilitates the mapping of the virtual links to the physical paths in the subsequent phase. The mapping problem is solved using a Mixed Integer Program (MIP) formulation. The authors also assume substrate support.

Several algorithms consider network migration and reconfiguration. Butt et al. [17] note the importance of differentiating physical network resources and argue that topology-aware mapping together with reoptimizing bottleneck mappings can improve the acceptance ratio. Schaffrath et al. [18] formalize the mapping problem as a linear mixed integer program and allow dynamic reconfiguration of existing mappings.

Of particular interest is the vnmFlib network mapping library implemented by Lischka and Karl [19]. Noting the relationship between the network mapping problem and subgraph isomorphism detection, they develop a backtracking algorithm based on the VF2 algorithm used in the pattern recognition community for finding subgraph isomorphisms in large graphs. VnmFlib maps virtual nodes and links in a single stage and achieves better and faster mappings than the two stage approach used by Yu et al. [5], and works especially well for large virtual networks with strong resource constraints.

While many algorithms (including VF2x) can produce optimal results (subject to some utility function), this frequently involves exhaustive search and is therefore expensive. Moreover, it is rarely required; in practice a near-optimal solution in reasonable time is preferable. Emulab's simulated annealing algorithm [11] is a good example of exploiting this property.

However, the Emulab approach suffers from two limitations: firstly, it does not always return the same result due to its use of randomness, which makes the debugging of the algorithm challenging. Furthermore, it sometimes fails to find a solution that satisfies all the constraints even if such a solution exists. This is illustrated by the "ugly" example included in the Emulab source code. In contrast, VF2x is deterministic in all its heuristics, and for this "ugly" mapping problem, can find a solution with no violation in constraints in considerably less time.

3   VF2x Algorithm and Implementation

Recent proposals for distributed testbeds such as GENI presume a federated, distributed physical infrastructure over which virtual networks ("slices") are instantiated. Low cross-sectional bandwidth is expected in such testbeds. At present, the various proposed GENI frameworks address the mapping problem in different ways: ProtoGENI [20] inherits the existing `assign` mapping algorithm from Emulab; ORCA-BEN [21] uses NDL-OWL ontology language to express substrate and a sequence of request and release operations, and relies on Jena RDF and OWL reasoning engines to perform topology mapping [22]. The cost of the mapping operation is not prohibitive since the BEN network is small.

We found vnmFlib [19] to be especially suitable for the network testbed mapping problem, as explained above. However, in the process of trying to apply vnmFlib directly to our testbed resource allocator, we find several limitations of both the algorithm and its implementation which we explain in detail below. This motivated us to develop VF2x, our own VF2-derived virtual network mapping algorithm.

3.1 Implementation Decisions

As with vnmFlib, VF2x extends VF2 with semantic constraints on virtual node and link attributes (a key requirement for testbed applications) and a pre-defined distance value ϵ which, unlike VF2, allows virtual links to be mapped to multi-hop *paths* in the physical network of length at most ϵ.

Algorithm 1 shows the main skeleton of VF2x mapping algorithm. Variable *depth* maintains account of how many nodes have been successfully mapped so far. At each step, a new pair of nodes (n, m) is generated to try to match against each other. The feasible(n, m) function checks the syntactic (structure of the graph) and semantic (node and link attributes) feasibility of the mapping. If it succeeds, the mapping is remembered; otherwise, we try the next pair until we reach a dead end and backtrack().

Algorithm 1. VF2x mapping algorithm

    Input: Attributed graph G_{vn} and G_{pn}
    Output: Mapping from $M(G_{vn})$ to G_{pn}

1 **while** $|M| \neq |G_{vn}|$ **and** $depth > 0$ **do**
2     $(n, m) \leftarrow$ genpair();
3   **if** $n < 0$ **or** $m < 0$ **then**
4   backtrack();
5        $depth \leftarrow depth - 1$;
6   **end**
7   **else if** feasible(n,m) **then**
8        $M(m) \leftarrow n$;
9        $depth \leftarrow depth + 1$;
10   **end**
11 **end**

VF2x improves dramatically over vnmFlib through a combination of careful implementation and several algorithmic improvements. The implementation techniques can be summarized as follows: VF2x is implemented entirely in C (about 1,500 lines) based on the existing igraph library [23] implementation of VF2; VF2x supports modelling of network topologies as both directed and undirected graphs, while vnmFlib is restricted to topologies modeled only as directed graphs; unlike vnmFlib, VF2x avoids non-tail recursion; and finally, VF2x computes neighbors in a lazy manner and populates the adjacent neighbor table on demand, while vnmFlib recomputes neighbors every time.

By themselves, these implementation decisions make a dramatic difference in performance. Table 1 compares our VF2x implementation to vnmFlib using two simple mapping problems. To fairly compare the two implementations, we turn off the "splittable" option (to map the flow in a virtual link to multiple paths in the physical network), solve the mapping problems for directed graphs only, and set ϵ to 2 for both implementations. The hardware used is the same as that used in Section 4.

As seen from Table 1, even these better implementation techniques by themselves allow VF2x_base to already solve the problems in roughly *two orders of magnitude* less time than vnmFlib, without employing vnmFlib's sorting heuristics.

We are not the first to observe the performance issues with vnmFlib [24], but our goal here is to demonstrate that VF2-based algorithms in general can be implemented with good performance for reasonable problem sizes.

Table 1. VF2x vs. vnmFlib

	Example1[a]		Example2[b]	
	Steps	Time(ms)	Steps	Time(ms)
vnmFlib	3	2.786	20	18.994
VF2x_base	10	0.130	29	0.370
VF2x_candi	9	0.117	16	0.329
VF2x_candi_sort	4	0.089	14	0.050

[a] VN: 3 nodes and 3 links; PN: 6 nodes and 9 links.
[b] VN: 11 nodes and 10 links; PN: 14 nodes and 15 links.

Besides careful implementation, VF2x_base can be further optimized through algorithmic changes which prune/reorganize the search space further and thus lead to a better solution in less time.

Table 1 includes two of the algorithmic changes we use in VF2x: using a *candidate queue* and applying *heuristic sorting*. With these changes, the number of matching steps is reduced. Details of these and other algorithmic changes, and their performance impact, are given in the rest of this section.

3.2 VF2x with a Candidate Queue

To map a virtual node n to the physical network, rather than matching n against every node available from the physical network, VF2 matches only against those nodes within ϵ hops of the physical nodes already mapped.

VF2x uses a *candidate queue* to prune the search space still further. We first find all the nodes that n's neighbors have been mapped to. In the example shown in Figure 1, n's neighbors n_1, n_2 are mapped to m_1, m_2. Then, we calculate the intersection of $E(m_1)$ and $E(m_2)$. Here, $E(m)$ is the set of nodes at most ϵ hops away from m in the physical network. In fact, the only possible candidates for n are elements of this intersection and we call it n's *candidate queue*. In Figure 1, the candidates are the light gray ones in the shadowed area. The candidate queue improves solving time by reducing the number of candidates to match: `genpair()` only generates candidate pairs (n, m) where m belongs to the candidate queue. Table 1 shows the improvement obtained (the VF2x_candi row).

3.3 Heuristic Sorting of Network Topologies

Like VF2, VF2x is based on a depth-first search strategy. The sequence of the candidate pairs generated depend on how the nodes are ordered in the virtual and physical

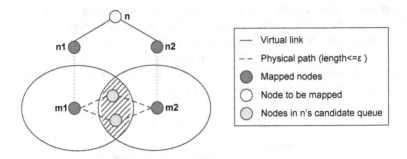

Fig. 1. The generation of n's candidate queue

networks. This suggests that sorting the nodes according to heuristics can reorganize the search tree, and find a better solution in less time.

Different heuristics can be applied. vnmFlib sorts the generated candidate pairs based on the resource consumption of the virtual nodes; VF2x sorts graph nodes such that *switches* are ordered before *hosts* (whether a graph node is a switch or a host is indicated by the additional "type" attribute which is introduced for a testbed environment), furthermore high-degree nodes are sorted ahead of low-degree ones. Figure 8(b) in Section 4.2 shows the effectiveness of this heuristic of mapping more-constrained resources first.

3.4   Batching

Another extension VF2x makes for a testbed environment is to support batch solving: mapping several virtual network requests in one solving process even though they share the same physical network resources. The original VF2 algorithm does not support this and can only detect isomorphism for the disconnected subgraphs (VN requests) by mapping the virtual nodes from these requests to different physical nodes. With this extension, the same physical switch can be shared by different requests even though different switches in the same request are mapped to different physical ones.

3.5   Timeout-and-Relax for ϵ

The vnmFlib authors propose two algorithms to pick an appropriate ϵ (recall that virtual links are only mapped to paths shorter than ϵ): VnmFlib-simple uses a fixed ϵ, while vnmFlib-advanced starts with $\epsilon = 1$, exhaustively searches for a mapping, and then successively increments ϵ until one is found or until ϵ reaches 10.

For smaller ϵ, fewer candidate nodes need be considered, but the tighter constraints can increase the required exploration of the search space. Informally, for small ϵ, if a solution exists, it is likely that it will be found early in the search.

This observation leads us to adopt an additional heuristic to mitigate occasional worst-case performance of VF2x (the general problem remains NP-hard), which we term *"timeout-and-relax"*. Instead of always running VF2x to completion, we start with small ϵ and impose a small time limit on the solving time, aborting the algorithm if it exceeds the limit. We then increase ϵ and the value of timeout, and retry. This approach attempts a good compromise between shorter solving time of a smaller ϵ, and higher success rate of a larger ϵ. As shown in Figure 9, this strategy brings down the average solving time considerably compared to fixed ϵ and timeout values.

3.6 Algorithm Analysis with Synthetic Workload

Using the GT-ITM tool, we generated 10 separate physical networks with 100, 150, 200, ..., 550 nodes. Each node pair is randomly connected with probability 0.1. In this way, the physical network with 100 nodes are connected by around 500 links. We also generated 200 virtual networks. The size of the virtual networks is uniformly distributed between 2 to 20 and the nodes are connected with probability 0.5. The CPU capacity and the link bandwidth follow a uniform distribution ranging from 1 to 100 for the physical networks and ranging from 1 to 50 for the virtual networks. While synthetic, these randomly generated virtual and physical networks are of the same characteristics as those used by other researchers [5, 13, 19].

To evaluate each algorithmic change introduced above, we run a set of experiments to map 200 virtual networks to each of the 10 physical networks using variants of VF2x. In these experiments, ϵ is fixed and set to 2 and *timeout* is set to 5s. The VF2x algorithm variants compared are: VF2x_base, VF2x_candi and VF2x_candi_sort. VF2x_base is an extended VF2 which supports semantics constraints and maps virtual links to multi-hop paths. VF2x_candi extends VF2x_base with a candidate queue which further prunes the search space. VF2x_candi_sort applies heuristic sorting to VF2x_candi and sorts the nodes by the degree. Heuristic sorting reorganizes the search space in a way to find a better mapping in less time.

We ran all the experiments on a machine with an Intel Core2 Q6700 (quad-core 2.66 GHz) CPU and 4GB memory. The machine was running Ubuntu Linux 10.04 LTS Lucid Lynx, and we used version 0.5.4 of the *igraph* library.

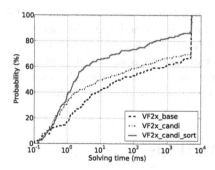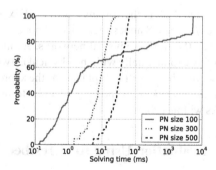

Fig. 2. Solving time CDF for VF2x variants   **Fig. 3.** Solving time CDF for various PN sizes

Figure 2 compares the three algorithm variants by mapping 200 virtual networks to the same 100-node physical network. As we can see, algorithmic improvements dramatically reduce the solving time and improve the mapping success rate: among 200 requests, within 5s, VF2x_base fails to map 65 requests, VF2x_candi fails to map 61 requests, while VF2x_candi_sort manages to bring the number down to 26. If we set the timeout to 500s, one request fails after exhausting the search space and 11 requests fails due to timeout.

Figure 3 plots the solving time of VF2x_candi_sort to map 200 randomly generated virtual networks to three different physical networks: 100 nodes with 483 links, 300 nodes with 4513 links, and 500 nodes with 12458 links. As shown in the figure, for more than 65% of the requests, VF2x uses less time to map them to the 100-node physical network. However, it takes substantially more time for about 20% of the requests, and even times out for 26 requests out of 200. Physical network size does play an important role in the algorithm and we investigate this subject further in Section 4.3. Moreover, within the same time limit, the *timeout-and-relax* strategy can improve the success rate significantly, as we show in Section 4.2.

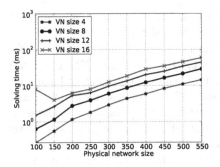
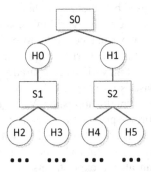

Fig. 4. Solving time CDF for various VN sizes   **Fig. 5.** Generated tree topology

Figure 4 plots the solving time of VF2x_candi_sort to map 4 virtual networks of 4 nodes / 4 links, 8 nodes / 12 links, 12 nodes / 34 links, and 16 nodes / 54 links separately to the 10 different physical networks. As the figure shows, the solving time increases roughly exponentially with the physical network size as well as the virtual network size. However, this is still acceptable for these problem sizes since VF2x is able to map the virtual network of 16 nodes / 54 links to the physical network of 500 nodes / 12458 links within 100*ms*.

4   Evaluation Using Real Testbed Workloads

Since networking testbeds are still relatively new, particular those which are distributed in nature and permit complex topological requests, it is not clear what kind of workload is representative for a testbed resource allocator. Much related work uses GT-ITM to simulate requests and testbed network topologies, as we have done to analyze different VF2x algorithm variants in Section 3.6.

However, these randomly generated undirected graphs cannot faithfully represent real testbed requests and infrastructures. Therefore, in this section, we describe the generation of a more plausible test workload and use it to evaluate VF2x. While we make no authoritative claims that the workload generated is representative, we do argue that it is based on plausible data and assumptions. The hardware used is the same as that used in Section 3.6.

4.1 Workload Generation

Physical Topology. We extracted physical topology information from ProtoGENI[1] and build our physical topology with 627 nodes (including switches and hosts) and 1163 links based on the resource information from the Utah ProtoGENI site. We simplify the topology by summing up the bandwidth of all links from the same host to the same switch instead of including all "duplicated" links. This physical topology is used for all the experiments shown in this section.

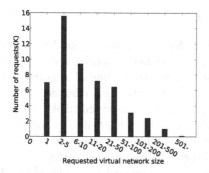
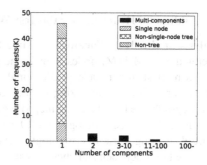

Fig. 6. Distribution of the requested VN size   **Fig. 7.** Topology of the requested VNs

Request Stream. We then derive a sequence of virtual network requests from a complete sequence of Emulab topology requests for 5 years up to June 2007, essentially covering every experiment submitted to Emulab before that date. This trace consists of 23818 projects, 127586 topology requests among which 52089 are unique (the Emulab .top files are not identical). Figure 6 shows the distribution of the requested network sizes.

Temporal Characteristics. We assume that virtual network requests arrive dynamically. The users submit "requests" stating desired network resources, when they are needed, and for how long. In response, the testbed resource allocator will decide whether to accept the requests and if so, which specific physical resources will be allocated.

In order to construct a realistic request workload, two important temporal variables must be modeled: the request *arrival rate* and *duration* which defines for how long the user actively uses the allocated resources.

---

[1] http://www.protogeni.net/trac/protogeni

The arrivals of the requests are modeled as a Poisson process with a mean of λ requests per time window. As a reference, we roughly calculate the request arrival rate for the Emulab request trace. Based on the fact that Emulab received 127586 top requests over 4 years, we conclude that Emulab received 4 requests per hour on average. Using 4 as a base value, in the following experiment, we vary λ to increase or decrease offered load. This distribution model naturally does not take into account load spikes on the system (such as before conference deadlines).

Request duration is modeled as a Gamma distribution. which have long been used for modeling demand distribution in queuing systems [25, 26]. We choose the parameters *shape* = 0.3 and *scale* = 20, and generate 1000 duration values with the distribution as follows: 266 values are less than 10 minutes, 117 between 10 and 30 minutes, 90 between 0.5 and 1 hour, 459 between 1 and 24 hours, 68 between 1 and 7 days.

Based on the distribution models, we annotate the Emulab request stream with two time parameters – when to request resources and when to release them – and generate our workload from this. The workload is used in Section 4.4 to evaluate our testbed resource allocation with VF2x mapping algorithm.

4.2   Additional Heuristics for the Test Workload

Analysis of the Test Workload. Unlike the random virtual and physical networks generated by GM-ITM, nodes both in the physical topology described above and in our new request stream have an additional "type" attribute indicating whether they are switches or nodes. By analyzing the number of components of the requested virtual network graph, we found that the majority of the requests are connected graphs. Among them, most have tree topology and 20% of the trees are single nodes, as shown in Figure 7. Among these tree-topology requests, the structure in Figure 5 is common, where the hosts between switches are running DummyNet and acting as delays.

To explore the best heuristics we can apply to the test workload, we use the physical network described in Section 4.1, and generate a series of trees of various sizes following the structure pattern shown in Figure 5. We ran the VF2x mapping algorithm with different ϵ values (the maximum length of the physical path that a virtual link can be mapped to) and different sorting heuristics.

ϵ values are 1, 2, 3 and 4. Our baseline for comparison is "doing nothing": ordering virtual and physical nodes as they are declared in the specification; the second heuristic is the one we describe in Section 3: sorting virtual and physical switches and hosts in descending order of their degrees: first switches from high to low degree, then hosts from high to low degree (so that switches are mapped first).

By comparing Figures 8(b) and 8(a), we can see that the heuristic to order/map switches and hosts based on their degrees can reduce the solving time and increase the success rate within a solving time limit of 10s.

These two experiments both show some interesting properties of ϵ. First, the smaller the ϵ value is, the fewer candidate nodes are to be considered, which results in less solving time. Second, the smaller the ϵ value is, the more constrained it is to find a satisfiable solution. This can result in longer solving time for the cases where a solution with smaller ϵ exists but requires more exploration of the search space, or when failing to find a mapping solution due to a timeout. Third, the smaller the ϵ value is, the more

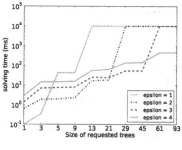

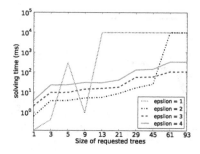

(a) "Doing nothing" heuristic sorting   (b) Degree-based heuristic sorting

Fig. 8. Solving time for trees of various sizes

sensitive the solving time is to the order of the nodes. In Figure 8(b), a tree of size 5 takes more time to solve than tree of size 9. The 5-tree orders the nodes as $S0, S1, S2, H0, H1$ while the 9-tree orders them as $S1, S2, S0, H0, H1, H2, ...H5$ according to the sorting heuristic. These observations led us to adopt the "timeout-and-relax" technique: we start with small ϵ and small timeout, and increase ϵ and the value of timeout after each timeout. This approach aims at a good compromise between faster average solving time of smaller ϵ, and higher success rate of larger ϵ.

Applying Heuristics to the Test Workload. Having shown the effectiveness of the sorting heuristic, in the next experiment we use our request stream to investigate the effectiveness of the "timeout-and-relax" strategy. We randomly choose 2000 requests out of 52089 Emulab requests and individually map each of them to the *same* physical topology introduced in Section 4.1. We compare two different strategies: the simple strategy in which ϵ is fixed and set to 4 with *timeout* = 10s; the timeout-and-relax strategy in which ϵ is dynamic with different timeouts: $(\epsilon = 2, 1s), (\epsilon = 3, 2s), (\epsilon = 4, 7s)$. In both experiments, the sorting heuristic described above is applied.

Figure 9(a) and Figure 9(b) plot the solving time against the virtual network size. Here, the virtual network size is defined as the total number of nodes and links. Figure 9(c) depicts the solving time CDF for fixed $\epsilon = 4$ and dynamic $\epsilon = [2, 3, 4]$. From these figures, we can see that: with timeout-and-relax, VF2x solves most (more than 85%) mapping problems in less time, while it also achieves a higher success rate and the number of timeout cases decreases from 119 to 74.

Figure 9(d) shows this comparison in more detail by plotting the solving time with *fixed* ϵ against the solving time with *dynamic* ϵ. As we can see, most of the mapping problems are solved in less time with *dynamic* ϵ and a majority of them are twice as fast. The dots plotted in the center right of the figure are the 45 requests which fail with fixed ϵ but succeed with dynamic ϵ. The dots plotted in the top right corner are the 74 requests (out of 2000) which fail to be mapped within 10s.

The algorithm used in all the next set of experiments is VF2x_candi with the above sorting heuristic and timeout-and-relax strategy applied.

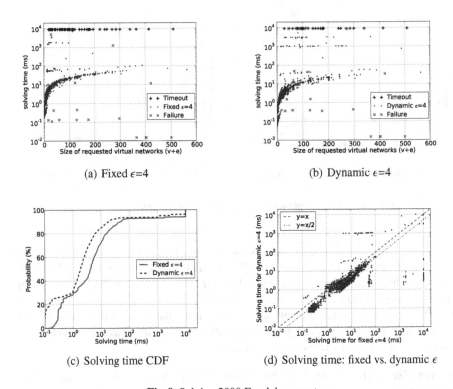

(a) Fixed $\epsilon=4$

(b) Dynamic $\epsilon=4$

(c) Solving time CDF

(d) Solving time: fixed vs. dynamic ϵ

Fig. 9. Solving 2000 Emulab requests

4.3 Repeated Requests to Exhaust Physical Resources

In this section, we use a simple test workload to investigate the *sequential* and *global* allocation strategies. The test workload is a round-robin sequence of four requests from Emulab request history which contain one node, 4 nodes, 7 nodes and 13 nodes separately. For the two allocation strategies, we investigate the solving time to map physical resources to the successive requests, as well as the total proportion of physical resources that are allocated. In the experiment, we deliberately repeat the request in order to investigate, for one specific request, the influence of the shrinking physical resource pool.

With the sequential solving strategy, we allocate resources to each request, mark the resources allocated as unavailable and never reallocate them, and continue until we exhaust all physical resources. During this process, physical resource utilization is increasing and the free physical resources are decreasing. Figure 10(a) plots the relationship between the solving time for one specific request and the shrinking physical network. It shows how, initially, the solving time decreses since the available resources are abundant the search space is shrinking. This trend stops in the middle when the platform has much fewer resources available and the solver has to nearly exhaust the (smaller) search space to find a solution.

With the global solving strategy, whenever we process a new request, we reassign resources to all the requests seen so far in one mapping process, without respecting any

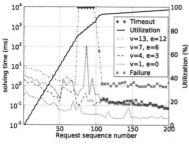
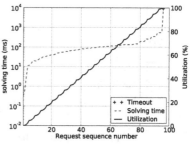

(a) Solving 4 requests repeatedly   (b) Solving accumulated requests

Fig. 10. Exhausting physical resources

previous resource assignment. As we have observed in [27], with global solving, the execution time increases exponentially as more constraint programs are solved simultaneously in the ECLiPSe solver we used [28]. To our surprise, with the batch solving described in Section 3.3, the solving time in VF2x does not increase exponentially. As shown in Figure 10(b), after a sharp increase at the beginning, the execution time increases linearly. This is due to the fact the requests are repeating themselves. At the beginning, VF2x takes some time (still within 10ms) to find mappings for the first 4 requests. Then, since successive requests are identical, they reuse the switch mappings generated beforehand and this significantly prunes the search space. This shows that batch solving is a surprising promising technique for solving a set of structurally recurring requests efficiently.

4.4   Long Trace Behavior

In this section, we use the full test workload generated in Section 4.1 to evaluate our testbed resource allocator with the VF2x mapping algorithm.

We run the simulations for 200 time windows with different request arrival rates: $\lambda = 4, 8, 16$ which correspond to $800, 1600, 3200$ requests in each simulation instance. The generation of the request workload and the physical network topology used in the simulations is described in Section 4.1. We use a client simulator to send resource requests and release requests to the allocator. Upon receiving a resource request, the allocator runs VF2x to decide whether or not to accept the request, if yes, it decides which physical resources to allocate and removes them from the physical network; upon receiving a release request, the allocator will revoke the resources and return them to the physical network.

In Figure 11, the dotted line depicts the utilization of the physical network (dividing the number of allocated hosts by the total number of physical hosts) under a request arrival rate of $\lambda = 4$. The solid line shows the utilization in an "ideal" scenario where all the requests are accepted and satisfied. Of 800 requests, the allocator refuses 69 due to resource insufficiency and fails to map 7 requests to the physical network within $10s$. For these timeout cases, we can relax their resource constraints and retry the mapping with VF2x.

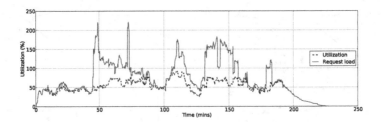

Fig. 11. Executing the generated trace of arrival rate $\lambda = 4$

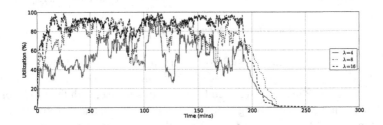

Fig. 12. Executing the generated trace of arrival rate $\lambda = 4, 8, 16$

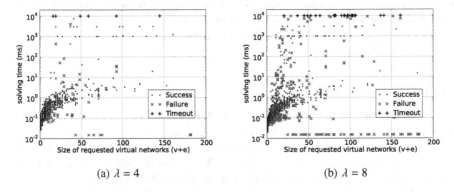

(a) $\lambda = 4$ (b) $\lambda = 8$

Fig. 13. Executing the generated trace of arrival rate $\lambda = 4, 8$

Figure 12 shows the physical network utilization under different request loads. After some warm-up time, the system enters a more steady state as leases are requested and released "evenly". In the end, when no more requests are received, the allocator gradually releases all the resources. By comparing the lines for different λ, we can see that the higher the load, the more likely it is that the allocator can fit small requests into the network and achieve higher utilization.

Figure 13 shows the solving time (including failures and timeouts) of VF2x in mapping the requests of different sizes to the changing physical network in the continuous resource allocation process. As we can see, with a bigger λ value, the provider receives more requests in a given time slot, and this results in a higher failure rate because of its limited capacity.

5   Conclusion

We have presented VF2x, a new virtual network mapping algorithm based on the VF2 subgraph isomorphism detection algorithm. VF2x supports semantic constraints and is able to map virtual links to multi-hop paths. Several algorithmic improvements are introduced: using a candidate queue, applying heuristic sorting and adopting timeout-and-relax strategy.

The design of suitable network mapping algorithms for network testbeds (and, indeed, similar scenarios such a datacenter networks and cloud facilities) is still in its infancy, and the idealized problem is, in theory, computationally hard.

However, we have shown that a combination of good choice of algorithm, pragmatism with regard to timeouts, and careful attention to implementation details can provide a fast way of embedding virtual networks in a physical substrate – when combining algorithmic optimizations, implementation, and heuristics like sorting and timeout-and-relax, VF2x is over two orders of magnitude faster than previous systems like VnmFlib.

References

1. Anderson, T., Peterson, L., Shenker, S., Turner, J.: Overcoming the internet impasse through virtualization. IEEE Computer Magazine 38, 34–41 (2005)
2. Turner, J., Taylor, D.: Diversifying the internet. In: GLOBECOM, pp. 755–760. IEEE (2005)
3. Mosharaf KabirChowdhury, N.M., Boutaba, R.: A survey of network virtualization. Comput. Netw. 54, 862–876 (2010)
4. GENI, http://www.geni.net/
5. Yu, M., Yi, Y., Rexford, J., Chiang, M.: Rethinking virtual network embedding: substrate support for path splitting and migration. SIGCOMM Comput. Commun. Rev. 38, 17–29 (2008)
6. Andersen, D.G.: Theoretical approaches to node assignment (December 2002) (unpublished manuscript)
7. Cordella, L.P., Foggia, P., Sansone, C., Vento, M.: A (sub)graph isomorphism algorithm for matching large graphs. IEEE Trans. Pattern Anal. Mach. Intell. 26, 1367–1372 (2004)
8. Lepreau, J.: Emulab - Network Emulation Testbed, http://www.emulab.net/
9. The DETER Testbed: Overview, www.isi.edu/deter/docs/testbed.overview.pdf
10. McGeer, R., Andersen, D.G., Schwab, S.: The Network Testbed Mapping Problem. In: Magedanz, T., Gavras, A., Thanh, N.H., Chase, J.S. (eds.) TridentCom 2010. LNICST, vol. 46, pp. 383–398. Springer, Heidelberg (2011)
11. Ricci, R., Alfeld, C., Lepreau, J.: A solver for the network testbed mapping problem. SIGCOMM Comput. Commun. Rev. 33, 65–81 (2003)
12. Hibler, M., Ricci, R., Stoller, L., Duerig, J., Guruprasad, S., Stack, T., Webb, K., Lepreau, J.: Large-scale virtualization in the emulab network testbed. In: USENIX 2008 Annual Technical Conference on Annual Technical Conference, Berkeley, CA, USA, pp. 113–128. USENIX Association (2008)

13. Zhu, Y., Ammar, M.H.: Algorithms for assigning substrate network resources to virtual network components. In: INFOCOM. IEEE (2006)
14. Lu, J., Turner, J.: Efficient mapping of virtual networks onto a shared substrate. Technical Report WUCSE-2006-35, Washington University (September 2006)
15. Razzaq, A., Rathore, M.S.: An approach towards resource efficient virtual network embedding. In: Proceedings of the 2010 2nd International Conference on Evolving Internet, INTERNET 2010, Washington, DC, USA, pp. 68–73 (2010)
16. Mosharaf Kabir Chowdhury, N.M., Rahman, M.R., Boutaba, R.: Virtual network embedding with coordinated node and link mapping. In: INFOCOM, pp. 783–791. IEEE (2009)
17. Farooq Butt, N., Chowdhury, M., Boutaba, R.: Topology-Awareness and Reoptimization Mechanism for Virtual Network Embedding. In: Crovella, M., Feeney, L.M., Rubenstein, D., Raghavan, S.V. (eds.) NETWORKING 2010. LNCS, vol. 6091, pp. 27–39. Springer, Heidelberg (2010)
18. Schaffrath, G., Schmid, S., Feldmann, A.: Generalized and resource-efficient vnet embeddings with migrations. CoRR, abs/1012.4066 (2010)
19. Lischka, J., Karl, H.: A virtual network mapping algorithm based on subgraph isomorphism detection. In: Proceedings of the 1st ACM Workshop on Virtualized Infrastructure Systems and Architectures, VISA 2009, New York, NY, USA, pp. 81–88. ACM (2009)
20. ProtoGENI, http://www.protogeni.net/trac/protogeni
21. Chase, J.: ORCA control framework architecture and internals. Technical report, Duke University (September 2009)
22. Baldine, I., Xin, Y., Evans, D., Heerman, C., Chase, J., Marupadi, V., Yumerefendi, A.: The missing link: Putting the network in networked cloud computing. In: International Conference on the Virtual Computing Initiative (ICVCI 2009) (October 2009)
23. The igraph library, http://igraph.sourceforge.net/
24. Guo, C., Lu, G., Wang, H.J., Yang, S., Kong, C., Sun, P., Wu, W., Zhang, Y.: Secondnet: a data center network virtualization architecture with bandwidth guarantees. In: Proceedings of the 6th International Conference, Co-NEXT 2010, New York, NY, USA, vol. 15, pp. 1–12. ACM (2010)
25. Smith, J.R., Golden, P.A., Appleton, B.: Airline: a strategic management simulation. Prentice Hall (1991)
26. Jain, R.K.: The art of computer systems performance analysis: Techniques for experimental design, measurement, simulation, and modeling, p. 720 (April 1991)
27. Yin, Q., Roscoe, T.: A better way to negotiate for testbed resources. In: Proceedings of the 2nd ACM SIGOPS Asia-Pacific Workshop on Systems (APSys 2011), Shanghai, China (July 2011)
28. Apt, K.R., Wallace, M.G.: Constraint Logic Programming using ECL^{i}PS^e. Cambridge University Press (2007)

How to Build a Better Testbed: Lessons from a Decade of Network Experiments on Emulab

Fabien Hermenier[1,2] and Robert Ricci[1]

[1] University of Utah School of Computing
[2] OASIS Team, INRIA - CNRS - I3S, Univ. Sophia-Antipolis
fabien.hermenier@inria.fr, ricci@cs.utah.edu

Abstract. The Emulab network testbed provides an environment in which researchers and educators can evaluate networked systems. Available to the public since 2000, Emulab is used by thousands of experimenters at hundreds of institutions around the world, and the research conducted on it has lead to hundreds of publications. The original Emulab facility at the University of Utah has been replicated at dozens of other sites.

The physical design of the Emulab facility, and many other testbeds like it, has been based on the facility operators' expectations regarding user needs and behavior. If operators' assumptions are incorrect, the resulting facility can exhibit inefficient use patterns and sub-optimal resource allocation. Our study, the first of its kind, gains insight into the needs and behaviors of networking researchers by analyzing more than 500,000 topologies from 13,000 experiments submitted to Emulab. Using this dataset, we re-visit the assumptions that went into the physical design of the Emulab facility and consider improvements to it. Through extensive simulations with real workloads, we evaluate alternative testbeds designs for their ability to improve testbed utilization and reduce hardware costs.

1 Introduction

Network emulation testbeds [2,3,11,15,14] have become environments of choice for evaluating network research. Their ability to provide highly customizable network topologies make them suitable for hosting a wide variety of experiments, including security, networking, and distributed systems research. One of the oldest and largest, the Utah Emulab facility [5,8,15], is currently built from more than 600 nodes having more than 3,000 network interfaces. It gives experimenters full administrator access to their allotted physical nodes and the ability to shape characteristics of dedicated network links. We estimate that worldwide, at least ten thousand experimenters, a substantial fraction of the network research community, use testbeds that are derived from, or similar to, the Utah Emulab facility, and are thus affected by the decisions that have gone into its design. In this paper, we examine user requests submitted to Emulab to gain insight into experimenters' behavior, and we use this information to inform the physical design of future testbed facilities.

The goals of network testbeds differ from general-purpose clusters, and thus traditional cluster and data center designs cannot be applied directly to this domain. Clusters typically concentrate on maximizing host-based metrics (such as compute power or

T. Korakis, M. Zink, and M. Ott (Eds.): TridentCom 2012, LNICST 44, pp. 287–304, 2012.
© Institute for Computer Sciences, Social Informatics and Telecommunications Engineering 2012

I/O operations) with the network playing only a supporting role. In a network testbed, these priorities are reversed: the network is the main object of study, and the physical infrastructure of the testbed must support embedding of a wide variety of experimenters' requested topologies. It is important to enable embeddings that avoid artifacts due to under-provisioned network links or devices. In most clusters, communications patterns on the network are not explicit; that is, any node may wish to communicate with any other node, and the existence and bandwidths of particular communication paths are not defined *a priori*. As a result, cluster networks must be provisioned based on measured load or built with full bisection bandwidth. In contrast, the networks in emulation testbeds are explicit, and it is possible to directly study whether the network substrate is capable of meeting the demands that are placed on it. Testbeds also have relaxed requirements for high-availability—downtime due to failure of non-redundant components represents an inconvenience, rather than a large loss of revenue.

Thus, while datacenter networks have received extensive study [1,7,9], a different approach is needed for testbed networks. Facilities such as the Utah Emulab [15], DETER [2], and StarBed [11] have independently designed their physical network topologies subject to budgetary constraints and *assumptions* regarding experimenters' needs. Such decisions impact the effectiveness of the testbed. Budgetary constraints necessitate tradeoffs between factors such as the number of nodes in a testbed (affecting the number and size of experiments that can be supported) and the degree of connectivity between them (affecting the types of topologies that can be instantiated). If the decisions made during testbed design are mismatched with user behavior, the result is a testbed that either does not meet user needs or is unnecessarily expensive.

Emulation testbeds are now mature enough to provide us with a large dataset showing how experimenters use them in *practice*; by studying this dataset, we can learn how to build better testbeds. To this end, we have analyzed the network topologies submitted to the Utah Emulab site, the largest and most widely-used emulation testbed, over a period of eight years: from 2003 to 2011.[1] This dataset consists of over 500,000 network topologies submitted by 500 projects as they ran 13,000 experiments. From our analysis, we form several hypotheses about the most effective ways to build future testbeds, and test these hypotheses with simulations using real workloads.

We begin in Section 2 with a description of the Emulab testbed and the dataset used for our study. In Section 3, we analyze the properties of experimenters' submitted topologies, including their size and edge-connectivity. Section 4 considers key decisions in the physical design of a network emulation testbed, taking into account the cost implications of these choices. Section 5 evaluates the effectiveness of different testbed designs through extensive simulation using real user-submitted topologies. Finally, Section 6 presents the high-level conclusions that we draw from the study.

2   The Emulab Testbed

To run an experiment on Emulab, a user submits a description written in a variant of the *ns-2* simulator language [6]. Included in this description is a *virtual topology* defining

---

[1] Topologies from Emulab's first years, 2000–2002, were not saved in enough detail for analysis.

the nodes, links, and LANs[2] on which the experiment is to be run. Emulab realizes this virtual topology on top of the hosts and switches in its *physical topology* by loading operating systems, configuring software, and creating VLANs.[3]

One of Emulab's primary goals is *scientific fidelity*: it only "accepts" experiments for which it has sufficient capacity. Bottlenecks in the physical topology (such as links between switches) should not lead to artifacts in experiments. Because Emulab is a multi-user facility, this means that interference between simultaneous experiments must be minimized and resources already allocated to other users must be taken into account. Emulab uses `assign` [12], a randomized solver, to find mappings from experimenters' virtual topologies onto the testbed's physical infrastructure. `assign` ensures that the mappings it produces do not violate constraints such as bandwidth on bottleneck links, and attempts to maximize the potential for future mappings by avoiding scarce resources when possible. Most experiments run on Emulab use "bare hardware" with a one-to-one mapping between nodes in the virtual topology and physical hosts. For the purposes of this paper, we refer to these as "isolated experiments." Emulab also supports "multiplexed experiments," in which multiple virtual machines can be placed on each physical host. Multiplexed experiments are less popular than isolated ones because Emulab users typically want high fidelity and low-level access to hardware. The primary use of multiplexing is to run experiments that are too large to be instantiated one-to-one on the testbed's limited physical resources.

Emulab's physical topology has two networks: each node connects to both. The first is a "control" network, over which testbed control tasks such a disk loading and network filesystem mounts occur. This network connects to the Internet, and is used for remote access to the nodes. The second is the "experimental" network: this network is isolated from the outside and is re-configured as needed to create the experimenter's virtual topology. In this paper, we focus on the experimental network, as it is the one in which the experimenter's topology is embedded, and which must be sufficiently provisioned to ensure scientific fidelity. Emulab supports "delay" nodes for traffic shaping on the experimental network: when an experiment requests a link with non-zero latency or with a bandwidth value not natively supported by Ethernet, Emulab inserts a node acting as a transparent bridge. These nodes bridge two interfaces together using FreeBSD's `dummynet` [13] to delay packets or limit their bandwidth. Because delaying a single link requires only two interfaces, physical nodes having an even number of interfaces can delay multiple links.

The Emulab facility at Utah has grown organically over the past twelve years: from an initial set of 10 nodes, it has now grown to approximately 600, connected by thirteen Ethernet switches. Nodes have been added over time in large, homogeneous batches, and old nodes are rarely removed from service. Most nodes have four connections to the experimental network. The rationale behind the use of homogeneous node groups is to achieve a high degree of flexibility: the more interchangeable nodes are, the more freedom there is in resource assignment. Old nodes are kept under the assumption that

---

[2] For Emulab's purposes, a LAN is defined as a clique of nodes with full bisection bandwidth.

[3] In this paper, we concentrate on Emulab's most heavily used resource: a "cluster" testbed made up of PCs and Ethernet switches. Emulab also supports a wide range of other physical devices, including wireless links, network processors, wide-area hosts and links, and Layer 1 switches.

since network researchers are interested primarily in the network, most can tolerate older, low-powered hosts. Emulab's physical topology is tree-like: because there is no need for redundancy, there is only a single path between any pair of switches. It is built primarily with large modular switches (supporting up to 384 ports per chassis), because full bisection bandwidth can be provided for modest cost within one switch. Emulab does not attempt to provide full bisection bandwidth across its entire physical topology due to the high cost of doing so. Instead, it relies on `assign` to map experiments in such a way as to minimize the use of inter-switch links, and rejects experiments that cannot fit within these limits. Switch interconnects are generally built from interfaces one order of magnitude faster than the node interfaces. For example, switches providing 100 Mbps Ethernet to nodes are interconnected using four to eight 1 Gbps ports, and gigabit switches are interconnected using four 10 Gbps ports. Older Emulab nodes have all interfaces connected to a single switch, while newer ones are "striped" across multiple switches as described in Section 4.

The Utah Emulab is one of the oldest and largest facilities of its kind, and its design has influenced many other facilities. Other testbeds built using the Emulab software [14], including DETER [2], use a similar physical topology. Unrelated testbeds, such as StarBed [11] and Grid'500 [3], also use fundamentally similar physical topologies.

2.1 Description of the Dataset

Each time a user creates, deletes, or modifies an experiment, Emulab records the action in a database and puts the resulting topology in an archive file. We extract from these records a *raw dataset* containing 619,504 topologies submitted by experimenters since 2003. These topologies are grouped into 22,266 different *experiments*: in Emulab, a single experiment may be instantiated on the testbed many times, because users typically release resources when not in active use. The experiments belong to 522 *projects*. A project is a group of experimenters collaborating on the same research topic, from the same lab, or in the same class.

Not every topology is relevant to our study, so we reduced the raw dataset in several ways. First, some topologies request only a single node or no network links. Such topologies are used by experimenters who are not studying the network, or to test the deployment of specific applications or operating system images in preparation for larger experiments. They are not relevant to the design of the testbed's physical network, so we ignore them for this study. Second, Emulab provides users with the ability to create or modify experiments without instantiating them on the physical hardware, and we excluded such topologies. Third, the operators of the testbed have several internal projects. As such projects are not representative of general research needs, we have excluded them. Finally, some experiments use resources that are not part of the main cluster testbed, such as wireless nodes or wide-area hosts embedded in campus or backbone networks [4]. While important, these types of experiments have little effect on the design of the cluster network, so we removed them from our study. Table 1 details the filtering performed to produce a *working dataset* composed of 477 projects, 13,057 experiments, and 504,226 topologies.

Table 1. Refinement performed on the raw dataset to form the working dataset

	Projects	Experiments	Topologies
Raw dataset	522	22,266	619,504
− empty topologies			553
− single node topologies			27,983
− unconnected nodes			24,454
− non-instantiated topologies			32,260
− internal projects	9	1,936	16,004
− non-cluster resources			14,024
Working dataset	477	13,057	504,226

3   Properties of Experimenters' Topologies

We begin our study by analyzing the topologies submitted by experimenters, concentrating on the properties that directly affect testbed design: the topologies' sizes, the types of nodes they request, and their connectivity.

3.1   Most Experiments Are Small

Figure 1 shows the distribution of experiment sizes in the dataset. The first fact evident from this figure is that most experiments are small: 80% of the isolated experiments use fewer than 20 nodes. There is a small, but significant, tail of large experiments: 4% (more than 20,000 topologies) requested 100 nodes or more. The large topologies belonged to 514 different experiments in 68 different projects, so while large experiments represent a small fraction of all experiments, 14% of projects run at least one. We believe this is because many projects conduct many small experiments in preparation for a few large ones. For example, they may run several experiments to develop and debug a distributed system before evaluating it at scale. Only 5% of experiments are multiplexed, but these tend to be large: 20% have 200 nodes or more. As a result, multiplexed nodes actually represent a sizable fraction (31%) of all node requests.

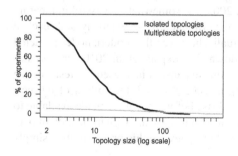

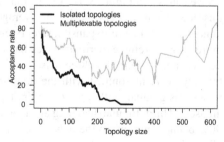

Fig. 1. Distribution of the number of nodes in experiments (note log-scale X axis)

Fig. 2. Percentage of experiments accepted by experiment size

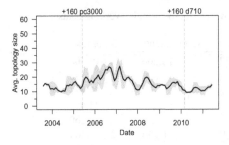

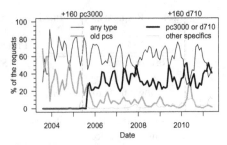

Fig. 3. Average isolated topology size; shaded region is the 95% confidence interval

Fig. 4. Types of nodes requested by experimenters over time

When a user submits an experiment to Emulab, it is "accepted" if there are enough nodes and network resources free to instantiate it. Otherwise, it is "rejected." Figure 2 shows the percentage of experiments that were accepted as a function of the experiment's size. We first observe the acceptance rate for isolated topologies is fairly low, even for small topologies: only 50% of submissions with 20 nodes are accepted, despite the fact that such a topology only uses 3% of the testbed. This shows that the testbed is used heavily, and frequently does not provide sufficient free resources to admit even small experiments. In order to cope with resource scarcity, some users turn to multiplexed experiments, deploying many VMs on the same physical node. Because they use fewer physical nodes, these experiments have a much higher acceptance rate, and even allow experiments larger than the physical testbed. Other users reduce the sizes of their experiments to increase the chance they will be accepted.

3.2   Attractive Physical Nodes Are the Bottleneck Resource

The Utah Emulab facility has gone through several major hardware expansions over its lifetime. Two such expansions occurred during the time covered by our dataset: in June 2005, 160 pc3000 nodes were added, approximately doubling the size of the testbed and bringing the first Gigabit Ethernet to Emulab. In early 2010, 160 d710 nodes were added, giving Emulab its first multi-core processors and greatly expanding its number of Gigabit network interfaces.

One objective of the expansions was to support the deployment of larger experiments. As we can see in Figure 3, the expansion in 2005 was somewhat successful in meeting this goal: for nearly two years, the average experiment size grew slowly and reached almost double the pre-expansion size. Eventually, however, the modern nodes attracted more users, forcing experiment sizes back down. The expansion in 2010 was less successful in this regard for three reasons. First, this expansion increased the testbed size by only 50%, in contrast with the doubling in 2005. Second, the rollout of the new nodes was gradual, with a period of limited release before they were made available to all users. Third, Emulab had long ago reached a saturation point, with utilization of over 90% being common, so the new nodes did little to alleviate this pressure: they simply allowed more experiments to be accepted.

Emulab allows users to request specific node types (such as pc3000 or d710), or to simply request nodes of any available type. Figure 4 shows how these requests have

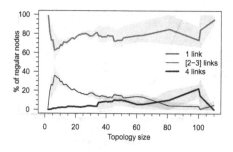

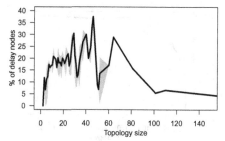

Fig. 5. Network interfaces per node   **Fig. 6.** Percent of delay nodes per experiment

evolved over time. The Utah Emulab facility has kept all old nodes in service after expansions, with two goals in mind: to keep the testbed as large as possible, and to support reproduction of results published using these nodes [5]. However, can be seen in the graph, specific requests for old nodes types have dropped near zero. Requests for "any" node type have declined slowly but steadily, presumably because users do not wish to be allocated the oldest nodes, which are now over a decade old. We conclude that the cause of the high rejection rates seen in Section 3.1 is not simply lack of available nodes, but more specifically a lack of attractive nodes.

3.3 Most Requests Use Few Interfaces

Emulab was built with fairly homogeneous node connectivity: with the exception of some d710s, most nodes have four interfaces available for experiments. The rationale behind this design was maximum flexibility: large blocks of identical nodes greatly simplify resource allocation. However, as we can see in Figure 5, requests using many interfaces are uncommon—the majority of requested nodes have only a single interface. This is in keeping with typical networks containing many edge hosts, which are typically not multihomed. The result, however, is that most interfaces in Emulab go unused most of the time. It is interesting to note that the popularity of 4-interface nodes grows up to experiments of size 100, then drops off sharply. Topologies at or right under 100 tend to be large trees, while topologies larger than 100 nodes are dominated by LANs, which require only one interface per node. It is also worth noting that users have clearly adapted to the physical constraints of the testbed: nearly all user requests have four or fewer interfaces. While some topologies requested five or more interfaces, the number was negligible, and is not shown in the figure. Anecdotal evidence suggests that if higher-degree nodes were available, some users would take advantage of them, but this effect cannot be measured from our dataset.

Figure 6 shows that delay nodes represent a significant proportion of the requests: up to 50 nodes, delay nodes represent 10% to 40% of the total. This not only shows that experimenters are interested in traffic shaping, but also the necessity of having numerous physical nodes with at least two network interfaces to act as delay nodes. We also observe that use of delay nodes decreases for large experiments. We believe this to be caused by two factors. First, as seen in Section 3.1, larger experiments are harder to instantiate, and removing delay nodes is one way of keeping the experiment

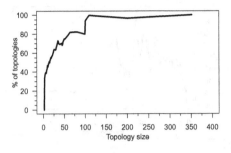
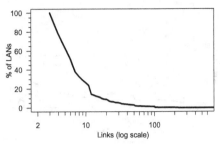

Fig. 7. Percentage of topologies having LANs   **Fig. 8.** Distribution of LAN size

size down. Second, multiplexed experiments are more common at large sizes, and these experiments perform traffic shaping on the hosts rather than using delay nodes.

3.4   LANs Are Common, But Most Are Small

LANs are of particular interest to testbed design: because they require full bisection bandwidth, they are much more difficult to instantiate than topologies comprised of links alone. Figure 7 shows the percentage of experiments that include at least one LAN. Figure 8 depicts the distribution of the sizes of those LANs. The most striking feature of Figure 7 is the fact that LANs dominate large experiments. Even at smaller sizes, they are quite common: 40% of 8-node experiments use at least one LAN. LANs are indeed primary components in many real networks, and experimenters who want representative topologies must consider these components when designing their experiments. While some experiments consist solely of a single LAN containing all nodes, this is not the dominant use case for LANs: only 20% of the experiments that contain them take this form. Finally, we observe from Figure 8 that a majority of LANs are small in practice: only 10% of LANs interconnect 20 or more nodes. This is explained by the small average experiment size.

4   Key Considerations for Network Testbed Design

Having seen the types of topologies that users submit to Emulab, we now turn our attention to the design of the physical facility: a well-designed facility should be matched to the types of experiments that are submitted to it.

4.1   A Cost Model for Physical Nodes

We begin with a model for the cost of a testbed's hardware. Of course, minimizing cost may not be the only factor influencing a testbed's design. It may be desirable, for example, to support certain rare but important types of experiments, even if the monetary cost of doing so is high. Nevertheless, it is important to understand the effect of design decisions on facility cost so that these decisions can be made with full awareness of

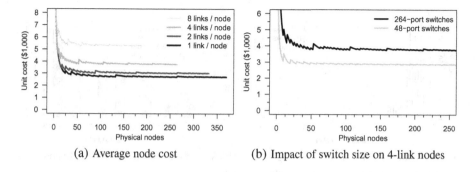

(a) Average node cost   (b) Impact of switch size on 4-link nodes

Fig. 9. Cost per node to build a testbed using a budget of up to $1M

their effect on the testbed's budget. In addition, spending limited money to support certain types of experiments may limit the type or quantity of other experiments that the testbed can support.

Our cost model takes into account all factors involved in the purchase of new nodes, including not only the nodes themselves, but also network interfaces, switches, inter-switch connectivity, infrastructure servers, racks, cabling, and power distribution. Prices for these items were determined from current market rates. An important consideration is that while nodes can be purchased individually, most supporting hardware must be purchased in larger units: for example, one rack may hold 20 servers, and a modular switch requires the purchase of a chassis plus some number of line cards. The result is that the average cost per node is not a simple linear function of the number of nodes, but instead exhibits a "sawtooth" pattern as seen in Figure 9(a). This figure also shows the effect of varying the number of interfaces per node: adding more interfaces both increases the cost (due to the expense of switch ports) and shortens the period of the sawtooth (as additional switches must be purchased more often).

Clear "sweet spots" are present in the graph, though their effects become less pronounced as the number of nodes increases. On a small scale, connectivity is not a large factor in average node cost: when purchasing 10 nodes, a node with four links costs only 14% more than a node with one link. At this scale, a strongly-connected testbed is warranted. At larger scales, the amortization of infrastructure costs results in a price more strongly influenced by connectivity: when purchasing 100 nodes, the difference between these two configurations widens to 30%. With a $1M budget, choosing one link rather than four allows the purchase of 100 additional nodes. As a result, large testbeds must plan their connectivity carefully to avoid spending money on unneeded interfaces.

A critical parameter to the cost model is the type and size of switches. Figure 9(b) compares two types of switches: a modular switch supporting up to 284 ports with 24-port modules, and a fixed-configuration switch supporting 48 ports. All switch ports that connect to nodes are 1 Gbps, and ports used for interconnects to other switches are 10 Gbps. The large switches have four 10 Gbps interfaces (leaving 264 ports available for the nodes), and the small switches have two.[4] Using smaller switches results in

---

[4] These switch configurations, and their prices, are based on current HP ProCurve products.

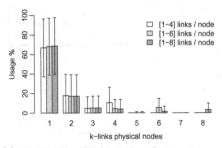
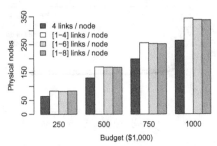

(a) Distribution of links on three heterogeneous testbeds; error bars show standard deviation

(b) Size of the testbed with respect to node connectivity.

Fig. 10. Impact of nodes' connectivity on testbed size

significant cost savings: 30% on average, and for a budget of $1M, a testbed built with small switches can acquire 70 additional nodes. The penalty is that the "islands" of full bisection bandwidth are much smaller, putting more demand on the interconnects between switches. As a result, a small-switch testbed will be unable to host large LANs and some strongly-connected topologies.

4.2 Heterogeneous Node Connectivity Enables Larger Testbeds

We now expand our model to consider configurations in which nodes have heterogeneous connectivity: some nodes have more interfaces than others. To do so, we ran a series of simulations. In each simulation, a set of experimenters' virtual topologies are mapped onto a physical testbed of infinite size. Nodes in testbed have differing numbers of physical interfaces, and each virtual node is mapped to a physical node having the minimum number of interfaces needed to satisfy it. We look at the resulting distribution of physical interfaces used by the mapping; this gives us a rough guideline of how many nodes of each type to include in a heterogeneous testbed. Figure 10(a) shows these distributions for three different testbeds: one having one to four interfaces per node, another having one to six, and a third having one to eight. On average, 67% of the physical nodes used have one interface, 20% have two interfaces, and very few nodes with more interfaces are needed. This correlates with our earlier statistics in Section 3.3, showing that nodes with few interfaces dominate testbed use.

We then construct testbeds using our previous cost model with different nodes having different numbers of interfaces. We use the distribution from Figure 10(a) to select the proportion of the physical nodes having each number of interfaces. Within a fixed budget, more nodes can be acquired, as the majority will only have a few links. Figure 10(b) compares the size of a homogeneous testbed with testbeds built using the heterogeneous distributions from Figure 10(a). The heterogeneous testbeds enable us to acquire 25% more nodes using the same budget. The gain is slightly reduced when the testbed is composed of nodes having more than four links. However, the loss is not significant as the number of high-interface nodes is small. Nodes with six or eight experimental links may be still useful in Emulab to support future users' needs.

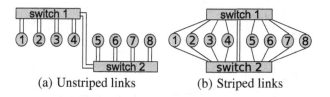

(a) Unstriped links   (b) Striped links

Fig. 11. Two network topologies connecting eight nodes, each with two gigabit interfaces

4.3 Alternatives for Switch Connectivity

Because providing full bisection bandwidth across the entire network is prohibitively expensive, bandwidth between switches (interswitch bandwidth) becomes a critical resource in distributed infrastructure [1,7]. In a network testbed, it is important to avoid oversubscription of these bottleneck links, which can lead to capacity artifacts and harm the scientific fidelity of the facility. Interswitch bandwidth imposes limits on the size of experiments that the testbed can host, and on LAN sizes in particular.

A traditional way to increase interswitch bandwidth is to purchase faster interconnects between the switches. This strategy, however, quickly becomes expensive. Because of their large number of network interfaces and explicit communications channels, an alternative strategy is available to network testbeds. This strategy is to *stripe* nodes' links across multiple switches; rather than connecting all of a node's interfaces to the same switch (as shown in Figure 11(a)), a node's interfaces are distributed across different switches, as shown in Figure 11(b). In a traditional datacenter network, a node may be connected to two switches for redundancy. Interface striping in a network testbed involves more interfaces per node and has a different purpose: it serves to align the switch connectivity with communication patterns. Intuitively, the motivation for connecting two interfaces to the same switch, rather than different switches, is to take advantage of the high bisection bandwidth within the switch. Two interfaces on the same node, however, rarely have a need to exchange traffic among themselves. It is much more likely that they will be connected to interfaces on other nodes, and striping ensures that, for any pair of nodes, there exists at least one switch on which both nodes have an interface. The result is a greatly decreased dependence on interswitch links and the ability to create large LANs, potentially connecting every node in the testbed. A disadvantage of striping is that it limits the number of nodes in the testbed to the maximum available switch size. Another disadvantage is that heterogeneous interface counts become more complicated to support, as they disrupt the symmetry of the striping.

We ran a simulation to discover how much interswitch bandwidth is used in practice on Emulab. We used the physical topology of Emulab's 160 pc3000 nodes, which are connected in an unstriped manner to two large switches connected by an 8 Gbps trunk. Our simulation re-played the user requests for the pc3000 nodes: after mapping each user topology to the testbed using Emulab's assign program, we examined the amount of bandwidth allocated on the interswitch trunks. The original submission time for each experiment was preserved, and we assumed that each experiment stayed instantiated on the testbed for 24 hours.

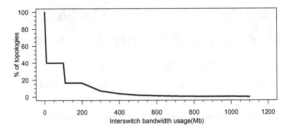

Fig. 12. Interswitch bandwidth between the switches connecting the `pc3000` nodes

Figure 12 shows the distribution of allocated interswitch bandwidth after each experiment is instantiated. We observe the usage is significantly below the maximum capacity of 8 Gbps: the maximum usage is 1.1 Gbps, and only 3% of instantiations result in consumption of more than 1 Gbps. The domain features of network testbeds explain this surprising result. Emulab relies on large switches with hundreds of ports to connect physical nodes. With 80% of submitted topologies being composed of fewer than 20 nodes, the probability of being able to fit a requested topology within a single switch are high. Furthermore, `assign` optimizes each topology mapping to keep the interswitch bandwidth usage as low as possible. This result suggests that it is worth investigating testbeds built with smaller switches. While such testbeds would rely more heavily on interswitch links, and possibly be unable to support some large experiments, the large switch topology is clearly over-provisioned in this respect. Since small switches typically cost much less than large ones, the savings would allow the testbed to add more nodes.

5   Evaluating Testbed Designs

We now combine the lessons of the two previous sections to evaluate new testbed designs: using information about users' requests and the costs of alternative topologies, we run simulations to find the topologies that are most effective on real workloads. The workload used for these simulations is a subset of the entire Emulab dataset: we use the 14,873 topologies that specifically requested Emulab's pc3000 nodes. We chose this subset to limit the runtime of the simulation, and to capture what could be considered a "sub testbed" of the full Emulab topology. This workload is processed through a FIFO batch queue and resource mappings are produced by Emulab's `assign` program. If resources are available, the experiment in the front of the queue is instantiated on the testbed, and those resources are marked as unavailable; otherwise, the queue blocks until sufficient resources are available. After instantiation, each experiment stays on the testbed for 24 hours of simulated time before terminating. We submit all experiments simultaneously at beginning of the simulation, and measure the total amount of simulated time until all experiments have been completed. We also measure the rejection rate: that is, the number of virtual topologies that cannot be mapped to the physical testbed under any conditions. This occurs when the physical topology being evaluated does not contain enough physical nodes, a sufficient distribution of interfaces, or satisfactory inter-switch bandwidth. This measure is important, since rejecting a large number of topologies would keep the completion time low, but indicate that the testbed does not meet the needs of at least some experimenters.

5.1 Heterogeneous Node Connectivity

As discussed in Section 3.3, most nodes in virtual topologies have few network interfaces, and the cost model in Section 4.1 shows us that it is possible to trade off fewer physical interfaces for more physical nodes. Choosing a distribution for network interfaces is a critical decision for improving the testbed's hosting capacity, but it is important to balance cost against variability in the workload. We evaluated the suitability of seven simulated testbeds which differ in the number of interfaces on each physical node. Each testbed was generated from the cost model using a $500,000 budget. Each has a different proportion of nodes having either two or four Gigabit Ethernet links on the experiment network. Interfaces are not striped across switches, and the inter-switch bandwidth capacity is set to 40 Gb (modeling four trunked 10 Gb ports). The configuration having only 4-link nodes is similar to that used on the Emulab facility at Utah.

Table 2. Simulation results for seven generated testbeds that differ in the proportion of two-interface and four-interface nodes. The "0%" case is similar to the topology of the Utah facility.

2-link nodes	Phys. nodes	Interswitch Bw.		Rejections	Time (days)
		avg.	max.		
0%	130	1.46 Gb	9 Gb	0 (0.0%)	1564
20%	135	1.41 Gb	10.1 Gb	0 (0%)	1510
40%	144	1.27 Gb	8 Gb	0 (0%)	1421
60%	148	1.11 Gb	8.1 Gb	0 (0%)	1394
80%	159	223 Mb	3 Gb	33 (0.2%)	1405
90%	161	30 Mb	4 Gb	33 (0.2%)	1487
100%	165	12 Mb	1 Gb	3,532 (23.8%)	995

Table 2 details the results. As expected, the number of physical nodes in the testbed increases with the proportion of nodes that have two links. For example, with 20% of nodes having two links, the testbed is 5 nodes larger than when all nodes are 4-link nodes. Around a proportion of 80%, 4-link nodes become scarce resources and experiments start to be rejected for requesting too many nodes with more than two links. When we increase the percentage of 2-link nodes to 90%, no additional topologies are rejected, but the completion time is increased by 5.8%. The small number of 4-link nodes is sufficient to map the same set of topologies, but because these nodes are scarcer, some topologies must wait a long time for them to become free, blocking the queue. In the extreme case, a testbed comprised of only 2-link nodes rejects nearly one quarter of all experiments.

We also observe that increasing the number of nodes with two interfaces reduces the average interswitch bandwidth usage. This is explained by the increasing number of physical nodes attached to the same switch. When all nodes have four links, a 264-port switch connects 66 nodes; when all nodes have two links, 132 nodes fit onto each switch. Thus, the probability that a topology is able to fit within a single switch increases with the percentage of 2-link nodes.

In this experiment, the testbed with a 60%/40% split between two- and four- link nodes is the most efficient: the 18 additional nodes afforded by this configuration reduces the completion time by 10.8% while still being able to host every topology in the workload.

5.2   Switch Connectivity

We now evaluate the alternate switch topologies from Section 4.3: striping the interfaces of each node across more than one switch, and building a testbed out of small 48-port switches. We compare to the best design from the previous evaluation, a heterogeneous testbed with a 60%/40% split. As before, all testbeds are built with a budget of $500,000.

Table 3. Simulation results for two generated testbed topologies, with and without interfaces striped across the switches

| Network configuration | Interswitch bw | | Rejections | Time (days) |
	avg.	max		
Unstriped	1.11 Gb	8.1 Gb	0	1394
Striped	85 Mb	2.1 Gb	0	1392

Table 3 shows the impact of a striped physical topology using two switches, with each node having two interfaces on each switch. Neither configuration rejects any experiments, and the difference in total completion time is negligible. The striped configuration uses much less interswtich bandwidth, giving it a clear advantage—only 7.7% as much on average, and 26% at the maximum. However, both configurations result in interswitch bandwidth comfortably below even a single 10 Gb link, meaning that from a practical perspective, either is capable of handing the workload in our simulation. Striping still has the potential to be advantageous if the submitted topologies are more strongly connected than those typically seen on Emulab. It can also provide a benefit if the cost of interconnects is high, as is the case when using the latest, and therefore most expensive, generation of Ethernet technology. Finally, striped connectivity is also meaningful when the ratio of node ports to interswitch ports is high. This can occur when when using large, high-density switches or small fixed-configuration switches with a limited number of "uplink" ports.

It can be difficult in practice to map virtual topologies to striped physical facilities. We repeated our previous simulation with five interfaces per node, necessitating an asymmetric striping pattern—each node had two interfaces on one switch and three on the other. The result of this experiment was a marked *increase* in the interswitch bandwidth used, to 800Mb. This can be explained by the fact that the irregularity introduced by asymmetric striping makes the mapping problem harder, and Emulab's solver, `assign` has not been tuned for this case. Making effective use of an asymmetric striped topology would require a new mapping algorithm.

We next turn our attention to the size of the switches used to build the testbed. As we have seen in Section 4.3, connectivity in Emulab experiments tends to be sparse, so small, cheap, switches may be an economical alternative to the large switches used in the Utah Emulab facility. The first two rows of Table 4 show simulations for two testbeds using 264-port and 48-port switches, respectively. As expected, the cheaper 48-port switches allows us to acquire more physical nodes, and the resulting testbed is 27% larger. However, we observe that 138 topologies (1%) were rejected as being unable to be fit on this testbed. An analysis of the rejected topologies confirms they were composed of LANs with more than 30 virtual nodes; these LANs fit on a single switch in the large-switch configuration. 85 of the rejections (60% of the total) were due to actual capacity limitations, while the remaining 57 are due to the fact that `assign` sometimes misses valid solutions due to its randomized, heuristic nature.

Table 4. Simulation results for testbeds using an 60%/40% split of two- and four-link nodes. 264-port switches and 48-port switches are connected through 40 GB and 20 GB uplinks, respectively.

Switches	Nodes	Interswitch bw avg.	max	Rejections	Time (days)	Cost
264 ports	148	1.11 Gb	8.1 Gb	0 (0%)	1394	$498,796
48 ports	186	1.06 Gb	8.1 Gb	138 (0.9%)	996	$498,354
48 ports	148	883 Mb	9 Gb	142 (0.9%)	1314	$390,268

The greater number of nodes in the small-switch testbed allows the workload to complete 28.5% faster. The cost of providing a network capable of hosting sizeable LANs is an increase in the completion time. Viewed from this perspective, when spending $500,000, the use of large switches allows us to host 1% more topologies, but at the cost of increasing the completion time of the whole workload by 40%.

In order to estimate the monetary cost of supporting this 1% of experiments, we ran another simulation, shown in the third row of Table 4. This time, we used small switches, but limited the number of nodes to 148, the number in the large-switch testbed. The result was a cheaper testbed, costing only $390,000. As with the previous simulation, the use of 48-port switches restricts the testbed's hosting capacity, and 142 topologies were rejected.[5] Comparing this configuration to the large-switch testbed, we see that the completion times are similar.[6] As both testbeds have the same number of nodes, this confirms that the network is the bottleneck that causes some experiments to be rejected. The usage of small switches reduces the testbed cost by $108,000. Thus, we can estimate that supporting these 142 experiments (0.95% of the total) raises the testbed cost by 28%. Put another way, the "easiest" 99% of experiments cost on average $33.5 each, while the "hardest" 1% cost $760.7 each. Note that these experiment costs should

---

[5] The difference with the previous experiment is explained by the nondeterminism of `assign`.
[6] The slightly higher time for the large-switch testbed is explained by the fact that it runs more experiments.

be interpreted as illustrative, rather than true costs: since our simulations only cover 6 years (less than the useful life of a node) and use a simple model for experiment duration, they should not be considered definitive costs.

The conclusion we draw from these simulations is that testbed design should take into consideration the relative costs of supporting certain types of experiments, and the research value of such experiments (in particular, large LANs) should be weighed against their increased infrastructure costs.

6 Conclusions

From our analysis of user topologies and simulations of alternative physical topologies, we draw the following conclusions:

While *experiments requiring few nodes dominate testbed usage*, there is also *a significant contingent of users who want to deploy experiments that are quite large*. The latter class of experimenters are likely limited by the number of nodes available on a shared-use testbed. The fraction of projects using at least one large experiment is greater than the fraction of experiments that are large, suggesting that projects use many small experiments to prepare for a relatively small number of large trials.

A *physical testbed topology need not have full bisection bandwidth*; on the contrary, a testbed is able to meet its users' needs with a surprisingly small amount of bandwidth between switches. This makes building testbeds out of small, cheap, switches more attractive than expected. The exception to the low edge-connectivity rule is *large LANs*, which are employed by some experimenters. This implies that a testbed built from small switches may find value in one large switch to support these LANs.

Striped topologies reduce the need for inter-switch connectivity. Though it is possible to build a testbed with modest bisection bandwidth even without striping, a striped configuration aligns the physical topology with common communication patterns, and can reduce the need for inter-switch bandwidth even further. The tradeoff is a more difficult mapping problem, requiring further work to use this configuration with maximum efficiency.

Nodes with few links are prevalent in users' requests. The result is that a homogeneous testbed, with an equal number of physical interfaces per node, makes inefficient use of resources. By varying the number of interfaces per host, it is possible to build a larger testbed, a cheaper testbed, or one with a significant number of high-degree nodes.

The savings from heterogeneous node connectivity vary with the scale of the testbed. For large testbeds, many costs amortize, and the cost of network ports becomes a dominant factor. Giving some nodes fewer interfaces results in substantial cost benefits. For small testbeds, this effect is much less pronounced, and a homogeneous testbed is preferable for its flexibility.

Some experiments require a more expensive testbed than others, so care should be taken when planning a testbed to decide how valuable these experiments are. In our simulations, we found that if Emulab were to intentionally exclude the 1% most "difficult" experiments, it could save 25% of hardware costs or could build a 32% larger testbed.

While users know what topologies they want, they also quickly *learn the limitations of the testbed*, and tend to adapt their expectations to what is realistic to instantiate on it.

For example, experimenters rarely request more network interfaces than Emulab nodes have. This is in keeping with earlier studies finding similar effects on the Internet infrastructure: the degree of connectivity of Internet routers is heavily influenced by available commercial offerings [10]. Experimenters also decrease the sizes of their experiments when nodes are scarce.

Multiplexed experiments are used primarily to support very large topologies. Though multiplexed experiments represent only 5% of submitted topologies, their large average size means that they account for 31% of all nodes allocated by Emulab, making them an important resource. The implication is that most users prefer "bare hardware," but are willing to tolerate virtualization in order to run large experiments. Testbeds aiming to appeal to the widest possible userbase should support non-virtualized experimentation, those aiming to support large experiments should support virtualization, and for maximum flexibility, it is desirable to support both.

In the Utah Emulab facility, demand always exceeds capacity, and expansions to the testbed hardware are met with increased usage. As a result of Emulab's "first come, first serve" policy, users tend towards small experiments. In order to support larger experiments, a testbed would need to be either significantly over-provisioned (and thus expensive and inefficient), or to implement allocation policies (such as advance scheduling) that favor large experiments.

References

1. Al-Fares, M., Loukissas, A., Vahdat, A.: A scalable, commodity data center network architecture. In: Proceedings ACM SIGCOMM (2008)
2. Benzel, T., Braden, R., Kim, D., Neuman, C., Joseph, A., Sklower, K., Ostrenga, R., Schwab, S.: Experience with DETER: a testbed for security research. In: Proceedings of Tridentcom (2006)
3. Bolze, R., Cappello, F., Caron, E., Daydé, M., Desprez, F., Jeannot, E., Jégou, Y., Lanteri, S., Leduc, J., Melab, N., Mornet, G., Namyst, R., Primet, P., Quetier, B., Richard, O., Talbi, E.-G., Touche, I.: Grid'5000: A large scale and highly reconfigurable experimental grid testbed. Int. J. High Perform. Comput. Appl. 20, 481–494 (2006)
4. Duerig, J., Ricci, R., Stoller, L., Wong, G., Chikkulapelly, S., Seok, W.: Designing a Federated Testbed as a Distributed System. In: Korakis, T., Zink, M., Ott, M. (eds.) TridentCom 2012. LNICST, vol. 44, pp. 321–337. Springer, Heidelberg (2012)
5. Eide, E., Stoller, L., Lepreau, J.: An experimentation workbench for replayable networking research. In: Proceedings of NSDI (2007)
6. Fall, K., Varadhan, K. (eds.): The ns Manual (November 2011)
7. Guo, C., Lu, G., Li, D., Wu, H., Zhang, X., Shi, Y., Tian, C., Zhang, Y., Lu, S.: BCube: a high performance, server-centric network architecture for modular data centers. ACM SIGCOMM Computuer Communication Review 39, 63–74 (2009)
8. Hibler, M., Ricci, R., Stoller, L., Duerig, J., Guruprasad, S., Stack, T., Webb, K., Lepreau, J.: Large-scale virtualization in the emulab network testbed. In: USENIX 2008 Annual Technical Conference, pp. 113–128 (2008)
9. Leiserson, C.E.: Fat-trees: Universal networks for hardware-efficient supercomputing. IEEE Trans. Comput. 34, 892–901 (1985)
10. Li, L., Alderson, D., Willinger, W., Doyle, J.: A first-principles approach to understanding the Internet's router-level topology. In: Proceedings of ACM SIGCOMM 2004 (2004)

11. Miyachi, T., Chinen, K.-I., Shinoda, Y.: StarBED and SpringOS: Large-scale general purpose network testbed and supporting software. In: Proceedings of VALUETOOLS (2006)
12. Ricci, R., Alfeld, C., Lepreau, J.: A solver for the network testbed mapping problem. ACM SIGCOMM Computer Communications Review 33, 65–81 (2003)
13. Rizzo, L.: Dummynet: a simple approach to the evaluation of network protocols. SIGCOMM Comput. Commun. Rev. 27, 31–41 (1997)
14. The University of Utah. Other Emulab testbeds, http://users.emulab.net/trac/emulab/wiki/OtherEmulabs
15. White, B., Lepreau, J., Stoller, L., Ricci, R., Guruprasad, S., Newbold, M., Hibler, M., Barb, C., Joglekar, A.: An integrated experimental environment for distributed systems and networks. In: Proceedings of SOSP (December 2002)

Federating Wired and Wireless Test Facilities through Emulab and OMF: The iLab.t Use Case

Stefan Bouckaert, Pieter Becue, Brecht Vermeulen, Bart Jooris, Ingrid
Moerman, and Piet Demeester

IBBT - Ghent University, Department of Information Technology (INTEC),
Gaston Crommenlaan 8, Bus 201, 9050 Ghent, Belgium
{firstname.lastname}@intec.ugent.be
http://ilabt.iLbL.be

Abstract. The IBBT iLab.t technology centre provides computing hardware, software tools and measurement equipment to support researchers
and developers in building their ICT solutions, and in measuring the performance of these solutions. Among other things, the iLab.t hosts several
generic Emulab-based wired test environments called the Virtual Walls,
and two wireless test environments which are grouped under the name
w-iLab.t. Until very recently, these wired and wireless test facilities each
had their own history: they were deployed and maintained by a different group of people, were operated using different tools, and each had
their own community of experimenters. This paper provides insight on
the origin and evolution of the Virtual Wall and w-iLab.t facilities. It
explains how these facilities were federated, by using the best parts of
both the OMF and Emulab frameworks. It discusses the benefits of our
local federation as well as our future federation plans.

Keywords: testbed, wireless, wired, emulab, omf, federation.

1 A Short History Behind the iLab.t

The history behind the iLab.t test facilities goes back to 1997, and starts with
a first experimental set-up consisting out of 1 ATM switch and 2 Windows PCs
deployed in the premises of the IBCN research group of the INTEC department
of the Ghent University, Belgium. One year later, the Atlantis testlab was born,
and over the years additional nodes, a diverse range of network equipment and
measurement equipment was added. After the IBBT (Interdisciplinary Institute
for Broadband Technology) was founded in 2004, the activities of the Atlantis
lab —at that point already counting well over 100 network nodes— were con-
tinued and significantly expanded under the flag of the IBBT iLab.t technology
centre. By 2006, the iLab.t counted over 300 rack mount PCs, a wide selection
of network devices and technologies, professional test and measurement equipment including wired and wireless sniffers, packet generators and QoS analysers.
Currently, about 120 40U racks are used. In 2007, it was decided to make the
testbeds more generic by installing the Emulab software [1] on 100 servers, that

T. Korakis, M. Zink, and M. Ott (Eds.): TridentCom 2012, LNICST 44, pp. 305–320, 2012.
© Institute for Computer Sciences, Social Informatics and Telecommunications Engineering 2012

we named 'the Virtual Wall'. In this way, people could use the same resources repeatedly and create also larger testbeds for experiments.

At that time, the popularity of wireless WLAN devices and sensor nodes was also significantly increasing. Being a research institute involved in multidisciplinary demand-driven research projects that often demand a proof-of-concept demonstrator, several small-scale desktop wireless testbeds with diverse types of hardware and wireless interfaces started to appear throughout the office building. However, it quickly became clear that there are significant drawbacks to maintaining several small-scale (wireless) testbeds; to name just a few drawbacks, with multiple individual test set-ups, it was often time-consuming to re-run 'old' experiments after the equipment had been stored in a cupboard for an extended period of time, especially if a certain experiment was not well-documented. Furthermore, re-using (parts of) previously programmed code and scripts is difficult, for example if one set-up is based on a COTS wireless Wi-Fi router and another set-up makes use of desktop PCs with Wi-Fi cards. As a final example, for scalability and efficiency reasons, in many cases it makes much more sense to build expertise on devices of a single type and buy a large amount of these nodes, than to have fragmented and more limited knowledge on operating a more diverse selection of hardware and have several testbeds of a smaller scale. These and other experiences led to the design and deployment of a 200-node wireless testbed, called the w-iLab.t in 2007 [2]. Since 2007, the w-iLab.t has been further developed and at this moment, there are two instances of the lab. Being deployed in the IBBT offices in Gent, Belgium, the original deployment is called the w-iLab.t office. The new location is known as w-iLab.t Zwijnaarde, after the town in which it is located, approximately 5 km away from the central IBBT offices.

In 2010 and 2012 respectively, a second and third Virtual Wall were installed. As a result, there are now 300 servers available in 3 Emulab configurations.

2   The Virtual Wall and w-iLab.t Facilities

To get a better understanding of the Virtual Wall and w-iLab.t facilities, a high-level description of both facilities is provided below. Next, Section 2.3 explains how both facilities are currently being used.

2.1   High-Level Description of the Virtual Wall

The iLab.t currently has 3 Virtual Wall testbeds. A Virtual Wall exists out of 100 servers, all connected with 4 or 6 Gigabit interfaces to a central switch (Force 10 E1200) which functions as a patch panel. Besides this, there is a control interface per node through which people can login. The testbed runs the Emulab software of the University of Utah [1]. Experimenters can build (large) experiments by drawing a topology in a graphical user interface or by creating NS2 files describing the topology of the experiment. One of the advantages of the Virtual Wall is that the Emulab software controls the switch as a virtual patch panel, so

Fig. 1. Emulab based Virtual Wall testbed

experimenters can remotely change topologies and configurations. There is no virtualisation involved, so the experiments run on the bare machine hardware, which is very important for performance experiments. As can be seen in Figure 1, 20 of the 100 nodes are connected to a display so that also visual feedback can be gathered, for example from large scale gaming experiments or video streaming experiments. As indicated above, in 2010 and 2012 two additional Virtual Walls were installed of 100 nodes. The advantage of having the testbed locally, is that we can also connect measurement hardware (e.g. Spirent Testcenter) or specific test devices besides getting visual feedback.

2.2   High-Level Description of the w-iLab.t

As indicated above, the original w-iLab.t deployment is located in an office building, and spans 3 floors of 90m x 18m. At 200 spots throughout offices, meeting rooms and hallways, wireless nodes are mounted to the ceiling. More precisely, at each of the spots, an embedded PC (PC Engines Alix3c3 [3]) is installed. All embedded PCs are connected over Ethernet to a central control server. Each embedded PC is equipped with two Wi-Fi a/b/g mini-PC interfaces. Moreover, a TelosB sensor node is connected via a custom-built so called 'environment emulator' to a USB port of the embedded PCs. This environment emulator allows experimenters to take more control over their sensor node experiments (e.g. emulation of sensor node inputs, reading/setting analog and digital I/O pins) and enables advanced logging functionality [4]. As a result, each node in the w-iLab.t office can be activated as a sensor node, a Wi-Fi node, or a combination of sensor and Wi-Fi, for example to act as a gateway. How the sensor nodes and/or Wi-Fi nodes behave is completely decided by (and reprogrammable by) the experimenter. For example, a Wi-Fi node uses the Madwifi [5] driver by default. As such, each Wi-Fi node can be programmed to behave as an access point, or as a station, or can be configured in monitor mode. It is also possible to install a different wireless driver, and/or to extend or modify any of the nodes in the same way as an experimenter would be able to do with a node that resides on his desktop, thus guaranteeing full flexibility in the experiments. The control software of the w-iLab.t office is based on the Motelab software [6] but has been extended over the years [2] to improve the functionality and usability.

The main driver for deploying a second w-iLab.t testbed, was the fact that the 2.4GHz ISM spectrum band in the office environment is at times heavily interfered by operational wireless networks, cordless phones and microwave ovens. Furthermore, since people are working in the office, the wireless link quality during daytime experiments may be very unpredictable. While for some experiments, this interference and unpredictability is a welcome challenge, it is obviously also very helpful to be able to execute experiments in an environment where no people are working and where no devices external to the experiment are causing interference. Such environment was found in a utility room above a cleanroom in Zwijnaarde. In this 66m x 20.5m room, 60 fixed nodes (Wi-Fi a/b/g/n, custom sensor node, Bluetooth) are installed. In addition, 20 mobile nodes based on a vacuum cleaning robot available with similar characteristics as the fixed nodes are soon to be added. The new nodes are more powerful than those in the office deployment [7]. While the low-power nodes in the office deployment are powered over Ethernet, the more powerful nodes in the Zwijnaarde testbed are powered via Power Distribution Units (PDUs). A high-level overview of w-iLab.t Zwijnaarde architecture is provided in Figure 2. While not listed on the figure, the w-iLab.t Zwijnaarde is also home to software defined radios and advanced spectrum sensing components.

When planning the new Zwijnaarde deployment during 2011, the requirements were determined based on the experience gained when installing and maintaining the w-iLab.t office environment. The wish list of new functionalities included expectations such as a more easy versioning system (to make it easier to go back to a previous version of the code under test and to specific parameter settings), easier sharing of experiments and code between users, a more uniform interface for including and manipulating sensor nodes and Wi-Fi based nodes in experiments, a more flexible way to share and comment on results, support for mobile nodes, and support for multi-site experiments. As such, it was clear the control software that was used for the office environment would have to be significantly extended. While such redesign would have been possible, or new and clean code could have been written from scratch, after studying the state of the art at that time we decided to start from and contribute to the OMF [8,9] control and management framework, since part of the functionality that was on our wish list became available with no or limited adjustments, by adopting OMF. Furthermore, while OMF does not fully support all functionalities available in the w-iLab.t testbed (e.g. environment emulator or our custom visualisation and processing extensions), we believe this lost functionality can easily be transfered

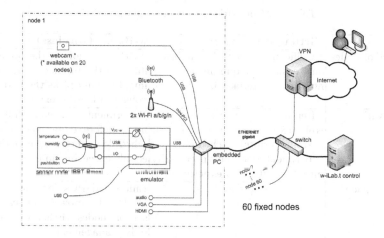

Fig. 2. High-level overview of the w-iLab.t Zwijnaarde architecture

to the OMF. To summarize: using the functionality provided by, and contributing to a well-known and widely used tool was found to be more useful than continuing to work on a custom code base. As will be described in Section 3, it is the OMF tool that is also used to enable the federation between the w-iLab.t Zwijnaarde and the Virtual Wall.

2.3   Role of the Facilities

Until recently, the (wired) Virtual Wall and (wireless) w-iLab.t facilities, although operated on the same physical location, were installed and largely maintained by different people. For each of the facilities, different user tools were/are provided, and in general, the knowledge on operating and using the platforms and the specific extensions was/is divided among two distinct user groups. In hindsight, the divide between the wired and wireless experimentation facilities grew in a natural way and is largely historically linked to the organization of our research in research clusters, such as 'wireless and mobile networks' and 'cloud computing'. As such, when initially implementing both facilities, the choice was made to start the Virtual Wall based on the the Emulab software, and the (original) w-iLab.t (office) on Motelab, based on multiple site visits of similar testbeds in the US and Europe. In 2007-2008, those choices fitted best our needs. Obviously, as the experimental facilities were further developed, the fact that different people were involved in setting up and maintaining the testbeds also means that the Virtual Wall and the w-iLab.t have grown to what they are today while fully focussing on their respective experimenter communities, without having to make compromises towards the other community. Table 1 summarizes the most important differences.

Table 1. Comparison of facility characteristics

	Virtual Wall (wired)	w-iLab.t (wireless)
Choice of nodes	Specific nodes are chosen based on technical requirements (e.g. number of interfaces).	As the location of the nodes influences the topology, the experimenter hand-picks the nodes involved in his/her experiment.
Reservation	After reserving nodes, user controls experiment via SSH (or custom scripts). Scheduling an experiment does not necessarily mean executing an experiment.	Experiment is usually fully defined before experiment can be scheduled; scheduling experiment equals executing an experiment.
Node capacities	Powerful multi-core PCs	Embedded PCs for control and Wi-Fi, low-power low-capacity sensor nodes. Ethernet usually only management.
Interfaces	Multiple identical Ethernet interfaces per node	Heterogeneous wireless interfaces (Wi-Fi, Bluetooth, IEEE 802.15.4)
Storage	NFS mounts, or custom solution by the experimenter	NFS mount, custom database solution for sensor nodes
Experiment life-cycle support	Support for swapping in images	Office: support for flashing/installing nodes, collecting, processing, visualising results, trigger events during experiments; Zwijnaarde: OMF/OML based deployment

Although, as will be described in Section 3, a federation between these wired and wireless experimentation facilities is now a fact (at the moment of writing, the final steps of the integration happened little over 2 weeks ago), so far the differences in experimentation communities are still reflected in the user accounts for the Virtual Wall and w-iLabt. When comparing the user account lists from both platforms, only 9 experimenters have an account for both testbeds, with the total number of accounts for the Virtual Wall and w-iLab.t being 120 and 60 respectively (excluding student group accounts and other generic accounts which are used by multiple users, for instance in the scope of a research project). An example experiment performed by a 'typical' Virtual Wall user on the w-iLab.t involved reasoning on top of sensor values that were dynamically obtained in real-time from the wireless sensor nodes of the office testbed. In this case, a central machine with a lot of processing power, which is not available in the 'normal' w-iLab.t set-up was required. The ad-hoc solution in this case was simply to add an external computing node to the control network of the w-iLab.t for the duration of the experiment. In addition to the accounts for individual experimenters, both iLab.t facilities are used in many national and international research projects, and are used by PhD and master students for research and educational purposes. An selection of international research projects and the role of the iLab.t is listed in Table 2.

Table 2. Selected projects in which the iLab.t facilities are used

Use and development of experimentation infrastructure	
BonFIRE www.bonfire-project.eu	BonFIRE designs, builds and operates a multi-site Cloud prototype Future Internet facility. The Virtual Wall is one of the facilities in the BonFIRE cloud, providing support for experiments with a need for a fully controllable network environment.
CREW www.crew-project.eu	The w-iLab.t is one of the core testbeds in the CREW federation. Among other things, the w-iLab.t test environment is used to create reproducible interference environments modelled according to the typical use of wireless networks at different locations, such as a home or an office.
OFELIA www.fp7-ofelia.eu/	The OFELIA project creates an experimental facility that allows researchers to not only experiment 'on' a test network but also to control and extend the network itself in a precise and dynamic way, using OpenFlow networking technology. Both the Virtual Wall and the w-iLab.t are part of the OFELIA facilities.
OpenLAB www.ict-openlab.eu/	OpenLab brings together the essential ingredients for an open, general purpose and sustainable large scale shared experimental facility. The w-iLab.t testbed is made available to selected experimenters as part of the OpenLab federation.
Research projects	
SPITFIRE www.spitfire-project.eu/	The w-iLab.t is used to evaluate the implementation and usage of embedded web service technology based on the IETF CoAP protocol. Novel solutions for facilitating sensor deployment, discovery and access are designed and evaluated.
SPARC www.fp7-sparc.eu/	The SPARC project studies carrier grade extensions to split architectures including OAM, restoration and reliability, network virtualization, and resource isolation in order to open up carrier networks to the benefits of split architectures. The iLab.t Virtual Wall is used to prototype carrier class applications of OpenFlow and to evaluate their scalability and performance.
EULER www.euler-fire-project.eu/	The main objective of the EULER research project is to investigate new routing paradigms so as to design, develop, and validate experimentally a distributed and dynamic routing scheme suitable for the future Internet and its evolution. The Virtual Wall is used for the prototyping, functional validation and performance measurements of the routing protocols.
CONSERN www.ict-consern.eu	CONCERN aims at developing and validating a novel paradigm of dedicated, purpose-driven small scale wireless networks that are characterized by energy awareness and service-centric evolution. Within this context, w-iLab.t is used to implement and experimentally measure the power savings that can be achieved by different cooperative mechanisms in heterogeneous network environments.

From this table, it can be seen that while the Virtual Wall and the w-iLab.t facilities are used in many projects, currently only the OFELIA project makes use of both facilities. Considering the above observations, it is a very valid question whether it makes sense to federate wireless and wired experimentation facilities. In the next section, it will be explained why we decided to federate our wireless and wired facilities, regardless of these observations.

3   Federating the Virtual Wall and w-iLab.t Facilities

3.1   Complimentary Experimentation Tools

As can be seen in the overview Table 3, both Emulab and OMF have specific functionality in the experiment life cycle. Some of the functionality is overlapping, while other functionality is unique for one of the frameworks. Especially the unique features of one of the frameworks are very interesting to share among all experimenters/experiments. Besides these, the standard OMF framework is lacking some functionality regarding secure use of nodes, which can be perfectly filled in by Emulab functionality. Because of these reasons, it was obvious for us to try to combine the functionality of both frameworks in a federated environment. For free, we got a similar environment for wired and wireless experiments, which is very interesting for both testbed administrators and experimenters. Customised code is limited to the minimum and fed back to the official frameworks. This means also that we can open up the testbeds more easily to the outside world, as e.g. APIs created for projects as Bonfire or Ofelia can now talk to wired and wireless testbeds.

Table 3. Comparison of facility characteristics

	Virtual Wall (Emulab)	w-iLab.t Zwijnaarde (OMF)
Resource dis-covery	proprietary + SFA	Inventory database on AM
Resource reser-vation	Only current availability on a first come, first served base	-
Resource ini-tialization	SFA/XMLRPC	Manual
Experiment control	ssh + startup scripts	ssh + OEDL scripts
Monitoring	-	OML
User storage	NFS (secure user and project home mounted)	NFS (user home mounted)
Authorization	webbased + XMLRPC + SFA Credential API	-
Experiment topology setup	Web interface or NS file	Ruby topology script
NIC config	done by Emulab	OEDL scripts

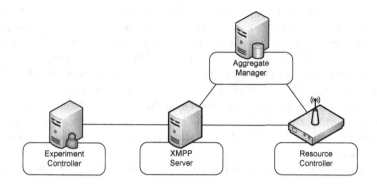

Fig. 3. OMF system architecture

3.2   iLab.t Federation: Building Blocks

The initial blocks for the federation are two separate facilities: the Virtual Wall, based on Emulab, and the w-iLab.t Zwijnaarde. The choice for federating with the w-iLab.t Zwijnaarde in this initial phase is made because this newer testbed is currently already equipped with OMF, while the w-iLab.t office is yet still managed by our older, Motelab-based management software. In a later phase, the w-iLab.t office is also to be integrated in the iLab.t federation. The remainder of this section is organized as follows: first, the Emulab and OMF frameworks and the relevant methodology are introduced in Sections 3.3 and 3.4. Next, the federation approach is explained in Section 3.5.

3.3   OMF Basics and Experimentation Lifecycle

The OMF framework consists of 4 major blocks, illustrated in Figure 3, that are interconnected over a wired control framework. First, there is the Aggregate Manager (AM), which can be considered as the main server of the testbed. The AM is responsible for initializing and configuring testbed resources. The AM also runs the OML (OMF Measurement Library) server [4] to collect results from the nodes during the experiment. Second, the Experiment Controller (EC) is the machine on which experimenters log in to run their experiments on the testbed. The EC can start and stop experiments and interact with the nodes by sending commands to the resource controllers during the experiment. Third, the Resource Controller (RC) is a software daemon which runs on each of the resources (which are in the case of w-iLab.t the wireless nodes) and waits for instructions from the experiment controller. Finally, there is an XMPP (Extensible Messaging and Presence Protocol) server, used to propagate the communication between the experiment controller and the resource controllers.

To understand the relevance of the proposed federation solution, it is important to understand the installation process and experiment lifecycle of an OMF testbed; The first step in **installing** an OMF testbed, is to install an aggregate manager (AM). This AM runs a DHCP, DNS and TFTP server. Whenever a node is added to the testbed, its specifications should be added to the inventory database on the AM. Every node should also be registered to a certain part of the testbed (also called a 'slice') via the XMPP server. The AM also runs a Frisbee server [6] to load images on the nodes. The second step is to install the experiment controller, and complete the EC configuration with the IP addresses of the AM and the XMPP server. Finally, the resource controllers are installed and configured on the nodes. In the corresponding configuration file, the control interface (e.g. eth0), the XMPP server address and the experiment slice the node operates in by default (e.g. the default slice, spanning the entire testbed) have to be specified.

After the installation, the **OMF experiment lifecycle** is the following.

- When a user wants to run an experiment on an OMF-enabled testbed, he first has to decide which image (OS, drivers, ...) he wants to configure the nodes with. By executing an *omf load* command on the EC, the image is multicast from the AM to the nodes that require that image.
- The second step for the user is to write an OEDL script (OMF Experiment Description Language). This script selects which nodes will be part of the experiment and what applications will be executed at what time during the experiment. We use the Human Readable Name (HRN) to define a node. This HRN is also listed in the inventory database and is registered to a slice in the XMPP server.
- Now the user can start the experiment by executing an omf exec command on the EC.
- The EC now checks the status (power on/off) of the nodes through the AM. The AM can then power on the nodes if necessary via a software component which is part of the so called Chassis Manager, responsible for the management of the power state of the nodes.
- Once the nodes are powered on, the EC sends commands to the resource controllers (RC) on the nodes through the XMPP server. Commands can be to install software, start scripts, configure wireless interface, ...
- During the experiment, results can be collected with OML [10]. The OML server runs on the AM. Resource nodes need to have the OML client library installed.

3.4   Emulab Basics and Experimentation Lifecycle

Figure 4 illustrates a basic view on an Emulab based testbed. There are 2 central servers (which run FreeBSD): BOSS is in charge of all configuration and organisation work, while OPS is the NFS server. Experimenters can login on OPS to get to the storage after their experiment was finished. Then there is a large switch to which all nodes are connected with as much as possible ethernet ports. This switch only functions as a patch panel, so it substitutes the manual patch cable connections. In this way, experimenters can use nodes as software based routers with multiple ports, use nodes as delay or packet loss nodes, and so on.

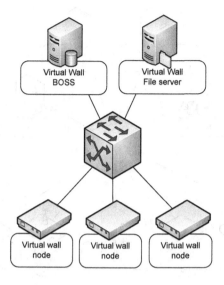

Fig. 4. Emulab architecture

Some nodes have 4 harddisks to make it possible to create RAID0 configurations for fast disk access. Emulab also has a user/group/project model which works by delegation. A user which is a 'grouproot' can admit other users to his experiments, so this makes the testbeds scalable to many users with a low sysadmin overhead. All experimenters in a group have access to the nodes of experiments of this group.

When starting an experiment, Emulab swaps in the right images on the right nodes, configures the IP addresses, the VLANs on the switch and the user passwords. There is also a very useful dynamic DNS system which makes that you can address your nodes in the experiment always through the same hostname, no matter which node is chosen for the experiment. At the end of swapping in the experiment, a script can be executed, or the experimenter can take manual control through SSH or RDP (remote desktop). Emulab has also a pubsub system with barriers, but experimenters tend to implement a similar thing in their experiment software, we have learned.

3.5   The iLab.t OMF-Emulab Federation

The basic approach of our federation solution is to extend the Virtual Wall (Emulab) testbed to support OMF experiments. Because no structural changes were made to the original setup, users can continue to use the testbed as before, as such guaranteeing backward compatibility and continuity of both experimentation environments. Figure 5 provides a high-level overview of the federation set-up.

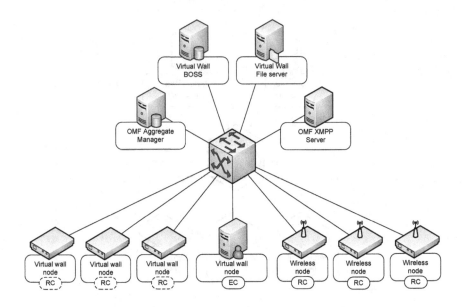

Fig. 5. The Virtual Wall – w-iLab.t federation

As shown in this Figure, two servers were added to the Virtual Wall set-up. One server acts as OMF Aggregate Manager, the other one as XMPP server. Although the OMF framework allows experimenters to install their own Experiment Controller on their local desktop, experimenters are assisted in setting up a joint experiment as follows. A specific script was created, that can be included when configuring a Virtual Wall experiment. By (automatically) executing this script, a regular Virtual Wall node is configured as an OMF Experiment Controller. As such, whenever users want to run an OMF experiment on the Wall, one of the Virtual Wall nodes can be swapped in, and this conversion script can be started automatically. The user home directory on the EC is persistent, as it is mounted on the home directory of the user on the Virtual Wall file server, which can be accessed at all times (also after the experiments are completed).

A similar approach is used for the nodes that are part of a joint experiment. Both Virtual Wall nodes and wireless nodes can be part of an OMF experiment. To accommodate this, a first requirement is that the nodes should run an OMF Resource Controller. We therefore provided a script that turns a regular (Virtual Wall or wireless) node into an OMF-enabled node. The RC configuration file only requires the address of the XMPP server, which is a static server added to the Emulab setup. As discussed in Section 3.3, the second requirement of the OMF framework is that all nodes should be listed in the inventory database and should be registered to a certain slice in the XMPP server. We therefore created a second script (started after the conversion script), which registers the node to the AM inventory and the XMPP server. For this we use the Emulab DNS system that generates a unique dynamic DNS name and IP address for every node that is swapped in for an experiment. Based on the MAC address, the register script inserts the IP address and HRN (a unique DNS name assigned by Emulab) in the inventory and uses the HRN again to add the node to an experiment slice in the XMPP server. After the experiment is finished, the nodes should be removed from the inventory and the XMPP server to avoid problems when re-scheduling an experiment, since Virtual Wall resource names can be different for every run of an experiment. Note that for wireless nodes, the Emulab software is configured to select specific nodes. This is needed because the location of a node is very important in wireless experiments. In this setup, the Virtual Wall can be considered as the core testbed, having the possibility to swap in the OMF framework when requested by the user. This loose coupling approach has the advantage of requiring very little effort to achieve and ensures the correct working of the core testbed software. Furthermore, the Virtual Wall users can now also make use of the OML functionality to log their experiment results. In the chosen implementation, the Virtual Wall replaces some of the AM functions: the AM normally has to check whether nodes are on or off when an experiment is started and switch them on if necessary. In this implementation, this functionality is not needed anymore, since the Emulab software ensures that the nodes are switched on once they are swapped in. In order to overrule the AM functionality, we configured the AM to use a dummy Chassis Manager, which informs the AM core that the resources are always on. Furthermore, the AM functionality to load images on nodes is now also performed by the Virtual Wall, which also uses the Frisbee disk loader. This means that previously configured images of the w-iLab.t can be reused in the federated testbed.

Figure 6 demonstrates the setup of an experiment, using the new federation possibilities. In this experiment two arbitrary Virtual Wall (pcX and pcY) nodes are swapped in. One is configured as OMF EC, the other node is part of the experiment and can run additional software (e.g. video streaming server for home security system). Two fixed wireless nodes are chosen to act as wireless access points. Note the difference between the Virtual Wall nodes (arbitrary chosen by the system) and the wireless nodes (specifically requested by the user). All the nodes in this example are running Ubuntu 11.04, but other operating systems can be used as well. The only requirement for the nodes is that they should be able to run the experiment or resource controller, programmed using ruby scripts

4   Discussion and Future Plans

The iLab.t federation approach explained above demonstrates that federation – although exactly defining the term 'federation' in the context of Future Internet infrastructures is a discussion on its own– should not always be a time consuming and complex process. The implemented loose coupling between the OMF and the Emulab framework results in benefits for both the experimenters and ourselves as testbed owners/maintainers. For experimenters, the federation means easy and unified access to both a wired and a wireless experimentation facility. Executing experiments which concurrently use (parts of) the Virtual Wall and (parts of)

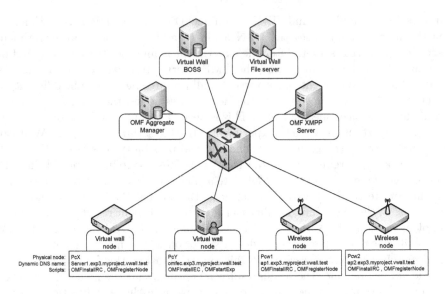

Fig. 6. Example federated experiment

the w-iLab.t is now possible. Even when combining nodes of both testbeds is not of importance to the experimenter, there is still the benefit of added functionality: Virtual Wall experimenters now have better control over their experiment lifecycle thanks to OMF, and the OML measurement library can be used to collect and process measurements. Vice versa, for experimenters using the w-iLab.t Zwijnaarde deployment, the federation means that nodes can now be configured via a user-friendly Emulab GUI. Furthermore, while in the 'normal' OMF deployment of the w-iLab.t Zwijnaarde, experimenters could (un)willingly destroy another experimenter's experimenter by executing an OMF-load command on a node that was already in use, this is now impossible, as an Emulab experiment cannot be swapped out by an other user. Also, the whole user/project delegation system of Emulab is now available to the wireless testbed, meaning that creation of accounts happens in a unified way, and, that secure use of storage is possible now.

Without any doubt, this functionality that was added by federating the Emulab and OMF approaches could also have been added by modifying or extending the code of either Emulab or OMF. The advantage of gaining the functionality through federation, is that there was very little implementation effort required to gain functionality while being assured of backwards compatibility. We also profit in this way of the best things of two standard frameworks with almost no customisation. It must be noted that enabling this local federation from a technical point of view is just one little aspect of the iLab.t federation story: having the technical possibility to let OMF and Emulab - wireless and wireless - experimentation facilities cooperate does not mean that experimenters will instantly be aware of the possible benefits and start scheduling federated experiments. However, for the administrators maintaining the Virtual Wall and w-iLab.t

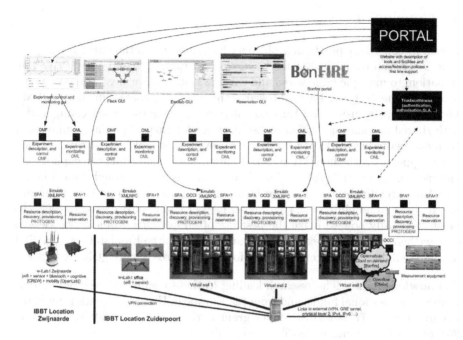

Fig. 7. Future federation vision: at the bottom we see the two wireless testbeds, the 3 Virtual Walls and measurement equipment. On top we see the resource provisioning through Emulab's Protogeni and an extension for future reservation. Also shown, is the OMF layer for experiment and monitoring control. On top, the different graphical user interfaces (community, platform or project specific as e.g. Bonfire) are shown together with a Portal pointing the experimenter towards the right tools and a distributed trustworthiness layer.

facilities, federating the facilities has been a trigger to promote discussion and to better cooperate on future extensions to the facilities. As an example, the adoption of SFA was one of the drivers: an SFA interface for OMF is still under development, while the Protogeni SFA interface on top of Emulab is already very stable. In this way, both our wired and wireless testbeds will be reachable through SFA (see Figure 7). The gain of OMF experiment control for the wired experimenters will be very important. In the near future, we plan to organize workshops targeted to the w-iLab.t and Virtual Wall communities, in which the federation approach is explained and example federated experiments are provided. It is expected that future extensions to the iLab.t facilities will be useful to both the Virtual Wall and w-iLab.t communities, and that the federation will further stimulate cooperation. Also from a technical point of view, the local Virtual Wall – w-iLab.t federation is not an endpoint. In the future, the federation exercise will be repeated continuously at a larger scale. A first step will be to also integrate the w-iLab.t office in the federation. Next, federation at a larger scale, with experimental facilities owned by other legal entities will be pursued.

5   Conclusion

Driven by some very practical problems which arose when the IBBT iLab.t grew from individual experimenter testbeds, over an Emulab based Virtual Wall installation, to multiple large wired and wireless testbeds, we have studied and implemented the best way forward towards the future for controlling our testbeds. We ended up by using the Emulab software in a multi-testbed configuration with shared accounting (which makes it easier for upgrading and maintenance than one really big testbed) for the node provisioning and account/project handling topped of with the OMF/OML framework for controlling the experiments and measurements themselves. This federation was rather straightforward compared to extending one or another framework, and seems to be very promising for the testbed administrators and experimenter communities as know-how can be shared easily now to make the best use of all available frameworks. Besides this, we believe that also external federation through the Emulab Protogeni SFA interface will be a very interesting way forward towards a more global federation.

Acknowledgment. The research leading to these results has received funding from various national funds, and from the European Union's Seventh Framework Programme (FP7/2007-2013) under grant agreements nr 258301 (CREW), nr 258365 (OFELIA) and nr 287581 (OpenLab).

References

1. Emulab. Home page, http://www.emulab.net
2. Bouckaert, S., Vandenberghe, W., Jooris, B., Moerman, I., Demeester, P.: The w-iLab.t Testbed. In: Magedanz, T., Gavras, A., Thanh, N.H., Chase, J.S. (eds.) TridentCom 2010. LNICST, vol. 46, pp. 145–154. Springer, Heidelberg (2011)
3. PC Engines. Alix system board, http://www.pcengines.ch/alix.html
4. Tytgat, L., Jooris, B., Mil, P.D., Latré, B., Moerman, I., Demeester, P.: Wilab, a real-life wireless sensor testbed with environment emulation. In: European Conference on WSNs, Cork, Ireland (February 2009)
5. Madwifi. Multiband atheros driver for wifi (2010), http://madwifi.org/
6. Werner-Allen, G., Swieskowski, P., Welsh, M.: Motelab: a wireless sensor network testbed. In: Fourth International Symposium on Information Processing in Sensor Networks, IPSN 2005, pp. 483–488 (April 2005)
7. The CREW project. w-ilab.t zwijnaarde, http://www.crew-project.eu/portal/wilab/open-environment-testbed-zwijnaarde
8. Rakotoarivelo, T., Ott, M., Jourjon, G., Seskar, I.: Omf: a control and management framework for networking testbeds. SIGOPS Oper. Syst. Rev. 43, 54–59 (2010)
9. OMF. The testbed control and management framework - home page, http://omf.mytestbed.net
10. White, J., Jourjon, G., Rakatoarivelo, T., Ott, M.: Measurement Architectures for Network Experiments with Disconnected Mobile Nodes. In: Magedanz, T., Gavras, A., Thanh, N.H., Chase, J.S. (eds.) TridentCom 2010. LNICST, vol. 46, pp. 315–330. Springer, Heidelberg (2011)

Designing a Federated Testbed as a Distributed System

Robert Ricci[1], Jonathon Duerig[1], Leigh Stoller[1], Gary Wong[1],
Srikanth Chikkulapelly[1], and Woojin Seok[2]

[1] University of Utah, School of Computing
{ricci,duerig,stoller,gtw,srikanth}@cs.utah.edu
[2] Korea Institute of Science and Technology Information
wjseok@kisti.re.kr

Abstract. Traditionally, testbeds for networking and systems research have been stand-alone facilities: each is owned and operated by a single administrative entity, and is intended to be used independently of other testbeds. However, this *isolated facility* model is at odds with researchers' ever-increasing needs for experiments at larger scale and with a broader diversity of network technologies. The research community will be much better served by a *federated* model. In this model, each federated testbed maintains its own autonomy and unique strengths, but all federates work together to make their resources available under a common framework.

Our challenge, then, is to design a federated testbed framework that balances competing needs: We must establish trust, but at the same time maintain the autonomy of each federated facility. While providing a unified interface to a broad set of resources, we need to expose the diversity that makes them valuable. Finally, our federation should work smoothly in a coordinated fashion, but avoid central points of failure and inter-facility dependencies. We argue that treating testbed design as a federated distributed systems problem is an effective approach to achieving this balance. The technique is illustrated through the example of *Proto-GENI*, a system we have designed, built, and operated according to the federated model.

1 Introduction

Testbeds for networking and systems research have traditionally been built as stand-alone facilities where each testbed is operated and managed by a single entity. The problems of building, running, and improving each individual testbed have received attention in the literature in preference to issues of coordination, trust, and cooperation between testbeds [30,18,17,1].

Increasingly, experimenters need to run larger experiments incorporating a broader diversity of devices and network technologies. It is difficult to satisfy this requirement with isolated testbeds, since each testbed is limited in size and tends to concentrate on a particular type of resource. If experimenters were able to treat a collection of testbeds as a single facility, this would enable them to run larger experiments and take advantage of diverse resources.

This leads to a *federated* model, in which individual testbeds work together to provide their users with a common framework for discovering, reserving, and using resources.

T. Korakis, M. Zink, and M. Ott (Eds.): TridentCom 2012, LNICST 44, pp. 321–337, 2012.

This common framework must meet a number of requirements. It must establish trust between federates, but allow each member of the federation to retain autonomy; each federate should have independent local control over usage policies and resource maintenance. The federation should support pre-existing testbeds, which are managed using a variety of software suites, and which were created to manage different kinds of resources. While accommodating this heterogeneity, the federation must present a single interface and provide the appearance of a single "virtual facility," giving users access to a richer set of resources than any one facility can provide by itself. Finally, the federation must provide coordination among members without sacrificing robustness, as a complex distributed system introduces many points where failures can occur.

This paper makes three contributions. First, it defines a set of five design principles that, together, meet the requirements of a federated testbed. Second, it presents a specific realization of these principles in the ProtoGENI federation. Third, it shares our experiences building and running this federation, which has been used by more than three hundred experimenters over the last three years. These include experiences that have caused us to re-think parts of the federation's design, an analysis of its robustness to failures, and an evaluation of the time required to set up experiments.

Our five design principles are:

- *Partitioned trust* between the federates: Each federate is responsible for its own resources and users, and only trusts other federates insofar as the peer's resources and users are concerned. Each federate retains the right to make local authorization and policy decisions, and no testbed occupies a privileged position in the federation.
- *Distributed knowledge*: No single entity has complete knowledge of the system. This enables local extensions, allowing federates to offer unique resources and to add new features without being limited by the global framework. It also aids in removing centralized points of failure and inter-facility dependencies.
- *Minimal abstraction*: The ProtoGENI framework provides a low-level API for resource access, rather than hiding the details of resources behind higher-level abstractions. This gives implementers of user tools the flexibility to define their own higher-level abstractions, tailoring them to specific user communities or use cases.
- *Decentralized architecture*: ProtoGENI has only one centralized entity, which is used for bootstrapping and convenience. Operation can proceed without it in most cases. There are no global locks in ProtoGENI; instead, we make use of local transactions to coordinate operations that span federates.
- *Minimal dependencies*: Each ProtoGENI call carries as much context with it as possible. This minimizes dependencies between services, which do not need to contact each other on-line for correct operation.

2   Related Work

Emulab [30] provides a diverse set of experimental resources such as wireless nodes, simulation, and real Internet resources through portals to the PlanetLab [29] and RON testbeds [1]. This control framework is built around a strong assumption of centralized management. There are dozens of testbeds around the world built on Emulab, but until we began work on ProtoGENI, each operated in isolation. The federation of these previously divided testbeds is the chief user-visible contribution of ProtoGENI, and has required significant architectural changes to the underlying software.

PlanetLab is also a large-scale testbed, distributed around the world. All sites run a common code base, and most maintenance and allocation is done by central entities, called PlanetLab Central (PLC).There are multiple instances of PLC, including one in Europe, another in Japan, and VINI [3], which extends PlanetLab's support for topology control. PlanetLab introduced the idea of "unbundled management," separating user tools from the management of the facility, and we make use of it in ProtoGENI. As part of the GENI project, this federation is evolving along a similar path to the one we present in this paper.

ORBIT [17] and StarBed [14] are built around a centralized use, policy, and maintenance model. ORBIT is a Radio Grid Testbed, providing wireless devices to its users. Due to the restrictions of its physical environment, ORBIT does not "slice" its testbed, but allocates all nodes in its testbed to one experiment at a time [21]. StarBed is specifically designed for virtualization, enabling users to build experimental topologies up to thousands of nodes.

The Open Resource Control Architecture (ORCA) is an extensible architecture which provisions heterogeneous virtual networked systems via secure and distributed management over federated substrate sites and domains [16]. ORCA focuses on mechanisms for providers and consumers (e.g. experimenters) to negotiate access to, configure, and use testbed resources. ORCA provides diverse environments on a pool of networked resources such as virtualized clusters, storage, and network elements which are maintained independently by each site. While ORCA shares many features with ProtoGENI, it uses a different set of fundamental design decisions.

Panlab [27,28] is a federated testbed with facilities distributed across Europe. While the Panlab and ProtoGENI architectures have many analogous elements, the philosophies behind them differ. Panlab's "Private Virtual Test Labs" (similar to GENI slices) are typically controlled and used through a centralized manager, called Teagle. In contrast, ProtoGENI's architecture emphasizes distributed systems aspects of testbed federation, avoiding centralized services almost entirely.

Namgon Kim et al. [10] have published work on connecting the FIRST@PC testbed with ORCA-BEN. They focus more on the stitching aspects of federation, while we examine the overall architecture and API.

SensLAB is a large scale wireless sensor network testbed, allowing researchers access to hundreds of sensor nodes distributed across multiple sites [24]. The system presents a single portal, through which users can schedule experiments across all the available networks. The current SensLAB installations operate highly homogeneous hardware platforms, but are working toward interoperability with OneLab [2], and we expect that this integration will result in sophisticated federation management facilities.

WISEBED [4] is another distributed system of interconnected testbeds, in which the hardware resources are large scale wireless sensor networks. Like GENI, WISEBED aims to produce a large and well organized structure by combining smaller scale testbeds; the chief difference is that WISEBED focuses on wireless sensor technology, while almost all networked GENI resources use wired links (with a minority of facilities choosing to make wireless resources available for special purposes).

Soner Sevinc [25] has developed an architecture for user authentication and trust in federations using Shibboleth as an identity provider. Our federation architecture provides mechanisms for federates to coordinate experimentation, and has been integrated with Soner Sevinc's system.

Grid [8] and Tier [13] systems share some goals with federated network testbeds, in that they are distributed systems able to connect heterogeneous, geographically distributed resources from multiple administrative domains. Grid systems provide dynamic allocation and management of resources via common tool kits such as Globus [7]. As with our system, each domain is responsible for its own maintenance and policy. The fundamental distinction is that in ProtoGENI, it is the network, rather than computing resources, that is the primary object of interest. Grid computing hides most resource heterogeneity and infrastructure behind abstract interfaces, where as we expose them whenever possible. Cloud computing takes this one step further with virtualization. In comparison, ProtoGENI provides users with more transparent control over the network and the ability to take advantage of the diversity of resources for experimentation. Researchers are investigating the integration of Grid and traditional network testbed resource management techniques [23]; such a combination is largely orthogonal to the peer-to-peer federation model we consider. Most grids are organized hierarchically, while ProtoGENI is decentralized, allowing its principals more autonomy; most clouds consist of resources owned by a single entity, and are thus not federated.

3   Architecture

The architecture of ProtoGENI builds on the GENI framework. In this section, we will describe the overall GENI structure before examining how ProtoGENI expands on that architecture.

3.1   GENI

GENI's architecture is based on the "Slice-based Federation Architecture" (SFA) [19], which has been developed by the GENI community. The SFA is so named because it centers around partitioning the physical facility into "slices," each of which can be running a different network architecture or experiment inside. Physical resources, such as PCs, routers, switches, links, and allocations of wireless spectrum are known as "components;" when a user allocates resources on a component, the set of resources they are given comprises a "sliver." This sliver could be a virtual machine, a VLAN, a virtual circuit, or even the entire component. Each sliver belongs to exactly one slice: in essence, a slice is a container for a set of slivers.

There are two main types of principals in GENI:

Aggregate Managers (AMs) are responsible for managing the resources (components) on which users will create networks and run experiments. AMs are responsible for the allocation of their resources, and may make decisions about who is authorized to use them. An individual AM may manage a collection of components, called an *aggregate*; in practice, each facility in GENI runs a single AM that manages all of its resources, and the largest aggregates contain hundreds of nodes and thousands of links.

Users access components from the federated testbed to run an experiment or a service. A user is free to create slices which span multiple AMs, and each user is authorized by one of the facilities in the federation.

Principals and many other objects in the system are uniquely named by a Uniform Resource Name (URN) [15]. The URN scheme that we use [26] is hierarchical—each authority is given its own namespace, which it can further subdivide if it chooses. To maintain *partitioned trust*, each authority is prohibited, through mechanisms described in [31], from creating URNs outside of its namespace. An example of a GENI URN is:

`urn:publicid:IDN+emulab.net+user+jay`

Because the URN contains the identity of the authority that issued it (in this example "`emulab.net`"), it is possible to tell which authority "owns" the object without resorting to a lookup service; this is in keeping with our *decentralized architecture* goal.

At a high level, testbeds federate in this framework by forming trust relationships: if facility A trusts facility B, then A is willing to trust B's statements about what users it has, what slices they have created, and what resources B offers. Note that this does not preclude A from having local allocation policies: just because it recognizes B's users does not obligate it to satisfy all requests they might make. Arrangements regarding "fair sharing," etc. can be made as part of the federation agreement. Trust relationships need not be symmetric: A may choose to trust B even if that trust is not reciprocated.

3.2 ProtoGENI Architecture

We build on the basic GENI architecture by adding two new kinds of entities into the federation, and by providing an expanded API for AMs.

Slice Authorities (SAs) are responsible for creating slice names and granting users the necessary credentials to manipulate these slices. By issuing a name for a slice, the SA agrees to be responsible for the actions taken within the slice. An SA may be an institution, a research group, a governmental agency, or other organization.

A user has an account with an SA, called the "home" SA; this SA vouches for the identity of the user, and in most cases, is willing to create slices for the user. The user is, however, free to create slices using any SA that, according to its own policies, is willing to be responsible for that user's actions.

Of course, establishing trust in this pairwise fashion does not scale well to large federations. ProtoGENI's sole centralized service, the **Clearinghouse** (CH), is used to make this process more convenient: it allows federates to publish the certificates that are used to establish trust, and to discover the certificates of other federates. It is important to note that this does *not* mandate specific trust relationships: as described in [31], a federate may choose not to trust some certificates stored at the clearinghouse, or may choose to trust additional certificates that are not registered there.

The clearinghouse also serves a second purpose: it acts as a registry where various objects can be looked up. Notably, users can ask the clearinghouse for a list of all registered federates to bootstrap the process of resource discovery, as described in the next section. In both of these roles, the information provided by the clearinghouse changes infrequently, and can be safely cached for long periods of time (days or weeks).

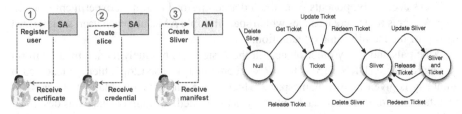

Fig. 1. Overall architecture detailing user interactions with entities in the federation

Fig. 2. Life cycle of a sliver. Edges are labeled with the name of the operation that causes the state transition.

ProtoGENI AMs also export an expanded interface relative to the GENI standard. Specifically, they can issue *tickets*, which are guarantees of resource provision for the owner of the ticket. When a user *redeems* one of these tickets with the AM, the AM creates a sliver, and the user can begin running an experiment. ProtoGENI AMs also support the ability to update existing slivers.

ProtoGENI has sophisticated requirements for authentication and authorization, complicated by the fact that different parts of the system are owned and operated by different organizations, each of which may need to enforce custom local policies.

The authentication system is based on the IETF PKIX model [5], while the authorization mechanism involves the presentation of cryptographically signed *credentials* (which behave analogously to X.509 Attribute Certificates [6]). Together, these primitives allow the warranting of identities, the granting and delegation of permissions, and the verification of identity and privilege. Most importantly, all of these operations may be performed by different principals, who need no direct knowledge of each other. ProtoGENI's authentication and authorisation system are detailed elsewhere [31].

3.3 Running an Experiment

Putting these pieces together, a user goes through the following steps to run an experiment (see Figure 1).

Creating a Slice: He contacts an SA (usually the "home" SA), and requests a new slice. If the request is granted, the SA gives him a name for the new slice and the credentials necessary to manipulate it. At this point, no resources are yet allocated.

Discovering Resources: Next, the user selects the components that he will use to build his network. This can be done in a number of different ways. The simplest is to ask each AM in the system to enumerate the resources it has available; the user asks the CH for a list of federated AMs (or uses a cached copy of this list), and then asks each AM for an "advertisement" describing its resources. Alternately, he may make use of network embedding tools [22] to help select appropriate components.

Creating Slivers: Once the user has selected a set of components, he creates a "request" describing the network to be built. The user sends this request to each AM from which he wants resources. When granting such a request, the AM returns a "ticket", promising the use of those resources. If not all ticket requests are granted, the user may keep the tickets he has and/or try to obtain new tickets to replace the failed requests. Once he is satisfied with the set of tickets held, those tickets may be "redeemed" at the AMs that issued them, causing slivers to be created.

Using Resources: The user may now log into the slivers and begin running experiments. Programming, configuring, or logging in to a sliver is done with component-specific methods; many components are accessed through ssh, but other access methods may be required for some components. The user may modify the slice while it is running, and releases all slivers when the experiment is complete.

4   Interactions between Federates

ProtoGENI has been designed to keep federates as loosely coupled as possible; they do not depend on central services, and the only parts of the system involved in a given operation are those directly affected by it. In the extreme case, if a federate is cut off from communication with the rest of the federation, users who can reach the federate are still able to create slices and slivers on it.

This is possible because, in keeping with the design principles of *decentralized architecture*, *minimization of dependencies*, and *distributed knowledge*, ProtoGENI goes to great lengths to ensure that *minimal state synchronization* is required between AMs, SAs, and the CH. This section describes the interactions these services have with each other and with users. We concentrate on where ProtoGENI stores state, how it avoids centralized services, and how failures are managed. Because the full ProtoGENI APIs [20] are too large to cover in depth here, we introduce only the calls necessary to understand state management.

4.1   Slice State

ProtoGENI does not attempt to guarantee a globally consistent view of the state of each slice. Instead, it uses a loose consistency model in which each of the individual authorities and managers maintain their own state.

The authoritative source for user and slice records is the SA that issued them, and the authoritative source for sliver information is the AM on which the sliver exists. Because the URNs used in ProtoGENI encode the issuing authority, it is possible to determine the correct authority to query simply by examining an object's name. If, for example, a AM wishes to find out more about a user who has created a slice on it, the AM may use the user's URN to identify and query the user's home SA.

When a sliver is created, the AM is *not* provided with a global picture of the slice: the sliver request (whose format is covered in Section 5) need only contain the resources on the AM in question and any links to directly adjacent AMs that need to be configured as part of the slice. Information about the rest of the slice is not needed for the AM to create its slivers, and maintaining a global view would require that the AM be notified of changes *anywhere* in the slice, even if those changes do not directly affect it.

As a convenience, SAs register users and their slices at the CH. Records at the CH are not considered authoritative, however, since a network partition might delay updates to them. Nor does the CH maintain a list of slivers; this list is constantly changing, and could never be completely up to date without adding a large amount of synchronization (and consequently delay) to the system. Each AM attempts to inform a slice's SA whenever a sliver is created or destroyed, but as with records in the CH, these data are advisory rather than authoritative.

Slice and Sliver Lifetimes. Because authoritative slice state is distributed across SAs and AMs, and we cannot guarantee that they remain in contact throughout the lifetime of the slice, we give each slice and sliver an expiration date. This way, we can be assured that all slivers are eventually cleaned up and their resources reclaimed.

There are important nuances, however, in the relationship between slice and sliver lifetimes. Because each sliver must belong to a slice, the sliver must not outlive its slice. If it did, this could lead to a situation in which the user would lose control of the sliver.

The first consequence of this requirement is straightforward: the expiration time for each sliver is bounded by the expiration time of the slice itself. The slice credential that is generated by an SA when then slice is created contains that slice's expiration time. When slivers are added to the slice, AMs must simply ensure that the slivers' expirations are no later than the slice's expiration.

The second consequence is that a slice cannot be deleted before it expires. It is possible that slivers exist that the SA is unaware of; a AM may have been unable to contact the SA to inform it of the sliver's existence. Therefore, the SA cannot know with certainty that deleting the slice is safe and will leave no orphaned slivers. As a result, slice names cannot be re-used by experimenters before they expire. Since the namespace for slices is effectively unbounded in size, this is not a major concern.

Both slices and slivers may be renewed before they expire; the slice's lifetime must be extended before the slivers'.

Resource Reservation across AMs. Slices that cross AMs present a dilemma: we would ideally like the process of allocating or updating slivers to be atomic across all AMs. As a concrete example, consider a slice with existing slivers from two different AMs. We would like to make a change on both slivers, but only if both of the changes succeed. If either one is denied, we want to roll back to the original configuration without losing existing resources or otherwise changing the slivers. However, the loosely-coupled nature of the federation precludes using global locks or global transactions.

Instead, we consider the resource allocation process on each AM to be a separate local transaction, and model the life cycle of each sliver as a state machine, shown in Figure 2. We designed the state machine with *minimal abstraction* in mind, allowing clients or other intermediaries to build a transactional abstraction across AMs on top of our lower-level per-AM API. Each sliver can be in one of four states:

1. The *Null* state, in which the sliver does not exist (has not yet been created, or has been destroyed).
2. The *Ticket* state, in which the user holds a ticket promising resources, but the sliver is not instantiated on the component.
3. The *Sliver* state, in which the sliver has been instantiated, but the user does not hold a valid ticket.

4. The *Sliver and Ticket* state, in which the user has both an instantiated sliver and a ticket.

This state machine makes sliver manipulation a three-step process:

1. Get the list of currently available resources from each AM.
2. Request a new ticket on each AM; this step obtains a *guarantee* of resources, but does does not actually instantiate a new sliver or modify an existing sliver.
3. Redeem the tickets at each AM to "commit" the resource change.

Steps 1 and 2 are not atomic: if other users are simultaneously trying to reserve resources to their own slices, the second step may fail. In a distributed system like Proto-GENI, it is not feasible to *lock* the resource lists for any length of time. Since contention for resources is generally rare in ProtoGENI, a form of *optimistic concurrency control* [11] is employed to both avoid locking and to ensure that users will find out if someone else has already reserved a resource.

If the second step fails on some AMs, but not others, the user has three options. First, he can decide to simply redeem the tickets that he *was* successful in getting. A user trying to get as many slivers as possible might employ this strategy. Second, he can abort the transaction by releasing the new tickets he obtained. This will return the slivers to their previous states (either *Null* or *Sliver*) without modifying them. Third, he can employ a more sophisticated strategy, in which he holds onto the tickets that he did receive, and requests tickets from a *new* set of AMs to replace those that were denied.

Our experience running the Emulab testbed [30] suggests that retries due to the race between steps 1 and 2 will be rare. Emulab uses a similar optimistic model in which the resource database is not locked during allocation, and despite the fact that Emulab sees heavy use, of 9,500 experiment swap-ins (analogous to ProtoGENI sliver creations) in the past year, only 21, or 0.2%, had to be retried due to contention for resources.

In addition to its lifetime, each ticket has a "redeem by" time, which is set to expire much sooner; typically, in a matter of minutes. If the user does not redeem the ticket in time, the resources are reclaimed. This guards against clients that do not complete their transactions in a timely fashion.

4.2   Behavior in the Face of Failures

ProtoGENI passes as much context as possible in API calls, so that they can be *self-contained*. While this does result in some extra overhead in the calls, the benefit is that the user can continue to make progress in the presence of network or service failures. For example, a user obtains authorisation credentials from his home SA, and these credentials are passed *by the user* to AMs when requesting tickets. As described in [31], the AM receiving this material can verify its authenticity without contacting the issuer.

The result is that users can continue to use the system in the face of failures in one or more services, including the CH. For example, if an SA is down, its users cannot create new slice names, but can continue to interact with any existing slices and slivers. As long as they do not lose the slice credentials obtained upon slice creation, there is no need to contact the SA to manipulate the slivers in the slice. The lone exception is to *extend* the life of a slice before it expires. However, this can be done at any time before the slice expires, so transient errors are not fatal.

While SAs attempt to register new slices at the CH, and AMs attempt to register new slivers with the slice's SA, failure to do so does not cause slice or sliver creation to fail. Making this registration mandatory would significantly increase the dependencies in the system, and reduce its ability to operate in the face of service failure.

5   Resource Specification

Resource specification is a core part of interacting with a testbed and must fulfill three functions: First, AMs must be able to describe their available resources. Second, users need to describe what resources they would like to acquire. Third, AMs must provide information required for users to make use of those resources.

To perform these functions, we have developed a new resource specification format, RSpec, which is an XML-formatted descriptive language. In keeping with the principle of *minimal abstraction*, our specification is declarative rather than imperative. While an imperative language would add descriptive power, it is more difficult to analyze and manipulate. Adopting a descriptive format makes it possible for many tools to process and transform resource descriptions, and encourages composition of tools.

One key principle behind our RSpec design is *distributed knowledge*. Because knowledge of resources is distributed, every entity in the system can independently provide information about resources. We use progressive annotation to allow a client to coordinate data from multiple sources: operations take a resource specification as input and yield that same specification annotated with additional information as output.

5.1   Annotation

Our specification format comes in three variants, each one designed to serve a slightly different function. Multiple entities in the system can provide knowledge about a single resource, and we allow calls to these entities to be composed by a client. An RSpec describes a topology made up of nodes, interfaces, and links that connect them. Annotations can provide additional information about the topology or resources.

Advertisements. Advertisements are used to describe the resources available on a AM. They contain information used by clients to choose components. The AM provides at least a minimal description of these resources. Our architecture then allows its advertisement to be passed to measurement services or others who may discover more information about the resources. At each such service, the advertisement is further annotated.

This progressive annotation of advertisements enables our *distributed knowledge* model. An AM can change the set of resources advertised without first notifying or negotiating with other federates. AMs provide their own authoritative information about which resources they manage and the availability of those resources.

At the same time, other entities can describe resources. A service might measure shared resources to determine which ones are the most heavily used. Or it might provide information about bandwidth and delay between networked components. Annotating services do not need to coordinate with any AMs, who need not even be aware of their existence.

Requests. Requests specify which resources a client is selecting from AMs. They contain a mapping between physical components and abstract nodes and links.

When the client has an advertisement with the information they need, they create a request describing which resources they require. Some requests, called bound requests, specify precisely which resources are needed—"I want pc42, pc81, and pc9." Other requests provide a more abstract, or unbound, description—"I want any three PCs."

Once the request is generated, it goes through an annotation process similar to that of the advertisement. If there are unbound resources in a request, it may be sent along with an advertisement to an embedding service which annotates the request with specific resource bindings. In order to *minimize dependencies*, embedding services are not associated with a particular AM and receive both a request and one or more advertisements from the client. The client then sends the bound request returned by the embedding service to a AM in order to acquire the resources. Each resource is tagged with the AM that should allocate it. This means that the client can simply send the same request to all relevant AMs and each one will allocate only those resources which it controls.

Manifests. Manifests provide information about slivers after they have been created by the AM. This information is typically needed by users so that they can make practical use of the resources: details such as host names, MAC addresses, ssh port numbers, and other useful data. This information may not be known until the sliver is actually created (e.g. dynamically assigned IP addresses). The manifest is returned to the user upon sliver creation.

5.2 Extensibility

To allow AMs to make unique resources available, we must provide a mechanism for allowing them to advertise new kinds of resources. Our core RSpec is therefore designed for *distributed knowledge*, allowing different federates to provide their own independent extensions. The base RSpec schema verifies within a single namespace and allows elements or attributes from other namespaces to be inserted anywhere. These fragments are then verified using extension-specific schemata. We allow extensions on any variant of the RSpec, thus allowing extensions to be created and used by any entity in the federation.

Our extensions have a number of useful properties:

1. *Extensions are safely ignored:* Not all clients or servers will support all extensions. If a client or server does not support a particular extension, then the tags which are part of that extension will be ignored. This allows extensions to be created and deployed incrementally with much greater ease than a change to the core RSpec.
2. *Extensions are modular:* Each extension can mix elements or attributes into the main RSpec, but those elements and attributes are explicitly tied to the extension namespace. Every extension can co-exist with every other extension.
3. *Extensions are validated:* In order to tag extensions, each one uses a unique XML namespace. We are thus able to validate any XML document using the core schema. The extensions themselves are also validated. We use independent schemata for each extension and validate the elements in the namespaces for each extension against its schema.

6   Experiences

The primary indicator of the success of our design is that ProtoGENI is a running, active system; the current federation contains sixteen AMs, and over 300 users have created more than 3000 slices. To evaluate our system more concretely, we first describe our experiences in creating and running the ProtoGENI federation, then show results from quantitative tests of the system.

6.1   Framework Design

ProtoGENI has been open to users and tool developers throughout its development. This allowed our experiences with actual users and experimenters to guide our design decisions. Described below are some of the lessons we have learned from seeing our system used by others.

Slice and Sliver Lifetimes: One area of the system that required very careful design was the lifetime of slices and slivers. We have found that this aspect of the system is consistently confusing to users; they expect to be able to delete *both* slivers and slices, and have trouble understanding why slice names cannot be deleted before they expire. However, as discussed in Section 4.1, this cannot be allowed, given the decentralized architecture of our system: an SA cannot be sure that all slivers are really gone until the expiration time on the slice (which bounds the expiration time on its slivers.)

Adding to the confusion is the fact that a slice name can be *reused* on an individual AM. In other words, the holder of a slice credential may create, destroy and then create a sliver again. As far as the AM is concerned, if no local sliver currently exists for a slice, then it is willing to create one. In fact, this is exactly what many users do.

Users will often create a slice name, and then use that credential to create and destroy many slivers on the same AM. This works since users usually know the state of their own experiments. It has also resulted in an unintended consequence: users may create a slice name, and set the expiration time to many months in the future. Since users often forget to destroy their slivers, resources can get tied up doing nothing for a long time. When this became a common problem, we established a policy which requires slices to be renewed every five days.

UUIDs: Our initial strategy was to use UUIDs [12] as identifiers. One advantage was that they can be generated by any party with a high confidence that they will be unique. They are also opaque, meaning that clients do not have to do any work in parsing or interpreting them. However, we discovered that using a flat namespace for all objects had one major drawback.

There is no inherent mapping between identifiers and authorities. A flat namespace requires a lookup service to resolve the authority issuing an identifier. For example, verifying that an identifier was issued by a particular authority would require one to first resolve the UUID to that authority. While decentralized resolvers for flat namespaces do exist (such as DHTs), we saw that including the authority in the identifier, and thus skipping this first step, was more in keeping with our minimization of dependencies principle, so that operations require contacting only the entities directly involved in them.

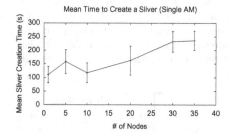

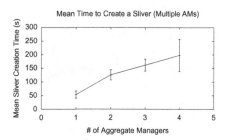

Fig. 3. Mean time to create slivers of various sizes

Fig. 4. Mean time to create slivers on multiple AMs

Sliver Lifecycle: When designing the ProtoGENI API, we tried to make it easy to use resources that are distributed geographically, under *different administrative domains*, and controlled by distinct management authorities. Users are faced not only with the task of deciding what resources they want, but they must also contact independent authorities to ask for those resources. As described in Section 4.1, dealing with resource allocation failures is complicated for both the system and the users. Worse still are sliver updates, especially those that span multiple AMs.

The *life cycle* diagram shown in Figure 2 was the result of user experience and multiple design iterations. An early version of the API used the same method to modify both an unredeemed ticket and an existing sliver. In the latter case, the user had to present the original ticket, even though the ticket had already been redeemed and was technically worthless. The user was also required to hang onto this ticket in case he wanted later modify the sliver. Furthermore, if the user decided to release this new ticket, he was left in an even less complete state, with an active sliver and no ticket to modify it later. As described in Section 4.1, this sequence is a common activity, as users allocate and modify resources across a set of AMs.

As more users signed up to run experiments with ProtoGENI, we received numerous questions about updating tickets and slivers. It was at this point that we decided to formalize the sliver lifecycle as a state machine, but our early attempts resulted in designs with a large number of states, making them difficult to understand. We finally arrived at the state machine in Figure 2, which puts the user in control of what to do with denied ticket requests, while minimising the size of the state machine.

6.2 Testing the System

In this section, we look at two metrics. We measured the time required to create slices both on a single AM and across multiple federates. In addition, we injected various faults and examined the behavior of the system when dealing with them.

Slice Creation Time. We have run tests on the federation to determine the duration of typical user tasks. For our experiment, we ran a test script using the following sequence of steps: get a user credential, create a slice, list component managers at CH, discover resources on one or more AMs, get a ticket, and finally redeem the ticket. We ran these

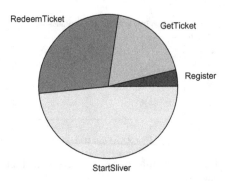

Fig. 5. Breakdown of time spent creating sliver

Table 1. Operability during failures. Each row is an attempted operation. Columns are component failures. Cells show if the given operation succeeds, *can* succeed if the client has cached the indicated object, or always fails (×).

Operation	Failed Entity		
	CH	SA	AM
Discover Res.	*AM List*	*Self Cred.*	×
Create Slice	Success	×	Success
Get Ticket	Success	*Slice Cred.*	×
Redeem Ticket	Success	*Slice Cred.*	×
Start Sliver	Success	*Slice Cred.*	×
Stop Sliver	Success	*Slice Cred.*	×
Delete Sliver	Success	*Slice Cred.*	×
Sliver Login	Success	Success	Success

tests with up to 35 nodes to see how increasing the size of the request affected the results. Figure 3 shows our results.

We also ran experiments using multiple AMs: between one and four. Figure 4 shows the time required to allocate nodes as the number of AMs increases. Each trial allocated 20 nodes total, but split the allocation of those nodes across a different number of AMs. As the number of AMs used increases, so does the time required to allocate nodes. This increase in time could be mitigated by contacting the AMs in parallel. The single AM case was run at a relatively lightly-loaded AM and so runs unusually fast relative to the times seen in Figure 3.

The time spent creating a ten node sliver (averaged over multiple runs) is detailed in Figure 5. The *Register* step accounts for all the negotiation with the SA to allocate the slice name and obtain slice credentials. All subsequent steps are carried out at the AM: *GetTicket* reserves components to the sliver, and is potentially expensive because it attempts sophisticated optimization not only to satisfy the immediate request, but also to maximize the proportion of *future* sliver demands which can be met [22].

The following *RedeemTicket* stage prepares the allocated components for use in the sliver: for instance, disk images are transferred [9] to nodes where necessary, and VLANs are programmed into switches (but not brought up). Our current implementation also performs auxiliary tasks for user convenience at this point (such as configuring DHCP servers with information about control network interfaces, and registering DNS names for nodes in the sliver). The final *StartSliver* period is frequently the lengthiest, although much of the operation is beyond the direct control of the AM. It involves rebooting each node in the sliver into the newly defined environment, as well as completing configuration tasks that are most easily deferred until boot time (such as configuring routing tables for the experimental networks).

Some of the time a client spends interacting with the system is spent gathering information it has already fetched during previous runs, such as the list of AMs, the user's "self credential," and credentials for slices that are being reused. In addition to providing additional robustness in the face of failure, caching these values can reduce the time it takes for a user to successfully create slivers. This provides a constant time speedup regardless of how many nodes or AMs are involved in creating a sliver. Our experiments show that this reduces the time taken to create a sliver by 17 seconds on average.

Behavior in the Face of Faults. Our federation was designed to cope with failure of one or more elements. In order to test this, we injected faults into the system in order to emulate a network partition. In each test, one federated entity was isolated from the federation and the client. We then attempted various operations to see whether they succeeded, failed, or required some cached client-side information to work. The results of these experiments are shown in Table 1.

If the CH fails or is isolated from the federation, the client can still perform operations on any AM it can reach, as well as the client's SA. In order to discover resources on a AM, the client would need to have a cached list of AMs in the federation; because this list does not change frequently, most clients will have a fairly recent copy. The only consequence of using an out-of date AM list is that the client may miss the opportunity to use AMs that have recently joined.

The SAs are responsible for managing users and their slices. If an SA fails, its users can no longer create slices or acquire credentials to manipulate existing slices. If a user already has a self credential, it can be invoked to discover resources on any AM in the federation. If the user has already created a slice, it has not expired, and the client has cached the slice credential, then the user can still create and manipulate slivers on any AM.

When a AM fails, the user cannot perform resource discovery or sliver creation, or any sliver manipulation calls on that *particular* AM. Depending on whether the failure is with the AM or the component itself, the user may still be able to log in to the slivers that have already been created. The failure of one AM does not affect the user's ability to use other AMs in the federation.

7   Conclusion

Federated testbeds provide new opportunities for experimentation, but also raise a number of design challenges. We applied five design principles to the design of ProtoGENI, resulting in a loosely coupled system that preserves local autonomy for federates. Proto-GENI provides a low-level interface to discovering and reserving testbed resources; our future work will build upon this fundamental framework to provide higher-level abstractions and services for experimenters.

Acknowledgments. Many people have been active participants in the GENI design process, which arrived at the basic design described in Section 3. While the total number of contributors to this process is large, we would like to specifically acknowledge the chairs of the GENI Facility Architecture Working Group and heads of the GENI control frameworks: Larry Peterson (PlanetLab), John Wroclawski (TIED), Jeff Chase (ORCA/BEN), and Max Ott (OMF). Others major contributors to the design process have included Aaron Falk, Ted Faber, Steve Schwab, and Ilia Baldine.

References

1. Anderson, D.G., Balakrishnan, H., Kaashoek, M.F., Morris, R.: Resilient overlay networks. In: Proc. of the ACM Symposium on Operating Systems Principles (SOSP), Banff, Canada (October 2001)
2. Antoniadis, P., Fdida, S., Friedman, T., Misra, V.: Federation of virtualized infrastructures: sharing the value of diversity. In: Proc. of the 6th International Conf. on Emerging Networking EXperiments and Technologies (CoNEXT), Philadelphia, PA (November 2010)
3. Bavier, A., Feamster, N., Huang, M., Rexford, J., Peterson, L.: In VINI veritas: Realistic and controlled network experimentation. In: Proc. of the ACM Special Interest Group on Data Communication (SIGCOMM), Pisa, Italy (August 2006)
4. Chatzigiannakis, I., Koninis, C., Mylonas, G., Fischer, S., Pfisterer, D.: WISEBED: an open large-scale wireless sensor network testbed. In: Proc. of the 1st International Conf. on Sensor Networks Applications, Experimentation and Logistics (September 2009)
5. Cooper, D., Santesson, S., Farrell, S., Boeyen, S., Housley, R., Polk, W.: Internet X.509 public key infrastructure certificate and certificate revocation list (CRL) profile. Request for Comments 5280, IETF (May 2008)
6. Farrell, S., Housley, R., Turner, S.: An internet attribute certificate profile for authorization. Request for Comments 5755, Internet Engineering Task Force (January 2010)
7. Foster, I., Kesselman, C.: Globus: A metacomputing infrastructure toolkit. International Journal of Supercomputer Applications 11(2) (summer 1997)
8. Foster, I., Kesselman, C., Tuecke, S.: The anatomy of the grid: Enabling scalable virtual organizations. International Journal of High Performance Computing Applications 15(3) (August 2001)
9. Hibler, M., Stoller, L., Lepreau, J., Ricci, R., Barb, C.: Fast, scalable disk imaging with Frisbee. In: Proc. of the 2003 USENIX Annual Technical Conf., San Antonio, TX, pp. 283–296 (June 2003)
10. Kim, N., Kim, J., Heermann, C., Baldine, I.: Interconnecting International Network Substrates for Networking Experiments. In: Korakis, T., Li, H., Tran-Gia, P., Park, H.-S. (eds.) TridentCom 2011. LNICST, vol. 90, pp. 116–125. Springer, Heidelberg (2012)
11. Kung, H.T., Robinson, J.T.: On optimistic methods for concurrency control. ACM Transactions on Database Systems 6(2) (June 1981)
12. Leach, P., Mealling, M., Salz, R.: A universally unique identifier (UUID) URN namespace. Request for Comments 4122, Internet Engineering Task Force (July 2005)
13. McKee, S.: The ATLAS computing model: status, plans and future possibilities. Computer Physics Communications 177(1–2) (July 2007)
14. Miyachi, T., Basuki, A., Mikawa, S., Miwa, S., Chinen, K., Shinoda, Y.: Educational environment on StarBED: case study of SOI Asia 2008 spring global E-Workshop. In: ACM Asian Conf. on Internet Engineering. Bangkok, Thailand (November 2008)
15. Moats, R.: URN syntax. Request for Comments 2141, Internet Engineering Task Force (May 1997)
16. The ORCA GENI control framework, http://www.nicl.cs.duke.edu/orca
17. Ott, M., Seskar, I., Siraccusa, R., Singh, M.: ORBIT testbed software architecture: Supporting experiments as a service. In: Proc. of the International ICST Conf. on Testbeds and Research Infrastructures for the Development of Networks and Communities (TridentCom),Trento, Italy (February 2005)

18. Peterson, L., Bavier, A., Fiuczynski, M.E., Muir, S.: Experiences building PlanetLab. In: Proc. of the USENIX Symposium on Operating Systems Design and Implementation (OSDI), Seattle, WA (November 2006)
19. Peterson, L., Ricci, R., Falk, A., Chase, J.: Slice-based federation architecture (June 2010), http://groups.geni.net/geni/wiki/SliceFedArch
20. ProtoGENI Project: ProtoGENI API (May 2012), http://www.protogeni.net/trac/protogeni/wiki/API
21. Rakotoarivelo, T., Jourjon, G., Ott, M., Seskar, I.: OMF: A control and management framework for networking testbeds. ACM SIGOPS Operating Systems Review 43(4) (January 2010)
22. Ricci, R., Alfeld, C., Lepreau, J.: A solver for the network testbed mapping problem. ACM SIGCOMM Computer Communication Review (CCR) 33(2), 65–81 (2003)
23. Ripeanu, M., Bowman, M., Chase, J.S., Foster, I., Milenkovic, M.: Globus and PlanetLab resource management solutions compared. In: Proc. of the 13th IEEE International Symposium on High-Performance Distributed Computing (HPDC 2004), Honolulu, HI (June 2004)
24. Burin des Roziers, C., Chelius, G., Ducrocq, T., Fleury, E., Fraboulet, A., Gallais, A., Mitton, N., Noél, T., Vandaele, J.: Using SensLAB as a First Class Scientific Tool for Large Scale Wireless Sensor Network Experiments. In: Domingo-Pascual, J., Manzoni, P., Palazzo, S., Pont, A., Scoglio, C. (eds.) NETWORKING 2011, Part I. LNCS, vol. 6640, pp. 147–159. Springer, Heidelberg (2011)
25. Sevinc, S.: A Path to Evolve to Federation of TestBeds. In: Korakis, T., Li, H., Tran-Gia, P., Park, H.-S. (eds.) TridentCom 2011. LNICST, vol. 90, pp. 126–141. Springer, Heidelberg (2012)
26. Viecco, C.: Use of URNs as GENI identifiers (June 2009), http://gmoc.grnoc.iu.edu/gmoc/file-bin/urn-proposal3.pdf
27. Wahle, S., Tranoris, C., Denazis, S., Gavras, A., Koutsopoulos, K., Magedanz, T., Tompros, S.: Emerging testing trends and the Panlab enabling infrastructure. IEEE Communications Magazine 49(3) (March 2011)
28. Wahle, S., Magedanz, T., Campowsky, K.: Interoperability in Heterogeneous Resource Federations. In: Magedanz, T., Gavras, A., Thanh, N.H., Chase, J.S. (eds.) TridentCom 2010. LNICST, vol. 46, pp. 35–50. Springer, Heidelberg (2011)
29. Webb, K., Hibler, M., Ricci, R., Clements, A., Lepreau, J.: Implementing the Emulab-PlanetLab portal: Experience and lessons learned. In: Proc. of the First Workshop on Real, Large Distributed Systems (USENIX WORLDS), San Francisco, CA (December 2004)
30. White, B., Lepreau, J., Stoller, L., Ricci, R., Guruprasad, S., Newbold, M., Hibler, M., Barb, C., Joglekar, A.: An integrated experimental environment for distributed systems and networks. In: Proc. of the USENIX Symposium on Operating Systems Design and Implementation (OSDI), Boston, MA (December 2002)
31. Wong, G., Ricci, R., Duerig, J., Stoller, L., Chikkulapelly, S., Seok, W.: Partitioning trust in network testbeds. In: Proc. of the 45th Hawaii International Conf. on System Sciences (HICSS-45), Wailea, HI (January 2012)

Experimentation in Heterogeneous European Testbeds through the Onelab Facility: The Case of PlanetLab Federation with the Wireless NITOS Testbed

Stratos Keranidis[1,2], Dimitris Giatsios[1,2], Thanasis Korakis[1,2],
Iordanis Koutsopoulos[1,2], Leandros Tassiulas[1,2],
Thierry Rakotoarivelo[3], and Thierry Parmentelat[4]

[1] Department of Computer Engineering and Telecommunications,
University of Thessaly, Greece
[2] Centre for Research and Technology, Hellas
[3] National ICT Australia (NICTA), Alexandria, Australia
[4] INRIA, Sophia Antipolis, France
{efkerani,gidimitr,korakis,jordan,leandros}@uth.gr,
thierry.rakotoarivelo@nicta.com.au, thierry.parmentelat@sophia.inria.fr

Abstract. The constantly increasing diversity of the infrastructure that is used to deliver Internet services to the end user, has created a demand for experimental network facilities featuring heterogeneous resources. Therefore, federation of existing network testbeds has been identified as a key goal in the experimental testbeds community, leading to a recent activity burst in this research field. In this paper, we present a federation scheme that was built during the Onelab 2 EU project. This scheme federates the NITOS wireless testbed with the wired PlanetLab Europe testbed, allowing researchers to access and use heterogeneous experimental facilities under an integrated environment. The usefulness of the resulting federated facility is demonstrated through the testing of an implemented end-to-end delay aware association scheme proposed for Wireless Mesh Networks. We present extensive experiments under both wired congestion and wireless channel contention conditions that demonstrate the effectiveness of the proposed approach in a realistic environment. Both the architectural building blocks that enable the federation of the testbeds and the execution of the experiment on combined resources, as well as the important insights obtained from the experimental results are described and analyzed, pointing out the importance of integrated experimental facilities for the design and development of the Future Internet.

Keywords: Testbed Federation, Wireless Mesh Networks, Experiments.

1 Introduction

Wireless Mesh Networks (WMNs) are currently considered as the default solution for delivering high-speed Internet access to users within the last few network

T. Korakis, M. Zink, and M. Ott (Eds.): TridentCom 2012, LNICST 44, pp. 338–354, 2012.
© Institute for Computer Sciences, Social Informatics and Telecommunications Engineering 2012

miles in non-urban areas. As a result, the interest of the research community in proposing WMN-related approaches has dramatically increased during the last few years. The inherent inability of simulation models to accurately estimate performance of wireless networks, in accordance with the unique characteristics introduced by the complex nature of WMNs [1] have directed research efforts towards implementation approaches and evaluation through experimentation in real world network scale and settings.

However, development of large scale WMN testbeds is a rather challenging task that requires careful design and induces high deployment and maintenance cost. Moreover, as WMNs are usually considered as a promising technology for Internet access provision, experimentation across global scale networks that feature real Internet characteristics is required, in order to conclude on realistic results under real congestion conditions. Such requirements have led the research community to create global large scale infrastructure that results from the federation of heterogeneous types of networks, such as wired (local, wide-area or optical) and wireless (local, mesh or sensor networks).

Federation between inherently heterogeneous testbeds introduces several issues that arise due to the difference in the nature of experimental resources, but more importantly due the use of different software frameworks for resources management and controlling. In this work we realize the federation between two well-established heterogeneous network testbeds, namely the NITOS wireless testbed and the planetary scale wired PlanetLab Europe (PLE) testbed. The utilization of a common experiment control framework, OMF [2] (cOntrol and Management Framework), and the adoption of the slice abstraction as the building block for the federation have made the testbeds' integration possible.

In order to demonstrate the usefulness of the resulting integrated architecture, we develop and implement an association scheme for WMNs that is aware of end-to-end delay, part of which is generated in the wired part (PLE) and part in the wireless part (NITOS). The implemented mechanism is based on novel association metrics [3] that consider wireless channel contention, which are further enhanced to take into account wired delay as well. The evaluation of the proposed mechanism is performed through extensive experiments conducted on the combined network architecture, which results from the federation of the two heterogeneous experimental facilities.

This paper is organized as follows. In section 2 we discuss research work related with both association in WMNs and federation of heterogeneous experimental facilities. In section 3 we describe the architecture of the two heterogeneous testbeds and moreover provide details about the approach followed and the tools used for the establishment of the testbed integration. In section 4 we analyze and discuss the proposed association approach. In section 5 we present and comment on the results obtained from the experimental evaluation of the implemented mechanism. Finally, in section 6 we summarize our work, by pointing out conclusions and directions for future work.

2   Related Work

2.1   Association in Wireless Mesh Networks

WMNs are composed of Mesh Routers (MRs), which form the wireless back-haul access network and Mesh Clients (MCs). MRs forward packets acting as intermediate relay nodes and may also provide wireless access services to MCs, in which case they are referred to as Mesh Access Points (MAPs). The WMN consists also of Internet Gateway nodes (IGWs) that provide Internet access to the network, through direct connection to wired infrastructure. MCs associate with a certain MAP in order to access the network and do not participate in packet forwarding.

The affordable cost and ease of deployment of IEEE 802.11 compliant equipment has led the majority of WMNs to be based on conventional IEEE 802.11 devices, although this does not limit the application of other standards. According to the IEEE 802.11 standard, which was originally proposed for infrastructure Wireless Local Area Networks (WLANs), MCs perform scanning to detect nearby MAPs and simply select to associate with the MAP that provides the highest Received Signal Strength Indication (RSSI) value. The performance of the standard association policy has been extensively studied [4] in the context of IEEE 802.11 WLANs and it is well known that it leads to inefficient use of the network resources. In WMNs, the entire path between the MC and the IGW is composed of two discrete wireless parts: the single-hop access link between the MC and the MAP it is associated with and the multi-hop backhaul part that connects the MAP with the IGW. As the standard policy considers only factors affecting performance on the wireless access link, its direct application on WMNs becomes inappropriate. As a result, more sophisticated association schemes are required to capture performance achieved in both the access and the backhaul network parts.

Trying to address the issues generated by the unique two-tier architecture introduced by WMNs, several approaches on MAP selection have been proposed in the recent literature. An innovative cross-layer association mechanism that considers not only the access link but also routing in the multi-hop backhaul part is proposed in [5]. The authors in [6] consider also the interaction of physical (PHY) layer transmission rate with the packet size and hop count and propose a signaling mechanism through which information about congestion on both parts is passed from the MAPs to the MCs. In [7], a new metric is proposed that takes into account the impact of 802.11 MAC layer contention on bandwidth sharing and results in accurate link throughput estimations. Another approach, proposed in [8], considers also estimation of real-time traffic load conditions trying to cope with the variability of network conditions, which is an inherent characteristic of WMNs. The common characteristic of the works referenced above is that they rely only on simulation based evaluation of the proposed mechanisms.

Recent research studies in the field of WMNs jointly consider problems that traditionally were considered in isolation, such as association and routing. However, as simulation models are not not able to capture the interaction among different layers [1], research related to WMNs is mainly performed in experimental facilities. A recent work in the field [9] proposes a cross-layer association mechanism, which is implemented and evaluated through experimentation in a wireless testbed. However, the evaluation of the implemented scheme is restricted in experiments conducted in a small scale testbed composed of conventional laptop computers and not in a customized large scale Mesh testbed.

At this point, we argue that approaches proposed for WMNs should be fully implemented and properly evaluated through extensive experimentation under real interference and congestion conditions. In an effort to support realistic and large-scale experimentation with heterogeneous network platforms, both the GENI initiative in the U.S. [10], as well as the FIRE initiative in Europe [11] are currently investigating federation of heterogeneous testbeds.

2.2 Integration of Heterogeneous Experimental Facilities

An initial effort on federation of testbeds was proposed in [12], where the wireless EmuLab testbed and the wired planetary-scale PlanetLab testbed [13] were integrated through the *EmuLab-PlanetLab portal*. The integrated interface provided useful extensions to the PlanetLab's management system. Moreover, several integration challenges were identified for the first time and appropriate solutions were provided. Another work, proposed in [14], aimed at integrating Planet-Lab with the ORBIT wireless testbed. The authors considered also the ability of performing experiments on the integrated framework concurrently. Although PlanetLab testbed provided support for virtualization of resources in the wired part, virtualization of the wireless part had to be further investigated in order to overcome the issues that the broadcast nature of the wireless medium generates. Two discrete integration models were proposed in this work, where the first one aimed to support PlanetLab users in extending their experimental topologies with wireless nodes, while the second one was introduced to provide users of the ORBIT testbed with the extra ability of adding wired network extensions to their experiments.

An important issue that the aforementioned federation approaches had to cope with was the scarcity of a common management system, as well as a common experiment description language. However, this issue was overcome with the introduction of OMF, which provides tools for the management and execution of experiments on testbed infrastructures. Nowadays, OMF has been deployed and maintained on multiple testbeds supporting many different types of technologies. The work proposed in [15] presented the integration of an OMF-controllable WiFi testbed and PLE, through the addition of an extra wireless interface in PLE nodes that were located within the range of the wireless testbed. This integration was achieved through the development of special tools that supported the definition of slice-specific routing table rules and the exclusive use of the wireless testbed by a single experimenter. Although this integration attempt provided an integrated environment, where all resources could be instrumented through OMF, it also faced the drawback of realizing the wireless testbed as a single resource and thus limited the access of the federated environment to a single user for each reservation slot.

In an effort to maximize the utilization of OMF-based experimental facilities, NITOS introduced a testbed Scheduler [16] that enables the assignment of different subsets of nodes and channels to different users during specific reservation slots. The work in [17] proposes an integration architecture, which combines an OMF-based wireless testbed supported by the NITOS scheduling mechanism with several PLE OMF-enabled nodes. The resulting federated environment formed a realistic global-scale WMN that supported the execution of multiple concurrent experiments, through NITOS Scheduler. Moreover, the authors demonstrated an experimental scenario that provided interesting insights regarding real-world experimentation with peer-to-peer systems.

3   OneLab Federation of NITOS and PlanetLab

OneLab [18] is an initiative to provide an open, general-purpose experimental facility, aimed at promoting innovation among network and ICT researchers in Europe, both in academia and industry. It is primarily based on the results of two EC FP7 projects, namely the Onelab and Onelab2 projects. One of the most important goals of the initiative is to establish a federated environment between different, possibly heterogeneous testbeds. As several testbeds have been deployed independently by research institutions across Europe during recent years, and each of them has developed or adopted a different control and management framework, a complex and inconvenient mosaic arises. In this mosaic, experimentation in different testbeds implies familiarization with the respective control frameworks, while combined experiments between different facilities are extremely difficult to setup. The federation between NITOS and PLE, two testbeds of entirely different architecture, which took place during the Onelab2 project, demonstrated that through agreements and collaborations among the involved administrative entities, it is possible to establish architectural paradigms that allow for combined experiments across heterogeneous platforms. In this section, after describing the two facilities, we analyze the components of the federated environment, which allowed for a combined experiment.

3.1   PlanetLab Europe

PlanetLab Europe is the European portion of the publicly available PlanetLab testbed, a global facility for the deployment of new network services. It is tightly federated with PlanetLab Central, offering a total of 1000+ nodes worldwide. Each node is a dedicated server that runs components of PlanetLab services.

Slices/Slivers. The notion of a slice is a rather central notion in PlanetLab; it typically allows to model resource allocation, by relating a set of users and a set of resources (nodes). Once created, the slice "owns" one private server (sliver) on each of the selected nodes, and to the designated users, being part of the slice means UNIX shell access to all these slivers. The PlanetLab software is tailored for smoothly orchestrating a complex workflow that involves a large number of people, with different roles (from the legal paperwork, down to locally vouching for users and remote IT management); it also needs to deal with accountability of the resulting network traffic, especially given its scale and diversity of usages, that by design often leads to untypical shapes of traffic; but it admittedly offers little help in managing a slice, and encourages users to leverage third-party tools for the actual experimentation phase.

MyPLC. MyPLC is the software that was packaged by the PlanetLab operators to let others run their own private PlanetLab system. It was created by Princeton University and is currently being codeveloped by Princeton and OneLab partner INRIA. It provides a ready-to-install set of packages, for both infrastucture-side (XMLRPC API, with related database, software server for securely booting and upgrading nodes), and node-side (slivers management, accountability, remote operations and monitoring). MyPLC is rather flexible, and several tens of instances of MyPLC have been deployed around the world, either for entirely local testbeds, or at the scale of a research consortium.

3.2 NITOS Testbed

NITOS is a wireless testbed featuring 50 WiFi-enabled outdoor nodes in the premises of a University of Thessaly campus building. It is remotely and publicly accessible to any researcher wishing to use its resources, after a registration and its approval by the testbed administrators. Below we describe the two basic software entities of the NITOS testbed, OMF/OML and NITOS Scheduler.

OMF/OML. NITOS has adopted OMF as its testbed control and management framework. The architecture of OMF is based on three main software components: the Aggregate Manager (AM), the Experiment Controller (EC) and the Resource Controller (RC). The AM provides a set of services to the testbed (inventory, image loading, etc.). The EC, which is the user's interface, receives and parses an experiment script describing configuration of resources and the actual experimental scenario. This script is written in a domain-specific language called OEDL (OMF Experiment Description Language). The instructions in the script are transferred to the RCs of the respective resources, which are responsible to perform the local configurations and application invocations. The different components communicate asynchronously through an XMPP publish-subscribe system, where each message is transferred to an XMPP server, which relays it to its intended destination.

OML (OMF Measurement Library), a companion framework for OMF, is responsible for handling measurements. It consists of two architectural components, the OML server and the OML client libraries. The client libraries are responsible for capturing measurements generated at the resources and, possibly after some manipulations, injecting them in streams headed towards the

OML server. The OML server receives the data and stores them in organized databases, one per experiment.

NITOS Scheduler. NITlab has developed a reservation and access control software tool for NITOS, called NITOS Scheduler. This tool provides a web-based reservation front-end for users of the testbed. In the Scheduler's backend, there are two main functionalities worth mentioning: the Scheduler's interaction with the XMPP framework used in OMF and the spectrum slicing framework. Both of them are utilized to create slicing of the testbed, that is, to enable simultaneous experimentation by multiple users through allocation of disjoint sets of resources. Each user at NITOS is associated with a slice. Unlike the typical PlanetLab setup where slices imply the existence of virtual machines, at NITOS a slice is an abstract entity. For each slice in NITOS, the PubSub nodes /OMF/<slicename> and /OMF/<slicename>/resources are always present.

When a reservation for a NITOS resource starts, an additional PubSub node /OMF/<slicename>/resources/ <resource_name> is created. When this reservation ends, this entry is deleted. As a result, access to NITOS nodes is restricted through this dynamic association and dissociation of resources to the corresponding slices, based on queries to the NITOS scheduler's database. Since all OMF communication takes place via XMPP, this mechanism is equivalent to OMF-based dynamic access control to the NITOS resources.

3.3   Federation Framework

In this subsection, we describe the basic components of the federated environment between NITOS and PLE. The development of these components took place during the project Onelab2 and enabled, from an architectural point of view, the conduction of the experiment presented in this paper.

Single Sign Up. One important characteristic of a federated environment is that a user of such a facility should not be obliged to register at its different components separately, but instead be able to use common credentials. To achieve this operation between NITOS and PLE, a single-sign up mechanism has been developed, so that any user of PLE can log into NITOS portal without going through any extra registration process. This single-sign up process is based on PlanetLab's standard XMLRPC user authentication API. In particular, when a user attempts to log into the NITOS portal, providing a username and a password, the portal's underlying code not only tries to match the credentials with an entry from the native user database, but also contacts the authorization server of PLE through the standard API. If a match is found among PLE's users, an affirmation is sent back to NITOS, which then automatically generates (in the case that id does not already exist) a slice in NITOS having the name of the PLE slice and moreover logs him in NITOS portal with the provided credentials. The process is transparent to the user and incurs no significant delay.

Deployment of OMF/OML at PLE Resources. A major difficulty when trying to run combined experiments using heterogeneous facilities is that different

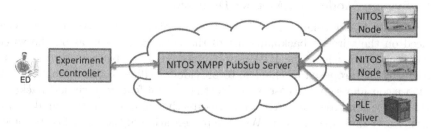

Fig. 1. XMPP Server Connectivity

languages are used to describe resource configurations and actions. There is the need for agreement to use a common language for experiment description, which must be able to handle the broadest range of resource types possible and easily add support for new resource types in a modular fashion. OEDL is a perfect candidate, as it meets these requirements. Therefore, PLE decided to incorporate OMF support on demand, in the form of so-called 'OMF-friendly' slices. For slices with this tag activated, an OMF Resource Controller is installed and initiated in the related slivers. In this way, a PLE resource can be viewed as any other resource of an OMF-based testbed and it can be configured through instructions issued by the experimenter in an experiment script written in OEDL.

XMPP Communication Using Slices. In order for all the resources to be able to communicate with the EC, they must be registered in the same XMPP server or to a set of XMPP servers peered with each other. Currently the XMPP servers of PLE and NITOS are not peered. As a result, we adopted the first choice of using a single XMPP server and more specifically the NITOS XMPP server, where the PLE node could be registered as if features a public IP address, which is not the case for NITOS nodes that use private IP addresses. We are currently working towards enabling the peering between these two XMPP servers. The architecture, used in our current work, is presented in Fig. 1. As for a next step, we logged into NITOS using the PLE slice credentials and statically associated the PLE resource to the automatically generated slice, by adding a corresponding entry to the NITOS XMPP server. In accordance with the functionality of NITOS Scheduler, the PLE resource could be accessed via NITOS only by the user related with the automatically generated slice and thus no unauthorized access issues were raised.

4   Proposed Association Mechanism

In order to demonstrate the usefulness of the federated environment that combines the wired PLE with the wireless NITOS testbeds, we developed a novel association mechanism proposed for WMNs that is end-to-end performance aware. In this section, we describe the developed association mechanism and moreover provide details about its driver level implementation.

4.1   System Model and Metrics Definition

As end-to-end performance in WMNs depends also on the performance experienced on the wireless backhaul part of the network, as well as on the wired infrastructure on which the IGWs are connected, both factors are taken into account by the proposed mechanism to provide for efficient associations. In this work, we consider a special case of WMNs that do not feature a wireless backhaul part, but are composed of MAPs that are directly connected to the wired infrastructure and thus operate as IGWs. A representation of the described topology is illustrated in Fig. 2.

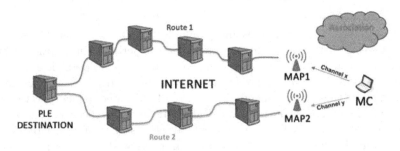

Fig. 2. Topology representation

Each MC chooses to associate with a single MAP among the MAPs that operate in its vicinity. Each network node n has a set of neighbors, that reside in its sensing area and operate on the same channel with n. This set of "1-hop" neighbors, that can be either MAPs or MCs, is denoted by A_n. In our previous work [3], we concluded to two discrete throughput based metrics for uplink and downlink communications that conform with the special case of infrastructure 802.11 networks. In this work, we consider only the case of uplink communications, which provides for a simple analysis of the proposed mechanism. In uplink communications, frames are transmitted by each MC and destined to the specific AP it is associated with. In our previous work, we arrived at an expression that considers the medium sharing of each MC_i with its "1-hop" neighbors (A_i) and estimates throughput on uplink as follows:

$$T_{ij}^{up} = \frac{1}{\dfrac{f_i}{R_{ij}} + \sum_{k=1}^{|A_i|} \dfrac{f_k}{R_k}}, \tag{1}$$

where R_{ij} and R_k denote the PHY rates used by MC_i and each node $k \in A_i$ accordingly, while f_i and f_k are defined as activity indicator factors reflecting the activity intensity of MC_i and node $k \in A_i$ in comparison with each other.

4.2   End-to-End Performance Aware Association Mechanism

Based on the analysis in the previous section, we are able to estimate throughput performance for the single-hop access link between the MC and each potential neighboring MAP. More specifically, the denominator of expression 1 estimates the average time duration required for a single bit of information to be transmitted over the access link. In this work, we develop an association framework that is based on Round-Trip Time (RTT) measurements. In order to estimate the RTT required for the initial transmission and subsequent retransmissions of a frame with specific length, we have to multiply the calculated delay with the number of bits that are transmitted over the access link and moreover double the resulting value to estimate the total delay required for both transmissions. Concluding, we estimate the RTT for a specific frame of M bits that is transmitted over the access link from MC_i to MAP_j and back again, as follows:

$$RTT_{ij}^A = 2 * M * \left(\frac{f_i}{R_{ij}} + \sum_{k=1}^{|A_i|} \frac{f_k}{R_k}\right) \tag{2}$$

In our approach, we develop a simple mechanism to estimate RTT experienced on the wired backhaul part of the network as well. More specifically, each MAP_j periodically transmits probe packets and measures RTT_j^B for the wired network backhaul. These values are broadcasted to all MCs in range and as a result each MC_i is able to estimate end-to-end RTT for each potential MAP_j, as follows:

$$RTT_{ij}^{total} = RTT_{ij}^A + RTT_j^B \tag{3}$$

4.3   Implementation Details

For the implementation of our mechanism, we used the Mad-WiFi open source driver. Details about the mechanism aiding in performance estimation on the wireless part can be found in our previous work [3]. In this section we will provide details about the developed mechanism that enables application layer information regarding wired RTT information to reach neighboring MCs. First of all, we use a simple application level program that runs at the APs and sends probe packets to the destination host to calculate RTT_j^B values. In order to broadcast this information to all neighboring MCs, we first had to make the RTT_j^B value available to the kernel level, as all MAC layer mechanisms are implemented as loadable kernel modules by the MAD-WiFi driver. An efficient way to transfer information to the kernel is through the proc virtual filesystem, which resides in the kernel memory. The proc files used by the MAD-WiFi driver are stored in /proc/sys/net/wlan/athX, where X denotes the specific interface. Another script running locally at the APs periodically writes values to the specified proc file and as soon as a new record is written the driver is informed. As for the next step we had to broadcast the RTT_j^B value to all neighboring MCs. In order to do this, we extended the *Beacon* and *Probe-Response* frames to carry this information. This frame extension does not affect the normal operation of the 802.11 protocol, as these frames feature a dynamic part that supports extension, according to the standard. The MCs constantly estimate the RTT_{ij}^A values for each potential MAP. The third step is also performed at the MC side, where the driver combines the RTT_j^B value with the RTT_{ij}^A and calculates the RTT_{ij}^{total}. Finally, each MC_i associates with the MAP_j that features the lowest RTT_{ij}^{total} value.

5   Experimental Evaluation

In this section, we evaluate several experimental scenarios that have been designed to demonstrate the effectiveness of association mechanisms that jointly consider factors affecting both wireless and wired performance, rather than presenting innovative research results. The execution of such combined experiments requires integrated testing, which would not be feasible without the existence of the federated environment.

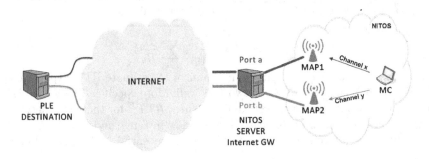

Fig. 3. Experimental topology representation

5.1   Measurement Methodology

Fig. 3 represents the actual topology used in our experiments. We consider a typical scenario, where one traffic flow is generated from the MC node and relayed through the two available APs to the final PLE destination node. The MAPs act as IGWs and get access to the wired network part through NITOS Server. As NITOS nodes are assigned private IP addresses, we had to enable a Network Address Translation (NAT) service at NITOS Server through proper IPtables [19] configurations, in order to provide Internet access to the two nodes operating as MAPs. We also followed a similar procedure to provide for proper relaying of traffic generated by the MC through the two MAPs.

As our association mechanism is end-to-end delay aware, we had to generate conditions of varying delay in both the wired and the wireless parts. In order to add artificial delay in the wired backhaul link, we used the *Dummynet* [20] tool, which is able to simulate queue and bandwidth limitations, delays, packet losses, and multi-path effects, by intercepting packets in their way through the protocol stack. As an outcome of the OneLab project, PLE natively supports dummynet as a kernel module in all nodes, configurable from the sliver through a command-line tool. As all packets received at the destination, share the same IP address of the NITOS Server, we base packet discrimination on the port numbers. To this aim, we used a simple *Nmap* [21] script to dynamically detect the specific ports used for incoming connections at the PLE node. For the wireless part, we enable a pair of nodes that operate on each of the channels used by the MAPs and generate

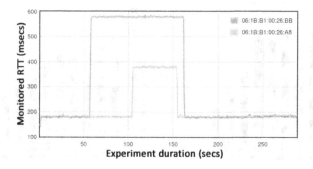

Fig. 4. Delay monitored at the PLE node for two flows generated by each MAP

channel contention conditions of varying traffic rate. Fig. 4 shows a screenshot of the OMF visualization tool representing delay emulation for two discrete flows generated by each one of the MAPs, as monitored at the PLE node.

The throughput performance of the experiments is measured by using Iperf [22]. In our experiments, we run an Iperf Client at the MC to generate TCP flows and UDP flows of varying rate and also an Iperf Server residing at the PLE node to receive traffic and collect the corresponding measurements. We run each experiment 10 times and each run lasts for 2 minutes.

5.2 Experiments

The conducted experiments are organized in two sets, where in the first set we generate conditions of varying delay in the wired backhaul part, while in the second set we vary the delay in the single hop wireless access link. Moreover, each experiment is performed in two discrete phases, where in the first one we compare the effect of injected delay on performance affecting either the wired (1st set) or wireless (2nd set) part solely, while in the second phase we consider the impact on the combined network architecture.

The conducted experiments aim at presenting the performance improvement that can be offered through the application of the proposed association mechanism and thus measure the performance for a static scenario, where the MC communicates with a specific MAP. Under this scenario we alter the delay induced in each part and monitor the resulting performance in terms of TCP /UDP throughput, packet loss and jitter values. The initial RTT in the wired part between NITOS Server and the PLE node residing in France is around 80 ms, while in the wireless part the reported RTT between the MC and each MAP without any external contention is below the value of 1 ms. In all the conducted experiments, the default Rate adaptation algorithm of the driver has been used.

Wired - Combined Set of Experiments. In this first set of experiments we use the *Dummynet* tool to generate artificial delay. Fig. 5(a) and Fig. 5(b) illustrate the TCP throughput achieved under various artificial delay values in

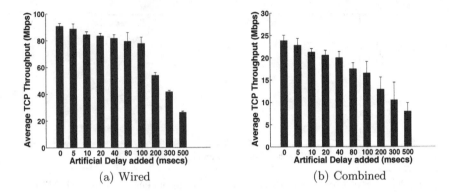

(a) Wired   (b) Combined

Fig. 5. TCP Throughput vs Artificial Delay

the wired and the combined architectures accordingly. We notice that even small variation of delay in the wired part significantly affects TCP throughput and therefore should be taken into account. Moreover, we notice that the wireless access link acts as the performance bottleneck that significantly limits yielded performance. A particular observation is that the same experiments provide higher deviation values when conducted in the combined topology, for the cases of 200, 300 and 500 msecs of injected delay, in comparison with the execution solely in the wired part. However, average throughput values show similar performance in the above cases. Based on the observed results, we remark that relatively high values of injected delay make TCP performance in the combined network highly unstable.

In Fig. 6(a) and Fig. 6(b), we present the duration required for the successful transmission of a file with size of 100 MBs in the wired and combined network accordingly. We easily notice that even a low increase in RTT values of 20 ms

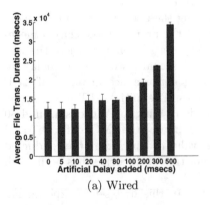
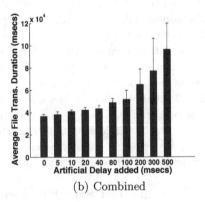

(a) Wired   (b) Combined

Fig. 6. TCP File Transmission Duration vs Artificial Delay

increases file transmission duration up to 5,5s (15%). Moreover, we notice that the effect regarding the increased deviation values is also clearly illustrated between Fig. 6(a) and Fig. 6(b). We also conducted experiments based on UDP transmissions. However, UDP performance in terms of throughput, packet loss and jitter is not affected by the artificially injected RTT delay. This comes from the fact that even high values of artificial delay cannot result in packet loss, as the high capacity of operational system buffers supports storage of packets that arrive during the artificial delay interval even at the maximum traffic rate of 90 Mbps that is used in our experiments.

Wireless - Combined Set of Experiments. The second set of experiments has been designed to demonstrate the impact on end-to-end performance of channel contention in the wireless access link . Fig. 7(a) and Fig. 7(b) illustrate TCP and UDP throughput achieved in the wireless access link and the combined network accordingly, under various values of traffic rate for the contending flow.

For the UDP case, we notice that even contending flows of low traffic rate highly impact performance in both cases. In addition, we observe that results obtained in the wireless and combined networks are very similar and both feature relatively low deviation values. Packet loss measurements illustrated in Fig. 8(a) and Fig. 8(b) show that UDP performance is directly related to loss of packets. As the MC injects packets with high traffic rate, the wireless network capacity is exceeded due to the simultaneous transmissions of the contending flow. The resulting channel contention yields packet loss, which cannot be detected by the UDP protocol and thus the rate of data entering the network is not restricted within the network capacity region.

However, in the TCP case, we observe lower throughput performance yielded in the combined network (Fig. 7(b)). This is due to the fact that the TCP protocol involves RTTs estimation in its adaptive retransmission procedure and thus upon the detection of increased RTT values that result from the augmented network range, limits the rate of traffic injected by the MC. Another

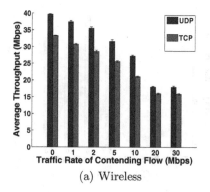

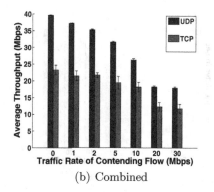

(a) Wireless   (b) Combined

Fig. 7. TCP - UDP Throughput vs Contention

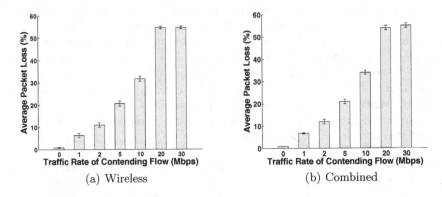

Fig. 8. UDP Packet Loss vs Contention

particular observation regarding the TCP case is related to the high deviation values observed among the multiple executions of the experiment in the combined architecture, compared with the low deviation values observed in the local wireless network. This is due to the fact that the generated traffic flows go over the Internet through PLE during experimentation in the combined architecture and thus high deviation values are recorded as a regular characteristic of experimentation on realistic planetary scale networks.

Concerning UDP packet loss values presented in Fig. 8(a) and Fig. 8(b), we observe similar performance between experimentation on the wireless link and the combined network. Similar results are also obtained in terms of UDP Jitter between experimentation on the two different network architectures, as illustrated in Fig. 9(a) and Fig. 9(b). Moreover, we used the OMF visualization tool, in Fig. 10, to plot RTT values reported from the two MAPs with red and blue colors and also yellow color for values reported from the MC. Particularly, we observe that the MC is always associated with the MAP that features the lowest

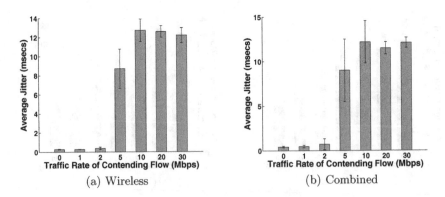

Fig. 9. UDP Jitter vs Contention

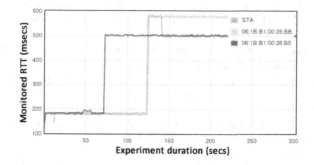

Fig. 10. Handoff demonstration

RTT delay and moreover notice a handoff that lasts between the 120 and 140 seconds of the experiment.

6 Conclusions and Future Work

The unique two-tier architecture introduced by WMNs has directed research efforts towards experimentation on global scale realistic environments that result from federation of heterogeneous networks. In this work, we present the federation of the wired PLE and the wireless NITOS testbeds. The resulting architecture has enabled the execution of realistic association experiments in the context of WMNs, which presented several characteristics of experimentation under real world scale and settings. As part of our future work, we plan on investigating performance of typical WMNs that also feature a wireless multi-hop backhaul in the aforementioned federated environment.

References

1. Pathak, P.H., Dutta, R.: A Survey of Network Design Problems and Joint Design Approaches in Wireless Mesh Networks. IEEE Communications Surveys Tutorials 13(3), 396–428 (2011)
2. Rakotoarivelo, T., Ott, M., Jourjon, G., Seskar, I.: OMF: A Control and Management Framework for Networking Testbeds. SIGOPS Oper. Syst. Rev. 43(4), 54–59 (2010)
3. Keranidis, S., Korakis, T., Koutsopoulos, I., Tassiulas, L.: Contention and Traffic load-aware Association in IEEE 802.11 WLANs: Algorithms and Implementation. In: Proceedings of WiOpt (2011)
4. Bejerano, Y., Han, S., Li, E.L.: Fairness and load balancing in wireless LANs using association control. In: Proceedings of MOBICOM (2004)
5. Athanasiou, G., Korakis, T., Ercetin, O., Tassiulas, L.: Dynamic cross-layer association in 802.11-based mesh networks. In: Proceedings of INFOCOM (2007)
6. Makhlouf, S., Chen, Y., Emeott, S., Baker, M.: A Network-Assisted Association Scheme for 802.11-Based Mesh Networks. In: Proceedings of WCNC (2008)

7. Luo, L., Raychaudhuri, D., Liu, H., Wu, M., Li, D.: End-to-End Performance Aware Association in Wireless Municipal Mesh Networks. In: Proceedings of Globecom (2009)

8. Wang, H., Wong, W., Soh, W., Motani, M.: Dynamic association in IEEE 802.11 based wireless mesh networks, 2009. In: Proceedings of ISWCS (2009)

9. He, Y., Perkins, D., Velaga, S.: Design and Implementation of CLASS: A Cross-Layer ASSociation Scheme for Wireless Mesh Networks. In: Proceedings of INFO-COM (2010)

10. Elliott, C.: GENI: Opening Up New Classes of Experiments in Global Neworking. IEEE Internet Computing 14(1), 39–42 (2010)

11. Gavras, A., Karila, A., Fdida, S., May, M., Potts, M.: Future Internet research and experimentation: the FIRE initiative. SIGCOMM Computer Communication Review 37(3), 89–92 (2007)

12. Webb, K., Hibler, M., Ricci, R., Clements, A., Lepreau, J.: Implementing the Emulab-PlanetLab portal: Experience and lessons learned. In: Workshop on Real, Large Distributed Systems, WORLDS (2004)

13. Chun, B., Culler, D., Roscoe, T., Bavier, A., Peterson, L., Wawrzoniak, M., Bowman, M.: PlanetLab: An Overlay Testbed for Broad-Coverage Services. ACM SIGCOMM Computer Communication Review 33(3), 3–12 (2003)

14. Mahindra, R., Bhanage, G., Hadjichristofi, G., Ganu, S., Kamat, P., Seskar, I., Raychaudhuri, D.: Integration of heterogeneous networking testbeds. In: Proceedings of TridentCom (2008)

15. Di Stasi, G., Avallone, S., Canonico, R.: Integration of OMF-based testbeds in a global scale networking facility. In: Proceedings of ICST QShine (2009)

16. Anadiotis, A.-C., Apostolaras, A., Syrivelis, D., Korakis, T., Tassiulas, L., Rodriguez, L., Seskar, I., Ott, M.: Towards Maximizing Wireless Testbed Utilization Using Spectrum Slicing. In: Magedanz, T., Gavras, A., Thanh, N.H., Chase, J.S. (eds.) TridentCom 2010. LNICST, vol. 46, pp. 299–314. Springer, Heidelberg (2011)

17. Di Stasi, G., Bifulco, R., D'Elia, F.P., Avallone, S., Canonico, R., Apostolaras, A., Giallelis, N., Korakis, T., Tassiulas, L.: Experimenting with P2P traffic optimization for wireless mesh networks in a federated OMF-PlanetLab environment. In: Proceedings of WCNC (2011)

18. Fdida, S., Friedman, T., Parmentelat, T.: OneLab: An Open Federated Facility for Experimentally Driven Future Internet Research. Springer (2010)

19. IPtables, http://netfilter.org

20. Dummynet, http://info.iet.unipi.it/~luigi/dummynet/

21. Nmap, http://nmap.org/

22. Iperf, http://dast.nlanr.net/Projects/Iperf/

Smart Information Network: A Testbed Architecture for Future Internet

Xiangyang Xue[1], Yi Li[2], Xiaoyuan Lu[2], Xin Wang[1], and Lingwei Chu[2,*]

[1] Fudan University, No.825 Zhangheng Road, Shanghai, China
[2] Shanghai Engineering Research Center for Broadband Technologies & Applications
No. 150 Honggu Road, Shanghai, China
{xyxue,xinw}@fudan.edu.cn, {yli,xylu,lwchu}@b-star.cn

Abstract. This paper introduces a testbed architecture for future Internet, which is called smart information network (SIN). The testbed opens up capabilities of network nodes through programmable platform, builds a uniform schedule system and various decision applications. The testbed can be easily employed to design and verify future Internet concepts.

Keywords: testbed, future network, cognitive network, programmability.

1   Introduction

Recently, future Internet research has attracted attentions, which is towards the design of new Internet architecture from clean slate. Many programs about future Internet research have been established, e.g. FIND [1], GENI [2], FIA [3], FIRE [4], and so on. In these programs, FIRE and GENI are two major initiatives for developing large scale future Internet testbeds.

One important trend in the field of testbed is programmability [5], which allows user to program network nodes. For example, OpenFlow [6] is employed in GENI to provide programmability. However, OpenFlow only provides a interface to modify flow table entries.

There are other trends in the field of testbed, e.g. virtualization and federation [5], which increase the complexity of testbed. As a result, the testbed is difficult to manage, and automatic management techniques are needed. Recently, cognitive network has been presented to decrease human intervention, which can sense current reality, plan for the future, make a decision and act accordingly [7]. We believe that it is beneficial to automate testbed management.

2   System Overview

SIN is presented in this paper, which exposures more capabilities, builds up a scheduler platform for different equipments, and establishes various programmable

---

* This work is supported by The National High Technology Research and Development Program of China (No. 2011AA01A109), and Foundation Project from Science and Technology Commission of Shanghai Municipality (No. 10dz1500107, No.10220711700).

T. Korakis, M. Zink, and M. Ott (Eds.): TridentCom 2012, LNICST 44, pp. 355–357, 2012.

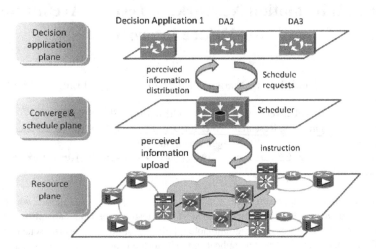

Fig. 1. The architecture of SIN

decision applications (DA) with cognitive loop, as shown in figure 1. SIN achieves smart configuration, control and information transmission.

2.1   Resource Plane

Resource plane is responsible for perceiving network status, transferring data flow and opening up network capabilities. Resource nodes can perceive the status of interior module, dada packet, link, path and so on. Rules are constructed inside network nodes, which denote the process manner of perceived information, such as forward, upload, modify, drop, and so on. For the information without a match rule, it will be delivered to scheduler to decide whether a rule should be added.

Network nodes with open capabilities can be constructed using NetMagic programmable platform [8]. Using pass through mode of NetMagic, all flows from input interface are transmitted to user module (UM). Capabilities are programmed and embedded in UM, such as perceive set, port management, route table control and so on. In control module of NetMagic, management functions can be called, and then configure and execution in network nodes can be changed.

Subsumption architecture [9] is employed in network nodes to decompose complicated intelligent behaviors into simple behavior modules, which can improve action speed and avoid conflict. Behavior module subsumes underlying modules, e.g. if two module's results have conflict, higher module's result will be accepted, and lower module's result will be rejected.

2.2   Converge and Schedule Plane

This plane distributes perceived information, controls network nodes, and maintains network topology view. For each DA, a distribution space is determined in this plane, which denotes that perceived information in such space should be transmitted to a DA, i.e. a mapping from a set of DAs to a set of perceived information field range.

Scheduler classifies perceived information, and distributes the information to DAs. To improve distribution speed by parallel processing, mapping from each perceived information field to DAs should be determined from above mentioned mapping. If perceived information is received by a scheduler, it will be analyzed by filed resolvers. Each resolver produces a set of DAs, and the intersection of all sets is the final set of DAs that should process the information.

2.3   Decision Application Plane

This plane is responsible for analyzing perceived information, making decision and invoking actions, which consists of various DAs. Diverse DAs can be constructed, such as energy efficiency DA, safe network DA, and so on. Energy efficiency DA can close low load ports, links and modules temporarily to reduce energy consumption. Safe network DA can determine if a host is attacked by flow rate analysis, e.g. DDOS attack, and suspend the attack flows.

3   Conclusion

The design and architecture of SIN is presented in this paper. Functions and characters of three planes of SIN are also illustrated. SIN is innovative for designing and verifying future Internet concepts. In the future, we will design key technologies and build the testbed.

References

1. http://www.nets-find.net/
2. GENI: Global Environment for Network Innovations, http://www.geni.net/
3. http://www.nets-fia.net/
4. FIRE: Future Internet Research and Experimentation, http://cordis.europa.eu/fp7/ict/fire/
5. Haque, M., Pawlikowski, K., Ray, S.: Challenges to Development of Multipurpose Global Federated Testbed for Future Internet Experimentation. In: 9th IEEE/ACS International Conference on Computer Systems and Applications (AICCSA), pp. 289–292 (2011)
6. McKeown, N., Anderson, T., Balakrishnan, H., et al.: OpenFlow: Enabling Innovation in Campus Networks. ACM SIGCOMM Computer Communication Review 38(2) (2008)
7. Fortuna, C., Mohorcic, M.: Trends in the development of communication networks: Cognitive networks. Computer Networks 53, 1354–1376 (2009)
8. NetMagic, http://netmagic.nudt.edu.cn
9. Amir, E., Maynard-Zhang, P.: Logic-based subsumption architecture 153(1), 167–237 (2004)

Photonic Services and Their Applications

Josef Vojtech[1], Vladimir Smotlacha[1], Stanislav Sima[1], and Pavel Skoda[1,2]

[1] CESNET z.s.p.o., Zikova 4, 160 00 Prague 6, The Czech Republic
[2] FEE CTU Praha, Technická 2, 160 00 Prague 6, The Czech Republic

Abstract. The poster addresses Photonic Services as a general approach to end-to-end connection over optical networks and possible types of applications that can benefit from them. Features and known challenges are highlighted. Also expected fields of application are listed and precise time transfer together with atomic clock comparison is discussed in detail with specific results.

Keywords: optical fibre communications, real-time transmission, all-optical, precise time transmission.

1 Photonic Services

In general, a Photonic Service can be defined as an end-to-end connection between two or more places in the network and can be described by its Photonic-path and allocated bandwidth. Photonic-path is a physical route that light travels from one end point to one or more other end point(s). Allocated bandwidth is part of system spectrum that is reserved for Photonic Service user all along the Photonic-path. It is important to carry signals over network with minimal impact, so the processing at the end point will depend just on the application. In present networks, delay is almost independent of capacity. It is a fundamental characteristic (constraint) of the data topology also in over-provisioned networks, where queuing and buffering are null or minimal. The requirements for delay minimization impact all communication layers, starting from fibre topology. All network application benefits from low latency, ranging from interactive (e.g. video conferences, of interaction between a user and a "cloud") to traditional data transfers. These are typically based of window confirmation network protocols (e.g. TCP) where performance of such protocols is inversely dependent on RTT (round trip time) value.

More demanding applications, especially in research community, even pose limits on latency jitter. This all is provided by well controlled all-optical network. Therefore an Optical-to-Electrical-to-Optical (OEO) conversion should be avoided to increase transparency of an optical network to Photonic Services, except for special cases.

2 Applications

Advent of many telecommunication services was driven by end-users and it is not different in case of Photonic Services. Photonic Services are called upon by

T. Korakis, M. Zink, and M. Ott (Eds.): TridentCom 2012, LNICST 44, pp. 358–362, 2012.

demanding applications that are not feasible (or are with significant complications) over traditional Internet Service Providers (ISP's) network. We identified crucial parameters that characterize specific applications and pose requirements on network. The jitter in network latency represents the changes in time between any two consecutive pieces of information that arrive to destination. The jitter in network latency is also caused by lags that are introduced by (de)serialization and buffering during OEO conversion in present networks where necessary QoS parameters are solved via so called over-provision of bandwidth. The penalty for not meeting the jitter limits or service failure is mild in most applications but there are also applications, where failure interrupts whole experiment or even endangers human life. Examples of demanding applications and relevant references follow.

Interactive Human Collaboration, High Definition Video and Cave-to-Cave

The simplest case of interactive collaboration is human speech. ITU-T recommendation G.114 defines transmission latency limit up to 150ms for high-quality communication. Nevertheless speech quality is complex matter and when the echo and loss are not present the latency can be higher; users don't perceive discomfort up to 300ms. However 200ms is an empiric valued cited in many documents. The most demanding examples of this application are probably remote fine arts lessons like piano or violin lesson, where teacher should be able guide her students according to visual and aural experience delivered over the network. The fine art lesson has been tested in Brazil across Atlantic Ocean (Brazil and Spain) with success and presented at Customer Empowered Fibre Workshop 2010 in Prague [11]. Moreover, we must distinguish negligible latency (e.g. sound propagation in air) from latency to which user can adapt, for example from about 5ms for chamber orchestra to 40ms for symphonic orchestra. Nevertheless 100ms is value which can user adapted to easily. Some experiments are described for example here [12]. The overall quality is strongly dependent on the codec used and generally two techniques are applied to improve a packet loss robustness and sensitivity to a variation in the delay of received packets. The packet loss concealment technique masks the effects of packet loss and the simplest forms are based on repeating the last received frame, the most sophisticated algorithms apply HMM (Hide Markov Models). An adaptive mode of play-out delay buffer dynamically adjusts to the amount of jitter present and the value is always calculated as duration of one frame multiplied by integer number.

Cave-to-cave and HD video have recently enabled doctors and students of medicine to see the real-time high resolution video of operation by their own eyes and enjoy the precise work of top surgeons in the world. These high bandwidth demanding application usually require a dedicated Lambda to provide users with full experience. Actually a practical demonstration of HD video transfer has been accomplished in the Czech Republic over dedicated 10Gb/s link on the distance of 150km. The data stream reached transfer rates of approximately 2.5 Gb/s and the signal delay was less than 1 ms, enabling the real-time broadcast [1].

Remote Instrument and Vehicles Control

New unique instruments and facilities are often built at the most suitable places in the world that may not be well accessible. To name just a few, the unique observatory in India, that was built over 4500 meters high above the sea level in the barren desert of Ladakh [2], or highly specialized robot-assisted surgery system da Vinci located just in the most famous hospitals in the world [3]. The remote control of such instruments can save time and expenses to relocate experts to work directly on the site. The hospital in Strasburg conducted a Tele-surgery already in 2001. The robotic Tele-surgery connected a surgeon from New York to a patient in Strasburg [4]. It is worth of mentioning that there were also experts on site ready to take the manual control of robot in case of network failure. The latency for a robotic surgery is considered negligible, when it is about 100ms, but the limit of adaptability can be up to 400ms. More detailed study can be found here [13]. Recently, professionals of CESNET and Masaryk Hospital in Ústí nad Labem have demonstrated their experience with transmission of robotic operations to their colleagues in Japan [5]. In general, this type of applications has mild requirements on bandwidth and network latency. Once the Tele-surgery proceed to regular use, it will be unacceptable to interrupt the connection, because the operation can discontinue and interruption can directly endanger patients' life. These prerequisites will hardly be met in standard over-provisioned networks and probably may require a dedicated optical channel.

Many projects all around the globe are investigating intelligent transportation systems that would assist or replace vehicle driver to increase transportation safety and efficiency. Numerous tasks in future vehicle communication have been identified. Some of them should warn a vehicle driver or operator and address environmental warnings like hazardous location, traffic signal violation or slow vehicle motion. Emergency warnings like pre-crash sensing have stringent latency requirements of around 50ms with unacceptable penalty of vehicle crash. Although exchange of information among vehicles and infrastructure will be wireless, the availability of data from a surrounding infrastructure will be essential [9].

Comparison of Atomic Clocks and Ultra-Stable Frequency Transfer

Time standards are usually represented by caesium clocks and other accurate clocks should be synchronized to them. The most accurate comparison of distant clocks was made by bidirectional radio transmission using dedicated satellite channels – it is an expensive method with that requires complex instruments. Advances in optical networking opened a new comparison option by utilization of optical channels. The accuracy in order of tenths of nanoseconds or better can be achieved. Example of such experiment is described in [6].Transfer of accurate time and stable frequency between two distant places is required by experts from fields of time and frequency metrology, astrophysics, particle accelerators and fundamental physics [7]. The straightforward and beneficial approach is to utilize NRENs that already connect many research institutes and universities [8]. Successful transfer of ultra-stable frequency has been demonstrated over an optical network with live traffic [10]. This application requires dedicated equipment in network nodes, but it is possible to run it next to standard long haul equipment. Optical clocks, that provide ultra-stable frequency, are developing into frequency standards. In this case, the frequency is not transferred as a modulated optical signal – instead, the frequency generated by optical clock is subject of transmission. Any usual O-E-O conversion would violate this service, since frequency transfer requires special continuous wave narrow single mode lasers.

3   Precise Time Transfer

One of typical applications, that proved the concept of Photonic service as a multi-domain end-to-end service, is highly accurate time transfer. Results of more than a year error-free operation of atomic clock comparison over distance of 550 km are presented at poster. More information can be found in [14][15].

4   Conclusions

Photonic services have a great potential to enhance many contemporary or future applications including real-time applications. Although described application may seem to be very specialized and useful for small community of scientists, it has great impact. Atomic clocks are representing local approximation of UTC time scales and are running in every country. The accurate comparison of these time scales is essential for maintain the universal time scale UTC.

Acknowledgements. This work was supported under the GN3 project and by Ministry of Education, Youth and Sport of the Czech Republic under The *CESNET Large Infrastructure* project.

References

[1] 3D Full HD Broadcast from a Robotic Surgery (in press release),
       http://www.ces.net/doc/press/2010/pr100618.html
[2] Indian Astronomical Observatory, http://www.iiap.res.in/centers/iao
[3] da Vinci® Surgical System, http://biomed.brown.edu/Courses/BI108/
       BI108_2005_Groups/04/davinci.html
[4] The cutting edge in surgery. EMBO Reports 3(4), 300–301 (2002), doi:10.1093/embo-reports/kvf083
[5] Assisted Robotic Operation to Japan (in press release),
       http://www.ces.net/doc/press/2010/pr101123.html
[6] A new method of accurate time signal transfer demonstrates the capabilities of all-optical networks (in press release),
       http://www.ces.net/doc/press/2010/pr100401.html

[7] Foreman, S.M., Holman, K.W., Hudson, D.D., Jones, D.J., Ye, J.: Remote transfer of ultrastable frequency references via fiber networks. Rev. Sci. Instrum. 78, 21101–21125 (2007)

[8] Kéfélian, F., Lopez, O., Jiang, H., Chardonnet, C., Amy-Klein, A., Santarelli, G.: High-resolution optical frequency dissemination on a telecommunication network with data traffic. Opt. Lett. 34, 1573–1575 (2009)

[9] ETSI TR 102 638: Intelligent Transport Systems, Vehicular Comm., Basic Set of Applications; Definitions, v 1.1 (June 2009)

[10] Lopez, O., Haboucha, A., Kéfélian, F., Jiang, H., Chanteau, B., Roncin, V., Chardonnet, C., Amy-Klein, A., Santarelli, G.: Cascaded multiplexed optical link on a telecommunication network for frequency dissemination. Opt. Exp. 18, 16849–16857 (2010)

[11] Carvalho, C.M.B.: Networking and remote mentoring. In: CEF 2010, Prague (2010), http://www.ces.net/events/2010/cef/p/carvalho.ppt

[12] LOLA (LOw LAtency audio visual streaming system), http://www.conservatorio.trieste.it/artistica/ricerca/progetto-lola-low-latency/ircam-lola-forweb.pdf?ref_uid=e98cac4a9c6a546ac9adebc9dea14f7b

[13] Technical Annex to FR: AAP20 Hapto-Audio-Visual Environments for Collaborative Tele-Surgery Training over Photonic Networking, http://www.photonics.uottawa.ca/HAVE/docs/public_progress_reports/C4_AAP20_HAVE_Public_Final_Report_Technical_Annex.pdf

[14] Parallel 100 Gbps transmissions in CESNET2 network (in press release), http://www.ces.net/doc/press/2011/pr110909.html

[15] Smotlacha, V., Kuna, A., Mache, W.: Time Transfer Using Fiber Links. In: EFTF 2010, Noordwijk, The Netherlands (2010)

An Instrumentation and Measurement Architecture Supporting Multiple Control Monitoring Frameworks

Marcelo M. Pinheiro[1], Igor L.E. Macêdo[1], Igor L.O. Souza[1],
Thiago S. Hohlenweger[1,3], Paulo R.R. Leite[1], Adriano L. Spínola[1],
Herbert Monteiro[1], Raphael A. Dourado[2], Leobino N. Sampaio[4],
José A. Suruagy Monteiro[2], and Joberto S.B. Martins[1]

[1] Salvador University (UNIFACS)
[2] Federal University of Pernambuco (UFPE)
[3] Federal Institute of Bahia (IFBA)
[4] Federal University of Bahia (UFBA)
{marcelo.mpinheiro,igorleoem,pauloricardorios,
hmsouza,raphaaugusto}@gmail.com, igorluiz@solic.com.br,
thiago@ifba.edu.br, adriano_spinola@hotmail.com,
leobino@ufba.br, suruagy@cin.ufpe.br, joberto@unifacs.br

Abstract. Virtual and/or experimental networks capable of supporting an entire new set of applications and services (Future Internet, Grids, Cloud Computing, other) use, typically, different Control and Monitoring Frameworks (CMFs). This poster addresses the multiple federated CMFs instrumentation and measurement problems. A monitoring architecture (FIBRE-BR I&M Architecture) is briefly introduced by illustrating its basic components and services and its capability to integrate different CMF's I&M Services. FIBRE-BR will use three different control and monitoring frameworks in its nine islands: OFELIA Control Framework, cOntrol and Management Framework (OMF) and ProtoGENI. Our target is to provide monitoring services, possibly, with a maximum reuse of the available CMFs I&M services over a new integrated and federated network structure. Some of the various aspects involved include the virtualized equipment, networks and monitored data; the collected data control access; and, finally, the multiple CMFs I&M data integration. This poster presents the FIBRE-BR I&M Architecture that integrates diverse I&M services, tools and facilities from multiple CMFs, allowing FIBRE-BR users, possibly transparently to each specific CMF, to benefit from the corresponding infrastructure and experiment specific measurement data.

FIBRE-BR Instrumentation and Measurement (I&M) Architecture

The FIBRE-BR I&M Architecture integrates diverse I&M services, tools and facilities from multiple CMFs, allowing FIBRE-BR users, possibly transparently to each specific CMF, to benefit from the corresponding infrastructure and experiment specific measurement data.

T. Korakis, M. Zink, and M. Ott (Eds.): TridentCom 2012, LNICST 44, pp. 363–364, 2012.
© Institute for Computer Sciences, Social Informatics and Telecommunications Engineering 2012

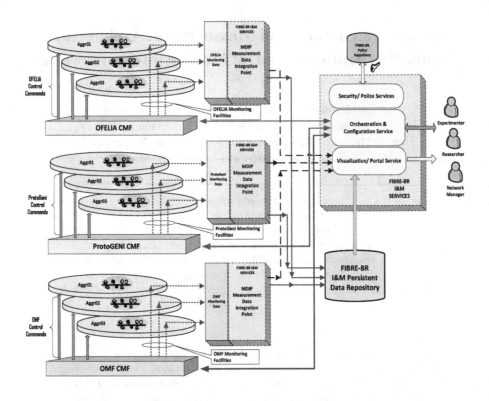

Fig. 1. FIBRE-BR I&M Architecture

The Measurement Data Integration Point (MDIP) conforms the collected data from the available CMFs to FIBRE-BR I&M standard format (NM-WG), representation and distribution (including visualization). This service includes all measurement data processing related aspects such as, message format, message transport protocol and/or service, access privileges and common data storage or on-the-fly data distribution.

The Orchestration and Configuration Services act on behalf of the users allowing them to configure, to define measurement points, and to orchestrate these measurement data collecting facilities according to each individual CMF.

The I&M Portal main functionality is to provide a user friendly interface to control and access the measured data, according to a defined policy.

The architecture has a storage strategy that allows users to retrieve data from their own or from others previous experiments, according to their access privileges. The persistent storage option is an experimenter decision that must comply with FIBRE-BR retention policy.

For additional information, please refer to: http://www.fibre-ict.eu/

Acknowledgments. This work makes use of results produced by the FIBRE project, co-funded by the Brazilian Council for Scientific and Technological Development (CNPq) and by the European Commission within its Seventh Framework Programme.

A Self-organized, Service-Oriented GMPLS Optical Network Testbed

Apostolis Siokis and Kyriakos Vlachos[*]

Computer Engineering and Informatics Dept. & Computer Technology Institute and Press,
University of Patras, GR26500, Rio Patras, Greece
{kvlachos,siokis}@ceid.upatras.gr

Abstract. In this paper, we detail the implementation of a self-organized GMPLS network using the DRAGON software suite to introduce service awareness in a GMPLS network. DRAGON daemon has been extended to support anycast routing to allow forwarding user (service) requests to the most suitable servers based on their advertised service attributes. Furthermore, OSPF daemon has been also extended to allow for these advertisements to propagate through the network and modify shortest paths based on these service attributes that can be network (i.e. bandwidth, delay etc) and non-network (storage capacity, CPU units, availability etc) resources.

Keywords: GMPLS, DRAGON, routing, path selection, anycast, service awareness.

1 Testbed Development and Testing

DRAGON (*Dynamic Resource Allocation in GMPLS Optical Networks*) project [1, 2] deploys the IP network infrastructure and creates a GMPLS optical core network to allow dynamic provisioning of dedicated LSPs (*Label Switched Paths*). *Virtual Label Switch Router* (VLSR) is a basic element of the control plane architecture of DRAGON. VLSR translates GMPLS protocols into device specific commands, to allow dynamic reconfiguration of non-GMPLS aware devices. The *Client System Agent* (CSA) is a software that runs on (or on behalf of) any system, which terminates the data plane link of the provisioned service.

There are four software daemons running at every VLSR node. OSPF and Zebra daemons are used for routing. RSVP daemon is used for signaling and DRAGON daemon provides all the necessary commands in order to request, delete and set the attributes of LSPs. We extended DRAGON daemon in order to support anycast routing to allow forwarding user (service) requests to the most suitable servers based on their advertised service attributes, [3]. OSPF daemon has been also extended to allow for these advertisements to propagate through the network (via LSAs - *Link State Advertisements*) and modify shortest paths based on these service attributes that can be network and non-network resources.

---

[*] Corresponding author.

T. Korakis, M. Zink, and M. Ott (Eds.): TridentCom 2012, LNICST 44, pp. 365–368, 2012.
© Institute for Computer Sciences, Social Informatics and Telecommunications Engineering 2012

A simple network testbed has been employed to test the extensions of OSPF and DRAGON daemon, see Fig. 1. It consists of three hosts/CSAs and one VLSR. In VLSR, DRAGON software is installed in Linux software switch mode. VLSR will use Linux commands in order to create or delete LSPs /VLANs (in the current setup). All CSAs run DRAGON in peer mode (CSAs have both RSVP and OSPF). Connectivity in the control plane is provided via a switch. GRE tunnels are setup for control plane messages. Two hosts are setup as service hosts that support two services, namely SERVICE 1 and SERVICE 2. A unique cost is associated for each service for each host. RSVP will ask local OSPF daemon for routing paths, in order to route the signaling messages.

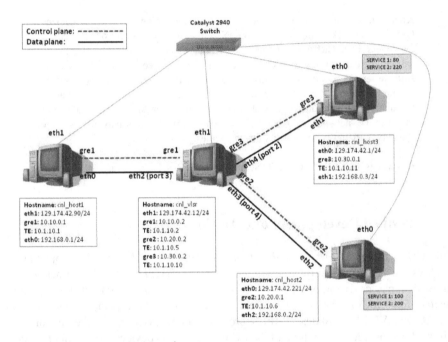

Fig. 1. Testbed design and development

2   Service Requests

For requesting a service, CLI (*Command Line Interface*) was used. Provision for SERVICE 1 is requested with the commands shown in Fig. 2, using "S1". The chosen service host is 129.174.42.221 (cnl_host2). "show lsp" allows the inspection of the LSPs. An LSP between cnl_host1 and cnl_host2 is created, as shown in Fig. 3a. The output of the added commands "show servers" (DRAGON daemon) and "show ip ospf servers" (OSPF daemon) can be seen in Fig. 4a. AGE column denotes the AGE of the respective LSA.

```
cnl_host1-dragon> edit lsp test
cnl_host1-dragon(edit-lsp-test)# set source ip-address 129.174.42.90 lsp-id 1000 destination ip-address 1.1.1.1
   tunnel-id 2000 S1
Chosen server id for service S1: 129.174.42.221 metric 100
cnl_host1-dragon(edit-lsp-test)# set bandwidth eth150M swcap l2sc encoding ethernet gpid ethernet
cnl_host1-dragon(edit-lsp-test)# set vtag any
cnl_host1-dragon(edit-lsp-test)# exit
cnl_host1-dragon> commit lsp test
cnl_host1-dragon> show lsp

                    **LSP status summary**

Name          Status    Dir   Source (IP/LSP ID)  Destination (IP/Tunnel ID)
-----------------------------------------------------------------------------
test          In Service <=>  129.174.42.90       129.174.42.221
                               1000                2000
```

Fig. 2. Commands for the provision of SERVICE 1

3   Service Host Failure

After having stopped cnl_host2, we requested provision for SERVICE 1 again. In such a case, host cnl_host3 was chosen as a destination (see Fig. 3b for LSP creation

(b)

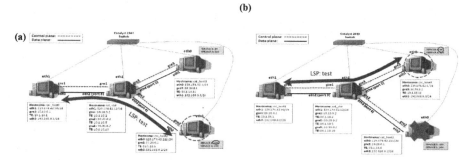

Fig. 3. a) LSP created for SERVICE 1. b) LSP created for SERVICE 1 after failure of cnl_host2.

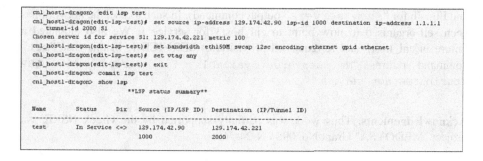

Fig. 4. Output of commands "show servers" (left) and "show ip ospf servers" (right) before (a) and after (b) a service failure in cnl_host2

and Fig. 4b for "`show servers`" output command). In such a case, the network has been self-organised to now point to cnl_host3 for service 1. We also emulated a failure in cnl_host3 and re-requested provision of SERVICE 1. In this case "`set`" command returns "`No servers available for service S1. LSP attributes not set`".

Acknowledgements. Thus work was partially supported by the Greek NSRF, via project "MEDOYSA" Grant No. 09SYN-24-769.

References

1. Yang, X., et al.: Policy-Based Resource Management and Service Provisioning in GMPLS Networks. In: Proceed. of IEEE INFOCOM 2006, pp. 1–12 (2006)
2. `http://dragon.maxgigapop.net/twiki/pub/DRAGON/VLSR/DRAGON_VLSR_Implement_v02.pdf`
3. Vlachos, K., Siokis, A.: A Service-Transparent and Self-Organized Optical Network Architecture. In: Proceed. of IEEE ICC, pp. 1–6 (June 2009)

A Framework for Multidimensional Measurements on an Experimental WiMAX Testbed*

Fraida Fund, Chen Dong, Thanasis Korakis, and Shivendra Panwar

Department of Electrical and Computer Engineering
Polytechnic Institute of New York University
Brooklyn, New York

Abstract. A major difficulty in the design, study, and implementation of wireless protocols and applications is the multitude of nondeterministic factors (e.g. interference, weather conditions, competing traffic) that can affect their performance. For this reason, testbeds that enable researchers to quantify these influences have become increasingly essential in the wireless research community. The growing sophistication of wireless testbeds and the wide array of services they can provide to researchers have advanced the field tremendously.

Toward this end, we present an early implementation of an instrumentation and measurement framework that we have deployed on an open-access 802.16e wireless research testbed at the Polytechnic Institute of NYU. We have created a set of tools to allow experimenters to routinely collect measurements of environmental conditions during experiment runtime. These tools integrate high volumes of multidimensional measurement data from a diverse array of sources, including measurements from software defined radio peripherals, sensors, and network device drivers. With this, we aim to give researchers the ability to conduct rigorous and repeatable over-the-air experiments. We also foresee potential applications for this framework beyond its use in experiments, such as in long-term testbed monitoring.

1 WiMAX Testbed at NYU-Poly

Current and proposed Internet protocols are mainly developed and tested over wired and WiFi networks, but Internet traffic is increasingly moving to new wireless broadband networks, including WiMAX and LTE. Because the properties of these networks are very different from traditional WiFi and wired networks, there exists a great need to evaluate Internet application and protocols over these networks. The WiMAX testbed at NYU-Poly supports this aim by providing an open-access, highly configurable wireless broadband network for use in research.

---

* This work is supported by GENI under WiMAX Mesoscale Deployment grant number 1751, the New York State Center for Advanced Technology in Telecommunications (CATT), the Wireless Internet Center for Advanced Technology (WICAT), and NYU WIRELESS.

T. Korakis, M. Zink, and M. Ott (Eds.): TridentCom 2012, LNICST 44, pp. 369–371, 2012.

2   Quantifying the Environment

It is difficult to conduct rigorous and repeatable over-the-air experiments because wireless signals are highly sensitive to the experimental environment. It is especially difficult for remote users of a wireless testbed to understand what is happening at the experiment site that may affect experimental results. Therefore, we provide a set of tools (built on top of OML [2], the OMF [1] measurement library) for experimenters to routinely collect measurements from a diverse array of sources, to help them quantify these environmental conditions.

3   Measurement Sources

Our measurement sources include:

- Software defined radio peripherals, which sense the RF environment and compute the FFT of raw WiMAX samples.
- Temperature and humidity sensors, which alert experimenters to extreme weather conditions that can affect the wireless signal, and light sensors, to indicate the level of human movement (which can contribute to multipath effects) in the area.
- WiMAX network cards, which are used for WiMAX connectivity and which also indicate signal strength and interference levels.

Each of these measurement sources can be configured to stream measurements to an OML server during experiment runtime.

4   Applications

The measurements are stored by OML together with experimental data and network configuration information, so that all relevant information about the experiment is archived in one place. They are also used for real-time feedback on network conditions during experiments, visualizations of multidimensional data, and long-term monitoring of testbed conditions.

References

1. Rakotoarivelo, T., Ott, M., Jourjon, G., Seskar, I.: OMF: a control and management framework for networking testbeds. SIGOPS Oper. Syst. Rev. 43(4), 54–59 (2010)
2. White, J., Jourjon, G., Rakatoarivelo, T., Ott, M.: Measurement Architectures for Network Experiments with Disconnected Mobile Nodes. In: Magedanz, T., Gavras, A., Thanh, N.H., Chase, J.S. (eds.) TridentCom 2010. LNICST, vol. 46, pp. 315–330. Springer, Heidelberg (2011)

NYU·poly
POLYTECHNIC INSTITUTE OF NYU

A Framework for Multidimensional Measurements on an Experimental WiMAX Testbed

Fraida Fund, Chen Dong, Thanasis Korakis, and Shivendra Panwar
Department of Electrical and Computer Engineering, Polytechnic Institute of NYU

 NYU

WiMAX Testbed

Current and proposed Internet protocols and applications have been developed and tested over wired and WiFi networks, but Internet traffic is moving to wireless broadband networks

- By 2016, global mobile data usage is predicted to reach 10.8 exabytes/month over 10 billion mobile devices
- The properties of wireless broadband networks (including WiMAX and LTE) are very different from WiFi or wired networks.

Controlled experimentation over wireless broadband is difficult:

- Over commercial networks, subject to changing carrier policies and competing traffic
- Simulations are only as good as their model
- Wireless broadband testbeds are costly to deploy

GENI WiMAX sites provide open-access, highly configurable, wireless broadband networks for use in research:

- 802.16e base station and computers with WiMAX network cards
- Open for use (by reservation) at http://witestlab.poly.edu

 NYU WIRELESS

Quantifying the Environment

Supporting the goal of **rigorous, repeatable over-the-air experiments**

- Wireless experiments are very sensitive to the environment
- Especially difficult for remote experimenters to understand how their experimental results will be affected

We provide a set of tools for experimenters to **routinely** collect measurements from a diverse array of sources.

- Built on top of OML framework
- Helps remote researchers quantify environmental conditions

Measurement Sources

Software Defined Radio

- USRP N210 with RFX 2400 daughter card at each node senses the RF environment
- GNU Radio script takes FFT of raw WiMAX samples and streams the results to OML server

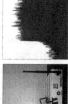

Sensors

- Temperature and humidity sensors alert experimenters to extreme weather conditions that affect wireless signal
- Light sensors give indication of movement in the room, which introduces multipath effects
- OMF experiment periodically retrieves measurements from AVR cards and stores results in OML server

WiMAX Network Cards

- Intel WiMAX 6250 cards used for WiMAX connectivity
- Driver API provides RSSI, CINR, Transmit Power

Applications

- Real-time feedback on network conditions during experiments

This graph shows the Received Signal strength (RSSI) on the WiMAX link.

- Visualizations of multidimensional data

- Long-term monitoring of testbed conditions

- Archive experimental results together with environmental data and network configuration

NSF   WICAT

http://wicat-poly.edu

FIBRE Project: Brazil and Europe Unite Forces and Testbeds for the Internet of the Future

Sebastia Sallent, Antonio Abelém, Iara Machado, Leonardo Bergesio, Serge Fdida,
Jose Rezende, Siamak Azodolmolky, Marcos Salvador, Leandro Ciuffo,
and Leandros Tassiulas

sebastia.sallent@i2cat.net, abelem@ufpa.br,
iara@rnp.br, leonardo.bergesio@i2cat.net,
serge.fdida@lip6.fr, rezende@gta.ufrj.br,
sazod@essex.ac.uk, marcosrs@cpqd.com.br,
leandro.ciuffo@rnp.br, leandros@uth.gr

Abstract. In October 2011 a new, ambitious project was launched, named FIBRE (Future Internet testbeds experimentation between Brazil and Europe). Its main goal is to create common space between Brazil and EU for Future Internet experimental research into network infrastructure and distributed applications, by building and operating a federated EU-Brazil Future Internet experimental facility. Apart from bridging partners from two continents, the project brings together different technologies, including OpenFlow, wireless and optical communications. To demonstrate the public utility of the facility, FIBRE will design and implement a set of pilot applications ranging from seamless wireless connectivity to high-definition content delivery. The poster to be presented describes FIBRE's goals, its testbed facilities and a schema of the envisioned architecture embracing the functionalities of the individual testbeds, as well as their federation. This schema has resulted from the collaborative work of the partners in order to define the functional requirements related to such an architecture. Our ambition with this poster is to attract new users for the facility from the experimental research community, but also to stimulate interest for FIBRE's activities among the conference's attendees.

T. Korakis, M. Zink, and M. Ott (Eds.): TridentCom 2012, LNICST 44, p. 372, 2012.
© Institute for Computer Sciences, Social Informatics and Telecommunications Engineering 2012

Cross-Testbed Experimentation Using the Planetlab-NITOS Federation[*,**]

Nikos Makris[1,2], Stratos Keranidis[1,2], Dimitris Giatsios[1,2],
Thanasis Korakis[1,2], Iordanis Koutsopoulos[1,2], Leandros Tassiulas[1,2],
Thierry Rakotoarivelo[3], and Thierry Parmentelat[4]

[1] Department of Computer Engineering and Telecommunications,
University of Thessaly, Greece
[2] Centre for Research and Technology, Hellas
[3] National ICT Australia (NICTA), Alexandria, Australia
[4] INRIA, Sophia Antipolis, France
{nimakris,efkerani,gidimitr,korakis,jordan,leandros}@uth.gr,
thierry.rakotoarivelo@nicta.com.au,
thierry.parmentelat@sophia.inria.fr

Abstract. Federation of network testbeds has been identified as a key goal in the experimental testbeds community, leading to a recent activity burst in this research field. In this demo, we describe a federated experiment between the NITOS wireless testbed and the Planetlab Europe (PLE) testbed. The federation scheme supporting this experiment was initially established during the Onelab2 EU project and was enhanced during the OpenLab EU project. The experiment constitutes in testing the implementation of an end-to-end delay aware Wi-Fi association scheme, in an environment where a wireless station situated at NITOS is sending traffic towards a remote PLE server.

1 Introduction

Federation between heterogeneous testbeds introduces several issues that arise due to the different nature of experimental resources, but more importantly due to the use of different software frameworks for resource control and management. In the present demo, we focus on the federation between Planetlab Europe (PLE) and NITOS testbeds, which took place during the Onelab2 project [1]. For the purposes of the demo, we present a simple Wi-Fi association experiment across the federated testbeds.

PLE [3] is the European portion of the publicly available PlanetLab testbed, a global distributed facility offering more than 1000 nodes worldwide. Each PLE

---

[*] This demo accompanies the paper submitted to the conference with title: Experimentation in Heterogeneous European Testbeds through the Onelab Facility: The case of PlanetLab federation with the wireless NITOS Testbed.

[**] The research leading to these results has received funding from the European Community's Seventh Framework Programme (FP7/2007-2013) under grant agreement n°287581 (Project name: OpenLab).

T. Korakis, M. Zink, and M. Ott (Eds.): TridentCom 2012, LNICST 44, pp. 373–376, 2012.

node is a dedicated server, hosting multiple virtual machines referred to as *slivers*. Users access a number of slivers by means of so-called *slices*. These are a central notion in the Planetlab software framework, which deals with all the complex management tasks, such as authentication, resource allocation and accountability. Experimentation per se, however, is not treated in the Planetlab software and users may use their own solutions to orchestrate an experiment.

NITOS [2] is a publicly available testbed, located in the premises of University of Thessaly, and is mainly focusing on wireless experimentation. It has adopted OMF [4] as its control and management framework. The basic building blocks of OMF are the Experiment Controller (EC) and the Resource Controller (RC). During an experiment, the user interacts with an EC instance, which orchestrates the behavior of the experiment resources, on which RCs are running. OML, a measurement software framework closely related to OMF, is being used to handle experiment measurements at NITOS.

2   The Federated PLE-NITOS Architecture

The federated framework between NITOS and PLE is based on three main architectural components:

- **Single sign up**: Any user of PLE can log into the NITOS testbed portal without having to go through any extra registration process.
- **Deployment of OMF/OML at PLE resources**: PLE has incorporated OMF support on demand. For PLE slices with this tag activated, an OMF RC is installed and initiated in the related slivers.
- **XMPP Communication using slices**: The resources in an OMF experiment must be registered in a set of peering XMPP pubsub servers, in order

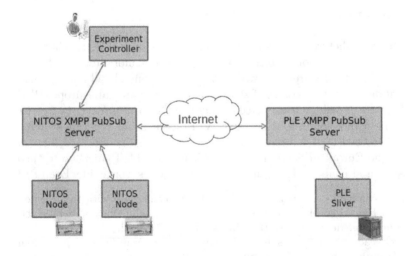

Fig. 1. PLE-NITOS federation architecture

to be able to communicate with the EC. Such a peering has taken place between the NITOS and PLE XMPP servers during the OpenLab project. This essentially means that an experimenter only needs to connect to a single testbed and has access to the resources of both testbeds through OMF commands. This architecture is depicted in Fig. 1.

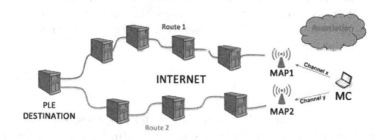

Fig. 2. Experiment topology

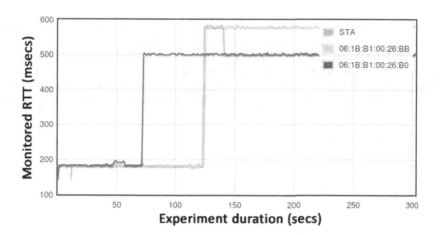

Fig. 3. Snapshot of experiment measurements

3   The Experiment

The experiment highlights the importance of association mechanisms in the general context of a network involving both wired and wireless (Wi-Fi) components. The scenario is that of Fig. 2. A wireless station (STA) operating in an environment with two available access-points (APs) is sending traffic to a remote destination through the Internet. In current 802.11 WLANs, the STA decides about upcoming associations by taking into account only RSSI measurements from neighboring APs. The goal of this experiment is to shed light on an important parameter, often neglected in this context, the fact that the perceived QoS of a station depends on end-to-end performance metrics, rather than AP-specific metrics. In particular, one specific metric is taken into account, the end-to-end delay.

In Fig. 3 we can see a snapshot of the observed measurements during the experiment. It is clear from the figure that the station is always associated with the access-point that offers the lowest end-to-end delay to the stream towards the remote destination.

4   Conclusion

The federation between the NITOS and PlanetLab Europe testbeds was demonstrated by means of an experiment spanning both testbeds. There is an ongoing effort to extend the federation bonds between the two testbeds, particularly those related to trust management and resource allocation functionalities.

References

1. Fdida, S., Friedman, T., Parmentelat, T.: OneLab: An Open Federated Facility for Experimentally Driven Future Internet Research. Springer (2010)
2. NITOS Wireless Testbed, http://nitlab.inf.uth.gr/NITlab/index.php/testbed
3. Planetlab Testbed, http://www.planet-lab.eu/
4. Rakotoarivelo, T., Ott, M., Jourjon, G., Seskar, I.: OMF: A Control and Management Framework for Networking Testbeds. SIGOPS Oper. Syst. Rev. 43(4), 54–59 (2010)

OpenFlow and P2P Integrated Testing, Project: OpenLab

Christos Tranoris and Spyros Denazis

University of Patras, Greece
tranoris@ece.upatras.gr, sdena@upatras.gr

Abstract. Facilities and resources are offered by testbed providers for creating richer and broader experimentation scenarios for future internet research. Federation among resource providers has emerged as a concept of enabling such rich experimentation scenarios. This demo presents the work in the context of OpenLab project by enabling with OpenLab tools Openflow experimentation

Keywords: Future Internet Research, Experimentation, federation, openflow.

1   Introduction

Figure 1 displays the current OpenFlow deployment in UoP. Currently 3 XEN servers have been deployed where each one is capable of hosting a number of virtual machines. On each machine Openvswitch is installed, replacing linux networking. This virtual switch is configured with two virtual bridges each one connected to a network interface of the host. There are 2 networks: i) One public Network for accessing each host (and eventually each vswitch) over internet. This is used also by experimenters for accessing machines for an experiment. ii) A data network for VM data traffic. This network is used to send traffic to and from an external VM on another host. When a VM is requested, networking XEN scripts configure this VM to have 2 virtual interfaces. Each one is attached to virtual bridges created on the openvswitch.

Figure 2 displays how we enabled the testbed for experimentation. We used technologies by the previous Panlab project.

Some Characteristics of the testbed are :

- Access Switches via Public IPs
- Install user software in VMs
- Experiment with user's own Openflow controllers
- Access testbed via elastic public IP
- SFA enabled to integrate with other resources (i.e. PlanetLab)

T. Korakis, M. Zink, and M. Ott (Eds.): TridentCom 2012, LNICST 44, pp. 377–378, 2012.

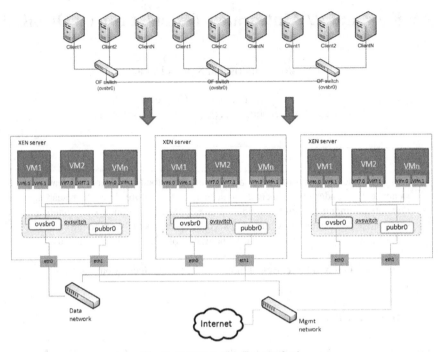

Fig. 1. The UoP openflow testbed

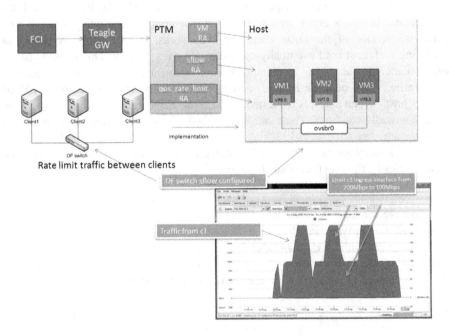

Fig. 2. Enabling the testbed for experimentation

An Integrated Chassis Manager Card Platform Featuring Multiple Sensor Modules*

Giannis Kazdaridis, Stratos Keranidis, Harris Niavis, Thanasis Korakis,
Iordanis Koutsopoulos, and Leandros Tassiulas

Department of Computer Engineering and Telecommunications,
University of Thessaly, Greece
Centre for Research and Technology, Hellas
{iokazdarid,efkerani,haniavis,korakis,jordan,leandros}@uth.gr

Abstract. The gradually growing demand for experimentation of protocols designed for wireless networks in real environments has resulted
in the development of experimental network facilities (testbeds). Most
currently deployed testbeds have been designed so as to offer services to
experimenters that lie within the testbed's premises, thus limiting the
accessibility to external users. The requirement for multi-user access of
network resources has led several large-scale testbeds to provide remote
access services to certified experimenters. However, management and
maintenance of large-scale remotely accessible testbeds is a rather challenging task that requires proper hardware, as well as software custom-
built tools. In order to provide for remote switching of testbed nodes,
NITOS has developed a new chassis manager (CM) card and also a custom framework that allows for monitoring and controlling of the nodes'
operational mode. In addition, NITOS CM card provides for gathering
of various types of sensor measurements, through the attached temperature, humidity and light intensity sensor modules. Another innovative
characteristic of the proposed card is that it provides the experimenters
with the ability to monitor the energy consumption of each testbed node,
which is rather important for experimentation with power optimization
schemes. In this demo, we will present the various functionalities of
the NITOS CM card and the developed control framework that accompanies it.

Keywords: Chassis Manager, Testbed administration, Wireless Sensor
Networks, Power Consumption Measurements.

1   Introduction

Remote administration of testbed resources requires proper custom-built solutions that are composed of both hardware and software parts. Toward, this

---

* The research leading to these results has received funding from the European Community's Seventh Framework Programme (FP7/2007-2013) under grant agreement
n°287581 (Project name: OpenLab).

T. Korakis, M. Zink, and M. Ott (Eds.): TridentCom 2012, LNICST 44, pp. 379–382, 2012.

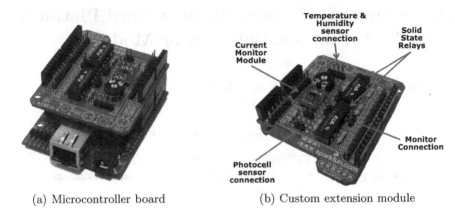

(a) Microcontroller board   (b) Custom extension module

Fig. 1. NITOS CM Card

direction, NITOS testbed has developed a custom framework that provides for remote controlling of the testbed nodes' operational mode. The hardware part consists of the newly introduced NITOS CM card, while the software part is composed of custom scripts that enable monitoring and controlling of the nodes' operational mode, through a graphical user interface.

2   NITOS Chassis Manager Framework

In this demo, we will present a framework that enables remote chassis management of testbed nodes, as well as gathering and analysis of various types of sensor measurements. The tool was developed for NITOS testbed [1], which is a large scale, remotely accessible testbed that currently consists of 50 operational WiFi nodes. NITOS is deployed at the Computer & Communication Dept. University of Thessaly building. Currently all testbed nodes are equipped with NITOS CM cards.

2.1   NITOS CM Card

The NITOS CM card is based on a micro-controller board, which is compatible with the Arduino programmable, open-source platform. The card features an Ethernet network interface, which provides connectivity through the transmission and reception of Ethernet frames. Moreover, the card features a custom-built extension module that consists of:

– two solid state relays used to short the power ON/OFF and reset jumper circuits of each node's motherboard,
– one monitor connection that gathers voltage values, which are used to determine the current operational mode (ON/OFF) of the node.

In Fig. 1(a) and Fig. 1(b), we present the developed CM card and the custom extension module accordingly.

As previously mentioned, NITOS CM card supports also gathering of various types of sensor measurements, such as temperature, humidity and light intensity. In order to gather humidity and temperature measurements, we use digital Sensirion SHT1x [2] series sensors, while for light intensity measurements, we use a properly calibrated analog photo-conductive cell. More specifically in Fig. 2(a) and Fig. 2(b), we present the two different types of sensors that are attached to the card.

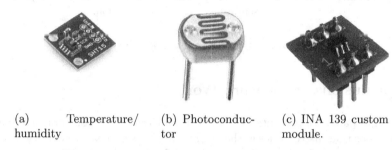

(a)   Temperature/   (b) Photoconduc-   (c) INA 139 custom
humidity   tor   module.

Fig. 2. Types of sensors attached to NITOS CM card

Another innovative characteristic that the NITOS CM card provides is the ability to estimate the energy consumption of each individual testbed node. More specifically, we use the INA 139 [3] integrated circuit to monitor the level of current across the motherboard's power supply pins. In order to estimate the power consumption a specified time interval, we also require the motherboard's constant voltage supply, which is acquired through the monitor connection of the CM card. In Fig. 2(c) we can see the custom module part that features the INA139 integrated circuit.

2.2   NITOS CM Framework

The NITOS CM framework consists of custom scripts that enable monitoring and controlling of the nodes' operational mode, as well as gathering of sensor measurements. In essence, the scripts that experimenters use to control the CM card, send corresponding http requests, which are destined to the static IP address that is assigned to each specific CM card. Then, the web server running at each CM card, executes the selected operation (power ON/OFF, reset, gathering of sensor measurement) and sends back an http response with details about the operational mode of the node, or the actual sensor measurement. Moreover, the CM framework is accompanied by a web graphical user interface that reports the operational mode of each node, which is presented in Fig. 3(a).

The user is also able to get a graphical representation of the various sensor measurements (temperature, humidity, light, power consumption) that have been stored in NITOS database. Various statistical measures can be extracted from the corresponding records, such as average and deviation values per each sensor. Fig. 3(b) and Fig. 3(c) show snapshots of the supported statistical measures.

Grid

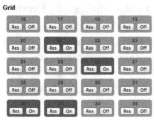

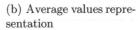

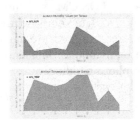

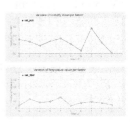

(a) Chassis Management Interface

(b) Average values representation

(c) Variation representation.

Fig. 3. NITOS CM Framework web GUI

3   Conclusions and Future Work

In this demo paper we presented a framework for remote chassis management of testbed nodes that also enables gathering and analysis of measurements gathered from various types of sensors. The developed framework is based on the newly designed NITOS CM card and features also a web GUI that further simplifies the experimentation process. Currently, we are in the process of extending the framework features by providing mechanisms able to estimate the actual power consumption of the wireless cards that are attached to each node. In Fig. 4 we present a prototype PCMCIA adapter that is able to connect directly to the CM current monitor input and calculate the energy consumed during the operation of the wireless card.

Fig. 4. NITOS PCMCIA prototype adapter for energy comsunption measurements

References

1. NITOS Wireless Testbed, http://nitlab.inf.uth.gr/NITlab/index.php/testbed
2. Sensirion SHT1x – Humidity and Temperature Sensors,
   http://www.sensirion.com/
3. TI INA 139 - Current Shunt Monitor, http://www.ti.com/product/ina139

An Experimental Framework for Channel Sensing through USRP/GNU Radios*

Virgilios Passas, Stratos Keranidis, Thanasis Korakis,
Iordanis Koutsopoulos, and Leandros Tassiulas

Department of Computer Engineering and Telecommunications,
University of Thessaly, Greece
Centre for Research and Technology, Hellas
{vipassas,efkerani,korakis,jordan,leandros}@uth.gr

Abstract. In the last decade testbeds have been set-up to evaluate network protocols and algorithms under realistic settings. In order to draw solid conclusions about the corresponding experimental results, it is important for the experimenter to have a detailed view of the existing channel conditions. Moreover, especially in the context of non-RF-isolated wireless testbeds, where external interference severely impacts the resulting performance, the requirement of experimenters for accurate channel monitoring becomes a prerequisite. Toward, this direction, various channel sensing platforms have been introduced, where each one offers different operational characteristics. In this demo, we propose the NITOS Channel Sensing framework, which is based on software-defined radio (SDR) devices that feature highly flexible wireless transceivers and are able to provide highly accurate channel sensing measurements. Through this framework, online measurement gathering is automated and further simplified using specifically developed scripts, so that it becomes a transparent process for the experimenter. The proposed framework is also accompanied by a web user interface that allows the user to get a graphical representation of the gathered measurements.

Keywords: GNU radios, channel sensing, experimental evaluation.

1 Introduction

The constantly growing demand for experimentation of protocols designed for wireless networks under realistic settings has resulted in the development of experimental network facilities (testbeds). In order to provide for accurate channel sensing during protocol validation in such experimental testbeds, the use of sophisticated and configurable spectrum sensing platforms is required. To this end, NITOS has developed a specific framework that provides experimenters with the ability of accurate channel sensing, based on SDRs and more specifically the USRP device [1] accompanied by the GNU radio platform [2].

---

* The research leading to these results has received funding from the European Community's Seventh Framework Programme (FP7/2007-2013) under grant agreement n°287581 (Project name: OpenLab).

T. Korakis, M. Zink, and M. Ott (Eds.): TridentCom 2012, LNICST 44, pp. 383–386, 2012.

2   NITOS Channel Sensing Framework

In this demo, we will present a framework for channel sensing through SDR systems. The tool was developed for NITOS testbed [3], which is a large scale wireless testbed that currently consists of 50 operational WiFi nodes. NITOS is deployed at the Computer & Communication Dept. University of Thessaly building. As NITOS is an outdoor deployed, non-RF-isolated testbed that offers rich interference conditions, it is important to provide NITOS users with a spectrum sensing platform that is able to provide accurate information regarding the dynamically varying channel conditions.

We implement this framework based on USRPs, which is a hardware platform for software radio, and is commonly used by research labs and universities, and the GNU Radio, which is a free, open-source software development toolkit that provides signal processing blocks to implement software radios. A total number of 9 wireless nodes are equipped with USRP1 and USRP N210 devices and are spread among the multiple floors of the testbed deployment. The main scope of the spectrum scanning procedure is to estimate the occupancy ratio per sampled frequency, regarding only Received Signal Strength (RSS) measurements that exceed a predefined RSS threshold. More details about the definition of the Channel Occupancy Ratio (COT) can be found in our previous work [4].

As for the first step, the reservation of the appropriate nodes that are equipped with USRPs is required. As for the second step, the experimenter simply executes specifically developed scripts that enable the definition of multiple sampling parameters, such as:

- the list of frequencies that will be sampled,
- the duration of sampling per individual frequency,
- the number of iterations of the repeated sensing procedure,
- the overall sampling period,
- and the RSS threshold that will be used for measurement filtering.

In the next step, the actual spectrum sensing is performed on each frequency among the list of frequencies that have been specified by the user and the gathered samples are saved locally at each node in an .out file format. Each frequency is sampled for duration equal to the provided duration and this sampling procedure is repeated for the specified number of iterations with interspace equal to the specified sampling period.

In the following step, all the locally saved files are filtered out, so that only values that are equal or above the specified threshold are taken into account. In order to accomplish this step, we set all values that are lower than the threshold equal to zero and save the filtered file into a new one. Afterwards, we calculate the average channel occupancy ratio per sampled frequency among the multiple measurements that have been gathered and store the corresponding results at the NITOS database, with a unique identification tag. A flowchart representation of the sensing procedure follows in Fig. 1.

Finally, the user is able to get a graphical representation of each measurement set that has been stored in NITOS database, through a web interface that is

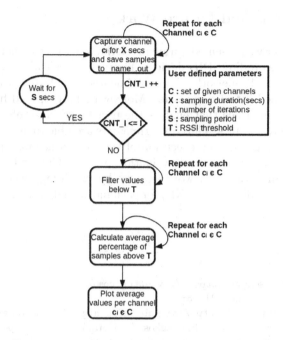

Fig. 1. Flowchart representation of the channel sensing procedure

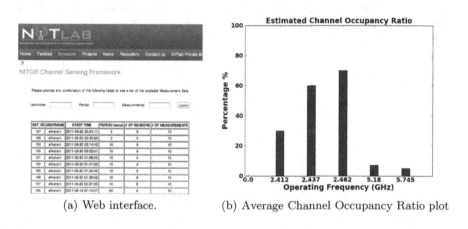

<table>
<tr><td>(a) Web interface.</td><td>(b) Average Channel Occupancy Ratio plot</td></tr>
</table>

Fig. 2. NITOS Channel Sensing Framework Graphical tools

illustrated in Fig. 2(a). Various statistical measures can be extracted from the corresponding records, such as average and deviation values per each frequency or per each individual iteration. Another important feature that the framework provides is the correlation matrix representation that provides an indication of how much the measurements of each USRP-enabled node are correlated with each other. Figure 2(b) shows a representation of average channel occupancy ratio values for the multiple frequencies that are being monitored.

3   Conclusions and Future Work

In this demo paper we presented a framework that enables channel sensing based on software-defined radio (SDR) devices. Through specifically developed scripts based on the GNU framework, the experimenter is able to gather RSS samples over a specified list of frequencies. Moreover, the proposed framework features a web user interface that enables the user to get a graphical representation of the gathered results. Thus, experimenters are able to accurately monitor channel conditions during the execution of their experiments, which results in improvement of the experimental evaluation process. Currently, we are in the process of extending the framework features by providing mechanisms able to estimate Signal to Noise Ratio (SNR) for each individual frequency that is being monitored.

References

1. USRP - Ettus Research, https://www.ettus.com/
2. GNU radio, http://gnuradio.org/
3. NITOS Wireless Testbed, http://nitlab.inf.uth.gr/NITlab/index.php/testbed
4. Kazdaridis, G., Keranidis, S., Fiamegkos, A., Korakis, T., Koutsopoulos, I., Tassiulas, L.: Novel metrics and experimentation insights for dynamic frequency selection in wireless LANs. In: Proceedings of the 6th ACM International Workshop on Wireless Network Testbeds, Experimental Evaluation and Characterization, WiNTECH 2011, New York, NY, USA, pp. 51–58. ACM (2011)

Integrating FlowVisor Access Control in a Publicly Available OpenFlow Testbed with Slicing Support*

Dimitris Giatsios, Kostas Choumas, Dimitris Syrivelis,
Thanasis Korakis, and Leandros Tassiulas

Department of Computer and Communication Engineering,
University of Thessaly, Greece
Centre for Research and Technology Hellas, CERTH, Greece
{gidimitr,kohoumas,jsyr,korakis,leandros}@uth.gr

Abstract. OpenFlow technology has recently attracted a lot of attention in the networking research community, as the ability to control the forwarding plane of a switch through software opens new exciting capabilities for protocol designers. Several network testbeds have added OpenFlow-capable switches to their equipment, while at the same time new OpenFlow-centric testbeds have been created. This demo describes a proposed approach to provide testbed slicing in a publicly available testbed featuring OpenFlow switching equipment. The approach leverages the slicing features of the FlowVisor software component and combines them with the NITOS Scheduler resource reservation framework. The resulting configuration was implemented and successfully integrated into the software framework of the publicly available testbed NITOS.

1 Introduction

OpenFlow (OF) technology, first introduced to the networking community in 2008 [1], has attracted a lot of attention both in the research community and in the industry. Several OF-centric testbeds have been deployed by research institutions, while international research projects, such as OFELIA [2] and FIBRE [3], have been launched, focusing on OF experimentation (either exclusively or as a main direction).

The NITOS testbed [4], a publicly available testbed in the premises of University of Thessaly (UTH) mainly focusing on wireless experimentation, has recently added two OF-capable switches to its equipment. The purpose of this demo is to describe the combination of two independent software components, the FlowVisor [5] and the NITOS Scheduler [6], in order to provide testbed slicing capabilities in the OF component of NITOS.

Testbed slicing constitutes in allowing multiple researchers to experiment in a testbed simultaneously, through the use of disjoint sets of resources. In an OF

---

* This work makes use of results produced by the FIBRE project, co-funded by the Brazilian Council for Scientific and Technological Development (CNPq) and by the European Commission within its Seventh Framework Programme.

T. Korakis, M. Zink, and M. Ott (Eds.): TridentCom 2012, LNICST 44, pp. 387–389, 2012.

context this can be translated to assigning disjoint flowspaces to different users, so that, for instance, a user can not direct a flow to a specific switch port, if this port does not belong to a slice assigned to the user.

2   Integration of FlowVisor and NITOS Scheduler

The Scheduler-FlowVisor framework provides the required functionalities in order to

- Reserve a flowspace (in the case of NITOS a set of ports in an OF switch)
- Restrict access of users to flows according to the reservations

The FlowVisor is a transparent proxy between OF switches and multiple OF controllers that correspond to multiple users. It creates slices of network resources and delegates control of each slice to a different controller or user. While the FlowVisor provides the required isolation of different slices within an OF switch, it doesn't provide any solutions on how these slices can be reserved and how each of them can be accessible by authorized users only. In order to provide these extra features, we combined the FlowVisor's functionalities with the NITOS Scheduler resource reservation tool.

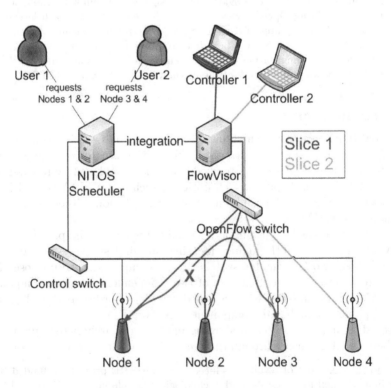

Fig. 1. NITOS Scheduler - FlowVisor integration

The NITOS Scheduler is a software framework dedicated to resource discovery, reservation and access control. It comprises a web frontend for reserving network resources for limited time intervals and a backend set of scripts to handle access to them.

The procedure can be summarized as follows:

1. When a slice is created in NITOS, a corresponding FlowVisor slice is also created and connected to a default NOX controller that instructs the OF switch to adopt standard switching behavior. At any later time a user in charge of this slice may redirect the controller to a new address where another, custom, OF controller has been setup and initialized.
2. A user reserves some nodes of the NITOS testbed. These nodes feature an experimental Ethernet interface connected to an OF switch. Along with the reservation of the nodes, a reservation of the flowspace corresponding to the switch ports connected to these nodes takes place (transparently to the user).
3. When the time interval of the reservation begins, the Scheduler backend submits a set of commands to the FlowVisor, instructing it to add the flowspace corresponding to these ports to the respective user's slice.
4. At the end of the reserved time interval the Scheduler instructs the FlowVisor to delete the added flowspace from the respective slice, so that users associated to the slice don't have access to the switch ports anymore.

3 Conclusion

We described the integration of testbed slicing capabilities in OF testbeds through the combination of FlowVisor and the NITOS Scheduler reservation software. This architecture, implemented as part of the NITOS testbed framework, can be readily applied to any other OF testbed.

References

1. McKeown, N., Anderson, T., Balakrishnan, H., Parulkar, G., Peterson, L., Rexford, J., Shenker, S., Turner, J.: OpenFlow: enabling innovation in campus networks. In: Proc. SIGCOMM (2008)
2. Ofelia - OpenFlow in Europe, http://www.fp7-ofelia.eu/
3. FIBRE - Future Internet testbeds/experimentation between Brazil and Europe, http://www.fibre-ict.eu/
4. UTH NITLab, http://nitlab.inf.uth.gr
5. Sherwood, R., Gibb, G., Yap, K., Appenzeller, G., Casado, M., McKeown, N., Parulkar, G.: Can the Production Network Be the Test-bed? In: Proc. OSDI (2010)
6. Anadiotis, A., Apostolaras, A., Syrivelis, D., Korakis, T., Tassiulas, L., Rodriguez, L., Ott, M.: A new slicing scheme for efficient use of wireless testbeds. In: Proc. WINTECH (2009)

A Demonstration of Video over an IEEE 802.11 Compliant Version of the Enhanced-Backpressure Algorithm*

Kostas Choumas, Thanasis Korakis, Iordanis Koutsopoulos, and Leandros Tassiulas

Department of Computer and Communication Engineering, University of Thessaly, Greece
Centre for Research and Technology Hellas, CERTH, Greece
{kohoumas,korakis,jordan,leandros}@uth.gr

Abstract. This demo presents a novel routing and scheduling scheme, named Enhanced-Backpressure over WiFi (EBoW), that obviously outperforms the dominant approach of a shortest-path routing (SRCR) combined with the classic CSMA/CA scheduling policy of 802.11 networks. The new scheme combines aspects of load-balancing and shortest-path routing and enhances the CSMA/CA scheduling, maximizing the throughput performance, while keeping low end-to-end delay. We perform a comparative demonstration of video streaming over an ad-hoc 802.11 network, using EBoW and SRCR, where the latter one is a state-of-the-art shortest-path routing algorithm. The new scheme delivers a smooth and jitter-free video playback experience, while the SRCR scheme experiences noticeable jitter and rather frequent distortions. The demo clearly demonstrates the performance superiority of the new implemented scheme, as compared to the other one. The implementation of both schemes relies on the well-known Click framework.

Keywords: Backpressure, wireless mesh, multi-path routing, testbed.

1 Introduction

The efficiency of a wireless mesh network is directly related to the applied routing and scheduling policy. Backpressure [1] is a throughput optimal scheme that instead of performing explicit path computation from source to destination, it forwards independently packets to less loaded nodes, while it requires TDMA and centralized scheduling. Enhanced-Backpressure (EBP) [1] is an improved version that reduces the average end-to-end delay performance. However, both schemes cannot be implemented on top of WiFi networks, due to the decentralized nature of 802.11 networks. In this paper, we present an 802.11 compliant version of EBP, named Enhanced-Backpressure over WiFi (EBoW) [2], which implements the EBP aspects in a manner that is compatible with WiFi networks. Particularly,

---

* This work was supported by European Commission under Marie Curie IRSES grant PIRSES-GA-2010-269132 AGILENet.

T. Korakis, M. Zink, and M. Ott (Eds.): TridentCom 2012, LNICST 44, pp. 390–393, 2012.

we introduce a scheme in which every node attempts to forward packets to less loaded and closer to the destination neighbors, in a similar way that EBP scheme schedules.

The implementation of the novel scheme is based on the Click framework [3], while the NITOS wireless testbed [4] is used for its experimental evaluation. As we mentioned above, we compare EBoW with SRCR [5] in terms of perceived video quality after streaming a video clip over a wireless mesh. We also use a GUI that shows at runtime which route the video stream followed in consecutive moments of time.

2   Enhanced-Backpressure over WiFi

EBoW is an 802.11 compliant routing and scheduling scheme, that attempts load-balancing routing retaining low end-to-end delay, while enhances CSMA/CA scheduling. More specifically, it maintains a set of internal network layer queues at each node, where each queue corresponds to a different destination. When a node receives or generates a packet that needs to be forwarded, it identifies the destination of the packet and pushes it to the corresponding queue. Moreover, each node that has packets in its queues, initiates a procedure to schedule the transmission of a packet. The node computes a weight per each pair of neighbor-destination, which grows when the neighbor is less loaded for this destination or is closer to this. Then the node chooses the maximum weighted pair and transmits a packet of the relative queue to the corresponding neighbor. This algorithm is the routing policy of the EBoW scheme. On the other hand, in case that every neighbor is more loaded for or in a longer distance to every destination, the node remains inactive and does not schedule transmissions. These requirements constitute the distributed scheduling policy of the EBoW scheme.

3   Demonstation of Video over the New Scheme

In this demo, we compare EBoW with SRCR, that is a state-of-the-art shortest-path routing algorithm. SRCR chooses always the shortest route, while EBoW creates parallel routes and therefore balances the traffic load in the network. A ring network (Figure 1) consisting of 5 NITOS nodes has been designed, featuring a 2-hop and a 3-hop path as well, that connect their common source and destination. The physical transmission rate for each node is fixed to 6 Mbps, while their frequency selection is the rarely used (in Greece) 802.11a frequency of 5280 MHz, in order to eliminate outside interference. The well known video of *foreman* is transmitted from source to destination, compressed as H.264 video with constant bitrate equal to 1Mbps. Simultaneously, an Iperf [6] high traffic stream runs from the intermediate node of the 2-hop path to destination, that overflows the intermediate node.

As illustrated in Figure 1, we use an external PC, which runs the VLC [7] client and server to generate and receive respectively the UDP/RTP/H.264 video stream. The server machine of the NITOS testbed is used as the connecting part of the actual network and the external PC. All frames delivered from the PC to the source node, are forwarded to the destination node through the wireless part of the network. Finally, the frames delivered at destination are further delivered back to the external PC. The forwarding procedures are implemented through Socat [8] connections.

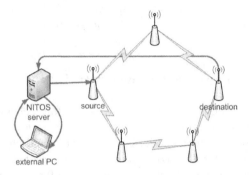

Fig. 1. Ring Network

SRCR forwards the video stream through the shortest two-hop path, although the fact that the intermediate node is overloaded. Because of this phenomenon, the majority of video packets are discarded and the delivered quality to the destination node is not satisfying. On the other hand, the proposed scheme detects the overload node and avoids forwarding towards it. The utilization of the parallel 3-hop is much more efficient in terms of throughput and perceived video quality. Eventually, we are able to compare the quality of the video resulting from transmissions that follow the previous mentioned protocols. In Figure 2, four screen shots are provided that clearly depict the superiority that the EBoW protocol achieves in terms of video quality.

Moreover, a Graphical User Interface (GUI) has been developed that gives a depicted representation of the whole topology and its state. GUI shows the path that video stream followed in average the last second. Figure 3 shows two snapshots of the GUI, which indicate that the video stream followed the 2-hop or the 3-hop path respectively. The GUI periodically collects the necessary data using appropriate questions at control TCP socket of Click.

(a) SRCR snapshot (b) EBoW snapshot (c) SRCR snapshot (d) EBoW snapshot

Fig. 2. *foreman* snapshots

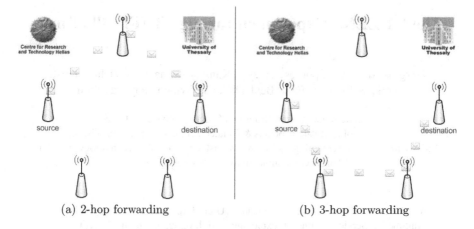

(a) 2-hop forwarding   (b) 3-hop forwarding

Fig. 3. GUI snapshots

4   Conclusion

In this demo paper we present a novel routing/scheduling scheme that dynamically avoids overloaded paths, creates parallel routes and therefore manages to balance the network traffic load, increasesing in this way its throughput efficiency. We used this scheme to stream a video over a double-path topology, and we observed that it outperforms the state of the art shortest-path routing protocol in terms of throughput and perceived video quality. A future direction is an improved scheduling policy based on prioritization schemes of 802.11, such as those proposed by the 802.11e amendment.

References

1. Georgiadis, L., Neely, M., Tassiulas, L.: Resource allocation and cross layer control in wireless networks. Foundations and Trends in Networking 1(1), 1–149 (2006)
2. Choumas, K., Korakis, T., Koutsopoulos, I., Tassiulas, L.: Implementation and end-to-end throughput evaluation of an ieee 802.11 compliant version of the enhanced-backpressure algorithm (submitted for publication, 2012)
3. Morris, R., Kohler, E., Jannotti, J., Kaashoek, M.F.: The click modular router. In: ACM SOSP
4. NITLab: Network Implementation Testbed Laboratory,
   http://nitlab.inf.uth.gr/NITlab/
5. Bicket, J., Aguayo, D., Biswas, S., Morris, R.: Architecture and evaluation of an unplanned 802.11b mesh network. In: ACM MobiCom (2005)
6. Iperf: The TCP/UDP Bandwidth Measurement Tool,
   http://dast.nlanr.net/Projects/Iperf/
7. VLC: The open source cross-platform multimedia framework,
   http://www.videolan.org/vlc/
8. Socat: Multipurpose relay (SOcket CAT),
   http://www.dest-unreach.org/socat/doc/socat.html

The QUEENS Experiment through TEFIS Platform

Georgios Aristomenopoulos[1], Argyris Kaninis[2], Panagiotis Vlahopoulos[2], Annika Sällström[3], Farid Benbadis[4], and Symeon Papavassiliou[1]

[1] Institute of Communications and Computer Systems, Greece
[2] VELTI SA of Software Products & Related Products & Services, Greece
[3] Lulea University of Technology – Centre for Distance-Spanning Technology, Sweden
[4] Thales Communications and Security, France

Abstract. QUEENS (Dynamic Quality User Experience ENabling Mobile Multimedia Services) aims at exploiting and leveraging on the benefits and flexibility provided by a novel dynamic real-time QoE provisioning framework in order to assess and establish a new era of user-centric mobile multimedia applications. To achieve that, QUEENS utilizes and builds on the TEFIS infrastructure (EC ICT FIRE initiative) that provides a unique integrated platform for supporting efficient Future Internet service experiment and development involving different actors and heterogeneous testbeds. The TEFIS tools and facilities for designing, planning and executing QUEENS experiment, along with a QoE-aware mobile multimedia application prototype will be demonstrated, forming the trends of future internet services and experimental procedures.

Keywords: Experimental testing Facilities, Quality of Experience, Multimedia Services.

1 The QUEENS Experiment and TEFIS Platform

QUEENS (Dynamic Quality User Experience ENabling Mobile Multimedia Services) aims at establishing, assessing, evolving and prototyping a novel framework for extending QoS (Quality of Service) to QoE (Quality of Experience) in mobile wireless networks, placing emphasis on mobile on-demand multimedia applications. Among the key features of the QUEENS framework is the joint consideration of user-centric QoE preferences and network-centric mechanisms to enable a novel cross-layering approach based on Network Utility Maximization (NUM) theory [1], which allows the operation optimization and the resource utilization maximization of: a) mobile application's server and b) underlying wireless network radio resource management processes.

To facilitate its goals the unique characteristics of TEFIS integrated testbed platform [2] is exploited by QUEENS experiment. TEFIS (FIRE Initiative), a TEstbed for Future Internet Services, provides a single point of access to a set of federated testbed resources, exploited by QUEENS towards enabling: a) real-time end-users' QoE provisioning (User Interface) experiments, b) performing large scale mobile emulation networking experiments and, c) validating application prototypes with currently existing standards (i.e., IMS, 3GPP/LTE).

T. Korakis, M. Zink, and M. Ott (Eds.): TridentCom 2012, LNICST 44, pp. 394–396, 2012.
© Institute for Computer Sciences, Social Informatics and Telecommunications Engineering 2012

2   Background and Demonstration Description

The TEFIS platform supports the overall experiment lifecycle, by providing a graphical user interface that allows for designing, planning, executing and evaluating the experiment results, eliminating the burden of managing, configuring and operating multiple heterogeneous testbeds, as described in Fig.1. The adoption of this platform for the description and the workflow of QUEENS experiment will be demonstrated.

The initial, part of the QUEENS experiment lays the foundations and the overall concepts of the proposed Dynamic QoE Provisioning mechanism that offers enhanced services to the end users, increased profits to the service and network providers, as well as overall system performance maximization.

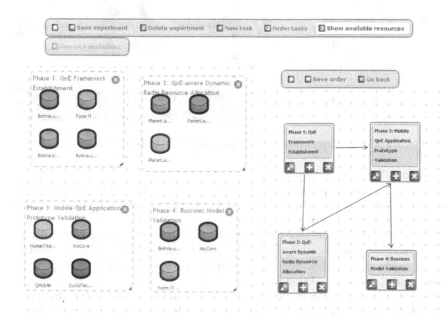

Fig. 1. The QUEENS experiment workflow as described at the TEFIS experiment manager

An interactive mechanism designed to support enhanced mobile multimedia applications by allowing users to interact with the video currently watched and request for different quality of service towards increasing their QoE will be demonstrated. Specifically, the developed android-based application will be demonstrated that offers a lightweight interactive graphical user interface that allows users to select and rate different video qualities of the same video clip (Fig.2), while providing context information and pricing incentives towards steering their decisions (Fig.3a). Testruns by Botnia Living Lab [3] users (as part of the overall TEFIS platform) provide a realistic and pragmatic view of users' requirements and expectations. Moreover, a proficient correlation between QoE, as derived by users' satisfaction rating (Fig.3b)) and QoS, by appropriately mapping video file

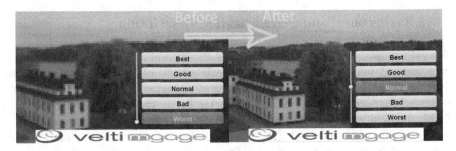

Fig. 2. QoE provisioning graphical user interface (within the mobile multimedia application)

Fig. 3. a) Context information and pricing incentives, **b)** QoE satisfaction rating

specifications, like codecs, bitrate or fps, to network metrics, like throughput or delay, expressed via the use of proper utility functions, will be illustrated. Finally, pricing incentives that drive users' behavior, as well as its effects on network operators' and service providers' profits will be highlighted.

The derived utility functions correlating QoS to QoE, as well as the knowledge of users' expectations and requirements that will be initially demonstrated, are used as feedback to the next phases. Specifically, regressive and stress tests in large scale environments offered by PlanetLab [4] evaluate the correctness, stability and scalability of the proposed dynamic QoE adaptation scheme in the resource allocation process of the wireless networks and video servers. Moreover, the mobile QoE-aware multimedia application will be prototyped and end-to-end validated via SQS IMS Testbed [5] towards assuring its compliance with the reference protocols and standards, as well as its interoperability on a realistic environment (e.g., 3GPP/LTE).

References

1. Aristomenopoulos, G., Kastrinogiannis, T., Kaldanis, V., Karantonis, G., Papavassiliou, S.: A Novel Framework for Dynamic Utility-Based QoE Provisioning in Wireless Networks. In: Proc. of IEEE Globecom (2010)
2. FP7 EU PROJECT TEFIS (TEstbed for Future Internet Services), http://www.tefisproject.eu/
3. Botnia living labs, http://www.openlivinglabs.eu/node/125
4. PlanetLab Europe, http://www.planet-lab.eu/
5. Software Quality Systems S.A., http://www.sqs.es/en/

Integrating Sensor Measurements through CM Cards as an OMF Service*

Vasilis Maglogiannis, Dimitris Giatsios, Giannis Kazdaridis,
Thanasis Korakis, Iordanis Koutsopoulos, and Leandros Tassiulas

Department of Computer and Communication Engineering
University of Thessaly
Centre for Research & Technology Hellas (CERTH)
Volos, Greece
{vamaglog,gidimitr,iokazdarid,korakis,jordan,leandros}@uth.gr

Abstract. Several OMF-based testbeds are using Chassis Manager (CM) cards for autonomously controlling and monitoring the status of nodes. CM cards are typically microcontroller boards and can be connected to different kinds of modules, including sensor modules. The NITOS testbed, which has recently adopted the use of CM cards, features various types of sensors connected to them. Measurements can be easily obtained through dedicated web services running on the microcontroller, through a network interface. This demo describes the implementation of an OMF service on top of these CM card measurement web services. This service can either be requested directly by an experimenter who wishes to obtain a specific sensor measurement, or it can be utilized in OMF experiment scripts.

1 Introduction

Chassis Manager (CM) cards have been introduced as an out-of-band management solution for experimental network testbeds, particularly for the purpose of remotely powering testbed nodes on or off. They are a relatively cost-efficient solution especially for wireless testbeds, where testbed nodes are typically distributed in a wide area rather than gathered in racks.

NITOS [1], a publicly available wireless testbed at the premises of University of Thessaly featuring almost 50 outdoor nodes, has recently adopted the use of CM cards. In particular, NITlab, the laboratory maintaining the NITOS testbed, developed a set of custom CM cards [2] for the nodes, based on AVR microcontrollers. The cards were supplied with several sensor modules, including temperature and humidity sensors as well as power meters. NITOS had already been featuring sensors among its equipment, connected to the nodes via USB, but the deassociation of sensor fucntionalities from the node itself offers several advantages, the most important being energy saving, as the node doesn't

---

* The research leading to these results has received funding from the European Community's Seventh Framework Programme (FP7/2007-2013) under grant agreement n°269179 (Project acronym: COOPLAB).

T. Korakis, M. Zink, and M. Ott (Eds.): TridentCom 2012, LNICST 44, pp. 397–399, 2012.

have to be powered on in order to get a sensor measurement. The microcontroller used for the NITOS CM cards features an Ethernet interface and a tiny webserver which allows programming of web services. Therefore, requesting a measurement from a sensor attached to the CM card can be easily done through a simple HTTP request to the webserver of the microcontroller.

2   OMF Sensor Measurement Service

NITOS has adopted OMF [3] as its control and management framework. OMF services are groups of specific tasks which operate on the testbed, such as loading a software image into a node or rebooting a set of nodes.

Leveraging on the measurement web service available on the CM cards of NITOS, we implemented a new OMF service called *measure*. It comprises a method for each type of measurement and each of these methods receives two arguments, the HRN of the node (each node features a CM card) and the domain, which is typically the testbed's domain name.

The new service can be utilized by a testbed user directly by invoking it in a browser, or indirectly through an OMF experiment script. In the second case, a user can schedule a measurement related experiment (e.g. monitor some measurement data for a given time interval) or use the measurement as feedback which may drive some kind of on-the-fly steering of a network experiment.

A pre-defined experiment script has been bundled as a new OMF command available at NITOS, called *omf measure*. This command has the following format:

omf   measure   [-s   SENSOR-MEASUREMENT]   [-h]   [-t   TOPOLOGY]
[-c AGGREGATE]

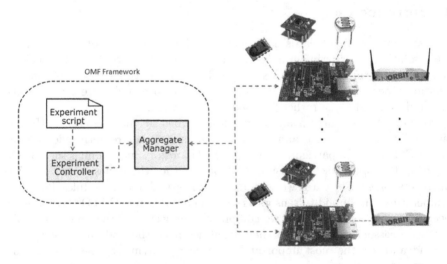

Fig. 1. Provision of measurement OMF service through CM cards

The argument SENSOR-MEAUREMENT specifies which measurement is requested from the CM card attached to the nodes in the TOPOLOGY argument. If not provided, a list of the available sensors for the specific card(s) is returned.

A scheme of the architecture of the OMF sensor measurement service can be seen in figure 1.

3 Conclusion

We described the implementation of a new OMF service available at the NITOS testbed, which provides measurements from sensors attached to the CM cards of the testbed nodes, upon request.

References

1. NITOS testbed, http://nitlab.inf.uth.gr/NITlab/index.php/testbed
2. NITOS CM cards, http://nitlab.inf.uth.gr/NITlab/index.php/testbed/hardware/cm-card
3. Rakotoarivelo, T., Ott, M., Jourjon, G., Seskar, I.: OMF: A Control and Management Framework for Networking Testbeds. ACM SIGOPS Operating Systems Review 43, 54–59 (2010)

Demonstrating an Information-Centric Network in an International Testbed

George Parisis[1], Ben Tagger[1], Dirk Trossen[1], Dimitris Syrivelis[2], Paris Flegkas[2], Leandros Tassiulas[2], Charilaos Stais[3], Christos Tsilopoulos[3], and George Xylomenos[3]

[1] Cambridge University, Computer Lab, Cambridge, UK
{georgios.parisis,ben.tagger,dirk.trossen}@cl.cam.ac.uk
[2] CERTH-ITI, Volos, Greece
{jsyr,pflegkas,leandros}@inf.uth.gr
[3] Athens University of Economics and Business, Athens, Greece
{stais,tsilochr,xgeorge}@aueb.gr

Abstract. Information-Centric Networking (ICN) has increasingly been attracting attention by the research community. In ICN the center of attention becomes the information itself and not the endpoints as in today's IP networks. In this demonstration we present applications that we developed as proof of concepts for our ICN approach. A video streaming as well as a voice and a HTTP over publish/subscribe application that run on top of our ICN prototype will be demonstrated running in an international testbed.

Information-centric networking has been touted as an alternative to the current Internet architecture by several research groups. Several technological solutions within a range of architectures have been proposed, such as in [1][2][3]. In this proposed demo we present three applications that we have implemented on top of the

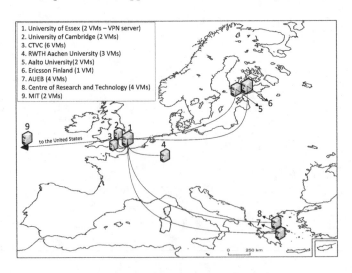

Fig. 1. PURSUIT International Testbed

T. Korakis, M. Zink, and M. Ott (Eds.): TridentCom 2012, LNICST 44, pp. 400–402, 2012.
© Institute for Computer Sciences, Social Informatics and Telecommunications Engineering 2012

network prototype, named Blackadder [8], which we have implemented in the context of the EU FP7 project PURSUIT [4]. Blackadder is based on the principles outlined in [1] and is implemented using the Click router project [5].

The Testbed. We have deployed our prototype in an international network in the context of the EU FP7 PURSUIT project [4]. As shown in Figure 1, eight sites across Europe as well as MIT in the US currently host 26 virtual machines, interconnected in an OpenVPN overlay. This enables us to emulate various topologies by assigning multiple link identifiers to the single network interface of each virtual machine. Note that forwarding in our prototype (called *Blackadder* in the following) is currently based on the LIPSIN approach [6], directly being implemented on top of Ethernet. A deployment tool has been developed in order to automate the deployment of network topologies and start experiments. This tool reads a configuration file that describes all nodes in the testbed along with their connections with other nodes and creates Click [5] configuration files for all testbed nodes, which in turn are copied to the respective nodes, initiating all testbed nodes.

Demonstrated Applications. In the proposed demonstration we will present a video streaming as well as a voice and a HTTP over publish/subscribe application that run on top of our Blackadder prototype, based on the high-level architecture outlined in [3].

Video Streaming: A video store across the network publishes an information item that represents a video catalogue. Whenever a subscriber subscribes to this catalogue, rendezvous takes place and, subsequently, the Topology Manager (TM) creates a forwarding identifier that is published to the publisher (the video store). The publisher then publishes the catalogue to the subscriber, which can then browse all published videos and subscribe to any one of them. Subscribers can calculate the identifiers of each video by hashing its name in the received catalogue. Therefore, an information identifier in this demo represents the channel used to publish the video with video fragments being published using the same identifier. The media server is a VLC server that streams the selected video via a local UDP socket. The publisher on same physical host as the video server receives the video through a UDP client socket. When subscribers for that specific information ID join the system, the publisher starts publishing the video. If no subscribers exist for the advertised information item, then the publisher remains idle. If all previously joined subscribers unsubscribe from the channel, the rendezvous system notifies the publisher to stop publishing the video. During the video transmission, subscribers may join or leave. Subscribers forward all received video fragments to a VLC client, via a loopback UDP socket, which reproduces the transmitted video. The demonstrated application is written in Java and C++.

Voice over Blackadder[7]: A voice connection in our demo is established similar to today's Voice over IP, with the callee being the subscriber and the caller being the publisher. The information identifiers of the caller and callee are calculated by applying a hash function on each name. Firstly, the caller publishes to the callee's identifier and includes in that message its own identifier, in order for the callee to be capable to send messages back to the caller. The callee publishes to the received caller identifier as an acknowledgement. With this, the participants are able to commence a two-way voice data message exchange. In order to identify successive voice messages exchanged between the two parties, we rely on information exchanged during the establishment of the connection as well as on sequence numbers. This provides some degree of flow control in that if a packet arrives with a sequence number less or equal to the previous one, we can drop it rather than push it to the audio component of the application. The demonstrated application is written in Java.

HTTP over Blackadder: We have implemented HTTP subscribe-GET and subscribe-POST operations for Blackadder. Each web content server, subscribes to its domain name where content browsers may publish subscribe-GET requests for a specific domain content. After publishing a request, the browser subscribes to an algorithmic identifier for that request and the web server publishes the requested content under the same request identifier. A similar transaction takes place for subscribe-POST requests. The s-GET and s-POST operations can be public or private. This is enabled by the metadata session identifier that standard HTTP requests carry. If a response data contains a session identifier, then the algorithmic content identifier for the s-GET and s-POST requests is uniquely formed to implement sessions. We have developed a python content proxy for IP browsers and a python-based Internet proxy server that fetches and publishes content directly from the Internet.

Acknowledgments. The research presented in the demo is supported by the EU FP7 project PURSUIT under grant FP7-INFSO-ICT 257217.

References

1. Jacobson, V., Smetters, D.K., Thornton, J.D., Plass, M., Briggs, N., Braynard, R.: Networking named content. Communications of the ACM 55(1) (2012)
2. Koponen, T., Chawla, M., Chun, B., Ermolinskiy, A., Kim, K., Shenker, S., Stoica, I.: A data-oriented (and beyond) network architecture. In: Proceedings of SIGCOMM (2007)
3. Trossen, D., Sarela, M., Sollins, K.: Arguments for an Information-Centric Internetworking Architecture. ACM Computer Communication Review (April 2010)
4. PURSUIT project (2011), http://www.fp7-pursuit.eu
5. Kohler, E., Morris, R., Chen, B., Jannotti, J., Kaashoek, M.F.: Click modular router. ACM Trans. on Computer Systems (TOCS) 18(3) (2000)
6. Jokela, P., Zahemszky, A., Arianfar, S., Nikander, P., Esteve, C.: LIPSIN: Line speed Publish/Subscribe Inter-Networking. In: ACM SIGCOMM (August 2009)
7. Stais, C., Diamantis, D., Aretha, C., Xylomenos, G.: VoPSI: Voice over a Publish-Subscribe Internetwork. Future Network & Mobile Summit (June 2011)
8. Kjällman, J. (ed.): First Lifecycle Prototype Implementation, PURSUIT Deliverable D3.2 (September 2011), http://www.fp7-pursuit.eu

Demonstration of a Vehicle-to-Infrastructure (V2I) Communication Network Featuring Heterogeneous Sensors and Delay Tolerant Network Capabilities*

Donatos Stavropoulos, Giannis Kazdaridis, Thanasis Korakis,
Dimitrios Katsaros, and Leandros Tassiulas

Department of Computer Engineering and Telecommunications,
University of Thessaly, Greece
Centre for Research and Technology, Hellas
{dostavro,iokazdarid,korakis,dkatsar,leandros}@uth.gr

Abstract. The development of applications based over vehicular networks, such as road safety, environmental information etc. require a complete testbed platform for research and evaluation. Such a platform will be provided by NITOS[1] testbed, that will include nodes mounted on cars and fixed nodes of the testbed operating as road side units (RSU). Besides the wireless infrastructure, there will be several sensors regarding the environmental conditions and the vehicle. These will gather measurements about air conditions and GPS data such as position and speed and will be collected in a central database, where the experimenter will be able to depict them in a Google map.

Keywords: Vehicular Network, Delay Tolerant Network, 802.11p, Sensors, Testbed, NITOS, NITlab, Wireless.

1 Introduction

Todays wireless communications testbeds, tend to expand their infrastructure to dynamic deployments, such as mobile and vehicular environments. In the presence of this scope, NITOS is being extended to incorporate nodes mounted on vehicles. Furthermore, we enhance the nodes' capabilities with a sensors framework, based on microcontroller boards. Testbed's users will be able to collect measurements regarding the environmental conditions, the vehicle's trajectory and the vehicle's internal status (e.g. fuel consumption, velocity etc.). These measurements include temperature, humidity and CO_2 indications. Measurement points will be localized according to the GPS coordinates and they will consist of data, concerning the vehicle's speed, elevation and position.

The methodology that will be used to collect sensors measurements, will be incorporated into an OML framework[2], which is currently available in

* The research leading to these results has received funding from the European Community's Seventh Framework Programme (FP7/2007-2013) under grant aggreement n°288254 (REDUCTION).

T. Korakis, M. Zink, and M. Ott (Eds.): TridentCom 2012, LNICST 44, pp. 403–405, 2012.

NITOS testbed to the experimenters, as a framework that collects measurements. The data collected from the sensors will be initially stored locally on the car-mounted node and afterwards, it will be uploaded to the testbed's central database through an RSU.

The above implies a delay tolerant network (DTN), which is achieved through an OML module, named OML-Proxy-Server[3] and acts as local buffer before the measurements are being sent to the central OML server of the testbed.

Finally the experimenter will be able to retrieve the database file during the experiment, so he can evaluate the received measurements as soon as they are collected and injected into the database. The network scheme is shown in Figure 1.

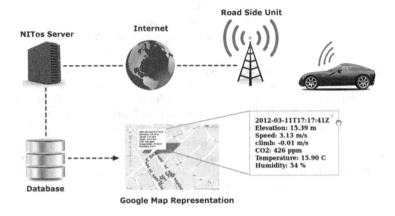

Fig. 1. The big picture

2   Network Components

The main components of the vehicular network contain the hardware parts, which are the sensors and the nodes. However, besides the necessary hardware, a bunch of software programs are used to collect measurements using OML. Additionally a web interface will be available to the experimenter to evaluate the car's route and measurements.

The connection between the car mounted node and the RSU is achieved through a WiFi interface. The communication protocol used for this set up is the 802.11p, using Mikrotik R52 wireless cards.

The RSU will be a static node of NITOS testbed. It will be responsible to forward the received measurements, from the car to the testbed's server, where the data will be stored in a sqlite3[4] database.

Regarding the sensors infrastructure, we exploit Arduino Uno[5] potential, which is a programmable microcontroller board and let us feature the car's node with CO_2 2(a), temperature and humidity 2(b) sensors. Additional, a GPS module is connected to the car node and enables measurements like *Latitude, Longitude, Altitude, Speed, Vertical Speed and Direction.*

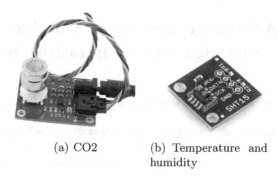

(a) CO2   (b) Temperature and
                           humidity

Fig. 2. Sensors

Fig. 3. Arduino Uno board

3   Conclusions and Future Work

In this demo, a vehicular network with multiple sensors and DTN capability is presented as part of the NITOS testbed. Temperature, humidity, CO2 and GPS measurements are collected through an OML framework and stored in a central database. During the experiment a dynamic Google map is created, depicting all the available data contained in the database so far. For future work, we plan to control the network's resources with the OMF[6] framework, which is featured on NITOS testbed for conducting experiments.

References

1. NITos testbed, http://nitlab.inf.uth.gr
2. OML project portal, http://omf.mytestbed.net/projects/oml/wiki
3. OML proxy server, http://omf.mytestbed.net/projects/oml/wiki/Proxy_Server
4. sqlite3 database, http://www.sqlite.org/
5. Arduino Uno board, http://arduino.cc/en/Main/arduinoBoardUno
6. OMF project portal, http://omf.mytestbed.net/

A Semantic Interface for OpenLab
Network Measurement Infrastructures

Jorge E. López de Vergara, Víctor Acero, Mario Poyato, and Javier Aracil

High Performance Computing and Networking Research Group,
Escuela Politécnica Superior, Universidad Autónoma de Madrid, Madrid, Spain
jorge.lopez_vergara@uam.es

Abstract. This demo presents a semantic approach to integrate network measurement information. For this, we use a common ontology for network measurements, taking the results of the ETSI Monitoring Ontology for the Internet (MOI). This ontology allows working with a common information model, but it is also necessary to define mappings to each measurement database schema. Finally, the user can get the integrated information by distributing a semantic query among every data sources containing the monitored information.

1 Introduction

OpenLab[1] is a European project that aims at providing large scale shared experimental network facilities. OpenLab is composed of several testbeds, where each one includes monitoring tools to obtain network measurements, such as packet delays and losses, link bandwidth usage, etc. It is important for the testbed users to have an integrated view of their experiments measurements. However, each monitoring tool provides its own view of the network measurements. Most times, these measurements deal with very similar information, but represented following different structures.

2 Demonstration Description

The proposed demonstration shows how the measurement information can be integrated from multiple measurement repositories. To get the information from them, a single integrated query will be needed. Using the concepts defined in the MOI ontology[2], the query will be distributed among the available repositories.

The information in the repositories is usually represented in different formats. For this reason, a mapping between each measurement repository schema and the MOI ontology concepts is defined. The researcher aiming to query network measurements will not have to know the underlying databases that contain such data, but only the MOI ontology.

---

[1] http://www.ict-openlab.eu/
[2] http://portal.etsi.org/portal/server.pt/community/MOI

T. Korakis, M. Zink, and M. Ott (Eds.): TridentCom 2012, LNICST 44, pp. 406–407, 2012.

To achieve the semantic integration, a system capable of querying multiple measurement repositories is needed. Users send integrated SPARQL[3] queries to an interface, which are then translated and distributed to the multiple measurement repositories. Each SQL repository has an SPARQL endpoint provided by a D2R server[4] that maps each database table to a set of ontology concepts. Then, a mapping file is defined for each repository.

In order to obtain a better performance when translating SPARQL queries into SQL ones, the code of the D2R server has been modified to use less redundant aliases in table joins. Another modification has also been done to automatically assign super-classes of a specified class in a `ClassMap`, making the mapping process easier.

The semantic query system has a graphical interface, shown in the figure below:

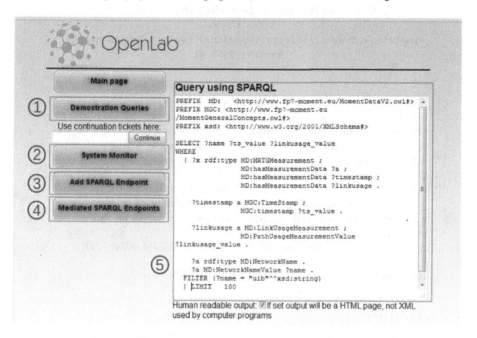

Fig. 1. OpenLab Semantic query interface

The elements of the interface (highlighted in Fig. 1) are the following:

1. In "Demonstration Queries", a set of predefined SPARQL queries can be executed.
2. In "System Monitor", currently executing queries can be checked.
3. In "Add SPARQL Endpoint", a new data repository can be added to the system.
4. In "Mediated SPARQL Endpoints", a list of available data repositories can be checked.
5. This area is the core of the system, allowing a user to write a SPARQL query for the requested network measurements.

---

[3] http://www.w3.org/TR/rdf-sparql-query/
[4] http://d2rq.org/d2r-serverD2

A Demonstration of a Relaying Selection Scheme for Maximizing a Diamond Network's Throughput*

Apostolos Apostolaras, Kostas Choumas, Ilias Syrigos, Giannis Kazdaridis,
Thanasis Korakis, Iordanis Koutsopoulos, Antonios Argyriou,
and Leandros Tassiulas

Department of Computer and Communication Engineering
University of Thessaly
Centre for Research & Technology Hellas (CERTH)
Volos, Greece
{apaposto,kohoumas,ilsirigo,iokazdarid,korakis,jordan,anargyr,
leandros}@uth.gr

Abstract. We demonstrate a queue-aware algorithm studied in a diamond network topology. This algorithm's decisions are obtained from an analytical optimization framework relying on our technical work [4] and we devise an implementation part by modifying the features of *ath9k* driver [3] and *click modular router* [5]. Performance evaluation is conducted through experimentation on the NITOS Wireless Testbed and it reveals a significant rise in total throughput considering a particular networking scenario while also it maintains stability of backlog queues when schedules indicated by Lyapunov-based technique as throughput optimal are selected.

NITOS Wireless Testbed website: *"http://nitlab.inf.uth.gr"* [2].

Keywords: Scheduling, Cooperation, Relay Selection.

1 Introduction

This work presents a maximum throughput and queue stable scheduling algorithm that exploits cooperative transmissions in order to forward traffic from source to destination through relays. With cooperative transmission, a packet can be scheduled to be forwarded to a potential helper node (relay) if the direct link from source to destination is worse than the links from source to relay and from relay to destination. We implement a scheduling algorithm by exploiting information on transmission queue lengths and channel quality to indicate the optimal scheduling decision. This scheduling algorithm is implemented by using the features of click modular router [5] and ath9k driver [3] in packet routing and forwarding mechanisms.

* The research leading to these results has received funding from the European Community's Seventh Framework Programme, CONECT (FP7/2007-2013) under grant agreement n°257616.

T. Korakis, M. Zink, and M. Ott (Eds.): TridentCom 2012, LNICST 44, pp. 408–410, 2012.

We consider the two-hop network depicted in Fig. 1 consisting of a source node S, two relay nodes R_1, R_2 and a destination D. The relays help the source node when channel conditions (or other factors such as queue congestion) do not favor direct source-destination transmission by carrying out traffic through alternative links. We assume that links are interference limited and impose the constraint that, at any time slot t, only one of the two sets of links (shown in Fig. 1.1 and in Fig. 1.2) can be activated. This is achieved by operating the network in different channels per hop and featuring relay nodes with two wireless interfaces.

We implement this scheduling decision algorithm and we verify its performance in the NITOS wireless testbed [2] . The algorithm quantifies metrics that are related to channel state information and queue lengths from all the network nodes. Every node broadcasts this information to other nodes in the vicinity, so as a common scheduling decision to be taken.

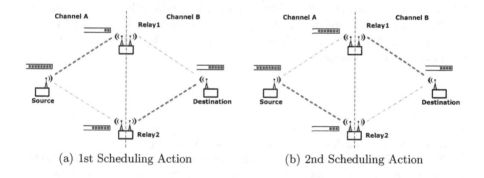

(a) 1st Scheduling Action   (b) 2nd Scheduling Action

Fig. 1. Scheduling Actions every Time Slot

2   Relay Scheduling

We describe briefly a simple algorithm that selects relays for forwarding the traffic and schedules transmissions relying on data backlog size. We denote by $Q_a^{(t)}$ the data length size in the queue transmission buffer on each node a at time slot t, and by $r_{ab}^{(t)}$ the transmission rate from node a to node b. Rate $r_{ab}^{(t)}$ is chosen so that to be the maximum of the feasible rates that the link can support subject to an acceptable packet error rate threshold. The algorithm performs its decisions for scheduling by quantifying the following metric Eq. 1. Its central decision relies on enabling a mechanism in the source for gathering information about queue lengths from relays. We elaborate this mechanism by exploiting features of the click modular router [5] . Then the source sends periodically to relays the scheduling activation decisions according to the following rule as given in Eq. 1.

$$Select\ 1^{st}\ Schedule\ if\ (Q_S^{(t)} - Q_{R_1}^{(t)})r_{SR_1}^{(t)} + Q_{R_2}^{(t)}r_{R_2D}^{(t)} > (Q_S^{(t)} - Q_{R_2}^{(t)})r_{SR_2}^{(t)} + Q_{R_1}^{(t)}r_{R_1D}^{(t)}$$

$$\tag{1}$$

Otherwise, select 2nd Schedule

Then the source node S and the activated relay (either R_1 or R_2) transmit packets in the forthcoming time slot t with the the respective transmission rate that was used in the aforementioned rule. Particularly, if the 1st Scheduling action is selected, then S transmits to R_1, and R_2 to D with rates $r_{SR_1}^{(t)}$ and $r_{R_2D}^{(t)}$ respectively, otherwise if the 2nd Scheduling action is selected, link activations and transmission rates change respectively.

3   Conclusion

We implement a scheduling decision control algorithm by using the *click modular router* along with the *ath9k* driver in order to enable relay assisted cooperative transmissions. Schedules are being activated towards maximizing the total throughput traffic, when networking conditions do not favor direct transmissions from source to destination.

References

1. IEEE 802.11-2007 Wireless LAN Medium Access Control and Physical
2. NITOS Wireless Testbed, http://nitlab.inf.uth.gr/NITlab/
3. The Ath9k Wireless Driver, http://linuxwireless.org/en/users/Drivers/ath9k
4. Apostolaras, A., Cottatellucci, L., Gatzianas, M., Koutsopoulos, I., Li, Q., Nikaein, N., Wang, L.: Cooperative Networking for High Capacity Transport Architectures CONECT. In: Project Deliverable, D2.2: Advances on Packet-level Cooperation Techniques for Unicast Traffic Transmission (2011)
5. Morris, R., Kohler, E., Jannotti, J., Kaashoek, M.F.: The click modular router. ACM SOSP 34(5), 217–231 (1999)

A Demonstration of Fast Failure Recovery
in Software Defined Networking

Sachin Sharma, Dimitri Staessens, Didier Colle, Mario Pickavet, and Piet Demeester

Department of Information Technology
Ghent University-IBBT
{firstname.lastname}@intec.ugent.be

Abstract. Software defined networking (SDN) is a recent architectural framework for networking, which aims at decoupling the network control plane from the physical topology and at having the forwarding element controlled through a uniform vendor-agnostic interface. A well-known implementation of SDN is OpenFlow. The core idea of OpenFlow is to provide direct programming of a router or switch to monitor and modify the way in which the individual packets are handled by the device. We describe our implemented fast failure recovery mechanisms (Restoration and Protection) in OpenFlow, capable of recovering from a link failure using an alternative path. In the demonstration, a video clip is streamed from a server to a remote client, which is connected by a network with an emulated German Backbone Network topology. We show switching of the video stream from the faulty path to the fault-free alternative path (restored or protected path) upon failure.

1   Introduction

Split architecture is a concept of decoupling the control functions from the forwarding elements and defining an open programmable interface between them. This split means that there are separated entities (physically) that remotely control several forwarding elements, which allows the independent design of control plane and leads to Software Defined Networking (SDN). One of the most known implementations of SDN is OpenFlow [1], which has gained significant interest from many research communities, and many of the research challenges behind it have been investigated in a number of projects all around the globe. In OpenFlow networks, one or more OpenFlow switches are controlled by separate devices (controllers) that communicate with the OpenFlow switches via the OpenFlow protocol. OpenFlow (specification 1.1 and beyond) provides the concept of FlowTables and a GroupTable [2], which is an abstraction of the Forwarding Information Base (FIB). We implemented fast failure recovery mechanisms in OpenFlow, capable of recovering from a link failure using an alternative path. We demonstrate the effectiveness of the implemented mechanisms by emulating a large scale German backbone network and achieving a recovery time of less than 50 ms.

T. Korakis, M. Zink, and M. Ott (Eds.): TridentCom 2012, LNICST 44, pp. 411–414, 2012.
© Institute for Computer Sciences, Social Informatics and Telecommunications Engineering 2012

2   Our implemented Mechanisms and Experiment on High Speed Testbed

One of the European projects named SPARC [3] studies how OpenFlow can be deployed in carrier-grade networks. The carrier-grade network should recover from the failure within 50 ms. We implement two well-known mechanisms of failure recovery i.e. restoration and protection in OpenFlow networks. In the case of restoration, the alternative path is established by the controller when it receives the failure notification from the OpenFlow switches [4,5]. In the case of protection, two disjoint paths (working and protected) are established by the controller before the failure occurs in the network. When the failure is detected in the working path, the traffic is switched to the protected path. We use a fast-failover type of the group-entry [2] to switch traffic between two different paths. This type is responsible for executing one of the action buckets of the group-entry as well as switching to another bucket upon failure. In our protection experiment, we establish an additional BFD session to monitor the failure in the working path. Once the BFD session stops receiving the BFD packets, the OpenFlow switch changes the associated alive-status.

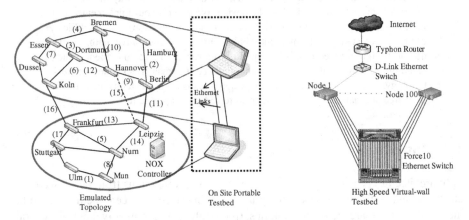

Fig. 1A. Emulated Topology and On Site Portable Testbed   B: Virtual-wall Testbed

We emulated our recovery mechanisms. in a nationwide German network topology (Fig. 1A). Each of the switches in Fig. 1A is also connected to a server (not shown) and has a dedicated interface to a switched LAN which establishes connection with the controller. Our testbed where this emulation is carried out is shown in Fig. 1B.

For the experimentation, we implement our recovery mechanisms in a NOX 1.1 controller and OpenFlow 1.1 software, recently developed by Ericsson [6]. We generate 182 different flows by using the Linux kernel module pktgen, break one link between switches and find recovery time. In our restoration experiment, the switches detect the failure due to loss of signal, which is approximately equal to the time when the first flow is restored in the network. On the other hand, the switches in the protection experiment detect the failure in 33 to 40 ms by establishing BFD sessions.

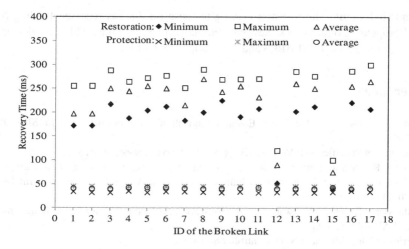

Fig. 2. Recovery Experiment

The results of the experiment are depicted in Fig. 2. In Fig. 2, the X-axis represents the broken link (the number in brackets of Fig. 1A).; the Y-axis represents the recovery time. The minimum value is the time it takes to recover the first flow; the maximum value is the time it takes to recover all the flows; and the average value is the expected time for any flow to be recovered after the failure. In our nodes, Hannover node where we break the link 12 or 15 (Fig. 1A) detects the failure within 50 ms in restoration. However, for other nodes, this value is between 167 to 210 ms (Fig. 2). The results show that restoration takes approximately 80 to 100 ms after detection of the failure (or after first flow is restored) and protection takes 1 to 3 ms.

3   Demonstration on Portable Testbed

In the on-site demonstration, we show our implemented restoration and protection in OpenFlow networks where a video server at one laptop streams a commercial video clip continuously, while the video client at other laptop receives and plays it in real time. We remove the link 15 (dotted link in Fig. 1A) from our emulated German topology to demonstrate it with two laptops, which consist of two Ethernet ports to communicate with each other. Mininet is used in the experiments to emulate this topology. We extend the Mininet software to send or receive the traffic from the physical port. For the demonstration, half of the topology is emulated in the first laptop and the other half is emulated in the second laptop (shown in Fig. 1A). In the topology, one NOX controller controls all the forwarding switches including switches emulated in the other laptop. Therefore, we use one Ethernet port for the working path; whereas other Ethernet port for the protected path and also for the communication between the controller and the switches of the other laptop. During the demonstration, we remove the Ethernet cable of the working path and show switching of traffic to the alternative path.

Acknowledgment. The research leading to these results has received funding from the European Community's Seventh Framework Programme (FP7) under grant agreement n° 258457 (SPARC) and n° 258365 (OFELIA).

References

1. McKeown, N., et al.: Openflow: Enabling innovation in campus networks. In: SIGCOMM (2008)
2. OpenFlow Specification: Version 1.1.0 (2011), http://www.openflow.org/
3. SPlit ARchitecture Carrier-Grade Networks (SPARC), http://www.fp7-sparc.eu/
4. Sharma, S., et al.: Enabling Fast Failure Recovery in OpenFlow Networks. In: DRCN (2011)
5. Staessens, D., et al.: Software Defined Networking: Meeting Carrier Grade Requirements. In: LANMAN (2011)
6. Ericsson OpenFlow and NOX Controller Software, https://github.com/TrafficLab

Controllable Packet Prioritization on PlanetLab Using NEPI

Alina Quereilhac, Claudio Daniel Freire, Thierry Turletti, and Walid Dabbous

INRIA, Sophia Antipolis, France
{alina.quereilhac,claudio-daniel.freire,thierry.turletti,
walid.dabbous}@inria.fr

Abstract. We present the extensions made to NEPI, the Network Experimentation Programming Interface, to allow easy creation and customization of routing overlays on top of PlanetLab. We particularly focus on demonstrating the traffic shaping capabilities provided by NEPI, with the use of customizable stream filters on PlanetLab overlays to induce controllable packet prioritization.

Keywords: networking, overlays, PlanetLab, NEPI.

1 Demonstration

This demonstration is intended to supplement the paper[1] accepted at TRIDENTCOM'12. We focus on demonstrating the experiment use case presented in that paper, in which we make use of stream filters as a means to control the characteristics of an overlay deployed in PlanetLab, [2] providing a realistic yet controllable environment where to test the POPI[4] tool.

NEPI [3] is an experiment management framework which provides support for design, deployment, control and gathering of results of network experiments. We added support for automating deployment and customization of routing overlays on PlanetLab, to alleviate the complexities of performing these tasks manually, and to more easily circumvent administrative limitations. NEPI automates resource discovery, node provisioning, application deployment, and creation of tunnels between the selected nodes to build the overlay network. It also provides the ability to customize traffic in the overlays by adding user defined *stream filters*, processing functions applied to packets traversing the overlay tunnels. They can be used to implement custom queues, packet filters or transformations, and tunnelling protocols.

To demonstrate NEPI's ability to provide a solution to existing problems when using PlanetLab, we selected a previously published experiment case [4]. In this experiment, researchers developed the POPI tool to attempt to infer packet priorities in the intervening routers between two endpoints, by inducing bulk traffic and analyzing point-to-point loss rates. However, in order to verify the results obtained after running POPI on PlanetLab, it was necessary to ask ISPs about their routing policies, because no other means were available to verify that the priorities reported by the tool corresponded to actual prioritization policies.

T. Korakis, M. Zink, and M. Ott (Eds.): TridentCom 2012, LNICST 44, pp. 415–416, 2012.
© Institute for Computer Sciences, Social Informatics and Telecommunications Engineering 2012

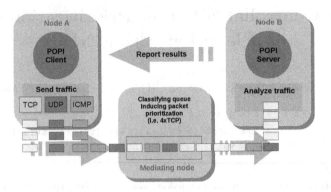

Fig. 1. POPI. An overlay is formed with 3 PlanetLab nodes. Traffic is sent by the POPI client, from node A to node B through a *mediating node*, where packets are processed by a classifying queue to induce class-dependent priorities. Traffic profiling results are then reported back and analyzed expecting to verify the classification.

The researcher's ability to verify the obtained results was limited, as not all providers responded, nor provided complete information.

In our demonstration we re-evaluate POPI, using NEPI to create a controlled routing overlay on PlanetLab to which we add stream filters to modify traffic behavior in a known way, by means of a classifying queue that induces packet prioritization. NEPI provides support for queues that implement queuing policies by inspecting the Type Of Service (TOS) field in the IPv4 header of the processed packets. Such queues can be easily attached to PlanetLab network devices, and thanks to this feature, designing this experiment was straightforward. Figure 1 depicts the design of our experiment consisting of 3 PlanetLab nodes connected in series. The node in the middle applies a controlled class of queuing, resulting in recognizable statistical bias to the packet stream. This method allows modification of overlay traffic behavior on PlanetLab in a controlled way, avoiding the need to request information regarding traffic policies to the ISPs.

With this experiment we demonstrate how the *stream filters* feature provided by NEPI enabled us to overcome existing limitations when experimenting with PlanetLab-base overlays. Moreover, apart from automating deployment of custom overlays in PlanetLab, NEPI also makes it possible to run numerous repetitions of a same experiment, or variations of it, enabling thorough experimentation.

References

1. Freire, C., et al.: Automated deployment and customization of routing overlays on PlanetLab
2. Chun, B., et al.: PlanetLab: an overlay testbed for broad-coverage services. SIG-COMM Comput. Commun. Rev. 33, 3–12 (2003)
3. Quereilhac, A., et al.: NEPI: An Integration Framework for Network Experimentation. Software, Telecommunications and Computer Networks 19, 1–5 (2011)
4. Lu, G., et al.: POPI: a user-level tool for inferring router packet forwarding priority. IEEE/ACM Trans. Netw. 18, 1–14 (2010)

Testing of LTE Configurations and Applications[*]

Francisco Javier Rivas[1], Almudena Diaz Zayas[2], and Pedro Merino Gomez[2]

[1] AT4 Wireless, Systems Division, Malaga, Spain
fjrivas@at4wireless.com
[2] Dpto. de Lenguajes y Ciencias de la Computación, University of Malaga, Spain
{almudiaz,pedro}@lcc.uma.es

Abstract. This paper introduces an experimental testbed developed at the University of Malaga to analyze the behavior of mobile applications and services over LTE (Long Term Evolution) networks. The novelty of the testbed is the ability to correlate the impact of radio propagation issues on LTE configurations and applications protocols and cross tuning LTE parameters and IP protocols from the point of view of the quality perceived by end users. In this work we focus on the evaluation of VoIP services over LTE networks.

Keywords: Testbed, LTE, mobile application and services, performance.

1 Introduction

LTE have proven to be the primary choice for network operators to provide high rate data services with an evolving path to 4G, which will be provided by LTE Advanced. As LTE is an All-IP data centered technology, there is no support for circuit switched voice services. However, LTE is expected to provide voice services over IP and IMS (IP Multimedia Subsystem), as intended by the VoLTE (Voice over LTE) initiative.
According to network operators, their customers are used to a high voice quality, and any migration path to LTE should not compromise the provided quality of service. Voice is still the core business for many operators, and obtaining accurate knowledge on the trade-offs involved in resource management and QoS over LTE will be critical for their success. With the aim of generating reference results, we suggest a novel approach that will hopefully help key market players in making decisions. Further details can be found in [1].

2 Testbed Architecture

In order to meet the target requirements, we suggest a test architecture based on high-end network emulation, open VoIP applications and standard voice quality estimation methods.

---

[*] This work has been funded by Spanish projects TIN 2008-05932 and WITLE2 IDI-20090382, by the Andalusian project P07-TIC3131 and ERDF from the European Commission.

T. Korakis, M. Zink, and M. Ott (Eds.): TridentCom 2012, LNICST 44, pp. 417–418, 2012.

A custom tool chain illustrated in Fig.1 has been integrated to allow automatic processing of received traffic parameters and voice quality. Voice calls are originated between a softphone SIP client, and a VoIP server. For clients deployed in a laptop, the internet connection is established by a commercial LTE USB device and Wireshark may be used to monitor the traffic at the client side. Alternatively, a VoIP client can be run at smartphones and the TestelDroid [2], a tool developed in our department to allow the acquisition of communication related measurements at different levels in Android devices, is used to monitor the traffic.

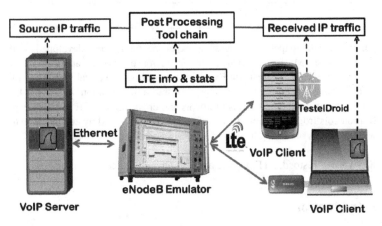

Fig. 1. Testbed setup deployment

An LTE network is created using an E2010 eNodeB emulator from AT4 wireless that allows fine configuration of radio network parameters using the S3110B LTE Mobile Test Application. Most of the features are exposed by the S3110B not only through a graphic interface but also via remote control commands. Using those commands, we plan to automate network configuration and measurement campaigns.

For that purpose, a data gateway application has been developed to communicate the external server with the E2010 external data interface. This gateway will also allow us to control the data flows in future works, e.g. restricting the available bandwidth or introducing packet losses, to emulate the effect of the core network transport.

References

1. Díaz, A., Merino, P., Rivas, F.J.: Test Environment for QoS Testing of VoIP over LTE. In: Proceedings of the 13th IEEE/IFIP Network Operations and Management Symposium (NOMS 2012), Maui, NV, USA (April 2012)
2. Álvarez, A., Díaz, A., Merino, P., Rivas, F.J.: Field measurements of mobile services with Android smartphones. In: Proceedings of the IEEE Consumer Communications and Networking Conference (CCNC), Las Vegas, NV, USA (2012)

TaaSOR – Testbed-as-a-Service Ontology Repository

Milorad Tosic[1], Ivan Seskar[2], and Filip Jelenkovic[1]

[1] Univeristy of Nis, Faculty of Electronic Engineering, 18000 Nis, Serbia
[2] Winlab, Rutgers The State University of New Jersey, NJ, USA
mbtosic@acm.org, seskar@winlab.rutgers.edu,
filip.jelenkovic@gmail.com

Abstract. This demonstration is introducing Testbed-as-a-Service (TaaS) infrastructure that illustrates use of community based approach to building experimental ontologies and generation of supporting testbed resources applied to OMF based testbed. While this TaaS demo is initially primarily targeting virtualization and community collaboration, the final objective is to support domain specific experimental description languages and resource management in federated testbeds.

Keywords: Web Services, Ontology Repository, Semantic Web, Interoperability, Testbed.

1 Introduction

The research question addressed by the presented demo is: could we facilitate the Testbed-as-a-Service federated infrastructure by using existing XML based aggregate managers (or services), generating ontologies out of their XML descriptions, then using these ontologies, enable semantic service annotations and facilitate humanized interaction with experiment controller and resources supporting the range of what-if scenarios (including "what parameters may I change?", "do I break some constraints?", "give me range of the parameter") . These new services are potentially leading to an experiment specification language, ontology and even automated (OEDL/Ruby) code generation for OMF testbed management framework.

We identify *two crucial facilitators for achieving the vision of total system scalability in federated testbeds*: Experiment Virtualization, and Community Growth. We propose to exploit Semantic Technologies in general and Semantic Web in particular to develop the facilitators.

2 Community-Driven TaaSOR

TaaSOR (available at http://www.orbit-lab.org:8080/tasor) currently targets OMF framework [1], and is limited to internal use while being externally available as a proof-of-concept only. Here, we demonstrate the following: 1) Importing XML service description and generating the corresponding set of resources; 2) Browsing the set of

T. Korakis, M. Zink, and M. Ott (Eds.): TridentCom 2012, LNICST 44, pp. 419–420, 2012.

resources; 3) Loading new domain (NDL) and application specific ontologies; 4) Context and domain adaptation of the GUI; 5) Resolving semantic conflicts within the loaded services; 6) Semantic annotation of services; 7) Publishing the created semantics as an ontology as well as Rubi source code; 8) Command line access to the RESTful API.

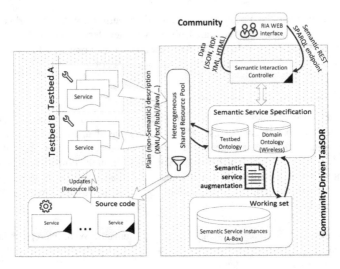

Fig. 1. Implementation architecture. Federation of services is built by importing plain service descriptions (XML or other) and transforming them into the corresponding set of RDF resources. The resources are further annotated by community using loaded domain (NDL) and application ontologies. The Working set developed that way may be published on the system's URL either as RDF ontology or Rubi code (a semantic positive feedback loop is created).

Fig. 2. RIA Web Interface: a) Drag-and-drop semantic statements builder with auto-complete. b) Hierarchical browsing of services' resources: All resources are clickable, draggable, and context sensitive. Knowledge pane presents convenient set of resources relevant for the last clicked resource. c) Working set of created semantic statements.

Reference

1. Rakotoarivelo, T., Ott, M., Jourjon, G., Seskar, I.: OMF: A Control and Management Framework for Networking Testbeds. ACM SIGOPS Operating Systems Review 43, 54–59 (2010)

Enabling Sensing and Mobility
on Wireless Testbeds*

Harris Niavis, Giannis Kazdaridis,
Thanasis Korakis, and Leandros Tassiulas

Department of Computer and Communication Engineering,
University of Thessaly, Greece
Centre for Research and Technology Hellas, CERTH, Greece
{haniavis,iokazdarid,korakis,leandros}@uth.gr

Abstract. The inherent inability of simulation models to adequately express factors such as wireless signal propagation etc., can lead to incomplete evaluation of wireless protocols and applications. Thus, testing of proposed schemes under real-life settings has become the de facto validation process. More specifically, in the context of testing scenarios that include mobility, evaluation in real environments becomes a prerequisite. Networking testbeds have recently extended their capabilities by providing the researchers with the ability to include mobile nodes in their experiments as well. Towards this direction, we have developed a prototype mobile node in NITOS, which features a mounted camera and wireless interfaces that enable remote access and control. The proposed mobility framework is also accompanied by a graphical user interface that allows the experimenter to observe the node's behavior remotely.

1 Introduction

As recent work has shown, mobility has positive impact on the behavior of wireless networks, as it improves coverage, helps security in ad hoc networks and helps with network congestion as well [7]. As a consequence, the extension of NITOS testbed with mobile nodes is indispensable, in order to allow for experimentation under real mobility conditions.

In this demo, we will present a custom mobile node, developed at NITlab which aims at upgrading NITOS, a large scale wireless testbed that currently consists of 50 operational WiFi nodes.

2 Mobile Node Parts

From a higher-level view, our mobile node consists of the following hardware parts:

---

* The research leading to these results has received funding from the European Community's Seventh Framework Programme (FP7/2007-2013) under grant agreement n°287581 (Project name: Open-Lab).

T. Korakis, M. Zink, and M. Ott (Eds.): TridentCom 2012, LNICST 44, pp. 421–424, 2012.

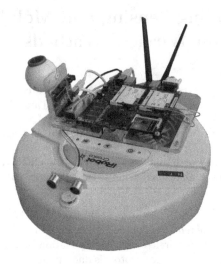

Fig. 1. Mobile node

- an iRobot Create [3,2]
- an Alix board alix2d2 [4], which is a single board computer, highly power efficient, small and capable of running operating systems
- a webcam mounted on top of the robot
- an Arduino Uno[1], which is a small-size, programmable microcontroller board that also features a digital accelometer and an ultrasonic sensor as well.

In particular, the prototype features a custom designed tray that enables the iRobot Create to carry the Alix board. The board communicates with the robot over the serial port and is supplied power through the robot's own battery. The Alix board runs the Voyage Linux distribution, but it is able to run any light Linux distribution. The mounted camera is facing upwards and thus is used to recognize specific patterns that are placed on the ceiling, which provide the robot with the ability to detect its position and navigate around the room.

In addition, the Arduino board is connected to the Alix board through the USB port, and thus it provides for gathering of measurements from the attached ultrasonic and accelerometer sensors. The ultrasonic sensor aids in avoiding obstacles that may appear in front of the robot, while the digital accelerometer is used to get acceleration measurements during the movement of the robot.

3   Programming the Robot

The Open Interface (OI) of iRobot Create consists of both an electronic and a software interface that enable the experimenter to manipulate the robot's behavior and access sensor measurements through a series of commands that are sent through the serial port by an external PC or micro-controller. In order to to interact with the robot we developed custom Python scripts [5], which are based on the iRobot Create Open Interface.

Regarding the image recognition we use the ARToolKit [6], which is a software library for building Augmented Reality(AR) applications. Using ARToolKit, our mobile node is able to recognize four different patterns that are placed on the ceiling and thus manages to detect its current position and send appropriate commands to the Robot.

4   Demonstration

In this demo, we will use one of the two available network interfaces of the Alix board, in order to wirelessly control our mobile node . This interface will be connected with an operating in range Access Point(AP) and will be used as the control interface. The second interface will be used for the actual experimentation from the NITOS testbed users. Through a graphical user interface, which is presented in Fig.2, we will be able to observe the node's movement around the NITlab laboratory premises. At the right part of the GUI, we can see direction indicators, as well as a representation of the currenlty recognized pattern.

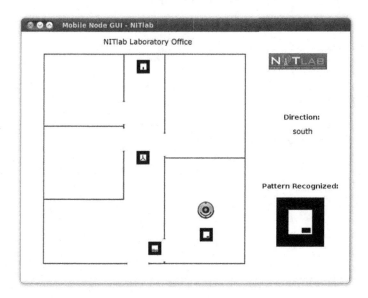

Fig. 2. GUI screenshot

5   Conclusion and Future Work

In this demo paper we will present an implementation of a location-aware mobile node that has been developed in NITOS wireless testbed. Expansion of the testbed capabilities with mobile nodes provides for more complex experiments in new research fields. Currently, we are in the process of expanding the abilities of our mobile node, by training the camera software so as to be able to recognize more patterns and moreover by using orientation tracking, in order to inform the user about the exact angle under which the specific pattern is detected.

References

1. Arduino Uno, http://arduino.cc/en/Main/arduinoBoardUno
2. iRobot Create Open Interface Manual, http://www.irobot.com/filelibrary/ pdfs/hrd/create/Create%20Open%20Interface_v2.pdf
3. iRobot Create Owners Guide, http://www.irobot.com/filelibrary/create/ Create%20Manual_Final.pdf
4. PC Engines alix2d2, http://www.pcengines.ch/alix2d2.html
5. Pyserial, http://pyserial.sourceforge.net/pyserial.html
6. Hirokazu Kato, I.P., Billinghurst, M.: Artoolkit, http://pyserial.sourceforge.net/pyserial.html
7. Schindelhauer, C.: Mobility in Wireless Networks. In: Wiedermann, J., Tel, G., Pokorný, J., Bieliková, M., Štuller, J. (eds.) SOFSEM 2006. LNCS, vol. 3831, pp. 100–116. Springer, Heidelberg (2006)

Remote Control of Robots for Setting Up Mobility Scenarios during Wireless Experiments in the IBBT w-iLab.t

Pieter Becue, Bart Jooris, Vincent Sercu, Stefan Bouckaert,
Ingrid Moerman, and Piet Demeester

IBBT - Ghent University, Gaston Crommenlaan 8 bus 201, 9050 Ghent, Belgium
pieter.becue@intec.ugent.be

Abstract. The w-iLab.t is a large-scale generic wireless experimentation facility. Two locations are equipped with in total over 260 wireless
nodes. In the w-iLab.t Zwijnaarde location mobile nodes are hosted. The
mobile nodes are mounted on top of robots, of which the movement can
be fully controlled by the experimenter. Due to a high accuracy positioning algorithm, the exact position of the robots is known at all time
during the experiments. This enables us to provide repeatable and controlled mobile experiments to our users.

Keywords: mobile, robots, experimentation, wireless, positioning,
testbed.

1 The IBBT w-iLab.t: Mobile Extensions

The w-iLab.t is a large-scale generic wireless experimentation facility. Two locations are equipped with in total over 260 wireless nodes (IEEE 802.15.4, Wi-
Fi a/b/g/n, Bluetooth). In the w-iLab.t Zwijnaarde location mobile nodes are
available. These mobile nodes are mounted on top of iRobot Roomba vacuum
cleaning robots. These nodes are identical to the fixed testbed nodes and are
fully configurable by the experimenter. To power the mobile nodes, an extra
battery pack was installed on the robot. Thanks to an in-house designed circuit
board, it is possible to recharge both the external battery pack and the robot
battery through the iRobot Roomba docking station. The board also serves as
a bridge between the robot and a wireless sensor node (eZ430) which is used
to control the robot movement. Finally, the board can also be used to remotely
power on/off the mobile node on the robot. Please see Figure 1 for an example
of the w-iLab.t robot configuration. The w-iLab.t is part of the IBBT iLab.t [1].

2 Accurate Positioning Algorithm

The exact position of the robots should be known at all times during the experiments. The basis of the positioning algorithm is dead reckoning: assuming
we know the starting position, we use the speed and the angle provided by the

T. Korakis, M. Zink, and M. Ott (Eds.): TridentCom 2012, LNICST 44, pp. 425–426, 2012.
© Institute for Computer Sciences, Social Informatics and Telecommunications Engineering 2012

Fig. 1. the IBBT w-iLab.t robot

internal Roomba logic to calculate the new position. Since this approach was not reliable on its own, corrections are made to the robot position by using a taped grid (with a cell size of 1 by 1 meter) on the floor of w-iLab.t Zwijnaarde. The horizontal and vertical lines of this grid are taped in different colours. Using the standard cliff sensors of the robot, the position of the robot is adjusted every time the robot crosses one of these grid lines. Empirical verification shows that the position of the robots never deviates more than 3 centimeters.

3   Controllable and Repeatable Mobile Experiments

The mobility solution is fully integrated into the testbed, which is OMF compatible [2]. Users can very easily include coordinate files into their OMF experiment description files, describing the exact path the robot has to follow during the experiment.

4   Conclusion

The w-iLab.t gives users the ability to easily include controlled mobility scenario's into their wireless experiments. By using the OMF framework, it is very easy for users to repeat these mobile experiments and analyze results afterwards.

Acknowledgments. The research leading to these results has received funding from various national funds, and from the EU's Seventh Framework Programme (FP7) under grant agreement nr 287581 (OpenLab).

References

1. IBBT iLab.t Technology center, http://ilabt.ibbt.be
2. Rakotoarivelo, T., Ott, M., Seskar, I., Jourjon, G.: OMF - a Control and Management Framework for Networking Testbeds. In: SOSP Workshop (ROADS 2009) (2009)

Author Index